JON BALSERAK — 07825-834-765

RECEIVED AT UNIV. OF BIRMINGHAM RIGHT AT
TIME (WAS LEAVING THERE FOR BRISTOL (AUG '08)

THE I TATTI
RENAISSANCE LIBRARY

James Hankins, General Editor

NICHOLAS OF CUSA
WRITINGS ON CHURCH AND REFORM

ITRL 33

NICHOLAS OF CUSA
✦ ✦ ✦
WRITINGS ON CHURCH AND REFORM

TRANSLATED BY

THOMAS M. IZBICKI

THE I TATTI RENAISSANCE LIBRARY

HARVARD UNIVERSITY PRESS

CAMBRIDGE, MASSACHUSETTS

LONDON, ENGLAND

2008

Series design by Dean Bornstein

Library of Congress Cataloging-in-Publication Data

Nicholas, of Cusa, Cardinal, 1401–1464.
[Selections. English & Latin. 2008]
Writings on church and reform / Nicholas of Cusa ;
translated by Thomas M. Izbicki.
p. cm. — (The I Tatti Renaissance library ; 33)
Includes bibliographical references (p.) and index.
ISBN 978-0-674-02524-0 (cloth : alk. paper)
1. Theology — Early works to 1800.
2. Sermons, Latin — Early works to 1800.
3. Sermons, Medieval — Translations into English.
I. Izbicki, Thomas M. II. Title.
B765.N51 2008
230'.2 — dc22   2008003075

Contents

ॐﬗ

REFORM AND *CHRISTIFORMITAS*

Introduction

꽃Ⴣᢞ

Nicholas of Cusa, widely considered the greatest philosopher and theologian of the fifteenth century, also holds an important position in the history of political and ecclesiological thought. His interest in issues of church governance and reform was a natural outgrowth of his career. He was born in Kues on the Moselle in 1401 into a middle-class family. He studied at the University of Heidelberg and became a doctor of canon law at the University of Padua in 1423 before entering the service of the Church. Nicholas taught at the University of Cologne, where he also studied theology. He participated in the Council of Basel (1431–1449), including its negotiations with the Hussite heretics in Bohemia. In this period he wrote *The Catholic Concordance* (1433),[1] the most important work to emerge from the Council's efforts to promote orthodoxy and reform in the Church. Cusanus, as he is usually known, gradually became alienated from the majority party in the council, which refused to move to Italy for a council of reunion with the Eastern churches for fear the pope would control it. Pope Eugenius IV (1431–1447), who was striving to defend his supreme authority against Basel's efforts to impose reforms, responded by inviting the Byzantine emperor and the patriarch of Constantinople to a council in Ferrara. Nicholas left Basel in 1437, siding with Eugenius and his Council of Union. The exact balance of principle and self-interest in Cusanus' decision is hard to determine.[2]

While bringing the Greeks to Eugenius' council, Cusanus had a shipboard experience in 1437–1438 that shifted his writing emphasis to speculative topics, including theology, philosophy and mathematics. Nicholas reported that he received a divine gift that showed him how to speak about God by embracing "incomprehensibles incomprehensibly." "Learned ignorance" would allow him

to transcend the limits of human abilities to discuss the divine.[3] This theological breakthrough, explication of which would occupy him for the rest of his life, did not, however, distance Nicholas from ecclesiastical politics. The papal Council of Ferrara-Florence (1438–1445) provoked a response from the Basel assembly, which declared Eugenius deposed and elected its own pope. Nicholas served as a papal diplomat in the ensuing struggle, an effort that earned him the nickname "The Hercules of the Eugenians." These labors culminated in his promotion to the cardinalate in 1450 by Pope Nicholas V (1447–1455), to whose authority the assembly at Basel yielded at long last. Nicholas then served as papal legate in Germany (1450–1452) and was made bishop of Brixen (1450–1464). The Brixen episcopate became Cusanus' worst experience. His efforts to impose reform aroused fierce — even armed — opposition, forcing the cardinal to flee to Rome. Nicholas served as papal vicar for Rome while Pius II (1458–1464) was at the Congress of Mantua (1459), trying to organize a crusade against the Turks. Cusanus died at Todi in 1464 while working for the failed crusade launched by Pius II, who also died in this effort. Nicholas is buried at San Pietro in Vincoli in Rome, but the hospital he founded in Bernkastel-Kues lives on.[4]

Cusanus' writing career is usually treated as having two phases. A short period, during which he wrote *The Catholic Concordance*, is succeeded by a long period of composing metaphysical works. This division is not entirely illusory. Nicholas never wrote another political work as substantial as *The Catholic Concordance* after departing from Basel. His most important metaphysical writings followed the shipboard experience. We must not, however, overstate this separation. Nicholas continued writing on issues related to the Church and its reform well into his final years. Moreover, his speculative writings show signs of development from an initial insight into a series of experiments intended to help the cardinal and

his readers strive for knowledge of a God Who eluded the limited human intellect.[5]

We are able to distinguish four groups of texts among Cusanus' various writings on political matters: those from the Basel years; those from the years spent on diplomatic missions for the papacy; a third group, overlapping chronologically with the second, where he applies new concepts to the problems afflicting the Church; and a last group, reflecting the cardinal's efforts to promote reform and obedience both as a diocesan bishop and as a cardinal working in the papal court. The chief themes treated in these four broad groups are suggested by the titles chosen for each section.

Council and Concord

The first phase of Nicholas' writing on the Church is the best known. He became active in the Council of Basel as an advocate in a dispute over the see of Trier, but he also involved himself in issues of orthodoxy, discipline and reform. His earliest intervention on these issues was focused on the Hussites, the heretics who dominated the kingdom of Bohemia. The Hussites demanded, among other things, that the clergy give communion under both species, bread and wine, to everyone. Nicholas replied to this demand in his treatise *To the Bohemians: On the Use of Communion* (text 1). This work, divided into two parts, argued that Eucharistic usage had to conform to the Church's judgment of the needs of the times. Hussite arguments based on the literal meaning of Scripture were rejected in favor of obedience to the considered decisions of the ecclesiastical authorities, who were presumed to know best what the laity needed. This argument, presented in an awkward Latin full of citations of authoritative texts, did not prevent Cusanus from participating in the Council's negotiations with the Hussites, leading to a compromise. The Basel Compacts of

1436 accepted liturgical diversity as the price of peace. The Bohemian laity were allowed access to the chalice at communion, not just to the bread. The council ratified this agreement, but the papacy never accepted it.[6]

In this same period, Nicholas began working on *The Catholic Concordance*. The short work *Is the Authority of the Holy Councils Greater Than That of the Pope?* (text 2) discusses one of the major themes of the larger and probably slightly later work: that Church councils are of greater authority than that of any individual, even the pope. The more representative the council was of the entire Church, as the great councils of antiquity had been, the more reliable their judgments.[7] These arguments would be combined in *The Catholic Concordance* with a plea for harmony among all the elements of Christendom, clergy and laity alike. Also added was an argument that reform extended to the empire, not just to ecclesiastical affairs.[8] Coupled with the polemics against Hussite error, these works on the Church and Christendom sketched an agenda — orthodoxy, reform and obedience, all within a harmonious whole — that helps explain Nicholas' eventual break with the Council of Basel.

The beginning of this break can be discerned in Nicholas' last major contribution during this period, *On Presidential Authority in a General Council* (text 3). This work is rooted in the doctrine of concord, but it addresses a divisive issue, the relationship of the pope to the majority at a general council. In 1434 the majority, having secured the agreement of Pope Eugenius to continuing at Basel, was faced with a group of presidents he had named to lead them. This led to an effort to impose on the presidents an oath of obedience to conciliar decisions. In this context Nicholas, supporting the more conciliatory agenda of Cardinal Giuliano Cesarini,[9] the original papal legate to the council, argued for unanimity and consent of all in conciliar affairs. Eventually he would conclude that

such unanimity was becoming impossible and would leave Basel. Like Cesarini, one of his mentors, Nicholas made his peace with the pope and supported him against the Basel assembly. That Eugenius was trying to hold a council of reunion with the Greeks may have helped persuade Cusanus that true concord might be achieved under the papal aegis.[10]

The Hercules of the Eugenians

Cusanus' second phase of writing on the Church, when he emerged as a champion of the pope, began with his mission to Constantinople. Thereafter, although deeply committed to working out the philosophical implications of his shipboard experience, in his public life Nicholas was representing Eugenius before the princes of the Holy Roman Empire.[11] In this context he began rewriting his ideas on representation and consent to show that Basel had lost its legitimacy, rejected by the Church at large and by the Christian princes. While working in defense of Eugenius, Nicholas composed orations and memoranda opposing conciliar supremacy as the Basel majority, in opposition to the papacy, had defined it. Even while Cusanus sojourned in Germany, events took place that were shaping the challenges he faced. The Council of Ferrara-Florence in 1439 not only negotiated a union of Eastern and Western churches but also reaffirmed papal primacy. The Council of Basel, in the same period, declared conciliar supremacy a dogma of the Church and declared Eugenius deposed. They elected in his place Amadeus VIII, duke of Savoy, who chose to reign as Felix V.[12]

The most important confrontation between the representatives of Basel's pope, Felix V, and those of Eugenius took place at the Diet of Frankfurt in 1442. The Amedeists, as Cusanus called them, were represented by the canon lawyer Nicholas de

Tudeschis, archbishop of Palermo, known as Panormitanus.[13] Nicholas himself spoke for the Eugenian party. Both delivered extensive orations that they later documented in writing, quoting from Scripture, theological works, legal sources and documents. Aeneas Sylvius Piccolomini, the later Pope Pius II, was present at this and later assemblies. He derided efforts to convince princes with books and long-winded speeches. (In fact, the princes went hunting and left their advisers to hear these orations, which went on for three days each.)[14] We must recall, however, that the failure of either party to present its case would have cost it dearly in the competition for support within the Empire. Moreover, the *Oration at the Diet of Frankurt* (text 4) marks a stage in the development of Nicholas of Cusa's thought on the Church. He defended papal sovereignty, backing it with his revised idea of representation. Representation no longer had to be via councils. The consent of the princes and peoples throughout Christendom provided representation and validated the continued reign of Pope Eugenius.[15]

During this period the German princes adhered to a form of neutrality, refusing to side with either claimant while implementing reforms enacted at Basel. This indecision was formalized in the so-called Acceptation of Mainz (1439).[16] Neutrality was unacceptable to either party represented at Frankfurt. Nicholas himself took the time to rebuke the Germans in two memoranda on neutrality (texts 5–6), declaring a choice of allegiance a religious necessity. The unity of Christ's flock did not suffer division, and that unity required acceptance of the legitimate pope as the visible head of the ecclesiastical body.

Nicholas undertook a defense of the Eugenian case in another form. He composed a dialogue refuting the errors of his opponents, using a less thorny style to present the same case for Eugenius, the same ideas about representation and obedience. The *Dialogue against the Amedeists* (text 7) has no clearly defined audi-

ence or target. It is possible that Nicholas used it to work out issues he faced at the imperial diets and other gatherings he attended. The legal precedents and historical arguments employed are the same as those found in the *Oration*. They simply are expressed in a more accessible style and with fewer references to legal texts. The *Dialogue* is especially worthy of attention as evidence that Cusanus was working out the implications of his break with Basel even as the council's apologists were quoting his earlier works against him.[17]

Although the papacy defeated the Council of Basel and Felix V resigned in favor of Nicholas V, Cusanus' labors on behalf of Rome did not end. His legation to the lands of the Holy Roman Empire (1451–1452) brought him once more into contact with the Hussites. The papacy still was not prepared to embrace the concessions Basel had made to the Bohemians, and extended negotiations by the legate about restoration of uniform liturgical practice failed. As legate, Cusanus pulled together his correspondence on liturgical conformity in a *Letter to the Bohemians on Church Unity* (text 9), which synthesizes points made throughout his correspondence with Bohemia.[18] The argument that the authority of the Church was superior to that of Scripture in the area of liturgy was a continuation of ideas the young Cusanus had expressed in his early years at Basel.

Explicatio Petri

The Eugenian labors of Cusanus were simultaneous with his turn toward metaphysical speculation. The emphasis on human limitations in grasping God can be found in both his treatises and his surviving sermons. Citing 1 Corinthians 13:12, Nicholas even wrote of the way in which "the truth is learned . . . only through mirror images and enigmas" in a sermon given at Koblenz in 1439–1440

(text 8). Christ was the means of attaining such knowledge as humans could attain.[19] This emphasis on limits is set alongside a discussion of the Church. The Church, he said, is "a union of rational spirits with Christ, the head." But this Christological emphasis did not prevent Cusanus from emphasizing obedience as an element in the Christian life within the Church Militant. This sermon is a bridge to a reconsideration by Nicholas of his views on the Church in the light of learned ignorance.

This reconsideration is most evident in Nicholas' *Letter to Rodrigo Sánchez de Arévalo* (text 10). This missive was composed on the eve of the Diet of Frankfurt in 1442. It reads very differently than does the *Oration*. The legal references are minimal, and the Church is seen through different eyes. It is described as a "conjectural Church" (*ecclesia coniecturalis*) which can be discerned by signs but cannot be fully grasped. The Church is described as unfolded from Peter (*explicatio Petri*). This permits a certain papalist "spin" to the letter, but the emphasis falls elsewhere. Peter's faith is more crucial in this letter than is his office. Peter's faith caused him to conform to Christ, and all Christians — including the pope — were expected to do the same. Here Cusanus looks beyond the Basel schism to ultimate things, to Christ, uniting humanity with divinity, and to a union in which human beings share through Petrine faith.[20]

This same theme emerges in Nicholas' sermons from the period (texts 11–14). Peter's faith, not his office, is most crucial in these sermons for feasts of the Prince of the Apostles. This reveals a certain ambivalence on Cusanus' part in the sermons about Peter. Even the pope is assessed, in Nicholas' thought, first as a believer conforming to Peter's faith. Nonetheless, when preaching on Peter's keys, the symbol of his authority, the cardinal was quick to remind his hearers that the human imperfection of the shepherd does not authorize rebellion by the sheep.[21] This latter emphasis, found most notably in Nicholas' preaching to his turbulent diocese

of Brixen, may reflect the experience of resistance to reform by
secular clergy, religious and laity alike.[22]

Reform and Christiformitas

The final phase of Nicholas' writing on the Church also overlaps
with its immediate predecessor. Nicholas had written extensively
on reform in *The Catholic Concordance*. Thereafter he had not written on the subject at length, despite his reforming labors as legate
and diocesan bishop. Nonetheless, the topic became crucial again
in Nicholas' last years. He preached reform from the pulpit in
Brixen and Rome. This later preaching on reform had a strong
theological bent. The Christian was expected to achieve reform by
Christiformitas, conforming his life and devotion to Jesus himself.
These sermons (texts 15–16) set a high standard for the believer,
one congruent with Nicholas' attack (as legate) on superstitious
veneration of relics, like the bleeding hosts of Wilsnack, as an im-
proper substitute for real belief.[23]

Nicholas also took part in an unsuccessful effort to reform the
Roman Curia. Pope Pius II proposed such a reform, although he
did not carry it through. His efforts to organize a crusade against
the Turks took precedence.[24] Nicholas, nonetheless, made a substantial contribution to reform thought in his *A General Reform of
the Church* (text 17), which Pius used in a draft bull of reform. This
proposal required that reform begin with the head. The pope was
to accept reform by a small group of respected ecclesiastics. After
that, reform would spread through the Curia by both authority
and example. From Rome the effort would spread throughout the
Church. A pope who accepted Christiform reformation would be
best able to implement this far-ranging reformation of the Church,
both in head and members.[25]

After Nicholas died at Todi in 1464, he would be better re-
membered at first for his metaphysical writings, but *The Catholic*

Concordance would reappear in the 1514 Paris edition, together with the *Letter to Rodrigo Sánchez de Arévalo* and excerpts from the sermons about Peter, putting Nicholas' thought on the Church back into circulation on the eve of the Reformation.

The translator is grateful to many people. Professor Hans Georg Senger kindly shared drafts of his editions of *De usu communionis*. The late Dr. Heinrich Paulli gave the translator typescript editions of sermons in the process of being edited. Gerald Christianson, Christopher Bellitto and Margaret Schaus read drafts of the introduction and the translations to help improve their clarity. Publishers permitted revision of translations previously published,[26] and members of the American Cusanus Society provided input concerning translations used at more than one of the Society's Gettysburg conferences. Colleagues in Germany provided guidance in finding texts not yet in the translator's hands. As at the Academy Awards, I could read a very long list of those worthy of sharing any praise. The blame for the remaining blemishes is my own.

The translator also owes a great debt of gratitude to editors and publishers. Permissions to republish translations already in print were readily granted, and the right to use Latin texts was conceded by several publishers and text editors. Nothing would have been possible without this kind cooperation.

NOTES

1. *The Catholic Concordance*, trans. Paul E. Sigmund (Cambridge: Cambridge University Press, 1991).

2. On the ecclesiastical politics of the Empire, see Joachim Stieber, *Pope Eugenius IV, the Council of Basel and the Secular and Ecclesiastical Authorities in the Empire: The Conflict over Supreme Authority and Power in the Church* (Leiden: Brill, 1978).

3. See the letter to Cardinal Giuliano Cesarini in Nicholas of Cusa, *Selected Spiritual Writings*, trans. H. Lawrence Bond (New York: Paulist Press, 1997), pp. 205–206.

4. For a brief biography, see Donald F. Duclow, "Nicholas of Cusa, 1401—August 11, 1464" in *The Dictionary of Literary Biography, Volume 115: Medieval Philosophers*, ed. Jeremiah Hackett (Detroit: Gale, 1992), pp. 289–305. For a more detailed introduction to Nicholas' life and thought, see *Nicholas of Cusa: A Guide to a Renaissance Man*, ed. Christopher M. Bellitto, Thomas M. Izbicki and Gerald Christianson (New York: Paulist Press, 2004).

5. F. Edward Cranz, "Development in Cusanus?" in idem, *Nicholas of Cusa and the Renaissance*, ed. Thomas M. Izbicki and Gerald Christianson (Aldershot: Ashgate, 2000), pp. 1–18.

6. E. F. Jacob, "The Bohemians at the Council of Basel," in *Prague Essays, Presented by a Group of British Historians to the Caroline University of Prague on the Occasion of its Six-Hundredth Anniversary*, ed. R. W. Seton-Watson (Oxford: Clarendon Press, 1949), pp. 81–123.

7. Thomas Prügl, "The Concept of Infallibility in Nicholas of Cusa," in *The Legacy of Learned Ignorance*, ed. Peter J. Casarella (Washington, D.C.: The Catholic University of America Press, 2006), pp. 150–177.

8. Paul E. Sigmund, *Nicholas of Cusa and Medieval Political Thought* (Cambridge, Mass.: Harvard University Press, 1963); Morimichi Watanabe, *The Political Ideas of Nicholas of Cusa with Special Reference to His De concordantia catholica* (Geneva: Droz, 1963); Giuseppe Alberigo, *Chiesa conciliare: Identità e significato del conciliarismo* (Brescia: Paideia, 1981).

9. Gerald Christianson, "Cusanus, Cesarini and the Crisis of Conciliarism," in *Conflict and Resolution: Perspectives on Nicholas of Cusa*, ed. Inigo Bocken (Leiden: Brill, 2004), pp. 91–103.

10. The reasons for Cusanus' change of allegiance remain controversial. See James E. Biechler, "Nicholas of Cusa and the End of the Conciliar Movement: A Humanist Crisis of Identity," *Church History* 44 (1975): 5–21; Joachim Stieber, "The Hercules of the Eugenians at the Crossroads: Nicholas of Cusa's Decision for the Pope and against the Council in 1436/37: Theological, Political, and Social Aspects," in *Nicholas of Cusa: In*

Search of God and Wisdom, ed. Gerald Christianson and Thomas M. Izbicki (Leiden: Brill, 1991), pp. 221–255.

11. On the ideological dimensions of this diplomatic conflict, see Antony Black, *Monarchy and Community: Political Ideas in the Later Conciliar Controversy 1430–1450* (Cambridge: Cambridge University Press, 1970), pp. 85–129.

12. On the events of this period, see Joseph Gill, *The Council of Florence* (Cambridge: Cambridge University Press, 1959).

13. Morimichi Watanabe, "Authority and Consent in Church Government: Panormitanus, Aeneas Sylvius, Cusanus," *Journal of the History of Ideas* 33 (1972): 217–236.

14. *Reject Aeneas, Accept Pius: Selected Letters of Aeneas Sylvius Piccolomini (Pope Pius II)*, ed. and trans. Thomas M. Izbicki, Gerald Christianson and Philip Krey (Washington, D.C.: The Catholic University of America Press, 2006), pp. 361–362, Letter 76.

15. Thomas M. Izbicki. "Representation in Nicholas of Cusa," in *Repraesentatio: Mapping a Keyword for Churches and Governance. Proceedings of the San Miniato International Workshop, October 13–16 2004*, ed. Massimo Faggioli and Alberto Melloni (Münster: Lit Verlag, 2006), pp. 61–78.

16. Morimichi Watanabe, "Nicholas of Cusa, the Council of Florence and the *Acceptatio* of Mainz (1439)," in *The Divine Life, Light and Love, Euntes in mundum universum: Festschrift in Honour of Petro B. T. Bilaniuk*, ed. Renate Pillinger and Erich Renhart (Graz: Andreas Schnider Verlags-Atelier, 1992), pp. 103–115.

17. On the use of excerpts from *The Catholic Concordance* and *On Presidential Authority in a General Council*, see Thomas M. Izbicki, "Auszüge aus Schriften des Nikolaus von Kues im Rahmen der Geschichte des Basler Konzils," *Mitteilungen und Forschungsbeiträge der Cusanus-Gesellschaft* 19 (1991): 117–135.

18. F. M. Bartos, "Cusanus and the Hussite Bishop M. Lupac," *Communio Viatorum* 5 (1962): 35–46.

19. Walter Andreas Euler, "Proclamation of Christ in Selected Sermons from Cusanus' Brixen Period," in *Nicholas of Cusa and His Age: Essays Dedi-*

cated to the Memory of F. Edward Cranz, Thomas P. McTighe and Charles Trinkaus, ed. Thomas M. Izbicki and Christopher M. Bellitto (Leiden: Brill, 2002), pp. 89–103.

20. Thomas M. Izbicki, "The Church in the Light of Learned Ignorance," Medieval Philosophy and Theology 3 (1993): 196–214.

21. Thomas M. Izbicki, "An Ambivalent Papalism: Peter in the Sermons of Nicholas of Cusa," in Perspectives on Early Modern and Modern Intellectual History: Essays in Honor of Nancy S. Struever, ed. Joseph Marino and Melinda W. Schlitt (Rochester, N.Y.: University of Rochester Press, 2001), pp. 49–65.

22. Morimichi Watanabe, "Nicholas of Cusa and the Tyrolese Monasteries: Reform and Resistance," History of Political Thought 7 (1986): 53–72.

23. Morimichi Watanabe, "The German Church Shortly Before the Reformation: Nicolaus Cusanus and the Veneration of the Bleeding Hosts at Wilsnack," in Reform and Renewal in the Middle Ages and the Renaissance: Studies in Honor of Louis Pascoe, SJ, ed. Thomas M. Izbicki and Christopher M. Bellitto (Leiden: Brill, 2000), pp. 210–223.

24. Robert H. Schwoebel, "Coexistence, Conversion and Crusade against the Turks," Studies in the Renaissance 12 (1965): 164–187. Cusanus' own attitude toward Islam has been explored by several scholars; see particularly James E. Biechler, "A New Face Toward Islam: Nicholas of Cusa and John of Segovia," in Nicholas of Cusa: In Search of God and Wisdom, pp. 185–202; Jasper Hopkins, "The Role of pia interpretatio in Nicholas of Cusa's Hermeneutical Approach to the Koran," in Concordia discors: Studi su Niccolò Cusano e l'umanesimo europeo offerti a Giovanni Santinello, ed. Gregorio Piaia (Padua: Editrice Antenore, 1993), pp. 251–273; James Hankins, "Renaissance Crusaders: Humanist Crusade Literature in the Age of Mehmed II," Dumbarton Oaks Papers 49 (1995), pp. 111–207 which puts Cusanus' attitude toward the Turks into a broader context. Also: Nancy Bisaha, Creating East and West: Renaissance Humanists and the Ottoman Turks (Philadelphia: University of Pennsylvania Press, 2004).

25. Morimichi Watanabe, "Nicholas of Cusa and the Reform of the Roman Curia," in Humanity and Divinity in Renaissance and Reformation: Essays in Honor of Charles Trinkaus, ed. John O'Malley, Thomas M. Izbicki and

Gerald Christianson (Leiden: Brill, 1993), pp. 185–203; Morimichi Watanabe and Thomas M. Izbicki, "Nicholas of Cusa, *A General Reform of the Church*," in *Nicholas of Cusa on Christ and the Church: Essays in Memory of Chandler McCuskey Brooks for the American Cusanus Society*, ed. Gerald Christianson and Thomas M. Izbicki (Leiden: Brill, 1996), pp. 155–202.

26. See H. Lawrence Bond, Gerald Christianson and Thomas M. Izbicki, "Nicholas of Cusa: On Presidential Authority in a General Council," *Church History* 59 (1990): 19–34 [text 3]; Izbicki, "The Church in the Light of Learned Ignorance" [text 10]; Watanabe and Izbicki. "Nicholas of Cusa, *A General Reform of the Church*" [text 17]. All the translations reprinted here have been thoroughly revised.

WRITINGS ON CHURCH
AND REFORM

De usu communionis ‹ad Bohemos›

‹Pars Prima›

Dirige, domine deus meus, in conspectu tuo viam meam!

1   Quoniam variae et innumerabiles sunt quaestiones, quae ad opera obscurissima dei sive ad scripturarum abditissimas latebras pertinent, quas aliquo genere complecti ac diffinire difficile est, et multa ibi ignorantur salva fide et alicubi erratur absque haeretico crimine, ut ait ille veritatis prudentissimus praedicator Augustinus secundo libro *De originali peccato*, hinc qui nimis amat sententiam suam usque ad praecisionem communionis et condendi schismatis vel haeresis sacrilegium diabolica praesumptione detineri dicatur. Est enim angelica perfectio in nullo aliter sapere quam se res habet. Recte, quamdiu per futuram resurrectionem istam angelicam perfectionem assecuti non fuerimus, nos admonet magnus Leo, evangelicae veritatis tuba, ne nos diabolica praesumptio apprehendat neque alia temptatio secundum apostolum quam humana; maxime hoc verum in fidei causa, quoniam, cum ipsa raro perfecta sit et nullibi periculosius erretur, temeraria praesumptio periculosissima est. Imbuti enim infidelitatis venenis animi non possunt impietatis suae glutinum abolere, si praesumptuositate virus infaustum inoleverit. Quare nervi sunt et quidam artus sapientiae in fidei causa non temere credere, uti Ambrosio ad Constantinum *Epistula XXXVII* placere videtur. Hinc sapientis Sophronii patriarchae Hierosolymitani sententiam in VI universali synodo prolatam amplectamur: non sibi quisquam credat, sed cum aliis pariter conferat Pauli exemplo, ne paternos terminos sua confidentia

To the Bohemians: On the Use of Communion

[First Part]

Lord and God, *direct my way in Thy sight.*[1]

There are various and innumerable questions pertaining to the 1
hidden works of God or the hidden recesses of the Scriptures
which are difficult to unfold and define in a particular genus, and
there are many things unknown therein except by faith. Occa-
sionally there is error without heretical crime, as Augustine, that
most prudent preacher of truth, says in the second book of *On
Original Sin.*[2] Therefore, whoever loves his own opinion to the
point of breaking communion and promoting the sacrilege of
schism or heresy is said to be possessed by diabolical presumption.
It is an angelic perfection to know things precisely as they are.
And rightly so, for until we shall attain this angelic perfection
through the future resurrection, Leo the Great,[3] trumpet of evangelical truth, warns us not to let diabolical presumption or any
temptation other than a human one lay hold of us, according to
the apostle; this is especially true in a matter of faith. Faith rarely
being perfect and error being nowhere more dangerous, rash presumption is most perilous [in matters of faith]. Souls steeped in
the poisons of infidelity cannot dissolve the glue of their impiety if
presumption implants the unfortunate venom. Wherefore, "these
are the sinews and joints of wisdom in a matter of faith, not to
believe rashly," as Ambrose appears to hold in his *Letter 37* to
Constantine.[4] Hence let us embrace the opinion of the wise
Sophronius, patriarch of Jerusalem, made known at the sixth universal synod.[5] No one should trust himself; but he should confer
with others, following the example of Paul, lest by trusting himself
he should overleap the ancestral boundaries. Then, having pre-

transiliat et tunc in quod—pace et unitate ecclesiae servata—pervenerit secure ambulare poterit.

2   Vos vero Bohemi, qui quadam singularitate sub religionis specie quoad usum divinissimae eucharistiae a reliquo corpore ecclesiae cum pacis et unitatis ruptura abscisi estis, contrarium huius agitis quod praedicatis. Nam cum hoc summum convivium non solum sit sacramentum unitatis corporis Christi in altaris sacramento, sed et etiam in pacis vinculo, ut vult Augustinus in *De ostensione ecclesiae ad Donatistas*—est enim mysterium unionis cum capite et membris Christi, ut idem ait de sacramentis fidelium, feria secunda Paschae—, non recte veneramini unitatis sacramentum, quo ipso in schismaticam divisionem utimini. Non rectam fidem sacramenti tenetis, si separati a corpore Christi vivere per ipsum putatis. Christus quidem, caput ecclesiae, vita est, quae non vivificat nisi unita membra. Quare, cum extra pacem et unitatem ecclesiae sitis, non vitam sed mortis iudicium exspectatis. Revertimini igitur ad ecclesiam a qua exivistis citius, ne id vobis contingat, quod Elias vicarius Hierosolymorum ad Theodorum Critinum spernentem venerandas imagines in octava generali synodo dixit, quoniam, qui diuturnae sectae inserviunt, difficile habent a mala qua tenentur opinione evelli. Ferreis enim catenis diabolus mentes ipsorum constrictas tenet. Ad memoriam revocate patrum gesta et comperietis in synodalibus gestis omnem particularem praesumptionem in fidei causa damnatam et demum afflante divino spiritu evanuisse.

served the peace and unity of the Church, he will be able to walk in it securely.

You Bohemians, however, are cut off from the rest of the 2 Church's body, rupturing its peace and unity, owing to a certain peculiarity, masquerading as religious scruple, in the use of the most divine Eucharist. But you do the opposite of what you preach. For since this supreme banquet is not just the sacrament of the unity of Christ's body in the sacrament of the altar but also in the bond of peace, as Augustine maintains in *On the Manifestation of the Church to the Donatists*[6] — it is the mystery of union with the head and members of Christ, as the same Father says [in his sermon] on the second day after Easter[7] concerning the sacraments of the faithful — we do not venerate the sacrament of unity rightly if we celebrate it in schismatic division. You do not hold the right belief about the sacrament if you think to live through it apart from the body of Christ. Christ, the head of the Church, is the Life who only gives life to members united to Him. Wherefore, when you are outside the peace and unity of the Church, you do not await life but the judgment of death. Return quickly, therefore, to the Church that you have left, lest you experience what Elias, the vicar of Jerusalem, said to Theodore Critinus at the Eighth General Synod in rejecting the veneration of images: that those who serve a long-standing sect have difficulty being uprooted from the evil opinion by which they are held fast.[8] The devil holds their minds bound tight with iron chains. Call to remembrance the deeds of the Fathers and you will find in conciliar records that every particular presumption has been condemned on behalf of the faith and has in the end vanished owing to the inspiration of the divine Spirit.

Argumenta Hussitarum pro diffessione erroris et haeresis suae

3   Forte dicitis: Christus 'via, veritas et vita' est. Per ipsum tantum ad beatitudinem pertingimus et summum bonum apprehendimus. Qui vero in veritate non ambulat, extra viam est. Qui extra viam et veritatem est, vitam aeternam non consequitur. Nos vero, cum via veritatis incedamus in vestigiis patrum nostrorum, qui cum Christo regnant, vitam attingemus, quam et ipsi assecuti sunt. Qui vero per hanc viam non pergit, sed breviorem quaerit, potius de seductione non tritae viae et praecipitatione et praesumptione timere habet, etiam si talis attingeret finem optatum. Cum non ambulet in semita sanctorum tamquam periculo se submittens, sequendus non est. Quid mali nobis ascribi potest, si nulla novitate utimur, si id agimus quod ceteri et insuper id addimus quod patres nostri in usu habuerunt? Si necessarium fuit vel ob Christi praeceptum aut quia ita ipse fecit iudicarunt sanctissimi praedecessores ita faciendum. Recte agimus eos sequendo. Sed apud eos sanguinis communio non necessitate praecepti Christi tradebatur populo. Inefficax tamen non fuit; aliquid gratiae recipienti accrevit. Non possumus reprehendi, si idem agimus. Nam etsi sine communione sacramentali vita haberi posset, non tamen is reprehensibilis est, qui ad communionem accedit, sicut nec corde crede‹n›s inutiliter ad fidei sacramentum accedit.

4   Cur nos manducantes iudicatis, cum vos ieiunantes minime iudicemus? Si credimus communionem nobis praeceptam et eam eapropter summopere tamquam nostram vitam extollimus et appetimus, in quo est delictum? Haec enim fides, quae in augmentum honoris tanti sacramenti tendit, ut credamus sine ipso vitam non esse, quomodo potest reprehendi, etiam si sine ipso vita haberi posset, sicuti habetur ubi affectus adest et deest opportunitas?

The Arguments of the Hussites Defending Their Error and Heresy

Perhaps you say, Christ is *the way, the truth and the life*,[9] through 3
whom alone we attain beatitude and grasp the supreme good.
Whoever does not walk in the truth is outside the way. Whoever
is outside the way and the truth does not attain eternal life. But
when we walk the way of the truth in the footsteps of our fathers
who reign with Christ, we obtain the life they attained. Whoever
does not walk this way but seeks a shortcut has to be afraid of being seduced by the untrodden way and of rashness and presumption, even if he attains the chosen end. Since he does not walk on
the narrow path of the saints, like a man taking risks, he is not to
be followed. What evil can be charged against us if we practice no
novelty, if we do what others do, and, moreover, if we are continuing the practice of our fathers? If it was necessary on account of
Christ's command or his example, our most holy predecessors
judged it must be done. We act rightly by following them. — But
[you say] according to them, communion of the Blood was not
necessarily, by Christ's command, given to the people. — Nevertheless, it was not inefficacious; some grace does accrue to the recipient. We cannot be rebuked if we do the same. For although
[eternal] life may be obtained without sacramental communion,
nevertheless, he is not worthy of rebuke who comes to communion, just as he who believes in his heart does not come uselessly
to the sacrament of faith.

Why do you pass judgment on those of us who eat, when we 4
pass no judgment at all on those of you who fast? If we believe
communion is enjoined upon us and on that account we extol and
desire it exceedingly, as our very life, where is the fault? This faith
then that tends to an increase of honor for so great a sacrament,
so that we believe that there is no life without it, how can it be rebuked, even if life may be had without it, as happens where the
disposition is present and the opportunity is lacking? Do we not

Nonne certum tenemus in hoc sacramento verum corpus Christi veramque vitam esse deum et hominem? Et manifestum est nos sine vita vivere non posse. Si igitur in hac peregrinatione Christus in ecclesia militanti sub sacramentalibus signis latet, quomodo dici potest non cadere sub praecepto ecclesiae dato vivere in Christo volentem ad cibationem istam non obligari? Sicut enim immundus et infirmus, dum per accessionem ad agnum sine macula per fidem mundatur et sanatur dum se ad salvatorem convertit, non tamen in ecclesia nisi signum huius manifeste appareat, ut huius sacramentum baptismus exsistit, ita et mundatus et sanatus in Christo absque refectione et spirituali cibatione vivere nequit. Et licet per internam caritatem Christo adhaereat et vivificante spiritu vegetetur per unionem amantis spiritus hominis et amati dei, non tamen in ecclesia censetur vivere posse absque sacramento in se vitam continente. Si enim gratum et acceptum est deo adhuc quod corde credatur ad iustitiam, quod etiam ore confessio fiat ad salutem, et oris confessio est signum fidei cordis, est clarum in ecclesia obligationem ad signa pertingere—licet signata tunc sufficiant, quando impossibilitas signum ademerit—, sicut amor proximi non sufficit mentalis, nisi opus ad signum accedat, ut compassio vulnerati circa viam non suffecit in sacerdote et levita, sed cum hoc exhibitio operis ut in Samaritano.

5   Impossibilitas autem excusat a signo, sicut egestas in non pascente fame morientem. Quare, cum lex sit possibilium, cadunt signa inquantum possibilia, sicut signata in praecepto: ‹diem sabbatis sanctifices›. Sanctificatio enim sabbati praecepta non recte expletur per separatam internam contemplationem, sed cum hoc

hold it as certain that in this sacrament are the true body and the true life of Christ, God and man? And it is obvious that we cannot live without life. If therefore Christ remains hidden in the Church Militant under sacramental signs while we are on this pilgrimage, how can it be said not to fall under a command given to the Church that anyone wishing to live in Christ is not obligated to this nourishment? Just as the unclean and infirm man, when by gaining access to the Lamb without spot is cleansed by faith and healed when converted to the Savior, is nevertheless not in the Church unless a sign of this manifestly appears, so that baptism exists as a sacrament of this [conversion], so the one cleansed and healed in Christ is not able to live without refreshment and spiritual nourishment. And although he may adhere to Christ by internal love and be quickened by the life-giving Spirit, through the union of the man's spirit that loves and the God who is loved, nevertheless, he is not deemed able to live in the Church without the sacrament containing life in itself. If then it is pleasing and acceptable to God that what is believed in the heart for justice is also confessed with the mouth for salvation, and the confession of the mouth is the sign of the heart's faith, it is clear that obligation in the Church pertains to signs (although the things signified may suffice at a time when it is impossible to use the sign),[10] just as mental love of neighbor does not suffice unless a deed is added to a gesture, just as compassion for the wounded man by the roadside did not suffice in the case of the priest and the Levite, but the performance of a deed along with it did, as in the case of the Samaritan.[11]

Impossibility, however, excuses from the sign, as in the case of a pauper who does not feed someone dying of hunger. So since law is a matter of possible things, signs apply insofar as they are possible, like the things signified in the command *Keep holy the Sabbath*.[12] The command to keep the Sabbath holy is not rightly fulfilled by internal contemplation in isolation, but along with that 5

requiritur huius internae sanctificationis explicata signa addere, ut sunt ecclesiasticae conventiones, sacrificii oblatio cum aliis multis, quae secundum tempus a deo inspirantur. Ita nec in honore parentes habet sufficienter, qui signo hoc non ostendit. Unde, cum deum teneamur quantum possibile est nobis supreme diligere et in ipsa dilectione quantum possibile est dilectioni dei, qua nos dilexit, ut unigenitum pro nobis morti traderet, conformare, erit necessarium huius dilectionis memoriam, mortis et passionis scilicet, nos habere, quoniam per ipsam vitam assequimur. Et huius caritatis, vivificationis, rememorationis mortis non aliud signum nobis relictum est quam communio eucharistiae, per quam mortem domini annuntiamus per memoriae reminiscentiam in nobis esse ac per ipsam nos vivere, donec veniat in alio adventu.

6   Hinc credimus nos recte obligari, dum in hac vita militamus, ad sacramentum divinissimum eucharistiae eo modo, quo perfectius significat passionem, hoc est sub utraque specie, quae corporis laniationem et sanguinis effusionem signat in praeteritum factam ac sub ipsis speciebus eundem sanguinem, idem corpus esse et sumenti per viam refectionis vitam praestare, ut, sicut in morte Christi liberati salvatique sumus, cuius sacramentum baptismus exsistit, ita in resurrectione Christi vivificati. Unde hoc sacramentum eucharistiae immortalis Christi sacramentum est, prout amplius non moritur, sed perenniter vivit, licet memoriam mortis esus, masticatio inter dentes, potatio sive fusio in os deglutitioque repraesentent. Et tamen, quia amplius non moritur, tunc sub signis memoriae mortis vita vivificans capitur. Et quia sacramentum baptismi per immersionem mortem et sepulturam figurat Christi, recte hoc sacramentum completum in se et mortis memoriam et resurrectionis vitam baptismum consequitur, quasi non sit fides,

it is required to add clear signs of this internal sanctification; thus there are ecclesiastical customs, the offering of sacrifice along with many other things, which are inspired by God according to the times. Thus a man does not honor his parents sufficiently who does not show it by means of some sign. Hence, since we are required to love God above all things insofar as is possible for us, and in that love to conform as much as possible to the love of God, who loved us so that he gave his only-begotten Son to die for us,[13] it will be necessary for us to have a memory of this love, that is, of his death and suffering, since through them we attain life. No sign of this love, of this giving of life, of this remembrance of death is left to us other than the communion of the Eucharist through which we proclaim that the death of the Lord exists in us by the recollection of his memorial, and that we live through it until He comes in another advent.

Hence we rightly believe ourselves to be obligated, while we 6 strive in this life, to this most divine sacrament of the Eucharist in the manner wherein it more perfectly signifies the Passion, that is, under both species, which signify the mutilation of the body and the shedding of the blood done in the past; and under these species are the same blood, the same body, offering life to the one who consumes it for refreshment along the way. Just as we were freed and saved in Christ's death, of which baptism is the sacrament, so we are revivified in the Resurrection of Christ. Hence this sacrament of the Eucharist is the sacrament of the immortal Christ, inasmuch as He dies no more but lives forever, although eating, chewing between the teeth and drinking, pouring or swallowing in the mouth represent the memorial of His death. Nevertheless, because he dies no more, at that moment life-giving life is grasped under the signs of the memory of His death. And as the sacrament of baptism by immersion represents the death and resurrection of Christ, this sacrament, complete in itself, both the memorial of His death and the life of His resurrection, rightly

quae vitam praestet, solum in morte Christi sed et resurrectio, qua cuncta completa sunt. Ita patres nostri infantibus et tradiderunt et tradi iusserunt corporis et sanguinis Christi post baptismum sacramenta, ut completam perfectamque fidem, salvationem simul et vitam consequeretur in Christo renatus.

7   Credimus etiam irreprehensibiliter hanc sacratissimam refectionem non tantum necessariam in anno semel, sed pro nostra infirmitate crebriter utilem. Habenti enim corpus debile tanta annalis abstinentia periculosa est a cibo ipsum confortante et vivificante. Ita iudicamus de spiritu nostro et eius alimento spirituali. Unde, si pluries accedimus ad hanc mensam — in hoc sanctiores et fortiores nobis, qui nunc cum Christo regnant, sequentes —, reprehendi non meremur manducantes a non manducante, sicuti nec nos reprehendimus non manducantes. Hoc enim in proba hominis latet, an abstinentia conferat sanitati potius quam cibatio et in medici providentia, cuius vicem pastores credimus gerere, qui ovibus alimenta ministrant aut subtrahunt, prout utilius iudicaverint.

8   Consideramus etiam omne sacramentum signum esse alicuius signati ac causam alicuius effectus gratiae et huiusmodi gratiae per sacramentum acquisitae. Necesse est quemlibet christianum fateri Christum operatorem gratiae esse tenerique christianum ad huius suae fidei sacramentum accedere. Et hoc est sacramentum sacramentorum: sacratissima eucharistia, quoniam adultus credit operatione divina Christi per signa, scilicet verba et elementum et lavationem, gratiam regenerationis et renovationis novi hominis, qui est secundum Christum, conferri; huius totius fidei quoad effectum sacramentalem gratiae eucharistia sacramentum est. Etenim virtute divina per verba ministri sub speciebus sensibilibus elementalibus plenitudo gratiae, veritas et vita, Christus dominus deus et homo, exsistit. Hoc itaque sacramentum est proprie sacramentum

follows after baptism, as though it were not faith alone in the death of Christ that guarantees life, but also the Resurrection, by which all things were fulfilled. Thus our fathers both gave and commanded to be given to infants the sacraments of the Body and Blood of Christ after baptism, so that the man reborn in Christ obtains all at once complete and perfect faith, salvation and life.

It is our irreproachable belief that this most holy nourishment 7 is necessary not just once a year but is useful, received frequently, for our infirmity. For anyone weak in body, such a year-long abstinence from the food that strengthens and gives him life is dangerous. We hold the same view with regard to our spirit and its spiritual feeding. So if we approach the table often — following in this men holier and braver than we, men who now reign with Christ — we who eat do not deserve reproach from those who not eat, just as we do not reproach those who do not eat. In the test of a man it is hidden whether abstinence contributes more to his health than eating; this lies within the providence of a doctor, in whose place we believe pastors act, who serve nourishment to their sheep or take it away, following the course they think most useful.

We consider every sacrament to be the sign of something signi- 8 fied and the cause of some effect of grace, and that graces of this kind are acquired through sacraments. It is necessary that each Christian confess Christ to be the worker of grace and a Christian is necessarily obligated to join in this sacrament of his faith. And this is the sacrament of sacraments, the Most Holy Eucharist, which an adult believes to be conferred by the divine work of Christ through signs (that is, words and element and washing) as the grace of regeneration and renewal of the new man who is a follower of Christ. The Eucharist is the sacrament of this entire faith as far as the sacramental effect of grace. The fullness of grace, truth and life, Christ the Lord, God and man, exists in very deed by divine power through the words of the minister under the sensible species of the elements. And so this sacrament properly is the

alterius cuiuscumque sacramenti et eius effectus. Unde sumitur pro complemento et confirmatione sacramenti alterius et eius effectus, sicut baptismus per catechumenos credentes. Unde fatemur, sicuti quodam loco praedicitur, hoc divinissimum sacramentum — prout datur in robur et complementum aliorum — minus necessarium, quia est ut signum signi et signati. Et cum signum signi legi possibilitatis subsit, signum signi minori necessitati subest; quare, ut est cibatio, fatemur textum 'Nisi manducaveritis carnem filii hominis et sanguinem eius biberitis' etc., cum possibilitate legis sacramentaliter obligatorium est, non tamen adeo obligatorium, dum sumitur pro sacramento sacramentorum, ubi faciliores excusationes admittimus. Et hinc non haesitamus puerum baptizatum, si ante sumptionem eucharistiae decesserit, per effectum prioris sacramenti regnum cum Christo consecuturum, cum hoc habeat, cuius eucharistia sacramentum esset, si sumpsisset.

9　　Laudamus tamen omnia sacramenta hoc sacramentum eapropter sequi, ut perfectissime et signatum et eius confirmatoriale signum per exuberantiorem gratiam consequamur, quoniam eucharistia est ipsa bona gratia simul et sacramentum. Quis in his omnibus simplex oculus nos errare iudicare ‹que› posset, ubi humiliter quantum valemus vestigia praedecessorum, praxim Christi et apostolorum insequimur?

‹Responsio Cusani›

10　Certe, quamquam his rationibus vos colorate nitemini defensare, multa tamen quae agitis reprehensibilia sunt, inter quae hoc maxime quod non cum pace ecclesiae, sed temere et vestra sponte, auctoritate prohibente etiam ecclesia, ritum communionis iam non sine causa quoad sanguinis speciem ad laicos inconsuetum reno-

sacrament of any other sacrament and its effect. Hence it is received for the completion and confirmation of another sacrament and its effect, such as baptism for believing catechumens.[14] Hence we confess, as is preached in a certain passage, that this most divine sacrament — insofar as it is given to strengthen and complete the others — is less necessary because it is like the sign of a sign and of a thing signified. And since a sign of a sign is subject to the law of possibility, a sign of a sign is subject to a lesser necessity; therefore, as it is a feeding, we confess that the text, *Except you eat the flesh of the Son of Man and drink His blood* etc.,[15] although it is obligatory sacramentally by the possibility of law, nevertheless, it is not so obligatory when it is eaten as the sacrament of the sacraments, where we admit easier excuses. Therefore, we do not doubt that a baptized child, if he dies before receiving the Eucharist, reaches the kingdom with Christ by the effect of the prior sacrament, since he had that of which the Eucharist is a sacrament, had he received it.[16]

Nevertheless, we praise the fact that this sacrament follows all 9 the sacraments, because through it we attain most perfectly by abounding grace the thing signified and its confirming sign, since the Eucharist is at the same time good grace itself and a sacrament. What simple eye could err and judge us in all these things when humbly, as best we can, we follow in the footsteps of our predecessors, the practice of Christ and the apostles?

[Cusanus' Reply]

Certainly, although you seek to defend yourselves colorably with 10 these arguments, nevertheless many things you do are deserving of reproach, among them this especially: that without the leave of the Church — even with its active disapproval — you have rashly and by your own will restored to the laity the rite of communion under the species of Blood which, not without cause, they had been un-

vastis, potius eligentes abscindi ab ecclesia quam a renovatione desistere; ubi haec egistis, putantes plus utilitatis vos ex bibitione calicis in separatione quam esu agni paschalis tantum in unitate et pace consecuturos, non recte iudicastis. Non enim utiliter calix domini unionis et pacis pro causa divisionis sumitur, nec vitam conferre potest extra ecclesiam, quae corpus Christi est, absciso membro, nisi reliquum corpus ecclesiae a vobis abscisum vosque veram ecclesiam in parvam Bohemiae portiunculam coartatam perniciosius assereretis.

11   In eadem quidem ecclesia remanente unitate varium posse ritum esse sine periculo nemo dubitat. Ubi vero praesumptuosa temeritas quemcumque ritum unitati et paci praefert, etiam si in se bonus, sanctus laudabilisque foret, damnabilis est. Dicitis praecepto Christi oboediendum esse primo loco, deinde ecclesiae. Et si aliud praeceperit ecclesia quam Christus, non ecclesiae, sed Christo oboediendum.

12   Certe in hoc est omnium praesumptionum initium, quando iudicant particulares suum sensum in divinis praeceptis voluntati divinae conformiorem quam universae ecclesiae. Audi huius similitudinem propinquam, quemadmodum Christus loquitur: 'Nisi manducaveritis carnem filii hominis et eius sanguinem biberitis, non habebitis vitam in vobis.' Ita idem loquitur: 'qui non' resignaverit 'omnibus quae possidet, non potest meus esse discipulus.' Origenes in ultima Homilia super Genesim praeceptum Christi esse ait et negat suum esse discipulum, quem viderit aliqua possidentem. Unde si est praeceptum, ut etiam Hieronymus in secundo *Dialogorum Attici et Critoboli* dicere videtur, tunc quia is solum habebit lumen vitae qui sequitur Christum, et is sequitur qui eius est discipulus, cur apostolici haeretici condemnati sunt, qui ita hoc

used to receive, and you have chosen to be cut off from the Church rather than desisting from reform. When you do these things, you are mistaken in thinking you will receive more utility from drinking the chalice in division than in eating only the Paschal Lamb in unity and peace. The chalice of the Lord, of union and of peace, is not drunk usefully in the cause of division; nor can it confer life on an amputated limb outside the Church, which is the body of Christ, unless you assert, even more perniciously, that the rest of the body of the Church is cut off from you and that you are the true Church, confined though you are to a tiny portion of Bohemia.

No one doubts a different rite could exist without danger and preserving unity within the same Church.[17] When, however, presumptuous rashness prefers some rite or other to unity and peace, even if that rite should be good, holy and praiseworthy in itself, it is damnable. You say: we must obey Christ's command first of all, then that of the Church. If the Church commands other than Christ does, we must obey not the Church but Christ.   11

Certainly in this lies the beginning of all presumption: when individuals judge their own understanding of divine commands to be more conformed to the divine will than that of the universal Church. Listen to a passage similar to the one where Christ says, *Except you eat the flesh of the Son of man and drink His blood, you shall not have eternal life in you.*[18] In like manner he says, *Every one of you that does not renounce all that he possesses cannot be my disciple.*[19] Origen, in his last homily on Genesis, says this is Christ's command and denies that anyone he sees owning something is His disciple.[20] Hence if it is a command, as Jerome too seems to say in the second book of the *Dialogue of Atticus and Critobulus*,[21] then supposing he who follows Christ alone will have the light of life, and whoever is His disciple follows him, why were the "apostolic heretics" condemned who understood the command in this way and carried it out, as Augustine says in the *Catalog of Heretics?*[22] Cer-   12

praeceptum intellexerunt et practicarunt, ut ait Augustinus in libro *Catalogi haereticorum?* Non alia certe de causa quam quod ipsi
se ab aliis possessoribus separarunt iudicantes ita stricte hoc praeceptum sub poena damnationis observandum et practicandum, licet non habere proprium in monachis et plurimis clericis laudabile
sit, ut ibidem Augustinus. Certe tunc laudabile, quando in unitate
ecclesiae huius intellectus praecepti practicatur. Et hoc sit exemplum, ubi pius etiam intellectus praeceptorum cum maceratione,
abstinentia et insecutione vestigiorum apostolorum et praxis
Christi extra unitatem damnatur. Sicut econverso rigorosus intellectus praecepti et devius non damnatur, si unitati ecclesiae non
praeponitur, uti fuit circa baptismum haereticorum sancti Cypriani et septuaginta episcoporum, de quo late per Augustinum
De baptismo et in aliis multis locis.

13   Unde si in symbolo et eius intellectu, praeceptis ac aliis etiam
omnibus sacramentis intra ab ecclesia separatos et ecclesiam
concordia foret, in hoc tantum discordia, quia non uniti cum ecclesia a qua recesserunt, vitam consequi non posse et sacramentorum effectum Augustinus *Contra Vincentium Rogatistam* aperte ostendit. Iste vero in ecclesia remanet, qui suum sensum
praesumptuose non elevat supra dictamen maioris partis sacerdotii, quibus verbum creditum est et qui Christi legatione funguntur.
In oboediendo enim illi sententiae nihil periculi incurrit christianus quam saniorem ecclesiae partem videt affirmare. Hanc quidem
sententiam ex Christi doctrina sanctus Cyprianus eleganter deducit ad Novatianum, ubi ait Christi veracem confessorum maiorem
melioremque partem in vera fide, lege et disciplina dominicae veritatis persistere, quoniam 'portae inferi non praevalebunt adversus

tainly for no other reason than because they separated themselves from others who have possessions, having concluded that this precept must be obeyed and carried out in so strict a way on pain of damnation—although it is praiseworthy for monks and many clerics not to have property, as Augustine says in the same place. Certainly, then, it is praiseworthy when one's understanding of this command is practiced within the unity of the Church. This is an example where a pious understanding of commands about chewing, abstinence and following in the footsteps of the apostles and the practice of Christ is condemned as outside the unity [of the Church]. Just as, to the contrary, a rigorous yet erroneous understanding of a precept is not condemned if it is not preferred to the unity of the Church, as was the opinion of Saint Cyprian and the seventy bishops concerning the baptism of heretics, on which Augustine[23] writes extensively in *On Baptism* and in many other places.

Hence, [even] if there should be concord between the Church 13 and those separated from the Church concerning the creed and how it is understood, her teachings and even all the other sacraments, and discord be confined to this one matter, the separated, since they are not united with the Church from which they withdrew, may not attain [eternal] life and the effect of the sacraments, as Augustine[24] explicitly shows in *Against Vincent the Rogatist*. But that man shall remain in the Church who does not presumptuously elevate his own opinion above the dictates of the greater part of the priesthood, to whom the Word has been entrusted and who represent Christ. In giving his obedience to the opinion which the sounder part of the Church seem to affirm, a Christian incurs no danger. Saint Cyprian, writing to Novatian,[25] elegantly deduces this very opinion from Christ's teaching where he says that the true, the greater and the better part of the confessors of Christ persists in the true faith, law and teaching of the Lord's truth, since *the gates of hell shall not prevail against it.*[26] Truth then inheres in

eam.' Veritas enim cathedrae adhaeret, quare membra cathedrae unita et pontifici coniuncta ecclesiam efficiunt, ut idem Cyprianus ad Florentium ‹et› Puppianum scribit, 'cuius pars habetur' ‹C.› 7 q. 1 ‹c. 7› *Scire debes*; hoc elegantissime Augustinus, Alipius et Fortunatus ad Generosum scribentes ostendunt, dicentes etiam angelo credi non debere potius quam ecclesiae dispersae per orbem, quae Romano pontifici et cathedrae Petri adhaeret. Et pro infallibili regula salutis nostrae Christus hanc tradidit ecclesiae potestatem et auctoritatem, ut, cum in unitate cum ipsa persistimus, quae cathedrae Petri adhaeret, per quam per successores etiam malorum Christo capiti alligatur, errare a via salutis non possimus, etiam si in ipsa ecclesia alius sic, alius sic vadat.

14   Dices fortassis: Ecclesia hodierna non ita ambulat in ritu communionis sicut ante tempora, quando sanctissimi viri utriusque speciei sacramentum necessarium esse vi praecepti Christi et verbo et opere astruebant. Potuitne tunc ecclesia errare? — Certe non. Quod si non, quomodo id hodie verum non est, quod tunc omnium opinione affirmabatur, cum non sit alia ecclesia ista quam illa? Certe hoc te non moveat quod diversis temporibus alius et alius ritus sacrificiorum, etiam sacramentorum stante veritate invenitur scripturasque esse et ad tempus adaptatas et varie intellectas, ita ut uno tempore secundum currentem universalem ritum exponerentur, mutato ritu iterum sententia mutaretur. Christus enim, cui pater regnum caeleste terrenumque tradidit, praesidens miro ordine angelorum hominumque mysteria pro temporum varietate dispensat, et quae singulis temporibus congruunt vel occulta inspiratione vel evidentiori illustratione suggerit. Haec est doctorum

the [episcopal] see, hence the members united to the see and joined to the pontiff make up the Church, "of which [that see] is held to be a part," as the same Cyprian writes to Florentius and Puppinian [in Gratian's *Decretum*], C. 1 q. 1 [c. 7], *Scire debes*. Augustine, Alipius and Fortunatus, writing to Generosus, show this most elegantly when they say that one should rather not believe an angel than the Church dispersed throughout the world, cleaving as it does to the Roman pontiff and the See of Peter.[27] And Christ gave this power and authority to the Church to be an infallible standard for our salvation, so that, when we persist in unity with her who cleaves to the See of Peter, through which — even through [Peter's] wicked successors — she is bound to Christ as her head, we cannot wander from the way of salvation, even if in this very Church one man goes this way, another that.

Perhaps you will say: today's Church does not walk in the rite of communion as in former times, when most holy men affirmed both by word and deed that the sacrament under both species, by the force of Christ's precept, was necessary. Could the Church have been in error at that time? Certainly not! If not, how is what was then universally affirmed not true today, since this Church is the same as that one? Certainly it should not disturb you that the rite of sacrifices — and even of the sacraments — is found to be different at different times, while the truth stands fast. The Scriptures are both adapted to the times and understood in various ways, so that they are set forth at one time according to the current universal rite, but when that rite changes, opinions about it change again. Christ, to whom the Father handed over the celestial and terrestrial kingdoms, ruling by means of a wondrous order of angels and men, dispenses mysteries according to the changing of the times; and He supplies what fits particular times by hidden inspiration or evident demonstration. This is the view of the doctors [of the Church]: Ambrose in his twelfth letter to Irenaeus,[28] and

14

sententia, Ambrosii XII epistola ad Irenaeum, Augustini ad Deogratias in secunda quaestione de mutatione sacrificiorum.

15   Quare, si hoc tempore distantiori a Christo, propinquiori ad
Antichristum ambulantibus nobis in descensu remoto aliorum
vestigiis, vestigiorum alius sit ritus quam fuerit, non tamen extra
veritatem eapropter sumus constituti, ut idem Augustinus ad Esi-
cium monachum de die novissimo scribens aperte declarat. Quare,
si etiam hodie alia fuerit interpretatio ecclesiae eiusdem praecepti
evangelici quam aliquando, tamen hic sensus nunc in usu currens,
ad regimen ecclesiae inspiratus uti tempori congruus, ut salutis via
debet acceptari, sicut de baptismi forma apostolorum tempore, ubi
'in Christi nomine,' et aliorum sequenti, ubi 'in trinitatis nomine',
et post hoc 'in nomine patris et filii et spiritus sancti' varietatem legimus secundum temporis congruentiam salutem praestitisse, ip-
sumque divinum praeceptum 'nisi quis renatus fuerit' et 'ite baptizate' etc. interpretationem tempori congruentem absque errore
recepisse uno tempore currente usu validam, alio invalidam. Cuius
sententiae etiam in septuaginta interpretibus Augustinum fuisse
XVIII libro *De civitate dei* legitur, arguens ex concordia tot inter-
pretum inspirationem divinam credi debere, etiam si inveniretur
aliud ab originalibus detractum vel additum, hoc eodem spiritu
instigante actum quo originale dictatum. Hanc sententiam radicem universalium conciliorum in omnibus paene conciliis reperimus canonizatam, quia ex unanimitate omnium etiam paucis resistentibus inspirationem divinam sententiam dictasse legitur.

16   Fatuum est ergo argumentum velle universalem ecclesiae ritum
ex scripturis praedecessorum arguere. Legitur enim apostolos non

Augustine [in his letter] to Deogratias, in the second question on the alteration of sacrifices.[29]

Hence, if in this time we are walking at a greater distance from Christ and nearer to the Antichrist, on a downward path remote from the footsteps of others, and our rite departs from their footsteps, we nevertheless are not for that reason placed outside the truth, as the same Augustine explicitly declares, writing to Hesychius the monk about the end of time.[30] Hence, even if today there is an interpretation by the Church of the same Gospel command differing from that of former times, nevertheless, the understanding now currently in use for the rule of the Church was inspired as befitting the times and should be accepted as the way of salvation. Just so we read that the variation in the form of baptism — in the time of the apostles it was performed "in the name of Christ;" in later times "in the name of the Trinity," and after that "in the name of the Father, the Son, and the Holy Ghost" — this variation, fitting to the times, brought salvation. And those divine commands *Unless someone be reborn*, and *Go forth and baptize*,[31] have taken on without error an interpretation befitting the times that was valid usage at one time, invalid at another. Augustine was of this opinion even in the case of the seventy translators,[32] as we read in Book 18 of *The City of God*, and argued from the harmony of so many translators that one should credit their divine inspiration, even if discrepancies with the original [Hebrew] should be found, as these discrepancies were dictated at the instigation of the very same Spirit who dictated the original.[33] We find this opinion, the root of the universal councils, canonized in almost all councils, since we read that divine inspiration had dictated the decision from the unanimity of all, even when a few resisted it.

Thus it is a foolish argument that aims to censure the universal rite of the Church from the writings of our predecessors. We read that the apostles did not transmit the faith through writings but

15

16

tradidisse fidem per scripturas, sed per vocalem impressionem bre-
vissimi symboli, ubi inter quae salvando necessaria narrantur ecclesiae sanctae ac sanctorum communio narratur. Unde scripturae
de bene esse regiminis ecclesiae, etiam inceptae et continuatae nequaquam de essentia exsistere possunt, quia per imperium tyranni
antichristiani omnes cremari et de mundo tolli possent, et quondam libri Veteris Testamenti per Esdram laboriose recuperati.
Unde cum possibile sit, non erunt de essentia scripturae cremabi-
les ecclesia semper persistente; et tunc manifestum est, cum in veritate persisteret hoc ut verius sequendum, quod universalius com-
muniusque foret, illisque ex Symbolo Apostolico necessario
communicandum, qui maiorem sanioremque ecclesiae partem effi-
cerent. Videmus etiam in scripturarum intelligentia varia hominum ingenia varios sensus explicare variamque auctoritatis scripturarum opinionem exsistere possibileque fore aut in auctoritate
earundem aut intellectu inextricabilem dubiositatem hominum
mentes suspendere. Ubi tunc erit solidum refugium peregrinantium? Certe in alio nullo quam in militantis ‹ecclesiae› usu atque
approbatione, sive hoc sit circa scripturam et eius auctoritatem
atque intellectum sive extra scripturam in consuetudine accepta
per ecclesiam. In his enim firmitas est, ut in solida petra ac veritatis columna lex exarata, quae talia dictat acceptanda aut sententia
cui oboediendum aut opere in quo concurrendum. Et ita via
cuiusque in ecclesia exsistentis est, ut per ecclesiam ad scripturam,
eius intellectum aut usum non scriptum convertat se, non ut per
eius scripturarum auctoritatem ad ecclesiam pergat et eam, si cum
scriptura non concordat, iuxta priscorum aut suum intellectum in
operis exercitio impune spernere possit et scripturae inhaerere.

by oral expression of a short creed, wherein are mentioned, among other things necessary for salvation, "the communion of Holy Church" and "of the saints."[34] Hence writings concerned with the well-being of Church government, even ones begun and continued, can by no means be essential, since they could all be burned up and removed from the world by the command of some anti-Christian tyrant, and [in fact] the books of the Old Testament were once laboriously recovered by Ezra. So since this is possible, writings that can be burned are not of the essence, while the Church lasts forever; and then it is obvious, since it will persist in the truth, that what is the more universal and common must be observed as the more true, and to those who make up the greater and sounder part of the Church this [greater truth] must be communicated of necessity from the Apostles' Creed. We see in the interpretation of the Scriptures the various minds of men explicating various meanings; we see various opinions existing about the authority of the Scriptures; we see it is possible for there to be inextricable doubt about their authority or their interpretation, leaving the minds of men in suspense. Where then will there be a reliable refuge for wayfarers? Surely it is to be found in nothing else than in the usage and approval of the Church Militant, whether the doubt is about Scripture, its authority and interpretation or, outside Scripture, about a custom accepted by the Church. There is firmness in these things, like a law carved in solid rock and on the column of truth, which dictates that such things must be accepted, either by a decree that must be obeyed or by an act with which we must concur. And so the way of anyone existing in the Church is that he converts himself through the Church to Scripture, her interpretation [of it] and her unwritten practice; he does not come to the Church through the authority of her Scriptures; and he may not spurn her with impunity if she is not in harmony with Scripture and stick to Scripture in his religious practice, according to his own interpretation [of it] or that of the ancients.

17   Haec enim est omnium sane intelligentium sententia, qui scripturarum auctoritatem aut intellectum, ut Augustinus de evangeliis
dicit, in ecclesiae approbatione fundant, quae unam accipit et
aliam spernit; et non econverso ecclesiae firmamentum in scripturarum auctoritate locant, licet etiam ecclesia ex scripturis per ipsam acceptis et approbatis ‹adversus eos›, qui ipsam impugnare
quaerunt, et non scripturis se iuvare consueverit. Et econverso
scripturae, si impugnentur in sua auctoritate per communionem
ecclesiae habente, pro sua validitate ad ecclesiae acceptationem refugium peta‹n›t, ut ita in communi medio disceptantes concordent
in veritate. Tamen possibile non est scripturam quamcumque
apud in ecclesia exsistentes — sive ipsa praeceptum sive consilium
contineat — plus auctoritatis ligandi habere aut solvendi fideles,
quam ipsa ecclesia voluerit aut verbo aut opere expresserit. Si enim
dictaverit praeceptum ut dei praeceptum in scriptis redactum ac-
ceptandum per medium ecclesiae, auctoritas manifestata reveren-
ter est amplectenda; si vero scripturam acceptat et ipsam per communem usum etiam aliter quam priores practicando intelligit, ita
cum tali intellectu auctoritatem habeat; si, ut concilium dixerit, ecclesia scripturam, etiam in verbis praeceptivis explicatam, verbo vel
praxi acceptandam, cum non habeat aliud auctoritatis quam uti
per ecclesiam, dictatur, non ad verba, sed ad experimentalem sensum ecclesiae obligor, quoniam ecclesia est quae non habet maculam neque rugam erroris et falsitatis. Est enim corpus Christi, qui
est veritas, et sic spiritu veritatis continue vegetatur et regitur, quia
in ecclesia loquitur Christus et in Christo ecclesia: Augustinus super Psalmo XXX et in sermone eiusdem *De die Pentecostes*. Et ipsa
ecclesia de se ipsa hoc testimonium perhibet in oratione quam pro
ordinatis fundit in die Parasceves.

This is decidedly the view of all persons of understanding. 17
They base the authority or interpretation of the Scriptures, as
Augustine says of the Gospels, on the Church's approval, which
accepts one and rejects another;[35] they do not, to the contrary, lo-
cate the stability of the Church in the authority of the Scriptures,
although the Church is accustomed to assist herself from the
Scriptures, accepted and approved by herself, against those who
seek to impugn her, and not from the Scriptures [alone]. To the
contrary, if the Scriptures are impugned in the authority they have
from their common use by the Church, they may take refuge for
their validity in their acceptance by the Church, so that those disagreeing about a common area of dispute may agree on the truth.
Nevertheless, it is not possible for any Scripture that exists in
the Church, whether it contains a command or a counsel, to have
in itself more authority to bind and loose the faithful than the
Church herself wishes or expresses in word or work. If it has dictated a command as a command of God, and produced it in writing, to be accepted through the Church as intermediary, the authority manifested is to be embraced reverently. If, however, it
accepts the Scripture and interprets it in practice through common use otherwise than as those who came before us did, it has
authority in this way with such an understanding. If the Church
dictates a scripture, for example in a council, even one spelled out
in explicit teaching, as something to be accepted in word and
deed, since it has no authority apart from the Church's I am not
bound to its words but to its meaning as experienced in the
Church, since it is the Church that is without *stain or wrinkle*[36] of
error and falsity. It is the body of Christ, who is Truth;[37] and so it
is continuously quickened and ruled by the spirit of truth, because
"Christ speaks in the Church and the Church in Christ": Augustine on Psalm 30 and in his sermon *On the Day of Pentecost*.[38] And
the Church herself bears witness concerning herself in the prayer
for those who are ordained, intoned on Good Friday.[39]

18   Dicetis forsitan: Praecepta Christi quomodo mutabuntur auctoritate ecclesiae, ut sint tunc obligatoria, quando ecclesiae placuerit? Dico nulla esse Christi praecepta quam per ecclesiam pro talibus accepta, ut praehabitum est. Si igitur constat ecclesiam illa
praecepta et talia laudare, illis ut praeceptis Christi oboediendum
esse nemo ambigit. Si vero circa praecepti intellectum et eius ex-
pletionem diversitas concurrat aut ex loco aut tempore, hic intellectus laudatus intelligitur, quem maior vel sanior pars verbo aut
opere approbat, non obstante quod aliquando alius intellectus in
practica viguit. Et non est haec mutatio tamquam a minori Christi
auctoritate praecipientis dependens, quoniam ecclesia, quae est
corpus Christi et eius Spiritu vegetatur, non aliud agit quam
Christus vult. Et ita mutatio ista interpretationis a Christi voluntate ita nunc volentis et inspirantis dependet, sicut praeceptum ipsum quondam iuxta illius temporis convenientiam aliter practicatum et propterea haec ligandi et solvendi potestas non minor est in
ecclesia quam in Christo. Unde Augustinus libro quarto De baptismo: 'Munus beatae vitae non nisi inter ecclesiam reperitur, quae
supra petram etiam fundata est, quae ligandi et solvendi claves accepit. Haec est una, quae tenet et possidet omnem sponsi sui et
domini potestatem.' Idem ipse in septimo libro ac aliis diversis locis. Ait enim ipsa Veritas: 'Non relinquam vos orphanos', sed 'vobiscum sum' omni tempore 'usque ad consummationem saeculi.'
Quare universa catholica ecclesia ad Petri cathedram conglobata a
Christo numquam recedet qui veritas est, cum qua Christus semper se mansurum pollicitus est. Varia sunt huius veritatis exempla.
Nonne praeceptum sabbati ante Christi adventum per ecclesiam,
quae tunc una fuit cum ista, intellectum et practicatum fuit de

Perhaps you will say: how is it that the commands of Christ are   18
to be changed by the authority of the Church, so that they are
binding only when it pleases the Church? I say there are no commands of Christ other than those accepted as such by the Church,
as was said above. If therefore it is evident that the Church ap-
plauds those commands and the like, no one can be in doubt that
he must obey them as commands of Christ. If, however, disagree-
ment arises concerning the interpretation of a command and its
execution on account of time or place, that interpretation is considered plausible which the greater or sounder part approves by
word or work, notwithstanding that at some time another interpretation prevailed in practice. And this change is not like depend-
ing on the lesser authority of Christ as teacher, since the Church,
which is the body of Christ and is quickened by His Spirit, does
nothing other than what Christ wishes. And so the change of interpretation depends on the will of Christ, who now wills it so by
His inspiration, just as once this very precept was practiced otherwise, according to the need of the time. And, therefore, this power
to bind and loose is no less in the Church than in Christ. Hence
Augustine in the fourth book of *On Baptism:* "The gift of a blessed
life is found only within the Church which is founded on the rock,
which receives the keys of binding and loosing. This is the one
that has and possesses all the power of its Spouse and Lord."[40] He
says the same in the seventh book and in several other places. The
Truth Himself says, *I will not leave you orphans,* but *I am with you
always even to the consummation of the world.*[41] Thus the universal
Catholic Church, gathered together at the See of Peter, never
withdraws from Christ, who is Truth, since Christ promised to remain with her always. There are various examples of this truth.
Was not the command to keep the Sabbath interpreted and kept
on the seventh day before the coming of Christ through the
Church, who at that time was together with her? After the coming
of Christ, however, it was kept on the first day, which is the first

septimo die? Post vero Christi adventum practicatum in prima feria, quae prima sabbati est, non sine maximo mysterio huius praecepti expletio ita introducta est a sancto spiritu, licet non constet
nobis hoc Christum voluisse aliter quam ex communi ecclesiae observantia, quae sibi displicere nequit. Et tamen non venit solvere
legem Christus sed adimplere. Unde praeceptum sabbati iuxta voluntatem praecipientis, licet non sic ut quondam servetur, non tamen solvitur sed adimpletur.

19   Idem in sacramento matrimonii probatur. Nonne deus dictus
est ab initio eos coniungere, qui intentione et consensu mutuo
concurrente contraxerunt praeceptumque est hominem separar‹e›
non debere, quos deus coniunxit? Et manifestum est, cum in paradiso institueretur, hoc sacramentum non habuisse quamcumque
graduum aut personarum exceptionem. Et tamen in temporis suc-
cessu opportunitate superveniente dictavit ecclesia infra certos gradus coniunctionem irrationabilem et iudicavit, si infra eos gradus
coniungerentur, amplius separandos esse, qui tamen ante tamquam a deo coniuncti non separabantur. Et communiter in novo
testamento visum fuit post aliquot tempora rationabile fore quod
in sacris ordinibus exsistentes non contraherent similiter nec solemniter voventes, quod si facerent, separandos esse, qui tamen
ante tamquam a deo coniuncti separari non potuissent; sic communiter de septimo gradu consanguinitatis et affinitatis et demum
de quinto gradu, et talia similia exempla plura tam in aliis sacramentis quam praeceptis.

20   Quare manifestum: Sicut non iudicamus deum eos coniungere,
quos ecclesia iuxta temporis qualitatem rationabiliter non iudicat
coniungibiles, licet hoc idem alio tempore ante et post rationabile

day of the Sabbath. Not without the greatest mystery was the fulfillment of this command thus introduced by the Holy Spirit, although it will not be evident to us that Christ willed this otherwise than through the common observance of the Church, which is unable to be displeasing to Him. Nevertheless, Christ did not come to abolish the law but to fulfill it; hence in accordance with the will of the Teacher the command about the Sabbath, although it is not now observed as it once was, is nevertheless not abolished but fulfilled.

The same is proved by the sacrament of matrimony. Did not 19 God declare from the beginning to join together those who, agreeing with intent and mutual consent, contract matrimony, and is it not commanded that man should not separate what God has joined? And it is obvious, since it was instituted in Paradise, that the sacrament did not make any exceptions regarding degrees of consanguinity.[42] Nevertheless, with the passing of time, as occasion arose, the Church ruled marriage within certain grades unreasonable; and it decreed that, if anyone married within those grades, they were to be separated afterwards, notwithstanding that previously they were not separated, as though joined by God. And it was generally seen in the New Testament after a certain time that it was unreasonable, similarly, for those in holy orders to make marriage contracts and take solemn vows [of matrimony], but if they did so, they were to be separated. Nevertheless, before that time, they could not have been separated, as if joined by God. Thus it happened, generally, with regard to the seventh degree of consanguinity and affinity,[43] and finally with regard to the fifth. And there are many similar examples to be found in the case of the other sacraments and commands.

So it is obvious: for just as we do not conclude that God joins 20 those whom the Church on reasonable grounds judges unable to marry in accordance with the circumstances of the times (although at another time, both before and after [the present time], it will

iudicaverit, ut de prohibitione usque ad septimum gradum, licet
etiam circa ipsas personas et qualitatem ipsarum nihil sit innova-
tum, sic et iudicamus deum per quaecumque praecepta non aliud
praecipere velle, quam quod ecclesia iuxta temporis condicionem
rationabile iudicaverit verbo vel opere, ut in primitiva ecclesia hoc
praeceptum proprium non habendi fuit per ecclesiam simpliciter
per omnes ut sonat acceptum, ut in Actibus Apostolorum et in libro Hieronymi *De illustribus viris,* ubi de Philone Iudaeo scribitur.
Hoc enim tunc conveniebat paucitati Christianorum et plantationi
ecclesiae. Post hoc vero intrante multitudine gentium non ita universaliter conveniebat. Unde secundum rationabilem temporis
congruentiam idem praeceptum absque errore tunc per omnes,
postea per aliquos, monachos scilicet, exstat adimpletum. Habemus itaque — si ab omnibus scrupulositatibus, quae circa praecepta
et eorum intelligentiam aut variam ecclesiae consuetudinem intelli-
gendi aut operandi secundum praecepta Christi aut patrum, erui
voluerimus —, scilicet quod ad ecclesiam firma fide et confidenter
concurramus, aliud extra ipsam si invenerimus pro nostra salute
minime curantes.

21   Forte cogitatis in his dictis meis hoc dubium remanere, ex quo
reprehensionis vestrae sumimus argumentum. Puta dicitis: De ecclesiae potestate nemo catholicus ambigit; sed quod illa veritatis
columna sit, quae cathedrae Petri ac Romanae sedi adhaeret, nondum probatum est sufficienter. Iam hoc per scripturas ab illa ecclesia approbatas, Augustini in allegato loco et alibi, Hieronymi ad
Damasum xxiiii, quaestione prima *Haec est fides,* per Ambrosium,
Athanasium ac alios laudatos doctores, sacratissima oecumenica
totius orbis concilia: Ecclesia a principio hoc ex ore Christi prola-
tum 'Tu es Petrus et super hanc petram' verum esse asseruit, do-

judge this same act to be reasonable, for example, a prohibition within the seventh degree, even supposing there is nothing different about those persons and their condition), in the same way we judge that God via commands of whatever sort wishes to command only what the Church shall judge by word or deed to be reasonable according to the condition of the time, just as in the primitive Church the command not to possess property was accepted by the Church simply and literally for everyone, as in the Acts of the Apostles and in Jerome's book *Concerning Illustrious Men*, where he is writing about Philo the Jew.[44] This precept was appropriate at that time given the small number of Christians and the need to establish the Church. Afterwards, however, when a multitude of nations had come into the Church, it was no longer universally fitting. Thus, in keeping with a reasonable sense of temporal fitness, the same command once fulfilled by all without error was fulfilled afterwards by some, namely monks. And so, if we wish to root out all scruples about teachings and their interpretation or the varied practice of the Church in interpreting or acting in accordance with the precepts of Christ or the Fathers, we have to have recourse to the Church with firm faith and confidence; if we find something apart from her, we care too little for our salvation.

Perhaps, having considered these words of mine, there remains some doubt about the basis for the assertion that you deserve rebuke. Consider, you say: no Catholic doubts the power of the Church, but it has not yet been sufficiently proven that sticking to the See of Peter and the Roman See is her column of truth. Now this has been shown already from writings approved by the Church in the passage cited from Augustine, and elsewhere in the words of Jerome to Damasus [in Gratian's *Decretum*], C. 24 q. 1 c. *Haec est fides* [c. 14]; by Ambrose, Athanasius and other approved doctors. The Church from the beginning asserted, taught and preached as true the statement promulgated from the mouth of

21

cuit et praedicavit. Et [quoniam] promissio Christi, quod ‹portae› inferi adversus ipsam numquam praevalebunt, hactenus ad eam ecclesiam, quae ad ipsam sedem tamquam primam unita est, veraciter tenuit. Licet non omnes in ea sede successive praesidentes primi in sanctitate praestitissent, non tamen hoc cathedrae obfuit neque obest, ut idem Augustinus in praeallegata epistola scribit. Veritas enim cathedrae per Christum alligata est, quando dixit 'Super cathedram Moysi' etc., non personis, quia ait: 'quae faciunt facere nolite.' Nolo tamen, ut ex loco auctoritatem arguamus, cum possibile sit aliquando ibi non futurum pontificem aut urbem opprimi ab infidelibus aut desolari, sed ex prioritate episcopi super ceteros, in quo prior principatus et altior super quosque exsistit.

22   Quare, cum nullo tempore a principio nascentis ecclesiae in alio cuiuscumque loci episcopo prior principatus fuerit quam in Petro, qui etsi in aliis locis ut transiens pontificis officio usus fuerit, in urbe tamen Romana ut in finali ad quam tendebat ipsum principatum erexit eamque sedem martyrio consecravit, hinc iubet Augustinus: Si scire velis an in ecclesia exsistas, hanc ut agas rationem, si cathedrae Romani pontificis adhaereas, quae per continuas successiones bonorum malorumque in Petrum principem continuatur. Credendum est hanc sedem sacratissimam quoad locum etiam inexterminabilem et tamen, si casu Romana ‹urbs› deficeret, ibi veritas ecclesiae remanebit, ubi principatus et Petri sedes modo praedicto. Cum enim episcopi succedant apostolis, primo apostolo recte primus succedit episcopus, ad quemcumque etiam particularem locum alium a Romana urbe fuerit sedes contracta. Nec potest haec quoquo modo cavillari iuxta sancti Cypriani sententiam, quia, cum populus adhaerens pontifici particularem constituat ec-

Christ, *Thou art Peter and upon this rock* [etc.].[45] And Christ's prom-ise [in the same passage] that *the gates of hell will* never *prevail against it* has thus far held true for that Church which is united to that see as her first see. Although not all those who presided successively in that see excelled as first in sanctity, this was still no bar to that see, nor is it so now, as the same Augustine writes in the letter previ-ously cited. Truth was tied to the see by Christ when He said, [*The scribes and Pharisees sit*] *on the seat of Moses*, not to persons, for He says, *Do not wish to do what they do*.[46] Nevertheless, I do not wish to affirm his authority on the basis of a place [i.e. Rome] — since it is possible that at some time a pontiff will not be there or that the City [Rome] will be oppressed by infidels or left deso-late — but from the priority of its bishop over all others, for in him is the first and higher principate, superior to any others.

Thus at no time from the beginning of the new-born Church   22 was there a principate higher than that of Peter in any other bishop of any other place. Peter, though passing through other places and exercising the office of pontiff, nevertheless erected that principate in the city of Rome, as the last city to which he directed his course, and he consecrated that see with his martyrdom. Hence Augustine decrees, "If you want to know whether you are in the Church, take account of whether you are holding fast to the see of the Roman pontiff, which through a continuous succession of good and bad men follows upon Peter as its prince." One must believe this most holy see is unlimited with respect to place, and nevertheless, if by chance the city of Rome should fail, the truth of the Church will remain where the principate and see of Peter shall be, in the aforesaid way. Since bishops stand in succession to apos-tles, the first bishop rightly stands in succession to the first apostle, even should the see be withdrawn from the city of Rome to any other place whatever. Nor can this be quibbled about in any way, according to the opinion of Saint Cyprian, because, as a people ad-hering to a pontiff constitute a particular church, and as there is

clesiam et cum unus sit per orbem episcopatus, qui suo priori adhaerere debeat, Romanae scilicet sedi, erit necessario catholica ecclesia illa, quae primae sedi Petri adhaeret. Et licet saepe multi
schismatica divisione ab illa Romana ecclesia recesserint, numquam tamen fuit, quin maior fidelium numerus in unitate illius
Romanae ecclesiae ex fidelibus et primo episcopo compactae per-
severaret, quare in ea nostrae saluti necessaria remansit hactenus et
remanebit veritatis columna.

23   Huius stabilis veritatis exempla plura legimus: Quotiens aliae
ecclesiae, maxime Constantinopolitana a fide erraverit et ab ipsa
Romana fatua praesumptione se absciderit et demum ad unitatem
ipsius et oboedientiam reducta sit? Si quis scire voluerit, libellum
Leonis IX *Contra praesumptiones Michaelis Constantinopolitani patriarchae* legat, simul et antiquorum conciliorum gesta in Constantinopoli, in urbe Romana ac Lugduno et alibi celebrata revol-
vat; ita de Alexandrina ac aliis patriarchalibus sedibus paria plura
inveniet. Nullum tamen eorum de Romana ecclesia aut quod ipsa
umquam a fide erraverit aut per quamcumque sedem fuerit reducta comperiet; sed sicut aliae ab ipsa aliquotiens recesserunt in
erroremque ceciderunt, ita per principatum fortissimum Petri de-
biles demum confortati in fide ad eius unionem reducti sunt.

24   Unde infallibilitatis refugium est in unione esse cum principe in
ecclesia, qui omnis principatus spiritualis tam Petri inter apostolos
et Iudaeos quam Pauli inter gentes uti legitimus successor
utriusque potestatem habet ob salutem Christi fidelium in aedificationem ecclesiae. Nec mysterio caret Romanum pontificem auctoritate principum Petri et Pauli ligare et solvere, quoniam horum

one episcopate throughout the world which ought to stick to its predecessor, that is, to the Roman see, the Holy Catholic Church necessarily will be the church that adheres to the first see of Peter. And although many may withdraw from that Roman church in schismatic division, nevertheless, the greater number of the faithful will always persevere in the unity of the Roman Church, made up of the faithful and their principal bishop. Hence the pillar of truth in those things necessary for our salvation has remained up to now and shall remain.

We read many examples of this fixed truth. How many times 23 have other churches, especially that of Constantinople, strayed from the faith and cut themselves off from the Roman church by foolish presumption, and were at last brought back to unity with and obedience to her? If anyone wants to know, let him read the book of Leo IX *Against the pretensions of Michael, the Patriarch of Constantinople*, and peruse in it the records of the ancient councils celebrated in Constantinople, in the city of Rome, in Lyons and elsewhere. He will also find many like things concerning Alexandria and other patriarchal sees. Yet he will find nothing like this in the case of the Roman church, either that it ever strayed from the faith or that it was brought back [to the true faith] by some other see. Just as others withdrew from it from time to time and fell into error, so they, weak as they were, in the end were strengthened in faith by Peter's most powerful principate and brought back to union with it.

Hence the refuge of infallibility is to be in union with the 24 prince in the Church, who holds universal power of spiritual rule as the legitimate successor both of Peter's power among the apostles and the Jews and of Paul's among the Gentiles, in the interests of the salvation of Christ's faithful in the building of the Church. Nor is it without mystery that the Roman pontiff by the authority of the princes Peter and Paul binds and looses, since he is their only successor. And both princes raised up the reputation of a sin-

unicus successor exsistit. Et ambo principes unius sedis et episcopatus titulum erexerunt, ut in universa ecclesia ex Iudaeis et gentibus congreganda tunc unus principatus in uno episcopatu ac una Christi ecclesia exsisteret. De utriusque tam Petri inter apostolos et Iudaeos quam Pauli inter gentes primatu immediate a Christo utrique collato Ambrosius eleganter explicat *Super epistolam ad Galatas*, quae hoc nobis insinuat. Potuit tamen uterque undique ecclesias fundare tam in circumcisione quam praeputio, licet principalis commissio cum primatu Petri fuerat in circumcisione et Pauli in praeputio. Nec in hoc alter alteri suberat, sed ambo sub Christo immediate, ut ait Ambrosius ibidem et secundo libro *De spiritu sancto*. Idem ait Augustinus super eadem epistola ad Galatas et Hieronymus ‹C.› 2 q. 7 ‹c. 33› *Paulus*. Tamen inter hos primatus prior erat Petri quam Pauli, qui meo iudicio, licet in circumcisione se primo dilataret, irrestrictus tamen erat ex consequenti quoad gentes. Et ita ex ipsa prioritate primatus Petri irrestrictaque potestate apostolatus, missionis et legationis Christi possemus dicere nihil Petro defuisse, quod singulariter Paulo collatum sit a Christo. Quare actum est divina ordinatione, ut, etiamsi quid fundandae sedi primatus in tota ecclesia Petro quoad gentes defuisset, Pauli primatus concurreret, qui una die tamquam unus communis principatus sedem glorioso martyrio consecraverunt, ut dicit Ambrosius ‹C.› 2 q. 7 ‹c. 37› *Beati*. Qui quidem unicus primatus per singulos successores in ecclesia viget cum plena ligandi solvendique potestate.

gle see and episcopate, so that in the universal Church gathered from the Jews and the Gentiles there should exist but one principate in one episcopate and one Church of Christ. In Ambrose's *Commentary on the Letter to the Galatians*,[47] he elegantly elucidates the primacy both of Peter among the apostles and the Jews and of Paul among the Gentiles, conferred immediately by Christ on both (a meaning implicit in [Paul's] letter). Nevertheless, both apostles could found churches everywhere both among the circumcised and the uncircumcised, although the principal commission in the case of Peter's primacy was to the circumcised and in the case of Paul to the uncircumcised. Nor was either one subject to the other in this; but both were immediately subject to Christ, as Ambrose says at the same place and in the second book of *On the Holy Spirit*.[48] Augustine says the same thing in explicating the same the epistle to the Galatians,[49] and Jerome too [in Gratian's *Decretum*] C. 2 q. 7 c. *Paulus* [c. 33]. Nevertheless, as between the two of them the primacy of Peter was prior to that of Paul. The former, in my opinion, although he spread the Gospel first among the circumcised, was nevertheless not restricted, by consequence, as regards the Gentiles. And so we can say from the very priority of Peter's primacy and the unrestricted power of the apostolate of Christ's mission and legation, that nothing was lacking to Peter that was conferred individually by Christ on Paul. Hence it was enacted by divine ordination that, even if in the whole of the church something was lacking to Peter with respect to the Gentiles in founding the primacy of his see, the primacy of Paul was joined to it. The two of them on a single day, as though they held a single principate in common, consecrated the see with glorious martyrdom, as Ambrose says [in Gratian's *Decretum*] C. 2 q. 7 c. *Beati* [c. 37]. This single primacy has flourished in the Church through each of their successors, with full power to bind and loose.

25   Nec est opus hoc loco investigare an ideo veritas infallibilis sit
in ea ecclesia: quia ad sedem illam unitur, tamquam a sede rivus
ille veritatis privilegialiter emanet, vel eapropter quia episcopatus
ille ecclesiam amplectitur, ideo ille episcopatus ab ecclesia infallibilitatem sortiatur aut neutrum horum, quoniam puto quod hoc
non sit ad nostrum propositum necessarium, licet credam ex mu-
tua adhaerentia exsurgere infallibilitatem sicut esse humanum ex
unione animae et corporis. Uti Cyprianus dicit ecclesiam esse in
episcopo et episcopum in ecclesia, ita et hic primatus amplectitur
ecclesiam, sine qua non est et ob quam est; ecclesia amplectitur
principem, sine quo una non est, nec bene persistere potest cum[1]
scissura in unitate. Quae quidem unitas est de essentia ecclesiae ut
primatus propter ipsam unitatem conservandam, ut ait Hieronymus Petro primatum traditum vitandi schismatis causa (*Contra Iovinianum*). Unde—etsi in ecclesia quaedam appareat materialitas,
inquantum subiective consideratur ad regimen principum, et in
primate[2] formalitas, ut ex ipsis tamquam materia et forma constituatur infallibilis illa ecclesia catholica quasi ex utroque consur-
gens—, tamen in parte ecclesiae quaedam prioritas videtur, ut
Hieronymus ait 95. di. *Olim* et 93. di. *Legimus*, sicut et in aliis naturalibus, ubi forma educitur de potentia materiae. Unde de potentia ecclesiae educitur ille primatus, qui eo ipso quod eductus
est, respective se habet ad ecclesiam, propter quam est, et divino
gaudet praesidentiali privilegio ex successione.

26   Et iam ista sufficiant quam breviter, ut sciamus ex mutuo com-
plexu ecclesiae et primatus veritatem ecclesiae persistere infallibili-
ter, sicut individua veritas ex unione naturali et concordanti ma-

There is no need in this place to investigate the reason why in-   25
fallible truth is in that [Catholic] Church: whether it is because it
is united to that see because from it a river of truth flows in a priv-
ileged manner, or because that episcopate embraces [all] the
Church, and so either the episcopate is alloted infallibility by the
Church or neither of them has it. I think it is not necessary [to decide this question] for our purpose, although it is my belief that
infallibility arises from mutual adherence, just as a human being
comes from the union of soul and body. As Cyprian says, the
Church is in the bishop and the bishop in the Church,[50] so also
this primacy embraces the Church, without which it is not and on
account of which it exists. The Church embraces the prince without whom it lacks unity, nor can it well endure with a split in its
unity. This unity is of the essence of the Church, so that the primacy must be preserved for the sake of that unity; as Jerome says
in *Against Jovinian*, the primacy was given to Peter for the sake of
avoiding schism.[51] Hence, although a certain material character is
manifest in the Church, insofar as it may be considered as a substrate in relation to princely rule, and the primacy has a formal
character, with the result that infallible Catholic Church is constituted of these like matter and form, as though arising from both,
there nevertheless seems to be a certain priority on the part of the
Church, as Jerome says [in Gratian's *Decretum*] D. 95 c. *Olim* [c. 5]
and D. 93 c. *Legimus* [c. 24], just as in the case of other natural
things, where the form is educed from the potency of matter.
Hence that primacy is educed from the potency of the Church,
which, from the very fact that it is educed from it, exists relative to
the Church on account of which it exists, and enjoys the divine
privilege of presiding by succession.

And now let these brief remarks suffice for us to know that the   26
truth of the Church persists infallibly from the mutual embrace of
the Church and its primate, just as the undivided [or whole] truth
persists from the natural union and concord of matter and form

teriae et formae de eius potentia eductae et in ipsa inchoatae. Nec
pati potest haec sententia calumniam quoad veritatem salvationis,
quoniam fides ab ecclesia numquam deficiet. Qui hoc non credit,
Christo et veritati non credit. Qui autem fidem habet et apud cor
suum irreprehensibilis est, cum fiducia impetrat, quia 'mandata
servat', 1 Io. c. 3. Quare ecclesia, pro tempore iudicans ita expedire
uti agit, irreprehensibiliter sequenda est, quia fidem habet et 'mandata servat', etiam si in hoc iudicio expedientis deciperetur, sicuti
cum iudex falso testimonio circumventus excommunicat insontem,
cum nihil agat, in quo cor suum eum reprehendat, adhuc mandata
non transgreditur, sed ipsa servat, cum dicant secundum allegata
et probata iudicandum. Et innocens oboediendo sententiae et se a
corpore domini eapropter separans non perdit gratiam aut vitam
quam ex sacramento consequeretur, sed ecclesiae etiam deceptae
oboediendo in omissione salutem consequitur.

27   Dico in omittendo alias licitum et sanctum, si non prohibitum,
sive ibi causa subsit sive non, sive illa causa quae subesse debet aut
propter quam vera sit sive non, quoniam in omittendo aliquem licitum meritorium actum non perditur salus, quae per internam
accessionem, ubi per se quis accedit 'ad deum semper viventem', in
perpetuum haberi potest (Ad Hebr. 7), et usque ad illum voluntatis internum liberum actum ecclesiae prohibitio non attingit. Et
ideo, cum absque periculo salutis omitti possit actus de genere bonorum, ne detur rebellandi potestas per inoboedientiam, potius
est oboedientia eligenda, sine qua nemo virtuosus esse potest,
quam ex praesumptione innocentiae prohibitus actus faciendus.
Non tamen ideo in faciendo aliud ex iudicis praecepto, quod illici-

and is educed from its potency and founded upon it. Nor can this opinion suffer calumny as far as the truth of salvation is concerned, since faith will never fail the Church. Whoever does not believe this does not believe Christ and the truth. Whoever has faith and is blameless in his heart prays with trust because *he keeps the commandments.*[52] Thus the Church, judging according to the times that it is expedient to act in such-and-such a way, must be followed blamelessly because it holds the faith and *keeps the commandments,* even if it is deceived in its judgement of expediency, just as when a judge, tricked by false testimony, excommunicates an innocent person. Although he does nothing for which his heart rebukes him, still he does not transgress the commandments but keeps them, since they say a man is to be judged according to what has been alleged and proved. And the innocent man by obeying the sentence (and for that reason separating himself from the body of the Lord), does not lose grace or the life that follows from the sacrament; but by obeying the Church even when it is deceived, he attains salvation by omission.

I say [he attains salvation] in omitting [to perform] an other-   27
wise licit and holy act [i.e., taking communion], if the act is not prohibited, whether or not the plea is admissible there, or whether it is a plea that should be admissible and relative to which it is true or not, since salvation is not lost by omitting some licit meritorious act, as perpetual salvation can be obtained by internal approach [i.e., by an inward act, without the sacrament], when on his own someone approaches *the ever-living* God (Hebrews 7[:25]); and the Church's prohibition does not affect that free internal act of the will. And so an act belonging to the genus of good acts can be omitted without peril to salvation, lest there be granted the power to rebel through disobedience. Obedience, without which no one can be virtuous, must be chosen in preference to performing a prohibited act from a presumption of its innocence. Nevertheless, I ought *not* to obey and do an illicit act in accordance with

tum est, oboedire debeo, ubi iudex circumventus hoc praecepit, quod ego eum praecepisse non praesumo, si veritatem scivisset, quoniam, si sine dei offensione peragi nequit, potius tunc deo quam iudici oboediendum, ne perdam salutem iuxta Iacobi apostoli sententiam: Qui 'in uno' offendit, 'omnium reus' erit, ut in c. *Literas, De restitutione spoliatorum, De sententia excommunicationis, Inquisitioni*; ‹C.› 11. q. 3 ‹c. 97›, *Qui resistit*, cum sequentibus ibi positis.

28   Dico, quando praesumo si veritatem scivisset, non mandasse, quoniam non est voluntas ecclesiae nisi ob causas propter quas, quibus cessantibus absque perplexitate — quoniam ita vult ecclesia — potius deo oboedire debeo, cuius mandatum propter causarum falsitatem non est per ecclesiam epieikeizatum. Secus igitur, si ecclesia divinum praeceptum limitaret aut interpretaretur epieikeizando ex causis quas rationabiles iudicaret et quae veritati subessent, impune is dispensatione ecclesiae tunc utitur, ubi causae concurrunt vel mandato sine animae detrimento parebit, immo impune non parere non poterit, uti probatur hoc quoad praeceptum sabbati in c. *Licet, De feriis.*

29   Quare manifestum est, quocumque modo constat de voluntate ecclesiae pura illi oboediendum est, tam in omittendo quam faciendo, alias ut ethnicus habendus qui ecclesiam non audit; si condicionalis fuerit voluntas, inquantum scilicet causae verae fuerint, quae causam praestant praecepto aut prohibitioni, si praeceptum alias illicitum foret et causae falsae, non vult ecclesia quod oboediatur. In prohibitionibus vero, etiam ex falsa causa, quae apud ecclesiam verum praesumitur, ob bonum oboedientiae etiam

a judge's commands, when a defrauded judge commands it, on the presumption that he would not have commanded it if he had known the truth, since, if it cannot be carried out without offense to God, then God must be obeyed rather than the judge, lest I lose salvation, according to the opinion of the Apostle James, *Whoever offends in one thing will be guilty of all*, as in [the *Decretals*] c. *Literas* [X 2.13.13], *De restitutione spoliatorum*, *De sententia excommunicationis*, c. *Inquisitioni* [X 5.39.44], [and Gratian's *Decretum*] C. 11 q. 3 c. *Qui restitit* [c. 97], with the texts following in that place.

I say "on the presumption that he would not have commanded 28 this if he knew the truth," because there is no will of the Church except in applicable cases, and when these are no longer in effect — since the Church wishes it so — I should rather, without perplexity, obey God, whose command the Church does not annul on grounds of equity because of false pleas. To the contrary, therefore, if the Church should limit the divine command or interpret it on grounds of equity from cases that it judges reasonable and which are subject to truth, the man then makes use of the Church's dispensation with impunity, where cases are parallel or he will obey without detriment to his soul; indeed he will not be able *not* to obey with impunity, as is proved in the case of the command to observe the Sabbath, [cited in the *Decretals*] c. *Licet, de feriis* [X 2.9.3].

Hence it is obvious that he must obey it in whatever way is 29 consistent with the pure will of the Church, in omitting as in doing, or be considered a heathen who does not heed the Church. If this will were conditional on the truth of the pleas presented for command or prohibition, if the command should be otherwise illicit and the pleas false, the Church does not want them obeyed. But in the case of prohibitions, even those based on a false plea which the Church assumes to be true, one must abstain even from licit things for the sake of the good of obedience, [as in Gratian's

a licitis est abstinendum, ‹C.› II. q. 3 *Quid ergo*, uti in iniusta excommunicatione ex falsa causa, ‹C.› II. q. 3 *Sententia pastoris*, et matrimonio prohibito in sacris exsistentibus seu prohibitis gradibus et aliis multis exempla patent.

30   Habemus itaque reprehensibilem esse omnem praesumptionem contra ecclesiae ritum inoboedientiamque usque ad schismaticam divisionem damnabilem non obstante quocumque colore — aut ex praxi aut scriptura quacumque — pro resistentia et inoboedientia allegato et assumpto. Ex qua conclusione evacuatur omnis vestra intentio cum suis quibuscumque rationibus, cum et usus universalis ecclesiae hodiernus ac Romanae et praeceptum in ipso usu rationabiliter fundatum nullam excusationem admittant.

‹Pars Secunda›

31   Quamquam satis aperte constet ex praehabitis non convenire vobis Bohemis ex quacumque causa non consentiente catholica ecclesia propria auctoritate communionem renovare sub utraque specie et hinc verum non est plus gratiae ex duplicis speciei communione vobis advenire, sed minus, quamdiu in schismate hoc agitis neque etiam patiente ecclesia plus aliis sub panis tantum specie communicantibus gratiae consequeremini, cum nihil usu ecclesiae approbante ipsis desit, quod recipere teneantur et non receperint, tamen hanc partem clariorem faciam brevi manuductione.

32   Arbitraria potestas ecclesiae credita irrestricte a sponso ligandi et solvendi iudicat et discernit inter meritoria opera. Et unum praefert alteri secundum locum et tempus iudicium variando, uti

Decretum] C. II q. 3 c. *Quid ergo* [c. 99].[53] Examples of this are clear in the case of an unjust excommunication because of a false plea, [as in Gratian's *Decretum*] C. II q. 3 c. *Sententia pastoris* [c. 1], and of marriage prohibited to those in holy orders or within prohibited degrees, and in many other things.

Thus we hold every presumption contrary to the rite of the   30 Church to be reprehensible and disobedience up to the point of schismatic division damnable, notwithstanding any colorable arguments — either from practice or scripture of any kind — cited and adopted for the purpose of resistence and disobedience. From this conclusion your every intention is voided with its arguments of whatever kind, since the current usage of the universal Church and the command of the Roman church, founded reasonably on this very usage, admit of no excuse.

[Second Part]

It will be sufficiently evident from the foregoing that it is not ap-   31 propriate for you Bohemians to restore communion under both species on your own authority for any reason without consent of the Catholic Church. Hence it is not true that more grace rather than less comes to you from receiving communion under both species. For as long as you do this in separation [from the Church], you do not obtain more grace than do others who communicate only under the species of bread with the permission of the Church, since the latter lack nothing, owing to their approval of the Church's usage, in that they are restrained from receiving [the cup] and do not receive [it]. Nevertheless, I shall make this part clearer by a brief overview.

The discretionary power of the Church to bind and loose, be-   32 lieved to have been conferred by her Spouse unrestrictedly, judges and discerns among meritorious works; and it prefers one to another by varying its judgment according to time and place, as the

quondam vita coniugalis virginali, post hoc virginalis coniugali praelata exsistit. Et de his multas ex tempore circa sacrificia et sacramenta mutationes legimus. Et non est dubium, quin pro tempore exsistens iuxta Salomonis doctrinam suum iudicium et sensum, ne propriae innitatur prudentiae, ecclesiae iudicio subicere et confirmare habeat; quam ergo secundum hoc iudicium operatur, per cordium et voluntatis scrutatorem remuneratur iuxta fervorem operantis. Quare necesse erit iudicium ecclesiae in illis conforme esse iudicio dei remunerantis ita ut, sicut quondam coniugium praeferebatur castitati per ecclesiam, ita et apud deum remunerantem, et postea mutato iudicio ecclesiae mutatum esse et dei iudicium. Si itaque ecclesia aliquem actum ob causas tunc temporis existentes iudicat actum magni meriti et alio tempore alium maioris — uti pro refectione pontis pacis tempore necessarii iudicat contributionem maximi meriti propter periculum totius rupturae incumbentis, non tanti si periculum non adesset; alio vero guerrarum tempore propter hostiles incursus, qui per pontem ipsum in patriae laesionem fiunt, iudicat magnum meritum contribuere pro destructione eiusdem pontis; et talis suum iudicium exprimit cum numero indulgentiarum temporis maioris et minoris, et operans seu contribuens nunc refectioni nunc destructioni secundum iudicium ecclesiae meritum per tempus mensuratum gradualiter, prout tempus sonat, consequitur — erit manifestum magnitudine meriti plurimum a iudicio ecclesiae dependere.

33   Quare, si ecclesia nunc iudicat contribuentem duos denarios pro aliquo pio opere consecuturum meritum ut decem, et alio tempore — aut paupertate hominum superveniente aut caritate refrigescente aut nemine ad pontem oculum habente ad hoc quod et

married life at one time was preferred to the virginal, and after that the virginal to the married. On these subjects we read about many changes in sacrifices and sacraments [that have been made] on account of the times; and there is no doubt that a person living at a given time, according to the teaching of Solomon, is required to subject and confirm his judgment and opinion to the Church's judgment and not rely on his own prudence. Whatever, therefore, is done according to this judgment will be rewarded by the Searcher of hearts and the will according to the fervor of the one who acts. Thus it will be necessary for the judgment of the Church to be conformable in these things to the judgment of the God who rewards us, so that, just as marriage once was preferred to chastity by the Church, and so too by the God who rewards, [yet] afterwards, when the judgment of the Church changed, God's judgment too changed. If, therefore, the Church judges some act of great merit on account of the causes existing at that time and a different act of greater merit at another time — as it judges a contribution of an obliging friend for the repair of a bridge in time of peace to be of the greatest merit when that bridge is in imminent danger of collapsing, less so if there is no such danger; but in wartime it judges it of great merit to contribute for the destruction of the same bridge when a hostile invasion might use the bridge to inflict injury on the fatherland — it expresses this judgment through a number of indulgences of longer or shorter duration. And the one working or contributing now for repair, now for destruction, acquires merit, according to the judgment of the Church, measured by gradations of time, as the times dictate. It will be manifest that, in respect of magnitude of merit, one depends very much on the judgment of the Church.

Thus if the Church now judges that someone who contributes 33 two pennies for some pious work should obtain merit like one who gives ten, and at another time, either because poverty has set in or charity has grown cold or because no one is keeping an eye

pons reficiatur et caritas reviviscat — iudicat unum denarium dantem idem meritum ut decem consecuturum, non dubium quin diverso tempore idem meritum sequatur opus simplex quod quondam duplum.

34   Pariformiter de gratia sacramentali. Si ecclesia quem excommunicat ut Paulus Corinthium, non hoc facit ut ipsum gratia et vita privet, quia non mortalis sed medicinalis est excommunicatio, sicut Paulus excommunicavit Corinthium, 'ut spiritus salvus fieret in die domini'. Si igitur ecclesia iudicat convenire saluti excommunicationem, manifestum est oboedientem gratia et vita non privari ex eo, quia ad participationem dominicae mensae non accedit, sed consequitur per actum oboedientiae eandem gratiam vitae. Et sic in oboedientibus ecclesiae eundem finem habet communicatio et excommunicatio.

35   Pariformiter ex eodem ecclesiae iudicio eundem finem gratiae et salutis oboedientes consequuntur ex communione sub una specie nunc sicut quondam sub diversis. Et similiter etiam oboedientes nunc et ecclesiae uniti per eius consensum sub duplici specie recipientes non plus consequuntur quam sub altera tantum usu communi ecclesiae acceptante et approbante.

36   Unde ex communione utriusque speciei, vobis Bohemis hodie illicita quia praesumpta cum scissura ecclesiae, si consentiente ecclesia inoleverit, non plus gratiae et vitae consequemini, quam ante renovationem ex communione sub panis specie fuistis consecuti. Nihil enim vobis tunc defuit, quod ecclesia opportunum iudicaret; quare nihil gratiae quam ex specie sanguinis separatim ex post re-

on the bridge because the bridge has been repaired and charity is flourishing, it judges that someone giving one penny should acquire the same merit as someone giving ten, there is no doubt that at different times the same merit may follow a onefold work that once followed a twofold one.

A similar form of reasoning may be followed with respect to sacramental grace: If the Church excommunicates someone, as Paul did the Corinthian, it does not do this to deprive him of grace and life, because excommunication is not mortal but medicinal, as Paul excommunicated the Corinthian *so that his soul would be saved on the day of the Lord.*[54] If, therefore, the Church judges that excommunication pertains to salvation, it is obvious that someone who obeys [the sentence of excommunication] is not deprived of grace and life by not taking part at the Lord's Table, but obtains the same grace of [eternal] life by the act of obedience. And so communication and excommunication have the same end for those who obey the Church.

By parity of reasoning, in accordance with the same judgment of the Church the obedient obtain the same end of grace and salvation now by communicating under one species as they formerly did by receiving under different ones. Similarly those currently obedient and united to the Church who receive under both species with her consent obtain no more [grace] than those who receive under one only, accepting and approving as they do the common practice of the Church.

Hence you would obtain no more grace and life from communion under both species (illicit for you Bohemians today because of your presumptuous split with the Church), if it were to come into use with the Church's consent, than you would have obtained from communion under the species of bread before that reform. At that [former] time you lacked nothing that the Church thought opportune, which is why there was no [additional] grace that you received afterwards from the species of Blood [which you took] in

34

35

36

cipietis. Unde etsi alia gratia per corpus sub panis specie, alia per sanguinem sub vini specie erogatur, non tamen alia sanguinis gratia futura post dominici corporis sacramentum exspectatur, quae non corporis sumptionem consecuta sit, ubi post communionem panis calicis communio approbante ecclesia non exspectatur. Recte, uti quondam temporibus Iulii papae, quando quidam propria auctoritate a ritu sub utraque specie communicandi recedentes, loco utriusque intinctum panem dederunt et non recte ritum sua auctoritate immutare poterant, quare per Iulium papam reprehendebantur, ut *De consecratione* di. 2 *Cum omne*, post hoc nihilominus in ecclesia catholica, licet novitati primo Iulius resisteret, ex certis rationabilibus causis ritus exstat introductus cum intincto communicand⟨i⟩ in multis locis, ut in concilio Turonensi statutum legitur, de quo in libro Burchardi V, c. *Ut omnis presbyter*, universali ecclesia demum approbante et non contradicente.

37   Quare illud gratiae, quod quondam servato priori ritu sub diversa specie christianus consequebatur, nunc comedendo separatim, tunc bibendo — illud postea ex unico actu communionis sub specie intincti panis exstat assecutus. Et licet tunc non parva altercatio in principio mutationis illius prioris ritus in ecclesia fuerit ob praxim Christi et priorum patrum, ut in eodem c. *Cum omne*, tamen universalis ecclesia, quia ita tempore congruebat, populum cum intincto pane communicare permisit. De qua re quidam religiosus frater Arnolfus ad quaestionem cuiusdam Lamberti circa illa tempora scribens dicit post principium: 'Prima ergo posita percontatio de altaris sacramento exstitit, cur hodierna consuetudo

a state of separation. So even if one grace was distributed by the Body under the species of bread, another by the Blood under the species of wine, nevertheless another, future grace of the Blood is not to be looked for, following upon the sacrament of the Lord's Body, that would not be obtained from receiving the Body, [as in cases] where, after communion of the bread, communion of the chalice is not looked for with the approval of the Church. Once in the time of Pope Julius, when some persons, departing by their own authority from the rite of communicating under both species, in place of both gave bread dipped in the chalice, and could not rightly change the rite by their own authority, they were deservedly rebuked by Pope Julius, as in [Gratian's *Decretum*], *De consecratione* D. 2 c. *Cum omne* [c. 7]. Nevertheless, afterwards in the Catholic Church, although Julius resisted this first innovation, the rite of communicating with dipped bread was introduced in many places for certain reasonable causes, as we read was established at the Council of Tours. We read this in the book of Burchard, Book V, c. *Ut omnis presbyter*:[55] the universal Church in the end approved and did not contradict [the practice].

Therefore the portion of grace that a Christian once obtained 37 by observing the prior rite under different species, now by eating alone and then by drinking afterwards, was secured by the single act of communicating under the species of dipped bread. And although there was no little dispute in the Church when the change in the prior rite began, owing to the practice of Christ and the earlier fathers, as [may be seen] in the same chapter [of Gratian's *Decretum*] *Cum omne*, nevertheless, the universal Church, because it was suitable to the times, permitted the people to communicate with dipped bread. Concerning this matter a certain religious, Brother Arnulf, writing about those times in response to a question of a certain Lambert, says, after the beginning [of the text], "First, therefore, having posited that the inquiry is about the sacrament of the altar, why should the present custom of the Church

ecclesiae censeat porrigi corpus dominicum aliter quam a domino in cena discipulis fuit distributum? Id enim quotidianus usus praetendit ecclesiae, ut porrigatur hostia sanguine intincta, cum a domino prius corpus, deinde sanguis porrectus fuisse memoretur, etiam Iulio papa hoc quondam prohibente. De cuius dubietatis ambiguitate quid intelligimus, quod a nostris doctoribus accepimus, respondere parati sumus. Redemptor noster veniens in mundum, quia propter hominum salutem inter homines apparuit quaeque reparationi humanae infirmitatis accommoda seu necessaria fore praevidit, sicut oportere vidit in sapientia sua, ita ab omnibus fieri et esse voluit in ecclesia sua; haec [eis] quae facienda erant eis, cum quibus conversari dignatus est, verbo vel exemplo insinuavit, certum, quo facienda erant, modum praefigere omittens'.

38 'Hinc esse videtur quod ait: "hoc facite in meam commemorationem", non ait "hoc modo facite"; et: "ite et baptizate" etc., non ait "hoc modo baptizate semel aut ter mergendo"; non ait: "scrutinium facite, chrisma conficite".' Quare insinuasse videtur circa modum mutationem ex causis rationabilibus accidere posse, sicuti haec experientia in multis comperimus, quia discipulis post cenam, nobis ieiunis traditur, ut Augustinus De consecratione di. 2 Liquido ad Ianuarium. Hieronymus narrat Super epistolam ad Titum, quomodo prius communi sacerdotum concilio ecclesia regebatur, 93 di. Legimus et 95 di. Olim. Imponitur aqua calici, quae per Christum imposita non legitur. Alius est ritus hodie conficiendi, alius fuit quondam.

conclude that the Lord's Body should be offered otherwise than it once was distributed by the Lord to the disciples at the Last Supper? That daily usage is placed before eyes of the Church, so that the host is offered dipped in the Blood (although it is recorded that the Body was offered by the Lord first and then the Blood), and Pope Julius once even prohibited this. We are prepared to say what we understand and what we have taken from our teachers about this doubtful and ambiguous matter. Coming into the world, our Redeemer, because He appeared among men for their salvation and foresaw there would be some accommodations or necessities for the repair of human infirmity, as he saw was necessary in His wisdom, He wished [these] to be carried out by everyone and to be [lodged] in His Church. The things they were to do He instilled in those whom He deigned to associate with by word and example [i.e., the Apostles], omitting to foreordain the way in which they were to be done."[56]

"It seems to be for this reason that he says, *do this in remem-* 38 *brance of me,*[57] not "do it in this [particular] manner;" and, *go forth and baptize,*[58] not "[go baptize] in this [particular] way, by immersing twice or thrice" or "conduct a scrutiny," or "prepare a chrism."[59] Thus He seems to have implied that changes in the modality [of the sacrament] could occur for reasonable causes, as we learn from experience in many cases, because [the Eucharist] was administered to the disciples after supper, [while] to us [it is administered] fasting, as Augustine says to Januarius [as in Gratian's *Decretum*] *De consecratione* D. 2 c. *Liquido* [c. 54]. Jerome relates in [his commentary] *On the Epistle to Titus* how the Church earlier was ruled by a common council of priests, [as in Gratian's *Decretum*] D. 93 c. *Legimus* [c. 24] and D. 95 c. *Olim* [c. 5]. Water is added to the chalice, and we do not read that this was enjoined by Christ. The rite of preparing the Eucharist is different today from what it once was.

39   Et post pauca dicit: ob honorem et reverentiam sacramenti et periculum effusionis ac ut sacerdos sine periculo ministrare posset, consuetudinem introductam panem intingendi. Ad decretum Iulii respondet: Quod, licet rationabiliter pro suo tempore fuerat institutum, praevaluit tamen ex post rationabilis ecclesiae consuetudo, quae cum invalescit decretis derogat, ut et decretis Telesphori de tempore celebrationis missae et aliorum de tempore baptizationis et chrismationis in fronte cum multis similibus per consuetudinem aliter introducta pro temporis convenientia reperimus. Ad hoc enim tendit voluntas pastoris, ut, quamdiu prodesse poterit saluti, observetur decretum, quare per rationabilem consuetudinem nemo dubitat ipsis statutis derogari.

40   Superaddit aliam rationem dicens: Quamdiu ob persecutionem fundendus fuit sanguis Christi fidelium, voluit Christus, dum fusionis memoriam sanguinis Christi per sumptionem calicis agerent, quod ad mortis et sanguinis fusionis tormenta viriliter confortarentur. Iuxta illud ad 'mensam magnam sedisti' scito, quoniam talia oportet te praeparare.

41   Ex quo videtur mihi, ut primo dicetur, colligendum usum sacramenti caritatem ecclesiae ad[3] Christum ostendere, ut tunc saepe et sub utraque specie, quando ardens est; tunc rarius in anno, quando calida est, et sub intincti panis specie; tunc rarissime in anno et sub una specie, quando tepida est, ut hoc tempore. Et quia tunc erant nonnulli, qui primum ritum utriusque speciei nondum reliquerant, qui tamen hos non iudicarunt, qui ritum mutarunt, ideo nec ecclesia eos, quod primum ritum observarunt. Quare ait

And, after a few words, [Arnulf] says: Out of honor and rever-   39
ence for the sacrament and owing to the danger of spilling the
wine, and so that a priest could minister without that danger, the
custom of dipping the bread was introduced.[60] In response to the
decree of Julius he says that, although [Julius' decree prohibiting
dipping the Eucharist] was instituted reasonably for its time, nevertheless a reasonable custom of the Church prevailed thereafter,
and when custom predominates it sets aside decrees; as also in the
case of [Pope] Telesphorus' decrees concerning the time for the celebration of Mass and in the case of decrees of other authorities
about the time of baptism and anointing the brow, along with many
similar things, we find alternative usages introduced through custom to suit the times.[61] The will of the Shepherd aims at the observance of a decree for as long as it can advance salvation. Thus no
one doubts that those statutes are set aside by reasonable custom.

[Arnulf] adds a further reason, saying: as long as the blood of   40
Christ's faithful had to be shed on account of persecution, Christ
wished that, when they enact the memory of the shedding of His
blood by drinking from the chalice, they should be comforted
manfully in the torments of death and bloodshed. According to
that text, *Thou are set at a great table*,[62] know that you should prepare for such things![63]

From this it seems to me, as is said above, that the practice of   41
the sacrament must be fashioned in such a way as to show the
Church's love [towards] Christ. It was once received often and under both species, when [that love] was ardent; later, when it was
warm, the sacrament was received more rarely in the year and under the species of dipped bread; still later, when love was tepid (as
at the present time), more rarely still in the year and under one
species. And although at that [earliest] time there were some who
had not yet left the original rite under both species, they nevertheless did not pass judgment on those who changed the rite; and so
neither did the Church pass judgment on them because they ob-

circa finem quaestionis huius: Omittimus de ea re ulterius loqui fautores dominici ordinis nequaquam arguentes, ecclesiasticae vero disciplinae cautelam minus providis commendantes. Videtis exemplum.

42   Notandum quomodo diversus ritus in concordanti unione ecclesiae catholicae aequaliter laudatur. Nec hic ideo melior, quia ordinem dominicum sequitur, quando alius ob ecclesiasticae[4] disciplinae cautelam per ecclesiam admissam per omnia ordinem ipsum sequi postposuit. Patet etiam quod, si comedere et bibere sacramentaliter caderent sub praecepto, non tamen obligarent ad aliter faciendum ipsam comestionem et bibitionem, quam habet ritus ecclesiae pro tempore, nunc separatis speciebus, nunc sub intincto pane et nunc sub altera specie, sub qua totus Christus est corpus et sanguis, licet ipsa specie non sit nisi aut edibilis aut potabilis, sicut intinctus panis non fuit potabilis, per quem tamen praecepto de bibendo, si praeceptum est, fuerat satisfactum.

43   Dixi: si sub divino praecepto caderet iuxta formam textus 'nisi manducaveritis' etc., quem tamen, ut infinita doctorum scripta vulgata transeam, non de sacramentali manducatione loqui sanctus Hilarius per communem nos instruit regulam in sexta generali synodo positam ex nono ipsius veritatis defensoris libro De sancta trinitate extractam, cuius haec sunt verba: 'Natus unigenitus deus ex virgine homo et secundum plenitudinem temporis in semetipso profecturus in deum hominem, hunc per omnia evangelici sermonis modum tenuit, ut se dei filium credi doceret, ut hominis filium praedicari admoneret. Locutus est et gerens homo universa quae dei sunt, loquens deinde et gerens deus universa quae hominis

served the original rite. Thus [Arnulf] says toward the end of this question: We omit speaking further of this thing, since supporters of the Lord's order never resist, commending an attitude of caution in ecclesiastical discipline to those less circumspect.[64] You see the example.

It should be noted how a different rite is equally laudable in achieving the union of the Catholic Church. Nor is one man the better because he follows the Lord's order when another prefers not to follow that order in all things owing to an attitude of caution, accepted as valid by the Church, with respect to ecclesiastical discipline. It is obvious that, if eating and drinking sacramentally falls under precept, [Christians] are nevertheless not obligated to perform that eating and drinking otherwise than the rite of the Church requires for the time, now [receiving] under separate species, now under dipped bread and now under one or the other species, under which is the whole Christ, Body and Blood, although He may not be in that particular species except as either edible or drinkable, just as dipped bread was not drinkable, yet the command about drinking (if it is commanded) was satified by that means.

I said, "if it falls under a divine command," according to the form of the text, *Except you eat* etc.,[65] which, to pass over the infinite, well-known writings of the doctors, does not refer to sacramental eating, as St. Hilary[66] instructs us, through a common rule posited in the sixth general synod, as extracted from the ninth book of *On the Holy Trinity* by that same defender of the faith, the words of which are: "The only-begotten Son of God, born a man from a virgin and in the fullness of time, in order to indicate the God-Man in Himself, held to this way of Gospel speech in all things, so that He might teach that He should be believed to be the Son of God; and so that He might urge that He be preached as the Son of Man. He spoke and enacted as a man all things that are of God, whilst speaking and enacting as God all

42

43

sunt. Ita tamen, ut in ipso utriusque generis sermone numquam nisi cum significatione hominis locutus et dei sit.' Haec ibi.

44 Cum igitur Christus haec verba cum in Capharnaum doceret locutus est, quare, cum de transitoria vita, quae per esum et potum praestatur, locutus fuisset, iuxta sui ipsius sententiam 'quia non in solo pane vivit homo, sed in verbo dei', ostendit se verbum vitae esse et vitam praestare hocque verbum incarnatum filium hominis. Quare dicit 'nisi manducaveritis carnem filii hominis' etc. Haec autem expositio non minus placet Augustino 26 homilia super Ioannem, quia dicit vitam de vita locutum, ut se ostendat vitam omnium sibi adhaerentium. Unde, ut ita intelligitur, tunc est prima et suprema veritas continens Christum deum et hominem, viam, veritatem et vitam omnium sibi adhaerentium. Et manifestum est hanc adhaesionem per fidem et caritatem fieri. Ait enim 'Qui credit in me, habebit vitam aeternam' et 'non morietur in aeternum'. Cuius adhaesionis excellentissima Pauli epistola ad Ephesios modum exprimit. Et Ambrosius, 16 epistola ad Herennium, admodum eleganter exponit, quomodo illa est per conversionem interni hominis per fidem ad Christum, sine qua est impossibile deo placere. Unde, sive illa adhaesio vocetur fides sive incorporalis ad corpus Christi sive spiritualis refectio, per quam vivit anima et ideo in vita et vita in ipsa, tunc est supremae necessitatis, antecedens omnia sacramenta, tanta distantia antecedens quod sine ista numquam vivere potuit nec poterit, licet multi, qui vivunt et qui vivent perenniter, omnibus caruerint visibilibus sacramentis. Non tamen nego secundum Augustinum, De verbis domini et super Psalmo 33, et alios, fidelibus in praefatis verbis sacramentum eucharistiae post hoc institutum commendatum. Sine quo tamen in-

things that are of man. Yet He never spoke unless His speech itself was of both sorts, signifying both the man and the God."
Thus Hilary.

When therefore Christ said these words while teaching at   44
Capernaum, for that reason, when He had spoken concerning this
transitory life which is sustained by eating and drinking, according
to His own statement that *not by bread alone does a man live, but by
the word of God*, he showed that He Himself was the Word of Life,
sustaining life, and that the Word Incarnate was the Son of
Man.[67] It was for that reason he said, *except you eat the flesh of the
Son of Man* etc. Augustine found this explanation equally attractive
in his twenty-sixth homily on John, since he says that Life spoke
about life so that he might show Himself to be the life of all those
who cleaved to Him.[68] Hence, understanding [the passage] in this
way, it then [refers to] the first and supreme truth, containing
Christ, God and man, *the way, and the truth, and the life* of all cleaving to Him.[69] And it is clear that this cleaving happens by faith
and love. He also says, *He that believeth in Me, hath everlasting life*
and *will never die*.[70] The most excellent letter of Paul to the Ephesians explains the manner of this cleaving. And Ambrose in *Letter
16* to Herennius quite elegantly explains how this cleaving is
through the conversion of the inward man to Christ by faith,
without which it is impossible to please God.[71] Thus, whether this
cleaving is called faith, or incorporeal or spiritual feeding on the
Body of Christ, through which the soul lives and in that way is in
life and life is in it, cleaving is then supremely necessary and precedes all the sacraments. It precedes them by such a distance that
without it no one was ever able to live nor could live, although
many who live and will live forever lack all visible sacraments. Yet I
do not deny that, according to Augustine in *On the Words of the
Lord* and [in his commentary] on Psalm 33, and others, the sacrament of the Eucharist, instituted after this, was commended to
the faithful in the aforesaid words.[72] Nevertheless, baptized in-

fantes baptizati vitam consequi possunt, quia Christo incorporati, quia id sunt, quod sacramentum significat, ut ait Augustinus sermone *De infantibus ad altare accedentibus*. Et sic cum hoc sacramentum, prout cibus est, sit grandium et iudicium rationis habentium, quod innuit apostolus per verba 'probet se ipsum homo', ibi 'non diiudicans', quoniam discreta ratio diiudicare sciens per hanc sapientiam et veritatem incarnatam pasci debet, quare ut sic infantibus non convenit, sed, ut superius asserebatis, aliquando ut sacramentum effectus prioris sacramenti, quasi ut ipsam confirmaret, tradebatur infantibus, sed non de necessitate salutis, ut dicit Augustinus, quia iam pueri id fuere consecuti, cuius hoc est sacramentum.

45   Unde manifestum est vitam sine hoc sacramento haberi et hinc textum praefatum dicentem 'non habebitis vitam in vobis' non posse de sacramentali esu intelligi, sine quo probatum est pueros auctoritate Augustini vivere; sed tamen, cum non sit dubium nullum sacramentum simpliciter necessarium et tamen quodlibet secundum suam condicionem et possibilitatem cum debita reverentia merito amplecti debeat, communes disputationes et auctoritates saepius allegatas hinc inde, ex quibus vos necessitatem praecepti probare, nos vero declinare contendimus, missa nunc facientes, quoniam superiora satis ostendunt auctoritatem ecclesiae praeferendam scriptoribus in finem, ut clarius conspiciatur veritas.

46   Altius prospicientes dicamus deo trino unum templum trinum ex angelicis spiritibus, ex beatis animabus ac peregrinantibus hominibus subordinatum, ut ait Augustinus 56 c. in *Enchiridion* et Ambrosius ad Herennium, pars vero militans ex trinitate est, sacramento ut spiritu, sacerdotio ut anima et fidelibus ut corpore.

fants can attain life without it, being incorporated with Christ, since they are what the sacrament signifies, as Augustine says in his sermon *On Infants Approaching the Altar*.[73] And so, since this sacrament, being food, is the food of those fully grown and having rational judgment, which the apostle [Paul] intimated in the words *a man proves himself*, [and brings judgement on himself for] *not distinguishing there* [i.e., in the Eucharist, *the* Body *of Christ*].[74] Since sound reason, knowing how to distinguish, should be fed by this incarnate wisdom and truth, it is for that reason not appropriate for infants. But, as was asserted above [§8], sometimes a sacrament is given to infants to confirm the effect of a prior sacrament, but not out of necessity for salvation, as Augustine says, because children already have obtained that of which [the Eucharist] is a sign.

So it is clear that [eternal] life can be had without this sacra-   45
ment and hence that the aforesaid text saying, *You shall not have life in you*, could not be understood of sacramental eating, as it has been proved from the authority of Augustine that children have [eternal] life without it. Yet, since there is no doubt that a sacrament is absolutely necessary and nevertheless that any [sacrament] should be worthily embraced with due reverence according to one's condition and ability, let us dismiss all the usual arguments and authorities so often alleged by which you try to prove, and we to avoid, the necessity of the command [to receive communion in both kinds]. The arguments above show sufficiently that the [living] authority of the Church is to be preferred in the end to that of writers, that the truth may be perceived more clearly.

From a more lofty perspective we may say that there is one tri-   46
une temple to the triune God, a temple constituted of angelic spirits, blessed souls and the wayfaring men below them, as Augustine says in c. 56 of the *Enchiridion*,[75] and Ambrose to Herennius.[76] But the Church Militant is made up of a trinity, with the sacraments as the spirit, the priesthood as the soul and the faithful as the

Postquam enim peregrinamur, nondum finem attingentes, in via positi, per signa tamquam in speculo et in aenigmate, quantum viae possibile est, capiti nostro spirituali coniungimur et ipsum, quem facie ad faciem videre nequimus, per fidem sub sacramentalibus signis attingimus. Quare ipsa sacramenta sunt in ecclesia peregrinanti tamquam Christus in patria, sacerdotibus ut ministris angelicis exsistentibus et fidelibus fidelium beatarum animarum typum gestantibus, ut tota ecclesia peregrinantium subsit toti triumphanti. Erit itaque prima et altior pars, spiritualior scilicet, sacramentorum primo loco, ecclesiae adeo necessaria quod sine ipsa ecclesia ut ecclesia medium unionis cum triumphanti ac Christo capiti habere non posset. Nec ecclesia, quae per fidem sub signis Christum amplectitur, ecclesia peregrinantium esse posset illa parte suprema et essentiali non exsistente. Unde, quamvis omnia ipsa sacramenta eiusdem capitis sint sacra signa ipsum secundum varios nostrae salutis respectus repraesentantia, tamen inter ipsa in ordine ad corpus ecclesiae graduatio necessitatis exsistit, uti in eodem rationali spiritu diversae potentiae sunt secundum sub et supra in ordine ad hominem se habentes.

47   Ex quo evenit quod sacramentum ordinis in ipsa ecclesia est de prioribus sacramentis, quoniam per ipsum sacerdotium constituitur et per sacerdotium alia sacramenta conficiuntur et ministrantur. Sacerdotium vero est ut anima, quae inter spiritum et corpus est vivificans et gubernans ipsum corpus per influentiam spiritus, ut eleganter Gregorius Nazianzenus in apologetico suo declarat. Unde, sicut in homine secundum Augustinum *Super symbolo* est spiritus rationalis deo proximior, deinde in infimo loco corpus et in medio tamquam partem capiens utriusque anima corpus animans tamquam medium, per quod spiritus vitam corpori influit, ita spiritualia sacramenta per medium ordinis sacerdotio coniun-

body. Since we are travelling as pilgrims and have not yet reached our end, situated on the way, we are joined to our spiritual head by signs as though in a mirror and an enigma, as much as is possible on the way, and we attain that spiritual head, which we are not able to see face to face, through faith under sacramental signs.[77] Hence those sacraments are in the Pilgrim Church like Christ in the fatherland, with the priests as angelic ministers and the faithful bearing the imprint of the blessed faithful souls, so that the whole Pilgrim Church is subject to the whole Church Triumphant. And so the first and higher part of the sacraments, namely the spiritual part, will be in the first place so necessary to the Church that without them the Church *qua* church could not have means of union with the Church Triumphant and with Christ as Head. Nor could the Church which embraces Christ by faith under signs exist as the Pilgrim Church if that supreme and essential part did not exist. Thus, although all these sacraments are sacred signs of the same Head, representing Him according to various aspects of our salvation, nevertheless a gradation necessarily exists among them in relationship to the body of the Church, just as there are different powers in the same rational spirit, ranked higher or lower in relationship to man.

That is why the sacrament of orders is among the earliest sacraments in the Church, since the priesthood is established by it and all the other sacraments are prepared and administered by the priesthood. The priesthood, however, is like the soul which gives life between body and spirit and governs that body by the influx of the spirit, as Gregory of Nazianzus elegantly declares in his apologetic book.[78] Therefore, just as in man, according to Augustine in *On the Creed*,[79] there is a rational spirit nearer to God, then the body in the lowest place and the soul in the middle, as if partaking of both, animating the body like a mean through which the spirit infuses life into the body, so the spiritual sacraments are joined to the priesthood by the mean of orders, and by the mean of the

47

guntur et per medium sacerdotii influunt vitam populo fidelium, ad instar ut in hierarchiis superioribus primus ordo illuminat, secundus illuminat et illuminatur, tertius illuminatur tantum. Unde concedatur necessarium quod ipsum sacerdotium continuetur per continuam successionem usque in primum et maximum sacerdotem, scilicet Christum, quoniam, si aliquando rupta fuisset talis continuatio, non esset idem Christi sacerdotium nec fuisset, qui eos subsequentes sacerdotes consecrasset. Nemo enim dare potuisset, quod non habuisset.

48   Quare ea, quae secundum Augustinum superius de cathedra Petri dicta sunt, ad hoc tendunt: Cum Christus Petrum primum sacerdotem cum plena potestate ligandi et solvendi constituisset et ita eum misisset, sicut ipse a vivente patre missus fuit, eidem tradidit alios successores eiusdem potestatis constituendi sacerdotes. Hoc quidem sacerdotium ita a capite inchoatum per successiones ad nos usque pertinet nec umquam deficiet talis successio legitima sacerdotii, quoniam necessario tota deficeret ecclesia; et hinc ecclesia, quae sacerdotem habet qui cum hac successione a Christo et Petro non descendit, non est de ecclesia catholica, quoniam non potest nec vere regi nec vera habere sacramenta. Christus enim per medium suorum latinorum sacerdotum, qui eius potestate et legatione funguntur, omni tempore renovat et conficit sacramenta et per medium ipsorum sacramentorum gratiam partitur fidelibus. Quare uti in Christo divinitatem, animam rationalem et corpus consideramus in unitate supposti, ita in una ecclesia sacramenta, sacerdotium et populum. Et sicut Christus secundum humanitatem fuit rex et sacerdos et haec humanitas rationalem animam principalius respicit, ita Christo succedunt legati sacerdotes regnum in ecclesia ac sacerdotium possidentes. Illi autem rationali animae Christi fuit hypostatice divinitas unita, secundum quam potuit ipsa anima rationalis in divinas et miraculosas operationes, supra naturam sanando aliquando signis mediantibus, ut quando

priesthood they infuse life into the [lay] people of faith, so that, reflecting the loftier hierarchies, the first rank illuminates, the second illuminates and is illuminated, the third is illuminated only. Thus it is conceded to be necessary that this priesthood should have continuity by continuous succession back to the first and greatest priest, that is, Christ, since if at some time such a continuity were broken, the priesthood of Christ would lose its identity and there would not be someone to consecrate the priests who follow them. For no one could have given what he did not have.

Thus the things which were said above, following Augustine, 48 about the see of Peter tend to this conclusion: When Christ made Peter the first priest with the full power to bind and loose and so sent him, as He himself was sent by the living Father, Christ gave Peter other successors with the same power of making priests. This priesthood, so begun by its Head, stretches by succession even down to us; nor shall such a legitimate succession of the priesthood ever fail, since the whole Church would then necessarily fail. And therefore a church which has a priest who does not descend in this succession from Christ and Peter does not belong to the Catholic Church, since it cannot truly be governed nor have true sacraments [from such a priest]. Christ then by means of His Latin priests, who exercise His power and represent Him, at all times prepares and renews the sacraments; and by means of those very sacraments He imparts grace to the faithful. Therefore, as we contemplate in Christ divinity, rational soul and body in the unity of a substrate, so in one Church we contemplate the sacraments, the priesthood and the people. And just as Christ according to His humanity was king and priest, and this humanity principally has regard to the rational soul, so His representatives, the priests, succeeding Christ, possess kingship and priesthood in the Church. As divinity was hypostatically united to the rational soul of Christ—thanks to which that rational soul could perform divine and miraculous works beyond nature by healing, sometimes by

manus posuit et verba locutus est, lutum fecit et oculos linivit, benedixit et fregit etc. huiusmodi; ita et voluit sacerdotio quandam divinam potestatem inesse, per quam et sacramenta conficerent, quae operationem supernaturalem haberent ac etiam ipsi operarentur ligando et solvendo virtute potestatis regiae et per medium sacramentorum virtute potestatis divinae ea, quae finaliter hominum saluti convenirent, propter quam quidem salutem Christus venit et factus est homo, rex et sacerdos. Unde cum hoc ita sit, manifestum est in potestate sacerdotii ministrationem sacramentorum esse, maxime huius divinissimi sacramenti eucharistiae, ut infra dicetur.

49   Oportet autem quod sacerdotium consideretur aut prout est de corpore fidelium et ita se habet pure passive in particularibus personis, quia sacerdo‹te›s ut privatae personae de corpore fidelium exsistentes ab aliis sacerdotibus publicam personam gerentibus ligantur et solvuntur; aut se habent ut officium sacerdotale publicum gerentes et tunc ligant et solvunt in virtute creditae potestatis et legationis; aut se habent ut ministri dei summi typum Christi gerentes et sic sanctificant et conficiunt sacramenta gratiam conferentia et sanctificantia. Quare sacerdotium materialiter ut est de corpore fidelium consideratum subest legibus fidelibus datis in recipiendo sacramenta ad Christum ac aeternam vitam ordinata. Unde, si praeceptum est fideles communionem eucharistiae sumere debere, hoc praeceptum, eo modo quo possibile est fieri, ita obligat sacerdotes sicut alios — dico 'modo possibili', quoniam lex possibilium est et ad impossibile nemo obligatur, quare, si praecipitur communio divinissimae eucharistiae sumi, debere — et non est dubium, cum consecrans per se capiat aut capere possit

means of signs, as when He touched someone, spoke words, made clay and anointed the eyes, blessed and broke and the like—so He willed a certain divine power to exist in the priesthood through which they can prepare sacraments which work supernaturally; and they too effect—by binding and loosing in virtue of their royal power and through the sacraments in virtue of their divine [priestly] power—the things that in the end are conducive to the salvation of men, for which salvation Christ came and was made man, king and priest. This being so, it is therefore obvious that the administration of the sacraments, especially of this most divine sacrament of the Eucharist, lies within the power of the priesthood, as will be said below.

It is necessary, however, that the priesthood should be considered either (1) as it pertains to the body of the faithful—and so its position is purely passive in particular persons, because priests, as private persons belonging to the body of the faithful, are bound and loosed by other priests, who act as public persons; or (2) priests are in the position of exercising the public priestly office, and then they bind and loose by virtue of the power and representation entrusted to them, or (3) they are in the position of ministers of the supreme God, bearing the mark of Christ, and so they sanctify and prepare the sacraments that confer grace and sanctify. Thus the priesthood, considered materially as belonging to the body of the faithful, is subject to the laws given to the faithful in receiving the sacraments ordered toward Christ and eternal life. Hence if the command is that the faithful are obliged to receive the communion of the Eucharist, this command obligates priests, like others, to carry it out in a possible way. I say "in a possible way," since law is concerned with the possible, and no one is obligated to the impossible, so if it is commanded that communion of the most divine Eucharist be received, it must be received. And there is no doubt, since the one consecrating receives or can receive the sacraments he has prepared, that he would not receive [the

49

confecta sacramenta, non capere[5] modo sibi possibili, si calicem di-
mitteret; quare, nisi sub utraque specie sumeret, reprehensibilis esset, ut declararunt patres nostri quamplures et ita vult textus *Comperimus, De consecratione* di. II. Si vero ipse sacerdos non conficeret
nec in sua potestate sacramenta haberet, sed in potestate tradentis
forent, manifestum est nec ipsum nec alium quemcumque ad aliter
accipiendum obligari posse quam ut sibi porrigerentur.

50   Unde haec est generalis regula omnium sacramentorum, quae
non sunt in potestate recipientis sed tradentis: ita tradere sicut li-
bet; ad alium modum non obligari—salva semper fide sine qua
impossibile est deo placere—quam ut sibi tradetur. Dico 'salva
fide' quae, si per sacramentum a deo tradi debet, necesse est, ut
forma ecclesiae servetur, mediante qua tantum gratia fidei in non
habentibus usum rationis creditur dari. In habentibus vero discretionem, ubi iam incorporatio praecessit, sufficit capere quaecumque sacramenta uti traduntur, adhibita tamen possibili cautela
per recipientem, ut ab eo capiat qui in communione ecclesiae exsistit et cuius modus tradendi se universae catholicae fidei et ecclesiae
conformat aut saltem diu scita, tolerata et confirmata per ecclesiam
exsistit. Tunc enim quando recipienti, ubi fides praecedit in se vel
parentibus quoad infantes et nihil sibi possibile impingi potest:
quis dubitat nec ob variam formam, modum aut ritum sacramentorum ab ecclesia tunc acceptum aut permissum salutem sibi ita
conformiter ad sententiam ecclesiae recipienti abesse posse? Nisi
dicere vellemus totam ecclesiam, cuius ille membrum factum est,
eiusdem ecclesiae iudicio iam penitus defecisse et ab omnimoda
salute cecidisse; quod est erroneum manifeste.

sacrament] in the way possible to him if he should forego the chalice. Therefore, unless he receives under both species, he would be reprehensible, as many of our Fathers declare; and the text of [Gratian's *Decretum*] *De consecratione* D. 2 c. *Comperimus* [c. 12] so opines. If, however, the priest himself does not prepare nor have in his power the sacraments, but they should be in the power of a server, it is obvious that neither he nor any other could be obligated to receive in any way other than as they are offered to him.

Hence there is a general rule for all the sacraments which are not in the power of the recipient but of a server: to serve as he wishes; not to be obligated [to serve] in any way (making exception always for faith, without which it is impossible to please God[80]) other than the way he is himself served. I say "making exception for faith," for if faith must be bestowed by God through the sacraments, is necessary that the form used by the Church be observed, by means of which the grace of faith is believed to be given even to those not having the use of reason. In those having discretion, where incorporation already precedes, it suffices to receive any sacraments as given; nevertheless, all possible caution must be applied by the recipient so that he receives from someone who is in the communion of the Church and whose way of bestowing conforms itself to the universal Catholic faith and the Church, or at least in a way that is long known, tolerated and confirmed by the Church. Then, when there is antecedent faith in the recipient or (in the case of children) his parents, and nothing can possibly be impugned against him, who can doubt that the recipient can lack, through the various forms, ways or rites of the sacraments then accepted or permitted by the Church, salvation conformably to the decision of the Church? — Unless we would say the entire Church, of which he has been made a member, by her very own judgement has already failed utterly and degenerated from salvation of any kind, which is plainly erroneous.

51   Quare non minus fuere aliquando in Christi nomine baptizati,
etiam infantes, quorum fides sana erat in omnibus articulis, etiam
Trinitatis, quam hodie in nomine patris et filii et spiritus sancti in
Christo renati; et ita de confirmatis, quondam per sacerdotes,
92 di. *Pervenit*, et nunc per episcopos; et ita de communicatis,
quondam infantibus, et extrema unctione etiam in infantili aetate
inunctis, et modo non; et de usu variae communionis, etiam
quoad adultos, penitus idem dico. Et hoc superius est manifestum
et satis est clarum, cum in adultis fidem habentibus sacramenta in
voto esse possint, eos ad spiritualem illam sacramentorum susceptionem in voto obligari, in receptione vero non aliter obligari,
quam sibi possibile est habere. Unde solum obligatio praeceptiva
sacramentorum quoad receptionem necessario refertur ad voluntatem tradentis, sic quod recipiens paratus sit ita recipere, uti traditur sibi per communionem habentem cum ecclesia. Et quia credita
est potestas sacerdotio praeposito populo sacramenta ad finem salutis prout convenientius iudicaverit ministrare—Levitici 14 et 27,
Deuteronmii 3, Ezechielis 4,4, I ad Corinthios 3, 6 et 9, II ad Corinthios 1, ad Epheseos 1, Lucae 17, Matthaei 24, Actuum 2, 5 di.
Praecipimus et maxime hoc casu ministrationis sacramenti eucharistiae, ut probant textus pulchre I Esdrae 2 et conformis Ne-
hemiae 7 et multa concilia, ‹C.› 26. q. 6 *Si quis* et de his cum aliis
De poenitentiis et remissionibus, *Omnis*, ibi ‘nisi de consilio sacerdotis’,
etc.—, tunc patet praeceptum communicandi necessario esse
condicionale, scilicet si animarum curam habenti visum fuerit.

Hence those who once were baptized "in the name of 51
Christ," — even infants — whose faith was sound on all the articles,
and also [those baptized in the name of] the Trinity, are no less
reborn in Christ than those today [who are baptized] "in the name
of the Father and of the Son and of the Holy Spirit."[81] So also
in the case of the confirmed, [a sacrament once performed] by
priests, [as in Gratian's *Decretum*] D. 93 c. *Pervenit* [c. 14], and now
by bishops; and in the case of communicants, [a class that] once
included infants, who were also anointed with Extreme Unction in
their infant years and now are not. And this was made manifest
above and sufficiently clear, since in adults of faith the [reception
of] sacraments could be [part of] a vow, [i.e.] that they were obligated by the vow to spiritual reception of the sacraments; but not
otherwise obligated [in the manner of] reception than that it be
possible for them to receive. Thus only a preceptive obligation to
the sacraments with respect to reception necessarily pertains to the
will of the server, such that the recipient is prepared to receive [the
sacrament] so that [it] is bestowed on him by someone in communion with the Church. And since it is believed that power is entrusted to the priesthood placed over the people to administer the
sacraments for the end of salvation in the way it shall think most
convenient — [as is shown by] Leviticus 14 and 27, Deuteronomy
3, Ezekiel 44, 1 Corinthians 3, 6 and 9, 2 Corinthians 1, Ephesians
1, Luke 17, Matthew 24, Acts 2, [Gratian's *Decretum*] D. 93 c.
Praecipimus [c. 26 fin.], especially in this case of the administration
of the Eucharist, as texts beautifully prove at 1 Esdras 2, and likewise at Nehemiah 7, and many councils [cited in Gratian's
Decretum], C. 26 q. 6 c. *Si quis* [c. 6], and on this, along with other
matters, *De poenitentiis et remissionibus*, c. *Omnis* [X 5.38.12], in the
passage "Only by the counsel of the priest" — it is then clear that
the command to communicate is, of necessity, conditional, that is,
[the manner of communication is determined] as seems best to
the one having cure of souls.

52   Quare receptio sacramentalis eucharistiae si sub praecepto dei
caderet, tunc in hoc praecepto aliquando homo, qui se ipsum probaret, ex humilitate secum posset dispensare per textum Pauli,
etiam per annos plures, sicut multi eremitae fecerunt ante praeceptum ecclesiae. Post vero praeceptum ecclesiae abstinere nihilominus quisque posset cum consilio sacerdotis, ut in c. *Omnis utriusque*
et aliis locis, et hoc totum propter salutem accedere debentis, ne
'iudicium sibi manducet et bibat'. In tradente vero similiter est potestas dandi et non dandi, ex causis rationabilibus vel sic et sic
dandi, prout viderit saluti expedire recipientis, quod nequaquam
verum foret, si tantae necessitatis sacramentum foret quod sine eo
vita haberi non posset sicut sacramentum fidei in discretione ca-
rentibus; quoniam nisi renati tales fuerint, regnum intrare nequeunt. Huius tam libere creditae potestatis tradendi ecclesiae sibi
commissae exempla multa legimus de Paulo excommunicante Corinthium; et non est dubium Paulum iuxta intentionem tunc
egisse, ut spiritus excommunicati 'salvus' fieret 'in die domini.' Aliquando non dabatur infantibus ante quintum annum, ut notatur
super 7 c. *Ecclesiasticae hierarchiae*, aliquando immediate post baptismum etiam infra illos annos, ut in libro primo Rabani *De institu-
tione clericorum*, cuius pars habetur *De consecratione* di. 4. *Post baptisma*, et similiter in libro Adelberti archiepiscopi Mediolanensis
De mysteriis baptismatis, ad interrogationem Caroli Magni, capitulo
ultimo. Post hoc in concilio generali, *Omnis utriusque sexus*, dicitur

Hence if sacramental reception of the Eucharist falls under 52
God's command, then, in light of this command at one time a
man who had tested himself could on his own dispense [with taking the Eucharist] out of humility, on the authority of Paul's
text,[82] even for many years, just as many hermits did before the
Church's command. After the command of the Church, nevertheless, someone could abstain with the counsel of the priest, as in
[the *Decretals*] c. *Omnis utriusque* [X 5.38.12] and in other places;
this is all on account of the salvation of the one who ought to approach [the sacrament], lest someone should *eat and drink judgment
upon himself.*[83] The server in similar fashion has the power of giving
and not giving [the sacrament] for reasonable causes, or giving in
such-and-such a way, as seems expedient for the salvation of the
recipient, something that would by no means be true if the sacrament were so necessary that without it [eternal] life could not be
obtained, like the sacrament of faith [i.e. baptism] in the case of
those lacking discretion [i.e. children], because unless they were
reborn, they could not enter the kingdom.[84] We read many examples of this power of disposing[85] being committed and freely entrusted to the Church for herself, [for example] when Paul excommunicated the Corinthian;[86] and there is no doubt that Paul acted
then with the intention that the spirit of the excommunicated man
would be saved on the day of the Lord. Sometimes [the Eucharist] is
not given to children before the age of five years, as is noted in the
seventh chapter of [Dionysius the Areopagite's] *Ecclesiastical Hierarchy,*[87] while sometimes it is given immediately after baptism even
to those below that age, as in the first book of Rabanus [Maurus]
On the Instruction of Clerics, part of which is found in [Gratian's
Decretum, under the rubric] *De consecratione* D. 4 c. *Post baptisma*
[c. 91], and similarly in the book of Adalbert, archbishop of Milan,[88] *On the Mysteries of Baptism,* written at the request of Charle-
magne, in the last chapter. After this, in the general council,[89] it is
said in [the *Decretals,* c.] *Omnis utriusque sexus* [X 5.38.12] that [a

quod 'postquam ad annos discretionis venerit' et sic communio puerorum cessavit et non deficiebant pro tempore rationes. Adultis dabatur aliquando omni die, ‹aliquando› pluries in anno, aliquando infirmis sub utraque specie, aliquando sub una, ut ista habentur *De consecratione* di. 2 *Peracta* et c. *Etsi non frequentius*, c. *Pervenit* et c. *Presbyter*, ubi sub specie panis, ‹C.› 26 q. 6 *His qui primo*, ubi sub specie vini, ut patet ex textu ibi 'eucharistia infundatur ori' etc., Cyprianus *De lapsis*; et ita confirmavit se illius dispositioni ministrare,[6] de cuius salute agebat, Daniel 4 'sicut populus, ita sacerdos'.

53   Hinc ex hominibus sumitur pontifex, ut eis compati possit, Ad Hebraeos 5. Saepe etiam nec sub una aut alia specie etiam in extremis constitutis et petentibus dabatur, ut *De poenitentia* di. 7 *Hoc autem*. Hoc fuit prohibitum in Nicaeno concilio, licet ante teneretur, ut late scribit Cyprianus ad Antonium et *De poenitentia* di. 3 *In tantam*, cum multis capitulis ibi positis, ‹C.› 26 q. 6 *De his*, et hoc secundum Innocentium papam I propter crebras persecutiones. Concessa enim poenitentia tunc fuit et negata communio; sed suis temporibus data pace ecclesiae prior durior observatio facta inclinatior, admittit simul et ad viaticum. Sardicense concilium statuit ambitiosos communione perpetuo privandos; ultimum capitulum Carthaginensium etiam viatico privat apostatas semel a voto et 63 c. Eleberitani concilii et 62 et 71 et 72, in quibus crimina enumerantur, ob quae confessis et contritis viaticum prohibebatur. Saepe etiam unus episcopus certis dabat, quibus alius nequaquam.

child communicates] "after he comes to the age of discretion." So communication of children ceased, and reasons were not lacking at the time. Communion sometimes was given to adults every day; sometimes several times a year; sometimes to the sick under both species; sometimes under one, as dicussed in [Gratian's *Decretum*], *De consecratione* D. 2 c. *Peracta* [c. 10] and c. *Etsi non frequentius* [c. 16], c. *Pervenit* [c. 29] and c. *Presbyter* [c. 93], where it is given under the species of bread; see also c. *His qui primo* C. 26 c. 6 [c. 8], where it is given under the species of wine, as is clear from the text there, "the Eucharist was poured into the mouth," and [from] Cyprian's *Concerning the Lapsed*.[90] And so he confirmed that he was ministering according to the disposition of those for whose salvation he acted, Daniel 4, *Just as the people, so the priest*.[91]

Hence the pontiff is drawn from among men, so that he might   53
have compassion for them, Hebrews 5[:1–2]. Often the sacrament is not given under one or the other species even to the dying who ask for it, as in [Gratian's *Decretum*], *De poenitentia* D. 7 *Hoc autem*. This was prohibited in the Nicene Council, although before it was obligatory, as Cyprian writes in great detail to Antoninus,[92] and [in Gratian's *Decretum*], *De poenitentia* D. 3 c. *In tantam* [c. 33] with the many chapters found there, [and in ibid.] C. 26 q. 6 c. *De his* [c. 9], and according to Pope Innocent I this [took place] on account of frequent persecution.[93] At that time penance was allowed and communion denied; but when in his time peace was given to the Church, the earlier, harsher observance became more merciful and simultaneously [the Eucharist] was permitted also as a viaticum. The Council of Sardica decreed that the ambitious were to be denied communion in perpetuity;[94] the last chapter of the Council of Carthage deprived of viaticum those who had been apostates from their vows on a single occasion;[95] and [so too] in c. 63 of the Council of Elvira,[96] and in chapters 62, 71 and 72, in which are listed crimes on account of which viaticum is prohibited to those who have confessed and repented. Often one bishop

Unde Cyprianus de hoc ad Antonium et post eum Augustinus ad Vincentium Rogatistam scribunt de certis episcopis, qui moechos etiam ad poenitentiam numquam admiserunt aliis admittentibus, nec propter hoc ab invicem et episcoporum collegio recesserunt nec ecclesiae unitatem duritie censurae ruperunt. 'Manente enim concordiae vinculo et perseverante ecclesiae catholicae individuo sacramento actum suum disponit et dirigit unusquisque episcopus, rationem propositi sui domino redditurus.' Haec ibi.

54   Quare nunc aperte satis ostensum puto propositum nostrum, scilicet nec ad sic vel sic tradendum sacerdotes praeceptum habere, sed medici fungi potestate in quid et cui et quando et qualiter ad finem salutis ministrando, habendo nunc respectum ad bonum publicum, quando ob facinora commissa contrito in terrorem aliorum tunc subtrahitur et nunc distribuitur aut etiam infirmitate et indiscretione considerata sic vel sic ministrando aut ob reverentiam sacramenti et cautelam disciplinae sub specie intincti panis aut altera specie tantum aut periculum infidelitatis crebrius vel rarius sic vel sic dando, semper respectum habendo ad id, quod sibi melius visum fuerit in credita legatione iuxta praeceptum Innocentii 90 di. *Praecipimus.*

55   Forte dicitis non posse negari ex rationabilibus causis ita, ut exemplis ostensum est, et factum esse et fieri posse. Sed cum non sint tales hodie, ob quas calix subtrahi debeat populo, irrationabile esse sine causa a Christo concessum non ministrare. Ad hoc luce

would give it to certain persons, but another bishop would not. Hence Cyprian, writing about this to Antonius, and Augustine writing after him to Vincent the Rogatist, describe certain bishops who never admitted adulterers to penance while others did, but they did not withdraw on this account from each another and from the college of bishops, nor did they rupture the unity of the Church owing to the harshness of their censure. "While the bond of concord lasts and the undivided sacrament of Catholic unity abides, any bishop disposes and directs his acts to be able to render an accounting for his way of life to the Lord."[97]

So I think now that our theme has been set out with sufficient clarity, namely, that priests are not commanded to administer [sacraments] in any particular way; but they act with the power of physicians, ministering for the end of salvation, [and have discretion to choose] in what [form], for whom, when and how [the sacraments are administered]. At one time, in the interest of the public good, the sacrament might, on account of crimes committed, be withheld the from the contrite as a terror to the rest, while on another occasion it might be distributed, taking account of infirmity and lack of discretion, ministering in such-and-such a way; or out of reverence for the sacrament and the need to preserve discipline, it might be administered under the species of dipped bread or under only one or the other of the species; or it might be given in a particular way, more frequently or more rarely, because of the danger of infidelity, always taking account of what seems better to the priest in the representation entrusted to him, according to the command of Innocent in [Gratian's *Decretum*], D. 90 c. *Praecipimus* [c. 11]. 54

Perhaps you will say that the chalice cannot be withheld in this way for reasonable causes, as is shown by examples; and that it has been and can be [given to the laity]; but since there is no reason why the chalice should be withheld from the people, it is unreasonable without cause not to administer [a sacrament] conceded 55

clarius responsum censeo in praecedentibus, quia commune sacerdotium, capiens sui regiminis motum a sancto spiritu, quoniam sanctissimum est ex Christi legatione, non obstante quod quidam peccatores sint, in ministratione errare non potest, quia ad communis sacerdotii errorem totam ecclesiam errare necesse foret; quare non cadit deceptio quoad fidelem populum etiam per malum sacerdotem rectum ex sui officii administratione, ut hoc clarissime videtur et Augustinus hoc ostendit ‹C.› 1. q. 1. *Per Ysaiam* et omnium haec est sententia. Alioqui, si in hoc haesitatio esse posset, duo inconvenientissima sequerentur, scilicet aut totam ecclesiam errare posse aut fidelem ad impossibilia obligari.

56   Et si ratio inquiri deberet huius communis ritus hodiernae communionis vera et indubia, ab eo nos sciscitari ipsam oporteret, qui sensum domini novit et consiliarius eius fuit. Persuasibile tamen est, sicut non sine mysterio casus et declivitatis ecclesiae diaconi in parochiis deficerunt, quorum officium erat prius eucharistiam sub panis specie per sacerdotem traditam cum sanguine confirmare, ut in ordinario Romano legitur, et Innocentius *De officio missae* ac sancti Laurentii legenda et notatur 93 di. *Diacones* et c. *Diaconi* et *De consecratione* di. 2 *Pervenit,* ac ob cautelam etiam et periculum effusionis et impossibilitatem diacono non exsistente, quia uni sacerdoti successive sub utraque specie ministrare tempus non suffecit. Quae omnia mysterio non carent, dum vix ecclesia tepescat in caritate ad ultimumque gradum descendens deducta, etiam ad ultimum gradum in ministerio pervenerit, ut ita rarius

by Christ. I think that a response to this argument [has already been given] in the foregoing, and one clearer than daylight: because the common priesthood, seizing the impetus of its rule from the Holy Spirit, and being most holy on account of its representation of Christ — notwithstanding that certain [priests] are sinners — cannot err in administration; because an error of the common priesthood means the whole Church necessarily would err. Hence deception does not affect the faithful laity, even in the case of a bad priest, [so long as he is] correct in the administration of his office. This seems utterly clear, and Augustine shows it in [a passage found in Gratian's Decretum], C. 1 q. 1 c. *Per Isaiam* [c. 98], and this is everyone's opinion. Otherwise, if there could be hesitation in this, two great disasters would follow, that is, either the whole Church could err or the faithful could be obligated to perform impossible things.

And if a true and indubitable reason need be sought for [what is] the common rite of communion at the present time, we ought to ask it of the man who knew the Lord's meaning and was His counselor [i.e., Peter]. Yet it is arguable that as parishes began to be left without deacons (a phenomenon belonging to the mystery of the Church's decline and fall), it being their office to strengthen with the Blood the Eucharist that had been offered by the priest under the species of the Bread — as is read in the Roman ordinal,[98] and as is said by Innocent in *On the Office of the Mass*,[99] and in the legend of St. Lawrence,[100] also noted in [Gratian's *Decretum*] D. 93 c. *Diacones* [c. 6] and c. *Diaconi* [c. 12] and in *De consecratione* D. 2 c. *Pervenit* [c. 29] — [communion in both kinds became] an impossibility owing to [the need to observe the required] precautions and the danger of spilling in the absence of a deacon, since time did not suffice for a single priest to administer both species in succession. All of this is not lacking in mystery, [for now], when the Church is scarcely warm with love and love has descended to its lowest degree, she has also arrived at the lowest degree in her

quam umquam et sub una specie tantum. Et hoc iuxta statum ecclesiae ad nostram salutem hunc usum inspiratum per Spiritum
Sanctum credere debemus, ut hic usus recte commensuratus cari-
tati ecclesiae ipsam sufficienter iuxta currentem caritatis appetitum
pascat, pauco fervore sitim divini sanguinis minime generante nisi
in ipsis pontificibus ad certam corporis et sanguinis oblationem
constitutis, ad Hebraeos 8. Et sacerdotibus populi peccata come-
dentibus et ex publico officio aliorum defectus supplentibus et
mortem domini, quousque in extremo iudicio denuo veniat, an-
nuntiantibus, qui ex merito officii publici et ex praecepto dei, ita
ecclesia interpretante *De consecratione* di. 2 *Relatum* et c. *Comperimus*, ad confectionem et sumptionem utriusque obligantur, in quibus persistat veritas et robur infallibilitatis, ratione commissae legationis, fidelium infirmitate non obstante; quibus fidelibus hoc
tempore tamquam ab hinc decessuris, sicut infirmis solitum fuit,
viaticum convenit ministrari sub una scilicet specie panis, ut probat textus *Presbyter* coniuncta glossa, *De consecratione* di. 2.

57   Solet etiam a vobis curiose, superflue tamen quaeri, quis Romanus pontifex aut quale concilium ritui unius speciei auctoritatem
primo praestitit. Et licet infallibilis nostrae salutis regula in istis
per Augustinum post Basilium 12 *De ecclesiasticarum conscripta* merito sufficeret, tamen, ut curiositati etiam superfluae satisfiat, dico
quod magna et plenaria totius orbis et universae ecclesiae synodus
anno Christi 1215 in ecclesia Lateranensi Romanae Innocentio illo
III, litteratissimo, divinae et humanae legis peritissimo praesidente

ministry, so that the sacrament is received more rarely than ever and under only one species. And we must believe that this usage was inspired by the Holy Spirit for our salvation owing to the state of the Church, so that this usage, rightly commensurate with the love of the Church, feeds her sufficiently according to the current appetite of love. Small fervor produces the minimal amount of thirst for the divine Blood, except in those pontiffs appointed to offer a fixed [amount of] the Body and Blood, Hebrews 8[:3]. And priests consume the sins of the people and make good the defects of others on account of their public office, proclaiming the death of the Lord until He comes again at the Last Judgment.[101] By the merit of their public office and by command of God, as the Church interprets [in Gratian's *Decretum*], *De consecratione* D. 2 c. *Relatum* [c. 11] and c. *Comperimus* [c. 12], they are obligated to the preparation and consumption of both species. Truth and the strength of infallibility persist in them by reason of the representation [of Christ] entrusted to them, notwithstanding the infirmity of the faithful. In these times the faithful are like persons departing this world, and it is appropriate to administer the viaticum to them, as used to be done in the case of the infirm, under the single species of Bread only, as the text of [Gratian's *Decretum*], c. *Presbyter* [c. 93], *De consecratione* D. 2, with the attached gloss, prove.[102]

You are wont to ask, curiously yet superfluously, which Roman 57 pontiff or what council first lent his authority to the rite of communion under one species. Although the infallible rule of our salvation in these matters, written down by Augustine,[103] following Basil *On the Enlisting of Clerics* 12,[104] should suffice in the matter, nevertheless, to satisfy superfluous curiosity, I say that a great and plenary synod of the whole world and the universal Church in the year of Christ 1215, in the Lateran church at Rome, with Innocent III, a man most learned in divine and human law, presiding, approved this rite of not communicating infants and communicating

hunc ritum non communicandi infantes et sub una specie fideles, per c. *Omnis utriusque sexus*, approbavit quoad infantes in verbo 'postquam ad discretionis annos', quoad unam speciem ibi 'eucharistiae sacramentum.' Et licet dici possit sacramentum calicis, quoniam etiam eucharistiae sacramentum est, comprehendi posse, ut in c. *Firmiter*, ❰ *Una*, *De summa trinitate*, tamen panis et vini sacramenta, prout sacramentum est vel sacrae rei signum vel complectitur signum cum re, licet sub utrisque speciebus idem Christus exsistat, nominantur sacramenta, ut in missarum complendis dicitur: 'Prosint nobis, quaesumus domine, sacramenta' et ne in hoc dubium remaneat, dicit ille textus a proprio sacerdote. Et iam superius manifestatum est numquam fuisse sacerdotis officium sanguinem populo ministrare. Et probatur idem in c. *Presbyter*, *De consecratione* di. ii iuncta glossa, ubi textus: 'Per sacramentum eucharistiae corpus tantum intelligit', ut ait glossa. Idem probatur in capitulo eiusdem generalis concilii *De custodia eucharistiae*, *Corpus*, ubi eodem termino, scilicet 'sacramento eucharistiae' utitur. Et tamen iuxta c. *Presbyter* cum glossa non potest ille textus concilii de sanguinis sacramento intelligi; et ita et ipse Innocentius ac omnes doctores post eum videntur intellexisse, qui⟨a⟩ ex omnibus, qui post ipsum concilium fuerunt, non invenitur aliquis, qui dicat fidelem ad communionem calicis obligari.

58   Et ita nihil amplius restat, de quo per divinae pietatis misericordiam non sit vobis abunde credo satisfactum. Quare amplius ab inceptis desistentes matrem vestram ecclesiam amplectimini, ut in eius unitatis pace peregrinantes simul ad aeternam pacem triumphantis ecclesiae Christo duce transferri mereamur. Amen.

the faithful only under one species [as in *Decretals*], c. *Omnis utriusque sexus* [X 5.38.12], with respect to infants in the passage "after the year of discretion"; with respect to [communicating in] one species at "the sacrament of the Eucharist." And although it could be called "the sacrament of the chalice," since it too is the sacrament of the Eucharist, it could be included, as in [the *Decretals*], c. *Firmiter* ❦ *Una* [X 1.1.1], *De summa Trinitate*. Nevertheless, the "sacraments" of bread and wine are named—insofar as a sacrament is either a sign of a sacred thing, or embraces the sign along with the thing—although the same Christ is under both species, as is said in the collect of the Mass,[105] "We ask, Lord, that the sacraments may benefit us." And to remove all doubt about this, that text says "from one's own priest." And as has been shown already above, it never was the duty of the priest to administer the Blood to the people. And the same is proved in [Gratian's *Decretum*], c. *Presbyter, De consecratione* D. 2 [c. 93], with the adjoining gloss, at the text "by the sacrament of the Eucharist he means the Body alone," as the gloss says.[106] The same thing is proved in the canon *Corpus* of the same general council, [in the *Decretals*], *De custodia eucharistiae* [X 3.44,1], where the same term, that is, "the sacrament of the Eucharist," is used. Nevertheless, according to c. *Presbyter* with its gloss, that text of the council cannot be understood to concern the sacrament of the Blood; and Innocent himself, and all the doctors after him, seem to have understood it in this way, because no one who lived after that council can be found who says that a faithful [lay] person is obligated to the communion of the chalice.

And so there remains nothing, I believe, about which, by the 58 mercy of divine piety, you have not been abundantly satisfied. So desist from any further undertakings and embrace your mother, the Church, so that, wayfaring in the peace of unity, we may deserve to cross over together, with Christ as our leader, to the eternal peace of the Church Triumphant. Amen.

‹Utrum auctoritas sacrorum conciliorum
sit major quam papae›

1 Quia varia oppinio hiis diebus exoritur de maioritate auctoritatis sacrorum conciliorum supra auctoritatem pape, ideo ex antiquis gestis pauca elicere curavi pro intrando fundamentum huius dubii.

2 Primo est consideranda varietas temporum et vocabulorum, quoniam iuxta temporum varietatem vocabula eciam variata sunt. Universale enim perfectum concilium a primo Niceno usque ad octavum generale, quod tempore Basilii imperatoris Constantinopolitani celebrabatur, per imperatores de omnibus sedibus colligebatur. Et ut habetur ex gestis Niceni primi concilii, tunc tantum tres sedes fuerunt antiquitus, scilicet Romana, Allexandrina et Antheocena, licet episcopus Helie sive Iherosolimorum semper honoraretur, ut habetur in vi c. concilii Niceni, et reputabatur patriarcha Ierosolimorum episcopus ex illo honore, unde post hoc eciam sedes nominatur, ut habetur in aliis gestis conciliorum. Unde scribitur in sexta universali synodo, que Constantinopoli fuit celebrata tempore Agathonis pape et Constantini imperatoris, quod imperator cum suis patriciis sedit, deinde legati Agathonis pape, deinde Allexandrinus, deinde Anthiocenus, deinde locum tenens vicarii Ierosolimorum, post hoc tres episcopi locum tenentes cxxv episcoporum synodi antique Rome, post hoc Rauennatensis locum tenens etc. Et sedebant patricii a dexteris imperatoris, legati et alii a sinistris, preter Constantinopolitanum, qui sedebat a dextris. Unde ex hoc habetur, quomodo Ierosolimitana sedes vocabatur sedes.

Is the Authority of the Holy Councils Greater Than That of the Pope?

Because various opinions have arisen in these days about the superiority of the authority of the holy councils over the authority of the pope, I have tried for that reason to elicit from the ancient records a few things to get to the bottom of this doubtful issue. 1

First one must consider the variation of times and terms, since terms too vary in accordance with the variation of times. Perfect universal councils were gathered by the authority of the emperors from all the [patriarchal] sees from the First Nicene to the Eighth General Council that was celebrated at the time of the Emperor Basil of Constantinople.[1] As is found in the records of the First Council of Nicaea, there were only three of these sees in ancient times, that is, those of Rome, Alexandria and Antioch, although the bishop of Jerusalem was always honored, as is found in c. 6 of the Council of Nicaea;[2] and the bishop of Jerusalem was regarded as a patriarch because of that honor. Hence after that time it too was called a [patriarchal] see, as is found in the other records of councils. Hence it is written in the sixth universal synod,[3] held in Constantinople at the time of Pope Agatho and the Emperor Constantine [IV], that the emperor sat with his patricians, then the representatives of Pope Agatho, then the patriarch of Alexandria, then that of Antioch, then the lieutenant of the bishop of Jerusalem, after that three bishops representing 125 bishops of the synod of Old Rome, after that the representative of Ravenna etc. And the patricians sat at the right of the emperor; and the legates and others sat at his left, except the bishop of Constantinople, who sat at his right. Hence it is supposed from this that the see of Jerusalem was called a [patriarchal] see. 2

3   Et similiter sciendum, quod Constantinopolitana ex eo, quia civitas nova Roma vocabatur, sedes eciam ex hoc patriarchalis facta est et longo tempore se universalem patriarcham scripsit. Unde in gestis sexte synodi, cum imperator ad eum scriberet, scribit: 'sanctissimo et beatissimo archiepiscopo nove Rome, patriarche universali.' Et contra illam presumpcionem illius tituli Gregorius nonus eleganter scribit in libro *Contra presumpciones Michaelis Constantinopolitani.* Tamen, ut in gestis Calcedonensis quarti universalis concilii legitur, tunc super illo, an universalis foret patriarcha Constantinopolitanus et supra Romanum, questio suborta fuit et allegaciones producte et lata est diffinitiva, quod Romana sedes primatum teneat primo loco et Constantinopolitanus, quia episcopus nove Rome, secundum locum, licet eisdem gaudeat privilegiis primacie. Et ita ante concilium illud Calcedonense et post legitur observatum, quod alie sedes orientales Constantinopolitanam tanquam supra se primam venerabantur, licet eciam in gestis varia multum inveniantur iam Allexandrinum Constantinopolitanum consecrasse, iam Romanum. Verum tamen Leo papa, qui fuit tempore concilii Calcedonensis, quoad illam partem, quod Constantinopolitanus secundum locum habere deberet, quia hoc fuit contra Nicenum primum concilium, nullomodo admisit, sed scripsit contra ad imperatorem et Pulcheriam augustam et alios, quomodo ordinacio concilii Niceni, que secundo loco Allexandrinum post Anthiocenum posuit, violari non potest. Tamen sentencia concilii Calcedonensis, que omnibus placuit, prevaluit, ut patet ex gestis omnium aliorum conciliorum post Calcedonense, quia semper precedit Constantinopolitanus Allexandrinum.

And similarly we know that the see of Constantinople, because   3
it is called the New Rome, was made patriarchal for this reason;
and the patriarch described himself for a long time as "the universal patriarch." Hence in the records of the sixth synod, when the
emperor writes to him, he writes, "To the most holy and blessed
archbishop of New Rome, universal patriarch."[4] And Gregory IX[5]
writes elegantly against this presumption in the book *Against the
Presumptions of Michael of Constantinople*.[6] Nevertheless, as we read
in the records of the fourth universal council at Chalcedon, a question arose on the topic whether the patriarch of Constantinople
should be a patriarch and above the one at Rome, and arguments
were presented. A definitive sentence[7] was issued that the Roman
see holds the primacy in the first place and the patriarch of Constantinople, because he is the bishop of New Rome, second place,
although they enjoyed the same privileges of primacy. And so we
read, before that Council of Constantinople and after, that it was
observed that the other Eastern sees venerated that of Constantinople as if first among them, although much variation is found in
the records, and at one time the patriarch of Alexandria, at another the patriarch of Rome consecrated the patriarch of Constantinople. Nevertheless, Pope Leo,[8] who reigned at the time of the
Council of Chalcedon, in no way accepted the decision that the
patriarch of Constantinople should have the second place, because
it was contrary to the First Council of Nicaea; but he wrote, on
the contrary, to the emperor and the empress Pulcheria and others
how the ordinance of the Council of Nicaea, which placed the patriarch of Alexandria in the second place after the patriarch of
Antioch, could not be violated. Nevertheless, the decision of the
Council of Chalcedon pleased everyone and prevailed, as is obvious from the records of all the councils after Chalcedon, because
the patriarch of Constantinople always preceded the patriarch of
Alexandria.

4   Et sic habemus quinque sedes in tota universali ecclesia, ut scribitur in gestis VIII universalis concilii septima accione, et vocantur quinque capita ecclesie in illis gestis. Et perfectum concilium tunc de illis omnibus sedibus per imperatores colligebatur, ut notat apocrisiarius apostolice sedis, qui octavum concilium transtulit de greco, quod imperatores nunquam nisi universalia concilia convocarunt. Et in illis conciliis usque ad octavum inclusive semper invenio convocacionem eciam primordialiter ab imperatoribus factam, ita convocando Romanum pontificem sicut alios patriarchas, licet legatur Marcianum Leonem papam advocasse et eum recusasse et demum consentisse convocacioni. Ex quo aliqui concludunt Marcianum auctoritate apostolica convocasse; quod tamen non potest ita intelligi, quod nisi auctoritas Romani pontificis in convocando intervenisset, quod tunc non fuisset verum concilium, quia in gestis aliorum conciliorum, scilicet sexti et octavi, manifeste habetur, quomodo Romanus pontifex Agatho in sexta et Adrianus in octava sacris imperialibus litteris vocati rescripserunt, quomodo propter obedire et parere preceptis divalibus miserunt suos legatos. Et eciam habetur in gestis sexti synodi, quomodo Constantinus ordinavit concilium, scribens de numero personarum, scilicet quot personas in concilio habere voluit de qualibet sede. Et ibidem et in gestis octave synodi colligitur, quod universale perfectum concilium est, quod ita collectum est de omnibus sedibus, id est de universali catholica ecclesia. Et tantum de primo principali etc.

5   Secundo notandum, quod aliud fuit universale consilium cuiuslibet patriarche, quia quilibet patriarcha ex antiqua consuetudine, ut in gestis concilii Niceni legitur et in c. vi, quod incipit *Antique consuetudines*, habuit omnium episcoporum sub eo existencium potestatem convocandi eos ad se pro synodo universali celebranda; et illa potestas solum se ad suas certas provincias extendebat. Sic et Romana sedes habuit concilium ex synodis subiacentibus. Unde

Thus we have five sees in the whole universal Church, as is   4
written in the records of the eighth universal council in the seventh proceeding,[9] and they are called the five heads of the Church
in those records. And a perfect council was gathered then by the
emperors from all those sees, as the envoy of the Apostolic See
who translated the eighth council from the Greek notes that the
emperors convoked nothing except universal councils.[10] In those
councils, up to the eighth inclusive, I find that from their inception they were always convoked by the emperors. Thus they summoned the Roman pontiff just like the other patriarchs, although
we read that Marcian summoned Pope Leo I and he refused, only
later consenting to the convocation.[11] From this some conclude
that Marcian convoked by apostolic authority. Nevertheless, it
cannot be understood this way, because at that time there was no
true council unless the authority of the Roman pontiff had inter-
vened in convoking it, since it is manifestly the case in the records
of some councils, that is, the sixth and the eighth, that the Roman
pontiffs, Agatho in the sixth[12] and Adrian I in the eighth,[13] when
summoned by holy imperial letters, replied that they sent their legates to obey and submit to imperial commands. And it is even
found in the records of the sixth synod how Constantine ordered
the council, writing concerning the number of persons, that is,
how many persons from each see he wished to have in the council.[14] Likewise it is implied in the records of the eighth synod that
it is a perfect universal council because it is gathered from all the
sees, that is, from the universal Catholic Church. So much for the
first principal point etc.

Second, we must note that a universal council of a given patri-   5
arch was something else, because any patriarch from ancient custom, as we read in the records of the Council of Nicaea and in
c. 6[15] which begins *Antique consuetudines*, had the power of summoning to himself all the bishops under him to celebrate a universal synod; but that power extended only to his own provinces.

scribit Constantinus Agathoni in gestis sexti universalis concilii in prima accione, ut mittat tres personas de sua ecclesia et de suo concilio mittat XII metropolitanos. Et idem scribit ad Constantinopolitanum, quomodo Agatho de toto suo concilio misit tres. Et Agatho scribit imperatori: 'iuxta defectum temporis ac servilis provincie qualitatem pro satisfaccione obediencie'; et infra: 'et nisi longus provinciarum ambitus, in quibus humilitatis nostre concilium constitutum est' etc.; et ibi 'septentrionales et occidentales episcopos de hoc concilio esse'. Et Flauianus Constantinopolitanus ad Leonem scribens dicit: 'omnibus, qui sub tua reverencia deo amantissimi episcopi constituti sunt' etc. Et Leo ad Theodosium et Hilarius ad Pulcheriam augustam etc. Et quod quilibet patriarcha tale concilium habuit, ibidem habetur in c. *Piissimus imperator.* Eciam aut quando concilium unius aut diversarum nacionum, dicitur universale quoad illas naciones, ut legitur in gestis Toletani concilii tempore Zenzilai regis celebrati. Et ita legitur sanctum Ambrosium heretico, contra quem in concilio Aquiliensi disputavit, respondisse, cum sibi obiceret non esse universale concilium, cum orientales non essent, quod congregacio occidentalium universale occidentalium concilium faceret sicut orientalium orientale.

6   Et dicitur pro tanto hoc concilium Romanum universale, quia duplex est synodus Romanus. Est enim synodus, que de propinquis et inmediate subiectis constituitur, et synodus, que de remotis provinciis congregatur, ut ex eadem parte sexti concilii colligitur, dum Agatho scribit: 'cum concilio confamulorum meorum episcoporum, tam de propinqua huius apostolice sedis synodo, quam de familiari clero' etc. Et sicut deprehenditur ex gestis, ad universale concilium Romanum non solebant omnes convenire episcopi, sed

Thus the Roman see also had a council of the synods subject to it. Hence Constantine writes to Agatho in the first proceeding of the sixth universal council[16] that he should send three persons from his church and twelve metropolitans from his council. And the same emperor[17] writes to [the patriarch of] Constantinople how Agatho had sent three from his entire council. And Agatho writes to the emperor, "[I sought out those who could be found, despite] a lack of time and the quality of an enslaved province, to satisfy the demands of obedience," and below, "[. . .] and if it were not for the great size of the province in which the council of our humility is set," etc.; and in that place, "northern and southern bishops belong to this council."[18] Flavian of Constantinople, writing to Leo, says, "To all the beloved bishops who are established under your reverence" etc.[19] And Leo to Theodosius,[20] and Hilary to the Empress Pulcheria etc.[21] It says in the chapter *Piissimus imperator*[22] that any patriarch had such a council. And even when a council is assembled from a single or different nations, it is called universal as far as it pertains to those nations, as is read in the records of the Council of Toledo celebrated at the time of King Chintila.[23] And so we read Saint Ambrose responded to the heretic against whom he disputed in a council at Aquileia, who objected against him that it was not a universal council since the easterners were not present, that an assembly of westerners made up a universal council of westerners, just as an assembly of easterners [made up a universal council of easterners].[24]

This Roman council is called universal inasmuch as the Roman 6 synod is double. There is a synod which is made up of nearby [prelates] and [those] immediately subject [to Rome], and a synod which congregates together from remote provinces. This is inferred from the same part of the sixth synod, when Agatho writes "with the council of the bishops, my fellow servants, both of the synod of those near to the Apostolic See and our familiar clergy" etc.[25] Just as we learn from the record that not all bishops are accustomed to convene at a universal Roman council, but — having

deliberati prius congregata synodo in provinciis aliquos legatos ad concilium et synodum Romanum miserunt, ut colligitur ex gestis variis illius sexti et octavi synodi, ubi invenitur de synodo Galliarum certos ad synodum Romanam missos, sic et de synodo Brittanorum etc. Et fuit ordinatum in viii° universali consilio, quod patriarche haberent potestatem archiepiscopos vocandi sive metropolitanos ad concilium, ut infra dicetur; et convocacionem huius generalis sive universalis concilii facere solum potest patriarcha, qui capud est huius consilii. Et sic intelligendum puto id, quod in variis locis invenitur, quod concilium absque auctoritate Romani pontificis congregari non possit. Hoc verum est de illo iam dicto concilio. Hoc autem concilium vocatur synodus sive ecclesia determinata ad capud, scilicet Romana vel Constantinopolitana, ut hoc legitur in gestis octavi concilii accione quinta, ubi, dum loqueretur de synodo Nicolai primi, scribitur: 'spiritus sanctus, qui locutus est in Romanorum ecclesia, locutus est et in nostris ecclesiis' etc.

7   Et de ista Romanorum ecclesia in variis gestis legitur, quomodo errare non possit in fide; et hoc privilegium habet ultra omnes alias ecclesias, quod in ipsa vera fides nunquam deficiet. Unde quando synodice et regulariter et unanimiter Romana ecclesia in materia fidei aliquid diffinit, hoc facit divina infallibili inspiracione, ut in septima accione octavi concilii legitur. Ibi, dum dicit de sentencia fidei Romani concilii, dicit: 'quam divina inspiracione depromptam esse credimus, dum unanimitate et concordia sancti synodi sit proculdubio promulgata.' Et in c. iii et vi, ubi dicit: 'Hec sunt, que sedes apostolica statuit, que synodice regulariterque decrevit.' Et infra: 'Que tanto studiosius oportet amplecti, tanto solicicius observare, quanto satis noscitis, que statuta fuerint ab ea,

deliberated previously at synods meeting in the provinces — they sent some legates to the Roman council and synod. This is inferred from various records of the sixth and eighth synods, where it is found that certain men were sent to the Roman synod from the synod of the Gauls and so also from the synod of the Britons etc.[26] And it was ordained in the eighth universal council[27] that the patriarchs have the power of convoking archbishops or metropolitans to a council, as will be said below. The patriarch, who alone is the head of the council, is the only one who can convoke this general or universal council. That is how I think we must understand what is found in various places, that a council cannot be gathered without the authority of the Roman pontiff. This is true of that aforesaid council. This council, however, is called a synod or an assembly ordered to its head, that is, the church of Rome or Constantinople, as we read in the records of the Eighth Council in the sixth proceeding, where, speaking of the synod of Nicholas I, it is written, "The Holy Spirit, Who has spoken in the Roman Church, has spoken in our churches" etc.[28]

We read in various records concerning this church of the 7 Romans that it cannot err in faith and that it has this privilege beyond all other churches, that the true faith shall never fail in it. Therefore, when the Roman church synodically, regularly and unanimously defines anything in a matter of faith, it does this by infallible divine inspiration, as we read in the seventh proceeding of the Eighth Council.[29] Speaking there of the sentence of the Roman council concerning the faith, it says, "[. . .] which we believe was prompted by divine inspiration, since it was, without a doubt, promulgated with the unanimity and concord of the holy synod," And in c. 3 and c. 6, where it says, "These are the things that the Holy See decided, which it decreed synodically and regularly."[30] And below, "[. . .] which should be embraced the more zealously and observed the more solicitously to the extent that you know well enough what it established: the things the universal Church

hec universalem semper tenuisse ecclesiam; ita ut contra singulos errores in ecclesia exortos prior hec secundum primatus sui auctoritatem sentencie terminum dederit, et ita demum universalis ecclesia, licet aliquando per aliquantum tempus in quibusdam reluctata sit, que illa tamen probavit, quantum probaverit, et que refutavit, refutaverit.' Et quomodo papa in suo concilio solebat decernere una cum aliis, ut in octava synodo septima accione legitur: 'deinde vero decernentibus nobiscum et similiter considerantibus sanctissimis fratribus coepiscopis nostris' etc. Et Agatho papa hoc probat in hiis, que habentur in principio sexti consilii, quod auctoritas Romane ecclesie consistit in hoc, quod est: 'Pasce oves', quoad fidem. Ergo cuncta catholica ecclesia eius fidem veneratur, et nunquam vera fides ibi deficiet in Romana ecclesia, ut probat ibidem, quia rogavit Christus, ut nunquam deficeret.

8 Et de hoc singulariter habetur in gestis octavi concilii scilicet Constantinopolitani in libello per omnes subscripto, qui incipit *Prima salus*, ubi dicitur, quod integra et vera religio christiana semper manet apud Romanam ecclesiam, et ergo illi non consencientes intra sacra misteria eorum nomina dicit non esse recitanda et sequestratos esse a communione katholicae ecclesie. In libro secundo Optati Milleuitani contemporanei Augustini, de quo eciam in conciliis Affricanis legitur — et scripsit contra Parmenianum septem libros, contra quem eciam Augustinus scripsit — ubi, cum de quinque dotibus tractaret catholice ecclesie, dicit cathedram esse primam dotem, in qua omnes sedere debent episcopi, cuius prior est in Romana urbe, ubi prior Petrus sedit et suo tempore Siricius; cui a Christo dictum est: 'Tibi dabo claves regni celorum et porte inferi' etc. Ubi deducit, quod, qui se in cathedra esse dicit

always held. Thus the Church set a limit to the sentence against individual errors that had earlier arisen in the Church in accordance with the authority of its primacy. Although sometimes for a short period it resists in certain matters, nevertheless the things it approves [remain approved] inasmuch as it approves them, and what it suppresses will be suppressed." And we read in the seventh proceeding of the Eighth Synod how the pope was accustomed to make decisions in his council together with others, "But then, having come to a decision with Ourselves and in like fashion in consultation with our our most holy brothers, our fellow bishops [. . .]."[31] And Pope Agatho proves this in these words spoken at the beginning of the sixth council:[32] that the authority of the Roman church consists in the statement, *Feed my sheep*,[33] as far as faith is concerned. Therefore, the whole Catholic Church venerates its faith; and the true faith will never fail in the Roman church, as the same passage proves, because Christ prayed it never would fail.[34]

Particularly relevant is a passage in the records of the Eighth 8 Council, that is, of Constantinople, in the pamphlet to which all subscribed, which begins, *Prima salus*,[35] where it is said that the whole and true Christian religion always endures within the Roman church. And, therefore, it says that the names of those not in agreement with the Roman church are not to be recited at the sacred mysteries and that they are to be cut off from the communion of the Catholic Church. In the second book of Optatus of Milevis,[36] a contemporary of Augustine, of whom we also read in the African councils — he wrote seven books against Parmenian, against whom Augustine also wrote — where, treating of the five gifts of the Catholic Church, he says that the first is the chair or see upon which all bishops should sit. The one having priority over [the rest] is in the city of Rome, where Peter first sat (and where Siricius sat in his time), to whom Christ said, *I will give to thee the keys of the kingdom of heaven, and the gates of hell* etc.[37] There

et non est in cathedra Petri Romana, errat. Et deducit ibidem, quomodo imperium Romanum est in ecclesia, hoc in Canticis exponendo: 'Veni, sponsa mea' inventa 'de Libano', id est, de imperio Romano; de quo ibi per eum.

9   Sed tamen sciendum secundum sanctum Ambrosium in sermone pastorali, quod licet ad Petrum hoc dictum est 'Pasce', tamen omnibus pastoribus ita a Christo per Petrum preceptum est. Unde non a Petro habent pastores pascendi potestatem, sed a Christo, licet in pascendo Petrus precedat. Et Ieronimus ad Damasum et ad eundem in decima questione De cathedra Petri, ubi dicit: 'Si quis kathedre Petri adheret, meus est' etc.; ubi, dum de triplici divisione ecclesie diceret, subiungit 'suum esse, qui cathedre Petri adheret,' etc. Unde hoc probat Leo ad Theodosium, et Valentinianus augustus ad Theodosium ita scribit: 'Beatissimus Romane civitatis episcopus, cui principatum sacerdocii super omnes antiquitas contulit, locum habeat ac facultatem de fide iudicare.' Et infra: 'Hec enim gracia secundum sollempnitatem conciliorum.' Et Constantinopolitanus episcopus eum per libellos appellavit propter intencionem que orta est de fide, item Marcianus et Valentinianus, Leoni 'archiepiscopo gloriose civitatis Rome: Tuam sanctitatem principatum in episcopatu divine fidei possidentem' etc. 12 d. Preceptis, 24 q. 1 Quociens, xvi q. 1 Frater noster, xxiii q. ult. Convenior, et aliis infinitis locis hoc potest probari, quod principatus Romani pontificis est in fide et, ut supra dictum est, ipse presidet in ecclesia Romana, que errare non potest in fide.

10   Quare universali catholice ecclesie quoad fidem presidet per sibi subiectam ecclesiam, quoniam synodice et regulariter sentenciam

he deduces that whoever says he is in his see and is not in the Roman see of Peter is in error. And he deduces in the same passage that the Roman empire is in the Church, expounding this passage in Canticles, *come, my spouse, from Lebanon*,[38] that is, from the Roman empire, of which [the text speaks] there.

Yet we should know that (according to Saint Ambrose in a pastoral sermon[39]), although *Feed* was said to Peter, Christ gave the command in this way to all the shepherds through Peter. Therefore the shepherds do not have the power of feeding from Peter but from Christ, although Peter had precedence in feeding. And Jerome to Damasus and the same father in the tenth question [of Gratian's *Decretum*], *De cathedra Petri*, says, "If someone adheres to the see of Peter, he is mine," etc.[40] There, speaking of the triple division of the Church, he added, "Whoever adheres to the see of Peter is His."[41] Hence Leo I[42] proves this [in a letter] to Theodosius, and Valentinian writes in this way to the emperor Theodosius: "the most blessed bishop of the city of Rome, on whom antiquity conferred the supreme principate over the priesthood, has the position and power of judging about the faith." And below, "And this grace [was conferred] in accordance with solemn councils." And the bishop of Constantinople sent petitions appealing on account of an accusation that had arisen about his faith, as did Marcian and Valentinian, to Leo, "the archbishop of the glorious city of Rome," [saying] "Your Holiness, who possesses the primacy in matters concerning our divine faith over the episcopate" etc. It also can be proved from [passages in Gratian's *Decretum* such as] D. 12 c. *Preceptis* [c. 2], C. 24 q. 1 c. *Quociens* [c. 12], C. 16 q. 1 c. *Frater noster* [c. 52], C. 23 q. 8 c. *Convenior* [c. 21] and numerous other places that the principate of the Roman pontiff is in matters of faith; and, as was said above, he presides in the Roman church that cannot err in faith.

Hence he presides in matters of faith over the universal Catholic Church through the church subject to himself [i.e. the Roman

fidei ferre debet ad hoc, ut divino spiritu inspirante non erret, ut dicitur in prima accione Calcedonensis concilii: 'non esse tutum et ubique absque sanctarum scripturarum presulibus questionem de fide tractare'; aliter errare posset, ut Honorius et Liberius erraverunt. Quod est notandum, quoniam, ut dicit sanctus Ciprianus in epistola ad Nouacianum et Augustinus et alii post eum tunc: 'Episcopatus unus est, cuius in singulis pars in solidum tenetur.' Et post multa dicit: 'Licet omnis homo sit mendax, deus tamen verax; ideo stat confessorum pars maior in fidei sue robore ac in lege ac discipline dominice veritate. Quare congregacio sacerdotum multum utilis, quia maior pars in lege fidei et discipline veritate tunc invenietur' etc.

11   Unde ex isto patet, quod concilium Romano pontifici subiectum est illud, quod constituitur ex episcopis provinciarum parcium septentrionalium et occidentalium et quondam eciam meridionalium, quando Affricani catholici fuerunt. Unde de toto illo concilio credo hoc verum esse, quod hoc universale concilium, quia subiectum fuit, non potest illa sua auctoritate papam iudicare, quia inferior superiorem non iudicat regulariter. Sic intelligo ea, que in gestis octavi de hoc diffuse contra Phocium, qui presumpsit Nicolaum papam iudicare, scribuntur. Et hoc probat textus 26 decreti octavi concilii: 'Quia, si quisque metropolitanus nec ab episcopis sue provincie nec vicinis metropolitis potest iudicari,' ut ibidem a forciori nec papa a suo subiecto concilio. Sed quia pape universale concilium ex omnibus sedibus congregatum vel indictum non subest pape, nisi quod sentenciam fidei regulariter prolatam acceptat,

see], because he is obliged to hand down, synodally and regularly, decisions regarding the faith, for the reason that, with the inspiration of the Divine Spirit, he will not err, as is said in the first proceeding of the Council of Chalcedon: "It is not safe to treat anywhere a question concerning the faith without the prelates [having authority over] the Holy Scriptures," otherwise one might err, as Honorius and Liberius erred.[43] This must be noted since, as Saint Cyprian says in the letter to Novatian (and Augustine and others after him) that at that time "The episcopate is one, and each part of it is obliged to be in solidarity with that one."[44] And much thereafter he says, "Although every man be a liar, nevertheless God is truthful, so the majority of the confessors stands in the strength of its faith, in the law and the truth of the Lord's teaching. Therefore the congregation of priests is very useful, because the majority of it will be found to be in the law of the faith and the truth of its teaching," etc.

Hence it is obvious that a council subject to the Roman pontiff 11 is made up of bishops from the northern and western provinces, and at one time even from the south, when there were African Catholics. Therefore, I believe it is true with respect to that entire council that a universal council, because it is subject to him, cannot judge the pope by its own authority, because an inferior as a rule cannot judge a superior. Thus I understand what is written at great length about this in the records of the Eighth Council[45] against Photius, who presumed to judge Pope Nicholas. And the text of the twenty-sixth decree of the Eighth Council[46] proves this, "Because, if any metropolitan cannot be judged by the bishops of his province or by the nearby metropolitans," then *a fortiori* neither is the pope subject to his council. But, since the pope's universal council, gathered from all the sees or proclaimed, is not subject to the pope unless it accepts a decision of faith published in a regular way, this council, superior to all in any given case has [the author-

ideo hoc concilium, tanquam supra omnes in quocunque casu, eum habet iudicare, ut est canon *Singularis* XXI octavi concilii.

12   Hodie autem, quia universalis catholica ‹ecclesia›, que quondam in quinque sedibus resedit, ut Bahanus patricius in septima accione octavi concilii predixit, redacta est ad sedem Romanam tantum, que in Christo capite alias revocabit, ut dicitur ibidem, tunc oportet dicere quod concilium universale Romanum sortitur duplicem naturam, quia subiectum est Romano pontifici, ut semper fuit, et cum representet universalem catholicam ecclesiam, quoad hoc est supra papam, ut eciam semper fuit, quia semper universalia concilia, que totam universalem catholicam ecclesiam representabant, fuerunt supra papam, ut in decreto allegato octavi concilii, licet tunc cum omni mansuetudine discussit, ut ibidem. Quare et hodie cum maiori mansuetudine et reverencia dubia apostolice sedis in generalibus conciliis discuti debent propter alterum respectum inmediate subiectorum, quod nota. Et iuxta hoc considerandum est, quod concilia universalia usque ad octavum generale tempore Adriani Constantinopoli celebratum satis sunt ponderanda, quia illa enim fuerunt celebrata per omnes sedes etc.

13   Et iuxta materiam nostram considerandum est primo, quod auctoritas conciliorum est supra omnem potestatem, quoniam in ipsis spiritus sanctus presidet. Unde hoc, licet in principio Ysodori de synodis et aliis multis locis declarari possit, tamen in concilio Calcedonensi dicitur spiritum sanctum manifeste consedisse patribus in Niceam congregatis. Unde dicitur 'spiritum sanctum ordinare, que ordinantur. Ergo qui retractat ea, spiritus cassat graciam.' Sancta synodus dixit: 'Omnes hoc dicimus; anathema, qui retractat.'

14   Similiter in sexta Constantinopolitana in multis passibus hoc legitur et in conclusione octavi concilii, ubi dicit causam, quare

ity] to judge him, as is [said] in the twenty-first canon, *Singularis*, of the Eighth Council.[47]

Today, however, because the universal Catholic Church, which 12 once resided in five sees, as the patrician Bahanes said in the seventh proceeding of the Eighth Council,[48] is reduced to the Roman see alone, which shall recall the others to Christ the Head, as is said in the same place, it is then necessary to say that the universal Roman council is alloted a double nature: [a first nature as] subject to the Roman pontiff, as it always was; and [a second nature], when it represents the universal Catholic Church, in respect of which it is superior to the pope, as it always was too, because the universal councils that used to represent the whole universal Catholic Church were always superior to the pope, as is discussed in the decree of the Eighth Council already cited, although with all mildness.[49] Therefore today too, doubts about the Apostolic See should be discussed in general councils with even greater mildness and reverence owing to the further respect due those immediately subject [to him]. Note that. And in light of this, universal councils, up to the Eighth celebrated in Constantinople at the time of Adrian, must be considered of sufficient weight because they were celebrated by all of the sees etc.

And in light of our subject matter, we must consider, first, that 13 the authority of councils is superior to any power, since the Holy Spirit presides in them. Hence, although the beginning of Isidore's *On Synods*[50] and many other places might be cited, nevertheless it is said in [the acts of] the Council of Chalcedon that the Holy Spirit clearly sat with the fathers gathered at Nicaea.[51] Hence it is said, "The Holy Spirit ordained what was ordained. Therefore the Holy Spirit withdraws grace from whoever withdraws those ordinations." The holy synod said, "All of us say this; let whoever draws back be anathema!'"

A similar statement may be read in many places in the Sixth 14 Council at Constantinople[52] and at the conclusion of the Eighth

conciliis omnino obediendum sit. Et dicunt patres: 'per datam nobis potestatem a spiritu sancto, a primo et magno pontifice nostro.'
Et infra: 'Quis enim nesciat, quod in medio sancte synodi fuerit
incomprehensibilis et incircumscriptus Christus et dominus, qui
dixit: Ubi sunt duo vel tres in nomine meo etc.?' Unde ex illa potestate, quam habent patres in sacro concilio iudicandi fidem et, ut
dixit Helpidius vir spectabilis in prima accione Calcedonensis
concilii, eciam verbum, salvatorem scilicet Christum nostrum, dicit: 'Hodie cunctorum dominus et deus, verbum, salvator vobis se
ad iudicandum tradidit et patitur iudicantes et honorat potestate
decreti.' Et hoc decretum explicatur ibi: *Quodcunque ligaveritis*, ut
habetur accione prima octavi concilii, et in 5ᵃ accione, ubi dicitur:
'Sanctissimi vicarii senioris Rome et nos, qui reliquarum sedium
vicarii sumus, hec omnia dissolvimus hodie gracia Iesu Christi, qui
nobis dedit summi sacerdocii potestatem iuste ac congrue ligandi
atque solvendi.'

15   Ideo manifestum est omnem viventem huic sanctissimo presidi,
sancto spiritu⟨i⟩ scilicet, et eius iudicio merito subici debere. Unde
in prima accione octavi concilii, quod non parens synodis anathe-
matus est et 'alienatus a christianorum gracia tanquam qui irridet
Christi veri dei nostri munificenciam, quam dedit sacerdotibus
suis docens: *Quecunque ligaveritis*.'

16   Quare nullum est dubium, quin universale concilium eciam papam iudicare possit, licet cum omni mansuetudine hoc facere debeat. Unde habetur in xxi decreto octavi concilii in ℭ *Porro*, ita:
'Porro si universalis synodus fuerit congregata et facta fuerit eciam
de sancta Romanorum ecclesia quevis ambiguitas et controversia,
oportet venerabiliter et cum convenienti reverencia de proposita
questione sciscitari et solucionem accipere et aut proficere aut pro-

Council,[53] where it states the reason why councils must be entirely obeyed. The Fathers say, "by the power given to us by the Holy Spirit, by our first and great pontiff [. . .]." And below, "Who does not know that the incomprehensible and illimitable Christ and Lord, who said *Where two or three are gathered in My name* etc., was in the midst of the holy synod?" Thence comes that power which the Fathers have in the holy council of passing judgment about the faith. As Helpidius, an outstanding man, says — and the Word, our Savior, that is, Christ, too says — in the first proceeding of the Council of Chalcedon,[54] "Today the Lord and God of all, the Word, the Savior, gave Himself over to you for judgment and suffers those who judge and honors them with the power of making decrees." And this decree is explicated there: *Whatever you bind*, as is found in the first proceeding of the Eighth Council and in the sixth proceeding, where it is said that "the most holy vicars of the Elder Rome and we, who are the vicars of the other sees, release all these things today by the grace of Jesus Christ, who gave us the power of the supreme priesthood to bind and loose justly and fittingly."[55]

So it is clear that anyone living rightly should be subject to this   15 most holy president, that is, the Holy Spirit, and its judgment. Hence we read in the light of the first proceeding of the eighth council[56] that anyone who does not obey synods is anathema and "alienated from the grace of Christians as one who mocks the munificence of our true God, Christ, which He gave to His priests, saying, *Whatever you bind*."

Therefore there is no doubt that a universal council even could   16 judge a pope, although it should do this with all mildness. Hence we find it is thus in the twenty-first decree of the Eighth Council in ℭ *Porro*, "Further, if a universal council were gathered and some sort of ambiguity and controversy arose even concerning the holy church of the Romans, it should treat the question raised respectfully and with due reverence, accept a solution and either proceed or cause proceedings [to be held]. Nevertheless, it should not au-

fectum facere. Non tamen audacter sentenciam dicere contra summos senioris Rome pontifices.' Ex hoc decreto manifestum est
eciam papam in quocunque dubio iudicari posse per concilium
universale, licet concilium non audacter, sed cum omni reverencia
procedere debeat; et plus hodie quam unquam ex causis supratac-
tis. Idem probat textus decimi capituli eiusdem concilii, qui vult,
'quod nullus ante diligentem examinacionem et synodicam sentenciam a communione se separet proprii patriarche, licet criminalem
quamlibet eius causam se nosse pretendat, et neque recuset nomen
eius inter sacra misteria referre' etc. Hoc c. loquitur manifeste in
quibuscunque criminalibus causis, non solum fidei etc. Et quod
hoc papa Nicolaus sensit, probant gesta octavi concilii accione septima, ubi ipse Nicolaus auctoritate Petri et Pauli, omnium sanctorum et sex conciliorum generalium tulit sentenciam etc., ubi se subesse conciliis fatebatur.

17   Sed quia aliqui Romani pontifices venerunt contra statuta
conciliorum ex certis causis, aliquando minus racionabilibus, dubium est, an hoc ne posset eis inhiberi cum irritante decreto. Circa
quod primo considerandum est, quod omnia statuta generalium
conciliorum ita antiquitus per Romanos pontifices stricte serva-
bantur, ac si eciam decretum irritans appositum fuisset. Non enim
videbatur eis, quod potestas eorum esset supra patrum statuta. Ita
scripsit Zozimus papa: 'Contra statuta patrum aliquid condere vel
mutare nec huius quidem sedis potest auctoritas. Apud nos enim
inconvulsis radicibus vivit antiquitas, cui decreta patrum sanxere
reverenciam.' Et habetur 25 q. 1 Contra statuta et c. Sunt quidam et

daciously deliver a sentence against the supreme pontiffs of the Elder Rome."[57] It is clear from this decree that the pope could be
judged by a universal council in any doubtful case, although the
council should not proceed rashly but with all reverence, and today more than ever, for the reasons touched upon above. The text
of the tenth decree of the same council proves the same thing,
which wills that "no one should separate himself from communion
with his own patriarch before a diligent examination and synodal
decision [is made of that patriarch], even if he claims to know
some criminal charge against [that patriarch], and he should not
refuse to mention his name when celebrating the sacred mysteries" etc.[58] This chapter speaks clearly about any and all criminal
causes, not just matters of faith etc. And what Pope Nicholas
thought of this, the records of the Eighth Synod, the seventh proceeding, prove, where Nicholas himself, by the authority of Peter
and Paul, all the saints and the six general councils, delivered the
sentence etc.; in this place he confessed himself to be subject to
councils.[59]

But because some Roman pontiffs have acted against the stat-   17
utes of the councils for certain causes, sometimes less reasonable
ones, there is doubt whether they could be restrained from these
actions by a voided decree. Concerning this we must first consider
that all statutes of general councils were observed so strictly by the
Roman pontiffs in olden times [that it was] as if [he believed]
even a voided decree were applicable [to him]. It did not seem to
these popes that their power was superior to the statutes of the
Fathers. Pope Zosimus wrote thus, "No authority, not even the
authority of this see, can lay down anything against the statutes of
the Fathers or change them. Antiquity lives firmly rooted in our
see, and the decrees of the Fathers confirm the reverence shown
her." We find this in [Gratian's *Decretum*], C. 25 q. 1 c. *Contra
statuta* [c. 7], c. *Sunt quidam* [c. 6] and c. *Omne* [c. 8], where there
are also many other texts on the subject. Hence it is said in the ru-

c. *Omne*, ubi et alii plures textus de hoc. Unde dicitur in rubrica dicti c. *Contra*, 'quod contra statuta sanctorum patrum apostolice sedis auctoritas aliquid concedere non valet.' Et c. *Contra statuta* dicit: 'Contra statuta patrum aliquid condere vel mutare' etc. ut supra. Concor‹dant› c. *Ridiculum* xii d. et ix q. iii *Conquestus*.

18   Et hoc eciam plene trahi potest ex epistola concilii Affricani ad Celestinum papam, qui quoniam certos in Affrica excommunicatos absolvit et admisit ad communionem, licet sub patriarchatu Romano forent, tamen concilium contra eum allegat Nicenum concilium, scribens ne hoc faciat. Unde papa non intendebat se cum sua potestate iuvare, quod non teneretur precise ad observanciam illorum decretorum, sed dicit alia esse Nicena statuta, licet compertum fuit Affricanos melius allegasse. Similiter in octavo concilio, et varia possent ad idem in epistolis Leonis et Bonefacii et aliorum haberi.

19   Unde patet, quod antiquitus[1] non licebat Romanis pontificibus, tanquam hoc iure non possent, contra statuta conciliorum facere. Et ita ipsi obligabantur ad servandum et exequendum statuta sicut alii subditi, quoniam et ipsi subditi sunt universalis concilii, licet papa dicat in accione prima octavi concilii secundum Gelasium papam, quod adhibita consideracione diligenti Romanus pontifex patrum et predecessorum statuta secundum temporum necessitatem moderari posse, ut eciam hoc legimus in pluribus passibus scripture et ita ex historiis factum comprehendimus. Quare ex ista ambiguitate dubium decreti irritantis oritur.

20   Et legitur in octavo concilio, septima accione, ubi papa loquitur: 'patrum ac predecessorum secuti vestigia qui soliti sunt eciam nu-

bric of the aforesaid canon *Contra* [*statuta*] that "The authority of the Apostolic See is not valid to grant something against the statutes of the holy Fathers." And *Contra statuta* says, "Against the statutes of the Fathers [the pope's authority cannot] lay down or change anything" etc., as above. Both c. *Ridiculum* D. 12 [c. 5] and C. 9 q. 3 c. *Conquestus* [c. 8, both in Gratian] agree.

And this also can be extracted fully from the letter of the African council to Pope Celestine, who had absolved certain excommunicated men in Africa and admitted them to communion. Even though they were subject to the Roman patriarchate, the council neverthess cited the Nicene Council against Celestine, writing that he should not do this. Whereupon the pope did not try to show that he could help the men with his power because he was not categorically bound to observe those decrees; but rather claimed that there were other Nicene statutes, although it was found that the Africans had cited [the statutes] more accurately. So too in the Eighth Council,[60] and various passages in the letters of Leo, Boniface and others could be cited to make the same point.   18

Hence it is obvious that in ancient times it was not permitted to the Roman pontiffs as though by right to act against the statutes of the councils. And so they were obligated to observe and execute the statutes, just like other persons subject [to them], since they themselves are subjects of a universal council—although the pope says in the first proceeding of the Eighth Council that, according to Pope Gelasius, the Roman pontiffs after careful consideration could moderate the statutes of the Fathers and of his predecessors according to the necessity of the time, as we also read in many passages of the Scriptures, and we understand from history that things have been done this way.[61] That is why doubt arose from this ambiguity about a voided decree.   19

We read in the seventh proceeding of the Eighth Council [a passage] where the pope says, "There are persons following in the footsteps of the Fathers and our predecessors who are accustomed   20

merosorum concilia nequiter celebrata cassare pontificum. Ex quo
trahitur papam eciam supra omnia concilia particularia posse' etc.
Huius habetur exemplum in sexta accione, quomodo Affricana synodus suam reprobavit sentenciam et Zozimo pape adhesit. Et
quod de tota ecclesia iudicare possit, ibidem loquitur papa ante locum predictum: 'Proinde nos, quia sedis apostolice de tota ecclesia
phas habentis iudicare moderamina tenemus.' Hec ibi. Ex quo patet pape iudicium universale esse ad totam ecclesiam. Tamen, ut
ante hoc legitur, idem Nicolaus papa dicit: 'Itaque denique volumus et ita decernimus istius, ymmo vero cunctorum sacerdotum,
causas examinare culpasve punire, ut paternos terminos non trans-
grediamur, sacros canones non conculcemus nec decretalia sedis
apostolice constituta, quibus ecclesia tota fulcitur atque unitur,
quoquomodo violemus' etc. Et in sexta accione, cum Zacharias a
Phocio Calcedonensis diceret: 'Et pape Nicolai ac ceterorum patriarcharum canon princeps est et secundum illum agentes nil faciunt extra id, quod decet. Cum vero extra hunc faciunt, sive papa
Nicolaus, sive alius quis, non acquiescimus,' nichil a concilio con-
tradicebatur, sed probacio, quod Nicolaus secundum canones iudi-
casset, fuit producta et ad argumenta responsum.

21   Unde pro hoc forte dicendum crederem, quod papa ante omnia
servare tenetur decreta de suo regimine et statu edita et regulariter
alios inferiores inpedire non debere; et pro hoc possit irritans decretum decerni, quod, quecunque per patrum et universalium
conciliorum statuta expressa sunt,[2] ad illa regulariter papa oblige-
tur eciam cum decreto irritanti, quod illa tollere aut inmutare non
possit. Sed si particulari casu, remanentibus decretis semper in

to annul the councils that were wickedly conducted by numerous pontiffs. From this it is inferred that the pope could be superior to every particular council" etc.[62] We have an example of this in the sixth proceeding, [in the passage about] how the African synod reproved his decision but remained loyal to Pope Zosimus.[63] In that same place, just before this passage, the pope says that he can pass judgment on the whole Church: "Consequently, because we hold the power of the Apostolic See, we have the right to pass judgment on the whole Church."[64] It is obvious from this that the judgment of the pope is universal for the entire Church. Nevertheless, as we read in the previous passage, the same Pope Nicholas says, "Finally, we will and so decide to examine the cases and punish the faults of this man, and indeed of all priests, in such a way as not to transgress paternal boundaries or trample underfoot the sacred canons or in any way violate the decretals laid down by the Apostolic See by which the entire Church is bolstered and united," etc.[65] And in the sixth proceeding, when Zachary of Chalcedon says, [representing] Photius, "The canon of Pope Nicholas and the other patriarchs is preeminent, and those acting according to it do nothing outside it, which is fitting; but when [anyone] acts outside it, whether that person is Pope Nicholas or anyone else, we do not willingly obey,"[66] the council contradicted nothing [in this statement], but [instead], in reply to the argument, produced a proof that Pope Nicholas had judged according to the canons.

Thus I am inclined to say in this regard that the pope is bound to observe before all things the decrees issued concerning his own regime and estate, and ought not as a rule hinder his inferiors. And in regard to the claim that he can decide to void a decree, the pope ordinarily is obligated to obey whatever statutes the fathers and the universal councils have issued, even in the case of a voided decree, because he may not change or set aside decrees. But in a particular case, so long as decrees remain always in force in all

21

aliis omnibus in suo robore, quod tunc habita diligenti consideracione secundum temporis necessitatem dispensare potest, sic tamen, quod illa dispensacio fiat ob necessitatem temporis et ob melius cum diligenti consideracione, servata semper quantum
possibile racione decreti. Si necessitas suadet, decretum servari
tunc non debere, et quod universali concilio tanquam superiori, de
hoc racionem reddat. Et si inventus fuerit absque causis illis per
Gelasium et Nicolaum Romanos pontifices in prefato loco positis
fecisse, tunc puniri possit tanquam abutens sua potestate, hoc sibi
licere putans, quod sibi minime licuit, quoniam eius potestas ad
edificandum data non debet prosilire contra canones nisi in edificacionem ecclesie et non alias.

22   Et pro hoc est advertendum, quod potestas Romani pontificis,
licet sit a deo, quoniam ita Christus ad Petrum locutus est:
'Quodcumque ligaveris' etc., tamen par eciam fuit omnium apostolorum potestas a Christo, quia omnibus dixit: 'Quodcumque ligaveritis,' ut scribit Ciprianus in epistola ad Nouacianum, et habetur eciam in c. *Loquitur* xxiiii q. i, et c. *In novo* xxi d. Si ergo par
potestas a Christo omnibus data est, tunc manifestum est papam a
Christo ultra alios episcopos nullam recipisse potestatem. Quare
in alios omnes non habet talem supraeminentem potestatem a
Christo, quin iudicari possit per congregatos in unum, ut predictum est. Sed a nullo particulari homine iudicari debet vel potest,
quia in ordine unius kathedre primum Petrus, deinde alii apostoli
sedebant. Unde prior a nullo posteriori iudicatur, sed prior de pos-
terioribus ‹iudicat›, quando sua potestate non in edificacionem
utuntur, sed abutuntur. Sic et collecti posteriores in actu vel po-

other respects, at that point, having carefully considered [everything] in accordance with the necessity of the time, he can dispense [an individual or collectivity from the force of decrees]. Nevertheless, the dispensation must be given in view of necessary circumstances and in order to improve the situation after careful consideration, preserving as far as possible the sense of the decree. If necessity should become persuasive, at that point let him explain why the decree ought not to be observed, and let him make this explanation to a universal council as though to his superior. And if it is found that he has acted without the causes posited by the Roman pontiffs Gelasius and Nicholas in the aforesaid place,[67] then he could be punished for abuse of power and for thinking he can licitly do what is entirely prohibited, since his power, given for building up the Church, ought not to overleap [boundaries and act] against the canons, unless to build up the Church — and not otherwise.

And in this regard it must be noted that the power of the Roman pontiff, although it is from God, since Christ spoke thus to Peter, *Whatsoever you shall bind* etc.,[68] nevertheless was equaled by the power of the apostles, also from Christ, because He said to all of them, *Whatsoever you shall bind,*[69] as Cyprian writes in the letter to Novatian;[70] and this also is found in [Gratian's *Decretum*], C. 24 q. 1 c. *Loquitur* [c. 18] and D. 21 c. *In novo* [c. 2]. If, therefore, equal power was given to all by Christ, then it is clear that the pope received no more power than did the other bishops. Therefore, he does not have from Christ such supereminent power over all the others that he could not be judged by them gathered together, as has been said. But he should or can be judged by no individual, because first Peter, then other apostles sat in order on the one see. Hence the prior is judged by no one posterior; but the prior judges the posterior when the latter use their power not to build up but to abuse. So also the posterior, gathered together, either in act or in potency judge the first.[71] So I understand that the

22

tencia iudicant primum. Sic intelligo, quod potestas pape sit a Christo et similiter potestas omnium aliorum. Sed cura, ut quisque recte utatur sua potestate, est principaliter in papa et successive in quolibet, secundum sibi ab antiquis determinatam provinciam vel locum.

23   Unde in concilio Calcedonensi, quando disputacio exorta est inter legatos pape et Constantinopolitanum super primacia et iudices concilii decreverunt, quod canones deberent produci, legati Leonis non produxerunt nisi sextum capitulum concilii Niceni. Et licet aliter hoc capitulum alibi habeatur, tamen in hiis verbis produxerunt: 'Ecclesia Romana semper habuit primatum, teneat autem' etc. Alibi tamen in octava universali synodo et in originali aliter habetur, ut infra dicetur. Tamen nullum habuerunt articulum legati nisi hoc, scilicet: Quia semper tenuit, tunc teneat. Et non dixerunt[3], quia a Christo recepit primatum. Et ut trahi potest ex diffinicione primi Constantinopolitani concilii centum quinquaginta patrum, tunc primatum habuit ab urbe Romana, ut eciam omnes alie civitates post Christum retinuerunt illas suas eminencias, ut prius quoad metropoliticas sedes et archiflamines, ut modicum infra dicetur. Dicitur enim sic in illo concilio, quod Constantinopolitanus episcopus sit secundus post Romanum, quia Constantinopolis secunda Roma. Et in diffinicione concilii Calcedonensis super controversia pretacta dicitur: 'Ex hiis, que gesta et ab unoquoque deposita, perpendimus ante omnia quidem primatum et honorem precipuum secundum canones antique Rome reverendissimo archiepiscopo conservari; oportere autem sanctissimum archiepiscopum regie urbis Constantinopolis nove Rome idem primatibus honoris dignum esse' etc. Ecce quod diffinicio di-

power of the pope is from Christ as likewise is the power of all the other [apostles]. But the responsibility to make sure each one uses his power rightly lies principally with the pope and by succession with anyone else [appointed by the pope, i.e. his representative], according to the province or place delimited for him by the ancients.

Therefore, when a dispute arose in the Council of Chalcedon 23 between the legates of the pope and the patriarch of Constantinople about primacy and the judges of the council decreed that the canons should be brought forth, the legates brought forth nothing except c. 6 of the Council of Nicaea.[72] Although this chapter is found quoted otherwise in other places, nevertheless, the words they quoted were these: "The Roman church always had primacy; let it hold" etc. Yet elsewhere in the Eighth Universal Synod we find it in the original text as quoted below.[73] Nevertheless, the legates had no other argument than this: Because it always held the primacy, then it should hold it; they did not say: because he received the primacy from Christ. And as can be inferred from the definition of the 150 fathers of the First Council of Constantinople, [the papacy] at that time held the primacy from the city of Rome, as all the other cities retained their eminence after the time of Christ, as earlier was true of metropolitan sees and their chief priests, as will be said a little below.[74] So it is said that in that council that the Bishop of Constantinople comes second after the Bishop of Rome, because Constantinople is the second Rome. And it is said about the aforesaid controversy in the definition of the Council of Chalcedon,[75] "We deem on the basis of these proceedings and the depositions of each one [of us] that primacy and particular honor are reserved according to the canons above all to the most reverend archbishop of the Elder Rome; and it is necessary that the most holy archbishop of the royal city of Constantinople, the New Rome, is likewise worthy of the same primacies of honor." Look: the definition says that according to the canons the

cit secundum canones antique Rome archiepiscopum primatum habere. Ex quo trahitur, quod canones inspecto loco, scilicet urbe Romana, que capud mundi fuit, et inspectis aliis mandatis per Petrum Clementi, ut infra dicetur, diffinierunt Romanum episcopum primatum habere debere.

24   Et per istum modum patet, quomodo archiepiscopus Romanus ex canonibus primatum habuit. Et quia canones spiritu dei conditi fuerunt, ita credendum est, quod a deo ita ordinatum sit. Unde Leo papa ad Anastasium Tessalonicensem: 'Etsi ordo, inquit, generalis est omnibus sacerdotibus, non tamen communis est dignitas omnibus, quia et inter beatissimos apostolos in similitudine honoris fuit quedam discrecio potestatis; et cum omnium par esset eleccio, uni tamen datum est, ut ceteris preeminaret.' Et per hoc faciliter consideratur, quod iudicium concilii universalis, quod est supra canones et canones condere habet universales, posset non obstantibus quibuscunque ante conditis canonibus ex inspiracione sancti spiritus alteri quam archiepiscopo Romano primatum tribuere, licet credamus, quod hoc nunquam evenire debeat propter diffinicionem sanctorum patrum et sancti spiritus, qui eis consedit in concilio Niceno, Constantinopolitano et Calcedonensi et aliis. Et videmus in multis particularibus conciliis Constantinopolitanis ad hoc longissimo tempore laboratum, quod Constantinopolitanus preferreretur Romano. Quod tamen nunquam in aliquo universali concilio potuit obtineri, eciam in celebratis Constantinopoli.

25   Ad autem aliquantulum probandum, quod archiepiscopus Romanus sortitus sit primatum ex primitivitate urbis, adductum prius in epistola Valentiniani ad Theodosium vocetur, ubi dicit: 'Antiquitas contulit sedi apostolice primatum.' Ecce dicit: 'Antiquitas contulit.' Quod est notandum. Item Galla Placidia augusta

archbishop of the Elder Rome has primacy. From this we conclude that the canons defined that the Roman bishop should have primacy in view of his situation, that is, in the city of Rome, which was the head of the world, and having taken cognizance of other commands given to Clement by Peter, as will be said below.

And in this way it is obvious that the archbishop of Rome had the primacy according to the canons. Because the canons were established by the Spirit of God, so we must believe that this was ordained thus by God. Hence Pope Leo says to Anastasius of Thessalonica,[76] "And if ordination is general in all priests, nevertheless, [the same] rank is not shared by all, because even among the most blessed apostles, despite a similarity of honor, there was a certain distinction of power. Although all are equally chosen, nevertheless it is given to one to be preeminent over the others." And from this it may be readily borne in mind that the judgment of the universal council, which is above the canons and has the power to establish universal canons, could, by the inspiration of the Holy Spirit, notwithstanding any canons made before, assign the primacy to someone other than the archbishop of Rome, although we may believe that would never happen on account of the pronouncement of the Holy Fathers and the Holy Spirit, who sat with them in the councils of Nicaea, Constantinople and Chalcedon, and other councils. And we see that in many local councils at Constantinople it was worked out over a long period of time that the bishop of Constantinople is given precedence over the bishop of Rome. Yet this state of affairs could never hold in any universal council, even in those celebrated in Constantinople.

The argument that the Roman archbishop was allotted the primacy because of the antiquity of his city is enunciated earlier in the letter of Valentinian addressed to Theodosius, where he says, "Antiquity confers privileges on the Apostolic See."[77] It should be noted that he says, "Antiquity confers." Likewise Galla Placidia the empress,[78] writing to her daughter, the empress Helena Pulcheria,

24

25

Helene Pulcherie auguste filie scribens in fine dicit: 'Debemus enim primatum in omnibus inmortali conversacioni tribuere ei, que totum mundum pie virtutis dominacione complevit.' Et Placidia filio augusto scribens dicit, quomodo Petrus in Roma principatum episcopatus ordinavit, quia maxima civitatum et domina omnium terrarum. Et ideo, sicut Petrus, qui fuit Cephas et capud, elegit caput orbis urbem Romanam, ita precipit Clementi, ut 'in civitatibus, in quibus olim apud ethnicos primi flamines et primi legis doctores erant, primates vel patriarche ponerentur, qui reliquorum episcoporum iudicia et maiora, quociens necesse fuerit, negocia in fide agitarent.' Et de hac ordinaria scribit Clemens ad Iacobum fratrem domini. Et Anacletus a Petro presbiter ordinatus in secunda epistola ad episcopos in Italia constitutos dicit: 'Provincie multo tempore ante Christum divise sunt maxima ex parte, et postea ab apostolis et Clemente predecessore nostro ipsa divisio est renovata; et in capite provinciarum, ubi dudum primates legis erant seculi ac prima iudiciaria potestas, patriarchas vel primates, qui unam formam tenent, licet diversa sint nomina, poni et esse iusserunt' etc. Et in tertia epistola: 'Quidam vestrum consuluerunt, an primates esse debuerant, an non' etc., ubi de hoc. Et brevissimis verbis hec omnia exprimuntur in decreto concilii Niceni, ubi dicit: 'Antiqua consuetudo teneat.' Quod exponit Hincmarus Remensis xv c. *Contra Hincmarum Laudunensem:* 'antiqua consuetudo, scilicet que fuit apud ethnicos.' Et pro hoc facit accio xii‹i› concilii Calcedonensis, ubi, dum Anastasius Nicee episcopus deducere vellet superioritatem sedis Nicee super Basianopolim, arguit ex curia, quoniam semper curia in Nicea habuit sub se Basianopolim sic, quod curialem ibi poneret, cum deficeret etc. Ubi de hoc plura.

says at the end that "we ought to grant primacy in all things to that acquaintance with the immortal, which fills the whole earth with the dominance of holy virtue." And writing to her son the Emperor she says that Peter established the primacy of the episcopate in Rome because it was the greatest of cities and the mistress of all the earth. And, therefore, just as Peter, who was Cephas and head, chose the head of the world, the city of Rome, so did he command Clement that "The primates and patriarchs are placed in the cities where once were the chief priests and doctors of the gentiles' law. They pass judgment over other bishops and deal with matters of faith, whenever necessary."[79] And Clement writes about this ordinary power to James, the brother of the Lord.[80] And Anacletus, who was ordained by Peter, says in the second letter to the bishops in Italy, "the provinces were mostly divided a long time before Christ; and that division was renewed afterwards by the apostles and Clement, our predecessor. In the head city of the provinces, in which once were those preeminent in secular law and the principal judicial power, they commanded that there be appointed patriarchs and primates who should hold one single form [of authority], although there are diverse names" etc.[81] And in the third letter [he says], "Some of you inquire whether there should be primates or not" etc, where [there is a discussion] of this.[82] All this is expressed in the briefest of words in a decree of the Nicene Council, where it says, "Let ancient custom bind."[83] Hincmar of Rheims expounds this in c. 15 of *Against Hincmar of Laon*, "'Ancient custom,' that is, the custom found among the gentiles."[84] And this is supported by the thirteenth proceeding of the Council of Chalcedon.[85] When Anastasius, bishop of Nicaea, wished to deduce the superiority of the see of Nicaea over that of Bassionopolis, he argued from jurisdiction, since the [secular] court in Nicaea always had Bassionopolis under it, given that it had placed a judicial representative there when it was lacking one, etc. One can find much on the subject in this passage.

26   Et ex istis patet, quod prioritas sedium omnium habet unam
regulam, scilicet Niceni concilii, in quo spiritus sanctus indubie
patribus consedit, scilicet: 'Antiqua consuetudo teneat,' scilicet que
fuit apud ethnicos; et talia privilegia sedium ex illo decreto perpetua sunt. Quare eadem racione, qua sedes Mediolanensis est me-
tropolitica, eadem et Romana prima omnium, quia consuetudo
antiqua teneri debet.

27   Sed non est ex hoc presumendum, quod pure humana ordinacione graduacio illa ortum cepit, ymmo et divina inspiracione
propter pacem ecclesiasticam conservandam. Unde Romana sedes
per hoc, quod Christus Petro loquebatur: 'Et super hanc petram,'
ex interpretacione sanctorum patrum et ob fidei constantissimam
firmitatem, quia in illa sede triginta successive martirio coronati
fuerunt propter fidem, credendum est illam sedem a domino primatum habere, sicut hoc Anacletus et multi sancti patres scripserunt. Nec est negandum, quando eciam alie sedes a domino gra-
duacionem suam acciperunt per ordinacionem sacri Niceni concilii
et aliorum, et plura concurrunt in sede apostolica ad eius firman-
dam primitivitatem, scilicet Romana urbs, mundi domini sedes,
principis apostolorum Petri etc., ut in simili scribit sanctus Inno-
cencius ad Allexandrum Antiocenum episcopum dicens: 'Revol-
ventes itaque auctoritatem Nicene synodi, que unam omnium per
orbem terrarum mentem explicat sacerdotum, que censuit de
Anthiocena ecclesia, cunctis fidelibus ne dixerim sacerdotibus esse
necessarium custodire.' Et infra: 'Unde advertimus non tam pro civitatis magnificencia hoc eidem attributum, quam quod prima
primi apostoli sedes esse monstretur, ubi et nomen accepit religio
christiana atque ‹propter› conventum apostolorum apud se fieri
meruit celeberrimum. Que urbis Rome sedi non cederet, nisi quod

It is obvious from these passages that the [Roman principle of] 26
priority over all sees [is based on] a single rule, that is, that of the
Nicene Council (wherein the Holy Spirit undoubtedly dwelt together with the Fathers), that is, "Let ancient custom bind," that
is, the ancient custom that existed among the Gentiles; and such
privileges of sees are perpetual from that decree. Therefore, for the
same reason that the see of Milan is metropolitan, Rome is the
first see of all, because ancient custom ought to bind.

But we must not presume from this that this ranking originated 27
in a purely human ordinance. Indeed it took its origin from a divine ordinance in order to preserve the peace of the Church.
Therefore, the Roman see, because Christ said to Peter, *And upon
this rock [I will build my Church],*[86] as interpreted by the holy fathers,
because of its utter firmness of faith — for thirty men who occupied that see were crowned in succession with martyrdom for their
faith — we must believe that see has its primacy from the Lord,
just as Anacletus and many other holy fathers wrote.[87] Nor is it
to be denied, since other sees too received their ranking from
the Lord through an ordinance of the Holy Council of Nicaea and
others; and many factors come together in confirming the first-
born status of the Apostolic See, namely, the city of Rome, the
seat of the lord of the world, the prince of the apostles etc., as in a
similar context Saint Innocent[88] writes to Alexander, the bishop of
Antioch, saying, "And turning to the authority of the Nicene
Synod, which unfolds the single mind of all priests throughout the
world, it is necessary that all the faithful, not just priests, keep to
its decisions regarding the church of Antioch." And below, "Hence
we remark that this [status] is to be attributed to [the Roman see]
not so much because of the magnificence of the city as because it
may be shown to be the first seat of the first apostle, and the
Christian religion first received its name there, and it deserves to
be the most celebrated on account of the meeting of the apostles in
it.[89] [Antioch] should yield to the see of the city of Rome just be-

illa in transitu meruit, ista susceptum et consummatum gaudet.' Idem scribit Leo ad Maximum Anthiocenum. Ex quo habemus urbem et Petrum primitivitatem Romane sedi dare.

28   Et quod magnificencia urbis plus operetur quam pontificis primi sanctitas aut precellencia aut prioritas, patet, quia Allexandria, ubi non fuit Petrus episcopus, sed Marcus, prefertur Anthiocene, sicut tunc Allexandria civitas Antiochie et loco Ierosolimorum, ubi pontifex maximus se obtulit pro nobis et ubi sanctus Iacobus primus archiepiscopus, ut legitur in gestis universalis Constantinopolitani concilii in prima accione in epistola patriarche Ierosolimorum, presedit. De quo in *Historia* Eusebii libro vii c. xvi habetur, ubi dicitur: 'Denique et Iacobi kathedra, qui primus in terris episcopus ab ipso Salvatore et apostolis in Ierosolimis est electus quemque fratrem Christi volumina designant, usque in hodiernum inibi conservatur, atque in ea sedent omnes, qui usque ad hoc tempus sedis illius sacerdocium sorciuntur. Servatur ergo cum ingenti studio vel a maioribus tradita memoria sanctitatis et cum magna veneracione habetur vel vetustatis vel primi sacerdocii obtentu.' Hec ille. Et doctores antiqui scribentes super epistolis canonicis querunt, cur epistole Iacobi preponantur, et pro causa una ponunt, quia ipse Ierosolimorum regendam suscepit ecclesiam, unde fons et origo euangelice predicacionis incipiens undique diffusa est, que prima sedes fuit christianitatis sicut et iudaismi, cuius cathedre dignitatem Paulus eos numerando venerans ait: 'Iacobus, Cephas, Iohannes, qui videbantur columpne esse ecclesie.' Hec dignitas transmutata est primum Antiochie, postea Rome, se-

cause what the former merited in passing [i.e., the presence of apostles], the latter rejoices in as a thing embraced and consummated." Leo writes the same thing to Maximus of Antioch.[90] From this passage we understand that the city and Peter granted first-born status to the Roman see.

And it is obvious that the magnificence of the city accounted 28 for more than the sanctity, the excellence or the priority of the first pontiff, because Alexandria, where Mark, not Peter, was bishop, is preferred to the Antiochene see, just as the city of Alexandria at that time had precedence over Antioch or Jerusalem, where the Supreme Pontiff [i.e. Christ] offered Himself for us and where Saint James was the first archbishop, as we read in the records of the universal Council of Constantinople, in the first proceeding, in the letter of the patriarch of Jerusalem.[91] This can be found in Book VII, chapter 16 of Eusebius' *History*,[92] where it is said: "Next, there is in Jerusalem the see of James — who was the first bishop on earth, chosen by the Savior Himself and the Apostles, whom the books designate 'the brother of the Lord' — preserved there down to the present day. And there sit all those who are allotted the priesthood of that see even to this time. It is therefore honored with great zeal either owing to the memory of its sanctity handed down by our ancestors and held in great veneration, or on the pretext of its antiquity and its first priesthood." Thus Eusebius. And the ancient doctors, writing about canonical letters, ask why the letter of James is placed first; and posit as one cause, because he took on the governance of the Christians of Jerusalem, the place from which sprang the preaching of the gospel, which began there and was diffused everywhere. It was the principal see of Christendom as of Judaism. Paul venerated the dignity of the see, listing them and saying: "James, Cephas, John, who seem to be the columns of the Church."[93] This dignity was transferred first to Antioch, afterwards to Rome, in accordance with the

cundum seculi dignitates. Quam adhuc obtinet apostolorum princeps Petrus, sicut sibi a domino concessum est. Hec ibi habentur. Unde licet omnibus mundi sedibus preferri deberet, habendo respectum ad sedentem et consecrantem illam sedem suo sanguine et ad predicta, tamen [propter] civitas⁴ Ierosolimorum, que tunc longe minor fuit quam Allexandria et Anthiochia in seculi dignitate, sequitur in ordine illas sedes, et Roma prefertur, sicut sibi a domino concessum est.

29   Similiter et Ephesum, ubi Iohannes sedit, merito deberet Allexandrine preferri ex sessione, quia Iohannes deo dilectus apostolus et evangelista, Marcus non apostolus. Quare concluditur, quod pax et utilitas ecclesie, que consideravit, quomodo fides augmentum habere potest, ita per spiritum sanctum ordinavit, ut maiori civitati ita honor conservacionis spiritualium daretur, sicut habuit temporalium, ut ex concordancia utriusque pax et conservacio fortis in ecclesia oriretur et stabiliretur, licet ad hoc eciam concurrerent alie divine cause in certis sedibus. Unde Ieronimus *Contra Iovinianum* libro primo, cum Iovinianus obiceret super Petrum uxoratum et non super Iohannem virginem ecclesiam fundatam, dicit: 'Licet id ipsum in alio loco super omnes apostolos fiat et cuncti claves regni celorum accipiant et ex equo super eos ecclesie fortitudo solidetur, propterea tamen inter duodecim unus eligitur, ut capite constituto scismatis tollatur occasio. Sed cur Iohannes virgo non est electus? Etati delatum est, quia Petrus senior erat, ne adhuc adolescens et pene puer progresse etatis hominibus preferreretur et magister bonus, qui occasionem iurgii debebat auferre discipulis, quibus dixit: "Pacem meam do vobis, pacem relin-

rankings of this world. Peter, the prince of the apostles, at last reached Rome, this being allowed him by the Lord. These events are contained therein. Hence, although [Jerusalem] should be preferred to all the sees of the world, having regard to its incumbent and the one who consecrated that see with His Blood and having regard to the aforesaid things, nevertheless the city of Jerusalem, which then was much less than Alexandria and Antioch in the ranking of this world, follows those sees in order with Rome leading the rest, as granted by the Lord.

Similarly Ephesus, where John made his see, by right should have precedence over the Alexandrian see on the basis of [the rank of its founder], since John was the apostle beloved by God and an evangelist, while Mark was not an apostle. Hence we conclude that the peace and utility of the Church, which considered how the faith could be increased, was so ordained by the Holy Spirit that the honor of safeguarding the things of the spirit was given to the greater city, along with rule over temporal things, so that from the harmony of both spiritual and temporal things there should be peace and stability in the Church, although other divine causes came together in the case of certain sees. Therefore, Jerome, in book 1 of *Against Jovinian*, replying to the objection of Jovinian that the Church was founded on Peter, who was married, and not on John, who was a virgin, says "Although Christ founded it in another place upon all the apostles, and they all received the keys of the kingdom of heaven, and the strength of the Church is rightly is founded on them equally, nevertheless, one of the twelve was chosen so that the opportunity for schism might be taken away by the selection of one of them as head. But why was the virginal John not chosen? It was entrusted to Peter on account of age, Peter being the older man, lest someone who was still a boy have precedence over men of advanced age. And the Good Teacher, who was obliged to take away any occasion for contention among his disciples — to whom He said; *Peace I leave with you; My peace I*

29

quo vobis," in adolescente quem dilexerat causam preberet invidie.'
Hec ille. Ex quo habetur conclusio, quod cunctus ordo et sedium
et presidencium in pace ecclesie fundatur, quod est notandum etc.

30   Item licet multi doctores valde egregie de summo sacerdocii Petri scribant, quomodo aliis prelatus fuit, tamen licet Romanus
pontifex eius teneat sedem, ex hoc tamen non est prioritas tantum
arguenda. Manifestum est enim episcopos apostolis succedere
eciam in illis locis, ubi apostoli non fuerunt. Quare successio ex
prima sessione non arguitur etc.

31   Item consequenter potest aliter persuaderi. Et prima considera-
cio est, quod sacros canones universalium conciliorum Romanus
pontifex et cuncti, qui catholici esse volunt, servare tenentur. Et
pro isto notandum illud, quod legitur in octava generali synodo in
primo canone, cuius rubrum est: 'De custodiendis et conservandis
omnino expositis antea et traditis ecclesie canonibus.' Et sequitur
canon: 'Per equam et regie divine iusticie viam inoffense incedere
volentes, veluti quasdam lampades semper lucentes et illuminantes
gressus nostros, qui secundum deum sunt, sanctorum patrum
diffiniciones et sensus retinere debemus. Quapropter et has ut secunda eloquia secundum magnum et sapientissimum Dionisium
estimantes et arbitrantes, eciam de eis cum divino Dauid enixe ca-
nimus: "Mandatum domini lucidum illuminans oculos," et: "Lucerna pedibus meis lex tua, et lumen semitis meis." Et cum prover-
biatore dicimus: "Mandatum lucerna est, et lex lux." Et cum
magnivoco Ysaia clamamus ad omnium deum, quia "lux precepta
tua super terram." Luci enim veraciter assimilate sunt divinorum
canonum hortaciones et dissuasiones, secundum quod discernitur
melius a peiori, et expediens atque proficuum ab eo, quod non expedire, sed obesse dinoscitur. Igitur regulas, que sancte catholice

give unto you— would not afford a cause for envy in the youth whom He loved."[94] Thus Jerome. The conclusion drawn from this is that the whole order of sees and presidents is based on the peace of the Church, which has been noted etc.

Again, although many doctors write with great distinction 30 about the supreme priesthood of Peter, how he was set over the others, nevertheless, although the Roman pontiff may hold Peter's see, his priority is not to be argued on this basis. For it is clear that the bishops succeed apostles in places where there were no apostles. Hence succession is not argued from the original foundation of the see.

Again, the case can be argued otherwise, as follows. The first 31 consideration is that the Roman pontiff and all who wish to be Catholics are bound to observe the sacred canons of the universal councils. And for this we must note what is said in the first canon of the Eighth Synod, whose rubric is, "On keeping and preserving entirely the canons previously set forth and given to the Church." The canon follows, "For those wishing to follow without stumbling the right and royal way of divine justice, like certain lamps always shining and illuminating our steps, which are according to God, we should hold fast to the definitions of the Holy Fathers and keep to their meaning. For that reason, esteeming and judging them like second pronouncements of God, according to the great and most wise Dionysius,[95] we earnestly sing of them with the divine David, *The commandment of the Lord is lightsome, enlightening the eyes;*[96] and *Thy law is a lamp to my feet, and a light unto my paths.*[97] And with the author of Proverbs we say, *The commandment is a lamp, and the law a light.*[98] And with Isaiah of the great voice we cry out to the God of all, "Your commandments are a light over the earth."[99] Truly the exhortations and warnings of the divine canons are like light, in accordance with which the better is distinguished from worse, what is expedient and useful is distinguished from what is not expedient but to be avoided. Therefore, we profess

atque apostolice ecclesie tam a sanctis famosissimis apostolis quam
ab orthodoxorum universalibus necnon localibus conciliis vel
eciam a quolibet deiloquo patre atque magistro ecclesie tradite
sunt, servare et custodire profitemur. Hiis et propriam vitam et
morem regentes et omnem sacerdocii cathalogum atque omnes,
qui cristiano censentur vocabulo, penis et dampnacionibus et e diverso recepcionibus et iustificacionibus, que per illas prolate sunt
atque diffinite, subici canonice decernentes. Tenere quippe tradi-
ciones quas accepimus, sive per sermonem, sive per epistolam
sanctorum, qui antea fulserunt, Paulus admonet aperte magnus
apostolus.'

32   Ex isto decreto, cui se vicarii senioris Rome et omnes alii patriarche et eorum vicarii et ceteri episcopi subscripserunt, apparet
professio de servandis canonibus et quod secundum eos propriam
vitam et mores regere quisque habet. Item decretum ligat omnes,
qui christiano vocabulo censentur, igitur et papam. Item ut ex ru-
bro et nigro apparet, canones traduntur ecclesie. Igitur, si per universale concilium traduntur universali ecclesie, quod universaliter
ab omnibus, qui in ecclesia sunt, servari debent, si in particulari et
locali concilio particulariter traduntur, ita et obligant. Ex quo manifeste apparet papam canonibus universalium conciliorum subici.
Hoc idem probari potest ex processu illius concilii, ubi Zacharias
in concilio dixit: 'Pape Nicolai et aliorum patriarcharum canon
princeps est et secundum illum agentes nil faciunt extra id, quod
decet. Cum vero extra hunc faciunt, sive papa Nicolaus, sive alius
quis, non acquiescimus' etc. De quo accione sexta.

33   Et quia universalia iura et canones universale concilium edere
potest, que eciam papam tenere necesse est, videlicet ex premissis,

that we observe and preserve the rules of the Holy Catholic and Apostolic Church given by the most famous apostles and by the universal councils of the orthodox, as well as the local councils, or even any father speaking for God and a teacher of the Church. We rule our own life and conduct by them, and we guide those enrolled in the priesthood and all who are listed under the Christian name with the penalties and condemnations, and, conversely, with the absolutions and acquittals which are promulgated and defined by them to be applicable canonically. Certainly Paul, the great apostle, explicitly warns us to hold fast to the traditions which we have accepted, whether by speech or a letter of the saints who previously were conspicuous."[100]

From that decree, to which the vicars of the Elder Rome and all the patriarchs, their vicars and the other bishops subscribed, there appears to be a promise to observe the canons, and everyone has to regulate his own life and conduct according to them. Again, the decree binds all who are enrolled under the name Christian; therefore, it binds the pope too. Again, as appears in the rubric and the text proper, the canons are handed down to the Church. Therefore, if they are handed down by a universal council to the universal Church, they should be observed universally by all who are in the Church. If they are handed down particularly in any particular and local council, they obligate [only the relevant part]. It appears clearly from this that the pope is subject to the canons of universal councils. This also can be proved from the proceedings of that very council, where Zachary said in the council, "This canon is the first one of Pope Nicholas and the other patriarchs, and those acting in accordance with it do nothing outside it, which is fitting. But when [anyone] acts outside it, whether that person is Pope Nicholas or anyone else, we do not willingly obey." The sixth proceeding discusses the matter.[101]

And because a universal council can issue universal laws and canons, which even the pope must necessarily keep (as is evident

tunc manifestum est universale concilium et eius synodicam sentenciam in omni casu omnem patriarcham ligare. Unde ita legitur
in x canone eiusdem concilii *Divina* et infra: 'Iuste ac congruenter
hec sancta et universalis synodus diffinit et statuit, quod nullus
laycorum vel monachorum aut aliquis ex cathalogo clericorum ante
diligentem examinacionem et synodicam sentenciam a communione se separet proprii patriarche, licet criminalem quamlibet eius
causam se nosse pretendat.' Et manifestum est ex canone, quod
non loquitur in heresi sola, sed quolibet crimine, pro quo patriarcha deponi potest, et quoad synodicam sentenciam omnes patriarchas equiparat. Licet quevis ambiguitas in universali concilio de
Romanorum sede discuti possit, non tamen audacter sentencia in
papam dici, sed venerabiliter cum convenienti reverencia, ut in 21
canone, qui incipit *Dominicum sermonem*, in ℭ *Porro* habetur.

34   Et quod conciliorum universalium canones insolubiles sunt,
Leo papa ad Anatholium Constantinopolitanum dicens: 'Illa Ni-
cenorum canonum per sanctum spiritum ordinata condicio nulla
est usquam ex parte solubilis,' et multa ibi, quomodo 'illi patres in
suis constitucionibus in toto orbe terrarum vivunt.' Ad idem Zosimus 25 q. 1: 'Contra sanctorum patrum statuta nec huius quidem
sedis potest auctoritas' etc. Et Gelasius ad episcopos per Darda-
niam: 'Confidimus,' inquit, 'quod nullus veraciter christianus ignoret uniuscuiusque synodi constitutum, quod universalis ecclesie
probaverit assensus, nullam magis exequi sedem pre ceteris oportere quam primam.' Item Leo de hoc ad Maximum Anthiocenum
patriarcham scribit, quod, 'si quid contra canones Niceni concilii
ad tempus est exortum, inviolabilibus canonibus nichil preiudicii
potest inferri.' Idem ad Marcianum augustum dicit, quod 'nulla
possunt inprobitate convelli, nulla novitate violari.' Et addit: 'In

from the aforesaid), it is then clear that a universal council and its synodal sentence bind every patriarch. Hence we read in canon 10, *Divina*, of the same council, "Justly and fittingly this holy and universal synod defines and decrees that no layman or monk or anyone from the ranks of the clergy can separate himself from communion with his own patriarch before diligent examination and a synodal sentence, although he may claim he knows of some crime of his own patriarch."[102] And it is clear from the canon that it is not speaking only about heresy but about any crime for which a patriarch can be deposed; and all patriarchs are equal before a synodal sentence. Although some ambiguity concerning the Roman see could be discussed in a universal council, nevertheless, a sentence cannot be imposed on the pope rashly, but with veneration and due reverence, as is found in canon 21,[103] beginning, *Dominicum sermonem* in ⁌ *Porro*.

The canons of universal councils are indissoluble. As Pope Leo says to Anatolius of Constantinople, "That condition of the canons of the Council of Nicaea ordained by the Holy Spirit never is dissoluble in any respect."[104] And he speaks much there about how "Those fathers live on in their constitutions throughout the whole world." Zosimus speaks to the same issue in [Gratian's *Decretum*], C. 25 q. 1 [c. 7], "Against the statutes of the holy fathers not even the authority of this see can" etc. And Gelasius says to the bishops throughout Dardania [in Gratian, C. 25 q. 1 c. 1], "We are confident that no true Christian will not know that a constitution of any synod whatever which has the assent of the universal church should [receive any less assent] than [a constitution] of the principal see." Likewise Leo writes this to Maximus, patriarch of Antioch, "If something arises for a time that is contrary to the canons of the Council of Nicaea, nothing prejudicial against the sacred canons can be inferred from it."[105] Likewise he says to the Emperor Marcian, "They can be removed by no depravity; they cannot be violated by any novelty." And he adds, "It is necessary

34

quo opere auxiliante Christo fideliter exequendo necesse est me
perseverantem exhibere famulatum, quoniam dispensacio michi
credita est et ad meum tendit reatum, si paternarum regule sanc-
cionum, que in synodo Nicena ad tocius ecclesie regimen spiritu
dei inspirante sunt condite, me, quod absit, connivente violentur'
etc. Ex quo habetur per Gelasium et Leonem executorem canonum papam esse etc.

35   Item contra eciam predicta sunt antiqua scripta, que sequuntur.
Ex libello Leonis noni *Contra presumpciones Michaelis Constantinopolitani et Leonis Archidani episcoporum* in c. x dicitur: 'Constantino et
concilio Niceno approbante ac subscribente diffinitum sit summam sedem a nemine iudicari debere. Et quarto anno baptismatis
Constantinus inviolabile privilegium, ut Romanus pontifex ita ab
omnibus mundi sacerdotibus caput habeatur, sicut rex ab omnibus
iudicibus; cuius sentenciam relique synodi universales, Constantinopolitana prima consensu pii augusti et religiosi Theodosii,
Ephesina prior sub iuniore Theodosio filio Archadii et Calcedonensis sub Marciano, secunda Constantinopolitana rogatu et
consensu iunioris Constantini, concorditer Romanam apostolicam
sedem post dominum Iesum capud esse omnium ecclesiarum dei
et hoc debere credi, confiteri, scribi ab omnibus veneratoribus Niceni concilii, cuius statutorum usque ad unum iota contemptori-
bus districtum anathema cautum est' etc.

36   Item in eodem libello c. 36: 'Quisquis Romane ecclesie auctoritatem vel privilegia evacuare seu minuere nititur, non hic unius ecclesie, sed tocius christianitatis subversionem et interitum machi-
natur. Cuius enim compassione vel sustentacione ulterius
respirabunt filie a quovis oppresse unica illa suffocata matre?

for me to persevere in showing loyalty in that work of carrying out the canons faithfully with the help of Christ. Dispensation is entrusted to me and fault would be found in me if the rules of the ancestral laws, which were established with the inspiration of the Spirit of God in the Synod of Nicaea for the rule of the whole Church, were violated through my connivance — God forbid!" etc. And on this basis it is held by Gelasius and Leo that the pope is the executor of the canons etc.

Again, there are ancient writings that contradict the aforesaid, as follows. It is said in the pamphlet of Leo IX *Against the Presumptions of the Bishops Michael of Constantinople and Leo of Achrida*, chapter 10, "It was defined, with the approval and subscription of Constantine and the Nicene Council, that the supreme see should be judged by no one."[106] And in the fourth year of the baptism of Constantine the inviolable privilege [was granted] "that the Roman pontiff is held by all the priests of the world to be their head, just as a king is by all the judges. The rest of the universal synods, the first of Constantinople with the consent of the pious and religious emperor Theodosius, the earlier one at Ephesus[107] under the younger Theodosius, son of Arcadius, and that of Chalcedon under Marcian, and the second of Constantinople, convoked at the request and with the consent of the younger Constantine, harmoniously shared this opinion that the Roman Apostolic See, after the Lord Jesus, is the head of all the churches of God and should be believed, confessed, and subscribed to by all those who venerate the Nicene Council. Anyone in contempt of its statutes, even in the least iota, is warned that he is bound by anathema" etc.

Again, in c. 36 of the same pamphlet, "Whoever strives to void or diminish the authority or privileges of the Roman church plots the subversion and destruction not just of one church but of all Christendom. By whose compassion or sustenance do daughters oppressed by anyone draw breath any longer when their one and only mother has been suffocated? To whom will they appeal for

35

36

Cuius refugium appellabunt? Ad quam confugium habebunt? Ipsa enim Athanasium, ipsa omnes catholicos suscepit, fovit, defendit et sedibus propriis pulsos restituit.'

refuge? Who will provide their sanctuary? It was she [the Roman church] that received, supported, and defended Athanasius and all Catholics; it was she who restored those to their sees [the bishops] who had been driven out."

Tractatus de auctoritate presidendi in concilio generali

1 In questione de presidentia primo considerandum occurrit, si queritur, quis concilio, aut quis in concilio presidere debeat. Prime questioni breviter respondet ipsa Veritas que dicit: Ubi duo vel tres congregati fuerint in nomine meo, in medio eorum sum. Et textus Chalcedonensis concilii qui dicit non dubium spiritum sanctum patribus in Nicea congregatis consedisse, sicut manifeste consedit. Et Christus dicit: Vobiscum sum omni tempore. Dicit: Vobiscum. Non hoc de omnibus particulariter dixit, cum quibus non semper fuit, quando ab eo per peccatum recesserunt. Nec dixit de ipsis tantum, qui non fuerint in omni tempore hic mansuri, sed de ipsa ecclesia sacerdotali que semper durabit. Et per textum Constantiensis decreti probatur, qui dicit concilii potestatem immediate a Christo esse, sicut patres in octava universali synodo in fine dixerunt: Per datam nobis potestatem in sancto spiritu a primo et magno pontifice nostro et [Dei] liberatore et salvatore. Et huiusmodi similibus multis patet, quod nullus homo presidet sacratissimo patrum conventui, qui rite adunati concilium faciunt, quoniam synodica auctoritas immediate est a Christo, qui in medio sedentium est, et a spiritu sancto, qui consedit patribus, et a potestate ligandi et solvendi sacerdotio tradita. Sic legitur actione prima octavi concilii, ubi, postquam anathematizantur resistentes diffinitioni concilii, dicitur: Anathema a patre, filio et spiritu sancto et privatus gloria Dei et heres eterni tormenti et coheres diaboli atque alienatus a Christianorum gratia, tamquam

On Presidential Authority in a General Council

Concerning the issue of the presidency, the first questions to be   1
considered are: who ought to preside over the council, and who
should preside in the council? To the first question, He who is
Truth Itself succinctly replies, *Where two or three are gathered together
in My name, I am in the midst of them.*[1] Also the text of the Council
of Chalcedon confirms that the Holy Spirit undoubtedly resided
with the fathers gathered at Nicaea, as "He manifestly resided."[2]
And Christ also says, *I am with you always.*[3] Note the phrase *with
you.* Now He did not refer to all men individually, for He had not
been with them always, because they withdrew from Him through
sin. Likewise, He did not mean just his immediate followers,
who would not sojourn on earth forever. He spoke in this way of
the priests of the Church, which is to endure forever. This is
demonstrated also by the text of the Constance decree, which says
that the power of the council is derived immediately from Christ.[4]
So also the fathers of the Eighth General Council concluded,
"Through the power given to us in the Holy Spirit by our first,
great Pontiff, by our Liberator and Savior.[5] And in many similar
places it is clear that no man presides over the most sacred convocation of the fathers, who, duly assembled, make up the council.
For the authority of the council issues directly from Christ, who is
in the midst of the assembly, and from the Holy Spirit, who resides with the fathers, and from the power of binding and loosing,
which has been given to the priesthood. In the first act of the
Eighth Council, after those who reject the council's definition are
anathematized, this is said, "Let them be accursed by the Father,
the Son, and the Holy Spirit and deprived of the glory of God.
Let them be heirs of eternal torment, coheirs with the Devil and

qui irridet Christi veri et Dei nostri munificentiam, quam dedit sacerdotibus suis, dicens: Quecumque ligaveritis super terram. Et infra: Qui enim vera esse Christi verba credit, et annuntiat, quod ea sunt ligata et soluta in celis, que per sacerdotes ligantur et solvuntur in terra, quomodo audebit solvere vel solutum ligare? Manifestum enim quod Deum contemnens huiusmodi et divinum magisterium irridens et honoranda precepta reprobans justam non effugiet penam. Hec ibi. Et actione prima Chalcedonensis concilii Helpidius vir spectabilis ad synodum dixit: Hodie cunctorum Deus verbum salvator vobis se ad judicandum tradidit et patitur judicantes et honorat potestate decreti. Hec ibi. Ego intelligo, illius decreti: quecumque alligaveritis etc. Nemo dubitat Petrum ac Paulum ac omnes fideles membra fuisse ecclesie, cuius Christus caput; ut sanctus Gregorius in registro deducit epistola 214 ad Johannem Constantinopolitanum. Sed vigor ipsius ecclesie non potest esse ab homine, sed a Christo vivificante per spiritum sanctum corpus suum per omnia membra. Igitur presidentia non est apud aliquem hominem, qui ecclesie universali presideat, tamquam ipsi ecclesia subjecta sit; ut idem Gregorius in registro loco preallegato et epistola 211 etc.

2   Quis autem in concilio de omnibus Christi membris presidere debeat aliis, dupliciter queri potest: aut quoad presidatum auctoritativum et judicativum aut quoad presidatum directivum, ordinativum et ministerialem. Et ad hoc, ut questionis solutio nota fiat, tunc oportet scire, quod plenarium concilium totius orbis ecclesiam representans habet maiorem auctoritatem, que est in ecclesia: ut probatur auctoritate Augustini 2 q. 7 *Puto*, § *Item: cum Petrus* et aliis multis locis. Sed non sic de aliis conciliis patriarchalibus, quia omnia illa subsunt concilio universalis ecclesie, quia etiam judicata

alienated from Christian grace, like those who scorn the munificence of the true Christ our God, which He gave to His priesthood, saying, *Whatever you have bound on earth.*"[6] It continues, "As to him who believes the words of Christ are true and asserts that those things which are bound and loosed in heaven are those which are bound and loosed on earth by priests, how will he dare to loose what is bound or to bind what is loosed? Indeed, it is clear that whoever so despises God, scorns this divine office and rejects the venerable precepts will not escape his just punishment."[7] And in the first act of the Council of Chalcedon the notable Helpidius explained to the synod, "On this day the God of all, the Word, the Savior, has given you the task of judgment and permits your doing the judging, and honors the power of that decree." (I understand "that decree" to refer to the passage, *Whatever you have bound*, etc.) No one doubts that Peter, Paul and all the faithful were members of the Church whose head is Christ, as Saint Gregory I sets forth in the *Register* in letter 214 to John of Constantinople.[8] The power of this Church, however, cannot come from a man, but only from Christ, who, through the Holy Spirit, gives life to its members. The presidency, therefore, is not with any man who would preside over the universal Church, as if the Church were subject to him, as the same Gregory states in the previously mentioned source and in letter 211, etc.[9]

But who, of all Christ's members, is to preside over the others in the council? This can be asked in two ways: either concerning a commanding, judging presidency or a directive, ordering and ministerial presidency. To answer this question, it is necessary to understand that the plenary council of the whole world, which represents the Church, possesses the greater authority in the Church, as is shown by the authority of Augustine in [Gratian's *Decretum*] C. 2 q. 7 *Puto* [c. 35] at *Item: cum Petrus* and in many other places. This, however, is not so of other, patriarchal councils, because all of these are subject to a council of the universal Church. We read

2

in conciliis Romanorum pontificum legimus in universali concilio iterum repetita et denuo examinata: sicut depositio Dioscori per Leonem papam facta fuit in Chalcedone examinata, et depositio Pyrrhi et Sergii per Martinum papam in synodo Romana facta fuit post hoc in Constantinopolitana sexta synodo examinata. Et depositio Phocii Constantinopolitani per Nicolaum et Hadrianum Romanos pontifices in synodis facta fuit examinata in octava Constantinopolitana. Et illi universali concilio omnis christianus subest, etiam Romanus pontifex, ut ad hoc allegavi auctoritates multas hoc probantes in opere *De catholica concordantia*.

3   Post hec oportet considerare in ecclesia tria, que semper manebunt et sunt partes ita essentiales, quod sine ipsis ecclesia non est nec erit, ut sunt sacramenta, sacerdotium et populus. Ex quibus unum corpus ecclesie tamquam ex spiritu, anima et corpore constituitur. Quod semper tales partes manebunt, patet ex decursu evangelii et Pauli: Fides non deficiet, et: Christus cum fidelibus manebit usque ad consummationem seculi. Et non tantum rogavit pro apostolis, sed omnibus credituris. Et quotiens calicem Domini biberint fideles, mortem Domini annuntiabunt, donec veniat. Remanebit ergo sacerdotium, per quod sacramenta conficiuntur, et sacramenta, donec veniat Dominus in judicium.

4   Sacerdotium autem habet a Christo commissionem regitivam populi fidelis, quia missum est sacerdotium a Christo, sicut Christus a patre vivente, et a spiritu sancto positi sunt sacerdotes ad regendum ecclesiam Dei. Et propter illam legationem, qua Christi legatione funguntur, habent a Deo potestatem judicandi inter lepram et lepram, Levitici 14 et 27, et sunt executores legis summi Dei, Ezechiel 44, et dispensatores mysteriorum 1. ad Cor. 4, et in

that those things which were decreed at the councils of the Roman pontiffs were taken up again and reexamined at a universal council. Thus the deposition of Dioscorus by Pope Leo was examined at Chalcedon.[10] The deposition of Pyrrhus and Sergius by Pope Martin at a Roman synod subsequently was examined in the Sixth General Council at Constantinople.[11] The deposition of Photius of Constantinople by Popes Nicholas and Adrian likewise was examined in the Eighth General Council at Constantinople.[12] Thus every Christian, even the Roman pontiff, is subject to the universal council; and I have cited many substantiating authorities in the work *The Catholic Concordance*.[13]

Next it is necessary to consider three things in the Church 3 which always will remain and so are essential parts without which the Church neither endures nor will endure. They are the sacraments, the priesthood, and the people. The one body of the Church is constituted of these, as its spirit, soul and body, as it were. That these parts always will remain is made clear by the testimony of the Gospel and of Paul, saying that *faith will not fail*[14] and that Christ will remain with the faithful *even to the consummation of the world*.[15] He has not petitioned on behalf of the Apostles alone but for all who henceforth would believe. Thus, as often as the faithful will drink the chalice of the Lord, they will *proclaim His death until He comes again*.[16] Therefore, both the priesthood, which dispenses the sacraments, and the sacraments themselves will endure until the Lord comes in judgement.

From Christ, the priesthood holds the commission to govern 4 the faithful, since it has been sent from Christ, as Christ was from the living Father. And the priests have been appointed by the Holy Spirit to govern the Church of God. And on the basis of this mission, by which they represent Christ, they have from God the power to judge between the clean and the unclean (Leviticus 14:57 and Deuteronomy 17:87);[17] they are the executors of the law of the most high God (Ezekiel 44:24), and the dispensers of the mys-

ipsis posuit Deus ministerium reconciliationis, Christi legationem
habentes, 2. ad Cor. 5. Et hec legatio est eis credita, 1. ad Cor. 9, ut
notum facerent sacramentum voluntatis sue, ad Eph. 1. Posuit eos
judices, 1. ad Cor. 6 et Luce 17, et quod ad verbum eorum omne
negotium penderet Deuteronomii 30. Et mandavit obediendum
verbis eorum quamquam mali, Matth. 23. Et Christus asseveravit
ecclesiam suam, quod veritas in doctrina eorum remanere deberet,
quia alias non dixisset: Que dicunt, facite. Unde assignavit sacerdotio cathedram unam Moysi legislatoris, in qua unitate cathedre
de veritate certificavit ecclesiam, non obstante malitia presiden-
tium, ut hoc per Augustinum probatum est in opere prefato. Ex
istis patet, quod potestas ligandi et solvendi a Christo sacerdotio
tradita est ipsis secundum premissa ex Christi missione et legatione quoad judicium credita. Et in hoc est una radix consideratio-
nis et prima.

5   Secunda consideratio est, quod ipsum sacerdotium, habens
hanc Christi regitivam legationem, constituit unum corpus mysticum, et hoc corpus habet unum episcopatum et unam cathedram.
De unitate sacerdotii ex evangelio: Vos unum in me, sicut ego in
patre. De unitate cathedre: Super cathedram Moysi sederunt. Dicit: cathedram, et: sederunt etc. De quo Optatus Milevitanus libro
II *Contra Parmenianum*, quomodo una fuit omnium apostolorum
cathedra. Et probatur per sanctum Gregorium in *Registro* ad Eulo-
gium Antiochenum epistola 199, qui dicit: In una Petri cathedra
tres episcopos, Romanum, Alexandrinum et Antiochenum, sedere; et quia non fuerunt antiquitus nisi tres sedes ille capitales, ad
quas constricti erant omnes episcopi, ut patet ex sexta diffinitione
Niceni concilii et aliis multis, patet, quod omnes episcopi in una

teries (1 Corinthians 4:1). And God has placed in them the ministry of reconciliation, for they represent Christ (2 Corinthians 5:19–20). He made them His representatives (1 Corinthians 9:17), so that they might make known the sacrament of His will (Ephesians 1:9). He has appointed them as judges (1 Corinthians 6:1–3 and Luke 17:14), so that every matter might weigh heavily on their word (Deuteronomy 30:16). God also has commanded obedience to their words, though they themselves might be evil (Matthew 23:3). But Christ has assured His Church that the truth always will remain in their doctrine; otherwise He would not have said, *What they say do.*[18] Therefore, He has assigned to the priesthood the one see of Moses, the lawgiver. In this unity of see, He has guaranteed the truth to the Church, notwithstanding the evil character of those who preside over it, as has been proven from Augustine in the previously mentioned work.[19] From these statements it is clear that the power of binding and loosing, given by Christ to the priesthood, has been entrusted to the priests for the task of judging through Christ's mission and legation. And therein lies one, and the first, root of our concern.

The second consideration thus follows: this same priesthood, which has its governing mission from Christ, established one mystical body; and this body has one episcopate and one see. So the unity of the priesthood is expressed in the Gospel, *You are in me as I am in the Father.*[20] It is written of the unity of the see, *They sit on the see of Moses.* Note the words *see* and *they sit.* Optatus of Milevis, in *Against Parmenian*, Book II, indicates that there was one see belonging to all the Apostles.[21] This also is demonstrated by Saint Gregory in the *Register* in letter 199 to Eulogius of Antioch, which says that three bishops, that is, of Rome, Alexandria and Antioch, sit in the one see of Peter.[22] From antiquity there have been only those three chief sees, to which all bishops are bound, as is evident from the sixth decree of the Council of Nicaea and from other sources.[23] It is clear that all the bishops have sat in one see. And,

5

cathedra sedebant. Et de uno episcopatu per sanctum Cyprianum ad Florentium et Puppianum 7 q. 1 *Novatianus* ❡*Item episcopatus*. Et sanctus Cyprianus de veritate illius episcopatus ibidem loquitur, et quomodo populus in illo episcopatu est, quia totum sacerdotium est ut anima una, habens ex obedientia et consensu fidelium, et ante omnia ex legatione Christi, potestatem regitivam et vivificativam. Sic sacerdotium errare non potest, cui illa legatio commissa est, quoniam per errorem sacerdotii erraret tota ecclesia. Quoniam omnis populus fidelis est in potentia sacerdotali, cui obedire tenetur et credere licet, non isti vel isti sacerdoti etc.

6 Tertia consideratio est, quod pro bono regimine corporis sacerdotalis, propter tollere scisma, sicut Petrus prelatus fuit aliis apostolis, ita episcopi sacerdotibus, archiepiscopi episcopis, patriarche archiepiscopis, ut sit unitas per mirabilem connexionem plurium per unum, ut demum deveniatur in unum per media proportionata. De Petro, quod propter hoc datus fuit prepositus a Christo et per apostolos electus, per Hieronymum *Contra Iovinianum*. De episcopis, quod illi ad instar Petri propter tollere scisma constituti sunt, per eundem Hieronymum 93 di. *Legimus*, 95 di. *Olim*. De archiepiscopis, quod ad instar Petri dati sunt, 22 di. *Sacrosancta*. De papa, quod Petro succedat, infinita sunt jura et auctoritates multe. Unde ex hoc habemus administrationes et dignitates ab episcopatu ad papatum inclusive a Christo, mediante ecclesia, ordinatas propter vitare scisma. Et non sunt de essentia, sed de bene esse ecclesie. Sacerdotium autem est de essentia. Et quia accidentaliter sunt administratorie dignitates in ecclesia, tunc ad radicem potestatis sacerdotalis ligandi et solvendi in se nihil conferunt, quoniam in illa

concerning the one episcopate, Saint Cyprian wrote to Florentius and Puppianus [in Gratian's *Decretum*] C. 7 q. 1 *Novatianus* [c. 6] at *Item episcopatus.* Here too Cyprian spoke the truth of the episcopate and of how the people are in the episcopate, since the whole priesthood is as one soul, having the power to govern and vivify, from the obedience and consent of the faithful, but above all from the legation of Christ. Thus the priesthood, to which the mission was entrusted, cannot err, since, through the error of the priesthood, the whole Church would err. The whole faithful people is under the sacerdotal power, which it must obey and freely should believe—not this or that particular priest.

There is then a third consideration: for the sake of good governance of the sacerdotal body and in order to abolish schism, just as when Peter was placed over the other apostles, so the bishops have been placed over the priests, the archbishops over the bishops, the patriarchs over the archbishops, so that there should be unity through the wonderful connection of many to one person and that, finally, unity should be accomplished through proportionate means. That Peter was given primacy by Christ and was elected by the apostles to this end is attested to by Jerome in *Against Jovinian.*[24] That the bishops were constituted after the fashion of Peter to abolish schism likewise is demonstrated by Jerome, [cited in Gratian's *Decretum*] D. 93 *Legimus* [c. 24], D. 95 *Olim* [c. 5]. That the archbishops were constituted after the fashion of Peter is found in [the *Decretum*] D. 22 *Sacrosancta* [c. 2]. And that the pope succeeds Peter is established by innumerable laws and by many other authorities. We then conclude that the offices and ranks, from the episcopacy to the papacy inclusive, were ordained by Christ, through the mediation of the Church, in order to avoid schism. Nevertheless, they are not essential to the existence of the Church, but to its well-being. The priesthood, however, is essential. And since the administrative ranks in the Church are accidental, they add nothing in themselves to the basis of the sacerdotal

6

omnes sunt equales. Pro quo 21 di. *In novo*, et in glo. 2 q. 7 *Puto*, et Hostiensis in *Summa*, *De ma[ioritate] et obe[dientia]*, et sanctus Augustinus super verbo: 'Pasce', et Hieronymus super verbo: 'Quodcumque ligaveris'.

7   Quarta consideratio, quod, quia illius unius episcopatus quilibet episcopus tenet partem suam secundum sanctum Cyprianum loco preallegato, et sic sacerdotium est dispersum et etiam episcopi sunt, necesse erat istas superintendentes dignitates ordinari, ut unitas et pax conservaretur per omnem ecclesiam. Hoc probat textus *Sacrosancta* 22 di. cum similibus. Et ideo, ad hoc, ut ipsa unitas conservaretur, considerarunt patres nostri, quod potestas ligandi et solvendi, que a Christo sacerdotio tradita est, illa habet a Christo unam assistentiam infallibilitatis in eo, quod dicit: 'Que dicunt, facite'. Et illam infallibilitatem considerarunt esse in sacerdotio; quoniam: ipsi sacerdotes plures dicunt, et quando congregati fuerint, quia tunc in medio eorum Christus esset. Et propter hoc, quia quisque particularis non habet in potestate sua ligandi et solvendi promissionem infallibilitatis, sunt superintendentes super quemlibet constituti, sicut episcopi super sacerdotes, et archiepiscopi super episcopos, et papa super archiepiscopos. Quare, cum quilibet de sacerdotio cuilibet in hac potestate equiparetur, considerarunt, quod verius judicium esse non posset quam synodicum. Unde constitutum fuit in Niceno concilio, quod quelibet provincia per synodum provincie in omnibus regi et judicari deberet. Unde ita synodice congregationes episcoporum ad provincialem synodum deferebantur. Et deinde fuit statutum in concilio Sardicensi ob memoriam Petri, quod judicia archiepiscopalium synodorum ad sedem apostolicam deferrentur, ut habetur 6 q. 4 *Quod si quis*. Et fuit datus ordo ad hoc, ut certo tempore episcopales synodi, certo

power of binding and loosing, because all priests are equal in this. Illustrative of this are [a canon of Gratian's *Decretum*] D. 21 *In novo* [c. 2], the glosses on [the same text] C. 2 q. 7 *Puto*,[25] Hostiensis in his *Summa* under the title *De maioritate et obedientia*,[26] Saint Augustine on the words *Feed my sheep*,[27] and Jerome on *Whatever you have bound*.[28]

The fourth consideration: whereas in that one episcopate every 7 bishop has his part, according to Saint Cyprian in the previously mentioned work, and so the priesthood and also the bishops are dispersed through the world, it is necessary that such ranks of superintendence be ordained so that unity and peace might be preserved by the whole Church. This is demonstrated in the text *Sacrosancta* D. 22 [from Gratian's *Decretum*] together with similar sources. Therefore, so that unity might be preserved, the Fathers considered that the power of binding and loosing, given by Christ to the priesthood, received from Him the single support of infallibility, contained in the words, *Whatever they say, do*. And they believed this infallibility is in the priesthood, for they said that priests in themselves are plural but, when they are gathered together, Christ is in the midst of them.[29] Therefore, since each individual has not been promised infallibility in his power of binding and loosing, rulers are placed over everyone; thus bishops are over priests, archbishops over bishops, and the pope over archbishops. And since all priests are equal in this power, the Fathers have considered that there can be no truer judgment than that of the council. It was established at the Council of Nicaea that each province should be governed and regulated by a provincial synod in every matter.[30] Wherefore synodal congregations of bishops have submitted to the provincial synod. And thus it was decreed in the Council of Sardica, in remembrance of Peter, that the judgments of archiepiscopal synods are to be submitted to the Apostolic See, as is recorded in [Gratian's *Decretum*] C. 6 q. 4 v. *Quod si quis* [c. 7]. Likewise, it was established that, at a certain time, epis-

provinciales, et omni anno patriarchales ad vocationem cuiuslibet patriarche, etiam sedis Romane, celebrarentur, ut in octavo universali Constantinopolitano concilio statutum invenitur. Et sic ad unitatem unius patriarchalis sedis omnia deferebantur, que sub patriarchatu erant. Et fiebant ordinationes in qualibet synodo ex communi omnium consensu, quia illa est vis synodica, prout statim dicetur etc.

8   Alia consideratio, quod supremum concilium est universalis totius catholice ecclesie, ubi conveniunt cum potestate per se vel legatos consentientes omnes episcopi, vel saltem vocati sunt et possunt interesse. Illud concilium universale omnes patres ac omnes Christi sacerdotes a domino legationem habentes regendi ecclesiam aut actu aut potentia comprehendit; unde in concilio Martine pape Rome tempore Constantini III contra Pyrrhum et Sergium celebrato de concilio Chalcedonensi legitur: Sancta Chalcedonensis synodus diffinivit, hoc est dicere: omnium sanctorum chorus, quoniam, quod una sanctorum patrum synodus judicare videtur, tam omnes synodi quam universi omnino confirmare patres noscuntur, utpote in eodem unoque verbo fidei sibi vicissim indissolubilem concordantiam concordantes. Hec ibi. Cuius quidem potestas est a Christo per verba: Quecumque alligaveritis juxta premissa. Et cuius judicium pendet ex unanimitate et omnium consensu, quia hec est diffinitio concilii 15 di. *Canones* ⟪*Synodus.* Dissentientes concilium non faciunt, et in octava synodo in fine legitur: Oportet quecumque ecclesiastica communi omnium consensu diffiniri et statui. Et hec est justitie regula cum aliis, que ibidem habentur, et de hoc sunt infinite concordantie. Et ob illam unanimitatem, a qua vigor dependet synodici actus, scimus spiritum sanctum dictare sententiam, qui est spiritus unionis et concordantie. Quare dicitur: Placuit spiritui sancto et nobis in

copal and provincial synods, and annual patriarchal synods, should be celebrated at the summons of each patriarch, and also of the Roman see, as is further decreed in the Eighth Council at Constantinople.[31] And so everything which took place within the patriarchate was submitted to the unity of the one patriarchal see. And the decrees were made in every synod by the common consent of all, for that is the power of the synod, as will be stated below.

Another consideration follows: the supreme council is that of the whole universal Church, where all the bishops convene, consenting either themselves or through their representatives. At any rate, they are called and can take part. Such a universal council comprises, in act or in potency, all the fathers and all Christ's priests, who have the duty of governing the Church. Wherefore in the Council of Pope Martin, held at the time of Constantine III against Pyrrhus and Sergius, one may read concerning the Council of Chalcedon: "Thus the holy Synod of Chalcedon has defined — that is, the chorus of all the holy ones — because whatever one synod of the holy fathers judges, all the synods and all the fathers everywhere are known to confirm, inasmuch as they concur in the same, the one word of faith in indissoluble concord."[32] That the council's power is from Christ is confirmed by the words, *Whatever you bind*, as argued above. Its judgment depends on the unanimity and consent of all, as this is the council's definition, [in Gratian's *Decretum*] D. 15 *Canones* ⊄ *Synodus* [c. 7]. Those who disagree do not make up a council. And in the Eighth Synod one reads at the end: "All ecclesiastical matters should be defined and resolved with the common consent of all."[33] This expression, with others in the same place, provides a legal norm; and there are innumerable other references which agree about this. And, because of the unanimity upon which the force of conciliar acts depends, we know that the Holy Spirit, the spirit of unity and harmony, has dictated the council's decision. Thus it was said in the apostolic council, "It pleased the Holy Spirit and us," for "they were

8

concilio apostolico, quia eorum erat cor unum et anima una. Et legitur in sexta actione octavi concilii universalis sic: Sanctissimi vicarii senioris Rome et nos, qui reliquarum sedium vicarii sumus, hec omnia dissolvimus hodie gratia Jesu Christi, qui nobis dedit summi sacerdotii potestatem ligandi atque solvendi. Et in eadem actione legitur sententiam divina inspiratione depromptam, quia unanimitate et concordia sancti concilii fuit promulgata.

9   Alia consideratio, quod Romanus pontifex, qui est membrum ecclesie, licet supremum in administratione, subest ipsi universali concilio et judicio eius. Quidquid enim universale plenarium concilium judicaverit, prefertur judicio unius hominis, etiam pape, in quocumque etiam casu. Hoc probatur per superiora et ex diffinitione concilii octavi, que dicit: Porro, si universalis synodus fuerit congregata et de Romanorum sede quevis ambiguitas suborta, oportet eam cum convenienti reverentia et in ea profectum facere etc. Probatur hoc ex auctoritate Augustini in epistola ad Glorium et Eleusium, ubi de judicio Melchiadis pape in causa Ceciliani Carthaginensis loquens dicit post judicium Melchiadis superesse judicium plenarii concilii. Probat hoc epistola, que creditur esse Damasi pape, in ordine epistolarum sancti Ambrosii 72, ubi dicit papa deputatos judices a synodo sibi preferri in judicando. Probant hoc gesta multa. Et per consequens papa ordinationibus et statutis universalis concilii subest, et antiquitus profitebatur illos canones se servaturum. Et se ipsis canonibus per se vel legatos subscripsit, et contra illa patrum instituta venire non potest 25 q. 1 *Contra.* Et canon est supra papam, ut Zacharias Chalcedonensis in octavo concilio legitur dixisse, quomodo pape Nicolai et omnium patriar-

one heart and one soul."[34] And in the sixth act of the Eighth General Council, "The most holy vicars of the elder Rome and we, who are the vicars of the other sees, annul all these things this day through the grace of Jesus Christ, who has given us the highest priesthood's power of binding and loosing."[35] And in the same act one reads that the decision was issued through divine inspiration, for it was promulgated with the unanimity and concord of the council.

Another consideration: the Roman pontiff, who is a member of 9 the Church, although supreme in administration, himself is subject to the universal council and its judgment. Indeed, whatever the universal, plenary council legislates concerning any matter is preferred to the judgment of one man, even the pope himself. This is proved by the above and from the definition of the Eighth Council which says, "Further, if the universal synod should be assembled and if there should arise any sort of discord with the Roman see, it is necessary that it be investigated and resolved with proper reverence."[36] Likewise, this is proved by the authority of Augustine in the letter to Glorius and Eleusius, where, speaking of the judgment of Pope Melchiades in the case of Caecilian of Carthage, he says that above the judgment of Melchiades there is the judgment of a plenary council.[37] This is demonstrated too in a letter attributed to Pope Damasus, no. 72 in the list of the letters of Saint Ambrose,[38] wherein the pope says that the judges delegated by the synod are ranked above him in judging. And many conciliar acts have proved this. Consequently, the pope is subject to the decrees and statutes of the universal council. In antiquity he was accustomed to promise that he would obey those canons. He also subscribed to them with his own hand or through representatives; and he was not able to act contrary to those things ordained by the fathers [according to Gratian's *Decretum*] C. 25 q. 1 *Contra* [c. 7]. A canon, therefore, is over the pope; as Zacharias of Chalcedon is recorded to have said at the Eighth Council, "The

charum canon princeps est; et probat c. 1 statutorum octavi concilii coniuncta superscriptione, ubi dicitur tales canones traditos esse universali ecclesie, et quemlibet fidelem perstringi per eos, et legati Romane sedis se subscripserunt illi capitulo. Et de hoc sunt auctoritates quam plures in collectione mea preallegata.

10   Et propter ista omnia potest ecclesia pro sua utilitate et necessitate de papatu, qualitercumque placuerit, disponere—quia non potest in hoc judicio tendente ad utilitatem ecclesie errare ipsa ecclesia—et non solum papam propter fidem deponere, sed quando inutilis esset et negligens; sicut Petrus Clementi dixit, quod propter negligentiam deponendus foret. Et in c. 1 De renuntiatione lib. VI papa dicit se cedere posse, quando se inutilem viderit. Sed hoc judicium de negligentia et inutilitate maius est in ecclesia, propter quam est papatus, quam in homine, qui est subiectum materiale ipsius papatus. Quare hoc non habet dubium, quin universaliter papa subsit omni judicio ecclesie, quando pro utilitate ipsius ecclesie aut canones aut leges etiam de ipso papa ordinaverit, aut quando ipsum propter inutilitatem deposuerit. Et licet sacerdotium collectum synodice non constituat totam ecclesiam, et licet papa representet totam ecclesiam, sicut concilium sacerdotium representat, tamen verior est ipsa representatio concilii quam pape, quia pape est remotissima, concilii proxima. Unde representatio concilii, cum plus appropinquet ad veritatem ecclesie et certiori modo representet eandem, tunc etiam prefertur confuse representationi papali in auctoritate et judicio. Insuper veritas non est tantum universali ecclesie promissa, sed ipsi etiam sacerdotio et parti illi ecclesie regitive; ad quam veritatem appropinquat universale

canon is ruler over Pope Nicholas and all the patriarchs."[39] This is proven also by c. 1 of the statutes of the Eighth Council together with its title, which says that "such canons are given to the universal Church and that every believer is obligated by them."[40] And the representatives of the Roman see set their signatures to that chapter. There are many more proofs of this in my previously mentioned treatise.[41]

For all these reasons, the Church—for the sake of its welfare and its needs—is able to dispose of the papacy in whatever way it pleases, because, in the case of a judgment bearing on the welfare of the Church, the Church itself cannot err. It can depose the pope not only for the sake of the faith but whenever he is incompetent and negligent. Thus Peter said to Clement that he would be deposed if he were negligent.[42] And in c. 1 *De renuntiatione* in the *Liber sextus*,[43] the pope says that he is able to resign when he deems himself incompetent. Nevertheless, the judgment concerning negligence and incompetence belongs more to the Church, for whose sake the papacy exists, than to a man, who only is the bearer of the papacy. Therefore, there can be no doubt that the pope universally is subject to every judgment of the Church, when it ordains canons or laws for the well-being of the Church, even those concerning the pope himself or deposing him because of incompetence. Even if the priesthood assembled at the council did not constitute the whole Church and even if the pope represented the whole Church, just as the council represents the priesthood, nevertheless, representation by the council is a truer representation than that by the pope, for his is most remote while the council's is nearest. And since the representation of the council comes closer to the truth of the Church and represents it in a surer and more definite manner, it is preferred in authority and judgment to papal representation, which is more indistinct. The truth, moreover, is promised not just to the universal Church, but also to the priesthood itself and to the governing part of the Church. The

concilium proxime, quia ibi sacerdotium totum est actu vel potentia. Ita ex hac radice representativa et veritatis approximatione per metropolitanos et papam solebant synodice congregationes patriarchales fieri; et cessante confluxu metropolitanorum, legati provinciarum, scilicet domini cardinales, in eorum locum successerunt, sine quorum judicio et subscriptione in causis universalis patriarchatus publicum pape judicium inefficax semper censebatur; ut de hoc in collectione pretacta.

11 Post hoc oportet scire, quod primum locum obtinens in concilio dicitur esse caput concilii ac etiam judex, sicut in episcopali episcopus, in provinciali archiepiscopus — ut 11 q. 1 *Si clericus*, ubi Archidiaconus, quomodo metropolitanus sit caput concilii — in patriarchali patriarcha, sicut legitur in octavo concilio universali quinque patriarchas quinque capita esse ecclesie etc. Et licet archiepiscopus sit judex provincie 9 q. 3 *Per singulas* et caput in concilio suo, tamen ex hoc non potest statuere canones, quos necesse sit recipere provinciam sine constitutione et consensu aliorum suffraganeorum, nec suffraganei sine ipso, ut ad hoc allegavi in eodem opere. Et ratio omnium illorum est, quia actus synodicus dependet a communi consensu eorum, qui debent et possunt interesse. Sed illa presidentia, qua caput presidet suo concilio, habet solum directionem talem, quia dirigit omnia facta concilii per interlocutiones et demum judicat et concludit ex votis singulorum ex communi consensu; licet unusquisque de concilio judicet et concludat pariformiter sicut primatum tenens. Et istud patet ex

universal Church comes closest to this truth, because there the whole priesthood is present actually or potentially. Thus, from this representative root and approximation of truth, it was the custom for metropolitans and the pope to hold synodal assemblies of their patriarchates. And when the metropolitans ceased to be convened, the representatives of the provinces, namely the lord cardinals, succeeded to their place. Without their judgment and signature in the affairs of the universal patriarchate, a public judgment of the pope always was viewed as without effect, as has been shown in my treatise mentioned above.[44]

Accordingly, it also is necessary to understand that whoever occupies the first place in a council is said to be the head of the council and also its judge, as the bishop is in the episcopal council and the archbishop in that of the province. Note what the Archdeacon[45] says [in Gratian's *Decretum*] at C. 11 q. 1 *Si clericus* [c. 46], that the metropolitan is head of his council, the patriarch of the patriarchal council—as it is written in the Eighth General Council that the five patriarchs are the five heads of the Church, etc.[46] Although the archbishop is judge in the province ([Gratian] C. 9 q. 3 *Per singulas* [c. 2]), and head of his council; nevertheless, he cannot establish canons which the province must receive without the ordinance and consent of the suffragans; nor can the suffragans do so without him, as I have argued, citing authorities in my treatise.[47] The rationale of all these things is that the synodal act depends on the common consent of those who should and can be present. But the presidential office, whereby a head presides over its council, only has such a guiding role that it directs all the affairs of the council for purposes of discussion. And it makes final judgments and conclusions in conformity with the opinions of the individual members on the basis of common consent. Each participant in the council freely judges, then, and concludes in the same manner as he who holds the primacy. And this

11

gestis omnium conciliorum et eorum, qui interfuerunt, subscriptionibus.

12   Deinde sciendum quod in universali concilio, ubi imperatores interfuerunt et non papa, semper invenio imperatores et judices suos cum senatu primatum habuisse et officium presidentie per interlocutiones et ex consensu synodi sive mandato conclusiones et judicia fecisse, et non reperitur instantia in octo conciliis; de quibus 16 di. *Sancta octo.* Preterquam in tertia actione Chalcedonensis concilii, ubi Paschasius, Lucentius et Bonifatius, Leonis pape vicem gerentes, quia nullus pro parte imperatoris interfuit, tunc synodo primatum leguntur tenuisse et presedisse et concilium direxisse per interlocutiones, et demum ex jussu synodi ex eo, quia primatum tenebant et eminentiorem locum, sententiam primo dixisse in Dioscorum ex communi consensu, aliis omnibus coniudicantibus. Et dixerunt omnes illi vicarii senioris Rome Leonis pape archiepiscopi per unum, scilicet Bonifatium, qui se in subscriptione presidentem solus vocat et alii non.

13   Ex istis est prima conclusio mea, quod primatum gerens in concilio, scilicet ipse Romanus pontifex, per se vel suos legatos communi consensu constituere habet, 2 q. 1 *Scelus;* 6 q. 4 *Quod si quis;* 36 q. 9 *Quod quis* cum similibus. Ita legitur Leonem ad synodum Ephesinam, ad quam Iulium episcopum, Renatum presbyterum et Hilarium diaconum misit, scripsisse: Mitto eos vice mea, ut sancto conventui fraternitatis vestre intersint et communi vobiscum sententia, que sunt Domino placitura, constituant. Et pro-

is obvious from the acts of all the councils and from the signatures of the participants.

One also should know that in the universal councils where the 12
emperors were present and not the pope, I have always found that the emperors and their judges, together with the senate, exercised the primacy and the office of presidency for purposes of discussion and made final conclusions and judgments with the consent of the synod, or with its mandate. No instance of the presence of a pope is found in the first eight councils; note [Gratian's *Decretum*] D. 16 *Sancta octo* [c. 8]. Only in the third act of the Council of Chalcedon, in which Paschasius, Lucentius and Boniface represented Pope Leo, is it recorded that the representatives held the primacy in the synod; since no one was present on the emperor's behalf, they presided and directed the council through interim judgments. And, in addition, by order of the synod, because they held the primacy and place of preeminence, they were the first to pronounce sentence on Dioscorus with common consent, all the others confirming the judgment. And all those representatives of the older Rome, of Pope Leo, the archbishop, spoke through one, namely through Boniface, who alone designated himself as president by signing the decrees; the others did not.[48]

On the basis of the foregoing, this is my first conclusion: he 13
who holds primacy in the council, that is the Roman pontiff, in person or through representatives, can legislate with common consent. Note [Gratian's *Decretum*] C. 2 q. 1 *Scelus* [c. 21], C. 6 q. 4 v. *Quod si aliquis* [c. 7], C. 35 q. 9 *Quod quis* [c. 3],[49] and similar places. Thus one reads that Leo I wrote the following to the synod of Ephesus, to which he sent Bishop Julian, Presbyter Renatus and Deacon Hilarius: I send them in my place "so that they may be present at the holy convening of your fraternity and that, in common opinion with you, they may so decree those things which will be pleasing to the Lord."[50] This again is demonstrated by the acts

bant hoc gesta omnium conciliorum et subscriptiones, ubi papa per se vel legatos interfuit.

14   Secunda conclusio est, quod legati apostolice sedis nullo modo sperni possunt, sed oportet eos necessario admitti; alias actus synodicus esset nullus. Sicut enim suffraganei sine metropolitano et judice provincie provincialia statuta edere non possunt, ita nec universalia sine papa, qui est judex universalis ecclesie. Quod papa sit judex universalis ecclesie, et sine eo synodus esse non possit, infinita pene sunt jura et exempla, quando saltem vellet et posset. Et quod alias actus esset nullus, probat epistola Damasi et episcoporum secum Rome congregatorum ad universos episcopos contra Ariminense concilium, et Leonis contra Ephesinam secundam synodum ad Theodosium, ubi se fundant in allegando nullitatem illorum, que actitata erant in illis conciliis, in exclusione episcoporum, qui debebant et volebant interesse. Et habentur ille auctoritates in collectione.

15   Tertia conclusio est, quod illa presidentia, qua omnes simul president, sicut unum papam representant, et eius personam induti sunt—ut legitur in principio sexti concilii in epistola Agathonis ad Constantinum tertium—sic etiam per unum loquentem et dirigentem eam exercere debent, ne confusio fiat, et ne plus possint legati quam principalis; quia principalis, si adesset, unum os tantum haberet. Et ita in Chalcedonensi concilio legitur practicatum.

16   Quarta conclusio: illa presidentia nullo modo aliquid habet auctoritatis ultra ministerium directivum per interlocutionem etc. Alioquin, si plus haberet aut coactionem aut punitionem aut jurisdictionem quamcumque in personas concilii, sublata esset essentialis forma a concilio, puta libertas in consultando, obstante coac-

and the lists of signatures of all the councils at which the pope was present in person or through representatives.

This then is the second conclusion: the representatives of the   14
Apostolic See cannot be rejected; rather they, of necessity, must be admitted to the council. Otherwise the synodal acts would be void. Just as the suffragans cannot establish provincial statutes without the metropolitan and judge of the province, neither can anyone establish universal statutes without the pope, who is judge of the universal Church. That the pope is the judge of the universal Church, and that without him there can be no synod — provided that he is willing and able to participate — is attested to by an almost limitless number of laws and examples. That otherwise the act of the council is invalid is proved in the letter of Damasus and the bishops assembled with him at Rome to all the bishops against the Council of Rimini,[51] and in the letter of Leo to Theodosius against the Second Synod of Ephesus.[52] Both of these argued the nullity of the things enacted at those councils because of the exclusion of bishops, who should be and wished to be present. And these too are included in my treatise.[53]

The third conclusion: the presidency is such that all the repre-   15
sentatives preside equally; since they represent one pope and have assumed his role, as one reads in the beginning of the Sixth Council in the letter of Agatho to Constantine III,[54] so that they exercise it through one spokesman and director, have no greater power than their sponsor. For, if he were present, the primate would have only one voice. And this was done likewise at the Council of Chalcedon.

The fourth conclusion: the president has no additional author-   16
ity beyond the ministry of directing through interim judgments, etc. If he had more power, that is compulsory or punitive power, or jurisdiction, over the persons of the council, then the essential requirement for a council, namely freedom of deliberation, would be taken away through obstruction by coercion. Thus everything

tione, et sic non omnes, sed unus omnia faceret; sicut Dioscorus in Ephesina synodo suam presidentiam sibi ab imperatore datam cum coactione exercens nulliter fecit, et synodus nullius efficacie fuit, ut Leo papa ad Theodosium scribit, et aliis multis locis etc.

would be done by one person, and not by all. In this manner, Dioscorus, at the Second Council of Ephesus, nullified his presidency, which was given to him by the emperor, by exercising it coercively; and his synod has no efficacy, as Pope Leo wrote to Theodosius,[55] and as can be found in many other places etc.

‹Oratio coram Dieta Francfordiensi›

1 Summa dictorum N‹icolai› de Cußa Francfordie 1442, 21. iunii
cum duobus diebus sequentibus contra olim Panormitanum et defensores scismatis Basilee facti.

‹Praefatio›

2 Dampnatis Amedistis in mangna ycumenica synodo, cui s‹anctissimum› d‹ominum› n‹ostrum› Eugenius papa legittima successione post mortem Martini pape sancti Petri sedem tenens presedit, non putabatur ipsos iudicatos amplius audiri debere,
prohibente hoc omni iure ecclesiastico et imperiali, maxime cum
ipsi, qui 'os in celum posuerunt, lingwa eorum transseunte super
terram', exemplo Calcedonensis sinodi audiri vetantur — 21. d. *In
tantum* —, sic et ex eo, quia scisma fecerunt — 23. q. 5. *Non vos* — et
suum intrusum defendere moliuntur — iii q. 1. ❡ *Patet.* Hiis enim
casibus 'audiencia denegatur', ut notat glo. 23. d. *In nomine domini*
super verbo *audiencia*, quoniam nichil subsistencie aut coloris contra ista enormia scelera iure adduci posse presupposuerunt. Nec
credebamus nos servuli apostolice sedis illos, qui more eorum, qui
recencia fundamenta inprimere satagunt, verbis deceptoriis habun-
dant, post tot concessas publicas et privatas audiencias in hac
dieta, ubi conclusio pollicita est, denuo audiri ad repeticionemque
sepissime dictorum redeundum. Credimus hanc ipsam omnium

Oration at the Diet of Frankfurt

A summary of what was said by Nicholas of Cusa at Frankfurt in   1
1442 on the twenty-first of June and the two days following in opposition to the former archbishop of Palermo[1] and the defenders
of the Basel schism.

[Preface]

In the great ecumenical synod, at which presided our most holy   2
lord Pope Eugenius, who holds the see of Saint Peter by legitimate
succession after the death of Pope Martin, it was not thought necessary that the accursed Amedeists,[2] once condemned, should be
heard any further. This is prohibited by every ecclesiastical and
imperial law, especially as those who *have set their mouth against
heaven, and their tongue hath passed through the earth*[3] are prohibited
from being heard by the example of the Council of Chalcedon
([Gratian] D. 21 *In tantum* [c. 9]), both because they brought on a
schism ([Gratian] C. 23 q. 5 c. *Non vos* [c. 42]) and because they
strive to defend their antipope ([Gratian] C. 3 q. 1 ❡ *Patet* [p.c. 6]).
In these cases, "he is denied a hearing" (as the gloss notes at
[Gratian] D. 23 c. *In nomine domini* on the word *audientia*),[4] since
they presuppose that no substantial or colorable grounds can be
adduced from the law to mitigate these enormous crimes. Nor do
we lesser servants of the Apostolic See believe that those who, after their fashion, have busied themselves with imposing the recent
foundations, overflowing with deceptive words, who have already
been allowed numerous public and private audiences at this Diet,
when they had promised to make an end, should once again be
heard so that they can repeat what they have said so often before.

eciam fuisse sentenciam garrulacionibus finem datum. Sed postquam importunissima et invericunda instancia eorum vicit cle-
mentissimum et invictissimum regem nostrum et gloriosissimos
principes electores, ut datis deputatis, coram quibus iterum et
finaliter, que vellent, dicerent, ad hoc deventum est, ut vos, r‹eve-
rendi› p‹atres› et magnifici et venerabiles domini ad hoc deputati,
eos triduo audiretis.

3   Deinde preter propositum, ne gloriarentur ex taciturnitate nostra iusticiam ecclesie per orbem disperse non posse ostendi, in
simplicitate sermonis veritatem rei geste atque pene omnibus no-
tissime pari triduo, eciam lectis publicis documentis, adeo dei gracia me ostendisse gaudeo, ut presumptuosissima iniusticia eorum,
qui Christi ecclesiam in partes scindere moliuntur, omnibus domi-
nacionibus v‹estris› patefacta sit. Verum quia in fine visi estis me-
moriale in scriptis desiderare de hiis auditis pro subsidio faciende
relacionis, quamvis nichil putem omnium prudentissimas domina-
ciones v‹estros› latere posse de omnibus per me enarratis, cum nichil alienum aut incognitum adduxerim, hic nunc pareo, ista suc-
cintissime annotando, que memoria administrat, non ista offerens,
quasi ecclesia per orbem dispersa aut sancta Romana ecclesia vel
ycumenica synodus opus habeat defensore alio quam sua auctoritate, aut quod hoc onus michi creditum quisque putet inter eos
infinicies doctiores perioresque sancte ecclesie filios, solum pro
modulo meo hoc ostendere cupiens, quod tam parvi momenti sunt
Amedistarum fundamenta, ut vir parvus ingenio et pericia facile
omnia comminuat, alciora et subtiliora maioribus remittens.

We believe that it was the opinion of all that such empty chatter should be brought to an end; but when their utterly impudent and disingenuous insistence had prevailed upon our most clement and invincible king[5] and the most glorious prince electors to assign deputies before whom they might say, once more and finally, what they wished, the result was that you, the reverend fathers and magnificent and venerable lords deputed to this purpose, have been hearing them out for three days.

Then, contrary to what they had planned, so that they could not boast from our silence that the justice of the Church spread throughout the world could not be demonstrated, by God's grace I rejoiced to have demonstrated, over a comparable period of three days, the truth of what had occurred, which is well known to almost everyone, in simplicity of speech, even reading documents aloud, so that the utterly presumptuous injustice of those who strive to cut Christ's Church to pieces may be made obvious to all your lordships. But since in the end it looked like you wanted a written memorandum of what you heard to help you report on what was said, although I think nothing of all that I recounted can possibly be hidden from your most prudent lordships, since I adduced nothing strange or unknown, I hereby submit these notes in succinct form as far as I remember them. I do not proffer them as though the Church spread throughout the world or the Holy Roman Church, or the ecumenical synod needs any other defender than its own authority. I have not undertaken this burden so that anyone should think me to be among the infinite number of more learned and experienced sons of holy Church. My only desire is to demonstrate this in accordance with my modest abilities, since the basis of the Amedeist party are so slight that a man of small intelligence and experience is easily able to shatter it all to bits, leaving higher and more subtle matters to greater men.

‹*Oratio*›

4   Incipio igitur sub influencia Christi capitis ecclesiam suam defensurus et dico: Recepto per universam ecclesiam sanctissimo domino nostro Eugenio pro unico indubitato pontifice, post plures annos regiminis eius quidam pauci Basilee residentes Amedeum Subaudie tunc ducem antipapam erexerunt. Hos scismaticos a iure et homine anathematizatos mandat apostolica sedes per hanc inclitam nacionem vitari, sicud alie christiane naciones illis communionem subtraxerunt, omnibus illis non obstantibus que per eos allegantur. Nam 'sermo eorum fumus est caligine plenus, oculos stolidorum obtenebrans', nichil habens de veritatis subsistencia. Si enim spiritum Christi, qui 'veritas' est, haberent, eius 'corpus, quod est ecclesia, non' tanto 'opere dilaniare' studerent — 24. q. 1. *Ubi sana* etc. *Hereticus.* Christus enim 'in eorum cordibus habitare non' potest, 'qui se a corporis Christi compage abrumpunt' — eadem C. et q. c. *Audivimus.* Erat enim unitas ecclesie ex capite Eugenio et membris fidelibus compaginata, et ibi 'post connexam et' undique 'coniunctam ecclesie unitatem' alium Nouacianum erigentes execrandum scisma fecerunt — 7. q. 1. *Nouacianus*, ubi de hoc; 24. q. 1. *Didicimus.* Hoc solum sufficit omnibus eorum fabulacionibus satisfaciens. Scisma enim nullam habet defenssionem, cum 'nulla' sit dabilis causa ad 'scisma necessitans', ut optime deducit sanctus Augustinus *Contra Parmenianum*. Eo ipso enim, quod scisma fecerunt, se ipsos impios, iniustos atque dampnatos esse ostenderunt — 23. q. 5, *Si vos*. Et hec est prohibicionis causa, cur scismatici audiri non debeant, cum causam habere nequeant excusantem; habet enim scisma intra se anathema inexcusabile.

5   Sed quoniam Amediste quodam caliginoso fumo defenssionis utuntur, dicentes se concilium universale fuisse, ecclesiam repre-

[Oration]

I begin, therefore, my defense of the Church under the influence   4
of Christ, its head, and I speak as follows: After our most holy
lord Eugenius had been accepted as the sole, undoubted pontiff
and had reigned for many years, a certain few residing at Basel set
up Amadeus, then the duke of Savoy,[6] as antipope. The Apostolic
See commands that those schismatics, accursed by the law and by
man, be shunned by this illustrious nation, just as the other
Christian nations have withdrawn from communion with them,
notwithstanding all their allegations. For "their speech is a cloud
full of smoke, blinding the eyes of fools,"[7] having nothing of
truth's substance. If they had the spirit of Christ, who is Truth,[8]
they would not attempt with such "effort to rend His body, which
is the Church" ([Gratian] C. 24 q. 1 c. *Ubi sana* [c. 29] and c.
Hereticus [c. 30]). Christ, therefore, can "not live in the hearts of
those who break away from the unity of the body of Christ" (ibid.,
c. *Audivimus* [p. c. 4 ⊄ 1]). The unity of the Church, then, was
bound together from the head, Eugenius, and the members, the
faithful; and there, "after being connected and" altogether "joined
to the unity of the Church," they started an execrable schism, setting up a new Novatian[9] (see [Gratian] C. 7 q. 1 c. *Novatianus* [c.
31], and C. 24 q. 1 c. *Didicimus* [c. 31]). This fact alone should
suffice to answer all their lies. For there is no defense for schism,
since there is "no attributable cause which makes schism a necessity," as Saint Augustine so well deduced in *Against Parmenian*.[10]
Insofar as they have started a schism, they show themselves impi-
ous, unjust and condemned ([Gratian] C. 23 q. 5 c. *Si vos* [c. 35]).
And this is the reason why it is prohibited to hear schismatics,
since they are unable to excuse their cause; for schism is intrinsically inexcusable and anathema.

But, since the Amedeists use for their defense "a cloud full of   5
smoke," saying that they constituted a general council, that they

sentasse et cum auctoritate plena conciliari, ab ipsis dominum nostrum depositum esse et Amedeum electum, ostendam hec omnia a
veritate aliena. Primo quidem patefaciam dudum omnem conciliarem auctoritatem desiisse Basilee ob concilii translacionem aut secundum ordinacionem olim Basiliensis concilii aut conventum patrum in Ferraria animo ycumenicum concilium celebrandi aut per
recessum presidentum et aliorum de Basilea aut per Grecorum
unionem aut translacionem per dominum nostrum factam. 2° loco
subiciam eciam, si hec non obstarent, processum contra d‹ominum› n‹ostrum› nequaquam fuisse synodicum. Primo quidem ipsum arrogantem ostendam et presumptuosum, cum nondum sit
per universam ecclesiam admissum contra unicum pontificem Romanum talem fieri posse. 2° etsi fieri posset, non erat ille legitti-
mus et synodicus, solvendo obieccionem de heresi. 3° contra eligentes Amedeum atque de inabilitate electi et nullitate pauca
adiciam. In omnibus plane et succinte progredi curabo. Premittam
autem summarium casum rerum gestarum, ex quo omnia, que in-
tendo, apparebunt, parvam quandam iustificacionem peticionis
s‹anctissimi› d‹omini› ‹nostri› annectendo, ut sic ordinacius cetera
attingam.

‹Summarium rerum gestarum›

6   Sanctissimus d‹ominum› n‹ostrum›, 'dum' esset 'in minoribus, reduccionem' orientalis ecclesie diligenter 'sollicitans', deinde ad Petri kathedram superna dissposicione perveniens, ex apostolico officio sibi nunc hanc curam commissam considerans, talem egit
diligenciam, ut conclusio capta esset de 'mittendo apostolico legato

represented the Church and had full conciliar authority, and that they have deposed our lord [Eugenius] and elected Amadeus, I shall show that all of these things are far from the truth. [I] First, I will make plain that all conciliar authority departed from Basel after the transfer of the council,[11] whether owing to the ordinance of the former Council of Basel,[12] the gathering of fathers at Ferrara with the intent of celebrating an ecumenical council, the withdrawal of the presidents and of others from Basel, the arrival of the Greeks, or the transfer carried out by our lord [Eugenius]. [II] In the second place, I will show, even if these things did not present an obstacle to them, that the process against our lord never was synodal. [IIa] First, I will show that it was arrogant and presumptuous, since the universal Church has never yet allowed such a thing to be done to a Roman pontiff when there was only one of them;[13] [IIb] second, even if it could be done, it was not legitimate and synodal in resolving its objection about heresy.[14] [III] Third, I will add a few remarks against those who elected Amadeus and about the ineligibility and nullity of the person elected. In all these things, I shall take care to proceed plainly and succinctly. I shall preface this, however, with a *summary* of the facts of the case, from which my whole intention will be apparent, adding a short *defense* in justification of the petition of our most holy lord, so that I may touch upon the other points in a more orderly fashion.

[Summary of Events]

Our most holy lord, "when" he was "in a lesser office, worked diligently to bring back" the Eastern church;[15] finally, succeeding to the see of Peter by divine disposition, now considering how to exercise the pastoral care entrusted to him by his apostolic office, he acted with such diligence that he decided to "send an apostolic legate[16] to Constantinople," with the necessary entourage for

6

Co‹n›stantinopolim' cum necessariis personis pro felici et facili consumacione unionis ecclesiarum dei. Sed eo nostro pontifice 'inscio' per patres, qui Basilee concilii causa convenerant, cum Grecis alii tractatus initi sunt. Anno enim domini MCCCCXXXIIII, VII idus septembris in concilio Basiliensi cum oratoribus Grecorum de unione eorum actum est. Qui cum eam extra ycumenicam synodum fieri non posse dixissent, fuit diucius tractatum, ut in Basileam pro loco consentirent. Et quia obstantibus 'instructionibus' hoc facere non poterant, 'iudicavit' concilium 'non expedire', quod 'propter locum tantum bonum negligeretur', sed obligavit se per iuramentum nomine concilii per apostolicum legatum et presidentem prestitum solempniter ad faciendum concilium ycumenicum in 'Calabria, Ancona vel alio' loco 'marit‹i›mo' aut in 'Bononia, Mediolano vel alio' loco 'in Ytalia, extra Ytaliam' in 'Buda in Vngaria' aut in 'Wyenna in Austria et ad ultimum' in 'Sabaudia', sic quod illud ycumenicum concilium in uno ex locis prefatis per concilium eligendo fiat ac quod oratores mittendi pro Grecis adducant 'quatuor galeas' et 'tricentos balistarios pro custodia civitatis Constantinopolitane' et 'nominent imperatori Grecorum locum unum ex nominatis' cum oblacione salvi conductus domini loci et civitatis, similiter et 'portum, ad quem ultimo debebit applicare', ad quem dum perveniret, concilium Basiliense 'infra mensem ad nominatum locum se transferret', accedente in omnibus 'expresso consenssu' Romani pontificis, qui eciam 'per se vel suos' ad hoc constitutos cum aliis 'patriarchis' et episcopis, qui 'similiter ibi esse debent vere vel representative', hoc concilium ycumenicum celebrabit.

7   Veniente igitur tempore eleccionis loci in concilio magnus numerus, qui tunc studiose pro faccione huius rei noviter ex coaccione adversariorum d‹omini› n‹ostri› advenerat ad hunc actum,

the fortunate and ready consummation of the union of God's churches. But our pontiff was unaware that the fathers who were assembled at Basel in council had also initiated negotiations with the Greeks. In the year of the Lord 1434, on the 7th of September, an agreement was made concerning the union in the Council of Basel with the envoys of the Greeks. Since the Greeks said the union could not be arranged outside of an ecumenical synod, there were further negotiations in order that they might agree to Basel as the site. Because they could not do this on account of their instructions, the council "judged it inexpedient" that "so great a good should not be accomplished because of the site;" but it bound itself, by an oath taken by the apostolic legate and president[17] in the name of the council, to hold an ecumenical council in "Calabria, Ancona or any other" place "near the sea" or "in Bologna, Milan or any other" place "in Italy; beyond Italy," in "Buda or Hungary," or in "Vienna in Austria and, lastly" in "Savoy." The ecumenical council was to be held in one of the aforesaid places, to be chosen by the council, and the envoys to be sent out to the Greeks would bring "four galleys" and "three hundred crossbow men for the protection of the city of Constantinople;" and "they would name one place among those named to the emperor of the Greeks"[18] with an offer of safe conduct from the lord of that place and city, and likewise they would name "a port to which the emperor will finally land." Once he had arrived, the Council of Basel "would translate itself to the chosen place within a month," with "the express consent" in all these matters of the Roman pontiff, who would celebrate this ecumenical council, either "by himself or through his" duly appointed legates, with the other "patriarchs"[19] and bishops, who "likewise should be there in person or through their representatives."

When therefore the time came for choosing the site in council, 7 a great number of persons at that time had arrived for this session with the express aim of bringing about a result not in accordance

de personis infimis et ad res synodicas tractandas ineptissimis inclinabatur pocius ad Auinionem, que civitas eciam pecunias obtulit necessarias mutuare. Addiderunt autem illi Basileam, iam a Grecis refutatam, et quia Auinio non fuit nominata, addiderunt et Sabaudiam. Hec autem duo loca ob fraudem adiunxerunt, ut postea compertum est. Presidentes apostolici et alii plures misteria intelligentes restiterunt. Auinionenses eciam petiverunt pro securitate suarum pecuniarum exponendarum decretacionem loci et portus et decime imponende. Multis resistentibus, ne hoc fieret, finaliter quidam domini pro concordia patrum conceperunt unum avisamentum, continens 'quod ambasiatores in' Constantinopolim 'ituri de Basilea, versus Auinionem' pergerent ac quod 'Auinionenses infra xxx dies' post recessum ipsorum deberent contentare 'capitaneum galearum de 30 800 florenis et residuum usque ad summam 70 000 florenorum' exsolverent ipsis 'ambasiatoribus realiter in pecunia numerata.' De quibus omnibus 'infra xii dies post xxx predictos certificari' deberet ipsum 'concilium' per litteras 'ambasiatorum predictorum; alioquin extunc posset et teneretur concilium procedere ad eleccionem alterius loci et aliunde universali ecclesie providere'. Hoc avisamentum fuit conclusum per deputaciones et congregacionem generalem.

8   Oratores Auinionem perrexerunt cum bullis et instruccionibus dominis presidentibus et eis adherentibus ignaris, inter cetera habentes potestatem portum nominandi, sicud eis videretur. Unde cum Auenionem venissent et Auinionenses multum dubitarent, an Greci ad eos venturi essent propter contradiccionem quam audierant Basilee factam, hoc argumento seducebantur, quia dicebatur ipsis Sabaudiam nominatam, quam Greci refutare non possent, esseque in potestate ipsorum oratorum portum ultimum nominare,

with tradition, under compulsion from the adversaries of our lord. The council, being now composed of low individuals unsuited to transacting the business of a council, inclined toward Avignon, a city which offered to advance the necessary funds. They added Basel [to the list of sites], which already had been refused by the Greeks; and, because Avignon was not listed, they added Savoy as well.[20] These places they listed fraudulently, as became obvious later. The apostolic presidents, however, and many others who understood the mysteries resisted. The men of Avignon even petitioned for the announcement of the place and port as security for the money they had laid out, and for the imposition of a tithe.[21] When many resisted doing this, some of the lords finally drafted an agreement to bring harmony among the council fathers, binding "the envoys who are going to set out from Basel" to Constantinople to head for "Avignon" [first] and that "the men of Avignon within thirty days" after their departure should engage "a captain of galleys for 30,800 florins and" pay "the rest, up to the sum of 70,000 florins," to those "envoys in money actually counted out."[22] The council was to "certify" all this "within twelve days after the aforesaid thirty" through the letters "of the aforesaid envoys; otherwise, thereafter, the council could and was obliged to proceed to the choice of another site and to provide otherwise for the universal Church." This agreement was accepted by the deputations and by the general congregation.[23]

The envoys left for Avignon with bulls and instructions unknown to the lord presidents and their adherents, giving, among other things, the power of choosing the port as they might see fit. They came to Avignon, and the men of Avignon were in grave doubt whether the Greeks were going to come to them owing to the denial that they heard had been made at Basel.[24] But they were seduced by the envoy's argument because they were told that Savoy was among the places listed and that the Greeks could not refuse to go there, and that it was in the power of the envoys to se-

8

et per hanc potestatem Grecos Auinionem conducerent, quia eos
ad portum propinquum circa Auinionem, scilicet Aquas Mortuas,
conducerent et, quando ita ad Auinionem fatigati Greci perveni-
rent, non instarent plus fatigari et ad Sabaudiam vehi, maxime
cum in Sabaudia nulla civitas specialiter nominata aut ad hoc ac-
comoda‹ta› esset, que preponeretur Auinioni cum incommodo iti-
neris et fatige. Unde ipsi oratores de non nominando alium portum se per iuramentum et alias solempniter Auinionensibus
astrinxerunt. Sed adhuc non bene securi pecuniam infra statutum
terminum non exbursarunt, ymmo lapso termino, ut prius, insta-
bant pro decretacione loci et decime et portus. Fraus hec de portu
occulte tenebatur, quia dabat pars illa Almanis ad intelligendum,
quomodo cum pecuniis Auinionensium concilium ycumenicum
finaliter Basilee constitueretur. Hec quidem fraudulenter dicebant,
ut sic Almanos ad favores allicerent.

9   Dum igitur hec sic Auinione agerentur, supervenit ex Grecia
orator imperatoris Iohannes Dissipatus, in generali congregacione
protestando nullum Grecorum per mare Siculum seu Tyrenum
venturum. Cum ipsis enim bona fide actum esset; sed illud mare
tale foret, quod imperator et patriarcha et alii senes prelati sine periculo vite per illud duci non possent, nec unquam in hoc consen-
sissent neque consentirent neque Auinionem approbassent, sed re-
futassent, protestando quod per hanc viam negocium unionis
destrueretur, expense perderentur, fides eis data et iurata non ser-
varetur. Et multa circa hoc dixit.

10   Videntes igitur domini presidentes negocium illud penitus in
fumum ire cum 'ignominia' ecclesie nostre, nisi ad aliam eleccionem procederetur, proposuerunt 'in generali congregacione' iuxta
'concordata' in concilio, quia 'Auinionenses infra terminum non sa-
tisfecissent, ad alterius loci eleccionem procedendum esse'; nam

lect the port of destination, and that they would use this power to bring the Greeks to Avignon. They would do this by bringing them to a port near Avignon, that is Aigues Mortes, and when the Greeks reached Avignon, they would be tired, and would not insist on the further fatigue of being brought to Savoy, especially as no particular city in Savoy had been named and none was as fit for this task as Avignon, quite apart from the journey and the fatigue it would involve. Therefore, the envoys bound themselves by oaths and solemn promises to the men of Avignon not to select any other port. But still, they would not pay the promised money within the stated term [without assurance of having the council]; so, after the term had elapsed, as before, they pushed for a declaration of the site, the tithe and the port. This act of deceit about the port was kept secret because that party had given the Germans to understand that the ecumenical council would in the end be held at Basel, using the money of the men of Avignon. This they declared deceitfully, so that the Germans would incline to their side.

While this was going on at Avignon, however, an orator of the emperor, John Dishypatus, arrived from Greece and testified in general congregation that none of the Greeks would come as far as the Sicilian or the Tyrrhenian seas. Although negotiations had been held with them in good faith, those seas were not acceptable because the emperor, the patriarch,[25] and other elderly prelates could not travel there without peril to their lives; neither had they assented, nor would they, to Avignon. They refused to go there, protesting that that choice would destroy the work of union. Their expenditures would be lost, and the promises and oaths given them would not be kept. And he said much on this subject.

The lord presidents, therefore, seeing that business virtually going up in smoke, with ignominy for our Church, unless the council should proceed to make another choice, proposed "in the general congregation," according to "the concordat" made in the council, that, since "the men of Avignon had not satisfied the

eleccio illa, eciamsi Auinio eligibilis fuisset per ordinacionem concilii Auinionensibus intimata, cassa et irrita facta esset per fluxum temporis, ita quod opus foret alia eleccione, exhortando ut illa fieret de loco Grecis grato et rebus gerendis accommodo. Post hanc exhortacionem aliquociens repetitam domini de XII secundum concilii formam avisarunt iuxta exhortacionem illam negociis Grecorum providendum esse, atque ita statuto die in deputacionibus ad alterius loci eleccionem deventum est, eligentibus quidem dominis presidentibus et aliis nonnullis regum et principum oratoribus et viris gravissimis, et tribus presidentibus trium deputacionum eleccionem concludentibus, aliis multis dominis deputacionibus interessentibus et non eligentibus, sed vota dantibus. Pro peticione Auinionensium, scilicet decretacione loci et decime etc., interposuit se Germanica nacio et cives Basilienses, et XII fuerunt media oblata et aliqua ex illis per olim archiepiscopum Panormitanum, qui favere tamen videbatur parti, que eligebat Auinionem, licet ipse palam allegasset solempniter ipsam non esse eligibilem tamquam non nominatam nec comprehensam in decreto convencionali. Omnia media per presidentes et eis adherentes admissa fuerunt cum una exuberantissima adieccione, quod omnis modus excogitabilis placeret pro desiderio alterius partis, sic quod negocium Grecorum non perderetur cum ignominia et infamia ecclesie et promissorum eius. Sed quia pars alia concordiam noluit, ita ut mala intencio ducum illius multitudinis facile intelligeretur, honor dei et ecclesie unitas et promissio bonos artabat, ne cederetur. Quare cum illa pars olim Arelatensis ad decretacionem festinaret, opus erat, ne veritas occumberet, quod ipsi domini presidentes pa-

agreement within the allotted time, it must proceed with the choice of another site;" for the former choice, even if Avignon had been eligible by the ordinance of the council intimated to the men of Avignon, was null and void because of the passage of time, so that deliberations on another site could proceed. The fathers were exhorted that it should be a place satisfactory to the Greeks and appropriate to the business to be transacted. After this exhortation had been repeatedly issued, the lords of the Twelve,[26] according to the council's procedures, announced that negotiations with the Greeks would be handled according to that exhortation; and so, on the appointed day, the deputations proceeded to the choice of another site. The electors were the lord presidents and a few others, the envoys of the kings and princes and the sounder men, and the presidents of the three deputations would conclude the election, while many other lord deputies were present and, though ineligible, gave their votes. The German nation and the citizens of Basel favored the petition of the men of Avignon about the choice of a site, the tithe, etc.; the Twelve offered compromise solutions, some of them suggested by the former archbishop of Palermo, who seemed to favor the party which preferred Avignon, although he argued solemnly in open session that it was not eligible, since it was not nominated nor included in the draft decree. All the compromises were admitted by the presidents and those adhering to them, along with an extremely liberal injunction that every means imaginable should be advanced to placate the desire of the other party, provided that the opportunity to negotiate with the Greeks should not be lost, to the ignominy and infamy of the Church and of its promises. But because the other party did not wish to agree — so much so that the bad motives of the leaders of that multitude were readily understood — the honor of God, the unity of the Church and its promise constrained the good men not to give in. Hence when the party of the former Cardinal of Arles[27] rushed to issue a decree, it was necessary for the lord presidents to

riformiter agerent. Decreta est igitur eleccio Vtini et Florencie aut alterius 'loci' ex nominatis grati Romano 'pontifici et Grecis', 'qui' prius 'necessaria paraverit'.

11 Missum est hoc decretum ad s‹anctitatem› d‹omini› n‹ostri›, qui audito processu, instante oratore Grecorum, communicato consilio dominorum cardinalium et prelatorum, qui in maiori numero, eciam ex Basilee quondam incorporatis, in curia tunc erant quam Basilee, gratam habuit ipsam eleccionem et eam in publico consistorio solempniter confirmavit atque ad exequendum eam, ut capud ecclesie et concilii, cum hiis, qui decretum illud s‹anctitati› sue presentarunt, oratores Constantinopolim misit.

12 Qui dum aliquamdiu in ea civitate Constantinopolitana fuissent, ex Auinione galeas venisse audiverunt, sine tamen balistariis. Unde, ne ob hoc Greci retraherentur a veniendo, dabant ipsi oratores s‹anctissimi› d‹omini› n‹ostri› et partis sue ad hoc speciale mandatum habentes Grecis potestatem cum illis galeis Auinionem veniendi aut per alium omnem modum eis gratum, sic tamen, quod omnino ad aliquam quamcumque civitatem ecclesie occidentalis venire non recusarent. Practicavit imperator Grecorum aliquibus diebus cum illis, et quia non poterant ad aliam viam consentire, quam quod per mare Tyrenum ad Aquas Mortuas descenderent in ultimum portum, ad quod Greci induci non poterant, redierunt ipsi vacui, Grecis Ferrariam venientibus, intimacione facta omnibus, que eciam ad noticiam Basilee remanencium pervenit, ex ultimo portu Veneciarum de eorum adventu.

13 Venit igitur dominus Iulianus cardinalis legatus apostolicus primus et ultimus, qui Basilee auctoritate apostolica presedit, et cum eo ex incorporatis prelatis Basilee multi viri doctissimi ad civitatem

act likewise so that the truth should not be laid low. They decreed, therefore, the choice of Udine and Florence or any other place, among those listed, satisfactory to the Roman "pontiff and to the Greeks, who already had made the necessary preparations."[28]

This decree was sent to our most holy lord, who, having learned what had occurred, on the urging of the envoy of the Greeks, took counsel with the lord cardinals and the prelates, of whom there was at that time a greater number in the papal curia, including some who once were incorporated into the Council of Basel, than remained at Basel; he found that choice most welcome and solemnly confirmed it in a public consistory.[29] For the execution of the decree, as head of the Church and of its council, the pope sent envoys to Constantinople, along with those who had presented that decree to His Holiness. 11

When they had been for some time in the city of Constantinople, they heard that the galleys had come from Avignon, but without the crossbow men. Hence, so that the Greeks would not withdraw from the journey on this account, these ambassadors of our most holy lord and of his party, having a special mandate for this, gave the Greeks the power of coming to Avignon on those galleys or any way they liked, so long as they did not refuse to come to some city of the Western church. The emperor of the Greeks negotiated with [the Avignonese party] for a few days; and, because they would not consent to any other route than that they should travel by way of the Tyrrhenian Sea to Aigues Mortes as the port of destination, and the Greeks could not be induced to take this route, they returned empty-handed. The Greeks came to Ferrara, having given notice to all of their coming at last to the port of the Venetians, and the remnant at Basel was also notified of this. 12

The lord cardinal Giuliano [Cesarini], the first and last apostolic legate who had presided at Basel with apostolic authority, came to the city of Ferrara; and with him, from among the prelates once incorporated into the Council of Basel, many highly 13

Ferrariensem, ita ut in fundacione illius ycumenici concilii in prima sessione plus quam in duplo plures prelati eciam ex olim Basilee incorporatis cum capite ecclesie et concilii, quam Basilee remanserint, reperti sint.

14 Verum quia olim Arelatensis et sui in finem, ut s‹anctitatem› d‹omini› n‹ostri› eciam apud Grecos diffamarent, ad inpediendum eorum adventum, audito quod s‹anctitas› sua confirmasset eleccionem partis presidencium, quoddam iniuriosissimum monitorium de facto decreverunt contra s‹anctitatem› suam et huius copiam oratores eorum Constantinopolim attulerunt, restiterunt presidentes apostolici atque alii gravissimi domini, eciam sancte memorie dominus imperator Sigismundus atque alii principes, ne tantum scandalum scisma resuscitaret. Et quia furori illorum, quem in multis ostenderunt, obviari nulla prece aut racione potuit, s‹anctissimus› d‹ominus› n‹oster›, ammonitus per re‹verendissimos› dominos cardinales et alios prelatos, ut ipsis furiosis gladium de manu tolleret, in cuius confidencia hoc attemptabant, scilicet auctoritatem concilii ab ipsis demeret, in finem, ne scisma fieret ac ne unio Grecorum impediretur, concilium eciam 'ante Grecorum adventum transtulit' cum condicione, si non desisterent ab illis presumptuosissimis scandalis, adiciens: 'in quo eciam sic translato talia auctore deo proponere et agere intendimus, ex quibus nostram innocenciam orbis totus cognoscere poterit' etc. Et quoniam illi ad cessandum et impetum refrenandum nulla prece principum induci poterant, ymmo magis intellecto Grecorum adventu ad Italiam inardescebant, hinc s‹anctissimus› d‹ominus› n‹oster›, congregatis non paucis prelatis Ferrarie, presidente domino cardinali sancte Crucis, congnosci fecit, an apud Basilee residentes et talia in fidei

learned men, so that at the start of the ecumenical council, at the first session, more than twice the number of prelates once incorporated into the former Council of Basel were found there, with the head of the Church [i.e. the pope] and of the council [i.e., Cardinal Cesarini].

The former Cardinal of Arles and those still with him, having   14
heard that His Holiness had confirmed the choice made by the party of the presidents, issued an utterly unjust admonition on this matter against His Holiness in order to defame His Holiness to the Greeks and to delay their arrival; and their envoys brought a copy of the admonition to Constantinople. The apostolic presidents and others among the weightiest lords, also the lord Emperor Sigismund of holy memory[30] and other princes, resisted this, so that so grave a scandal might not bring the schism to life again. And, because the fury of those men, which they showed in many things, could not be deflected by any prayer or argument, our most holy lord, as advised by the most reverend lord cardinals and other prelates, in order to take the sword [of conciliar authority] out of the hands of these madmen, trusting in which they had committed this outrage, took away from them the authority of a council, so that schism would not result nor union with the Greeks be impeded. Even "before the arrival of the Greeks, he translated" the council, with the condition that this would occur if they did not desist from their most presumptuous scandals. He added "in the translated council, with God as our authority, we intend to propose and carry out such acts that all the world will be able to recognize our innocence." And, since those at Basel could not be induced by any plea of the princes to cease and to refrain from rash acts, and indeed the news of the arrival of the Greeks in Italy inflamed them still more, our most holy lord, having gathered no small number of prelates at Ferrara under the presidency of the Cardinal of Santa Croce,[31] made an inquiry into the question of whether the authority of a council remained among the persons in

preiudicium et scismatis fomentum attemptantes concilii maneret auctoritas vel non. Tunc concilium legittime translatum fore de Basilea ad Ferrariam communi omnium sentencia diffinitum est, ac quod per lapsum termini ad hoc statuti concilium esset 'legittime Ferrarie stabilitum'.

15   Post hec illi, qui in Basilea erant, hiis omnibus non obstantibus, postquam ad ora Ytalie Grecos adventasse sensserant, d‹omini› n‹ostri› s‹anctitatem› nisi sunt diabolica presumpcione 'ab omni administracione suspendere et sibi ipsam papalem administracionem sub privacionis pena' vendicare, citando omnes cardinales et alios, ut 'ad' Basileam 'concurrant', precipiendo omnibus prelatis et principibus, ne eidem domino nostro pareant aut obediant.

16   Inchoata est autem felicissima sancta ycumenica synodus, sathanicis illis impedimentis non obstantibus, secundum ordinacionem olim Basiliensis concilii, et de reduccione Grecorum diligencia facta est, qualis in tali arduissima materia fieri debuit, ita quod dei dono immenso orientalis ecclesia ad fidem Romane ecclesie cum pace conducta est, ut nunc una sit Romane ecclesie atque Constantinopolitane, ymmo et Armenorum, Hyberorum, Afrorum, Iacobinorum atque Indorum fides.

17   Illi vero, qui Basilee remanserunt, in profundum malorum continue plus ruentes, bono unitatis invidentes, ad horrendum scisma sua sponte properarunt, contradicentibus omnibus nacionibus et prelatis, regum et principum oratoribus de contrario in faciem eorum protestantibus, cum hiis pene omnibus et multo maiori parte prelatorum, qui tunc Basilee erant, concurrentibus et de congregacionibus se absentantibus, ita quod inter omnes cardinales, archiepiscopos et episcopos, qui tunc Basilee erant, quasi ad numerum xxx, minus quam decem passionatissimi emuli, quorum vix quatuor aliud quam nudum usurpatum titulum habebant,

session at Basel, who were attempting to foment schism to the detriment of the faith. At that time it was formally decided by universal consent that the council was legitimately translated from Basel to Ferrara, and that owing to the lapse of the term set [for the response of the Avignonese] the council "would be established [anew] at Ferrara."[32]

After this, those who were at Basel, all this notwithstanding,   15 after hearing that the Greeks had arrived on the shores of Italy, attempted with diabolical presumption "to suspend" His Holiness "from all administration and claimed for themselves the papal administration on pain of deprivation of office," summoning all the cardinals and others "to gather at" Basel, and instructing all prelates and princes not to heed or obey our lord.[33]

The most fortunate and holy synod, however, began, notwith-   16 standing these satanic impediments, according to the ordinance of the former Council of Basel; and diligent work was carried out for the reunion of the Greeks of the kind required in such difficult matters, so that, by the immense gift of God, the Eastern church was reunited to the faith of the Roman church in peace, with the result that now the churches of Rome and Constantinople are one. Likewise, the Armenians, Hyperboreans, Africans, Jacobites and Indians share that faith.[34]

But those who remained at Basel, rushing ever downward into   17 the abyss of the wicked, envying the good of unity, hastened to the horror of schism by their own will, contradicting all the nations and prelates, as well as the protests offered to their face by the envoys of kings and princes. Almost all of the envoys and the greater part of the prelates who were at Basel were in agreement [with Eugenius] and absented themselves from the general congregations, so that, of all the cardinals, archbishops and bishops who were at Basel — about thirty in number —, fewer than ten, and those among the most passionately envious of the lot — of whom scarcely four had more than the bare title of a usurper — tried to

nisi sunt dominum nostrum deponere et universam per orbem dispersam ecclesiam scandalizare. Inter eos autem, qui huic nepharie faccioni se opposuerunt, post cardinalem Terraconensem, archiepiscopum Mediolanensem et alios maximos viros fuit ille olim Panormitanus, qui singulariter et in scriptis de iniusticia protestatus est. Ingratissimus vir tot iuramentorum apostolice sedi prestitorum, sue doctrine et protestacionum immemor partem scismaticam assumpsit, nunc hic pro defenssione capelli pseudocardinalatus sui cum ignominia militans. Posuerunt autem in pretensa sentencia dominum nostrum 'hereticum' esse ex eo, quia concilium transtulit Ferraream, licet neque super heresi citatus esset neque ante citacionem concilium eciam transtulisset, sibi Amedeum olim ducem Sabaudie in caput preficientes — novam rem ex laico aliquem ad monarchiam ecclesie velle erigere! — ecclesia per orbem diffusa dissenciente, ymmo anathematizante, nichilominus eciam omnes, cuiuscumque dignitatis ecclesiastice seu secularis, ac universitates honoribus privantes et anathematizantes tamquam heresis et scismatis fautores, qui domino nostro depost favores in pontificatu prestarent. Sed deus, qui non sinit veritatem opprimi, ecclesiam suam per orbem dispersam, cui inspiravit, ut Basiliensibus contradiceret, conservavit absque scismate, ita ut omnes naciones, usque in istam, hanc Basiliensem faccionem tamquam presumptuosissimam dampnent.

⟨*Iustificacio peticionis pape*⟩

18 In hac autem nacione, in qua 'propter dubium' translacionis tempore eleccionis bone memorie regis Alberti deliberacio ad tempus capta fuit cum protestacionibus bonis respectibus, maxime ne interim aut 'eleccio' illa 'cavillaretur', aut nacio Germanica 'scindere-

depose our lord and to scandalize the Church spread throughout the world.[35] Among those, however, who opposed themselves to this nefarious faction, along with the Cardinal of Tarragona,[36] the archbishop of Milan,[37] and others of the greatest men, was the former archbishop of Palermo, who lodged a separate protest, and in writing, about the injustice of the deposition.[38] That most unjust man [nevertheless] took the side of the schismatics, unmindful of the many oaths he had taken to the Apostolic See,[39] his own learning and his protests, and now was fighting ignominiously to defend his pseudo-cardinal's hat.[40] They called our lord a heretic in the pretended sentence because he translated the council to Ferrara, although he never was cited for heresy, nor had he even translated the council before being cited. They made Amadeus, formerly Duke of Savoy, their head. Now here was a revolutionary act: raising a layman to the monarchy of the Church! Despite the dissent and anathemas of the Church spread throughout the world, they nevertheless set about depriving of their honors everyone holding any kind of ecclesiastical or secular dignity, as well as collective bodies, and were anathematizing as supporters of heresy and schism whoever should show favor to our lord in his pontificate thereafter. But God, Who does not permit truth to be suppressed, inspired His Church spread throughout the world to contradict those at Basel. He kept it from schism so that all nations, except this [German] one, condemn the Basel faction as utterly presumptuous.

[Defense of the Pope's Petition]

In this nation, however, "by reason of doubt" about the translation, deliberation was put on hold with protestations of good intentions at the time of the election of King Albert of happy memory,[41] mostly to prevent that "election being quibbled over" in the meantime or the German nation "being cut off" [from the body of

18

tur', nunc agitur de conclusione illius deliberacionis et declaracione 'obediencie', cum continuacio perniciem pariat. Unde s‹anctissi-mus› d‹ominus› n‹oster› serenissimum Romanorum regem nos-trum et r‹everendissimos› patres et illustrissimos principes electo-res exhortatur, ut tollant de medio animorum susspe‹n›ssionem et in obediencia, in qua erant quo ad apostolicam sedem et s‹anctita-tem› suam, ut decet constantes fideles principes, se remanere de-clarent, hiis non obstantibus, que Basilee presumpta sunt.

19   Quod autem necessarium sit pro dei honore, salute animarum, ecclesie unitate ac inclite huius nacionis honoris conservacione de-claracionem absque protraccione taliter fieri, ex hoc manifestissi-mum est, quia, cum obediencia sit de necessitate salutis quo ad apostolicam sedem et Romanum pontificem — lxxxi d. *Si qui presbi-teri, De maioritate et obediencia, Solite* et in Extravagante *Unam sanctam* ❡ *Porro* cum similibus — tunc, cum principes nostri Ger-mani cum aliis orbis regibus ea, que Basilee contra d‹ominum› n‹ostrum› acta sunt, tamquam scandalosa et scismatica iuste non receperint, non possunt ex eo, contra quod protestati sunt, cum aliquo honore occasionem non obediendi recipere. Ymmo si sua-rum protestacionum immemores esse vellent, tunc, adhuc attento quod pene universa christianitas, illis que Basilee acta sunt non obstantibus, dominum nostrum Eugenium pro indubitato papa colit, non possunt dicere non esse dubium, an Basilienses rite pro-cesserint. Sed in dubio nequaquam, qui fuit indubitatus, 'deseren-dus' est — viii q. iiii *Nonne*; et est conciliariter diffinitum — xvii d. ❡ *Hinc eciam* — quod recedentes ob dubium ab obediencia 'scisma faciunt', ubi coniunctis ❡ *Item Simachus*, ii q. vii *Item cum Balaham* et glo. casus esse videtur. Probatur idem 24. q. 1. *Scisma*, ubi de

the Church]. Now action is being taken to conclude this period of deliberation and to make a declaration of obedience, since a continuation of neutrality would lead to disaster. Therefore, our most holy lord exhorts our most serene King of the Romans and the most reverend lord fathers and the most illustrious prince electors to remove from their midst the suspension of their allegiance and to declare that they remain in their former obedience to the Apostolic See and to His Holiness, as befits faithful princes, notwithstanding those things done presumptuously at Basel.

That it is necessary, however, for the salvation of souls, the unity of the Church and the preservation of the honor of this illustrious nation to make such a declaration without delay is obvious from the fact that obedience to the Apostolic See and the Roman pontiff is necessary for salvation ([Gratian] D. 81 c. *Si qui presbiteri* [c. 15]; [*Decretals* of Gregory IX], *De maioritate et obedientia* c. *Solite* [X. 1.33.6]; and in the constitution *Unam sanctam* ⟨ *Porro* [Extrav. Commun. 1.8.1] with similar texts). Then too, since our German princes, together with the other kings of the earth, may not justly accept the scandalous and schismatic acts performed at Basel against our lord, they cannot honorably accept the occasion of disobedience [these acts afford] while protesting against them. Indeed, if they are inclined to forget their own protests, they should still be aware that almost all Christendom, notwithstanding the actions taken at Basel, reverences the lord Eugenius as undoubted pope, so they cannot say they are in a state of doubt whether those at Basel acted correctly. In case of doubt, the undoubted pope never is "to be abandoned" ([Gratian] C. 8 q. 4 c. *Nonne* [c. 1].[42]), and it was defined at a council ([ibid.] D. 17 ⟨ *Hinc eciam* [p.c. 6 ⟨ 2]) that those who withdraw from obedience out of doubt "are making a schism"—combining the texts *Item Symmachus*, C. 2 q. 7 and ⟨ *Item cum Balaham* and the glosses[43] on the case. The same is proved by [Gratian] C. 24 q. 1 c. *Scisma* [c. 34], where there is a discussion of the matter. Hence we con-

hoc. Hinc concluditur peticionem domini nostri non solum esse iustam et honestam, sed et necessariam detestandosque esse Amedistas, quoniam 'omnis catholicus securus eam partem detestatur, cui ecclesiam universalem apostolicis sedibus roboratam non communicare congnoscit'; sunt verba sancti Augustini posita in c. allegato. Communicare enim illis est ecclesiam destruere, ut optime sanctus Petrus Clementem instruxit — 93. d. *Si inimicus.*

20   Dudum autem cessasse dubium, propter quod susspenssio animorum facta fuit, manifestum est. Nam dubitabant domini principes, an Basilee esset concilium, obstante translacione que eis per dominum episcopum Vrbinatensem fuit eo tunc Franckfordie insinuata. Si enim concilium Basiliense pro indubitato habuissent, quomodo fuisset iustum protestari de non obediendo eidem? Si autem translacio certa fuisset, non minus iniustum fuisset de non obediendo mandatis domini pape protestari. Causa igitur protestacionis fuit ambiguitas translacionis; sed quando post hoc Basilienses ab universa ecclesia per orbem dispersa ac a nostris principibus de contrario protestantibus et a capite ecclesie Romano pontifice se scismatice separarunt, Amedeum ducem in capud sibi preficiendo, cessavit dubium, an Basilee sit concilium, apud principes nostros et universam ecclesiam, que Amedeum non recepit. 'Una' enim 'ecclesia' non habet nisi 'unum' pastorem — vii q. 1. *Non autem* in glo. —, et ecclesia est 'grex pastori' unitus — ibidem in c. *Scire debes.* Quare illi nec ecclesia nec concilium esse potuerunt — 24. q. i *Didicimus* et q. iii *Clericus* et c. *Cum quibus.* Cessare igitur debuit protestacio ab eo tempore citra. Sed quia hoc per dominos principes hucusque declarari non potuit, quia eis oportunitas conveniendi cum serenissimo rege nostro data non fuit, excusati habiti

clude that our lord's petition is not only just and honorable but also necessary. The Amedeists are to be detested, since "every peaceful Catholic detests that party, which he knows to be not in communion with the universal Church corroborated by the Apostolic See." These are the words of Saint Augustine in the aforesaid chapter. To stand in communion with them is to destroy the Church, as Saint Peter taught Clement ([Gratian] D. 93 c. *Si inimicus* [c. 1]).

However, it is clear that the doubts for whose sake they had suspended their allegiance have at length come to an end. The lord princes were in doubt as to whether Basel was a council, in the face of the translation which had been made known to them by the bishop of Urbino,[44] who was then at Frankfurt.[45] If they had regarded Basel's conciliar status as beyond doubt, how could it be just to protest that they would not obey it? If, however, the translation [to Ferrara] was definite and certain, it was no less unjust to protest that they would not obey the mandates of the lord pope. The cause of the protest, therefore, was ambiguity about the translation; but when afterwards those at Basel, making Duke Amadeus their head, schismatically separated themselves from the universal Church spread throughout the world and from our princes, who protested against this, and from the head of the Church, doubt whether Basel was a council ceased among our princes and the universal Church, which did not accept Amadeus. "One Church," therefore, has only "one" shepherd (the gloss on [Gratian] C. 7 q. 1 c. *Non autem*);[46] and the Church is "a flock" united "to its shepherd" (ibid., c. *Scire debes*).[47] Therefore they cannot be either the Church or a council ([Gratian], C. 24 q. 1 c. *Didicimus* [c. 31] and C. 24 q. 3 c. *Clericus* [c. 35] and c. *Cum quibus* [c. 36]). The protest ought therefore to have ceased from that time onwards. But, because this could not be declared by the lord princes at that time, since an opportunity had not been given them for conferring with the most serene king, our most holy lord

sunt apud s‹anctitatem› d‹omini› n‹ostri›. Nunc autem omnis occasio retardacionis finem cepit. Hinc id fieri supplicatur, quod statuta dies promittit.

‹I›

21 Quamvis hoc solum sufficeret proposito nostro, maxime quando
iniusticiam Amedistarum fructus eorum pandunt, qui post promissionem augmenti fidei, pacis et reformacionis in turpissimam
ecclesie divisionem ruentes, hiis omnibus sacris premissis amplius
sathanice invidentes, ut casus habet, se 'spiritum' domini 'caritatis'
et 'unitatis' perdidisse opere manifestarunt—ut dicit textus
24. q. 1. *Ubi sana*, c. *Heretici*, c. *Audivimus* et c. *Scisma*, ubi ostenditur scissuram procurantes spiritum 'Christi' non habere, cuius 'corpus dilaniant', xxiii q. v *De Liguribus* cum similibus—et ipsum spiritum sanctum in ycumenica synodo cum domino nostro fuisse,
qui tam admirabilem unitatis fructum operatus est, tamen ad hoc,
ut garrulacionibus eorum sufficientissime videatur satisfactum,
dico quod, Romanus pontifex si iudicari posset, a concilio universali tantum hoc possibile est—ii q. vii *Sicud inquit* in glo., v q. iiii
Nullus episcopus.

22 Sed nullum fuit universale concilium Basilee tempore, quo
Amediste s‹anctitatem› d‹omini› n‹ostri› nisi sunt deponere, quia
fuit translatum secundum ordinacionem concilii ad Ferrariam, ut
patet ex casu. Igitur irrita est deposicio, que translacionem secuta
est. Non possunt Amediste casum negare, quem in ea parte cedule
concordate ac non-satisfaccione Auinionensium infra terminum
confessi sunt, quando anno domini MCCCCXXXVII in Reuß feria
IIII ante pentecosten magistrum Thomam de Corcellis ad princi-

holds them as excused.⁴⁸ Now, however, every occasion for delay has come to an end. Hence supplication is made that the appointed day [for submission] be fixed.

[I]

This alone would suffice for our purpose, especially when the 21
fruits of the Amedeists make known their injustice. After a promise to build up the faith, peace and reform,⁴⁹ they rushed into creating the most shameful dissension within the Church; in their satanic envy of all the aforesaid holy rites, as it turned out, they show by their works that they have lost "the spirit" of the Lord, "of charity and of unity,"⁵⁰ as the text says in [Gratian] C. 24 q. 1 c. *Ubi sana*, c. *Heretici*, c. *Audivimus* and c. *Scisma* [c. 29, c. 30, p.c. 4 ℂ 1, c. 34], where it is shown that those who promote schism lack the spirit "of Christ," whose "body they rend" ([Gratian] C. 23 q. 5 c. *De Liguribus* [c. 43], with similar ones); and the same Holy Spirit was in the ecumenical synod with our lord, which brought forth the Union as its admirable fruit. Nevertheless, so that a fully satisfactory reply may be given to their idle chatter, I say that if the Roman pontiff could be judged, this is possible only in a universal council ([Gratian] C. 2 q. 7 c. *Sicut inquit* in the gloss;⁵¹ C. 5 q. 4 c. *Nullus episcopus* [c. 1]).

But there was no universal council at Basel at the time when 22
the Amedeists attempted to depose our most holy lord, because it was translated to Ferrara in accordance with the ordinance of the council, as is evident from the summary of events. Therefore, the deposition which followed the translation is void. The Amedeists cannot deny the facts, which they affirmed in that part of the memorandum of agreement,⁵² and which were confirmed by the failure of the men of Avignon to satisfy its conditions within the time limit, when, in the year of the Lord 1437, on the fourth day before Pentecost, they sent Master Thomas de Courcelles to

pes nostros dominos electores miserunt ad impetrandum assistenciam pro Auinione; cum quo pro parte presidencium concurrebat dominus Iohannes senior abbas de Mulbrunno.

23   Sed soliti sunt dicere numerum ‹maiorem›[1] eorum quo ad Auinionem debuisse prevalere. Dicitur eis, quod, si post illam concilii ordinacionem, per quam Auinionensis civitatis eleccio in eventum non-solucionis cassabatur, et ante eleccionem presidencium et eis adherencium per novam ordinacionem prima immutata fuisset, hoc forte possent allegare. Sed ut casus habet, nulla mutacione conciliari facta de prima ordinacione ad eleccionem deventum est. Si igitur ipsi ad eleccionem per concilii presidentes vocati et moniti in deputacionibus existentes non voluerunt eligere quando potuerunt, hoc eligentibus non obest — De eleccione, Quia propter, ibi: Qui volunt et possunt, ubi glo. concorditer allegat. Ipsi non negant se eligere noluisse; sed quod potuerunt, concilium dicit in cedula concordata, quomodo Auinionensibus deficientibus concilium ‘potest et tenetur’. Potuerunt igitur cum aliis eligere alium locum; et quia non fecerunt, sibi imputent! Et per hoc omnia sophismata eorum sunt soluta.

24   Unde, cum dicunt concilium potuisse immutasse ordinacionem suam — et in hoc est resolucio omnium suorum argumentorum —, dicitur: Eciamsi maior pars concilii hoc potuisset, conciliariter tamen hoc ante eleccionem actum non est; ymmo tres presidentes trium deputacionum pro eleccione concluserunt, ut casus habet. Si habent immutacionem ante factam conciliariter, illam in medium ducant! Sed quia non habent, ‘fumus est caligine plenus obtenebrans oculos stolidorum sermo eorum’.

our prince electors at Reuss[53] to seek assistance for Avignon, with which lord Johann, senior abbot of Maulbronn,[54] concurred for the party of the presidents.

But they are accustomed to say that the majority ought to 23 have prevailed with respect to [the choice of] Avignon [as a site for the council].[55] It may be said to them that, if after that ordinance of the council through which the choice of the city of Avignon was cancelled because of non-payment of the subsidy, and before the choice of the site by the presidents and by those adhering to them, the first choice had been changed by a new ordinance, they might perhaps have alleged this. But it is in fact the case that they arrived at the choice of site from the first ordinance without the council making any change. If therefore those persons [i.e., the Amedeists] who were called and summoned by the presidents of the council from among the deputations did not wish to choose when they could have chosen, this did not form an impediment to those who did choose ([see the *Decretals* of Gregory IX], *De electionibus*, c. *Quia propter*, at *Qui volunt et possunt*, where the gloss[56] argues to the same end). They do not deny that they did not wish to choose; but the council said in the concordat that they could, as the council "was able and was bound to" [make a choice] once the men of Avignon had failed to make their payment. [The Amedeists] could therefore have chosen another site along with the others, and they claim credit for themselves for not having done so! This argument breaks down all their sophisms.

Hence when they say the council might have changed its ordi- 24 nance, we say this as the answer to all their arguments: Even if the majority of the council could have done this, what was done before the selection of the site was not done in a conciliar fashion, and in fact the presidents of three deputations[57] came to this conclusion before the new selection. If they made the previous change in a conciliar manner, let them publish it! But since they cannot, "their speech is a cloud full of smoke, blinding the eyes of fools."[58]

25   Sed advertendum, quod eciam illud verum non est ipsos contradicentibus presidentibus et eis adherentibus potuisse illam
concordem ordinacionem inmutasse. Primo, cum vigor conciliaris
dependeat a 'consenssu' omnium — xv d. *Canones* ❧ *Synodus* et c. *Si-*
cud sancti in fine cum similibus —, non potuisset fuisse tanta potestas ad tollendum ordinacionem contradicentibus primis et eis adherentibus, sicud fuit in ordinacione unanimi. 2° quia expressus
consenssus domini nostri pape debebat intervenire, ut habet casus
et ponitur in decreto convencionali 19ᵉ sessionis. Sed quia constat
ex omnibus bullis d‹omini› n‹ostri›, quod solum id promittit 'ratum et gratum se habiturum, quod per presidentes cum consilio
aut consensu concilii ordinatur aut concluditur', igitur in hoc casu
numerus maior contradicentibus presidentibus et parti eorum adherentibus locum non habuisset. Unde quia ad primum et supremum privilegium apostolice sedis spectare dinoscitur concilia indi-
cere — xvii d. *Regula* cum capitulis sequenti‹bus›, iii q. vi *Dudum,*
De eleccione, Significasti cum similibus — et hoc erat in pactum de-
ductum, quod erat iuris quo ad constitucionem novi ycumenici
concilii, hinc nequaquam maior numerus concilii, papa non
consenciente, hoc casu prevaluisset. Ubi enim concilium eligere
debuit et papa expresse consentire, minor pars cum papa necessario prevaluisset, ut quisque palpabiliter conspicit. Sed quia papa
consensit et approbavit eleccionem dominorum presidencium et
eis adherencium, qui hoc casu totum concilium fecerunt in execu-
cione ordinatorum per concilium aliis nolentibus, hinc patet concilium ycumenicum secundum ordinacionem consilii Basiliensis rite
fundatum; et cum duo universalia concilia universalem ecclesiam

But it must be noted that even this cannot be true, that [a majority] could have changed an ordinance requiring concord with the presidents and their adherents in opposition. First, since the effectiveness of a council depends on the consent of all ([Gratian] D. 15 c. *Canones* ❡ *Synodus* [c. 1 ❡. 7] and c. *Sicut sancti* [c. 2] at the end with similar texts), there cannot be a power great enough [in a majority] to undo an ordinance when the leaders and those agreeing with them oppose this, as the council was unanimous in making the ordinance. Second, this is true because the express consent of our lord the pope ought to have been brought into play, as the case required and as was laid down in the conventional decree issued in the nineteenth session.[59] But since it is apparent from all of the bulls of our lord that he promised "to regard as ratified and acceptable only what was ordained and concluded by the presidents with the counsel or with the consent of the council,"[60] therefore, in this case, the majority has no standing in opposition to the presidents and the party adhering to them. Hence, because convocation of councils is recognized as pertaining to the first and supreme privilege of the Apostolic See ([Gratian] D. 17 c. *Regula,* with the following chapters [cc. 5–7]; [ibid.] C. 3 q. 6 c. *Dudum* [c. 9]; [*Decretals* of Gregory IX] *De electionibus, c. Significasti* [X 1.6.4] with similar ones), and this privilege was taken into the pact as part of the law covering establishment of a new ecumenical council, the majority of a council could not have prevailed in this case without the consent of the pope. Where, therefore, the council should choose and the pope expressly consents, the minority together with the pope must necessarily prevail, as anyone can see with their own eyes. But because the pope consented to and approved the choice of the lord presidents and of those adhering to them, who made up the entire council in this case in that they carried out the council's ordinances when the others refused to do so, it is thus obvious that the ecumenical council was acting in an authorized fashion according to the ordinance of the Council of

25

representancia esse non possint simul et semel, ut est clarum et adversarii fatentur, hinc inchoato concilio ycumenico Ferrarie Basilee concilium defecisse est manifestum.

26   Adhuc[2] adicio, quod si fortassis nulla loci eleccio per concilium valida fuisset, nichilominus ycumenici concilii constitucio per papam tantum facta, ordinacione concilii facta fuisset; nam ut ex casu patet et in bulla d‹omini› n‹ostri›, ubi eleccio loci confirmatur, illud ipsum continetur, dominus noster ordinaverat reduccionem in Constantinopoli fieri debere. Sed concilium Basiliense, cui ipse acquievit, voluit, quod in hiis occidentalibus partibus fieret in uno ex nominatis locis; et quamvis ipsum concilium in xi[a] sessione exhortaretur omnes incorporatos, ne ante reformacionem in concilii translacionem consentirent, iudicabat nichilominus in 19[a] sessione causam reduccionis Grecorum esse talem, quod eciam ob ipsam concilium transferri deberet. Si igitur hoc ita est, quomodo poterit negari papam in uno ex locis, concilio in eleccione deficiente, constituere potuisse synodum, cum sit 'caput concilii' et 'ecclesie', ut ipsum concilium fatetur in responsione que incipit *Cogitanti* et in xiiii sessione? Nam dicere eum non posse uti omni potestate constituendi ad edificacionem ecclesie, hereticum est, ut notant doctores — xix d. *Nulli fas, De eleccione, Generali* li. VI, xxv q. ii *Si quis dogmata*. Pascenciam enim in fide illimitate a deo habet, ita quod nulla conciliari potestate in hoc impediri potest. Si igitur secundum ordinacionem concilii necessarium erat concilium in uno ex locis congregari propter hanc laudatissimam causam et approbatam in 19[a] et 24[a] sessionibus, nemo sane mentis dicere potest papam id, quod per concilium in edificacionem ec-

Basel; and, since there cannot be two universal councils representing the universal Church at one and the same time, as is clear and as our adversaries admit, it is therefore obvious that the council at Basel ceased when the ecumenical council at Ferrara began.

Besides, I add that if [you think] perhaps no choice of site   26
made by the council would have been valid, nonetheless, the establishing of the ecumenical council [at Ferrara] by the pope alone was done by ordinance of the council; for, as is obvious from the summary and from what is contained in the bull of our lord, where the choice of site was confirmed,[61] our lord had ordained that it should be held in Constantinople. The Council of Basel, however, to which he acquiesced, wished that it should be held at a Western site in one of the places named. Although that council, in the eleventh session,[62] exhorted all its incorporated members not to consent to the translation of the council before reform, nonetheless, in the nineteenth session,[63] it judged the affair of the Greeks to be of such consequence that the council should be translated for that reason. If therefore this is so, how can it be denied that the pope, since the council failed in the choice of a site, could convoke a synod in one of those places, since he is "head of the council" and "of the Church," as that very council admitted in its response which begins *Cogitanti*[64] and in the fourteenth session?[65] For it is heretical to say he cannot use all his power of convocation to build up the Church, as the doctors say ([Gratian] D. 19 c. *Nulli fas* [c. 5]; *De electione*, c. *Generali* in the *Liber sextus* [VI. 1.6.13]; [idem] C. 25 q. 2 c. *Si quis dogmata* [c. 18]). His pastoral power in the faith is so unlimited by God that he cannot be impeded in this by any conciliar power. If, therefore, according to the ordinance of the council, approved in the nineteenth and twenty-fourth sessions,[66] it was necessary to gather a council in one of those places for this laudable cause, no one of sound mind can say that the pope could not do what the council judged ought

clesie iudicatum est omnino fieri debere, facere non potuisse in defectum eciam concilii.

27   Adhuc dico, si hec differencia, que erat ob locum inter patres concilii, discuti debuit, ad capud concilii, scilicet Romanum pontificem, appellacione remota recurrendum erat — xvii d. *Multis,* vi q. iiii *Si inter.* Si enim disenssiones episcoporum in provinciali concilio ad capud provincie mandantur referri, tunc et dissenssiones episcoporum in universali concilio ad caput eius, scilicet Romanum pontificem. Hoc enim argumentum facit synodus xcvi d. *Bene quidem* et glo. in allegato c. *Multis,* scilicet quod ea habitudine se habet metropolitanus ad provincialem synodum, qua papa ad universalem; et pro hoc est textus optimus xxiii q. v *De Liguribus.* Et in hoc casu, quando de constitucione ycumenici concilii agebatur, hoc est indubitatum penitus, cum sit de maximis illi sedi propriis 'privilegiis' — ii q. vi *Ideo,* ubi de hoc, et in allegato c. *Multis* xvii d. Quare eius 'consultum' intervenire debuit, ut ibidem et c. *Huic sedi* et c. *Concilia* eadem d.

28   Deinde si nec concilium Basiliense nec Romanus pontifex locum Grecis deputassent, quomodo potest negari concilium ycumenicum fuisse, quando 'persone necessarie' secundum determinacionem xix sessionis animo concilium celebrandi concurrerunt? Si enim papa et patriarche ac alii episcopi per se aut representative animo celebrandi concilium ycumenicum Ferrarie conveniebant, nonne omnia necessaria ad concilii illius celebracionem concurrebant secundum determinata in illa sessione? Hinc impungnacio est frivola. Non est enim de essencia concilii, quod sit in tali vel

in every way to be done for the building up of the Church, once the council had failed to do so.

Besides, I say, if the difference which arose among the fathers   27 about the site required discussion, it should have been referred to the head of the Church, the Roman pontiff, setting aside the appeal process ([Gratian] D. 17 c. *Multis* [c. 5]; C. 6 q. 4 c. *Si inter* [c. 3]). If the dissensions of the bishops in a provincial council have to be referred to the head of the province, then the dissensions of the bishops in a universal council have to be referred to its head, the Roman pontiff. The synod makes this argument in [Gratian] D. 96, c. *Bene quidem* [c. 1] and in the gloss on the aforesaid c. *Multis*,[67] namely that the metropolitan has the same relationship to the provincial synod as the pope has to a universal one; and the best text about this is [Gratian] C. 23 q. 5 c. *De Liguribus* [c. 43]. And in this case, in discussing the establishment of a ecumenical council, there is simply no doubt at all, since this pertains to the most important and peculiar "privileges" of his see (compare [Gratian] C. 2 q. 6 c. *Ideo* [c. 17] concerning this and the aforesaid c. *Multis* in D. 17 [c. 5]). Therefore, his "decision" is necessary, as is stated in the same distinction [17] c. *Huic sedi* and c. *Concilia* [cc. 3 and 6].

Then again, if neither the Council of Basel nor the Roman   28 pontiff had assigned a site to the Greeks, how can it be denied that the council [of Ferrara] was ecumenical, when "the necessary persons," according to the determination of the nineteenth session,[68] assembled with the intention of celebrating a council? If the pope, patriarchs and other bishops gathered, in person or through representatives, with the intention of celebrating an ecumenical council at Ferrara, were not all the conditions necessary for the celebration of that council brought together, according to what was determined in that session? Hence to impugn its authenticity is frivolous. It is not of the essence of a council that it should be at such or such a site; but it is necessary that there be present certain per-

tali loco, sed quod sint tales persone animo concilium celebrandi et conciliariter procedant, sicuti Ferrarie actum est.

29 Preterea si Basiliense concilium millesies ordinasset quod dissolvi non deberet, nonne si de facto illi necessarii ad concilii celebracionem recessissent, concilium de facto fuisset dissolutum? Hoc enim dicitur in concilio Toletano hera v^clxxxi celebrato, quod nemo concilium solvat ante expedicionem agendorum, hoc est, recedat; recedere enim est dissolvere concilia. Si igitur presidentes apostolici, cardinales et alii maximi et primi et necessarii ad concilii celebracionem, et qui concilium fundarunt et rexerunt, recesserunt de Basilea, concurrentes pro celebrando ycumenico concilio Grecis in ultimo portu existentibus, quomodo dici potest concilium Basiliense tunc non fuisse dissolutum, quamvis civitas Basiliensis remanserit et aliqui prelati in ea? Absque enim illo loco Basiliensi et sine omnibus illis personis, que ibi remanserant, potuit esse concilium. Nichil enim remansit, quod de essencia esset concilii. Nam aliquando fuit Basilee concilium sine omnibus illis prelatis, qui remanserant, sed non sine illis presidentibus, qui recesserant. Ubi enim papa non est presens 'nec' eius 'legacio', non est regulare 'concilium' — 17. d. *Regula* et c. *Concilia*, ubi de hoc — ; sed pocius est 'acephalum' — xxi d. *Submittitur*, 93. d. *Nulla* —, maxime in hoc casu, ubi legittima causa, scilicet reduccionis Grecorum, et concilii Basiliensis ordinacio in convencionali decreto legatos abire compulit. Deficit igitur conciliaris auctoritas Basilee necessariis personis abeuntibus.

30 Postremo dico, quod Grecis reductis qualitercumque non potuit Basilee concilium esse universalem militantem ecclesiam representans. Solum enim 'plenarium' tocius 'orbis concilium' tale

sons who have the intention of celebrating a council and who proceed in a conciliar manner, as was done at Ferrara.

Moreover, even if the Council of Basel had ordained a thou-   29
sand times that it could not be dissolved, if *de facto* those necessary
for the celebration of a council had left, would not the council *de
facto* be dissolved? This was said in the Council of Toledo, celebrated in 581 of the era,[69] that no one may dissolve a council (that
is, depart) before the completion of its business; to depart is to
dissolve the council. If, therefore, the apostolic presidents, the cardinals and others of the most important and leading persons necessary for the celebration of the council, who established and directed the council, departed from Basel, agreeing to celebrate an
ecumenical council with the Greeks, who then were at their port
of destination,[70] how can it be said that the Council of Basel was
not dissolved, although the city of Basel had remained behind
with some prelates in it? There can be a council away from that
site in Basel and without all those persons who remained there.
Nothing essential for a council remains there. After all, at one
time there was a council at Basel without all those prelates who remained but not without its presidents, who have departed. Where
the pope is not present, "nor his legation," there is no regular
"council" (see [Gratian] D. 17 c. *Regula* and c. *Concilia* [cc. 2 and 6]
where this is discussed); but rather it is acephalous or headless
([Gratian] D. 21 c. *Submittuntur* [c. 8]; [ibid.] D. 93 c. *Nulla* [c. 8]),
especially in this case where there is a legitimate cause, that is,
bringing the Greeks back to unity, and an ordinance of the Council of Basel, in a decree of a general congregation, compelled the
legates to leave. The conciliar authority of Basel, therefore, becomes defective with the departure of the necessary persons.

Finally, I say that, once the Greeks had been reunited, the as-   30
sembly at Basel could in no way whatever be a council representing the universal Church Militant. The only plenary council of the
entire world is that which is gathered from all Christendom, as

est, quod ex tota cristianitate colligitur, ut ait sanctus Augustinus *De unico baptismo*. Greci autem non recognoverunt Basiliense concilium nisi pro Romano et patriarchali, ut in bulla patriarche habetur, que inseritur 19ᵉ sessioni. Quapropter si nos Grecos pro catholicis habuissemus, ab inicio eis non concurrentibus incongrue dixissemus Basiliense concilium universam ecclesiam representare, cum solum occidentalem representasset. Ita et post Grecorum reduccionem non potuit universam ecclesiam representare, eciamsi concilium fuisset. Sed cum solum 'concilium' universam 'militantem ecclesiam representans' sit illud plenarium, de quo loquitur concilium Constanciense, 'cui' omnis, 'eciamsi papalis dignitatis' fuerit, 'obedire tenetur', ut eciam Basilienses semper confessi sunt, hinc patet ipsos post Grecorum unionem eciam secundum sua principia in d‹ominum› n‹ostrum› papam nichil potuisse.

31   Scientes hoc se evadere aliter non posse, non verentur spiritum sanctum, sanctam Romanam ecclesiam et sacram ycumenicam synodum de mendacio arguere, dicentes hoc non esse verum, quod Greci sint reducti. Sed bulla aurea imperatoris Grecorum cum subscripcione apocrisariorum et xxviii archiepiscoporum Grecorum et bulla sanctissimi d‹omini› nostri pape atque diffinicio synodica ycumenici concilii, quam principes nostri ab apostolica sede receperunt, contrarium ostendunt. Quibus pocius credendum est quam illis talibus viris, qui eciam fingunt d‹ominum› n‹ostrum› omnia simulate cum Grecis egisse propter destruere auctoritatem conciliorum, cum constet, ut eciam casus habet, preter intencionem d‹omini› n‹ostri› concilium in occidente habitum, quoniam ordinaverat in Constantinopoli reduccionem fieri, si concilium Basiliense acquievisset.

32   Solent obicere d‹ominum› n‹ostrum› 'ante Grecorum adventum concilium transtulisse Ferrariam'. Sed casus tollit argumentum.

Saint Augustine says in *On the Only Baptism*.[71] The Greeks, however, did not recognize the Council of Basel either as Roman or patriarchal, as is found in the patriarch's bull, which was inserted into the records of the nineteenth session.[72] For which reason, if we should regard the Greeks as Catholics, it would be unfitting to start out by disagreeing with them and saying that the Council of Basel represented the universal Church, when it only represented the Western church. Likewise, once the Greeks were reunited, Basel could not represent the universal Church, even if it were a council. But since the only "council representing" the universal "Church Militant" is that plenary council of which the Council of Constance spoke, "which" everyone, "even if he were of the papal dignity, is bound to obey,"[73] as even those at Basel always claimed, it is therefore obvious that, after the union with the Greeks, even according to its own principles, it could do nothing against our lord the pope.

Knowing that they cannot evade this otherwise, they are not 31 afraid of accusing the Holy Spirit, the Holy Roman Church and the holy ecumenical synod of lying, saying that it not true that the Greeks have been reunited. But the golden bull of the emperor of the Greeks, with the subscriptions of his deputies and of twenty-eight Greek archbishops, the bull of our most holy lord the pope and the synodal definition of the ecumenical council,[74] which our princes have received from the Apostolic See, demonstrate the opposite. These are more worthy of credit than the men who even fabricated their claim that our lord faked everything with the Greeks to destroy the authority of the council [of Basel], when it is evident, as the outcome showed, that the council [of Ferrara] was held in the West against our lord's intention, since he had ordained that the reunion occur in Constantinople, if the Council of Basel had acquiesced.

The Amedeists are accustomed to object against our lord that 32 "he translated the council to Ferrara before the arrival of the

Nemo sane mentis negare potest summo pontifici in tali casu pro conservacione unitatis et ne Grecorum reduccio inpediretur hoc potuisse, maxime qui ad casum et ad translacionis bullam advertit. Quando enim ecclesia per orbem diffusa et principes contradixerunt, ne hoc fieret, et illi pauci emuli passionatissimi propter confirmacionem eleccionis partis presidencium in suum capud ita sevire sub nomine concilii attemptarunt et se scismaticos in illa particularitate constituerunt, in summum pontificem iudicis et actoris partes sua sponte sibi vendicando, se ipsos ad concilii celebracionem inabilitando, universalis ecclesie consenssu eis deficiente, dominus noster pocius ostendit eos non facere concilium, qui ad scisma properarunt, quam ab eis conciliarem auctoritatem auferret, qua se indignos effecerunt. Et ut ecclesia sciret pontificem iniuste diffamari, adiecit papa se velle ostendere 'innocenciam' in concilio, ad quod eos, qui ipsum diffamaverunt, cum salvo conductu advocavit. Non igitur facta est translacio illa sine causa, sed ob urgentissimas necessarias et laudatissimas vitandi scismatis causas per omnes orbis christiani naciones, reges et principes acceptas. Nec fugere voluit, qui se obtulit id acturum, per quod de sua innocencia constaret, et in eo loco, ubi hoc potuit. Nam non tenetur accusatus accusatores sequi, sed e converso, dicit textus iii q. vi *Neminem* cum sequentibus, ubi de hoc. Ita egit Gregorius papa sanctus — ii q. vii *Si quis*. Unde postquam hoc solum viderant illi viri presumptuosissimi, gaudere debuerant de principis ecclesie piissima mansuetudine, et dum nullam notorietatem incorrigibili-

Greeks." But the facts take away that argument. No one of sound mind can deny that the supreme pontiff could have done what he did in this case for the conservation of unity and so that the re-union of the Greeks should not be blocked, especially if anyone consults the summary of the case and the bull of translation. When the Church spread throughout the world and the princes opposed their doing this, and those few envious and highly pas-sionate men attempted to rage against their own head in the name of the council because he had confirmed the choice made by the party of the presidents, they established themselves as schismatics by usurping to themselves, of their own free will, the role of prose-cuting and judging the supreme pontiff. By so doing they disquali-fied themselves from conciliar celebrations, lacking as they do the consent of the universal Church. Hence our lord [merely] pointed out that those who rush into schism do not constitute a council, rather than depriving them of conciliar authority on the grounds of unworthiness. And so that the Church would know that the pontiff was defamed unjustly, the pope added that he wished to demonstrate his innocence before a council, and he summoned to it those who had defamed him, offering them a safe conduct.[75] The translation, therefore, was not made without cause, but owing to the most urgent necessities and the most praiseworthy of rea-sons, that of uprooting schism from all the nations of the Chris-tian world, reasons to which kings and princes are sympathetic. Nor [is their charge just, that] he wished to flee, as he [in fact] offered himself up for trial to prove his innocence; nor [is it rele-vant that] he was in a place where he could take refuge. For the ac-cused is not obliged to follow his accuser but vice versa, as the text at [Gratian] C. 3 q. 6 c. *Neminem* [c. 16], with the following ones, states. Pope Saint Gregory says the same in [Gratian] C. 2 q. 7 c. *Si quis* [c. 42]. Hence, once those highly presumptuous men had seen this, they should have rejoiced in the holy gentleness of the prince of the Church; and, when they found in him no notorious

tatis in eo invenirent, deum laudare debuerant et amplius a processu abstinere, eciamsi crimina ficta non fuissent. Omnium enim doctorum una est sentencia concilium nichil posse in pontificem corrigibilem, ut notat glo. xl d. *Si papa*, ubi de hoc. Sed ipsi ostenderunt se nec salutem ecclesie nec capitis eius querere, sed facciones dyabolicas scismaticas. Hinc nulla racione aut prece principum furor eorum sedari potuit.

33   Obiciunt xi^{am} sessionem, que susspendit transferentem, quam dicunt d‹ominum› n‹ostrum› per bullam approbasse. Dico sessionem illam non loqui in casu 'nostro', sed de 'futuris' conciliis iuxta disposicionem c. *Frequens*, ut patet in textu, nec ligasse pontificis manus ad conservacionem unitatis ecclesie. Intelligi enim debuit, si absque causa racionabili hoc ageret. Nec fuit illa sessio accepta aut approbata per d‹ominum› n‹ostrum›; nam forma data s‹anctititi› sue in xiiii sessione habet, quomodo s‹anctitas› sua declaret concilium prosecucionem habuisse in illis tribus, scilicet fide, scismate et reformacione, non approbando sessiones. Fuit eciam approbacio illa per d‹ominum› n‹ostrum› facta concilio se offerente in illa xiiii sessione, quod eum pro 'capite' haberet et 'eius pedes ut Petri oscularetur'. Sed postquam illi pauci se erexerunt contra capud, immemores eorum que concilium unanimiter tunc promisit, eciamsi d‹ominus› n‹oster› approbasset illam sessionem, eam tamen servare fidei fractoribus non tenebatur nec quovis modo debebat, nisi et ipsi ab istis scandalis cessassent. Videbitur eciam statim infra, quam iniquus atque nullus ille citacionis seu monicionis actus fuerit, ut luce clarius constet obieccionem illam non esse nisi 'fumum caligine plenum, oculos stolidorum obtenebrantem'. Et hoc de primo.

crime of incorrigibility, they ought to have praised God and abstained from any further trial, even if the crimes alleged had not been fictitious. The opinion of the doctors is unanimous that a council can do nothing against a pope who will accept correction, as the gloss on [Gratian] D. 40 c. *Si papa,* says of this.[76] But they show themselves to be seeking neither the welfare of the Church nor of its head but the creation of diabolical and schismatic factions. Hence their fury cannot be abated by any argument or plea of the princes.

They throw up to us the eleventh session, which suspends 33 someone who translates a council, which they say our lord approved by means of a bull.[77] I say that this session did not address our case but that of future councils, according to the decree *Frequens,*[78] as is obvious from the text; nor did it bind the hands of the pontiff when acting to preserve the Church's unity. This should be understood whether or not it did this without rational cause. Nor was that session accepted or approved by our lord; for the form given His Holiness in the fourteenth session says that he should declare that the council can conduct prosecutions in these three areas, that is faith, schism and reform, not in the area of approving sessions. There was also the approval given by our lord, which the council itself offered in that fourteenth session, that the council should regard him as "head" and that "it should kiss his feet like those of Peter."[79] But after those few set themselves up against the head, unmindful of those things which the council at that time had promised unanimously, even if our lord had approved that session, he was not obliged to observe a promise made to oath breakers; nor should he have done so in any way, unless they too had abstained from creating scandal. And it will be seen immediately below how unjust and null that act of citation or monition was, so that it will become clearer than light that this objection is "nothing but a cloud full of smoke, blinding the eyes of fools."[80] So much for the first point in this memorandum.

‹IIa›

34 Circa 2ᵐ est primo considerandum, si in summum pontificem unicum et indubitatum, qui se non submisit, sentencia per sinodum
ferri potest, extra casum ubi in dampnatam heresim incidit. Hoc
oportet absque hesitacione certum esse; in dubio enim hoc non licere manifestum est. Oportet enim iudicis cuiuscumque fundatam
esse iudicandi potestatem. Sed quia Basilienses dicunt universali
concilio hanc esse indultam potestatem, ipsi habent hoc probare,
cum hoc nondum sit notorium nec per universam ecclesiam sit receptum nec sit in practica, de qua constet, hoc visum, quod scilicet
unquam synodus unicum indubitatum pontificem synodica auctoritate iudicaverit, nisi se sponte submitteret. Adducunt eciam illi
huius sentencie pro se ritum patrum atque synodicas diffiniciones
simul et raciones. Nam papam 'ad' ius 'vocari posse' per synodum
'non' legitur in 'canonibus'; sed ipsi sunt 'canones', qui dicunt Romanum pontificem 'ad nullius commeare iudicium'—ix q. iii *Ipsi
sunt* et xxii d. *Qua tradicione*—, et sanctus Iulius papa in epistola ad
orientales, que incipit *Decuerat,* hoc ostendit. Non enim potest iudicari princeps et capud ecclesie et concilii a concilio; tale enim
'acephalum concilium' foret—21. d. *Submittitur.* 'Totum' enim 'corpus ecclesie habet auctoritatem' ab illo 'principatu', quem deus 'posuit' in pontifice Romano—xi d. *Nolite errare, De consecracione*
d. i *Basilicas*—, et nichil est in ecclesia, quod non sit prioriter 'in
Petro' et eius successore et per eius medium in aliis—xix d. *Ita dominus.* Fluit igitur a capite ecclesie, ubi est 'plenitudo potestatis'—
De usu pallii Ad honorem, ii q. vi *Decreto* et c. *Qui se scit*—, omnis

[IIa]

Regarding the second point, we must first consider whether a sen-   34
tence can be imposed by a synod on a supreme pontiff when he
alone is indubitably the pope and has not submitted himself for
judgment, apart from cases where he has fallen into a damnable
heresy. The latter must unhesitatingly be considered certain, for it
is manifestly illicit to be in doubt about it. Necessarily the power
of judging must be based in some judge or other. But since those
at Basel say a universal council has been conceded this power, the
burden of proof is on them, since this power of judging of theirs
does not yet enjoy notoriety nor has it yet been accepted by the
entire Church nor has ever been seen in practice that a synod has
ever judged with its synodal authority an unchallenged and undoubted Roman pontiff, unless he submitted himself to it of his
own free will.[81] [The Eugenians] adduce also in support of this
the usages of the Fathers and synodal definitions, together with
arguments from reason. There are no canons that say the pope
can be summoned by a synod; but there are canons which say that
the Roman pontiff "can be summoned to judgment by no one"
([Gratian] C. 9 q. 3 c. *Ipsi sunt* [c. 16] and D. 22 c. *Qua traditione* [c.
5]). And Saint Julius the pope demonstrates this in the letter to
the Easterners which begins *Decuerat*.[82] The prince and head of
the Church and of the council cannot be judged by a council, for
such a council [by definition] would be acephalous ([Gratian] D.
21 c. *Submittuntur* [c. 8]). "The entire body of the Church has its
authority" from that "principate," which God "established" in the
Roman pontiff ([Gratian] D. 11 c. *Nolite errare* [c. 3]; *De consecratione* D. 1 c. *Basilicas* [c. 6]. And nothing is in the Church which
was not "in Peter" and his successor first, and in the others by
means of him ([Gratian] D. 19 c. *Ita dominus* [c. 7]). Authority
thus flows from the head of the Church where "plenitude of
power" is located (*De usu palii*, c. *Ad honorem* [X 1.8.4 in the

potestas contractaque est in ecclesia, ut probatur ibidem et optime in c. '*Significasti, De eleccione.* Ipse enim 'imponit prelaturas' aliis atque ipse est 'capud' illius ecclesie prelatorum, qui regimen ecclesie habent, et omnes rectores eius 'membra', ut ibidem.

35   Si in ecclesia est iudicandi potestas, in ipso est ut in principe. Et forte ob hoc Marcellus papa et martir dicit in v c. suorum decretorum ipsum esse iudicem tocius ecclesie. Non est igitur intelligibile, quomodo iudex iudicetur ab hiis, quorum iurisdiccio ab ipso primo derivatur seu medio eius, cuius potestas ligandi et solvendi a deo est inmediate et in aliis nonnisi eo mediante, ut ait sanctus Leo. Ita nemo nisi in 'unitate' cum eo videtur aliquid posse, cum ipse sit in omnibus principatum tenens, que in ecclesia reperiuntur — facit 24. q. i. *Quicumque,* 7. q. i. *Scire debes,* xciii di. *Qui kathedram.* Et ob hoc ait Optatus Mileuitanus *Contra Parmenianum* li. ii, quod 'qui contra Petri kathedram militant', se a potestate ligandi et solvendi subtrahunt, quia inde fluit. Et ob hoc, ut scribit Leo ix^us contra presumpciones Michaelis Constantinopolitani in x c., sacra Nicena synodus statuit Romanum pontificem non posse iudicari a quoquam. Hoc probatur ii q. vii *In sancta Nicena,* ubi racio ponitur illius Nicene constitucionis, cur summus pontifex iudicari non possit. Idem probatur xvii d. ⊄ *Hinc eciam,* 21. d. *Nunc autem,* ubi concilia fatentur papam 'iudicari' non posse et 'in ipsum sentenciam proferre non licere', sed 'causam eius' aut 'deo' aut sibi remittendam. Ita dicit glo. ii q. v *Mandastis,* et legitur in Romano concilio presidente Siluestro, ubi et Constantinus im-

Decretals of Gregory IX]; [Gratian] C. 2 q. 6 c. *Decreto* [c. 11] and
c. *Qui se scit* [c. 12]); all power and contract is in the Church—as is
proved in the same place and, best of all, in *De electionibus* [X 1.6.4
ibid.], c. *Significasti*. The pope "imposed prelacies" on the others;
he is the "head" of that church of prelates who have the rule of the
Church; and all rectors are his "members," as in the same passages.

If the power of judging is in the Church, it is in it as in its   35
prince. Perhaps that is why Marcellus the pope and martyr says in
the fifth chapter of his decrees[83] that his judgment is that of the
whole Church. It is unintelligible, therefore, how a judge may be
judged by those whose jurisdiction derives in the first instance
from him or through the intermediation of the man whose power
of binding and loosing comes immediately from God, and which
is given to others only through him mediately, as Saint Leo says.[84]
Thus no one seems able to do anything unless in unity with him
who holds the principate in all things which are found in the
Church, as [Gratian] C. 24 q. 1 c. *Quicunque* [c. 27], [idem] C. 7 q.
1 c. *Scire debes* [c. 7], [idem] D. 93 c. *Qui cathedram* [c. 3] prove. To
this end, Optatus of Milevis[85] says in Book II of *Against Parmenian*
that "those who fight against Peter's see" separate themselves from
the power of binding and loosing, because it flows from there.
And to this end, as Leo IX[86] wrote against the presumption of
Michael of Constantinople in c. 10, the holy synod of Nicaea decreed that the Roman pontiff cannot be judged by anyone; this
is proved by [Gratian] C. 2 q. 7 c. *In sancta Nicena* [c. 4], where
an explanation of this Nicene constitution is given, saying why
the supreme pontiff cannot be judged. The same is proved by
[Gratian] D. 17 ⁋ *Hinc etiam* [p.c. 6], [idem] D. 21 c. *Nunc autem*
[c. 7], where the councils admit the pope cannot be judged and "it
is not permissible to impose a sentence on him," but "his case"
must be remitted to God or to the pope himself. The gloss[87] says
the same thing at [idem] C. 7 q. 5 c. *Mandastis*; and we read that,
in the Roman council at which Silvester presided, where the Em-

perator interfuit cum CCLXXXIII episcopis, hoc diffinitum per racionem, quia nemo iudicari debet, nisi accusetur, 'accusari' autem
superior ab inferiori non debet, sed a pari, ut est textus ii q. vii
Clericus eiusdem concilii Siluestri et c. *Ipsi apostoli,* quapropter
summus iudicari nequit. Hoc eciam ex 'sentencia' sancti Dionisii
ad Demophilum probatur, qui ait non esse iusticiam in 'perversi-
tate ordinis', scilicet ubi eciam criminosus a minori in gradu iudi-
caretur. Et ob hoc ait textus xcvi d. *Quis dubitet:* 'Nonne miserabilis
insanie esse cognoscitur, si filius patrem, discipulus magistrum sibi
conetur subiugare et iniquis obligacionibus illum sue potestati subicere, a quo credit non solum in terra, sed in celis se ligari posse?'
Hinc 'presumptuositatem Dioscori' in Ephesina 2ª synodo presidentis concessione imperiali et sibi adherencium 'in tantum
da‹m›pnavit sancta Calcedonensis' synodus — xxi d. *In tantum.* Et
Augustinus ait Sardicense concilium pocius hereticorum fuisse
quam catholicorum, quia in sanctum Iulium papam sentenciam
dare presumpsit.

36   Multos doctissimos viros huius sentencie esse constat pro hac
parte scribentes et allegantes, maxime occasionem recipientes ex
scissura, que Basilee concilii nomine facta est, dicentes multo
consulcius esse in unitate ecclesie pati malum prelatum quam au-
daciam auctoritativam prestare cuicumque congregacioni rebellandi et ecclesiam scindendi et se ipsos in regimen intrudendi, ut
nunc factum est. Illi ea, que ab adversa parte obiciuntur, faciliter
solvi posse arbitrantur. Nam ubi alia pars ait omnia illa dicta,
quod nemo iudicare potest primam sedem, intelligi debere distri-

peror Constantine was also present along with 283 bishops,[88] it was argued and defined that, since no one should be judged unless he is accused, and a superior should not be judged by an inferior, but by an equal (as in the text of [Gratian] C. 2 q. 7 c. *Clericis* [c. 10], from the same council of Silvester and c. *Ipsi apostoli* [C. 2 q. 7 c. 38]), for this reason, the highest cannot be judged. The same may be proven from the judgment of Saint Dionysius to Demophilus:[89] he says there is no justice in a perversion of order, that is, in cases where even a criminal prelate is judged by one of a lesser rank. And, about this, the text of [Gratian] D. 96 c. *Quis debuit* [c. 9] says, "Is it not known to be mark of wretched insanity if a son tries to subject a father to himself; or a disciple, a teacher; and likewise if a man who believes himself bound by a person not only on earth but in heaven tries to subject that person to his own power by means of unjust restraints." Hence "the holy synod of Chalcedon condemned" the "presumption of Dioscorus," who presided in the Second Council of Ephesus by imperial grant, and of those who adhered to him, [for unjustly deposing a superior] ([Gratian] D. 21 c. *In tantum* [c. 9]), and Augustine says the Council of Sardica had more heretics than Catholics because it presumed to impose a sentence on Saint Julius, the pope.[90]

That many highly learned men are of this opinion is obvious 36 from their writings and pleas on behalf of the Eugenian party, most of them occasioned by the split which was started in the name of the Council of Basel. They say that it is more advisable to put up with a bad prelate for the sake of Church unity than to authorize any meeting to have the audacity to rebel and divide the Church and intrude themselves into its governance, as has been done now. These learned men think it an easy thing to break down the objections made by the opposing party. For when the other party says that all those statements—the ones about no one being able pass judgment on the first see—ought to be understood of the Church spread throughout the world, not gathered together or in synod,

butive, non collective seu synodice, respondent illam glo. non posse stare; nam diffinitum fuit 'in Nicena' synodo, quomodo 'accusaciones' clericorum in conciliis diffiniri debent—iii q. vi *Neminem*, similiter v q. iiii *Nullus episcopus* cum similibus. Si igitur diffinitum est generaliter nullum episcopum nisi in legittima synodo iudicari posse et dicitur papam a nemine iudicandum, manifestum est hoc necessario eciam de concilio intelligendum, uti concilia intellexerunt—xvii d. ⦅ *Hinc eciam*, ibi: *Cognita*[3] *auctoritate Symachi pape* etc., et xxi d. *Nunc autem*, ubi pro causa concilia illa allegant.

37   Ad id vero, quod alia pars octavam synodum allegat in c. *Diffinimus* in ⦅ *Porro*, ubi dicitur, 'si universalis synodus fuerit congregata et quevis ambiguitas de Romanorum ecclesia' exorta, 'oportet' eam 'cum convenienti reverencia' discutere et in ea 'proficere aut profectum facere', respondent isti id, quod sequitur, solvere argumentum. Nam additur: 'Non tamen audacter sentenciam dicere in Romanorum papam.' Nam discutere et videre possunt patres 'cum convenienti reverencia' ea, que obiciuntur, ut dicitur eciam ii q. v *Mandastis*, sed non sentenciam ferre, quia 'deus' sibi 'reservavit' potestatem sentenciandi, ut dicit textus ix q. iii *Aliorum* et c. *Facta*. Et ob hoc patres in concilio, de quo in § *Hinc eciam*, 'causam deo' remiserunt per viam statuti, ut patet in subscripcione ibidem posita. Probatur illud optime iii q. vi *Quamvis*, ubi concilium discutere potest, sed non sentenciare, quia papa, qui est supra concilium illud, sibi reservavit potestatem sentenciandi et terminandi.

38   Ad hoc autem, quod de Augustino obicitur ad Glorium et Eleusium scribente, quomodo 'restabat plenarium concilium' post

the learned reply that this gloss[91] cannot be interpreted that way. For it was defined in the Nicene synod how accusations against clerics ought to be settled in councils ([Gratian] C. 3 q. 6 c. *Neminem* [c. 16], similarly C. 5 q. 4 c. *Nullus episcopus* [c. 1] with similar texts). If, therefore, it was settled generally that no bishop could be judged except in a legitimate synod, and it is said that the pope can be judged by no one, it is obvious that this must necessarily be understood even of a council, as the councils [themselves] understood ([e.g. Gratian] D. 17 ℭ *Hinc etiam* at *Cognita auctoritate Symachi pape* etc. [p.c. 6 ℭ 1] and [idem] D. 21 c. *Nunc autem* [c. 7], where those councils cite these texts for the same reason).

The other party cites the eighth synod in c. *Diffinimus* ℭ *Porro*   37 [Gratian C. 18 q. 2 c. 21 ℭ 3], where it says, "If the universal synod is assembled and some ambiguity concerning the church of the Romans" has arisen, "it is necessary" that it "should hold discussions with due reverence" and, in that case, "proceed or cause proceedings to happen." But the wise reply that what follows this passage overturns their argument. For it continues, "It should not however audaciously pass sentence on the pope of the Romans." For the [council] fathers can discuss and take cognizance "with due reverence" of matters brought before them, as is said also in [Gratian] C. 2 q. 5 c. *Mandastis* [c. 10], but not pass sentence, because "God has reserved" the power of sentencing to Himself, as is said in the text of [idem] C. 9 q. 3 c. *Aliorum* [c. 14] and c. *Facta* [c. 15]. And for this reason, the council fathers (concerning whom see ℭ *Hinc etiam* [idem, D. 17 p.c. 6]) are to remit "the case to God" by way of a statute, as is obvious in the subscription put in the same place. This is proved best in [Gratian] C. 3 q. 6 c. *Quamvis* [c. 7], where the council can debate but not sentence, because the pope is above that council, and reserves to himself the power of sentencing and deposing.

The Amedeists object, citing Augustine in a work sent to   38 Glorius and Eleusius,[92] that "there remained a plenary council" af-

iudicium Melchiadis pape, in quo de ipso iudice et iudicio eius iudicari potuisset etc., respondent non illam fuisse intencionem Augustini, quasi iudicandi potestas supra summum pontificem sit in plenario concilio; nam ipse fatetur 'post' Christum 'omnes causas magisterii in Petro' principe ecclesie esse, ut in libro *Questionum veteris et novi testamenti* q. lxxix ait. Si igitur in Petro et eius successore eadem est potestas—ut idem videtur affirmare in epistola quam ipse, Alipius et Fortunatus scribunt ad Generosum, et per omnes hoc tenetur 19. d. *Sic omnes*, xxiiii q. 1. *Quoniam vetus* et c. *Hec est fides*, vii q. 1. *Factus est* cum infinitis similibus—, tunc omnis potestas, que est explicata in ecclesia, est in papa ut in principio causali complicatorie, ut ipse possit omnia, que omnes et plures, si essent. Quare non est sentencia Augustini superioritatem esse in concilio super papam; sed pocius videtur voluisse in ea questione allegata omnem concilii potestatem in suo magisterio a causa omnis magisterii Petri fluere, ut dicit c. *Significasti* et veteres doctores theologi pene omnes. Sed de Melchiade hoc dixit, quia datus fuit commissarius a Constantino et post sentenciam heresim obiciebant Melchiadi. Poterant igitur in hoc recursum habuisse ad universalem synodum, cuius hec sunt verba *De unico baptismo* quasi circa finem: 'Huc accedit, quia[4] Melchiade tunc episcopo Romane ecclesie presidente ex precepto Constantini imperatoris, ad quem totam illam causam accusatores episcopi Carthaginensis ecclesie Ceciliani per Anulium[5] proconsulem detulerunt, idem Cecilianus innocens pronunciatus est; de quo iudicio cum maiores istorum importunissima pervicacia memorato imperatori quererentur',

ter the judgment of Pope Melchiades, in which there remained the possibility of judging the judge and his judgment. To this citation the learned reply that it was not the intention of Augustine to suggest that the power of judging the supreme pontiff was in a plenary council; for he himself confesses that "after" Christ "all cases of the magisterium belong to Peter," the prince of the Church, as he says in the book of *Questions on the Old and New Testaments*, q. 79.[93] If, therefore, the same power is in Peter and his successor — as Augustine seems to affirm in the epistle which he, Alipius and Fortunatus wrote to Generosus,[94] and this is held by all these texts — [Gratian] D. 19 c. *Sic omnes* [c. 2], [idem] C. 24 q. 1 c. *Quoniam vetus* [c. 25] and c. *Hec est fides* [c. 13], [idem] C. 7 q. 1 c. *Factus est* [c. 5] with an infinite number of similar ones — then all power which is unfolded in the Church is in the pope in an enfolded manner, as if in a causal principle, so that he can do all things which everyone and a majority can do if they are present. It is not, therefore, the opinion of Augustine that a council is superior to the pope; but rather he seems to have meant, in the question cited, that every power of a council in its teaching authority is derived from Peter as from the cause of all teaching authority, as he says in c. *Significasti* [in the *Decretals* of Gregory IX, X 1.6.4], and as do almost all the old doctors and theologians. But he said this of Melchiades because the latter had been sent by Constantine as his delegated judge; and, after sentencing, they charged Melchiades with heresy. In this matter [of heresy] therefore, they could have had recourse to a universal synod; these are his words on the subject in *On the Only Baptism* near the end:[95] "Moreover, the same Caecilianus was pronounced innocent when Melchiades, then bishop of the Roman Church, was presiding as instructed by the Emperor Constantine, before whom the accusers of Caecilianus, bishop of the church of Carthage, had brought their case through the proconsul Anulius. The majority of these complained about the judgment before the aforesaid emperor with

quomodo 'non plene neque recte fuerat examinatum atque de-
promptum, nichil de Melchiadis tradicione vel thurificacione dixerunt. Ad cuius audienciam nec venire utique debuerunt, hoc pocius ante suggerentes imperatori aut, ut suggereretur instantes,
quod apud traditorem codicum divinorum et ydolorum sacrificiis
coinquinatum causam suam agere non deberent.' Hec ibi. De hoc
idem Augustinus *Contra Parmenianum* et in aliis locis.

39   Ad id autem, quod de Constanciensi concilio obiciunt, quomodo ibi diffinitum sit eum, 'qui papalis dignitatis' est, 'obedire'
debere concilio 'in fide, scismate et reformacione' et, ubi 'contumaciter' resisteret, eum puniri posse 'ad iuris' remedia 'recurrendo',
respondent illud intelligendum esse secundum tunc currentem casum, quia dicit: in 'presenti scismate et de reformacione in capite
et membris' quo ad tempus illud scismatis; nam tunc omnia remedia, ut ad unitatem deveniretur, iuris fuere propter dubium iuris
contendencium. Obediendum enim erat tunc in illo antiquo scismate, quando universa per orbem ecclesia nullum contendencium
unquam pro unico pontifice receperat, ut in eo dubio ad unitatem
devenit. Si igitur illa ordinacio facta fuit, ut 'facilius et securius ad'
unitatem deveniretur, ut dicit sessio quinta eiusdem concilii, ubi
hec acta sunt — quo casu intelligi debet id quod dicitur ibidem de
punicione et remediis iuris —, non 'debet' hoc ibi 'pro remedio' in-
ventum tempore scismatis ad tempus unitatis extendi — i q. vii
Quod pro remedio —, ne pariat contrarium effectum, scilicet ne id,
quod pro unitate adipiscenda ordinatum fuit, scisma faciat, uti
modo vidimus Basilee. Et ita visi sunt patres illud intellexisse.
Eciam Martinus papa propter illam ordinacionem non mutavit
formam celebrandi concilia, quando dedit potestatem presidentibus Senis, ut sua 'auctoritate concilium dissolverent aut transfer-

importunate obstinacy, saying that the case had not been fully nor rightly examined and set forth, [but] they said nothing of the betrayal and sacrifices [to idols] of Melchiades. They should never have come to this audience, but should rather have suggested to the emperor, or insisted on its being suggested, that they ought not to try their case before a traitor to the divine books and one stained with sacrifices to idols." Augustine says the same thing in *Against Parmenian*[96] and in other places.

The Amedeists raise another point about the Council of Constance, namely, how it was defined there that he who has "the papal dignity" ought to "obey" the council "in faith, schism and reform," and where he resists "contumaciously," he can be punished "by resorting" to the remedies "of law." The learned reply to this citation by saying that it must be understood according to the situation then existing, since the Council of Constance says in "the present schism and about reform in head and members," with reference to that time of schism; for then all legal remedies could be employed for the Church to achieve unity because of doubt about the rights of the contenders. The council, then, had to be obeyed in that past schism, when the Church spread throughout the world never accepted any of the contenders as sole pope, in order that the Church might achieve unity in that doubtful affair. If, therefore, that ordinance was made so that the Church might achieve union "more easily and more surely" (as the fifth session of the Council, where these things were enacted, said), in that case, what was said there about punishment and remedies of law, meant as a remedy in time of schism, ought not to be extended to a time of unity ([Gratian] C. 1 q. 7 c. *Quod pro remedio* [c. 7]), lest it yield the contrary effect, that what was ordained for the achievement of unity should cause a schism, as we saw done at Basel. And so the fathers seemed to have understood it. Even Pope Martin did not change the form of celebrating a council because of that ordinance when he gave the presidents at Siena[97] the power, by his "author-

rent', et quando non aliud 'gratum habere' voluit, quam quod sui presidentes de consilio concilii aut consenssu diffinirent. Ex quibus clare conspicitur Martinum papam non intellexisse per illam ordinacionem observanciam antiquam mutatam et se nunc plus concilio subesse, quam ante concilium Constanciense Romani pontifices subfuerunt, quorum vestigiis inherebat; nec tamen ob hoc, quasi male intelligeret Constanciense concilium, reprehensus legitur.

40   Dicunt igitur, si ille ordinaciones tempore unitatis locum habere debent, tunc oportet, ut referantur termini ad papam et alios secundum cuiusque condicionem; nam iuris remedium in papa criminoso non reperitur esse sentencie prolacio, que sepius pareret scisma quam remedium. Si igitur hoc remedium prolacionis sentencie non reperitur in iure aliquo cautum, non possumus hoc ita contra iuris determinacionem interpretari. Unde cum remedium iuris sit non obedire prelato in hiis, que contra deum et universalem statum ecclesie Christi existunt, ut est concors omnium sentencia, tunc prelato ecclesie eciam pessimo per non-obedienciam resistitur, ubi ecclesiam destruere vellet; et hoc est remedium sine scismatis periculo, et est optimum et equissimum. Quare illi conclusioni papam iudicari non posse non propter personam pontificis, sed conservacionem unitatis ecclesie, nichil, ut illi aiunt, videtur obstare posse.

41   Cum autem causam superioritatis concilii super papam vel Basilienses vel alii assignare volunt, dicunt: Christo convenit indeviabilitas ex natura, ecclesie ex gracia, et ita concilio ecclesiam representanti; papa autem hoc privilegium non habet, quia peccare et deviare potest, sicud aliqui deviarunt. Ad hoc respondent, quomodo certum est multa concilia errasse; sed concilia universalem ecclesie consenssum habencia in hiis, que sunt de necessitate salu-

ity, to dissolve or translate the council;" and he wished nothing
else "to be welcome" than what his presidents should decide with
the advice and consent of the council. From this it is evident that
Pope Martin did not understand that ordinance to have changed
ancient observance, nor that he was now more subject to the council than the Roman pontiffs in whose footsteps he followed were
before the Council of Constance. Nor do we read that he was reproved for having misunderstood [the decrees of] the Council of
Constance.

The wise say, therefore, if those ordinances should have a place   40
in a time of unity, then it is necessary that they refer to the pope
and others according to the condition of each; for the remedy of
law against a criminal pope is not found to be the imposition of a
sentence [on him], which more often brings forth schism than it
does a remedy. If therefore this remedy of imposition of sentence
is not found secured in any law, we cannot interpret this against
the fixed limits of the law. Hence, since the remedy of the law is
not to obey a prelate in those things which are against God and
the universal status of the Church of Christ, as is the harmonious
opinion of all, then one resists a prelate of the Church, even the
worst one, by means of non-obedience when he wishes to destroy
the Church. This is a remedy without peril of schism, and it is the
best and most equitable. Hence it seems that nothing, as they
themselves say, stands in the way of the conclusion that it is impossible to pass judgment on a pope, not because of the papal person but to preserve the unity of the Church.

When, however, those at Basel or others wish to assign a rea-   41
son why a council is superior to a pope, they say: The inability to
stray belongs to Christ by nature; to the Church by grace; and
thus to a council representing the Church. The pope, however,
does not have this privilege, because he can sin and stray, as some
have [in fact] strayed. To this the wise reply that it is certain that
many councils have erred, but councils which have the consent of

tis, non errant. Ymmo si errarent, adhuc est ibi salus; non enim potest fidelis ad impossibile obligari. Hinc decipi nequit in eo, quod tota ecclesia recepit, eciamsi alio tempore hoc correccionem receperit. 'Concilia' autem 'posteriora' corrigere 'priora' admittit Augustinus *De unico baptismo.* Sed sicud papa est deviabilis, ita quisque aliorum; ymmo presumi debet papam minus deviabilem. 'Pro' Petro enim 'rogavit' Christus. Que efficax oracio obtinuit doctrinam veritatis in sede Petri numquam 'defecisse' — xxiiii q. 1. *Quodcumque* in glo. et c. *A recta* infra q. 1. quali. Quapropter si papa est deviabilis, qui est capud concilii, omnia alia membra deviare posse non est negandum, ut optime probatur ex dicto Augustini *De nupciis et concupiscencia* dicentis: Id quod dicitur 'ecclesiam non habere maculam' neque 'rugam', de 'futura, non' de 'ista' intelligendum est; 'nam qui modo eam talem esse dicunt, et tamen in illa sunt, quoniam et ipsi fatentur ‹se›[6] habere peccata, si verum dicunt, profecto, quoniam mundi non sunt a peccatis, habet in hiis ecclesia maculam; si autem falsum dicunt, quia corde duplici loquuntur, habet in hiis ecclesia rugam. Si autem se dicunt habere ista, non ipsam; ergo se non esse membra eius, nec se ad corpus eius pertinere fatentur, ut eciam sua confessione dampnentur.' Hec ille. Ecce, quod patres in concilio, qui sunt membra concilii peccabilia, non possunt dicere concilium esse ecclesiam non habentem maculam neque rugam aut indeviabilitatem, cum concilium non sit corpus mathematicum, sed ex membris peccabilibus unitum, ita quod concilium in ipsis habet deviabilitatem. Nec prodest eis allegacio sancti Ieronimi xxiiii q. 1. *Omnibus consideratis,* quoniam si hoc dictum de sacerdocio, quod est in ecclesia, intelligitur, tunc de officio sacerdotali, a quo procedit 'ligandi sol-

the universal Church do not err in those things which are necessary for salvation. Indeed, if they err, there is still salvation there; for the faithful cannot be obliged to the impossible. Hence we cannot be deceived in what the whole Church accepts, even if it shall have received correction at another time. Later "councils," however, "correct earlier ones," as Augustine admits in *On the Only Baptism*.[98] But, just as the pope can waver, so any one of these others; indeed, the pope ought to be presumed less likely to stray; for Christ prayed for Peter.[99] That efficacious prayer maintained the teaching of truth in the see of Peter, which never has failed (see the gloss[100] to [Gratian] C. 24 q. 1 *Quodcunque* [c. 6] and, likewise, in c. *A recta* below in the same question [C. 24 q. 1 c. 9]). For this reason, if the pope, who is the head of the council, can stray, then that the other members can stray cannot be denied, as is best proved from the dictum of Augustine in *On Marriages and Concupiscence*,[101] who says that the statement, "the Church has neither stain nor wrinkle,"[102] must be understood of the future Church, not the Church of this age. "For those who say that she is so now and nonetheless are [themselves] in her, since they too confess themselves to have sin, if they speak the truth, surely, since they are not clean of sin, the Church has a stain in these men; if they speak falsely, because they speak it with a duplicitous heart, the Church has a wrinkle in these men. If, however, they say that they have sins, but the Church does not, they thereby confess that they are not members of her body, so that they are condemned even by their confession." Look: the council fathers, being prone to sin as members of the council, cannot say that the council is the Church having neither stain nor wrinkle, and unable to stray, since the council is not a mathematical body, but is a unity composed of sinful members, so that the council has the ability to stray in these men. Nor does the citation of Saint Jerome (in [Gratian] C. 24 q. 1 c. *Omnibus consideratis* [c. 20]) help them, since if this is understood to mean the priesthood, which is in the Church, it is necessarily under-

vendique potestas', intelligi necesse est, quoniam est 'sine macula et ruga', cum Christus per 'ministros' operetur eciam 'malos', ut optime probatur *De consecracione* d. iiii *Baptismus*, ita scilicet, quod illi in hiis, que sunt de necessitate salutis, non errant, in quibus consensserint. Sed quod quisque tamen eorum atque omnes sint peccabiles et deviabiles, probatur per eundem Ieronimum xi q. 3. *Quando* et xxxii q. 5. *Si Paulus*, ubi ex dictis Ieronimi clare habes iniusticias et impietates in ea, que est domus domini, esse posse.

42   Nonne hec sentencia gravissimorum virorum talis est, quod adhuc non videtur certum sentenciam dari posse in unicum Romanum pontificem? Ymmo aliis[7] videtur papam subesse et iudicari posse, quia canonibus sanctorum tamquam membrum ecclesie subest et penis in eis contentis subicitur, excepto casu epikeie, ubi ut princeps ecclesie disspensatorie agit ob alciorem finem utilitatis vel necessitatis ecclesiam edificando; tamen hoc non potest equum videri, nisi ubi ex hoc iudicio subinferretur maior publica ecclesie utilitas, sicud et primis. Nam quamvis papa prius fuerit 'filius ecclesie' et sit sub legibus matris, antequam in 'principem' erigatur — lxviii d. *Quorum vices* —, et quamvis eciam ipse principatus non eximat eum ab observancia legum matris ecclesie, nisi ubi in casu dato non servit lex fini principatus, qui est edificare, tamen non est 'recedendum' a papa 'ante sentenciam' — ut viii q. iiii *Nonne* et in sepe allegato ℭ *Hinc eciam* xvii d. — excepta heresi notoria, ut infra dicetur. 'Sentencia' autem numquam potest iuste ferri in eum,

stood to mean the priestly office from which proceeds "the power of binding and loosing," since it is "without stain and wrinkle" when Christ works through "ministers," even "bad ones," as is best proved by *De consecratione* [in Gratian, Pars III] D. 4 c. *Baptismus* [c. 26]: so they do not err in matters necessary for salvation, in matters where they shall have achieved consensus. But that each and every one of them may sin and stray is proved by the same Jerome (in [Gratian] C. 11 q. 3 c. *Quando* [c. 23] and [idem] C. 32 q. 5 c. *Si Paulus* [c. 11]), where you can infer clearly from the dicta of Jerome that injustices and impieties can exist in the Lord's house.

Is this opinion of the gravest of men not such that thus far it does not seem certain that a sentence can be imposed on an unchallenged Roman pontiff? Yet, it appears to the others that the pope is under a council and can be judged because he is under the canons of the saints and the penalties contained in them, like a member of the Church—except in a case involving equity, where, as the prince of the Church, he gives dispensations for the higher end of the utility or necessity of building up the Church. Nonetheless, this [dispensatory power] cannot appear equitable, unless where the greater public utility of the Church is served by this judgment, as in the first. For, although the pope was at an earlier point [merely] a "son of the Church" and was under the laws of his Mother before he was raised up as prince ([Gratian] D. 68 c. *Quoniam vices* [c. 6]) and, although even that principate does not exempt him from the observance of the laws of the Church, unless where, in the given case, the law does not serve the end of the principate, which is building up, nevertheless, there is no appeal from the pope "before a sentence" (as in [Gratian] C. 8 q. 4 c. *Nonne* [c. 1] and in the often cited ℭ *Hinc etiam* D. 17 [p.c. 6]), except in a case of notorious heresy, as will be said below. "Sentence," however, never can be imposed on him justly, when "he has the multitude on his side," so that there is fear of "schism"

42

quando 'habet sociam multitudinem', ut 'scisma' timeatur — xxiii q. iiii *Cum quisquis*. Quare ante omnium concordanciam, ita ut scismatis periculum sit sublatum, non potest iuste sentencia ferri. Iniuriaretur enim ecclesie, que ob correccionem cuiuscumque scindi non meretur, maxime attento quod malus prelatus non potest ecclesie tantum obesse quantum scissura. Et quia raro potest hoc accidere, quod pontifex 'non habeat defenssores' adherentes et 'sociam multitudinem', ita ut vix cum pace ecclesie iudicari possit, hinc eciam secundum illorum opinionem rarissime sentencia dari potest in eum. Concluditur igitur: Cum in unum Romanum pontificem propter hoc, aut quia non putabant veteres hoc fieri posse, aut propter evitare periculum, non reperitur efficaciter sentenciam conciliarem datam, sed datam pocius reprehensam, omnino Basilienses hoc tempore exemplis maiorum abstinere debuissent.

⟨IIb⟩

43 Processum illum Amedistarum, si fieri potuisset prefatis non obstantibus, adhuc scismaticum fuisse ex hoc habetur. Nam universalia 'concilia universali tradicione et consenssu fiunt et recipiuntur', ut olim Basiliense concilium diffinitive posuit in ressponssione illa famosa, que incipit *Cogitanti*, allegans ad hoc dictum sancti Gregorii 15. d. *Sicud sancti* in fine, adiciens ibidem, quod 'unitas ecclesie' conciliaris ex eo 'multo maior et perfeccior est quam unitas regis unius aut imperatoris terreni. Hic enim et errat et in varias sepe sentencias scinditur; ecclesia autem nec errat nec sibi ipsi contradicit.' Hoc idem dicit textus *Canones* 15. d. in fine, dicens 'dissencientes non' facere 'concilium'. Ita diffinitum est in octava synodo opor-

([Gratian] C. 23 q. 4 c. *Cum quisquis* [c. 19]), so that schism may be feared. Therefore, so as to avoid the perils of schism, a sentence cannot be imposed justly until universal agreement is reached. It would injure the Church, which does not deserve to be divided in order to correct any individual, especially granted that a bad prelate cannot undermine the Church as badly as schism can. And since it rarely happens that a pontiff will not have his defenders, adherents and the multitude on his side, so that he scarcely can be judged without disturbing the peace of the Church, this too is a reason, according to the opinion of the learned, why sentence very rarely can be imposed on him. We conclude, therefore, since it is unexampled that a conciliar sentence was imposed efficaciously on an unchallenged Roman pontiff, but rather was condemned if attempted, either because of this last consideration [of enforceability] or because the ancient authorities did not think that this could be done, or in order to avoid danger [of schism], the Basel gathering ought to have abstained at this time and followed the examples of our forefathers.

[IIb]

That trial by the Amedeists, if it could be held notwithstanding the aforesaid, is considered schismatic because of the following considerations. Universal "councils are held and accepted by universal tradition and consent," as the former Council of Basel decreed as a definition in that famous response which begins *Cogitanti*.[103] It cites to this end the dictum of Saint Gregory (in [Gratian] D. 15 c. *Sicut sancti* [c. 2], at the end), adding there, on the basis of this dictum, that "the unity of the Church in council is much greater and more perfect than the unity of a single king or terrestrial emperor. For the latter errs and is often of two minds, but the Church neither errs nor contradicts itself."[104] The text of c. *Canones* [in Gratian] D. 15 [c. 1] says the same thing at the end,

43

tere omnia illa, que de ecclesiasticis rebus synodice aguntur, omnium consenssu et unanimitate fieri. Ait enim Basilius imperator ad synodum: 'Dicat nunc sancta et universalis synodus, si omnibus sanctissimis episcopis concordantibus atque consencientibus presens terminus depromptus est; oportet enim divina queque cum universorum conse‹n›ssu et' concordancia 'in ecclesiasticis predicari et confirmari collegiis. Sacra synodus dixit: Omnes ita sapimus, omnes ita predicamus, omnes concinentes et consencientes sponte subscribimus; hoc est veritatis iudicium, hoc est iusticie decretum.' Ad idem legitur in consilio Toletano tempore Sisinandi regis celebrato, ubi post ordinem additur: 'Concilium' autem 'nullus solvere audeat, nisi fuerint cuncta determinata, ita ut quecumque deliberacione communi finiuntur, episcoporum singulorum manibus subscribantur. Tunc enim deus suorum sacerdotum interesse credendus est' conventu‹i›, 'si tumultu omni abiecto solicite atque tranquille ecclesiastica negocia terminentur'. Hec ibi; facit v q. iiii *In loco benediccionis.* Ad idem legitur in concilio sancti Martini pape tempore Constantini tercii celebrato Rome, ubi ita de concilio Calcedonensi ponitur: 'Sancta Calcedonensis synodus diffinivit, hoc est dicere: omnium sanctorum chorus', quoniam, 'quod una sanctorum patrum synodus iudicare videtur, tam omnes synodi quam universi omnino patres confirmare noscuntur, utpote in eodem unoque verbo sibi vicissim per indissolubilem' concordiam 'concordantes'. Hec ibi. Synodus igitur est consonancia— 1. q. vii *Convenientibus* ❡ *Item Terasius* ibi: 'Si vero synodalis consonancia', et c. *Si qui voluerint* ibi: 'Fateantur se communi consenssu catholice ecclesie statuta observaturos', et Augustinus ii q. vii *Puto* ibi: 'Per universe ecclesie statuta firmatum', 79. d. *Si duo contra fas,*

saying, "those in a state of dissension do not" constitute "a council." Thus it was defined in the Eighth Synod that everything done synodally in regard to ecclesiastical affairs must be done with the consent of all and with unanimity. The Emperor Basil said to the synod,[105] "Now let the holy and universal synod declare, with all the most holy bishops agreeing and consenting, whether the present boundary has been set out. All matters divine should be preached and confirmed with the consent and" agreement "of all in ecclesiastical colleges." The holy synod said, "Thus all of us know; thus all of us preach; all, agreeing and consenting of our own will, subscribe. This judgment is true; this decree is just." On the same subject, we read that the Council of Toledo, celebrated in the time of King Sisinance[106] added at the end, "No one, however, should dare to dissolve a council unless all things have been determined, so that whatsoever things have been completed by common deliberation can be subscribed to by the hands of the individual bishops. For then God must be believed to have been present in the gathering of His priests, if ecclesiastical business has been transacted without any tumult and in a careful, tranquil manner." [Gratian] C. 5 q. 4 c. *In loco benedictionis* [c. 3] agrees. On the same subject we read in the council of Pope Saint Martin celebrated in Rome at the time of Constantine III, where it speaks thus of the Council of Chalcedon:[107] "The holy synod of Chalcedon, that is the chorus of all the saints, defined," since "what one synod of the holy fathers appears to judge, all synods as well as all the Fathers are known to confirm in its entirety, inasmuch as in one and the same word they agree with each other in turn by indissoluble" concord. A synod, therefore, is a harmony ([Gratian] C. 1 q. 7 c. *Convenientibus* ❰ *Item Terasius* [c. 4 ❰ 17] at: "But if synodal harmony" and c. *Si qui voluerint* [c. 8] at: "They claim to have observed all the statutes of the Catholic Church with common consent" and Augustine [in Gratian] C. 2 q. 7 c. *Puto* [c. 35] at: "Confirmed by the statutes of the universal Church" and [Gratian]

ubi communis 'consenssus' est idem quod concilium. Idem probatur 24. q. 1. *Maiores* ibi: *Coacta synodus*, et c. *Acacius'* ii et xxv q. 1.
Confidimus, et optime 50. d. *De eo*, 20. d. *De quibus*.

44   Oportet igitur, quod persone, que consenssum cum subscripcione prebent, sint tales, quod ecclesiam ipsam, cuius hoc est
concilium, representent; scilicet si est concilium provinciale, interesse debent persone provinciam representantes. Legitur enim in
c. viii Affricani concilii: 'Placuit propter ecclesiasticas causas, que
ad perniciem plebium sepe veterescunt, concilium' fieri, 'ad quod
omnes provincie, que primas sedes habent, de conciliis suis binos
aut quantos eligerunt episcopos legatos mittant, ut congregato
conventu plena possit esse auctoritas.' Ita diffinitum est in octava
synodo in patriarchalibus synodis metropolitanos per se vel representative esse debere, 'in universalibus autem papam et patriarchas'
cum 'aliis', ut in 19ᵃ sessione olim Basiliensis concilii eciam habetur. Legitur enim in accione nona octavi concilii in adventu vicarii
troni Allexandrini synodum dixisse: 'Glorificamus deum universorum, qui, quod deerat universali synodo, supplevit et nunc fecit
eam perfectissimam.' Representacio autem per legatos fit — xciiii d.
c. 1., ubi Simachus papa ait: 'Ubi nos presentes esse non possumus, nostra per' nostros 'representetur auctoritas.' Facit xciii d. c.
finale. Et ob hoc in Affricano concilio statutum legitur et in omnibus conciliis observatum, quod patres se propriis manibus in sen-
tenciis et statutis cum titulo suo subscripserunt ad ostendendum
consenssum eorum intervenisse, qui ecclesiam representabant,
cuius erat concilium. Legitur enim in fine octavi concilii vicarios
senioris Rome dixisse: 'Quoniam providencia dei in prosperum

D. 79 c. *Si duo contra fas* [c. 8], where common consent is the same
as a council). The same is proved by [Gratian] C. 24 q. 1 c. *Maiores*
[c. 2] at: *Coacta synodus* and the second c. *Acacius* [c. 3], and [idem]
C. 25 q. 1 c. *Confidimus* [c. 1], and, best of all, [idem] D. 50 c. *De eo*
[c. 35], D. 20 c. *De quibus* [c. 3].

It is necessary, therefore, that the persons who give their con-   44
sent with their subscription are such who may represent the
Church itself of which they are the council; that is, if it is a provincial council, persons representing the provincial church ought
to be present. We read in c. 8 of the African council,[108] "Because
of the ecclesiastical cases which are often put off to the harm of
the people, it has been decided" to hold "a council to which all
provinces which have primatial sees may send as representatives
from its councils two bishops, or as many as they may elect, so
that full authority can be present at the gathered assembly." Thus
it was defined at the Eighth Synod[109] that in patriarchal synods
the metropolitans ought to be present in person or through representatives; "in universal councils, however, the pope and the patriarchs," with "others," as is found in the nineteenth session of the
former Council of Basel.[110] We read in the ninth action of the
Eighth Council, upon the arrival of the vicar of the see of Alexandria, that the synod said,[111] "Let us glorify the God of all, who has
provided what was lacking for a universal synod and now has
made it most perfect." The representation, however, was provided
by legates; see [Gratian] D. 94 c. 1, where Pope Symmachus said,
"Where we cannot be present, our authority is represented by"
our legates. The last chapter of [idem] D. 93 [c. 26] makes the
same point. And we read that on this account it was established in
the African council[112] and observed in all councils, that the fathers
subscribed themselves with their own hands under their own titles
to the sentences and decrees in order to show that they who represented the church, whose council it was, had given their consent.
We read at the end of the Eighth Council that the vicars of the el-

finem omnia devenerunt negocia, oportet nos in scriptis manu propria hec roborare secundum synodicam consequenciam.' Hec ibi. Ecce, quomodo subscripcio quasi de essencia videtur esse synodi propter ostenssionem consensus.

45   Est autem hic consensus in hoc iudicio presertim necessarius, quoniam non vincit maior pars — vi q. iiii c. i, ii et iii, 65. d. *Episcopum* in glo. —; sed ubi episcopus a synodo venit iudicandus, concors omnium sentencia requiritur — vi q. iiii *Si quis episcopus* ii, glo. in c. *Multis* xvii d. Quare si papa ab universali synodo iudicari potest, omnium illius synodi consenssus debet intervenire. Et quoniam ipsum olim Basiliense concilium ex universali representacione ecclesie catholice sibi vendicabat in papam iudicandi potestatem, docere habet personas ecclesiam representantes interfuisse et consenssisse, si secundum suum eciam principium processus debet esse alicuius momenti. Sed ut ex casu habetur, prelati maiores, imperator nomine regnorum suorum et subditorum, rex Francie, rex Castelle, rex Arragonum, domini electores, nacio Italica, dux Mediolani et pene omnes ecclesiam catholicam representantes contradixerunt. Igitur aliorum nomine episcoporum processus non potest dici synodicus, sed est 'irritus' — argumentum lxiii d. *Obeuntibus* in textu et glo. lxvi d. *Archiepiscopus*. Nec possunt Amediste dicere connivenciam ecclesie catholice quovis modo intervenisse, licet connivencia in requirentibus expressum consenssum, ut in actibus conciliaribus, non sufficeret, cum ibi subscripcio requiratur. Nam 'connivencia' proprie secundum Laurencium est, quando 'scitur et non contradicitur' — lxiii d. *Adrianus*, 24. d. *Episcopus*. Hic autem constabat de contradiccione et protestacione iam

der Rome said,[113] "Since the providence of God has brought all business to a prosperous end, it is necessary that we ratify these things with our own hands according to synodal procedure." You see how subscription is, as it were, of the essence of a synod in order to manifest its consensus.

This consensus, however, is particularly necessary in this judg- 45 ment [i.e., the one deposing Eugenius IV], since the majority does not rule ([Gratian] C. 6 q. 4 cc. 1, 2 and 3, and the gloss at [idem] D. 65 c. *Episcopum*[114]); but when the bishop has come to be judged by a synod, the sentence requires the agreement of all ([Gratian] C. 6 q. 4 in the second c. *Si quis episcopus* [c. 2], and the gloss on [idem] D. 17 c. *Multis*[115]). Therefore, if the pope can be judged by a universal synod, the consent of all at the synod ought to be involved. And, since that former Council of Basel claims for itself the power of judging the pope as the universal representative of the Catholic Church, it has to show that the persons representing the Church were present and gave consent if the trial is to be of any weight according to its own premise. But in fact we find that major prelates, the emperor (in the name of his kingdoms and subjects), the king of France, the king of Castile, the king of Aragon, the lord electors, the Italian nation, the duke of Milan and almost all of those who represented the Catholic Church contradicted [the council on this point]. Therefore, the trial in the name of the other bishops cannot be called synodal; but it is "null" (see the argument in [Gratian] D. 63 c. *Obeuntibus* [c. 35] in the text and by the gloss at D. 66 c. *Archiepiscopus*[116]). Nor can the Amedeists say connivance of the Catholic Church was involved in any way, as turning a blind eye would not suffice in place of the requirement for express consent, as in conciliar acts, since a subscription is required there. For there is "connivance" properly, according to Laurentius,[117] when something "is known and not contradicted" ([Gratian] D. 63 c. *Adrianus* [c. 22], [idem] D. 24 c. *Episcopus* [c. 6]). In the present case, however, there was evidently

dictorum. Pretensa eciam sentencia eorum ostendit reges, cardinales, episcopos et universitates non consenssisse, quia eis sub horribilibus penis ibi mandatur, ut sentencie acquiescant.

46   Adhuc dico, quod in hoc iudicio, ubi supremus pontifex debet iudicari, tanto plus consenssus est necessarius, quanto scisma in ecclesia, si consenssus deest, est periculosius. Nam cum sanctus Augustinus *Contra Parmenianum* nos instruat insolubilibus racionibus nichil posse malum pontificem ecclesie obesse et ob hoc nullam omnino dabilem necessariam scismatis causam, concludit numquam ob correccionem iuste scisma fieri posse. Ita est textus supra allegatus 23. q. 4. *Cum quisque fratrum*. Quapropter, quando illi pauci videbant ob contradiccionem se procedere non posse, nisi scisma fieret, 'diabolica presumpcione' ducti sunt, ut dicit glo. ad Cor. x: 'Temptacio vos non apprehendat nisi humana'. Et est dictum sancti Augustini *De unico baptismo*; dicit enim 'dyabolicam presumpcionem' esse sue opinioni inherere usque ad ecclesie scissuram. Et bene possumus hoc dicere de istis Amedistis, qui nulla imperatoris, regum et principum humiliacione et prece, nulla presidencium persuasione sanctissima, nulla catholici populi supplicacione, ne in matrem ecclesiam et Christi corpus sevirent, flecti potuerunt, quasi ab omnibus prelatis et nacionibus ac ab ipsa sancta Romana ecclesia 'spiritus' sani 'consilii' esset sublatus et ipsis miseris datus!

47   O presumpcio luciferiana, demens et insana, qualis in ecclesia in paucis numquam legitur fuisse sub concilii specie! Et quia omnis scriptura et sanctorum doctrina eis adversabatur, ad solum Constanciense concilium refugium habuerunt, et tamen non intellexerunt id, quod allegarunt. Nam illa synodus ait, quomodo uni-

contradiction and protest on the part of the aforesaid. Even their pretended sentence shows that the kings, cardinals, bishops and universities did not consent, because they are commanded under horrible penalties to acquiesce in the sentence.

Besides, I say that in this judgment, where the supreme pontiff   46
is to be judged, consent is the more required as the danger of schism in the Church where consent is lacking is that much more dangerous. For when Saint Augustine in *Against Parmenian* taught us with irrefutable reasons that an evil Roman pontiff can offer no hindrance to the Church, and because of this no necessary cause ever can be given for schism, he concluded that it was never just to create schism simply to correct him. So says the text of the aforesaid [text of Gratian] C. 23 q. 4 c. *Cum quisque fratrum* [c. 19]. For this reason, when those few [remaining at Basel] saw that, because they had been contradicted [by the aforesaid representatives of the Church], they could not proceed without causing a schism, they were led on by "diabolical presumption," as the gloss says at 1 Cor. 10,[118] "No temptation may take you but such as is common to humanity." And this is the maxim of Saint Augustine in *On the Only Baptism*.[119] He says it is "a diabolical presumption" to adhere to one's own opinion even to the point of dividing the Church. We can say this very well about these Amedeists, who could not be turned from rending Holy Mother Church and the body of Christ by the humility and prayers of emperors, kings and princes, by the the holiest persuasions of the presidents, or by the supplications of the Catholic people—as though "the spirit of sound council"[120] had been taken away from all these prelates and nations and from the Holy Roman Church herself and given to these wretches!

O Satanic presumption, what madness, what insanity! We have   47
never heard of such presumption in the Church, so few masquerading as a council! Because all Scripture and the teaching of the saints is against them, they take refuge in the Council of Constance alone, yet do not understand what it is that they are citing.

versale 'concilium' universalem 'militantem ecclesiam representans a Christo habet potestatem'. Hoc enim concilium non facit scisma, quoniam intra se habet militantis ecclesie consenssum; quale non fuit illud malignancium scismaticorum conventiculum, ecclesia per orbem dispersa contradicente, a qua se separantes 'corpus Christi' nisi sunt 'laniare' et 'scismatici' facti sunt — 23. q. 5. *Non vos* cum similibus. Dicunt se universalem synodum sicud et illi, qui ante septimam ycumenicam synodum in Constantinopoli congregati errorem suum, quem circa ymagines habuerunt, sub nomine mangni concilii auctorizare pretendebant. Quibus in ipsa catholica septima synodo in vi[a] accione sic formaliter respondetur: Quomodo magna et universalis' fuit illa synodus, 'quam neque receperunt reliquarum presules ecclesiarum, sed anathemati hanc transmiserunt? Non enim habuit adiutorem illius temporis Romanorum papam vel eos, qui circa ipsum sunt sacerdotes, nec eciam per vicarios eius neque per hemicicliam epistolam, quemadmodum lex dictat conciliorum, sed nec consencientes patriarchas Orientis, Allexandrie scilicet' ac 'Anthiochie et sancte civitatis, vel conministros et summos sacerdotes, qui cum ipsis existunt. Vere fumus caligine plenus obtenebrans oculos stolidorum est sermo eorum.' Hec ibi.

48   Et in libro *De equitate potestatis*,[8] ubi investigat auctor, quid ad universale concilium requiratur, centesimoprimo capitulo ad summum propositum hanc concilii universalis per ecclesiam recepti adducit diffinicionem, per quam convincitur apertissime figmenta Amedistarum, quibus nomine universalis concilii aures hominum obtundunt, non esse nisi 'fumum caligine plenum stolidorum oculos obtenebrantem'. Nam loquuntur de ecclesia mathematice et abstracte, non respiciendo ad corpus aut eius membra, et de concilio geometrice, tantum ad locum respicientes, non ad personas consencientes — propter hoc eorum processus est arismetri-

For the synod says that the universal "council, representing the Church Militant, has power from Christ."[121] For this council did not create a schism, since it had within it the consent of the Church Militant, unlike that conventicle of wicked schismatics. The latter separated itself from the Church spread throughout the world, which was contradicting it, and tried to "rend the Body of Christ," and became "schismatics" ([Gratian] C. 23 q. 5 c. *Non vos* [c. 42] with similar texts). They call themselves a universal synod, like those who gathered before the Seventh Ecumenical Synod in Constantinople and pretended to authorize under the guise of a great council their error regarding images.[122] To them it was replied formally, in the sixth session of that Seventh Catholic Synod: "In what way" was that synod "great and universal, when the bishops of other churches did not accept it but anathematized it? For it did not have as a helper the pope of the Romans of that time or those priests who surrounded him, neither through his vicars nor through an encyclical letter, in the manner in which the law of councils requires; nor the consent of the patriarchs of the East, that is of Alexandria, Antioch and of the Holy City [i.e. Jerusalem], or of the co-ministers and the chief priests who dwelt with them. Truly, their words are a cloud full of smoke, blinding the eyes of fools."[123]

And in the book *On Ecclesiastical Power*,[124] where the author investigates what is required for a universal council, in c. 101, he adduces in summary a definition of a universal council received by the Church which refutes in the most obvious way the fictions that the Amedeists use, in the name of a universal council, to belabor the ears of men, showing them to be nothing but "a cloud full of smoke, blinding the eyes of fools." For they speak of the Church mathematically and abstractly, and not with regard to its body or its members, and of the council geometrically, looking only at the place rather than at persons in consensus. Because of this their error is arithmetical, and they come to conclusions through majori-

cus —, per pluralitatem indifferenter concludentes, credentes ar-
monica verbali modulacione fideles ita posse allicere, ut ipsi eis
ducuntur. Sed 'fumus eorum' detectus est.

49   Adhuc processum non fuisse synodicum ex eo eciam constat,
quia synodus illa ad certos fines fuit per dominum Martinum
atque post per dominum Eugenium instituta, ut in prima sessione
fundacionis olim concilii Basiliensis continetur, nequaquam autem
ad talem processum instaurandum; quare non synodice processerunt. Oportet enim, dicit, synodus actu congregata ad accusan-
dum pontificem specialiter 'sinodum convocare' — 17. d. ❲ Hinc
eciam, ii q. v Mandastis, in quibus locis hoc probatur in Romano
pontifice. Et quod non sufficeret generalis concilii convocacio, nisi
de hoc in convocacione specialiter esset cautum, quoad iudicium
episcopi cuiuscumque probari videtur v q. iiii Nullus episcopus coniuncta glo. et c. Duodecim. Patet igitur,[9] cum illi pauci synodice
non processerint, sed contra apostolicam sedem rebellaverint,
quod nemo de eorum iudicio timere debet, ‹ut› dicit textus sancti
Gregorii xix d. Nulli phas.

50   Dico nec illum processum contra minimum episcopum fuisse
legittimum. De essencia enim ibi 'necessario xii' sunt 'episcopi per'
reum 'electi' cum eorum superiore — iii q. viii — cui ius in
agendo — v q. iiii Duodecim —, et non potest synodice nisi ab illa
electa synodo iudicari — ii q. iiii Nullam. Debent enim illi electi xii
omnibus et singulis negociis interesse et cum gravitate et subscripcione propria procedere et concordare. Hic autem nec fuerunt 13,
nec illi, qui erant, fuerunt electi, sed suspectissimi, ut ex condi-

ties without distinction [of persons], believing that they can ensnare the faithful by a verbal harmonics, so that they can lead them.[125] But their cloud has been detected.

Besides, that the trial was not synodal is evident from the fact 49 that the synod was instituted by the lord [Pope] Martin [V] and afterwards by the lord [Pope] Eugenius [IV] to achieve particular ends, as contained in the first session inaugurating the former Council of Basel;[126] it was not reestablished to pursue such a process [as the trial of a pope]; therefore, they have not proceeded in a synodal manner. [Gratian] says that an active synod must convoke a special synod to accuse the pontiff (D. 17 ❡ *Hinc etiam* [p.c. 6], C. 2 q. 5 c. *Mandastis* [c. 10]); in these passages this is proved in the case of the Roman pontiff. And that the convocation of a general council would not suffice [for this purpose], unless it was specified in the [act of] convocation, seems to be proved with respect to the judging of bishops of any sort in [Gratian] C. 5 q. 4 c. *Nullus episcopus*, together with the gloss,[127] and [idem] c. *Duodecim* [C. 2 q. 4 c. 2]. It is obvious, therefore, since these few [prelates at Basel] have not proceeded in a synodal manner, but have rebelled against the Apostolic See, that no one should be afraid of their judicial acts, as the text of Saint Gregory says at D. 19 c. *Nulli fas* [c. 5].

I say that the trial would not have been legitimate against the 50 least of the bishops. For it is of the essence there and necessary that twelve bishops be chosen by the accused, together with their superior ([Gratian] C. 3 q. 8) to whom the right of acting is given ([idem] C. 5 q. 4 c. *Duodecim* [c. 2]). And he cannot be judged in a synodal manner except by that chosen synod [of twelve bishops] ([Gratian] C. 2 q. 4 c. *Nullam* [c. 3]). The twelve chosen ought then to be involved in each and every item of business and proceed and come to consensus with gravity and by their own signature. Here, however, there were not thirteen [i.e. the twelve bishops and their superior]; nor were those who were present chosen [by the

cione et presumpcione eorum hoc est plus quam notorium. Manifestum est autem, si universalis synodus propter presidentem tantum suspecta esset, nichil valere, quod agit contra episcopum eciam 'ter' contumacem, ut de Calcedonensi exemplum habetur — iii q. v *Quia suspecti*. Videte, an 'testes' fuerunt, ut ius vult — ii q. vii *Testes* —, quando idem actores, iudices et testes esse presumpserunt, ut iniustior processus esse non posset. Quapropter irritum et temerarium fecerunt contra suum dominum Christi vicarium scismaticum processum.

51   Est consuetudo Amedistarum omni excogitabili modo absque erubescencia per figmenta male acta colorare. Hinc dicunt: Non potest negari in heresi anathema esse et hereticum se ipsum ab ecclesia abscindere — i. q. i.: 'Si quis, inquit, de ecclesia heretica presumpcione exierit, a se ipso dampnatur', iiii q. v c. i., xxiiii q. i. c. i, ii et iii. Sed sic est, quod Eugenius est hereticus; quare omne id, quod contra processum obicitur, non prodest. Nituntur autem minorem probare ex suis confictis 'tribus veritatibus' et translacione concilii, ex decreto, quod incipit *Moyses*, et bulla, ut dicunt, studio Tolosano missa.

52   Ad hoc facilis est responsio, quia dum miseri illi Amediste in pontificem diabolice sevientes et propter conservare conciliorum auctoritatem se omnia agere dixissent, tunc pessimam intencionem suam propalarunt. Nam dum se deficere conspexissent in processu, quem super certis excogitatis criminibus sua sponte instaurarunt, dicente olim Panormitano relacione audita ex x locis se probaturum ex illo iniquo processu nichil fieri posse in iure contra d‹ominum› n‹ostrum›, statim ad heresim refugium quesiverunt,

accused], but were rather highly suspect persons, as is notorious from their condition[128] and presumption. It is obvious if the universal council were so much suspect because of the president, that what it does against a bishop would be worthless, even if he were thrice contumacious, as may be known from the example of Chalcedon ([Gratian] C. 3 q. 5 c. *Quia suspecti* [c. 15]). Look, were these men "witnesses," as the law requires ([Gratian] C. 2 q. 7 c. *Testes* [c. 39]), when the same persons had the presumption to act as accusers, judges and witnesses, so that the trial could not have been more unjust? For this reason, the schismatic trial they held against their lord, the vicar of Christ, was reckless and void.

It is the custom of the Amedeists to use fictions shamelessly 51 and in every imaginable way in order to give color to their wicked acts. Hence they say: it cannot be denied that one accursed as a heretic cuts himself off from the Church, citing [Gratian] C. 1 q. 1 c. [*Si quis* c. 70]: "If anyone should depart from the Church through heretical presumption, he has condemned himself by the very act." They also cite [idem] C. 4 q. 5 c. 1, C. 24 q. 1 cc. 1, 2 and 3. But [they argue] Eugenius is a heretic. Therefore all that is objected against their trial is profitless. They seek, however, to prove the minor premise from their confected "three truths:"[129] the translation of the council, from the decree which begins *Moses*,[130] and from the bull they claim was sent to the University of Toulouse.[131]

To this there is an easy answer, since while those wretched 52 Amedeists have been diabolically savaging the pontiff, saying they have acted in all things to preserve the authority of councils, they reveal that their motivations are the worst. For when they saw that they had failed in the trial they had begun of their own accord over the crimes they had imagined, and had heard the former archbishop of Palermo's report,[132] saying he would prove from ten passages that nothing could be legally done in that iniquitous trial against our lord, they at once took refuge in [the charge of] heresy,

ne in proposito maligno deficerent. Et quia non repererunt d‹ominum› n‹ostrum› citatum super heresi neque causam ipsum hereti-
candi, novos quosdam articulos, quos 'veritates' vocant, more suo
fantastico 'veritates fidei', tunc primo decreverunt pro medio here-
ticandi principem fidei Romanum pontificem, quasi dicerent: Si
necessarium est ad hoc, ut ipse abiciatur, quod sit hereticus, eum
faciemus hereticum, sive velit sive nolit. Et dum in hiis faccionibus
vigilarent, contradictum est ducibus malignis per eos, qui ecclesiam representarunt, ac per prelatos tunc Basilee existentes pene
omnes, per olim Panormitanum et longe maiorem partem, qui palam de iniusticia eorum, qui sine illorum prelatorum consenssu in
materia fidei attemptabantur, solempniter protestabatur, ut pridie
domini deputati, dum subscripta protestacio manu notarii concilii
legeretur, clare intellexerunt. Nichil est igitur id, quod dicitur de
illis veritatibus in subsidium complecionis perverse intencionis fa-
bricatis; et inimici nostri id ipsum tunc et iudices et prelati iudicarunt hoc iniustum. Verecundentur igitur et sileant; nam quare ad
heresim confugerunt miseri, qui ostendere atte‹m›ptarunt in alio
quam heresis casu papam per concilium deponi posse? Nonne per
hoc, quod sue faccioni heresim necessariam estimarunt, ad quam
confugerunt, auctoritatem conciliorum, quam ut novam edificare
se dixerunt, dereliquerunt et ad indubitatum casum heresis reversi
sunt, se in personam pontificis sevire pocius quam de conciliorum
auctoritate curam agere opere inefficaci ostendentes?

53   Dicunt d‹ominum› n‹ostrum› ex eo hereticum, quia transtulit
concilium. Tale argumentum paucissimi senssus homines non fe-
cissent. Ponatur papam actum prohibitum fecisse: Quomodo ex

so as not to fail in their malicious plan. And, since they could not find that our lord had been cited for heresy nor had given cause for being adjudged a heretic, they first decreed certain new articles, which they called "truths" — in their fantasies "truths of the faith" — as a means of declaring the prince of the faith, the Roman pontiff, a heretic. It was as if they had said: If it is necessary for him to be a heretic to cast him out, let us make him a heretic, whether he wishes it or not. And, while they kept themselves awake at night over their cabals, their malicious leaders were denounced by those who represented the Church and by almost all of the prelates then at Basel, by the former archbishop of Palermo and by the great majority, who issued a solemn protest against the injustice of the men who attacked [the pope] in matters of faith without the consent of those prelates. Yesterday, the lords deputed to hear our arguments understood this clearly when a signed protest in the hand of the notary of the council was read out.[133] There is nothing therefore that may be said of these "truths," which were fabricated to help them compass their perverted intentions. That is the very thing our enemies did at that moment; and the judges and prelates found it unjust. Thus they were shamed and fell silent. For how can these wretches take refuge in a charge of heresy when they [already] had tried to show that a pope can be deposed by a council in a case other than that of heresy? Have they not, by the very fact that they think taking refuge in the charge of heresy is necessary to their cabals, left behind the authority of councils, which they say they are building up anew, and turned to an "indubitable" charge of heresy, showing by this ineffective action that they are attacking the person of the pontiff rather than showing concern for the authority of councils?

They call our lord a heretic because he translated the council. 53 Even men of very little sense would not use that argument. It is posited that the pope had performed a forbidden act. How can one arrive at a conclusion of heresy in faith and rational judgment

peccato in facto concludi potest heresis in fide et in racionis iudicio? Si omnis prohibicionem transgrediens argui debet tamquam male de prohibitoris potestate senciens hereticus, non erit peccatum mortale sine heresi. Ad hoc autem, ut calumpnia eorum apercius aspiciatur, considerandum, quoniam ipsi Amediste d‹ominum› n‹ostrum› diffamarunt, quasi ipse pro libito concilia transferre et dissolvere posse crederet, hoc inconveniens arguentes: quia subesse tenetur in tribus, ut Constancie determinatum reperitur, igitur non debet esse in potestate illius, qui subest, concilium ad libitum mutare. Sed d‹ominus› n‹oster› numquam pro libito sibi licere dissolvere concilia aut transferre dixit; sed non dubitat decretis concilii Constanciensis non obstantibus, que hoc eciam nullibi prohibent, hoc sibi licere 'causis racionabilibus' existentibus. Causas autem 'in translacione' allegat racionabiles, non dicens 'pro libito', ut fingunt Amediste. Ita et Martinus papa credidit, qui suis presidentibus dedit 'facultatem' sua 'auctoritate concilium dissolvendi et transferendi', ut in bulla eius inserta prime sessioni Basiliensis concilii continetur.

54 Unde cum multa leguntur concilia eciam rite congregata propter malum processum oberrasse, 'ut' exemplum de '2ª Ephisina synodo' legimus, 'quam Leo papa ammovit et Calcedonensem instituit', tunc, si apud principem ecclesie non esset potestas malis conciliis resistendi ex iustis et optimis causis, non esset in ecclesia principatus cum plenitudine potestatis in edificacionem, nec esset ecclesie bene provisum et sufficienter. Est igitur illud, propter quod nisi sunt illi dominum nostrum hereticare, in ipsis da‹m›pnatissima heresis, non credentes, ymmo dampnantes pa-

from a sinful act? If everyone who transgresses a prohibition should be accused of heresy on the grounds that he has held wrong opinions about the authority of the one who issued the prohibition, there will be no mortal sin without heresy. Moreover, to make their calumny all the more evident, the following point must be considered. The Amedeists defame our lord, charging him with undue behavior in acting as though he believed he could translate or dissolve councils at his pleasure, whereas he is bound to be subject in three things [i.e., faith, schism and reform], as was determined at Constance;[134] therefore [they say], it ought not to be in the power of someone who is subordinate [to a council] to change a council at his pleasure. But our lord never said he was allowed to dissolve or translate councils at his pleasure; but he did not doubt, notwithstanding the decrees of the Council of Constance, which nowhere prohibited this, that he was allowed to dissolve or translate councils when rational reasons to do so existed. He cited rational causes "for translating" [the council] and did not claim he could do so "at his pleasure," as the Amedeists pretend. Pope Martin also believed he could do this, who gave his presidents, by his "authority, the power of dissolving and translating the council," as is contained in his bull inserted into the acts of the first session of the Council of Basel.[135]

Hence, since we read that many councils have fallen into error, 54 even when rightly constituted, through bad procedure—for example "the Second Council of Ephesus, which," we read, "Pope Leo annulled, instituting the Council of Chalcedon" [instead][136]—then, if the prince of the Church did not possess the power to resist evil councils for just and good causes, there would not exist in the Church a principate with plenitude of power for building up, and the Church would not be well and sufficiently provided for, [which is impossible]. Therefore, in the fact that they try to make our lord a heretic they fall into a most damnable heresy themselves, for they do not trust, but rather condemn the pope for his ability to

pam resistere posse destructoribus unitatis, pacis et fidei ecclesie, negantes in ipso omnem potestatis plenitudinem ad conservacionem et edificacionem ecclesie. An autem cause translacionis racionabiles fuerint, exitus docuit. A 'fructu' enim iuxta Christi doctrinam 'congnicionem' accipientes, negare non possumus translacionem eciam pro auctoritatis conciliorum conservacione necessariam. Nam si translacio scisma Basilee factum non precessisset, ita quod dici posset concilium fecisse scisma, quo malo nichil in ecclesia peius, ut probat Ieronimus 24. q. i *Non afferamus*, quis amplius veneraretur concilia quasi sancta, postquam talem fructum pessimum concilium Basiliense visum fuisset peperisse? Aut quis magnam auctoritatem conciliis inesse crederet, postquam compertum est omnes reges, principes et prelatos in faciem contradixisse concilio Basiliensi? Nonne translacio auctoritatem salvat, ut nunc dicatur: Non erat concilium, quod scisma fecit aut cui contradictum est, sed ante fuit translatum?

55   Loquuntur eciam de conciliorum dissolucione fantastice, non advertentes dissolucionem quo ad capud concilii, cuius mandato collectio facta est, aliud non esse quam mandati sublacionem et absolucionem, ut quisque ad propria redire possit. Quomodo potest papa notari quasi horrendum crimen incidisse, quia prelatis libertatem redeundi ad pastoralem curam prestitit? Si quis gesta conciliorum veterum canonice celebratorum legerit, ita reperiet et eos, qui in hoc fundamentum vanum locarunt, iuste deridebit. Nec obstat, quod patres Constancie sibi ipsis legem statuerunt, quod dissolvi nollent unione non peracta. Ita enim poterant facere, et necessitas procurande unionis ita fieri exposcebat nullo uno indubitato pontifice in universa ecclesia presidente.

resist destroyers of the unity, peace and faith of the Church, and they deny him the full plenitude of power to preserve and build up the Church. The outcome has taught us whether there were reasonable causes for the translation. For "from their fruit," according to the doctrine of Christ, "you shall know them,"[137] and we cannot deny that the translation was necessary even to preserve the authority of councils. For if the translation had not preceded the schism started at Basel, so that it might have been said that a council started a schism — an evil than which none could be worse for the Church, as Jerome proved ([Gratian] C. 24 q. 1 c. *Non afferamus* [c. 21]) — who would venerate holy councils any more after the Council of Basel had been seen to bear such evil fruit? Or who would believe great authority inheres in councils once it was found out that all kings, princes and prelates had denounced the Council of Basel to its face? Did not the translation save the authority of councils, so that now it may be said: It was not a council that made the schism or that has been denounced; it was translated before these things occurred?

They even talk deludedly of the dissolution of the council [by the pope], not noticing that the dissolution as regards the head of the council, by whose mandate the assembly was gathered, is nothing else than a cancellation and completion, so that anyone could return home. How can the pope be branded as having fallen into a horrendous crime simply because he gave the prelates the freedom of returning to pastoral care? If anyone should read the records of the ancient councils canonically celebrated, he will find it so; and he will be right to deride those who build on this weak foundation. Nor does it matter that the fathers at Constance decreed it as a law for themselves that they could not be dissolved without union being accomplished. For they had the power to do so, and the necessity of seeing to the unity of the Church demanded this be done while there was no one, uncontested pope presiding over the universal Church.

55

56   Hic secus dicunt de bullis prenominatis, post eorum dampnatam sentenciam editis, in quibus aiunt papam male de concilii auctoritate sentire, suam sentenciam ex noviter productis iustificando.
Sed hec eorum dicta, ut alia omnia, sunt 'fumus caligine plenus'.
Non enim in bulla *Moyses* aut alia conciliorum auctoritatem aut
decreta Constanciensis concilii dampnat, sed hereticum intellectum Amedistarum; nam Amediste per totum orbem suas inepcias
ad Constanciense concilium pro colore suo reducere nituntur,
quasi ipsis scisma faciendi Constanciense concilium auctoritatem
prestiterit. Hoc non est honorare, sed blasphemare pocius sacrum
Constanciense concilium.

57   Dicunt ipsi: 'Concilium' universale universalem 'militantem ecclesiam representans immediate ex Christo habet potestatem.' Hoc
ad sanum intellectum secundum verba concilii nemo negaret, quia
papa eciam de concilio illo est, ymmo 'capud' eius, ut non negavit
eciam olim Basiliense concilium. Si enim est capud ecclesie, vere a
maiori et representate in concilio. Sed dum subiciunt olim Arelatensis et sui sequaces: nos constituimus illud concilium, quia sumus Basilee, non obstante contradiccione ecclesie Romane, Ytalice,
Gallice, Germanice, Hispanice et Anglice; hinc possumus de papatu, imperio et omnibus regnis disponere, et omnes tenentur nobis obedire—certe istud est falsissimum et hereticum. Quod autem hunc intellectum habuerint illi pauci, opere ostenderunt,
presertim in pretensa sentencia contra d‹ominum› n‹ostrum› lata,
ubi non obstante contradiccione omnium sentenciam deposicionis
eciam in contradicentes nisi sunt promulgare. Tales presumpciones
et alias multas contra veritatem in praxi ostenssas 'caligine plenas'
dominus noster dampnat, non concilium Constanciense, quamvis
per unam obedienciam hoc sit determinatum, de qua s‹anctitas›

Here they speak otherwise of the aforementioned bulls, pub- 56
lished after their accursed sentence in which they say the pope
held a wrong opinion about the authority of the council, justifying
their sentence from the newly produced bulls.[138] But these sayings
of theirs, like all the rest, are "a cloud full of smoke." For neither in
the bull *Moses* nor in the other[139] did he condemn the authority of
councils or the decrees of the Council of Constance but the
Amedeists' heretical understanding of them; for the Amedeists
strive throughout the world to give color to their nonsense by referring to the Council of Constance, as if the Council of Constance gave them the authority to start a schism. This is not to
honor, but to blaspheme the holy Council of Constance.

They say: A universal "council representing the universal 57
Church Militant has power immediately from Christ." No one
may deny that this is a sound understanding of the words of the
council, because the pope too is a member of the council; indeed
he is its head, as even the former Council of Basel did not deny,
and if he is indeed head of the Church, truly the Church is represented by its greater [part]. But when the former Cardinal of
Arles and his followers add: We constitute that council because we
are at Basel, notwithstanding the denials of the Roman Church
and those in Italy, France, Germany, Spain and England; hence we
can dispose of the papacy, the empire and all kingdoms and all are
obliged to obey us — certainly that is most false and heretical. The
understanding those few have [of the Council of Constance] they
show by their deeds, especially in the pretended sentence issued
against our lord, where, notwithstanding the contradiction of everyone, they tried to promulgate a sentence of deposition even
against those who were contradicting them. Such were the presumptuous acts and the many other errors of commission against
the truth that our lord condemned as "full of smoke," not the
Council of Constance, even though [the decree *Haec sancta*] was
determined by a single obedience, to which His Holiness did not

sua tunc non erat, ex quo Amediste errorum suorum fulcimentum elicere satagunt; ymmo in bono et vero intellectu pocius illas ordinaciones, quas s‹anctitas› sua conciliares affirmat, laudat et approbat quam inficiat, ut ex tenore bulle *Moyses* rectum iudicium habens clare poterit intueri.

‹III›

58 Pudet amplius de intrusione Amedei olim Sabaudie ducis verba fundere, quam universus christianus orbis detestatur. Nam illi temerarii viri primo absque omni sentencia omnia papalia nomine superioritatis concilii sibi usurparunt, quod ante numquam legitur factum. Et quoniam cum ipsis adhuc apostolica sedes, quam penitus extingwere non poterant, concurrebat, cogitarunt per quandam pretenssissimam susspensionem ad se omnem papalem auctoritatem sua sponte attrahere, semper ecclesia per orbem dispersa contradicente. Sed ut se in principatu sic usurpato conservarent, post iniuriosissimam sentenciam ad eleccionem antipape 'more symearum', ut ait sanctus Ciprianus, processerunt. Simee enim aliquid simile habent et operantur ut homines; bestie tamen sunt racione carentes. Ita quidem et scismatici isti egerunt.

59   Tamen si hic locus esset cuncta impugnandi, fumositates 'caligine plenas' in omnibus eorum operibus facile patefacerem. Nam primo tres elegerunt, qui habebant omnium potestatem; illi alios, qui synodi auctoritatem in eligendo haberent, et multas tales fantasias ludibriosas et ridendas in praxi posuerunt scismatico. Primo notorium est ecclesiam, ut sepe dictum est, illis contradixisse. Cum ergo in electoribus debeat consenssus esse ecclesie, cui prefi-

at that time belong.[140] It is from this decree that the Amedeists seek to elicit a prop for their errors; and indeed His Holiness affirms, praises and approves those ordinances as conciliar in status, rightly understood, rather than regarding them as tainted, as anyone having right judgment can understand clearly from the tenor of the bull *Moses*.[141]

[III]

It is a shame to expend many words on the intrusion of Amadeus, the former Duke of Savoy, which the whole Christian world detests. For those rash men, first, thoughtlessly usurped all papal prerogatives for themselves in the name of the superiority of the council, an act utterly unexampled in written records. And since the Apostolic See, which they could not entirely extinguish, was still in existence along with them, they thought by an extremely high-handed act of suspension to draw to themselves of their own accord all papal authority, although the Church spread throughout the world always vetoed this. But to keep themselves in the principate they had usurped, after handing down an utterly unjust sentence, they proceeded to the election of an antipope, "in the manner of apes," as Saint Cyprian says.[142] For apes look and act somewhat like men; nevertheless, they are beasts lacking reason. And indeed these schismatics did act this way.

Still, if this were the place for impugning all their acts, I might easily clear up the clouds "full of smoke" in their deeds. For first they chose three men who were to have the power of all; and these selected others who would have the authority of the synod to elect [an antipope], and they laid down many such absurd and laughable delusions in the course of their schismatic activities. First, it is notorious that the Church, as often had been said, vetoed them. Since, therefore, the consent of the Church, over which a prelate must be set, ought to be present in the electors [of that prelate],

ciendus est prelatus, quia 'nullus invitis[10] debet dari episcopus' —
lxi d. *Nullus invitis* — et 'nulla racio sinit' papam aliquem 'inter episcopos haberi, qui non est per clerum' Romanum 'electus' de 'populi
consenssu' — 23. d. *In nomine domini,* lxii d. *Nulla racio* —, si igitur
hoc est verum — et negari nequeat, quia infinita sunt iura ad hoc —
, quomodo vendicabant sibi illi pauci potestatem universe ecclesie
antistitem eligendi, qui numquam illam habuerunt et ex eo, quia
Basilee erant, eam minime acquirere potuerunt ecclesia eis expresse contradicente? Dicunt: Nos omnes citavimus, ut venirent.
Fatua allegacio! Putabat olim Arelatensis ex eo, quia ipse fuit Basilee, quod ideo ipse et sibi adherentes in cardinales et pontifices
suis faccionibus malis non acquiescentes citandi aut cohercendi
potestatem acquisivissent. Mira res de tam caliginoso 'fumo'! Non
enim ex loco concilii cuiquam in concilio aut omnibus simul potestas accrescit, sed ex omnium consenssu. Unde nisi Romani
pontificis interesset auctoritas, cui omnes obedire tenentur, nemo
ad conveniendum in episcopos cohercionem haberet. Ita quidem
de metropolitano dicitur in provinciali ‹concilio›, et optime, concilium — 96. d. *Bene quidem* — hanc comparacionem facit de papa
quo ad universale concilium et de metropolitano quo ad provinciale, dicens utriusque consenssum in suo concilio necessarium. Et
quia abierat apostolicus legatus ex causa racionabili et non interfuit
apostolica censura, nec consenssus ecclesie fuit in hiis, que attemptabantur, dignum risu est olim Arelatensem cum suis citacionem
allegare, que emanavit a nullam potestatem habente.

because "no bishop ought to be given to the unwilling" ([Gratian] D. 61 c. *Nullus invitis* [c. 13]) and "no argument permits" any pope "to be placed among the bishops, who was not elected by" the Roman "clergy" with "popular consent" ([idem] D. 23 c. *In nomine Domini* [c. 1]; [idem] D. 62 c. *Nulla ratio* [c. 1]), if this is true, then—and it cannot be denied, because there are infinite legal rights to this effect—how can those few, who never had it, claim for themselves the power of electing a primate of the universal church, who never had such a power? Do they claim to have acquired it from the fact that they are at Basel, when the Church has expressly denied them this power? They say: "We summoned everyone to come." A fatuous argument! The former Cardinal of Arles thought, from the fact that he was at Basel, that he and his adherents had thus acquired a power of citing and coercing cardinals and bishops who did not acquiesce in their cabals. A wondrous power to come from such a "cloud full of smoke"! Power cannot accrue from the [mere] location of a council to any individual in a council or all members of it simultaneously, but only from the consent of all. Therefore, unless the authority of the Roman pontiff, whom everyone is obliged to obey, were involved, no one would have the coercive power to convene the bishops. Thus it is well said of a metropolitan in a provincial council, that the council (according to [Gratian] D. 96 c. *Bene quidem* [c. 1]) provides this comparison between a pope with respect to a universal council and a metropolitan with respect to a provincial council, saying the consent of each primate is necessary in his [respective] council. And since the apostolic legate[143] was absent for a reasonable cause and apostolic oversight was [therefore] not present, nor was the consent of the Church present in the actions they attempted, the former Cardinal of Arles is laughable when he and his supporters mention a summons which emanated from a body having no power.

60   Deinde si persone ille, qui de eleccione se intromiserunt, consi-
derantur, nonne eo ipso periuri et scismatici et excommunicati
fuerunt, non solum quia contra prestitum iuramentum apostolice
sedi de unitate conservanda iuxta c. *Significasti, De eleccione* eligere
antipapam attemptarunt, sed eciam quia contra iuramentum in
concilio prestitum temere venerunt? Iurarunt enim in sua incorpo-
racione 'sanum consilium dare' in hiis, ad que synodus congregata
fuit secundum nomina deputacionum de pace, fide et reformacione, et accesserunt contra pacem et unitatem ecclesie ad scissuram peragendam. Nonne de Sabaudiensi dominio omnes maiores
fuerunt accurrentes eleccionis tempore? Quis cogitasset posse viros ecclesiasticos ita fascinari, ut non verecundarentur cum iuramento intrare conclave ad illum eligendum, quem eligere non potuerunt, quem dudum populus prescivit hac arte preficiendum?
Cogitare debuissent deum aliquando vindicaturum hoc grande ne-
phas. Scio neminem eorum unquam legisse aliquem unicum Romanum pontificem valide et synodice deiectum et eo vivente alium
electum. Ait enim textus *Sicud vir* — vii q. 1. — 'ecclesiam', que recedit a pontifice sponso suo propter 'fornicacionem eo vivente accipere alium non' debere. Ita arguit sanctus Ciprianus Nouacianum
vivente Cornelio eligi non potuisse in c. *Factus est* eadem C. et q.
Dico notanter: quando ecclesia se separat ab episcopo suo propter
fornicacionem episcopi, illamet ecclesia se alteri copulare non debet, ut ibidem. Quam provide et caute hoc dictum sit, quisque
bene intelligit.

61   Sed non quesiverunt Amediste ecclesie salutem; alias abstinuis-
sent ab eleccione. Sed se ipsos semper quesiverunt. Hinc illum
contra sanctorum patrum canones erigere nisi sunt, cuius potencia

Then, if one takes into account the persons who injected them-   60
selves into the election, are they not by that very act perjurers,
schismatics and excommunicates, not only because they attempted
to elect an antipope, against the oath they swore to the Apostolic
See about safeguarding unity, as in *De electione* c. *Significasti* [in the
Decretals of Gregory IX, X 1.6.4], but because they even went
rashly against the oath they had sworn in the council? They swore
at their incorporation "to give sound counsel" in those matters[144]
for which the synod had been gathered, according to the names of
the deputations concerning peace, faith and reform; but they proceeded to initiate a schism, acting against the peace and unity of
the Church. Were not all the major figures rushing in from the
domain of Savoy at the time of the election? Who would have
thought that ecclesiastics could be so bewitched that they were not
ashamed to enter a conclave upon oath to elect a man they could
not elect, whom the people long knew would be elected by this de-
vice? They ought to have considered that God would avenge so
great an iniquity some day. I know that none of them ever read
that any unchallenged Roman pontiff was deposed in a valid and
synodal manner and that a new one was elected while his predecessor still was alive. The text of [Gratian] C. 7 q. 1 c. *Sicut vir*
[c. 11] says that "the Church" which withdraws from her spouse,
the pontiff, because of "fornication" ought "not to accept another
while he still lives." Thus Saint Cyprian argued that, with
Cornelius still alive, Novatian could not be elected (see the same
cause and question c. *Factus est* [C. 7 q. 1 c. 5]). Mark my words:
When the Church separates herself from her bishop because of
the bishop's fornication, that Church ought not to join herself to
another, as in the same place. Anyone can well understand how
advisedly and carefully this was laid down.

But the Amedeists were not looking out for the health of the   61
Church; otherwise, they would have refrained from the election.
But they always looked out for their own interests. That was why

ad assequendum propositum iuvarentur. Eligerunt enim laicum, quem omnia iura dicunt ineligibilem, maxime ad pontificatum Romanum—79. d. *Si quis*, 23. d. *In nomine Domini*—, et ob hoc anathematizati et antichristiani censendi sunt, ut ibidem. Et ait sancta magna octava ycumenica synodus, de patriarcha Romano eciam hoc ipsum disponens, in canone‹m› renovantes, quod 'nemo de senatoria dignitate vel mundana conversacione nuper tonsus sub intencione vel exspectacione patriarchatus honoris clericus vel monachus factus ad huiusmodi gradum scandere' possit, 'licet per singulos ordines divini sacerdocii plurimum temporis fecisse probetur. Neque enim propter timorem aut amorem dei aut propter exspectacionem transseundi viam virtutum, sed ob amorem glorie ac principatus tonsus huiusmodi reperitur. Si vero quis per nullam susspicionem predicte concupiscencie et exspectacionis, sed propter ipsum bonum humilitatis, que est circa Christum Ihesum, abrenuncians mundo fiat clericus aut monachus et omnem gradum ecclesiasticum transsigens per diffinita nunc tempora irreprehensibilis inventus extiterit et probatus, ita ut in gradu lectoris annum compleat, in subdiaconi vero duos, sitque dyaconus tribus, presbiter quatuor annis, bene placuit sancte et universali sinodo eligi hunc atque admitti.' Et infra: 'Si vero preter hanc diffinicionem nostram quisquam ad iam fatum supremum honorem provectus extiterit, reprobetur et ab omni sacerdotali operacione prorsus abiciatur, utpote qui extra sacros canones sit promotus.' Hec ibi.

62   An autem Amedeus quandam religionem laicalem assumens evaserit suspicionem, de qua in iam dicto canone, orbi notissimum est; dudum ante annos plures omnes audivimus sub spe papatus

they tried to set up Amadeus against the canons of the holy fathers, by whose power they were aided in following out their plan. For they chose a layman, whom all laws say is unelectable, especially to the Roman pontificate ([Gratian] D. 79 c. *Si quis* [c. 5], D. 23 c. *In nomine Domini* [c. 1]), and on this account they must be adjudged accursed and anti-Christian, as is said in the same place. And the holy Eighth Ecumenical Synod,[145] in dealing with this very matter regarding the Roman patriarch, against those who were renovating the canon, said that "no one of senatorial dignity or of a worldly lifestyle, newly tonsured, or made a cleric or a monk with the intention or expectation of the honor of the patriarchate" can "ascend to this rank, although it may be approved for someone who has spent a great deal of time in the individual ranks of the priesthood. For [the former kind of candidate] has not been found [to seek this office] because of fear or love of God or expectation of following the way of the virtues, but from lust for glory and of the principate. If, however, someone with no suspicion of the aforesaid lust and expectation, but, because of the virtue of humility which was in Christ Jesus, renounces the world and is made a cleric or monk and has passed through every ecclesiastical grade and has been found and proved to be irreproachable within the periods of time as now defined, such that he has completed a year in the grade of lector, two in that of subdeacon, three in that of deacon, and four in that of presbyter, it has well pleased the holy and universal synod that he be elected and admitted to office." And below, "But if, against this our definition, anyone already has been advanced to the aforesaid supreme honor, he is to be condemned and entirely cast out from every sacerdotal function inasmuch as he was promoted outside the sacred canons."

Whether, however, Amadeus, in assuming a lay form of religious life, has evaded the suspicion of what is prohibited in the aforesaid canon, is well known to the world; we have all heard for a long time that the man assumed this way of life many years ago 62

257

ipsum talem vitam assumpsisse. Elegerunt igitur illum in supremum rectorem ecclesie, qui numquam ecclesiasticam subintravit miliciam, contra ea, que habentur 61. d. *In sacerdotibus* et c. *Miramur* et per totum, et quem magna synodus reprobari et deponi iubet et quem illi, qui se concilium reformatoriale in capite et membris predicant, abicere debuissent, si eum Petri sedem occupare reperissent.

63   Hec sic summarie dixerim, ut constet domino nostro sanctissimo Eugenio obiecciones Basiliensium non obesse, quia vere 'fumus est caligine plenus obtenebrans oculos stolidorum sermo eorum.' Finit.

in the hope of the papacy. They chose therefore as supreme ruler of the Church a man who never had enrolled as a soldier of the Church, against the canons in [Gratian] D. 61 c. *In sacerdotibus* and c. *Miramur* [cc. 2 and 5] and throughout. He is a man whom the great synod [of Ferrara-Florence] ordered to be censured and deposed and whom they, who declare themselves a reforming council in head and members, ought to have cast out if they had found him occupying the See of Peter.

I have spoken in so summary a fashion to make it evident that the objections of those at Basel against our most holy lord Eugenius are no obstacle to him, because truly "their speech is a cloud full of smoke, blinding the eyes of fools."[146] The End.

63

Quod recedere de neutralitate seu ultralitate sit necessarium

1 Fides catholica habet 'unam' esse 'catholicam et apostolicam ecclesiam' et in illa 'remissionem peccatorum'. Que ita una est ex unitate 'gregis et pastoris', quod ille extra ecclesiam est, qui non cum pontifice est. Quapropter adherere summo 'pontifici' et ei obedire est 'de necessitate salutis'.

2 Item 'unitas' ecclesie 'non' patitur 'divisionem'. Non potest igitur vera catholica et apostolica ecclesia esse ex grege et capite Basilee erecto, si est ecclesia vera ex 'grege et pastore' Eugenio. Sed necessarium est, si est cum uno, quod non sit cum alio. Nec potest in ecclesia esse, qui nec sit cum uno nec cum alio, eciam ob quamcunque causam 'ignorancie vel simplicitatis'.

3 Sequitur quod, quamvis, ‹dummodo›[1] se compaciantur concilium et papa in unitate ecclesie et ante erectionem alterius capitis in Basilea, principum protestacio cum animorum suspensione salva fide unitatis ecclesie catholice et apostolice propter vitare scisma tollerari poterat, tamen post erectionem capitis Basilee contra Eugenium fides nec ultralitatem nec neutralitatem patitur. Urget igitur fidei necessitas, ut, qui in ecclesia esse velit, cum altero sit et ei obediat et quod credat alios extra unam ecclesiam catholicam et apostolicam esse et non habere potestatem ligandi et solvendi et quod eorum 'sacrificia' et communio vitanda sunt.

That It Is Necessary to Withdraw from Neutrality or Indecision

The catholic faith holds that there is "one Catholic and Apostolic 1
Church" and that in it is "remission of sins."[1] Thus there is one
Church from the unity of sheep and shepherd, and whoever is not
with the pope is outside the Church. For that reason, adhering to the
supreme "pontiff" and obeying him is "necessary for salvation."[2]

Again, "the unity" of the Church does "not" suffer "division."[3] 2
The true Catholic and Apostolic Church, therefore, cannot be
composed of the flock and the head set up at Basel, if [in fact] the
true Church is composed of "the flock and its shepherd,"
Eugenius. But of necessity he who is with one [head] is not with
the other. Nor can anyone be in the Church who is neither with
the one nor with the other head, even by any reason whatever "of
ignorance and simpleness."[4]

It follows that, although the protest of the [German] princes[5] 3
and the suspension of their allegiance in order to avoid schism
could be tolerated — saving the faith of the united Catholic and
Apostolic Church — as long as pope and council mutually tolerated each other, before the election of another head at Basel, nevertheless, the faith can tolerate neither indecision nor neutrality after the election of an antipope at Basel in opposition to Eugenius.
The necessity of faith should bring pressure on whoever wishes to
be in the Church to side with the latter and to obey him, and he
should believe that the others are outside the one Catholic and
Apostolic Church, and that they do not have the power of binding
and loosing, and that "sacrifices" and communion [with them] are
to be avoided.

Quod 'de necessitate salutis' sit esse cum domino Eugenio.

4 'Necessitas salutis' est esse in 'una ecclesia catholica', ut habet fides. Sed catholica sive universalis ecclesia per orbem diffusa habuit et habet dominum Eugenium pro pontifice summo. Qui igitur in unitate cum illa catholica ecclesia non est, sed in separata ab illa, scilicet in ecclesia Amedistarum, que exivit ab illa catholica ecclesia per orbem diffusa, extra ecclesiam veram esse necesse est.

5 Item 'necessitas salutis' est esse in 'apostolica ecclesia'. Sed dominum Eugenium legitima successione apostolicam sedem per mortem domini Martini vacantem intrasse consensu universe ecclesie eum recipiente manifestum est. Non potest igitur in ecclesia apostolica esse, qui cum domino apostolico non est. Nec potest quemquam id excusare, quod Basilee per quosdam presumptum est contra dominum apostolicum, contradicente apostolica ecclesia per orbem diffusa, que adhuc domino Eugenio communicat, cum in temeraria credulitate contra apostolicum ac in dubio quocunque nemo excusetur, presertim hoc casu, quando id, quod Basilee presumptum est, per maiorem partem episcoporum christianitatis et ecclesie per orbem diffuse non est receptum.

That it is "necessary for salvation" to side with Eugenius.

The faith holds that it is "necessary for salvation" to be "in one 4
Catholic Church." But the Catholic or universal Church spread
through the world accepted and accepts Eugenius as its supreme
pontiff. Whoever therefore is not united to that Catholic Church,
but is in a church separated from it, that is, in the church of the
Amedeists,[6] which has left behind the Church spread throughout
the world, necessarily is outside the true Church.

   Again, it is "necessary for salvation" to be in the "Apostolic 5
Church." But it is obvious that the lord Eugenius entered into the
Apostolic See by legitimate succession during the vacancy following the death of the lord Martin with the consent and acceptance
of the universal Church. No one, therefore, can be in the Apostolic Church who is not with the apostolic lord. Nor can it excuse
anyone that some persons at Basel have presumed to act against
the apostolic lord when the Church spread throughout the world
contradicted this act — the same Church which is still in communion with Eugenius. No one may be excused [being in opposition
to the apostolic lord] because of rash credulity and doubt of any
kind, especially in this case, when what was done presumptuously
at Basel has been accepted neither by the greater part of the bishops of Christendom nor by the Church spread throughout the
world.

: 6 :

‹Contra suspensionem animorum›

1 Dicis nonnullos eciam theologos asserere animorum suspensionem, que neutralitas dicitur, posse licite absque peccato continuari; ymo ais eos pro continuacione persuadere. De qua re satis mirandum esset, si illi ita re sicut nomine theologi forent; nam manifestum est dominos principes nostros sub spe conservacionis unitatis nacionis Germanice in quadam ordinacione convenisse ante electionem alicuius in Basilea, in qua 'propter dubium' translacionis concilii ad Ferrariam primo voluerunt sibi providere cum quadam suspensione animorum quo ad 'processus' hincinde, 2° noluerunt alicui legem dare in concernentibus forum penitencie.

2 Ista duo sunt ante novam electionem; videbantur eis licita 'propter dubium' translacionis, nam tunc iam annis multis in ecclesia viderunt concilium et papam, et hoc unitati ecclesie non disconvenit, ut sit concilium et papa unus. Quare 'propter dubium' in hiis, in quibus non videbant periculum scissure ecclesie Germanice, pape et concilio iudicabant obediendum, ut in foro penitencie, quousque deliberacio super veritate translacionis concilii sciretur. Habuit igitur illa conclusio duas partes, scilicet quandam neutralitatem in foro exteriori propter vitare scissuram nacionis considerata contrarietate pape et concilii, et in aliis penitencialibus quandam ultralitatem, ne non obediretur, ubi sine periculo scissure obediri posset.

Against Suspension of Allegiance

You say that some theologians too maintain that suspension of al- 1
legiance, which is called neutrality, may be licitly continued without sin; indeed, you say that they argue for continuance of this
suspension. This makes one wonder a bit whether they are theologians in fact as well as in name. It is obvious that our lord princes,
in hope of preserving the unity of the German nation, agreed before the election of anyone at Basel on a certain ordinance.[1] In this
ordinance, owing to doubts concerning the translation of the
council to Ferrara,[2] they first wanted to provide for themselves
some form of suspension of allegiance with respect to the trial
arising therefrom; and second, they did not wish to legislate for
anyone in things pertaining to the forum of penance [i.e. in matters of conscience].

These two considerations exist[ed] before the new election. 2
They seemed licit to them "because of doubt" concerning the
translation [of the council], for at that time they had seen a pope
and a council in the Church for many years, and it was not incon-
venient for the unity of the Church that there was council and a
single pope. Hence, because of their doubts about things which
did not seem to threaten a fracture in the German church, they
decided that [both] pope and council should be obeyed, as in the
forum of penance, until the deliberations about the validity of the
council's translation should be made known. This conclusion had
two parts, namely, a kind of neutrality in the exterior forum [i.e.
in law] in order to avoid splitting the nation in view of the conflict
between pope and council; and a kind of indecision in penitential
matters [i.e., in conscience], lest there be disobedience where one
could obey without danger of division.

3   Post hoc mutata est condicio,[1] quia Basilienses ad erectionem
capitis processerunt; et in hoc casu modo sumus. Et nunc est
questio, an unio predicta principum locum habere possit, et manifestum est, quod nullo modo fides unitatis catholice et apostolice
ecclesie ipsam amplius patitur. Nam si fide credere tenemur 'unam'
esse 'ecclesiam catholicam et apostolicam' et quod unius ecclesie
non possit esse nisi unum caput et unus pastor et unus summus
pontifex, manifestum est 'unam ecclesiam in duo dividi non posse
aut in plura', ut ait textus in c. *Scisma* circa finem 24. q. 1. Quapropter si apud dominum Eugenium est, apud alium Basilee erec-
tum esse non posse manifestum est. Hoc enim agit unitas eius, ut
apud unum et alium esse non possit; et ideo qui in una est ecclesia, que est in Eugenio, extra aliam esse necesse est, ut elegantissime et clarissime ostendit sanctus Cyprianus 24. q. 1 *Didicimus*
et in aliis locis multis.

4   Quapropter si 'ecclesia non est nulla', ut dicitur in allegato c. *Pudenda*, et fides nos docet eam esse 'et unam esse', et si non potest
divisa esse, quia 'unitas' eius 'divisionem non' patitur, ut in c. *Loquitur* 24. q. 1., manifestum est eam aut per gregem unitam pastori
Eugenio constitui aut per Basilienses suo capiti adherentes constitui, quoniam ecclesia non aliter constituitur quam per unionem
'gregis et pastoris'—7. q. 1 *Scire debes*—et non reperiuntur alii
quam hii duo pro summis pontificibus se gerentes. Necesse igitur
erit unam ecclesiam apud alterum tantum esse posse, et qui cum
neutro horum talium pontificum est, nequaquam 'in ecclesia esse',
ut ait sanctus Cyprianus in allegato c. *Scire debes*, dicens hunc 'non
esse in ecclesia, qui non est cum episcopo'; et idem sanctus ⟨Cy-
prianus⟩ 93. di. *Qui kathedram*. Unde credere, quod in utraque ec-

After this the situation changed, because those at Basel pro- 3
ceeded to set up an antipope; and now we are in our present state.
Now the question is whether the aforesaid compact among the
princes is applicable; and it is obvious that our faith in Catholic
unity and the Apostolic Church can in no way allow it. For if we
are obliged by faith to believe that there is "one catholic and apostolic Church,"[3] and that this faith cannot belong to one Church
unless there is one head, one shepherd and one supreme pontiff, it
is obvious that "the one Church cannot be divided into two or
more," as the text [of Gratian] says in the canon *Scisma* near the
end, in [Gratian] C. 24 q. 1 [c. 34]. For this reason it is obvious
that if the Church is with Eugenius, it cannot be with another
[pope] set up in Basel. Its unity requires that it cannot be with
both; and therefore whoever is in the one Church with Eugenius
must necessarily be outside the other, as Saint Cyprian elegantly
and clearly demonstrated in the canon *Didicimus* [in Gratian] C.
24 q. 1 [c. 32] and in many other places.

For this reason, if "the Church is not nothing," as is said in the 4
cited canon *Pudenda* [in Gratian, C. 24 q. 1 c. 33], and the faith
teaches us that it is "also one being," and if it cannot be divided,
because its "unity does not" suffer "division," as in the canon *Loquitur* [in Gratian] C. 24 q. 1 [c. 18], it is obvious that it is constituted
either by the flock united to the shepherd, Eugenius, or by those
at Basel who are adhering to their head, since the Church is constituted in no other way than by a union "of flock and shepherd"
([Gratian] c. *Scire debes* C. 7 q. 1 [c. 7]). No others can be found
conducting themselves as pope. It will therefore be necessary that
the one Church can be with only one of them, and whoever is
with neither one of these pontiffs cannot "be in the Church," as
Saint Cyprian says in the aforesaid canon *Scires debes*, where he
says "that man is not in the Church who is not with a bishop."
And Saint Cyprian says the same thing at [Gratian] D. 93 c. *Qui
cathedram* [c. 3]. Hence to believe that in both churches there is

clesia sit 'remissio peccatorum', prout in foro penitencie illa unio dominorum principum permisit quondam, ut prefertur, est contra fidem, que habet, quod in 'una ecclesia catholica et apostolica' sit 'remissio peccatorum'; 1. q. 1 *Extra catholicam*, 24. q. 1. *Quia ex sola*. Quare asserere, quod 'utrorumque sacrificiis' posset quis 'sociari', non est catholicum, ut 24. q. 1 *Scisma*, circa finem.

5   Dicis: Fatentur illi magistri ecclesiam unam 'esse, que est in apostolica radice fundata', ut dicit c. *Pudenda*; sed dubitant, an apud unum vel alium sit, quapropter in dubio videtur ultralitas excusari. Respondeo: Si dicunt se dubitare, ubi sit, an apud Eugenium vel alium, queratur, an illi theologi se credant in ecclesia esse. Si sic, quia ecclesia una est, erunt necessario in unitate cum uno aut cum alio, cum probatum sit ecclesiam sine altero esse non posse; et pariformiter probatum est utrimque esse non posse, et iterum ut prius. Patet igitur clarissime eo ipso, quod se dicunt in ecclesia esse, non posse ultralitatem defendere.

6   Dicis: Fatentur illi theologi ultralitatem non debere defendi, quia esset nutrire scisma; sed dicunt a communione utriusque suspensionem 'propter dubium' fieri debere, quousque 'dubium' declaretur, et ita ad neutralitatem pergunt. Respondeo hoc non esse catholicum; nam eo ipso, quod fatentur hoc dubium, non possunt se ab obediencia illius subtrahere, in cuius obediencia fuerunt, cum obediencia quo ad unum Romanum pontificem sit 'de necessitate salutis', ut post concordantes omnes veteres sanctos in Extrava. *Unam sanctam* determinatum extitit, et in 'dubio' non est obediencia quovismodo subtrahenda, ut omnes dicunt doctores —

"remission of sins," as that compact of the princes formerly allowed in the penitential forum [i.e. in the confessional or in conscience], as has been said, is against the faith, which holds that in "the one, catholic and apostolic Church" there is the "remission of sins" ([Gratian] C. 1 q. 1 c. *Extra catholicam* [c. 71], c. *Quia ex sola* [C. 24 q. 1 c. 22]). Hence asserting that someone can "associate with the sacrifices of either one" is not catholic, as in the canon *Scisma* [in Gratian] C. 24 q. 1 [c. 34], near the end.

You say: those masters [of theology] confess that there is one 5 Church, "which is founded on the apostolic root," as it says in the canon *Pudenda* [Gratian, C. 24 q. 1 c. 33]; but they are in doubt whether it is with the one or the other, and on this account indecision seems to be excused by doubt. I reply: if they say they are in doubt where the Church is, with Eugenius or with the other, it may be asked whether these theologians believe themselves to be in the Church. If so, since the Church is one, they are of necessity in union with one or the other, since it is proven that the Church cannot exist without one or the other, and likewise it is proven that it cannot exist with both; see the texts above. It is perfectly obvious from this, therefore, that if they claim they are in the Church, they cannot defend indecision.

You say: these theologians confess that indecision should not be 6 defended, since it would feed schism; but they say that a suspension of communion with both [obediences] ought to be made "because of doubt" until the "doubt" is resolved, and so they proceed to neutrality. I reply that this is not catholic, for the very act of confessing their doubt does not justify their withdrawal from the obedience of the church to which they belonged, since obedience as regards a single Roman pontiff is "necessary for salvation," as was decreed in the constitution[4] *Unam sanctam* [Extrav. commun. 1.8.1], following the harmonious opinion of all the old saints. And "doubt" does not permit withdrawal from obedience in any way, as all the doctors say ([Gratian] D. 17 ⁋ *Hinc etiam* [p.c. 6], C. 8 q. 4

17. di. ⦅ *Hinc eciam*, viii q. iiii *Nonne*. Et hoc clarissimum est, nam si obediencia est necessitatis, in dubio tucius est eligendum. Unde notabilissime ait textus 24. q. 1. *Scisma*, circa medium, de quibusdam, qui 'aut ignorancia aut' ex 'simplicitate se a communione' Romani pontificis subtraxerunt, dicens 'id ipsum magis esse, propter quod scismatici sunt' illi. Unde ille textus coniuncta glo. concludit apertissime illos theologos se 'separantes ab' obediencia, aut propter 'simplicitatem' intellectus aut ignoranciam, 'magis scismaticos esse quam illi, qui subtilitate' racionum convincti sunt per adhesionem non veri capitis errare.

7   Confortare igitur illos theologos, ut non 'evomantur', si 'tepidi' fuerint! Securi enim sunt, si tenuerint illam obedienciam, quam semel in universa catholica ecclesia viderunt et tenuerunt, et si 'eam partem detestantur', quam 'ecclesiam' per orbem diffusam in 'apostolicis sedibus roboratam' vident detestari, quos 'temere' credulitatis 'opinio contra apostolicam sedem divisit' a successore Petri, ut hic probatur in c. *Scisma* et c. *Pudenda* per Augustinum ibidem allegatum. Quem Cyprianus sanctissimus, si viveret, antechristianum vocaret in c. *Didicimus* allegato.

c. *Nonne.* [c. 1]). And this is utterly clear, for if obedience is a matter of necessity, it is safer to choose when in a state of doubt. Hence the text of [Gratian] C. 24 q. 1 c. *Scisma* [c. 34] notably says, near the middle [of the canon], of certain persons who either "from ignorance or simple-mindedness" withdrew "themselves from communion" with the Roman pontiff, that "[their disobedience] is all the greater, because they are schismatics." Hence that text, with its gloss,[5] deduces very clearly that those theologians who "separate themselves from" obedience, either from "simple-mindedness" or from ignorance, "are more schismatic than those who by subtlety" of reasoning have been proven to have erred by adhering to one who was not the true head.

Let those theologians take courage, lest they be "vomited out" if   7
they remain "lukewarm."[6] They are secure if they cling to that obedience which once they recognized and clung to in the universal Catholic Church, and if they "detest that party" which they see is detested by "the Church" spread throughout the world and "corroborated by the Apostolic See," if they detest those whom a "rash" and credulous "opinion against the Apostolic See has divided" from Peter's successor, as is proven in the canons *Scisma* and *Pudenda* [in Gratian, C. 24 q. 1 cc. 34 and 33] by Augustine, who is cited in those places. If the most holy Cyprian lived now, he would call him an Antichrist, as in the aforesaid canon *Didicimus* [in Gratian C. 24 q. 1 c. 33].

Dialogus concludens Amedistarum errorem
ex gestis et doctrina concilii Basiliensis

1 *Discipulus.* Oportune paternitas tua nunc advenit, ut me antiquum discipulum informet de certis, que michi adversari videntur in vobis.

Magister. Que sunt illa, diu amate discipule?

Discipulus. Recordor, quando post disputationem in sacro Basiliensi concilio cum Bohemis habitam ad nos rediistis, quomodo magna nobis de illius synodi Basiliensis sanctitate retulistis. Nunc autem, postquam de synodo Florentina, ubi dicitis Grecos unitos Romane ecclesie, rediistis, non cessatis enarrare, quanta fuerit sanctimonia illius concilii et quomodo numero episcoporum aliquando Basilee incorporatorum fuit ibi maior numerus quam aliorum, qui advenerant aut qui Basilee remanserant. Primum rogo, ut dicat reverentia tua, quomodo est hoc actum, quod patres concilii Basiliensis, qui se Florentiam transtulerunt, contra synodum Basiliensem dampnationis sententiam dederunt. Se ipsos igitur dampnasse videntur.

Magister. Sacra synodus Florentina non dampnavit sacram Basiliensem synodum, sed quosdam, qui adversantur synodo Basiliensi et veritati catholice.

2 *Discipulus.* Tu forte vis dicere, quod illi, qui Basilee remanserunt, sint illi, qui sunt dampnati, et ex eo, quia recesserunt a synodo Basiliensi? Hoc doce, nam non videtur hoc intelligibile.

A Dialogue against the Amedeists

*A dialogue deducing the error of the Amedeists
from the acts and teaching of the Council of Basel*

Disciple. Your Paternity comes now at an opportune time to instruct me, an old disciple, about certain things which seem to me contradictory in you.

Master. What are these things, long-beloved disciple?

Disciple. I remember when, after a disputation held with the Bohemians at the sacred Council of Basel, you returned to us and informed us of the great sanctity of that synod at Basel. Now, however, after you returned from the synod at Florence, where you say the Greeks were united to the Roman church, you have not ceased to tell us how sacred that council was and how a greater number was there than the number of the bishops formerly incorporated at Basel, a number greater than the number of bishops who have gone to or remained at Basel. I ask first that Your Reverence would say how this has happened, that the fathers of the Council of Basel, who transferred themselves to Florence, issued a sentence of condemnation against the synod at Basel.[1] They seem in this way to have condemned themselves.

Master. The holy synod of Florence did not condemn the holy synod at Basel but certain persons who opposed the synod at Basel and Catholic truth.[2]

Disciple. Perhaps you wish to say that those who remained at Basel are those who have been condemned, and that was because they departed from the synod at Basel? Explain this, for it does not seem intelligible.

Magister. Recessus a veritate dampnat, locus non dampnat aut sanctificat. Quare, etsi aliqui videantur Basilee remansisse, poterant nichillominus a veritate recessisse.

Discipulus. Igitur synodus, que fuit sancta, potest desinere esse sancta?

Magister. Non est synodus sancta, nisi sit in veritate, a qua dum cadit, sancta esse desinit, et quia nomine synodi venit sanctorum congregatio, hinc desinit esse synodus, quando recedit a veritate.

3 *Discipulus.* Si synodus a veritate recedit, ipsam ab ea veritate declarata et recepta per ecclesiam recedere neccesse est. Dic igitur, quomodo iudicaverunt patres synodi Florentine synodum Basiliensem aliquando sanctam et nunc recessisse a veritate?

Magister. Visum est patribus Florentini concilii, quod synodus Basiliensis, que congregata fuit rite et legittime, recte sentiisset et sancte, quando non dedit pravum intellectum decretis Constantiensis concilii; sed quando illis dedit alium intellectum quam ipsa Constantiensis synodus et tota catholica ecclesia cum capite et membris, tunc in errorem incidit et ex erroneo intellectu presumpsit facere multa, que iuste dampnata fuerunt Florentie.

4 *Discipulus.* Si ita foret, quod sacra Basiliensis synodus aliquando habuisset sanum intellectum decretorum concilii Constantiensis cum tota ecclesia catholica et postea a suo proprio intellectu recessissent aliqui, illi sine dubio iuste dampnati fuissent. Nam dissentientes non faciunt concilium. Concilium enim sibi ipsi non contradicit, ut dixit ipsa synodus Basiliensis in responsione, que incipit *Cogitanti.* Sed, queso, declara ista!

Magister. Sacra Constantiensis synodus in sessione quarta, antequam Gregorius et eum pro papa habentes aut Benedictus

Master. Withdrawal from the truth condemns a man; a place does not condemn or sanctify. Hence, even if some men seem to have remained at Basel, nevertheless, they could have departed from the truth.

Disciple. Therefore a synod which was holy can cease to be holy?

Master. It is not a holy synod unless it adheres to the truth; when it falls away from truth, it ceases to be holy. Since the congregation of the saints arrives under the name of a synod, it ceases to be a synod, therefore, when it departs from the truth.

Disciple. If the synod departed from the truth, it has necessarily 3 departed from the truth as declared and accepted by the Church. Explain then how the fathers of the Florentine synod made the judgment that the synod at Basel was once holy and now has departed from the truth.

Master. It seemed to the fathers of the Florentine council that the synod at Basel, which was gathered with due formality and legitimately, held just and holy opinions when it did not give a depraved interpretation to the decrees of the Council of Constance; but, when it gave them another interpretation than did the synod at Constance itself and the entire Catholic Church, head and members, it then fell into error and on the basis of its erroneous interpretation presumed to do many things which were with justice condemned at Florence.

Disciple. If it were so that the holy synod at Basel once had a 4 sound interpretation of the decrees of the Council of Constance with the whole Catholic Church, but afterwards some of them departed from its proper interpretation, doubtless they were condemned justly. For dissidents do not constitute a council; a council does not contradict itself, as that synod at Basel said in the responsory letter which begins *Cogitanti*.³ But I beg you to explain this!

Master. The holy synod at Constance in the fourth session, before Gregory XII and those who regarded him as pope or Benedict

et sibi obedientes concilium Constantie recognoscerent, anno 1415 sexta aprilis presente domino Sigismundo Romanorum rege sic decrevit:

In nomine sancte et individue trinitatis, patris et filii et spiritus sancti. Amen. Hec sancta synodus Constantiensis generale concilium faciens pro exstirpatione presentis scismatis et unione et reformatione ecclesie dei in capite et membris fienda ad laudem omnipotentis dei in spiritu sancto legittime congregata ad consequendum facilius, securius, uberius et liberius unionem ac reformationem ecclesie dei ordinat, diffinit, statuit et declarat, ut sequitur. Et primo, quod ipsa in spiritu sancto legittime congregata generale concilium faciens, ecclesiam catholicam militantem representans, potestatem habet immediate a Christo, cui quilibet, cuiuscumque status vel dignitatis, etiam si papalis existat, obedire tenetur in hiis, que pertinent ad fidem et extirpationem dicti scismatis et ad generalem reformationem ecclesie dei in capite et membris. Item declarat, quod quicumque, cuiuscumque status vel dignitatis, etiam si papalis existat, qui mandatis, statutis seu ordinationibus et preceptis huius sacre synodi et cuiuscumque alterius concilii generalis legittime congregati super premissis seu ad ea pertinentibus factis vel faciendis obedire contumaciter contempserit, nisi resipuerit, condigne penitentie subiciatur et debite puniatur, etiam ad alia iuris subsidia, si opus fuerit, recurrendo.

Ista est Constantiensis concilii ordinatio, quam aliquando Basiliense concilium sane intellexit, a quo intellectu aliqui recesserunt, qui ecclesiam turbant.

XIII and those obeying him recognized the Council of Constance, on April 6, 1415, with the lord Sigismund king of the Romans present, decreed this:[4]

In the name of the Holy and Undivided Trinity, Father, Son and Holy Spirit. Amen. This holy synod at Constance, making up a general council for the extirpation of the present schism, and to promote union and reform of the Church in head and members, to the praise of almighty God, legitimately gathered in the Holy Spirit to pursue more easily, securely, abundantly and freely the union and reform of the Church of God, ordains, defines, decrees and declares as follows. And first, that it is legitimately gathered in the Holy Spirit, making up a general council representing the Catholic Church Militant; that it has power immediately from Christ, which anyone of whatever estate or dignity, even the papal one, is bound to obey in those things which pertain to the faith, extirpation of the present schism and the general reform of the Church of God in head and members. Likewise, it declares that anyone of any estate or dignity, even a pope, who contumaciously spurns obeying any mandates, statutes, ordinances and precepts of this holy synod, or those of any other general council legitimately gathered, that it makes or shall make about the aforesaid matters or pertaining to them, unless he repents, is subject to a fitting penance and is to be punished rightly, even having recourse to other legal measures, if that is needed.

This is the ordinance of the Council of Constance, which the Council of Basel once interpreted rightly, and from which correct interpretation some who now disturb the Church departed.

5 *Discipulus.* Antequam progrediaris, queso, dubium ex dictis tuis exortum evacua. Est hocne ita, quod una obedientia, scilicet Iohannis xxiii nuncupati, hec decrevit?

Magister. Dico quod sic; ymmo plus dico, quod ipsum tunc concilium Constantiense de obedientia Iohannis expresse consensit ad eundem finem, ad quem fecit illa decreta predicta, scilicet propter unionem consequendam, quod per alias obedientias tunc primo censeretur concilium et teneretur pro tali, quando auctoritate Gregorii et consentiente ecclesia, que erat sub Benedicto, de novo convocaretur et indiceretur. Ita in gestis eiusdem synodi habes et in concordatis cum rege Aragonum.

6 *Discipulus.* Quare ergo dixit synodus se representare ecclesiam catholicam?

Magister. Quamvis tunc Constantie non essent alie obedientie, tamen, quia obedientia Iohannis non venit Constantiam, ut sola concilium faceret, sed ut omnes fideles concurrerent, usa est synodus titulo concilii congregandi, nondum plene congregati.

7 *Discipulus.* Procede nunc et doce, quem sensum illorum decretorum habuit ecclesia catholica et synodus Basiliensis a principio.

Magister. Ecclesia catholica et ipsa Basiliensis synodus non intellexerunt illa decreta aliter quam ratio constitutionis, que apponitur, ipsa intelligi debere exprimit, scilicet quod ad finem illum facilius consequendi unionem pro tunc synodus talia pro medio statuere potuit, non intendens nisi consequi unionem et quod ad illum finem illis decretis uti voluit. Hoc certe etiam ante plenam congregationem licuit. Postquam enim ad hoc synodus convenit, ut unionem faceret, qua in ecclesia nichil preferri potest, omnia, que ad illum finem consequendum

Disciple. Before you proceed, please resolve a doubt arising from   5
your words. Is it not true that [only] one obedience, namely the
obedience of the one called John XXIII, decreed this?

Master. I say yes; indeed, I would say further that the Council of
Constance, then made up of John's obedience, expressly consented to the same purpose for which it made that aforesaid decree, namely, achieving unity, and that it was considered a council and held as such by the other obediences for the first time
when by the authority of Gregory and with the consent of the
church subject to Benedict it was convoked and proclaimed
anew. Thus you have it in the records of the same synod and in
the concordats with the king of Aragon.[5]

Disciple. Why then did the synod say it represented the Catholic   6
Church [before being proclaimed anew]?

Master. Although the other obediences were not yet at Constance,
nevertheless, because John's obedience did not come to Constance so that it alone might constitute a council but so that all
the faithful would gather [there], the synod used the title of the
council that was to be gathered, not of the one that was not as
yet fully gathered.

Disciple. Proceed now, and explain what understanding the Catho-   7
lic Church and the synod at Basel had of the decrees of Constance from the beginning.

Master. The Catholic Church and that synod at Basel did not
understand those decrees otherwise than as a justification for
constituting a council that itself set out how it should be understood; namely, that for that specific time, for the specific purpose of pursuing union more easily, the synod could decree
such things as means, not intending anything except achieving
unity, and that it wanted to use those decrees for that purpose.
Certainly this was permissible even before a full congregation
had met. After the synod had met for the purpose of achieving
unity, than which nothing is more important in the Church, all

servire poterant, sanctissima erant, nec propterea intendebat illa synodus ritum sacrorum conciliorum immutare vel supremam apostolice sedis potestatem a Christo datam, usque ad illa tempora per catholicam ecclesiam et sanctos doctores bene intellectam et observatam, diminuere aut intellectum ecclesie et doctorum de illa dampnare.

8 *Discipulus.* Clarum est hoc, quod dicis, quod intelligentia capi debet ex ratione dicendi et quod omnia intelligere debemus in eo sensu, in quo ecclesiam et doctores concurrere conspicimus. Maxime non est opinandum synodum Constantiensem voluisse in aliquo derogare privilegiis apostolice sedis. Nam dicit Basiliensis synodus in responsione *Cogitanti,* quod 'ipsa sentit firmiter, quod, qui privilegio ecclesie Romane detrahit, in heresim incidit'. Privilegium enim eius a deo est et non ab homine. Edissere, queso, quomodo aliqui, qui Basilee remanserunt, a sano intellectu recesserunt!

9 *Magister.* Doctrina et practica illorum ostendit, quomodo ipsi intelligunt congregationem qualemcumque, etiam si desit legatus apostolicus, dummodo ab initio concurrebat in congregando auctoritas pape, representare ecclesiam, et sive consensus ecclesie concurrat in dictandis sive non, quod adhuc id, quod pauci illi fecerint, universalis synodi auctoritatem habeat. Nam dicunt: ad esse concilii requiritur, quod legittime sit congregatum, scilicet auctoritate Romani pontificis; quo facto, qui conveniunt, synodum faciunt. Si synodum faciunt universalem, igitur secundum decretum concilii Constantiensis a Christo immediate habent potestatem et representant universalem ecclesiam. Quare omnis christianus tenetur tali

things which served to achieve that end were most holy. Nor on this account did that synod intend to change the usage of the holy councils or to reduce the supreme power given the Apostolic See by Christ, which had been well understood and observed up to that time by the Catholic Church and the holy doctors, or to condemn the [previous] interpretation of the Church and the doctors concerning that power.

Disciple. What you have said is clear: an understanding of a decree 8 ought to be derived from the reason for its being pronounced, and we ought to interpret everything in the sense which enjoys the concurrence of the Church and its doctors. Especially one must not opine that the synod at Constance wished to derogate in any degree from the privileges of the Apostolic See. For the synod at Basel says in the responsory letter *Cogitanti* that "it firmly believes that whoever detracts from the privilege of the Roman church falls into heresy."[6] For its privilege is from God and not from men. Please discuss how those who remain at Basel have departed from sound understanding [of this principle].

Master. Their doctrine and practice show their understanding that 9 any sort of meeting represents the Church, even if the apostolic legate is absent, so long as the authority of the pope at the outset had agreed to its meeting and whether or not the consent of the Church concurs in its dictates; they understand such a meeting to have the authority of a universal synod to do what those few [gathered at Basel] are still doing. For they say that the existence of a council requires that it be gathered legitimately, that is, by the authority of the Roman pontiff; once that has been done, those who meet constitute a synod. If they constitute a universal synod, then according to the decree of the Council of Constance they have power immediately from Christ and represent the universal Church. Hence every Christian is bound to obey such a council, and whoever does not

concilio obedire, et qui non obedit, dei ordinationi resistit et
spiritui sancto seu potestati Christi, qua patres solum in
synodis utuntur. Sicut igitur obediendum est Christo et eius
mandatis, quando scimus illa Christi esse, sive illa nobis per
paucos aut multos propalentur, sic synodo sive paucorum sive
multorum episcoporum, postquam constat ex decreto concilii
Constantiensis omnem universalem synodum a Christo immediate potestatem habere, cui omnes fideles obedire tenentur.

10   *Discipulus.* Coloratus videtur iste intellectus. Potestne sanus esse?
     Magister. Nequaquam. Nam ex gestis sacri concilii Calcedonensis
     nos scimus concilium Ephesinum secundum per Leonem
     papam rite congregatum et patres Ephesum convenisse et
     finaliter non consentientibus apostolicis legatis erroneam
     sententiam in catholica fide dictasse. Ita quidem de aliis etiam
     legitur rite congregatis conciliis ipsa finaliter errasse. Non est
     igitur verum, quod ad hoc, quod concilium represente
     universalem ecclesiam et potestatem a Christo immediate
     habeat, solum sufficiat, quod sit recte indictum; sed requiritur,
     quod et vera sit ibi representatio catholice ecclesie, si debet
     censeri concilium catholice ecclesie, ac quod rite procedat. Ita
     quidem vides, quomodo in idem coincidunt concilium et
     representatio, ut ibi affirmemus verum concilium, ubi videmus
     veram representationem, presumendo de processu, si
     concorditer concluditur; et ibi dicamus non esse concilium, ubi
     deficit vera representatio.

     Et hinc iste intellectus fantasticus est, quod locus aliquis det
     tribus aut centum personis de una natione vel regione aut
     diversis ad ipsum confluentibus potestatem representativam,
     quam extra illum locum, si convenirent, non haberent. Et hic
     est dampnatorum intellectus. Vera autem Basiliensis synodus

obey resists God's ordinances and the Holy Spirit or the power of Christ, of which only fathers in synods make use. Therefore, just as Christ and His commands must be obeyed when we know them to be Christ's, whether they are proclaimed by a few or by many men, so one must obey a synod, whether it contain few bishops or many, since it is evident from the decree of the Council of Constance that every universal synod has power immediately from Christ, which all the faithful are bound to obey.

Disciple. This interpretation seems colorable. Can it be sound?   10

Master. By no means. For we know from the records of the Council of Chalcedon that the Second Council of Ephesus was gathered with the due formalities by Pope Leo and the fathers met at Ephesus and, without the consent of the apostolic legates, issued an erroneous sentence concerning the Catholic faith.[7] So, we read, other councils too were convoked with the due formalities but erred in the end. It is therefore untrue that the fact of its being rightly proclaimed is alone sufficient for a council to represent the universal Church and to have power immediately from Christ. It is also required that there should be present a true representation of the Catholic Church, if it is to be considered a council of the Catholic Church, and that it should proceed with due formalities. So you can see how a council and its representation come down to the same thing, so that where we see true representation, there we may affirm the existence of a council, presuming this from the proceedings, if they are concluded in harmony; and where representation is defective, there we say there is no council.

And hence that interpretation is deluded which says that some place could give three or a hundred persons, gathering there from one nation or region or several, a representative power they would not have were they to meet outside that place. And this is the interpretation of those who have been

intellexit synodum debere censeri representare ecclesiam, quando in loco et tempore instituto tales persone concurrunt, que representant ecclesiam in capite et membris, ita quod ille persone ibi sint, quibus ecclesia, quam ibi debet synodus representare, obedire teneatur, etiam si in eo loco non essent.

Sic dicitur: de neccessitate concilii provincialis est, ut sit metropolitanus, cui alias etiam provincia subiecta est, cum membris provincie. Membra autem provincie, sicut extra locum concilii non haberent potestatem in provinciam, ita si quid de provincia concernentibus decerneret provincialium congregatio non consentiente metropolitano, non obligaret provinciam. Sic de generali concilio quoad papam pariformiter. Quare representatio debet mensurari ex potestate eorum, qui conveniunt, quam secum dignitas ad synodum adducit. Non enim aliud synodus est quam conventio potestatem regitivam habentium, ut communi consilio et consensu casibus occurrentibus in edificationem ecclesie consulatur. Ita dicit sanctus Cyprianus papa de lapsis ad Antoninum scribens: 'De eo autem, quod statuendum esset circa causam lapsorum, distuli, ut, cum quies et tranquillitas data esset et episcopos in unum indulgentia divina convenire permitteret, tunc communicato et ‹de›liberato[1] de omnium collatione consilio statuerem, quid fieri oporteret. Si quis autem ante concilium nostrum et ante sententiam de omnium consilio statutam temere lapsis communicare voluisset, ipse a communione abstineat'. Et habetur 1 d. *De eo*. Simile xx d. *De quibus*.

condemned. The true synod at Basel, however, understood that a synod should be considered to represent the Church when such persons as represent the Church in head and members assemble at a place and time, such that those persons are present whom the Church, which the synod ought to represent there, is bound to obey, even if they are not in that place.

That is why it is said to be necessary for a provincial council that the metropolitan [or archbishop] be present, to whom the province [or archbishopric] is also subject at other times, along with members of the province. The members of the province, however, just as they would have no power in the province outside the place of the council, so, if they decided anything regarding provincial matters without the consent of the metropolitan, it would not bind the province. This is so, likewise, of the pope in relation to a general council. Hence representation ought to be measured from the power of those who gather, the power which their rank brings with it to the council. For a synod is nothing else than a gathering of those who have the power to rule, so that there is consultation with common counsel and consent in building up the Church with respect to the cases that are brought before it. Thus Saint Cyprian says, writing to Antonius concerning the lapsed: "Concerning what must be decided about the case of the lapsed, I am putting it off, so that, when one is given quiet and tranquility and one may be permitted by divine indulgence to gather bishops together, I may decide at that time, after informing and collating the considered counsel of them all, what ought to be done. If, however, anyone would wish rashly to communicate with the lapsed before our council and before sentence has been passed with everyone's counsel, let him abstain from communion." And this is found in [Gratian] D. 50 c. *De eo* [c. 35]; similarly, in [idem] D. 20 c. *De quibus* [c. 3].

11   *Discipulus.* Rationabiliter me instruis, ita ut dissentire nequeam. Nam scio hoc diffinitum in iure, quomodo synodus provincialis non est integra, si metropolita, qui caput eius est, deest; ita etiam a fortiori de generali concilio quoad papam arguit textus synodi (*Bene quidem* 96 d.). Et ob hoc dicitur concilium nullum (17 d. *Regula*), ubi legatio apostolice sedis non interfuit. Et ita arguit textus sextam synodum recipiendam, quia 'octo concilia professione Romani pontificis sunt roborata' (16 d. *Sextam*). Ita senserunt omnes antiqui, quod robur conciliorum decreta non haberent, si summi pontificis pro tempore, qui habet super ecclesiam pastoralem potestatem, non interveniret auctoritas, quoniam, sicut in ipso solum est plenitudo potestatis et universalis super universalem ecclesiam, in aliis autem vocatis in partem sollicitudinis secundum particularem sollicitudinem restricta potestas, ita non potest constitutio universalis, universalem ecclesiam universaliter et generaliter potestative obligans, ab alia potestate quam universali exoriri. Hec me aliquando docuisti, et mente teneo, per hoc tamen non volebas excludere potestatem ab aliis orbis episcopis, quin suis necessitatibus in negligentia primi pontificis consulere possint.

In quo quidem casu in pontificem Romanum aut Romanam ecclesiam nichil eos posse manifestum est, quoniam nec quidquam potestatis haberent in quemcumque metropolitam aut suam provinciam universi alii episcopi per se congregati, quibus auctoritas supremi iudicis deesset, scilicet pontificis maximi. Unde potentia illorum mensuraretur secundum consensum, sicuti videmus multa particularia concilia, que nullam habebant ligandi potestatem in ecclesia universali, per

Disciple. You instruct me in a rational fashion so that I am not   II
able to disagree. I know that this is defined in [canon] law, that
a provincial synod is not whole if the metropolitan, who is its
head, is absent; so too the text of a synod in the canon *Bene
quidem* [in Gratian] D. 96 [c. 1] argues the same thing *a fortiori*
of the general council in relationship to the pope. For this reason [Gratian, in] D. 17 c. *Regula* [c. 2], says that there is no
council when a representative of the Apostolic See is not present. And thus the text of [idem] D. 16 c. *Sexta* [c. 8–9] argues
that the sixth synod must be accepted because "eight councils
were ratified by declaration of the Roman pontiff." So all the
ancients thought that the decrees of the councils do not have
force if the authority of the reigning Roman pontiff, who has
pastoral power over the Church, is not in evidence, since, just as
in him alone is plenitude of universal power over the universal
Church, while in the others summoned there is a restricted
power towards part of a concern according to that particular
concern; so there cannot be a universal institution that has the
power to oblige the universal Church universally and generally
which arises from any power other than the universal one. You
taught me these things at one point and I remember them. Yet
you used not to wish on this account to exclude the other bishops of the world from power, in such a way that they might not
consult their own needs in cases where the first pontiff might
be negligent.

In such a case it is obvious that they could do nothing
against the Roman pontiff or the Roman church, since all the
other bishops, gathering by themselves, could not have any
power over any metropolitan or his province since they lacked
the authority of the supreme judge, that is, the first pontiff.
Hence their power should be measured according to consent,
just as we see many particular councils, which have no power of
binding over the universal Church, can extend their force

consensum ecclesie universalis robur suum extendisse
secundum magnitudinem consensus. Et hec videtur solida et
pacifica doctrina, quam putabam synodum Basiliensem semper
tenuisse. Rogo, instruas, quando habuit et quomodo deseruit
hanc intelligentiam.

12 *Magister.* Illam intelligentiam Basiliensis synodus habuit in prima
sessione, quando dixit:

> Cum enim finis instaret septennii, quod est tempus ex prein-
> serto decreto concilii Constantiensis celebrationi huius
> concilii prefinitum, felicis recordationis Martinus papa quin-
> tus, sancte Romane et universalis ecclesie tunc presidens
> pontifex, volens celebrationem generalis concilii fieri iuxta
> prememoratum decretum, cui tamen propter etatem decrepi-
> tam et multiplices sui corporis morbos in propria persona
> non poterat presidere, dictum dominum Iulianum, sancte
> Romane ecclesie sancti Angeli dyaconum cardinalem, de fra-
> trum suorum consilio ad celebrandum ipsum concilium et
> eidem vice et loco summi pontificis presidendi suum ac sedis
> apostolice destinavit legatum per suas apostolicas litteras te-
> noris subsequentis.

> Et deinde ponitur bulla potestatis, in qua datur facultas
> eidem domino legato presidendi eidem concilio et omnia cum
> consilio concilii determinandi, legato potestate coherciva
> tantum observata, et hoc solum gratum et ratum habere se velle
> dicit, quod per legatum cum consilio concilii sic fuerit factum.
> Approbat hoc sanctissimus dominus noster dominus Eugenius
> papa, et concludit synodus: 'Cum igitur tempus sit effluxum
> septennii et sacrosancte sedis apostolice non desit auctoritas',

through the consent of the universal Church in accordance with the magnitude of that consent. And this seems to be solid and peaceful doctrine, which I used to think the synod at Basel always held. Please explain to me when and how it abandoned this interpretation.

Master. The synod at Basel had that interpretation in the first session, when it said,[8]   12

Since the end of the seven-year period was impending, which was the predefined time set forth in the decree of the Council of Constance[9] for the celebration of this council, Pope Martin V of blessed memory, then the pontiff presiding over the holy Roman and universal Church, wishing the celebration of the general council to be carried out according to the aforementioned decree, nevertheless, since he could not preside in his own person because of advanced age and the multiple ailments of his body, designated, with the counsel of his brothers, the said lord Giuliano, cardinal deacon of the holy Roman church of the title of Sant' Angelo, as his legate and that of the Apostolic See to celebrate that council and to preside with the same power and in the place of the supreme pontiff through his apostolic letters of the following import.

And then the bull of empowerment was put out, in which the power was given the same lord legate of presiding over the same council and of determining all things with the advice of the council, coercive power being reserved only to the legate, and the pope said that he would regard as acceptable and approved only what was done by the legate with the advice of the council. Our most holy lord Pope Eugenius approved this, and the synod concludes,[10] "Since, therefore, the period of seven years has elapsed and the authority of the Apostolic See is not absent," it is concluded therefrom that "the Council of Basel

hinc concluditur 'concilium Basiliense stabilitum'. Ecce fundamentum stabilimenti concilii Basiliensis, ubi vides, quomodo cepit arguere synodus sic, quia Martinus papa, qui presedit universali ecclesie, voluit quod synodus celebraretur et per se non potuit, misit legatum qui celebraret concilium; approbavit dominus noster Eugenius ista, et quia adest legatus, qui presidere debet concilio, et sic adest auctoritas apostolice sedis et tempus statutum est effluxum et locus Basiliensis est electus, ideo est Basilee concilium.

Idem etiam probatur in omnibus bullis presidentum sanctissimi domini nostri Eugenii, qui, licet plus restringeret potestatem presidentum, quia voluit, quod approbante concilio decernerent, tamen non aliud se gratum habiturum promittit quam ea, que sic per presidentes statuantur. Et has bullas sacra synodus Basiliensis admisit et inseruit gestis et nunquam quoad illam partem ratihabitionis quidquam contradixit, admittens, sicuti hactenus in concilio Senensi et aliis omnibus usque ad ista tempora observatum fuit, vigorem et auctoritatem decreti universalis synodi ‹subesse›[2] universali presidenti ecclesie ac quod ipse pontifex non obligaretur ad observantiam alicuius decreti, cuius constitutio ex auctoritate apostolica per consensum ipsum representantis robur non recepisset; immo admisit synodus ipsa, ut ex iam dictis audisti, quod celebratio concilii fieret per legatum, ita quod non censeretur synodale decretum, quod auctoritate apostolica per ipsum non promulgaretur, sed solum illud, quod de consilio concilii aut consensu decerneretur per apostolicum legatum, admisit synodale decretum censendum.

Ex hiis patet presentiam legati apostolici necessariam in celebratione concilii; qui quidem legatus ita presidet concilio,

was established." Behold the basis for the establishment of the Council of Basel, where you see how the synod began by affirming this: since Pope Martin, who presided over the universal Church, wished that the synod should be celebrated but could not preside himself, he sent a legate who would celebrate the council; our lord Eugenius approved these things; and because the legate is present who should preside over the council, and thus the authority of the Apostolic See is present, and the allotted time has expired and the site at Basel has been chosen, therefore, the council is [established] at Basel.

The same even is proved in all the bulls of the presidents appointed by our most holy lord Eugenius.[11] Although he restricted the power of the presidents more, because he wished that they should make decisions with the approval of the council, nevertheless, he promised that he would regard as acceptable only what was decreed in this way through the presidents. And the holy synod at Basel admitted these bulls, inserted them into their acts,[12] and never contradicted anything with respect to that part of their ratification, admitting, as once was observed at the Council of Siena and in all other councils up to that time, that the force and authority of the decree of a universal synod [is subject to] the universal president of the Church and that the pontiff himself is not obliged to observe any decree whose establishment had not received its force from apostolic authority by the consent of the one representing it; indeed, that very synod admitted, as you heard from what has already been said, that the celebration of the council was accomplished by the legate, so that a decree not promulgated by him with apostolic authority is not regarded as synodal; but it admitted that only a decree decided by the apostolic legate with the counsel or consent of the council must be considered a synodal decree.

From this it follows that the presence of the legate of the Apostolic See is necessary for the celebration of a council; thus

sicut papa universali ecclesie. Hanc necessitatem pape aut ipsum representantis admisit universalis synodus Basiliensis in 19ª sessione, quando Greci ycumenicam sive universalem synodum describentes dixerunt, quod in illa synodo papa et patriarche sint per se vel suos procuratores, similiter alii prelati sint ibi vere vel representative.

Ex hoc habes, quomodo representatio debet esse vera in concilio universali, et ob hoc, quando dieta fuit Maguntie, Basilee residentes, audientes Grecorum reductionem in proximo esse, bullam quandam nomine concilii Basiliensis scripserunt ad principes electores, ut finem darent deliberationi, quia si contingeret Grecos reduci, tunc sine ipsis patriarchis orientalibus non posset universalis synodus totius christiani orbis congregari. Et quia Romanus pontifex non teneretur revereri nisi plenaria concilia, tunc per ista concilia occidentalia nichil posset fieri contra ipsum. Ad excitandum igitur principes, ut concurrerent eorum factioni, scismatice ista scripserunt et hec asseruerunt, que secundum pretactam diffinitionem ycumenici concilii negare non potuerunt.

13 *Discipulus.* Sufficienter deduxisti sacrum Basiliense concilium ecclesie representationem intellexisse realiter per presentiam personarum et consensum, inter quas papa est de necessitate aut eius legatus. Sed dic, queso, cum Constantie solum esset una obedientia Iohannis, cur dixit synodus se representare ecclesiam militantem?

Magister. Non legitur ante Constantiensem synodum aliquod concilium scripsisse se representare universalem ecclesiam, sed hunc titulum assumpsit sibi illa synodus propter finem unionis.

whoever is legate presides over the council like the pope over the universal Church. And this need for the pope or someone representing him was admitted by the universal synod at Basel in the nineteenth session,[13] when, describing an ecumenical or universal synod, the Greeks said that in that synod the pope and the patriarchs are present, themselves or through their procurators; similarly other prelates are present in reality or through representatives.

From this you may learn how true representation ought to exist in a universal council; and on this account, when the Diet was held at Mainz,[14] those residing at Basel, hearing that reunion with the Greeks was imminent, wrote a bull in the name of the Council of Basel to the prince electors[15] to put an end to their deliberations, because, if it should happen that the Greeks rejoined the Church, then there could not be a universal synod gathering all the Christian world without those Eastern patriarchs. And since the Roman pontiffs were not obliged to respect any but plenary councils, nothing could be done against him at that time by those Western councils. Therefore, to stir up the princes so that they would concur with their faction, they wrote these things in a schismatic spirit and asserted things they could not deny in accordance with the definition of an ecumenical council already touched upon.

Disciple. You have deduced sufficiently that the Council of Basel interpreted representation of the Church in its actual practice by the presence and consent of persons among whom are necessarily the pope or his legate. But tell me, please, when at Constance there was only the one obedience, that of [antipope] John [XXIII], why did the synod say it represented the Church Militant? 13

Master. We do not read, before the synod at Constance, that any council described itself as representing the universal Church; but that synod assumed this title for itself for the purpose of

Nam si concilium illud se dixisset ab aliquo trium de papatu contendentium auctoritatem habuisse, non fuisset concilium unionis. Congregata est igitur, non ut obedientia unius, sed ut representans non unam, sed omnes obedientias et ita universalem ecclesiam, et non sub uno trium contendentium, sed immediate sub Christo, a quo se scripsit potestatem habere ad illa, que ad unionem facere potuerunt. Aliter enim non fuisset possibile, quod concilium potuisset ecclesie per unicum pontificem pacem dare sublato scismate, nisi tolleret diversitatem obedientiarum et pluralitatem pontificum. Quod si hec tollere debuit, tunc ille titulus erat sibi ad finem unitatis aptissimus. Et nunc vides, quomodo illi decipiuntur, qui arguunt de concilio Constantiensi ad concilium aliud, ubi non est eadem ratio, et quia ad finem, ut alias obedientias attraherent, hunc titulum representationis universalis ecclesie premiserunt.

Et ita nota, quod ante adventum aliarum obedientiarum eas non representarunt, sed laborarunt per dominum Sigismundum et suos oratores, ut concurrerent non ad concilium unius obedientie, sed universe ecclesie. Titulus igitur ille non conveniebat illis, qui fuerunt Constantie, ante consensum aliarum obedientiarum secundum opinionem aliarum obedientiarum, que se in ecclesia esse et cum capite credebant, sed secundum opinionem eorum, qui credebant extra obedientiam Iohannis non esse ecclesiam, titulus erat verus. Sed ad hoc, ut ad finem unitatis perveniretur, laborabant, ut universaliter verus esset per accessum aliarum obedientiarum, et in hoc consenserunt, ut alie nationes non solum titulum illum, sed nec concilium acceptarent, quousque de novo indiceretur, consentientes post longam celebrationem concilii

union.[16] For if that council had claimed it had authority from any one of the three men contending for the papacy, it would not have been a council of union. It was gathered, therefore, not as one obedience but as representing not one but all obediences, and thus the universal Church; and not under one of the three contenders, but immediately under Christ, from Whom it described itself as having power to do whatever things could bring unity. Otherwise, indeed, it would not have been possible for the council to give peace to the Church through a sole Roman pontiff and end the schism, unless it took away diversity of obediences and plurality of pontiffs. But if the council was obliged to take away these [obstacles], then that claim was most apposite to its purpose of unity. And now you see how those who argue from the Council of Constance to another council are deceived where there is not the same reason, since [the council fathers at Constance] put forth this claim to represent the universal Church for the purpose of drawing in the other obediences.

Notice that, before the arrival of the other obediences, they did not represent them; but they labored through the lord Sigismund and his envoys for them to come, not to a council of one obedience, but to one of the entire Church. That claim, therefore, did not fit those who were at Constance before the consent of the other obediences according to the opinion of the other obediences, which believed themselves to be in the Church and with its head; but according to the opinion of those who believed there was no Church outside the obedience of John, the claim was true. But in order to arrive at unity, they labored that it should become true universally by the accession of the other obediences; and they agreed, with the proviso that the other nations would not accept either the claim or even the council until it were proclaimed anew, and they agreed that after the council had long been celebrated it should be proclaimed

ipsum primo de novo indici, omnia et illa solum licita scientes, que proposito procreande unionis congruebant.

14   *Discipulus.* Satis est de hoc. Dic nunc, ubi non observarunt Basilienses hanc doctrinam.

Magister. Quando spreto apostolico legato, quem in prima sessione dicebant celebrare concilium, sua sponte actus conciliares nisi fuerunt facere. Et quando eodem legato propter causam fidei et reductionis Grecorum, necessitante eum promissione facta Grecis, ad ycumenicum concilium Ferrariam eunte, ipsi, adhuc temerario ausu apostolice sedis auctoritatem ex fantastica representatione ecclesie sibi vendicantes, universale concilium se facere presumpserunt. Quando apud Ferrariam senserunt non solum Romanum pontificem et ecclesiam orientalem esse, sed et in triplo plures prelatos ex Basilee incorporatis, quam Basilee remanserunt, et se ad illam synodum Ferrariensem scientes vocatos, immemores iuramenti Romano pontifici prestiti non obedierunt, sed potestate synodica ab eis translata in Ferrariam per auctoritatem apostolicam et recessum legati abuti non destiterunt. Quando in furiam conversi se erexerunt contra caput ecclesie et conciliorum et universam ecclesiam non audiverunt, ymmo prelatorum et principum supplicationes humiles et oppositiones contempserunt, vendicantes sibi ex eo, quia Basilee erant, quendam principatum Luciferi supra universam ecclesiam. Quando in sua scismatica sententia contra Christi vicarium prolata non ipsum tantum, sed omnes universi orbis principes ecclesiasticos et seculares, quos contradixisse in faciem eorum audiverunt, dampnare nisi sunt, si scismatice factioni eorum

anew, knowing that all things and only those things were licit which were congruent with the purpose of begetting unity.

Disciple. Enough about this. Tell me now wherein the ecclesiastics   14
at Basel did not observe this doctrine.

Master. It happened when they spurned the apostolic legate—whom in the first session[17] they said [had the power] to celebrate the council—and tried to perform conciliar acts of their own free will. It happened when the same legate, owing to a situation regarding the faith and reunion with the Greeks and impelled by a promise made to the Greeks, went to the ecumenical council at Ferrara, and they claimed the authority of the Apostolic See for themselves, rashly basing themselves on a delusory understanding of church representation, and presuming to make themselves a universal council. It happened when they learned that not just the Roman pontiff and the Eastern church were present at Ferrara but three times the number of prelates formerly incorporated with Basel as remained at Basel; knowing that they themselves were summoned to that synod at Ferrara and unmindful of the oath they had sworn to the Roman pontiff, they refused to obey, but did not cease abusing the synodal power already transferred away from them to Ferrara by apostolic authority and the departure of the legate. It happened when, reduced to fury, they set themselves up against the head of the Church and of councils and would not listen to the universal Church; indeed, they held in contempt the humble supplications and the opposition of the prelates and the princes, claiming for themselves, because they were at Basel, a sort of principate of Lucifer over the universal Church. It happened when, in their schismatic sentence issued against Christ's vicar, they tried to condemn not only him, but all the ecclesiastical and secular princes of the whole world, whom they heard denouncing them to their faces, if those princes refused their consent to this schismatic faction. All this followed, as you see,

consensum non prebeant: Omnia ista, nescio an magis fatua quam erronea, ex pravo intellectu illo representationis secuta sunt, ut vides.

15 *Discipulus*. Optime video ex hoc uno pravo intellectu illos ad tantam presumptionem devenisse, et de hoc satis est mirandum. Nam in responsione *Cogitanti*, quando synodus dicit, quomodo universale concilium ob representationem ecclesie habet eandem potestatem quam ecclesia, subiungit, concilia universalia universali traditione et consensu fiunt. Deinde post multa dicit, quomodo unitati fidelium principatus ecclesie convenit. Allegat post hoc Gelasium: 'Confidimus, quod nullus iam christianus ignoret uniuscuiusque synodi constitutum, quod universalis ecclesie probavit assensus', et Gregorium de conciliis loquens 'quia dum universali consensu constituta sint' etc.

Quomodo ergo devenerunt aliqui ad illam insaniam, ut contra dictionem Romane ecclesie, legati apostolici, omnium pontificum, regum et principum consensum interpretentur? Nam si illa est synodus universalis, que ea, que facit, universali consensu facit et cuius constitutum universalis ecclesie probavit assensus, necesse est quod dicatur, quod ubi consensus deest, synodalem deesse censuram.

Mirari non sufficio, quomodo illi, qui prius dixerunt conciliarem traditionem in universali consensu fundari, ad hanc cecitatem deducti sint, ut ex eorum paucorum voluntate putent omnem ecclesie potestatem dependere, et hoc mirabilius videtur, quod dudum ipsi quasi contra veritatem et propriam professionem talia predicantes et practicantes non sunt eliminati et spreti ab omnibus fidelibus veritatem et unitatem diligentibus.

from that depraved understanding of representation [in the Church]. I hardly know whether to call their actions silly or erroneous.

Disciple. I see very well how they arrived at such presumption 15 from this perverted interpretation, and it's really rather surprising. For in the responsory letter *Cogitanti*,[18] when the synod says that the universal council has the same power as the Church through representation of the Church, it adds that universal councils are made universal by universal tradition and consent. Then, after a long discussion, it says how the principate of the Church belongs to the unity of the faithful.[19] Then it cites Gelasius:[20] "We trust that no one already a Christian can ignore a decision of any synod which the assent of the universal Church has approved," and also Gregory on the subject of councils: "since, so long as they are decided with universal consent," etc.

How then did some of them arrive at that pitch of insanity that they interpreted consent in a way contrary to the declarations of the Roman church, the apostolic legate, and all pontiffs, kings and princes? For if that is a universal synod which does what it does by universal consent, whose decisions have the approval of the universal synod, it must necessarily be said that, where consent is absent, there can be no synodal censure.

I feel unequal to wondering how those who once said the conciliar tradition was founded in universal consent have been led into this state of blindness, so that they think the whole Church depends on the will of a few of them; but it seems more wondrous still that the men who have been preaching and practicing such things against the truth and their own admissions for so long have not been thrown out and spurned by all the faithful who love truth and unity.

16 *Magister.* Illi viri, qui pro reductione Bohemorum et reformatione
ecclesie laborarunt Basilee, ab initio secuti sunt veritatem,
convertentes se ad veram intelligentiam in ea et unitate ecclesie
persteterunt; qui autem post hoc advenerunt Basileam, hec
mala operati sunt. Alii enim sunt ita, ut presumendum sit
deum eos permisisse cadere in reprobum sensum, quia corrupta
intentione accurrerunt, qui, ut sunt alii in personis et
intentione, ita et potius alia congregatio quam Basiliense
concilium faciunt et ob hoc non conciliares fructus protulerunt.

17 *Discipulus.* Procede! Si aliam erroneam intelligentiam decreti illius
habent, enarra!

Magister. Habent multas malas et erroneas intelligentias, que
tamen ex prefata exoriuntur. Nam arguunt ex illo decreto
papam non esse super ecclesiam congregatam, quia dicitur in
decreto, quod 'etiam si papalis dignitatis fuerit, obedire tenetur'.
Si igitur obedire tenetur, ergo non est supra, sed infra, quia
obedientia fit superiori.

18 *Discipulus.* Quam rationem assignant superioritatis?

Magister. Infallibilitatis, quoniam aiunt ecclesiam deviare non
posse, sed bene papam, concilium autem representare ecclesiam.
Et quia necesse est, quod sit eadem potestas in representante et
representato, ideo et infallibilitas est in concilio.

Discipulus. Satis concipio eos in hoc errare, cum notissimum sit
aliqua concilia errasse, etiam rite congregata; et hic error
exoritur a priori, quia non recte intelligunt representationem.

19 *Magister.* Fateor ad sanum intellectum illa omnia posse salvari, scilicet quod universale concilium universalem militantem

Master. The men who labored at Basel to return the Bohemians to   16
the fold and to reform the Church have followed the truth from
the beginning, converting themselves to a right understanding
in those matters, and they have persevered in the unity of the
Church. It is those who came to Basel later who have worked
these evil deeds. These others are such that one must presume
that God permitted them to fall into a reprobate understanding
because they arrived [in Basel] with corrupt intentions. These
men, being different in their persons and their intentions,
formed a gathering that was quite different from the Council of
Basel and for this reason produced fruit that was not conciliar
in its nature.

Disciple. Go on—tell me if they have another, erroneous interpre-   17
tation of the Constance decree.

Master. They have many wicked and erroneous interpretations,
which nevertheless arise from the aforesaid misinterpretation
[of the decree]. For they argue from that decree that the pope is
not above the assembled Church, because it is said in the decree, "even if he should be of papal rank he is bound to obey." If
then he is bound to obey, he is not above, but below [a council],
since obedience is to a superior.

Disciple. What explanation do they give for its superiority?   18

Master. One of infallibility,[21] since they say the Church cannot
stray, but the pope very well can; the council, however, represents the Church. And since it is necessary that the same power
be in the representer and the represented, the infallibility [of
the Church] is therefore in the council.

Disciple. I understand well enough that they err in this, since it is
very well known that some councils have erred, even those
gathered with due formality; and this error arises from the earlier one, their incorrect understanding of representation.

Master. I allow that all this could be salvaged in accordance with a   19
sound understanding, that is, that a universal council represent-

ecclesiam representans ita est supra papam, quod bene ibi
diffinita papa amplecti debet et illis uti in edificationem ecclesie.
Ita videmus papam obedire canonibus disponentibus de vita et
moribus episcoporum in habitu, tonsura, officio divino,
observantiis ecclesie quoad alia, et indubie peccaret
transgrediendo sicut alius, ymmo et plus propter altitudinem
gradus.

Sed quia Romanus pontifex a deo habet pastoratum gregis
dominici, tunc nulla constitutione manus eius claudi possunt,
quin potestas super omnem canonem sit apud ipsum, scilicet
quod si viderit expedire, ut non servetur canon in aliquo casu,
dispensatorie potest interpretari canonem non obstare aut locum non habere. Sic etiam puto, quod universalis synodus non
erret in hiis, que sunt de necessitate salutis. Nam universalis
synodus amplectitur consensum universalis ecclesie, capitis et
membrorum, ut dicitur etiam in responsione *Cogitanti*. Unde si
enim universa ecclesia consenserit in aliquo, non est possibile,
etiam si illud alio tempore corrigi contingat per subsequens
concilium, quod pro tempore observantie seducere aliquem
possit. Nemo enim ad impossibile obligatur, et in omnibus
obligatur unusquisque catholice ecclesie se conformare. Nemo
igitur decipitur quoad anime salutem, qui ecclesiam sequitur.

20 *Discipulus.* Tu dicis ea, que intelligibilia sunt. Audivi et ego
aliquando Basilee introductam disputationem de decreto
irritanti et obtentum a prudentioribus non esse possibile
Romanum pontificem ligari posse, ita quod in contrarium non
possit, quoniam hoc esset potius contra ecclesiam quam pro; si
enim non esset in terris, qui libere posset consulere saluti

ing the universal Church Militant is above the pope in this way:
that a pope ought to embrace things well defined [in council]
and use them to build up the Church. Thus we see the pope
obeying [conciliar] canons regulating the life and behavior of
bishops in matters of habit, tonsure, divine office, and church
observances regarding other matters; and he would indubitably
sin by transgressing them, just like any other person, indeed
even more so on account of his lofty rank.

But since the Roman pontiff has from God the duty of shep-
herding the Lord's flock, his hands cannot be tied by any
constitution, such that he has no power over each canon. That
is to say, if it seems to him expedient that a canon should not
be observed in some case, he can interpret the canon in a
dispensatory manner so that it is set aside or made irrelevant.
So I even think that a universal synod may not err in matters
necessary for salvation. For a universal synod embraces the
consent of the universal Church, head and members, as is said
in the responsory letter *Cogitanti*.[22] Therefore, if the universal
Church should reach consensus in some matter, it is not possible, even if that matter should, at some other time, happen to
be corrected by a subsequent council, that it can seduce anyone
[from the faith] during the period of its temporary observance.
For no one is obliged to do what is impossible; and everyone
is obliged to conform himself in all things to the Catholic
Church. No one, therefore, is deceived in what pertains to the
salvation of souls by following the Church.

Disciple. You say things that I can understand. I too heard when I   20
was at Basel a disputation introduced about making decrees,
and it was maintained by the wiser men that it is not possible
for the Roman pontiff to be bound in such a way that he cannot act to the contrary, since this [restriction on his power]
would be against the Church, rather than for it. For if there
were no one on earth who could freely look out for the salva-

fidelium ob prohibitionem canonis, contingeret canonem pro
bono publico a patribus adinventum effici vinculum
prohibitorium boni. Videmus enim rationes canonum sepe in
occurrentibus casibus cessare et malum esse, si dispensatio
credita non foret primo pontifici. Unde non possum videre,
quod statutum concilii sit supra papam, nisi eo modo quod
papa bene diffinita custodire debet, quamdiu serviunt
edificationi. Hoc quidem est de canonibus editis a
predecessoribus in conciliis; sed si celebratur concilium, non
video quomodo sit concilium supra eum, cum ipse presideat
concilio et celebret ipsum.

21 *Magister.* Nec dicit synodus Constantiensis, quod papa subsit, sed
dicit: etiam si papalis dignitatis fuerit, obedire tenetur. 'Papalis
dignitatis' tunc dicebatur, quando illa dignitas per plures
occupabatur, que tamen unica esse debet. Cui nunc[3] in unitate
non convenit hoc dictum 'etiam si papalis dignitatis'. Voluit
igitur concilium, quod illi tres, qui se papalis dignitatis
asserebant, obedire tenerentur. Hoc quidem neccessarium fuit,
si ad unitatem deveniri debuit.

Unde ad hoc, ut videas non posse congrue dici papam
subesse concilio, adverte: nam aut concilium est plenarium, et
tunc complectitur papam, qui est caput concilii, et non potest
dici, quod illud concilium sit supra papam, sed est de papa, ut
de capite, et de aliis, ut de membris [*lac.*].[4] Ymmo etiam
incongrue diceretur concilium esse supra patriarcham aut
archiepiscopum, quia est de patriarcha et archiepiscopo etc. Si
autem consideras concilium secluso capite et eo non
consentiente aut auctorizante ea, que ita per membra fiunt,
tunc illud concilium diceretur potius acephalum quam
perfectum et vigorosum, ut dicit textus *Submittitur* xxi d. Unde

tion of the faithful in connection with a canonical prohibition, it might happen that a canon formulated by the fathers for the public good could become a chain, preventing that good. Often we see that reasons behind canons cease to be relevant to current cases, and it would be bad if a power of dispensation were not entrusted to the pope. For this reason I cannot see that the statute of a council is above the pope unless in such a way that the pope ought to keep those canons that have been well defined as long as they serve to build up the Church. The same is the case with canons published in councils by his predecessors; but, if a council is celebrated, I do not see how a council may be above him when he presides at a council and celebrates it.

Master. And the synod of Constance does not say that the pope is   21 under a council, but it says, "even if he should be of papal rank, he is bound to obey." The expression "papal rank" was spoken at a time when this rank, which ought to be unique, was being occupied by several popes. The phrase does not apply to it now, when it is unique. The council therefore wished those three popes, who claimed the papal rank for themselves, to be bound to obey. This was necessary, if that rank was to be reduced to unity.

Notice in this connection that the pope cannot fittingly be said to be under the council, for either it is a plenary council, and thus includes the pope, who is head of the council, and it cannot be said that this council is over the pope, but that it is constituted of the pope, as its head, and of the others, as its members, [or it is not a true council]. Indeed, it would even be unfitting to say that a council is above a patriarch or an archbishop, because it is constituted of the patriarch or the archbishop, etc. If you bracket the head of the council and his consent and authorization of what is done by the council's members, then that council should rather be called acephalous than perfect and effective, as the text of [Gratian] D. 21

tunc ei non solum papa non subest, sed nec quisquam patriarcha aut archiepiscopus. Omnes enim archiepiscopi, si convenerint et eis apostolice sedis consensus defuerit, archiepiscopum iudicare et dampnare tanquam superiores non poterunt.

Vides, quomodo non potest congrue dici papam subesse concilio; sed papam se subicere posse congregatis episcopis et tunc subesse iudicio eorum, non arguit ipsum semper subiectum, quasi alii episcopi inferiores eo caput ecclesie, quia convenerunt in loco aliquo, iudicare possint. Locus enim eis non subicit Christi vicarium nec alium prius eis non subiectum. Oportet igitur, quod ad hoc episcopi sint convocati per iudicandum, ut sic censeatur se subiecisse, ut dicit textus ❲ Hinc etiam xvii d.

Adverte igitur, quomodo ex fantastico intellectu decreti Constantiensis hic error exoritur, quia eos, qui convenerunt in loco concilii, ex loco arguunt ecclesiam representare, que includit caput et membra. Ideo arguunt consensum includi. Tu autem vides hunc intellectum verum non esse. Si enim locus hoc faceret, scilicet quod illi, qui subiecti erant extra locum, sint in loco supra caput et caput sub et infra, locus operaretur contrarios effectus, scilicet superioritatem in subiectis et subiectionem in prepositis, quod, sicut nec intelligibile, ita dicere erroneum est. Ex hoc autem errore subsumunt papam concilium transferre non posse, quia subest.

22 *Discipulus.* Audivi omnem contentionem ex hoc exortam dicentibus Basiliensibus papam concilium transferre non posse, cum ei subsit, papa contrarium affirmante. Sed ego aliquando legens fundationem concilii Basiliensis reperi Martinum papam

c. *Submittuntur* [c. 8] says. At that point, therefore, not only is the pope not subject to the council, but neither is any patriarch or archbishop. For all the archbishops, if they gathered but lacked the consent of the Apostolic See, could not judge and condemn another archbishop as his superiors.

You see how it cannot be fitting to say that the pope is under the council; but that the pope could submit himself to the gathered bishops and then be subject to their judgment does not argue that he always is subject to them, as if the other bishops, inferior to him, can judge the head of the Church just because they are gathered in a certain place. For the place does not subject the vicar of Christ to them, nor anyone else not previously subject to them. It is necessary, therefore, when bishops are convoked for the purpose of judging him, that the pope be reckoned to have submitted himself to them, as in the text of ℂ *Hinc etiam* in D. 17 [p.c. 6].

Note, therefore, how this error arose from a delusional understanding of the decree of Constance: because they argue on the basis of the site that those who were gathered at the site of the council represented the Church, which includes head and members; thus, they argue, consent is implied. You see, however, that this interpretation is not a true one. For if the place could do this, that is, make those who were subject outside the place be above the head in that place, and the head beneath and below them, the place would bring about contrary effects, that is, superiority in subjects and subjection in leaders. Since this is unintelligible, it is erroneous to say it. Yet from this error they deduce the conclusion that the pope cannot transfer the council because he is subject to it.

Disciple. I heard that all the contention at Basel arose from those 22 who said that the pope cannot transfer the council, since he is subject to it, while the pope affirmed the contrary. But once, when reading about the foundation of the Council of Basel, I

dedisse legatis suis in Senensi concilio potestatem transferendi concilium ex rationabilibus causis, et hoc auctoritate ipsius Martini. Si igitur Martinus papa non obstantibus decretis concilii Constantiensis, que ipse maxime observare studuit, hanc potestatem non intellexit ab apostolica sede per illa decreta sublatam, quin posset ex rationabilibus causis sua auctoritate concilium transferre, et hunc intellectum Senense concilium admisit et per ipsum concilium Basiliense est Basilee stabilitum, quomodo illi contra hoc nunc os in celum levant, dicentes hanc potestatem transferendi concilium pape ut pape non convenire?

23 *Magister.* Dicunt ista[5] illi, quos passio non sinit respicere ad veritatem. Nam etsi dicant: aliquando transtulit concilium Bononiam et demum oportebat declarare translationem nullam, hoc non processit ex defectu potentie, sed causarum. Concilium enim Basiliense in responsione *Cogitanti* causas expressas in translatione non se in facto ita habere dicit et ob hoc supplicat ibi, cum cause rationabiles non sint, ut transferatur, sed ut remaneat Basilee, quod tunc tollat translationem. Hoc comperto papa complacuit patribus.

Nunc autem, quando reductio Grecorum instabat, propter conservare unitatem ecclesie et reducere Grecos transtulit concilium. Ille enim cause tam in illa responsione *Cogitanti* quam in 19 sessione et aliis sessionibus concilii approbatissime et rationabilissime iudicate sunt, sicut et eas unusquisque catholicus merito rationabiles iudicat. Quare translatio fieri

discovered that Pope Martin had given his legates at the Council of Siena[23] the power to transfer the council for reasonable cause, and that by the authority of Martin himself. If therefore Pope Martin, notwithstanding the decrees of the Council of Constance,[24] which he made every effort to observe, did not understand this power to have been taken away from the Apostolic See by those decrees, but thought that he could transfer the council on his own authority for reasonable causes; and the Council of Siena admitted this interpretation, and it was by that council that the Council of Basel was fixed at Basel, how can these men now raise their mouth against heaven[25] and oppose this, saying that this power of transferring the council does not befit the pope *qua* pope?

Master. Those who say such things have passions which permit no   23
respect for the truth. For although they say that [Eugenius IV] at one time transferred the council to Bologna and was at length obliged to declare that there had been no translation, this [reversal] did not proceed from a defect of [papal] power but from a causal defect. Indeed, the Council of Basel, in the responsory letter *Cogitanti*,[26] said that the causes expressed in [the act of] translation were invalid and on this account entreated that the council should [not] be transferred there, as rational reasons for doing so were lacking, but rather that they might remain at Basel, which would then override the translation. Once he learned of this, the pope granted the fathers' request.

Lately, however, when reunion with the Greeks became of pressing concern, the pope transferred the council in order to preserve the unity of the Church and to reunite the Greeks. Those causes quoted in the responsory letter *Cogitanti* and in the nineteenth session[27] and in other sessions of the council were judged most appropriate and reasonable, just as any catholic might judge them sound on their merits. Hence the transla-

potuit per eum, qui a Christo creditam habet potestatem super universam ecclesiam ad edificandum, cui nulla sanctio cuiuscumque concilii resistere potest.

24 *Discipulus.* Michi videtur, quod contradicere huic sententie sit dicere Christum non habere vicarium cum plenitudine potestatis in ecclesia et sit tollere privilegium apostolice sedi a deo datum.

Magister. Optime dicis. Et quando adverto ad propria decreta et responsa atque admissa Basilee et ad ista, que illi dicunt, quod papa sic concilio subsit, reperio multas contradictiones. Nam in prima sessione sacra synodus vocat sanctissimum dominum nostrum Martinum presidentem universalis ecclesie, vocat Eugenium papam dominum nostrum, dicit in responsione *Cogitanti*, quod sit Christi vicarius, caput ecclesie et concilii. Et cum dominus Tarantinus dixisset ipsum solum plenitudinem potestatis habere et alios vocatos in partem sollicitudinis, respondit synodus: 'ista fatemur'. Offert etiam, quomodo unusquisque sibi pedes osculabitur etc. Et in xiv sessione idem.

Adhuc, quando cum Bohemis disputatio fiebat de auctoritate et potestate Romani pontificis in articulo 'de libertate predicationis verbi dei', dictum fuit Bohemis presente synodo per doctorem unum, qui nichil dixit prius non approbatum per synodum, quomodo secundum sanctum Bernhardum ad Eugenium tertium, sicut in celo omnes angeli, archangeli etc. 'sub uno capite deo ordinantur, ita hic sub uno summo pontifice primates, patriarche, archiepiscopi' etc., et quod Christus solum dixit Petro: 'pasce oves', 'et quod nullus nisi auctoritate Petri habet pascere vel regere ubicumque, et quod omnis iurisdictio a papa dependet secundum Augustinum de Ancona, et etiam auctoritate sua quilibet plebanus suam

tion could be made by the pope, who has the power entrusted to him by Christ over the universal Church to build it up, which no sanction of any council can block.

Disciple. It seems to me that to contradict this opinion is to say   24
that Christ did not have a vicar with plenitude of power in the Church and to take away the privilege given by God to the Apostolic See.

Master. You are exactly right. And when I turn to their own decrees, the responses and admissions made at Basel, and [then] to the things they [now] say, that the pope is under the council, I find many contradictions. For in the first session the holy synod calls "our most holy lord Martin" the president of the universal Church; it calls Pope Eugenius "lord;" it says in the responsory letter *Cogitanti*[28] that he is the vicar of Christ, head of the Church and of the council. And when the lord [archbishop of] Taranto[29] had said that the pope alone has plenitude of power and others are called to a share in the responsibility, the synod replied, "We confess these things."[30] And it says the same in the fourteenth session.[31]

Besides, when a disputation was held with the Bohemians concerning the authority and power of the Roman pontiff in the article "On the freedom of preaching the word of God," one of the doctors told the Bohemians in the presence of the synod — a man who spoke on prior approval by the synod — how according to Saint Bernard [in his treatise *On Consideration*, dedicated] to Eugenius III,[32] just as in heaven all the angels, archangels etc. "are ordered under one head, God, so here the primates, patriarchs, archbishops etc. are under one supreme pontiff," and that Christ said to Peter alone, *Feed my sheep*,[33] "and that no one except by authority of Peter has the power to feed, or rule, in any place, and that all jurisdiction depends on the pope, according to Augustine of Ancona, and that every little parish priest governs his church by this authority.[34] And

regit ecclesiam; et quia ipse est vicarius Christi, ideo, sicut
nemo est christianus, qui non teneatur obedire Christo, sic et
pape; et sicut Christus recepit a patre ducatum et sceptrum
ecclesie gentium ex Israel egrediens super omnem principatum
et potestatem et super omne quodcumque est, ut ei genua
curventur, sic ipse Petro et eius successoribus plenissimam
potestatem commisit, ut ait Cyrillus'. Item pape potestas prope
Christum attingit ita, quod ei nulla in terris potestas comparari
possit, cum sit maior dignitate, causalitate et auctoritate. Ei,
secundum sanctum Bernhardum, 'cum sit pastor pastorum,
universe oves credite sunt, singuli greges aliis'.

Talia quidem et similia multa Basilee pro doctrina Bohemis
errantibus dicta sunt, que adhuc in scriptis undique reperiuntur
in librariis. Quomodo illa, rogo, concordant cum eo, quod
modo illi errantes predicant, scilicet quod papa subsit illis
patriarchis, archiepiscopis et episcopis in concilio? Si
quereretur ab illis: quis absolvit prelatos et pastores in loco
concilii ab obedientia pastoris pastorum, principe ecclesie et
Christi vicario, et cur magis ipsi prelati sint tunc absoluti ab
obedientia sui superioris quam eorum prelatorum inferiores a
sua obedientia? — nichil haberent, quod dicerent, nisi quod
solent dicere: papa non subest illi vel illi, sed concilio, quasi
concilium sit quid aliud quam illi et illi, qui membra sunt
concilii. Hec responsio est eorum, qui nichil firmitatis habent,
sed omnia in mathematicam abstractionem resolvunt.

Contra quos dicit sanctus Augustinus, *De nuptiis et
concupiscentia*, reprehendens 'eos, qui dicunt ecclesiam non
habere maculam', licet ipsi sint de ecclesia et maculati, dicens:

since he is himself the vicar of Christ, just as there is no Christian who is not bound to obey Christ, so too [all Christians] must obey the pope;[35] and just as Christ received command from the Father and the scepter of the Church, ruling the nations rising out of Israel, which is above every principate and power, and above everything that exists, so that every knee bends to Him, so He committed plenitude of power to Peter and his successors, as Cyril says."[36] Likewise, "the power of the pope touches Christ so closely that no power on earth can be compared to him, since he is greater in dignity, causality and authority."[37] According to Saint Bernard, since "he is the pastor of pastors, all sheep are entrusted to him, while individual flocks are entrusted to other pastors."[38]

Such speeches and many similar ones, now found in written form at the stationers everywhere, were given at Basel for the instruction of the erring Bohemians. I ask how they harmonize with what those erring men now preach, that is, that the pope is under those patriarchs, archbishops and bishops in council? If one could ask them who freed the prelates and pastors at the site of the council from obedience to the pastor of pastors, the prince of the Church and the vicar of Christ, and why those prelates are freer to disobey their superior than their inferiors are to obey those prelates themselves, they would have nothing to say, except what they always say, that the pope is not subject to this or that person, but to the council, as though the council were something other than this and that person, who [severally] form the members of the council. This is the response of men who lack stability and reduce everything to a mathematical abstraction.

Against them Saint Augustine says in *On Marriage and Concupiscence*,[39] criticizing "those who say that the Church has no stain" although they themselves belong the Church and carry stains: "If, however, they say that they have [stains] but the

'Si autem se dicunt habere ista, non ipsam, ergo se non esse membra eius nec se ad corpus eius pertinere fatentur, ut etiam sua confessione dampnentur'. Sic vides dicendum prelatis singularibus in concilio, si ipsi dicunt se singulariter subiectos pape, non concilium. Ergo fatentur se non esse membra concilii etc. Hoc iam diffinitum legitur xxi d. *Nunc autem* in fine, ubi clare constat synodum dicere non posse sententiam dare in papam synodum, quia omnes eo sunt inferiores et minores. Ex quibus habes, quantum errant isti dampnati a sententia catholica etiam synodi Basiliensis, qui nituntur ex pravo intellectu decreti Constantiensis omnem ordinem pervertere.

25 *Discipulus*. Satis clare ostendisti illos contradicere synodo Basiliensi et doctrine vere eius, sed nondum ad rationem infallibilitatis, in qua fundant superioritatem, respondisti.

Magister. Adeo parvi momenti apud me est, quod eam preterire statui. Ecce, ego facio argumentum sancti Augustini contra ipsos tale: papa potest errare et singuli de concilio; igitur infallibilitas non potest convenire concilio, que non potest alicui membro concilii convenire. Non est ergo verum, quod infallibilitas conveniat concilio.

26 *Discipulus*. Infallibilitatem dicunt convenire concilio, quia representat ecclesiam.

Magister. Dico, quod, si ecclesiam representat, non fallit in hiis, que sunt ad salutem, ut premisi, etiam si omnes mali forent. Nam cum auctoritas, que data est rectoribus ecclesie, sit gratia gratis data propter ecclesiam, ob malitiam prelati non minuitur, ut docuit synodus Basiliensis Bohemos.

Church does not, they admit thereby that they are not its members nor do they belong to its body, so they are condemned even by their own confession." That, you see, is what should be said to the individual prelates in council, if they say that they are subject to the pope individually but that the council is not: that they thereby confess themselves not to be members of the council etc. We read that this was already defined at the end of [Gratian] D. 21 c. *Nunc autem* [c. 7], where it is clearly established that the synod cannot say that it imposes a sentence on the pope, because all in it are inferior to and less than him. From this passage you can see how far these accursed men are wandering from the catholic position even of [the former] Council of Basel,[40] when they try to pervert all right order with their perverted interpretation of the decree of Constance.

Disciple. You have shown clearly enough that they contradict the   25
synod at Basel and its true doctrine, but you have yet to respond to the argument about infallibility on which they base their claim to superiority.

Master. It matters so little to me that I decided to pass over it. Look, I use against them an argument of Saint Augustine like this:[41] the pope can err, as can individuals in a council; therefore, infallibility cannot befit a council, since it cannot befit any member of the council; it is therefore untrue that infallibility befits a council.

Disciple. They say that infallibility befits a council because it represents the Church.   26

Master. I say that, if it represents the Church, it does not deceive in matters pertaining to salvation, as I stipulated, even if all its members should be wicked. For since authority, which is given to the rulers of the Church, is a grace freely granted for the sake of the Church, it is not diminished through the malice of a prelate, as the synod at Basel taught the Bohemians.

27 *Discipulus.* Videtur ex tuo argumento, quod tota ecclesia errare possit, cum unusquisque errare possit.

 Magister. Iam dixi tibi, quod possibile est, quod tota ecclesia aliquid nunc teneat et postea illud prohibeat, nec propter hoc est periculum salutis animarum. Aliquando enim tota ecclesia habuit unam formam baptizandi, secundum quam omnes salvabantur; post hoc alia est introducta, et tunc, si quis secundum priorem baptizatus fuisset, non salvabatur. In hiis igitur mutationibus saluti nichil deperiit. Augustinus autem *De nuptiis et concupiscentia* non intelligit ecclesiam sine macula et ruga esse istam ut hic, sed istam ut in futuro seculo.

28 *Discipulus.* Satis ego ex hiis intelligo argumentum infallibilitatis nichil facere. Nam etsi magnus numerus episcoporum presumatur minus errare, tamen compertum est in Arimino contrarium. Nichil igitur infallibilitatis dicit numerositas, ut propter infallibilitatem prima sedes subici debeat, ymmo, si hoc hactenus observatum fuisset, diu fides defecisset.

 ‹*Magister.*› Tradita fuit in Basiliensi synodo Bohemis doctrina in articulo De communione, quomodo in ecclesia Romana esset plus infallibilitatis, ita dicens: Apostolus Paulus vocat ecclesiam columpnam et firmamentum veritatis, ita scribens Thimotheo: 'Scias, quomodo oporteat te in domo dei conversari, que est ecclesia dei vivi, columpna et firmamentum veritatis.' Super quo Ambrosius in expositione illius epistole dicit: 'Cum totus mundus dei sit, ecclesia tamen domus eius dicitur, cuius hodie rector est Damasus. Mundus enim in prevaricatione eius diverso est turbatus errore; ideo illic neccesse est dicatur domus

Disciple. It seems from your argument that the whole Church   27
could err, since any member of it can err.

Master. I have already told you that it is possible for the entire
Church to hold some doctrine now and afterwards to prohibit
it, but there is no peril to the salvation of souls in this. Once
the whole Church had one form of baptism according to which
all were saved; after this time another was introduced, and at
that point, if someone were baptized according to the old rite,
he was not saved. In these changes, therefore, nothing relevant
to salvation was lost. And Augustine in *On Marriage and
Concupiscence*[42] did not understand the Church *without stain or
wrinkle* to be the Church of this world but the one to come in
the future age.

Disciple. I understand enough from the foregoing to dismiss the   28
argument from infallibility. For even if a great number of bishops may be presumed to err less, the contrary was nevertheless
found at the synod of Rimini.[43] Number, therefore, says nothing about infallibility, to the effect that the principal see ought
to be subject to a synod because of infallibility. Indeed, if this
had been observed up to now, the faith would have ceased to
exist long ago.

Master. At the synod in Basel the teaching was handed down to
the Bohemians in the article "Concerning communion" that
there was more infallibility in the Roman church, saying,[44]
"The apostle Paul calls the Church the pillar and foundation of
truth, writing thus to Timothy, *Thou mayest know how thou
oughtest behave thyself in the house of God, which is the Church of the
living God, the pillar and ground of the truth.*[45] On this text,
Ambrose says in his exposition of this text: 'Although the whole
world belongs to God, nevertheless, the Church is called His
house, whose rector today is Damasus. For the world in its
falseness has been disturbed by a different error; wherefore of
necessity the house of God and the truth may be said to be

dei et veritas.' Hec Ambrosius. Subiungitur in doctrina in concilio tradita Bohemis: 'Ecce quam aperte hic doctor declarat, ubi sit ecclesia, que est domus dei, illa scilicet et ibi, cui tempore suo Damasus papa presidebat, scilicet ecclesia Romana. Tenendum itaque est fide inconcussa ecclesiam Christi et Petri naviculam, quamvis agitetur multis turbinibus in hoc tempestuoso mari et procelloso, nunquam privari presentia Christi et gubernaculo spiritus sancti, qui eam non sinit errare in hiis, que fidei sunt et neccessaria ad salutem'. Hec ibi. Secundum hoc igitur, quod Bohemis pro doctrina Basilee traditum est, ecclesia illa, cui papa presidet, a veritate fidei et hiis, que ad salutem sunt neccessaria, minus recedit. Quare argumentum infallibilitatis potius debet Romanum pontificem preferre quam submittere concilii membris.

29 *Discipulus.* Ista clarissime ostendunt argumentum infallibilitatis potius concludere pro Romano pontifice et Romana ecclesia quam pro aliis membris ecclesie aut concilii ac quod ipsa Petri sedes etiam propter demeritum presidentis nunquam conculcari deberet.

Magister. Optime dicis. Nam sanctus Augustinus, confirmans prius dictum, ait 'Christum in cathedra unitatis posuisse doctrinam veritatis pro nostra salute, cum sit suum id, quod ibi docetur, non docentium'. Et idem contra Petilianum libro secundo respondendo Petiliano, qui christianos cathedram pestilentie habere dixit, dicit: 'Si omnes per totum orbem tales essent, quales vanissime criminaris, kathedra tibi quid fecit ecclesie Romane, in qua Petrus sedit et hodie Anastasius sedet, cui nos in catholica unitate connectimur et a qua vos nephario favore[6] separastis? Quare appellas cathedram pestilentie

there [in the Roman Church].'" It was added in the teaching handed down to the Bohemians in council: "See how openly this doctor here declares where the Church which is the house of God may be found: it is where it was in the time of Pope Damasus, namely, in the Roman church. And so we must cling with unshaken faith to the Church of Christ and the bark of Peter. Although tossed about by many storms on this tempestuous and wave-tossed sea, it never can be deprived of the presence of Christ and the governance of the Holy Spirit, who does not permit it to err in those things which pertain to faith and are necessary for salvation." According therefore to that which was handed down as doctrine at Basel to the Bohemians, the Church over which the pope presides cannot depart from the truth of the faith and from those things necessary for salvation. Hence the argument from infallibility ought rather to favor the Roman pontiff than subject him to the members of a council.

Disciple. These considerations show with the utmost clarity that   29 the argument from infallibility should come to a conclusion that favors the Roman pontiff and the Roman church rather than other members of the Church or the council, and that the see of Peter ought never to be trodden down even on the grounds of an undeserving president.

Master. You are exactly right. For Saint Augustine,[46] confirming what was said before, says Christ "placed the doctrine of truth in the seat of unity for our salvation, since what is taught there is His teaching, not that of teachers." And he says the same in the second book *Against Petellian*,[47] replying to Petellian (who said Christians "have the see of pestilence"): "If all of them throughout the whole world were like this — an utterly empty charge — what did the see of the Roman church do as far as you are concerned, the see on which Peter sat and Anastasius sits today, to which we are connected in Catholic unity and from which you are separated by a wicked partiality? Why are you

cathedram apostolicam? Si propter homines, quos putas legem loqui et non facere, numquid dominus Iesus Christus propter Phariseos, de quibus ait: 'Dicunt enim et non faciunt', ‹cathedre, in qua sedebant,›[7] ullam fecit iniuriam? Nonne illam cathedram Moysi commendavit et illos servato cathedre honore redarguit? Ait enim: "‹Super› cathedram Moysi sedent; que dicunt, facite, que autem faciunt, facere nolite. Dicunt enim et non faciunt." Hec si cogitaretis, non propter homines, quos infamastis, blasphemaretis cathedram apostolicam, cui non communicatis.' Hec ille. Ista verba recte dici possunt istis dampnatis Basiliensibus, qui cathedre apostolice et universe ecclesie iniuriantur.

30 *Discipulus.* Habeo nunc clarissime ex istis papam non subesse membris concilii, et ad hoc ostendendum suffecisset allegare, quomodo Martinus et Eugenius nichil ratum habere voluerunt, nisi illud per legatos et presidentes eorum vice apostolice sedis ageretur, et ita nichil ratum esse voluerunt, nisi quod ipsi statuerent. Et ex hoc capite dominus noster Eugenius papa per apostolicam bullam incipientem *Pastoralis cura*, datam anno domini m° quadringentesimo xxxiii in kalendis iunii, omnia cassavit, que Basilee facta fuerunt, preter ea, ad que synodus ipsa apostolica auctoritate fuit congregata.

Et quoniam talia synodus prius Senensis et post Basiliensis admisit et non reprehendit, quia de iure reprehendi non poterant, secundum omnem omnium conciliorum ob-servantiam, que nichil extra casum convocationis attemptarunt et ratum nichil presumpserunt, in quod vicem apostolici gerens per speciales commonitoriales litteras fulcitus non consensit, ut patet ex epistola synodi Calcedonensis ad Leonem papam, ut aliqua capitula, ad que apostolici legati non consenserant,

calling the Apostolic See the see of pestilence? If it's because of men who, you think, lay down the law but don't follow it, surely it's not possible that the Lord Jesus Christ did any injustice to the see in which the Pharisees sat when he says of them: *They say, and do not do?* Did He not commend the see of Moses and contradict the Pharisees, while honoring the see? For He says: they *sit upon the chair of Moses; do what they say, but do not wish to do what they do; for they say, and do not do.* If you think these things, but not because of the men you are defaming, you are blaspheming the Apostolic See with which you are not in communion." These words can be correctly applied to those accursed men in Basel who do injury to the Apostolic See and the universal Church.

Disciple. Now I understand with perfect clarity from the above that the pope is not subject to the members of the council, and to prove this, it suffices to cite how Martin and Eugenius wished to regard nothing as valid except what was done by the legates and presidents on behalf of the Apostolic See; and so they wished nothing to be valid except what they themselves decreed. And on this principle our lord Eugenius through the apostolic bull beginning *Pastoralis cura*,[48] issued on the first day of July in the year of our Lord 1433, canceled everything which had been done at Basel except the things for which that synod had been gathered by apostolic authority.

First the synod at Siena and then the one at Basel admitted and did not condemn actions like these because they could not condemn them legally, in accordance with every observance of every council, none of which attempted anything outside their original remit or claimed anything to be valid to which someone acting in the place of the pope, supported by special admonitory letters, had not consented. This is obvious from the letter of the synod at Chalcedon to Pope Leo,[49] which shows how some provisos to which the apostolic legates had not con-

30

dignaretur rata habere, hinc praxis illa unumquemque instruit te dixisse verum.

Sed quia mos est Basiliensium exclamatione quadam multos inducere, ut credant synodum papam posse iudicare, dicentes: papa potest esse pessimus et non potest per particulares iudicari; si igitur nec per synodum posset obviari malitie sue, non esset ecclesie sufficienter provisum, quando in manu devastatoris esset, cui nec synodus dicere possit: cur ita facis? — rogo, quid ad hoc dicendum?

31 *Magister.* Hoc est potius seditiosum quam rationabile argumentum. Nam si diceretur Basiliensibus illis: si ad obviandum malitie pape iudicatis necessarium ut synodus sit supra papam, quare ad obviandum malitie synodi non est admittendum papam esse super concilium? non haberent, quid responderent. Sicut enim papa potest esse malus, ita et unusquisque, qui in synodo est. Multa enim hereticorum et scismaticorum conventicula fuerunt, de quorum numero est ultimum illud, quod Basilee residens ecclesiam perturbat.

32 *Discipulus.* Secundum hoc posset forte dici, quod concilium est supra papam papa errante et papa super concilium concilio errante.

Magister. In synodo Basiliensi fuit Bohemis doctrina tradita nullum peccatum facere papam minorem, sed heresis faceret eum non-papam. Non ergo extra heresim inferioribus subicitur. Synodus autem, cum sine papa universalis esse nequeat, non dicitur proprie pape subici, quia membra cum papa capite concilium faciunt; sed papa supra statuta synodi potestatem principis habet epikeiiam, scilicet interpretationem in ecclesie edificationem. Sic dicitur supra concilium, hoc est conciliorum statuta, existere. Est igitur papa supra concilii statuta et

sented [the pope] deigned to consider valid. Hence church practice teaches everyone that you spoke the truth.

But it is the practice of those at Basel by a kind of outcry to induce many to believe a synod can judge the pope, saying that the pope can be the worst of men and cannot be judged by individuals; if therefore his wicked deeds could not be blocked even by a synod, provision would not be made sufficiently for the Church,[50] since it would be in the hands of a destroyer, to whom not even a synod could say, "Why are you doing this?" Now how would you reply to this claim?

Master. This is a seditious more than a rational argument. For 31 those at Basel would have no reply if it were said to them: if you judge it necessary for the synod to be above the pope to obviate the wicked deeds of the pope, why must it not be admitted that the pope is above the council to obviate the wicked deeds of a synod? Just as the pope can be wicked, so also anyone who is at a synod. There have been many conventicles of heretics and schismatics, including this latest one which resides at Basel and disturbs the Church.

Disciple. According to this reasoning, it might perhaps be said 32 that the council is above a pope when the pope errs, and the pope over the council when the council errs.

Master. In the synod at Basel the doctrine was handed down to the Bohemians that no sin can diminish the pope [*qua* pope], but heresy can make him a non-pope. Therefore, the pope is not subject to an inferior except in a case of heresy.[51] The synod, however, since it cannot exist as universal without a pope, is not said properly to be subject to the pope, because its members with the pope as their head make up the council; but the pope has the power of a prince in equity above the statutes of a synod, that is, in the interpretation of the statutes in order to build up the Church. Thus the pope is said to be above the council, that is, the statutes of councils. The pope, therefore, is

membra concilii universaliter. Sic vides, quo casu hoc potest admitti, quod dicis.

33 *Discipulus.* Quomodo est ergo extra heresim ecclesie provisum contra pape malitiam?

Magister. Si dixero tibi sanctos dicere non esse aliud remedium quam ad deum recurrere et orare, ut ipsum de medio tollat, ut sancti doctores dicunt, ridebis fortassis, sicut et illi Basilienses, qui humanam solum ecclesiam credunt, quasi non sit remedium, quod non humano commissum sit iudicio.

Sed ego tibi dico: per nullum remedium humanum ecclesie utilius potuisset provisum esse, quam per deum providetur. Primo quidem deus, ut ait Augustinus, providit ecclesie de malis prelatis, qui ait: 'que dicunt, facite, que faciunt, facere nolite.' Non enim diceret: 'que dicunt, facite, si in eorum doctrina non penderet salus tua', nec diceret: 'que faciunt, facere nolite, nisi mali esse possent'. Malitia igitur eorum non obest ecclesie.

Ecce optimam provisionem, ubi salus ecclesie concurrit cum malitia prelati. Nichil [igitur] periculi advenit ecclesie ex malitia prelati, nulla est igitur provisio contra eius malitiam iusta, que posset in perniciem ecclesie tendere. Nam si dicis quod, si synodus iudicare et cohercere eum posset, quod hoc sit iustum, primo habes ostendere deum non velle ipsum regnare. Nam pro salute populi peccantis permittit deus ypocritam regnare. Potest igitur ecclesie utilitatem prestare malitia regnantis, nunquam autem salutem impedire.

Si vero non expedit malum regnare, non credas remedium deficere. Nam si tunc oratur pro eo per universam ecclesiam,

above the statutes of a council and the members of a council in a universal way. Thus you see what can be admitted in the case which you cited.

Disciple. How then, outside the case of heresy, is provision made   33
for the Church against the wickedness of a pope?

Master. If I were to tell you that the saints say that there is no other remedy than to have recourse to God and pray that he be taken away from our midst, as the holy doctors say, perhaps you would laugh, just as those at Basel do, who believe the Church to be only a human institution, as though it were not a remedy that is not entrusted to human judgment.

But I tell you that no human remedy could have been provided for the Church more useful than the one God has provided. First, as Augustine says,[52] God has provided for the Church in the case of wicked prelates, since He says, *Do what they say, but do not will to do what they do.* He did not say, "Do what they say, if your salvation does not depend on their doctrine;" nor did He say, "Do not will to do what they do, unless they could be wicked." Their wickedness, therefore, does not impede the Church.

Look, the best provision [for the health of the Church] is when the health of the Church coexists with the wickedness of the prelate. No peril comes to the Church from the wickedness of the prelate; there is therefore no just provision against his wickedness, for such a provision could tend to the injury of the Church. For if you say it is just that a synod could judge and coerce him, you first have to show that God did not wish him to reign. For God permits a hypocrite to reign for the salvation of a sinful people. God therefore can promote the good of the Church despite the wickedness of the ruler; but he can never stand in the way of salvation.

But if it is not expedient for a wicked man to reign, you shouldn't believe that a remedy is lacking. For if prayer is

quomodo potest deus non exaudire ecclesiam pro sua salute orantem, et tunc, quando talis est, quod peccata sua non sunt tanta, ut merito ei tyrannus dominetur? Unde proprie illud dictum: 'si duo vel tres convenerint in nomine meo' secundum sanctorum expositionem loquitur de efficacia orationis ecclesie, que concurrit in orando pro sua salute, et tunc verificetur illud: 'quodcumque petieritis patrem meum in nomine meo', scilicet Christi, qui caput est ecclesie, pro ecclesia, inquantum est utile ecclesie: 'dabitur vobis'. Et sicut deus stante ecclesia in illa doctrina eam sub malis non permisit periclitari, ita nec permittet; et qui aliud credunt, Christo non credunt, qui assistentiam ecclesie promisit.

34 *Discipulus.* Sic igitur tu non excludis, quin etiam deus per medium concilii providere possit hoc casu?

Magister. 'Iudicia dei abissus multa!' Sic crede, quod, quamvis ordinarium remedium dari nequeat absque maiori periculo ecclesie, tamen deus, qui ad nullam formam astringitur, innumerabiles habet providendi modos pro tempore congruos.

35 *Discipulus.* Debet ergo presumi omnis ille modus ex divina ordinatione procedere, qui tyrannum de medio tollit?

Magister. Si notoria esset tyrannides et malitia, que universam ecclesiam scandalizaret, et remedium cum pace ecclesie exoriretur, qualecumque hoc esset, de divina ordinatione pro exauditione ecclesie provenisse iudicarem. Nec per hoc dico aliquod per me enarrari posse remedium ante factum, quod tunc deberet censeri iustum, cum 'dei iudicia incomprehensibilia et inenarrabilia' sint.

36 *Discipulus.* Intelligo mentem tuam papam dei iudici‹o› remissum in multo periculosiori stare iudicio quam synodi que per unam

offered for him then by the whole Church, how could God not respond to the Church praying for its salvation, and at a time when it is in such a condition that its sins are not so great as to merit its being dominated by a tyrant? Therefore, the saying, *Where two or three gathered together in My name*,[53] applies, according to the exposition of the saints, to the efficacy of the Church's prayer when it comes together to pray for its salvation; and it is in this case that the saying is proven true: *Whatsoever you shall ask the Father in my name*, that is, that of Christ who is the head of the Church, for the Church, in so far as it is good for the Church, *it shall be done to you*.[54] And, just as God (the Church having persevered in that doctrine) has not permitted it to be endangered, neither will He permit this; and those who believe anything else do not believe in Christ, who promised to help his Church.

Disciple. So then you don't exclude that even God could make provision for this case by means of a council?   34

Master. *The judgments of God are like the great deep.*[55] You should believe that, although a regular remedy could not be given without greater peril to the Church, nevertheless, God, who is bound to no form, has innumerable fitting modes of providing in accordance with the times.

Disciple. Every mode therefore should be presumed to proceed from divine ordination that takes a tyrant from our midst?   35

Master. If his tyranny and wickedness were notorious and scandalizing the whole Church, and a remedy were to arise consistent with the peace of the Church, of whatever sort it might be, I would judge it to come from divine ordinance in answer to the prayers of the Church. And I don't mean by this I could set out a remedy before the fact, which might then be approved as just, since *the judgments of God are incomprehensible and past setting out.*[56]

Disciple. I take it your sense is that a pope given over to the judgment of God faces a much more perilous judgment than that of   36

formam procedit. Sed declara, quomodo absque maiori periculo ordinarium humanum remedium dari nequeat.

Magister. Dixi divinum iudicium pace ecclesie salva presumendum; ex quo habes nullum iudicium iustum, ubi pax seu unitas ecclesie leditur, ut etiam in Basiliensi synodo Bohemi edocti sunt. Si igitur synodo ordinario iure illa facultas concederetur, quomodo foret possibile pacem ecclesie posse conservari, ymmo impossibile humanitus? Propter quam impossibilitatem unus omnibus prepositus est, quia alias unitas et pax ecclesie conservari non posset tollereturque ab inferioribus timor et ordo obedientie et a papa libertas potentatus in correctionibus, ne illis gravis esset, qui congregati ipsum suo arbitrio iudicarent; confunderetur ordo ecclesie et armonia concordantie nequaquam subsistere posset. Ex hiis vides, quomodo Basilienses in confusionem intelligentie incidunt, quando nituntur derelictis viis patrum humanam constituere ecclesiam et sic fantastice construendo potius destruunt quam edificent.

37 *Discipulus.* Satis est nunc, quia nichil restat non clare expositum. Non te tedeat pauca hiis addicere; nam audio multos alios errores ex pravo intellectu decreti Constantiensis sequi et illos clamare ad principes, ut auctoritatem ecclesie habeant recommissam, quasi ipsi sint ecclesia.

Magister. Verum dicis: dicunt se ecclesiam representare cum plena potestate ecclesie, et ergo auctoritatem et nomen ecclesie falso sibi usurpant. Iste est primus error omnium hereticorum. Omnes enim heretici extra ecclesiam salutem non esse scientes

a synod, which proceeds through a single form. But explain why an ordinary human remedy cannot be granted without greater peril [to the Church].

Master. I said divine judgment must be presumed, saving the peace of the Church; hence, where the peace or unity of the Church is harmed, you have no just judgment, as the Bohemians were taught even in the synod at Basel. If therefore that faculty were conceded the synod by ordinary law, how would it be possible for the peace of the Church to be preserved? Indeed, it would be impossible in human terms.[57] Because of that impossibility, one man is set over all, because otherwise the peace and unity of the Church could not be preserved; and fear and the order of obedience would be taken away from inferiors, and from the pope that liberty with which he is empowered for correction, lest it should weigh upon those who have gathered together in judgment over him. The order of the Church would be confounded and the harmony of concord would be unable to survive.[58] From these considerations you see how those at Basel fall into confusion of understanding when they try to constitute the Church as a human institution, abandoning the ways of the fathers; and by construing the Church in such a delusional manner they destroy it rather than build it up.

Disciple. I am now satisfied; nothing remains that has not been clearly explained. I hope it won't weary you to add a little more. For I hear about many other errors following from their perverted interpretation of the decree of Constance; and I hear them crying out to the princes that they should have the authority of the Church recommitted [to themselves], as if they themselves were the Church.

Master. You're right. They say that they represent the Church with the full power of the Church; and therefore they falsely usurp for themselves the authority and name of the Church. This is the first error of all heretics. For all heretics, knowing

37

se ecclesiam facere presumunt. Contra quem sancti doctores constantissime predicaverunt, quoniam non potest dici ecclesia katholica nisi ea, que communicat omnibus per orbem christianis. Dicere ecclesiam esse contractam, anathema est, et sanctus Augustinus 2° libro *Contra Petilianum* exponens, quid sit catholica ecclesia, dicit: 'Ego quidem Grece lingue perparum assecutus sum, et prope nichil. Non tamen impudenter dico me nosse *olon* non esse "unum" sed "totum" et *catholon* "secundum totum", unde "catholica" nomen accepit, que declaratur per Christum dicentem: "Non est vestrum scire tempora, que posuit Pater in sua potestate; sed accipietis virtutem supervenientis spiritus sancti in vos et eritis michi testes in Ierusalem et in totam Iudeam et Samariam usque in totam terram". Ecce unde catholica dicitur'. Hec ille. Et idem ad Vincentium de Rogatistis ac Donatistis: 'Quaslibet quisque ansas et uncos adversus simplicitatem veritatis intexat, quaslibet nebulas callide falsitatis effundat, sicut anathema erit, qui anunciaverit Christum neque passum esse neque tertia die resurrexisse, quoniam in veritate evangelica accepimus: "Oportebat Christum pati et resurgere a mortuis tertia die"; sic erit anathema quisque annuntiaverit ecclesiam preter communionem omnium gentium'. Hec ille.

Infinita testimonia scripturarum de hoc sunt, et quia tu scis, quomodo isti, qui de communione domini nostri pape et universe ecclesie exiverunt et sibi Amedeum quondam Subaudie ducem caput constituerunt, scismatici facti sunt, itaque eis ecclesie nomen nulla ratione competere potest. Ideo propter hos et alios exorbitantissimos errores iuste dampnati sunt a sancta sede apostolica approbante sancta synodo Florentina.

there is no salvation outside the Church, presume to make themselves the Church. Against this error the holy doctors have preached with great constancy that the only Catholic Church is the one that is in communion with all Christians throughout the world. To say that the Church is limited [to one place] is anathema; and Saint Augustine, in the second book *Against Petellian*,[59] expounding what the Catholic Church is, says, "I can follow little or nothing of the Greek tongue, yet I am not ashamed to state that I know *olon* doesn't mean 'one' but 'all,' and *catholicon* means 'according to the whole;' whence the name 'catholic' originated, which is set out by Christ when he says: *It is not for you to know the times which the Father has put in His own power. But receive the virtue of the overshadowing Holy Spirit in you; and you shall be witnesses unto Me in Jerusalem, and in all Judaea, and Samaria, and even to the uttermost part of the earth.* See what 'catholic' means." And the same Father says to Vincent about the Rogatists and Donatists,[60] "Whatever loops and hooks someone might join together against the simplicity of the truth, whatever clouds of cunning falsehood he might pour forth, just as he will be anathema who announces Christ neither suffered nor arose on the third day, since we accept in gospel truth, *It behoved Christ to suffer and to rise again from the dead, the third day*, so too will anyone be anathema who shall announce that the Church is outside the communion of all nations."

There are infinite testimonies to this in Scripture; and you know how those have become schismatics who departed from communion with our lord the pope and the universal Church and made their head Amadeus, once duke of Savoy, so they cannot for any reason appropriate the name of the Church to themselves. Therefore, because of these and other egregious errors, they are justly condemned by the Apostolic See with the approval of the synod at Florence.

38 *Discipulus.* Regratior tibi, magister, quia nichil hesitationis in me dereliquisti. Vitabo illos homines et eorum pestiferam doctrinam et cathedre Petri, ubi video solidam fidei doctrinam, constanter adherebo. Age tu, ut detegatur undique venenum seductorium perfidorum, qui quadam apparenti sanctimonia se ingerunt! Novitas enim ac quod detrahatur potestati primi et sublimentur inferiores, vulgo insipienti gratum est. In tempore resistere, ne heresis crescat et populares argumentis sophisticis istorum armati principatum omnem supprimant!

39 *Magister.* Recte consulis, sed non audior. Quo vis, ut pergam? Undique habet error iste aliquos defensores pertinaces, ita ut prudentia rerum imbutus facile conspiciat hunc errorem eversionem principatuum et effusionem maxime sanguinis pariturum, nisi deus omnipotens de celo provideat, quem oremus, ut pro sua pietate ecclesiam suam tueatur protegatque. Amen.

Disciple. I thank you again, master: you have left me with no   38
doubts or hesitations. I will avoid those men and their pestifer-
ous doctrine; and I shall stick loyally to the see of Peter,
wherein, I see, lies the solid doctrine of the faith. And you must
act to reveal everywhere the poisonous seduction of the
perfidious, who conduct themselves with the appearance of
sanctity! For novelty and what detracts from the power of the
leader and raises inferiors on high is pleasing to the foolish
mob. Resist promptly to prevent heresy from increasing and to
stop the populists, armed with their sophistical arguments,
from putting down every principate!

Master. Your advice is good, but I shall not take it. Where would   39
you wish me to go? Everywhere this error has some pertinacious defenders, so that a person who has acquired some prudence in affairs may see that this error will bring about the subversion of principates and great bloodshed, unless Almighty
God, to whom we pray, should look down from heaven and of
his mercy guard and protect His Church. Amen.

Sermo XXI: Intrantes domum

1 *Intrantes domum invenerunt puerum cum Maria, matre eius, et procidentes adoraverunt eum.* Matth. 2.

Primo, quo modo magi intraverunt domum etc., ut alibi, secundum historiam cum suis annexis. Et quia 'domus' capitur pro ecclesia militante — I Ad Tim.: 'Scias, quo modo oporteat te in domo Domini conversari,' et Sap. 9: 'Sapientia sibi aedificavit domum' — et pro ecclesia triumphante — Joh. 14: 'In domo Patris mei mansiones multae sunt,' et in Psalmo: 'Beati, qui habitant in domo tua, Domine' et alibi: 'Dilexi decorem domus tuae' — et capitur 'domus' pro ecclesia manufacta — 'Domus mea domus orationis vocabitur,' et Is. 2: 'Venite, ascendamus ad montem Domini et ad domum Dei Jacob' —, ideo secundo loco de ecclesia secundum hoc aliquid dicendum, quia hodie festum ecclesiae etc. Et quia etiam 'domus' est fidelis anima — Psalmo: 'Domum tuam decet sanctitudo,' et Ad Hebr. 3: 'Filius in domo sua' est, 'quae domus sumus nos' —, ideo de hac domo, et quo modo ipsam nostram domum intrare debeamus, ut inveniamus puerum cum Maria, matre eius, et quo modo procidentes adorare eum debemus, tertio loco dicendum est brevissime.

Sermon 21: *"Entering into the house"*

[Epiphany 1439 or 1440, possibly at Koblenz]

And entering into the house, they found the child with Mary His mother, 1
and falling down they adored Him. Matthew 2 [11].

First, how the Magi entered the house etc., as elsewhere, according to the story with its additions. And that "house" is to be understood as the Church Militant—I Timothy [3:15]: *Thou knowest how thou oughtest to behave thyself in the house of God,* and Proverbs 9[1]: *Wisdom hath built herself a house*—and on behalf of the Church Triumphant—John 14 [2]: *In My Father's house there are many mansions,* and in the Psalm [83:5] *Blessed are they that dwell in thy house, O Lord* and elsewhere [Psalm 25:8]: *I have loved the beauty of Thy house*—and "house" is to be understood as the church built by hands—[Mark 11: 17] *My house shall be called the house of prayer,* and Isaiah 2 [3]: *Come and let us go up to the mountain of the Lord, and to the house of the God of Jacob*—and so, in the second place, something must be said about the Church in this respect, because today is the feast of the Church etc. And that "house" is the faithful soul—Psalm [92:5]: *Holiness becometh Thy house,* and Hebrews 3 [6]: He is *the Son in His own house, which house are we*—and so, in the third place, something must be said briefly about this house, and how we ought to enter this our house, so that we might find the child with Mary, His mother, and how, falling down, we should adore him.[1]

Pars secunda: De ecclesia tamquam rationabilium spirituum
ad Christum caput unione, et quo modo in eam intretur.

a) In ecclesia militante, cuius finis est triumphans,
in unitate oboedientiae peregrinandum esse.

2 Intrantes ecclesiam inveniunt puerum etc., ad quam intratur per
fidem; nam 'ecclesia est congregatio fidelium.' Est verum, quod ecclesia militans est congregatio fidelium, ubi est unio christianorum
ad suum caput per fidem; nam ibi veritas non apprehenditur nisi
'in speculo et in aenigmate.'

3 In triumphante vero cessat fides, ubi 'facie ad faciem' videtur
Christus etc. Quare ecclesia est unio rationabilium spirituum ad
caput suum Christum. Et ideo notandum est, quo modo Deo nostro omnis creatura absque praesumptione aliqua de se ipsa pure et
simpliciter credere et oboedire tenetur tamquam infallibili sapientiae et per oboedientiam concordanter adhaeret praeceptori et
consequitur finem suum. Nam Deus omnia creavit propter se. Et
quoniam ipsa 'sapientia' aeterna 'domum' rationalis creaturae 'sibi
aedificavit,' in quo centraliter habitare deliciatur, tunc ipsa rationalis creatura gustare potest per adhaesionem ad ipsam creatricem
Sapientiam refectionem illius supercaelestis sapientiae, panem et
vinum.

Hoc autem fit per ipsam unitatem oboedientiae et caritatis, per
quam ipsi rationales spiritus unum sunt cum Christo et per ipsum
Deo Patri, sicut Filius est unum cum Patre. Et haec quidem unio,
quando est perpetua et infallibilis in patria, dicitur ecclesia triumphans; quando adhuc est in terra et peregrina, multis oppressa
tempestatibus et periculis separationis, dicitur militans; si se habet
medio modo, dicitur dormiens. Unde quanta sit ista conexio omnium spirituum cum Christo in patria, Ambrosius in Epist. 17 ad
Irenaeum eleganter ostendit.

Second Part:[2] *Concerning the Church as a union of rational spirits*
with Christ, the head; and how we may enter it.

a) In the Church Militant, whose end is the Triumphant one, we must
make the pilgrimage in the unity of obedience.

Entering the Church, which they entered through faith, they 2
found the boy etc., for "the Church is the congregation of the
faithful."[3] It is true that the Church Militant is the congregation
of the faithful where there is the union of Christians to their head
by faith;[4] for the truth is learned there only *through mirror image and*
enigma.[5]

In the Church Triumphant, however, where Christ is seen *face*
to face, etc., faith ceases. Therefore, the Church is the union of rational spirits to their head, Christ.[6] And so we must note how ev- 3
ery creature of itself is obliged to believe and obey our God, purely
and simply without any presumption, as infallible wisdom, and to
adhere to its teacher harmoniously through obedience and to pursue its end.[7] For God created everything for Himself.[8] And, since
that eternal *Wisdom hath built herself a house*[9] in the rational creature, in which it delights to dwell centrally, then that rational creature can taste the refection of that supercelestial wisdom, the
bread and wine,[10] through adhesion to that creative wisdom.

However, this is done through that unity of obedience and
charity through which those rational spirits are one with Christ
and through Him with God the Father, just as the Son is one with
the Father.[11] This union, indeed, when it is perpetual and infallible in the fatherland, is called the Church Triumphant; while still
on earth and a pilgrim, oppressed by many storms and perils of
separation, it is called Militant. If it is in the middle mode, it is
called the Church Sleeping.[12] Hence Ambrose elegantly shows, in
Epistle [16] to Irenaeus,[13] how great is this connection of all spirits
with Christ in the fatherland.

4   Ecclesia vero triumphans, quae iam exivit peregrinationis istius metas, primo ex oboedientibus angelis cum Verbo aeterno conexa est, segregatis praesumptuosis apostatis et inoboedientibus, qui similes esse voluerunt Altissimo. Inter quos angelos ad instar ut in ipsa Trinitate mirabilis ordo est, ita ut sint tres ordines ad instar Trinitatis, et in quolibet tres chori; et superior ad instar Patris illuminans etc. Unde ista congregatio deiformis multum intrinsece unitur Deo secundum suos gradus.

Et sicut istis spiritibus beatis alii rationales humani spiritus accesserunt in locum daemonum expulsorum, ita etiam 'ecclesia malignantium' contrario modo se habet absque ordine cum turbatione daemoniorum cum Lucifero capite eorum, ad quos etiam praesumptuosi et rebelles increduli humani spiritus descenderunt perpetuo mansuri.

Sunt vero in medio duae ecclesiae, scilicet militans et dormiens, quae nondum pervenerunt ad terminum. Et est dormiens propter certitudinem praemii exaltata supra militantem, licet sit tamquam peregrina secum adhuc unita, ita quod eius suffragiis adiuvetur; est tamen magis propinqua triumphanti ex certitudine victoriae aeternae mortis. Militans vero est congregata ex hominibus, quorum aliqui perveniunt per mortem immediate ad ecclesiam triumphantem, aliqui ad ecclesiam malignantium perditorum, aliqui ad ecclesiam dormientium purgandorum.

5   Huic ecclesiae militanti, quae 'sponsa' immaculata dicitur, promissa est transductio ad regnum aeternum, ad unionem triumphantium, si perfecerit per oboedientiam viam peregrinationis, ut Paulus attestatur ad Ephesios. Et ista est ecclesia 'mater nostra,' quam ab initio Verbum Dei et Patris Sapientia sibi desponsavit.

The Church Triumphant, however, which already has left the   4
boundaries of this pilgrimage, first is joined via the obedient angels with the eternal Word, cut off from the presumptuous, apostate and disobedient ones, who wish to be like the Most High.[14]
Among those angels there is a wondrous order reflecting that in
the Trinity, so that there are three orders in the image of the Trinity; and in each there are three choirs; and the highest is in the image of the Father, enlightening etc. Therefore, this congregation of
the deiform is united most intrinsically to God, each according to
its grade.[15]

And just like these blessed spirits, other rational human spirits
go to the place of the expelled demons, so that *the church of the
evildoers*[16] in the opposite way exists without order in the tumult of
demonic spirits, with Lucifer their head, to whom also the presumptuous and rebellious unbelieving human spirits[17] descend to
remain eternally.

There are, however, in the middle two Churches, those Militant and Sleeping, which have not yet reached their goal. And the
Sleeping one, exalted over the Militant because of the certitude of
its reward, although it is like the pilgrim church and still united
within itself, so that it is aided by the prayers [of the Church Mili-
tant]; it is, nevertheless, much nearer to the Triumphant by its
certitude of eternal victory over death. The Militant one, however,
is gathered from among men, some of whom come by means of
death immediately to the Church Triumphant; others, to the
church of the wicked and the lost; others, to the Church Sleeping,
undergoing purgation.[18]

The promise of passing over to the eternal kingdom, to union   5
with the triumphant souls, is made to the Church Militant, which
is called the immaculate spouse,[19] if it shall perfect the way of pilgrimage through obedience, as Paul attests in his letter to the
Ephesians [4:17–6:20]. And this is the Church, our mother, whom
the word of God and Wisdom of the Father espoused from the

Quod in paradiso figurabatur, dum ex latere Adae Eva creata, matrimonium est institutum cum mandato oboediendi subsequente. Nam sicut, ut ait Hieronymus, Eva ex costa Adae, ita ecclesia per Evam significata ex Christo, quam ut ad Adam sibi desponsavit, etc.

Quoniam vero homo se etiam erexit per praesumptionem contra oboedientiam, secundus Adam, scilicet Christus, venit, et hanc maculam contractam 'per inoboedientiam,' ut mereretur homo transire ad consortia caelestia, ad ecclesiam triumphantem, sponsam immaculatam, lavit sanguine suo, etc.

b) Ecclesiam militantem ad instar
triumphantis hierarchice ordinatam esse.

6 Quo modo vero ista militans ecclesia sit mirabiliter ordinata ad instar angelicae, Dionysius *De ecclesiastica hierarchia* tractat. Nam ita ordo reperitur hierarchicus, etc. Gregorius IX *Contra praesumptiones Michaelis*, etc. (Vide in libro tuo *De concordantia ecclesiastica*).

Quo modo sicut in corpore humano, ita in ipsa est spiritus, anima et corpus. Sicut in caelesti Deus, angeli et homines, sacramenta illuminantia et purgantia, est sacerdotium pastorale purgatum et purgans, est fidelis populus, qui purgatur.

Item, quo modo est mirabilis hierarchia in sacramentis usque ad sacramentum sacramentorum. Nam sicut 'facie ad faciem' in patria Deus se communicat, ita sub speciebus hic. Et hic, quo modo sicut sacramenta sunt ut ecclesia triumphans, ita etiam quodlibet gestat imaginem Trinitatis, quia est sacramentum tantum, est res tantum et res et sacramentum.

beginning.[20] That was prefigured in Paradise, when Eve was created from Adam's side; matrimony was instituted with the subsequent command to obey.[21] For, just as Eve was drawn out of Adam's rib, the Church, signified by Eve, is drawn out of Christ, Who espoused her just like Adam, as Jerome says.[22]

Since, however, man raised himself up by his presumption against obedience, the second Adam, that is Christ, came; and [He washed] this stain, contracted through disobedience, with His blood, so that man should merit to pass to the celestial company, to the Church Triumphant, the immaculate spouse, etc.[23]

> b) *The Church Militant is ordered after the example*
> *of the hierarchy of the Church Triumphant.*

How, however, the Church Militant is wondrously ordered after the example of the angelic hierarchy Dionysius treats in *On the Ecclesiastical Hierarchy*.[24] For there is found a hierarchical order etc. Gregory IX[25] *Against the Presumptions of Michael* etc.[26] (Refer to your book *On Ecclesiastical Concord*.)[27]

Now, however, just as in the human body, so in the Church there are spirit, soul and body. Just as in the celestial hierarchy there are God, the angels and men, in the Church Militant there are the sacraments, illuminating and purifying; the pastoral priesthood, purified and purifying; and the faithful people, which is purified.[28]

Likewise, how the wondrous hierarchy is in the sacraments up to the sacrament of sacraments [i.e., Christ].[29] For just as God communicates Himself *face to face*[30] in the fatherland, so under the species [of the sacraments, i.e., bread and wine] here. And here, just as the sacraments are like the Church Triumphant, so also whatever bears the image of the Trinity, because it is a great sacrament, is a great thing, both thing and sacrament.[31]

7   Ordo sacerdotii per sacramentum characterizatur, scilicet ordinis, ad superiora divina. Et in hoc sacerdotio est hierarchia ordinata a pontificatu summo usque ad laicum. Nam sunt quidam superioris ordinis, quidam inferioris, quidam medii, et in quolibet
tres chori sicut in angelis. Et habent se sacramenta ut spiritus, sacerdotium ut anima, populus ut corpus. Gregorius Nazianzenus
in *Apologetico* in principio: Sacerdotium in corpore ecclesiae officium gerit, quod anima in corpore. Et ita convenit eis illuminare,
vivificare, regere. Illuminare sicut rationi lumen dare etc., quia 'lux
mundi' et 'sal terrae.' Cyprianus *De aleatore.*

Est praeterea in primo choro pontificum ordo hierarchicus,
quia in uno episcopatu per orbem diffuso propter unitatem est
differentia cum concordantia plurium in uno, ut Cyprianus ad Novatianum, Hieronymus *Contra Iovinianum.* Et nota, quod necessario devenitur ad primum maximum pontificem, qui in terra habet
potestatem summi hierarchae ut summus minister, scilicet angelus
summus in caelo. Fungitur autem totum sacerdotium 'legatione
pro Christo,' quia dixit: 'Sicut misit me vivens Pater,' ita 'mitto
vos.' Sicut angeli sunt nuntii Dei, etc.

8   Et consequenter ipsum sacerdotium consideratur dupliciter: aut
quoad ordinem, quem habet ad regimen ecclesiae, uti est necessitatis, aut quoad unionem, quia anima regit et unit corpus.

Quoad primum sunt ordines hierarchici usque ad pontificatum;
quoad secundum sunt pro unione, ut sit unitas. In ecclesia est potestas dispensativa regulata, quae est iurisdictionis. Et haec potestas sacerdotalis habet cathedram unam, sicut habet unum episcopatum, etc. Et in illa cathedra est ordo hierarchicus quoad

The order of the priesthood is marked out by the sacrament,   7
that is, the sacrament of ordination, for higher, divine things. And
in this priesthood there is a hierarchy from the supreme pontiff
down to the lay person.[32] For there are some of a superior order,
some of an inferior one, some of a middle one; and in each there
are three choirs, just as among the angels. And they are arranged
so that the sacraments are as the spirit, the priesthood is as the
soul, and the people are as the body. Gregory Nazianzen says in
the beginning of the *Apologetic Oration*[33] that the priesthood in the
body of the Church exercises an office, that of the soul in the
body; and so it befits them to illuminate, vivify, rule. To illuminate is like bringing light to the reason etc., because [the priesthood is] *the light of the world* and *the salt of the earth*.[34] Cyprian, *On
the Gamester*.[35]

There is, furthermore, a hierarchical order in the first choir of
the pontiffs, because in one episcopate diffused throughout the
world, on account of unity, there is a difference with the concord
of many in one, as Cyprian says to Novatian,[36] and Jerome in
Against Jovinian.[37] And note that, of necessity, it comes down to the
first, greatest pontiff, who as the highest minister has on earth the
power of the supreme hierarch, that is, the supreme angel in
heaven.[38] He exercises, however, the full priesthood "by legation
for Christ,"[39] because He said, *as the father*, giving life, *hath sent Me*,
so *send I you*.[40] Just as the angels are the messengers of God, etc.[41]

And, consequently, that priesthood is considered in two ways: 8
with respect to orders, which it has for the rule of the Church, as
is necessary, or with respect to union, because the soul rules and
unites the body.

As to the first, there are hierarchic orders up to the pontificate;
as to the second, they are for union, as the priesthood is a unity.
In the Church there is a regular dispensing power, the power of
jurisdiction. And this priestly power has one see, just as it has one
episcopate etc. And in that see there is a hierarchic order with re-

praesidentes in illa. Et ibi notetur dictum Optati Milevitani de angelo, qui praeest cathedrae, etc. Et habet cathedra Petri promissionem veritatis, ut dicunt sanctus Augustinus, Alipius et Fortunatus
9 ad Generosum etc. Et ibi est notandum, quo modo non est potestas ligandi et solvendi nisi adhaerenti Apostolicae Sedi, quo modo non est censendus in ecclesia nisi Apostolicae Sedi adhaerens.

Item, quo modo omnes episcopi sunt ut anima populi ex communi consensu, et quo modo parochiani in plebano, et plebani in episcopo, et episcopi in papa, et per papam Petro, et per Petrum, qui est lapis et fundamentum ecclesiae, Christo, qui est petra, etc.

Item, quo modo consequenter est hierarchia in fidelibus de summo imperatore usque ad agricolas. Et de triplici ordine regum, etc. Item de triplici regimine monarchico, aristocratico et politico, et etiam oeconomico et contrariis istis, etc. Item de hierarchia cuiuslibet personae in se: de spiritu, anima et corpore, etc. Ista est dispositio differentialis in mirabili conexione. — 83 D. *Ad hoc.*

c) In ecclesiam per fidem intrandum esse.

10 Et quo modo ab Abel iusto usque ad ultimum est una ecclesia. Et quo modo hodie ecclesia est lavata in Jordane, ac quo modo hodie gentes intrarunt ad eam; quo modo ipsa est navis sive arca Noe, extra quam non fuit salus, et quo modo patitur fluctuationes, sed non submersiones, quia fides Petri non peribit. Et 'haec est domus Domini firmiter aedificata, bene fundata super firmam petram,' et intrare ad eam est de necessitate salutis.

11 Intratur vero in eam per fidem. Oportet enim unumquemque ablutum esse per sacramentum baptismatis aut per rem sacramenti

spect to those presiding over it.[42] And there one should note the saying of Optatus of Milevis about the angel who presides over the see, etc.[43] And the see of Peter has Peter's promise of truth, as Augustine, Alypius and Fortunatus say to Generosus etc.[44] And there it is to be noted how there is no power of binding and loosing except by adhering to the Apostolic See; how one is not enrolled in the Church except by adhering to the Apostolic See.[45]

Likewise, how all the bishops are like the soul of the people by common consent, and how parishioners are in the parish priest, and the parish priest in the bishop, and the bishops in the pope, and, through the pope, in Peter, and through Peter, who is the cornerstone and foundation of the Church, in Christ, who is the Rock, etc.[46]

Likewise, how in consequence the hierarchy is in the faithful from the supreme pontiff even to the farmers. And concerning the threefold order of kings etc. Likewise, of the threefold regime, monarchy, aristocratic and polity, and even household management, and concerning their contraries etc.[47] Likewise, concerning the hierarchy of each person within himself, concerning the spirit, the soul and the body etc.[48] This is a differential disposition in a wondrous connection ([Gratian] D. 89 c. *Ad hoc* [c. 7]).[49]

c) One must enter into the Church through faith.

And how there is one Church from Abel the Just down to the last man.[50] And how today the Church is washed in the Jordan,[51] and how today the gentiles enter it;[52] how it is the ship or ark of Noah, outside of which there is no salvation;[53] and how it suffers from the waves but is not sunk, because the faith of Peter will not perish.[54] And *this is the house the Lord hath firmly built, well founded upon the firm rock,*[55] and to enter into it is necessary for salvation.

We enter into it through faith. It is necessary that each person be washed by the sacrament of baptism, or by the essence of the

tollente necessitate sacramentum. Et sic per fidem adhaereat Christo hodie baptizato! Oportet eum signo illius summi capitanei esse signatum, ut sit de exercitu illius. Exercitus est ecclesia. Oportet esse fidelem et victoriosum et non traditorem, ut, cum vicerit, habeat sedem cum capitaneo, 'Deo et Agno,' et in hoc oportet esse oboedientem, etc.

Item, quo modo desponsatio capitis cum anima cuiuslibet est, ut si rex Alemannorum desponsaret reginam Franciae cum condicione, ut totum regnum Franciae sibi subiugaret, et tunc eum traducere vellet et sibi uniri. Et ita obligatur anima ad difficile et non ⟨ad⟩ impossibile. Et si fecerit per subiectionem corporis sibi et se spiritui subiciendo, tunc invenit 'puerum cum Maria,' etc.

12 Habeas menti inter alia declarare, quo modo Deus rationali spiritui communicavit regitivam potentiam; item, quo modo rectorum actus, etiam malorum, efficaciam habet a Spiritu Sancto quoad recipientem etc.; item de legibus et regulis ecclesiae etc.

Pars tertia: De intrando in se ipsum et fide in humilitate servanda.

13 Tertio est videndum quo modo quis intrare debet intra se ipsum, ut *puerum inveniat cum Maria,* etc.

Statim dictum est, quod anima fidelis per caput ecclesiae est sub condicione desponsata, ut scilicet fidelis remaneat et corpus sibi subiciat et in servitutem redigat. Alioquin non poterit intrare in tabernaculum Domini et adorare etc. Per fidelitatem intellegere debemus, ne anima sit adultera et alios amatores quaerat quam suum sponsum. Quaerit autem anima alios amatores, quando se

sacraments when necessity prevents performance of the rite.[56] And thus through faith he adheres to Christ, who was baptized today! It is necessary to be signed with the sign of the supreme captain,[57] so that he may belong to his army. The army is the Church. It has to be faithful, victorious and loyal, so that he may have a seat with the captain, *God and the Lamb*,[58] when He conquers; and he must be obedient etc.

Likewise, how the espousal of the Head with anyone's soul occurs, as if the king of the Germans espoused the queen of France with the condition that all the kingdom of France became subject to him and then she wished to bring him over and to be united with him. And so the soul is obligated to what is difficult and not to what is impossible. And if someone subjects the body to himself and subjects himself to the spirit,[59] then he will find *the child with Mary* etc.[60]

You should have in mind, among other things, to declare how God communicated ruling power to the rational spirit; likewise, how the acts of the rulers, even of the wicked ones, have efficacy from the Holy Spirit as far as receiving, etc.;[61] likewise, concerning the laws and rules of the Church etc.   12

*Third Part: Concerning entering into oneself
and serving Him with faith in humility.*

Third, one must see how one ought to enter into oneself, so that he may find *the child with Mary*, etc.   13

It must be said at once that the faithful soul[62] is espoused through the Head of the Church under this condition, that she remains faithful and her body be subject to her and be brought into servitude.[63] Otherwise it could not enter into the tabernacle of the Lord and adore etc.[64] By fidelity we ought to understand that the soul may not be an adulteress and seek other lovers than her Spouse. The soul, however, seeks other lovers when she turns her-

convertit per electionem ad creaturam; et quanto plus creaturae adhaeserit, tanto minus Deo.

Potest autem ista adhaesio esse duplex ad creaturam, scilicet vel quia in creatura aliquid divinitatis quaerit et illud in creatura amplectitur tamquam tale — et est idolatria — vel quaerit in ipsa creatura salutem aliquam tamquam a creatura, et tunc aut concurrit ratio medii ad hoc, ut in medicinalibus et certis astrologicis, et non recedit propterea a Deo; vel non concurrit ut in physicis ligaturis, tunc, quia ratio medii deficit et se diabolus in istis saepe immiscet, ab istis est abstinendum per christianum. Unde Exod. 13 de hoc.

14   Aliquando quis ex pura malitia non servat fidem Deo, sicut blasphemus, qui attribuit Deo, quod ei non convenit, vel negat ei convenire, quod convenit, vel usurpat, quod Dei est. Et aliquando ingerit se cordi ex diaboli inspiratione vel ex frequenti timore offensae Dei, sicut timor adducit terribilia cordi in loco tenebroso. Aliquando diabolus loquitur per hominem blasphemiam, et illa non inficit. Unde vilipendi debent tales cogitationes et labores expelli, etc. Blasphemia oris, quando quis verbum contumeliosum loquitur contra Deum volens se vindicare de Deo et nominat membra non nominanda.

Et est maximum peccatum propter intentionem pessimam lingua perforando Deum, etc. Neque Judaei neque haeretici habent talem intentionem, quia putant se bene facere etc. Est maximum, quia minus homo inclinatur ad hoc peccatum, est contra optimum, nobilissimum. Ideo Thomas (II^a/II^{ae} q. 13) tenet, quod est maius peccatum quam homicidium, quia contra praeceptum primae tabulae.

self by choice to a created thing; and the more she adheres to a creature, the less she adheres to God.

This adhesion to a creature, however, can be understood in two senses: either that the soul seeks something of divinity in a creature and embraces it in the creature as though it were divine—and that is idolatry—or it seeks in that creature some salvation as if [salvation came ultimately] from the creature, and then either the calculation of means concurs with this, as in the case of medicines and sure astrological predictions, and it does not consequently depart from God, or it does not concur, as in the case of amulets. In the latter case, because the calculation of means fails and the devil often interplicates himself into those things, the Christian must abstain from such things; whence Exodus 13 on this.[65]

Sometimes someone, like a blasphemer, attributing to God   14 what does not belong to Him or denying Him that which befits Him, or usurping what belongs to God, does not keep faith with God out of pure malice.[66] And sometimes someone feels in his heart, from the devil's usurpation, frequent fear of having offended God, just as fear breeds terrible things in the dark places of the heart. And sometimes the devil speaks blasphemy through a man, and that does not poison him. Therefore, they should despise such thoughts and cast out those labors, etc.[67] Blasphemy with the mouth is when someone speaks insulting words against God, wishing to avenge himself against God, and names members which should not be named.[68]

And it is a very great sin because of the wicked intention of wounding God with one's tongue, etc. Neither the Jews nor the heretics have such an intention, because they think they do well, etc. It is a very great sin because a lesser man is inclined to this sin; it is against the best, the most noble being. Thus Thomas in the [*Summa theologiae*], IIa IIae, qu. 13 [art. 3], holds that it is a greater sin than homicide, since it is against a precept of the first tablet.[69]

Quia patri et matri maledicere est poena mortis (Matth. 5), igitur blasphemus est dignus morte corporali et spirituali. Deus despicitur. *De haereticis, Vergentis.* Regi maledicere est poena mortis (*Codex: Ne quis imperatori maledicat* leg. 1). Similiter est eadem poena maledicere sanctis (In *Authentica: Ne luxurietur contra*) propter unionem cum Deo. Est maxima ingratitudo.

Distinguit filios Dei et diaboli. Est linguagium inferni. Inde audientes obturare debent aures, etc. Et pessimus homo tunc cognoscitur, cui omnes creaturae maledicunt. Inde corporaliter, spiritualiter et aeternaliter punitur (*De maledicis* cap. 2).

Exempla punitionis: in puero, de quo sanctus Gregorius, et de milite etc., et qui blasphemavit oculum beatae Mariae etc. (vide alibi), de sagitta etc., in territorio Mediolanensi etc., Romae suspensus, de denario comitis Hugonis, etc.

Unde tales, licet videantur esse in ecclesia, tamen, quia non sunt fideles, non sunt membra Christi, sed diaboli. Ideo, licet omnes in peccato mortali Deo fidem non servent, tamen isti maxime infideles Deo sunt et plus ipsum offendunt.

15 Oportet ergo volentem in ecclesia esse intra se ipsum intrare et fidem in humilitate servare. Secundo oportet, quod subiciat corpus animae, ut sensus sit sub ratione, et hoc fit, si intraverit intra se per cognitionem sui ipsius. Quando enim praevaricatores recedunt, tunc redeunt ad cor; et ita non est melior ars neque salubrior quam se ipsum cognoscere.

Because cursing a father and mother is punishable by death (Matthew 5[22]), a blasphemer therefore deserves a corporeal and spiritual death. God is despised. *De haereticis* c. *Vergentis* [in the *Decretals* of Gregory IX, X 5.7.10]. To curse the king carries the death penalty; *Codex: Ne quis imperatori maledicat, l.1.*[70] Similarly, it is the same penalty to curse the saints (in *Authenticum: Ne luxurietur contra*)[71] because of their union with God. This is the greatest ingratitude.

It distinguishes between God's sons and the devil's. It is the language of hell.[72] Thereafter the hearers ought to stop up their ears. etc. And then the worst of men, whom all men curse, is known. Therefore, he is punished corporally, spiritually and eternally (*De maledicis*, cap. 2 [in the *Decretals* of Gregory IX, X 5.26.2]).

Examples of punishment: the boy of whom Saint Gregory speaks,[73] and of the knight etc., and the one who blasphemed the eye of blessed Mary etc. (see elsewhere), about the arrow,[74] etc., in the territory of Milan etc., the man hanged at Rome, of the coin of Count Hugh etc.[75]

Therefore, such persons, although they seem to be in the Church, nevertheless, since they are not faithful, they are not members of Christ's Church, but of the devil's. Therefore, although all in mortal sin do not keep faith with God, nevertheless, they are the greatest infidels before God and they offend Him more.

It is necessary, therefore, that anyone wishing to be in the 15 Church should enter within himself and keep faith with humility.[76] Second, it is necessary that he should subject the body to the soul, so that sense may be under reason; and he does this if he enters into himself through knowledge of himself. When the liars depart [from the faith], then they return to their heart;[77] and so there is no better art, nor anything more salubrious, than to know oneself.[78]

Quando enim homo praeponit se sibi et respicit suam vilitatem, suas miserias atque peccati plagas cognoscat, ut doleat; respicit praesentium vanitatem, ut contemnat, beneficia Dei, ut gratus exsistat, misericordiam, ut speret, iustitiam eius, ut timeat, finis incertitudinem, ut sollicitum se gerat et paratum se semper exhibeat. Et sic, qui primo a Deo et se alienatus dixit: 'Cor meum dereliquit me,' iam reversus per introitum intra se: 'Invenit servus tuus cor suum.'

16   Reperimus autem nos gratuitis spoliatos, naturalibus vulneratos, ratione caecatos, voluntate curvatos, memoria inquinatos, et dicemus, cum haec profundius viderimus: 'Peccavi super numerum arenae' etc. Et tunc veniet illud Sapientiae 8: 'Intrans in domum meam conquiescam cum illa' sapientia, scilicet Jesu nostro. Nam ipse lux est; in nobis habitat per fidem. Et tunc audiemus, quid loquatur in nobis, etc. Is. 30: 'In silentio et spe erit fortitudo.' Nam tunc non est multiloquium, etc. Humiliatio sequitur etc.

Et postquam intra se sic intraverit homo, invenit 'puerum cum Maria' in templo, id est ecclesia, in deserto, id est loco paenitentiae, in domo ordinatae conscientiae, in praesepio, id est humilitate.

17   Ille vere Deum reperit, qui intrat intra se ipsum, ut dicitur *De spiritu et anima* cap. 20. Tunc ad vitam accedit, quando per amorem in sic invento intra se figitur. Unde oportet exire omne sensibile et omne imaginabile et omne intellegibile et redire centraliter ad se, ut solo desiderio summe desiderabilis attingatur.

Et cum puerum sic inveneris, accedes ad eum, adorabis eum tamquam servus dominum, mendicus indigens, infirmus humili

When a man places his own self before him and regards his vileness, he knows his miseries and the blows of sin so that he may suffers pain; he regards the vanity of present things so that he may contemn them; the benefits of God, so that he may be grateful; His mercy, so that he may hope; His justice, so that he may fear; the uncertainty of his end, so that he may conduct himself with care and always show himself prepared.[79] And so in the case of anyone who at first was alienated from God and himself says, *My heart hath forsaken me*,[80] then turning back through entering into himself, says, *Thy servant hath found his heart.*[81]

We find ourselves despoiled by profitless things, wounded by natural ones, blinded by reason, bent by the will, befouled by memory; and we say, when we see these things more profoundly, "I have sinned beyond the number of the sands" etc.[82] Then will come the text of Wisdom 8 [16], *When I go into my house, I repose myself with her*, wisdom, that is, our Jesus. For He Himself is the light; He dwells in us through faith.[83] And then shall we hear what is spoken in us etc. Isaiah 30 [15], *In silence and in hope shall your strength be*. For then there is no loquacity etc. Humiliation follows etc.

And after a man shall so enter within himself, he finds *the child with Mary* in the temple, that is, the Church, in the desert, that is, in the place of penitence, in the house of the ordered conscience, in the manger, that is, through humility.

Truly he who enters within himself finds God, as is said in *On the Spirit and the Soul*, c. 20.[84] Then he approaches unto life, when he is fashioned by love thus found within himself. Hence it is necessary to leave behind everything sensible and everything imaginable and everything intelligible and to return to the center of oneself, so that one may attain his only desire for the supremely desirable.

And when you shall find the [Christ] child in this way, you will approach Him, adore Him as a servant does his master, a needy

16

17

mentis prostratione, nudo affectu cum magnitudine desiderii et 'gemitu cordis,' 'in simplicitate et sinceritate.' Et exponis omnia tua cum fiducia et offers et committis sibi. Et tu te proicis in ipsum: 'Fiat voluntas tua' etc. Tunc attingis ultimum desiderium.

In hac tamen praegustatione vitae futurae intellegis, quam dulcia oscula sunt Mariae et Filii et tui etc., ut habes alibi, etc.

beggar, shaking with the humble prostration of the mind, naked of affection with greatness of desire and *with the groaning of my heart*,[85] *in simplicity [of heart] and sincerity*.[86] And you will set out all that is yours with trust and offer and commit yourself to Him. And you will throw yourself upon Him: *Thy will be done*.[87] Then you attain your ultimate desire.

In this foretaste of future life, nevertheless, you understand how sweet are the kisses exchanged by you with Mary and the Son — as you have cited elsewhere etc.

Contra Bohemos

1   Nicolaus miseratione diuina tituli sancti Petri ad uincula sacrosancte romane ecclesie presbiter cardinalis, apostolice sedis legatus, episcopus Brixinensis, magnificis, nobilibus, prudentibusque uiris, dominis, gubernatori, concilio, regentibus, et uniuersis incolis regni Bohemie veram pacem assequi et in ea perseueranter permanere.

2   Voluit diuina pietas ut ordinatione sanctissimi et piissimi pontificis nostri Nicolai pape quinti, summe pro uestra ac omnium salute uigilantis, uestre ad apostolicam sedem unitatis reintegratio, post multos longe nobis aptiores legatos, ad nos nunc perueniret ‹et› qualiscunque sollicitudo, et quamuis tam admonitione apostoli quam sanctorum conciliorum atque doctorum imbuti merito retraheremur, maxime quia auersio animorum non repperit hactenus efficax remedium, quasi iam tales animi in seruitute principis tenebrarum redacti nequeant intelligere ut bene agant, nihilominus nonnullis literis ex regno ad principes uicinos atque ad nos missis, in quibus sanctus dominus noster notatur quasi compactatis certis per Basilienses uobiscum initis detrahat, medio religiosi fratris Iohannis de Capistrano respondere distulimus, sperantes Iacobellianos qui Iacobelli uesaniam sequentes communionem utriusque speciei quo ad populum laicalem sua sponte contra ritum ecclesie catholice continuant, de proximo ad ecclesiam unde exiuerunt reuersuros, aut nos cum ipsis conuentum aliquem de proximo pro instauranda et firmanda pace habituros fuimus, de

Letter to the Bohemians on Church Unity

Against the Bohemians

Nicholas, by divine mercy Cardinal Priest of San Pietro in Vincoli   1
of the Holy Roman Church, Legate of the Apostolic See, Bishop
of Brixen, bids the magnificent nobles and wise men, the lords, the
governor, council, regents and all the inhabitants of the Kingdom
of Bohemia to follow true peace and remain in it perseveringly.

Through the ordinance of our most holy and most pious   2
pontiff, Pope Nicholas V, vigilant for your and for everyone's salvation, divine piety willed that some sort of responsibility for your
reunion with the Apostolic See should fall upon us now, after
many legates far more capable than us. Instructed by the warnings
of the apostle, the holy councils and the doctors, we rightly drew
back, especially because an efficacious remedy for the alienation of
souls has not been found up to this point, as if such souls, already
reduced to servitude to the prince of darkness, do not wish to understand so that they may do well. Nevertheless, we decided to respond to a few letters from the Kingdom to the neighboring
princes and to us, in which our holy lord is branded as though he
were withdrawing from certain Compacts entered into with you
by those at Basel. Through the intermediary of a religious,
Brother John Capistran, we deferred responding, hoping that the
Jacobellians, who, following the madness of Jacobellus, continue
giving communion under both species to the lay populace by their
own will, against the rite of the Catholic Church, eventually
would return to the Church whence they had departed; or that we
might soon make some covenant with them for the establishment
and confirmation of peace. And we were consoled no little in this

hoc non parum ex his optimis uerbis oratorum uestrorum qui nobiscum Ratispane conuenerant consolati.

3   Sed nobis inquirentibus quid singuli uestrum de sancte unionis
repetitione sentiant, comperimus nondum omnium intentionem
confractam ut ueram catholicam uelint unionem amplecti. Considerauimus autem Iacobelli sequaces sue diuisionis materiam plurimum ex compactatis firmari, post hec se praxim primitiue ecclesie
atque subsequentis, ac etiam sacras allegare scripturas, et quia uisi
sunt suis ultimis ad multos datis scripturis penitus in compactatis
residere, nos uolentes experiri an illa desinere uellent que nihil utilitatis contribuunt, deliberauimus primum nostris scriptis ostendere eos superuacue compactatis inherere, cum non seruiant ipsis
in aliquo, sed potius nobis catholicis contra eos, proponentes in
euentum indurationis alias eorum circa praxim primorum nostrorum enodare fallacias, atque demum nihil eos fulcimenti habere ex
sacris literis pro nostro modulo manifestare, quamquam fateamur
longe sufficientius a nostris predecessoribus et, qui adhuc super-
sunt, doctissimis fidelibus ad singula Iacobellianorum assumpta
responsum. Misimus autem primum ex Ratispana literas tenoris
subsequentis.

4   Nicolaus miseratione diuina tituli sancti Petri ad uincula sacrosancte Romane ecclesie presbiter cardinalis, apostolice sedis legatus, episcopus Brixinensis uniuersis et singulis nobilibus, uenerabilibus, strennuis, honorabilibus prudentibusque
baronibus, prelatis, militibus, presbiteris, religiosis, militari-
bus, magistris ciuium, et opidanis, et cunctis ecclesiasticis et

by the favorable words of your envoys who met with us at Regensburg.

But in asking what some of you think about seeking restoration 3 of holy union, we discovered it was not yet the contrite intention of all that they wished to embrace true Catholic union. We supposed that the followers of Jacobellus strongly confirm the subject matter of their division arising from the Compacts.[1] Afterwards they cited the praxis of the primitive Church and of the one that followed, and even the Holy Scriptures. And because they seem in their most recent, widely distributed writings to rest their case entirely on the Compacts, we wished to test whether they would want to stop doing things that were yielding them no advantage, and we decided first to show them in our writings that it is useless to stick to the Compacts, since they are not observing them in any particular, but that they should rather adhere to us, the Catholics, against them. We proposed in the event of obstinacy to unravel their other fallacies about the practices of our first ancestors, and to show from Sacred Scripture, so far as our small capacity allows, that in the end they have no foundation — although we admit that the response made to the individual propositions of the Jacobellians was made in a far more satisfactory way by our predecessors and by the learned among those of the faithful who are still left [among you]. We, however, first sent from Regensburg a letter of the following tenor:

Nicholas, by divine mercy Cardinal Priest of San Pietro in 4 Vincoli of the Holy Roman Church, Legate of the Apostolic See, Bishop of Brixen, to all and each of the noble, the venerable, vigorous, honorable and prudent barons, prelates, knights, priests, religious, soldiers and masters of the citizens and town dwellers, and to all ecclesiastical and secular persons inhabiting the famous Kingdom of Bohemia and the

secularibus inclitum regnum Bohemie, et marchionatum
Morauie inhabitantibus, uere pacis desideria feliciter adipisci.

5   Postquam diuina pietas statuit uti firmiter speramus regnum et marchionatum predictos hoc tempore ad obedientiam sacrosancte Romane et catholice ecclesie reuocare, sanctissimus dominus noster dominus Nicolaus papa quintus
nobis curam et sollicitudinem tam sancti operis commisit et
legati de latere plenam tribuit facultatem. Et quoniam nuper
ex nobilibus regni ipsius oratoribus in dieta Ratispanensi la-
tenter intelleximus desideria omnium uestrorum diuina inspiratione nunc ad ueram et effectualem unionem inclinari, et
quod eapropter apostolicam legationem in regno ipso constitui optatis pro complemento tam sancti propositi, mox operam dedimus ut hoc summo pontifici nostro quantocius pa-
tefaceret. Et quoniam ad rem ipsam feliciter conducendam
necesse est ut, ante accessum apostolici legati ad regnum, de
mente singulorum, aut saltem maioris et sanioris partis inha-
bitantium, quo ad puram ueram et effectualem obedientiam
et subiectionem simus certiorati — nam si foret propositi uestri uos uelle conformare progenitoribus uestris, qui ante
hanc differentiam catholicam uitam duxerunt, qui fidem or-
thodoxam ab apostolica sede atque priuilegia metropolitice
sedis et generalis studii pro sua deuotione et obedientia ad
matrem suam ipsam, scilicet sedem romanam, meruerunt,
quemadmodum et alia christiana regna que adhuc in eadem
obedientia perseuerant, superuacue apostolicus legatus in-
quietaretur, ut[1] re non peracta in non paruum omnium uestrorum dedecus rediret — quare ut experiamur quem fructum introitus legati efficere queat, honorabilem Iohannem
Dursmit presentium latorem capellanum nostrum deuotum
dilectum, ad uos omnes et singulos transmisimus, cui dedi-

March of Moravia, may they obtain happily their desire for true peace.

After divine piety established that we should firmly hope   5
at this time to recall the aforesaid Kingdom and March to obedience to the Holy Roman and Catholic Church, our most holy lord, Lord Pope Nicholas V, committed to us the responsibility and care for this holy work and gave us the power of a legate *de latere*. Since lately we had confidential information from the noble envoys of that Kingdom to the Diet of Regensburg that the desires of all of you now incline by divine inspiration to true and effective union, and for that reason you wish that an apostolic legation be appointed for your kingdom, to accomplish so holy a purpose we undertook that this should be made known to our supreme pontiff as quickly as possible. It is necessary for the felicitous conduct of this business, that, before the arrival of the apostolic legate in the Kingdom, we may be assured concerning the attitudes of every individual, or at least of the greater and sounder part of the inhabitants, with respect to true and effectual obedience and submission. For if it is your intention to conform to your ancestors, who before the present differences arose led a Catholic life, who merited the orthodox faith from the Apostolic See and the privileges of a metropolitan see and a university in return for your devotion and obedience to their Mother, that is, the Roman See, just like the other Christian kingdoms which still persevere in that obedience, it would be superfluous for the apostolic legate to worry that he might have to return with nothing accomplished, which would bring no little disgrace to you all. Hence, so that we may test what fruit the entry of a legate might be able to yield, we have sent to each and every one of you John Dursmit, the bearer of this letter, our devoted and

mus in mandatis ut his nostris patentibus litteris ostensis uniuscuiusque mentem et intentionem inuestiget circa iam dictam obedientiam prestandam, et que circa ipsam atque securum accessum apostolici legati fuerunt oportuna, prout de hoc per nos latius est informatus.

6   Quare rogamus uos et in domino exhortamur ut ipsum capellanum nostrum admittere, benigne audire et, que menti geritis, scripto patefacere uelitis, nec putetis nos a uobis rem magni ponderis leuiter exigere. Nam cum impossibile in ueram pacem ecclesiasticam constitui posse, quamdiu non est omnimoda conformitas corporis et membrorum — turpis enim est omnis pars, que toti non congruit — hinc in ea re ubi, qui non est cum uniuersali ecclesia, contra eam esse constat, necesse est pure et simpliciter absque pacto et conditione omnium conformitatem obedientie amplecti. Neque quenquam moueat, quod, cum oratores tunc Basiliensis concilii de pace ecclesiastica Prage tractarent, ad compactata deuentum. Nam experimento compertum est modum illum integram pacem et unitatem cum sancta Romana ecclesia non effecisse, que cum sit piissima mater omnium fidelium, redeunti quem in fide genuit gremium claudere nequit, et omnia que filii sui postulant, si salutaria sunt, liberaliter concedit. Sicut enim mater ipsa per quecunque pacta non possit trahi ad consentiendum in his que filiorum suorum saluti sciret obuiare, ita etiam ea que salutis sunt sine pactis assensum nequit denegare.

7   Unde, si qui sunt nimium fortassis solliciti, hos admonitos esse uolumus ne in catholica fide tali onere se frustra fati-

beloved chaplain. We gave him the mandate, after showing you these letters patent, to investigate the mind and intention of everyone concerning the aforesaid offer of obedience, and the matters relative to it and to the secure arrival of the apostolic legate, as we have informed him in more detail.

Therefore, we ask and exhort you in the Lord that you would grant our chaplain an audience, hear him with good will, and make clear in writing what you have in mind. Nor should you think we are asking of you lightly a matter of such great weight. For since it is impossible that true ecclesiastical peace can be achieved as long as there is not full conformity of body and members — for every part that does not fit with the whole is shameful — hence, in a matter where he who is not with the universal Church is evidently against it, it is necessary, purely and simply, without pact and condition, to embrace conformity of all in obedience.[2] Nor should it distress anyone that, when the envoys of the former Council of Basel negotiated the ecclesiastical peace in Prague, they agreed upon the Compacts. For it has been discovered by experience that this method did not bring about full peace and unity with the Holy Roman Church, which, since it is the most pious Mother of all the faithful, is unable to close its bosom to someone returning to her to whom she has given birth in faith. She freely grants everything her sons ask, if they are salutary. For just as that Mother could not be drawn by agreements of any kind to consent to those things that she knows would stand in the way of the salvation of her sons, so too she is unable to refuse her assent without agreements to those things pertaining to salvation.

Hence, if there are some who are perhaps unduly solicitous, we wish them to be warned not to weary themselves in vain with such a burden in the Catholic faith, while [at the

gent, sed matri fidei, cui hoc onus a sponso Christo domino creditum est, derelinquant. Scit enim mater illa, quibus nos debeat pascere fidei cibis, que sola in his talibus alimentis, que administrat pro salute nostra, errare nequit. Oportet igitur omnem christianum per puram obedientiam pasci cibo uite a matre sua, sancta romana et catholica ecclesia, que eum regenerauit, et nequaquam inniti proprie prudentie.

8   Experti estis quanta mala passi estis quod nonnullos qui contra Romane ecclesie fidem et obseruantiam nouitates introduxerunt, monitis matris uestre presuppositis. Hi enim degeneres filii iactabant se christianos et fratres nostros eiusdemque matris sancte Romane et catholice ecclesie filios, extra quam non est salus, et matrem spreuerunt. Et hodie aliqui se ei anteponunt, de quibus recte ait: Filios nutriui et ipsi spreuerunt me, hi uero nimium suo ingenio confidebant.

9   Nolite igitur tales pro fratribus honorare qui se matris uestre filios nominari uerecundantur. Aperite queso oculos, et considerate unde excidistis et quo perducti estis, et per quos, et credite plus matri uestre a quo omnia que salutis et honoris sunt recepistis, quam seductoribus illis, qui adeo ceci sunt quod lumen non uident, adeo bestiales quod matrem non cognoscunt. Paruifacite omnia que ipsi de compactatis ingerunt. Nam ad illorum sciolorum confusionem deus illa sic fieri permisit.

same time] abandoning the Mother of the faith, to whom this burden was entrusted by her spouse, Christ. For that Mother knows with what foods of the faith she should feed us, she who alone cannot err in the nourishments she provides for our salvation. It is necessary therefore for every Christian through pure obedience to feed on the food of life given him by his Mother, the Holy Roman and Catholic Church, who has regenerated him; and by no means to rely on his own prudence.

You know how great are the evils you have suffered because you preferred to the advice of your Mother certain men who introduced novelties contrary to the faith and observance of the Roman church. These degenerate sons boast that they are Christians, our brothers and sons of the same Mother, the Holy Roman and Catholic Church, outside of which there is no salvation; yet they spurn their Mother. Even today some put themselves before her, of whom the Scriptures rightly say, *I nourished sons, and they spurned me;*[3] but they trusted overmuch in their own wits.

Do not then honor such men as brothers who are ashamed to be called sons of your Mother. Please, open your eyes and consider from what you have been cut off and whither you have been drawn and by whom; and trust more in your Mother, from whom you have received all things that pertain to salvation and honor, rather than in those seducers, who are so blind that they do not see the light, so bestial that they do not know their own Mother. Dismiss everything they keep saying concerning the Compacts. For God has permitted those Compacts to be made for the confusion of these know-it-alls.

10   Neque religiosus frater Iohannes de Capistrano, uir utique zelum dei habens cum scientia, nec alius quisquam asserit, compactata heresim in se continere, sed constanter negatur in compactatis talia concedi, que uobis falso suggeruntur. Poteritis si uolueritis ex compactatis ipsis seductores uestros facile conuincere. Nam cum extra uniuersalem ecclesiam, que catholica grece dicitur, non sit salus, et, ut ipsi negare non possunt, uidete in compactatis, ubi est illa catholica ecclesia, et reperietis in capitulo primi articuli esse scriptum quod regnum Bohemie et marchionatus in fide conformare se debent uniuersali ecclesie, et non potest intellectus alius dari quam quod illa sit uniuersalis ecclesia, cui se debent regnum et marchionatus conformare. Si igitur illam admiserint esse uniuersalem ecclesiam cui se debent regnum et marchionatus conformare, clare intelligitis quod ipsi uestri sacerdotes, qui in concordata consenserunt, confessi sunt uos extra uniuersalem ecclesiam eorum ignorantia seductos. Nonne clarissimum est illam uniuersalem ecclesiam, de qua loquuntur compactata, in fide tenere communionem sub utraque specie non esse de necessitate salutis quo ad non consecrantes. Videte si illi, qui compactata allegant, sic credunt, ut etiam secundum textum compactatorum tenentur, et ostenditur manifeste ex compactatis ipsis, ubi dicitur quod post 'conformitatem fidei et rituum, illi et ille, qui usum habent sub utraque specie communicandi, communicent', etc. Admiserunt igitur sacerdotes illi quod communio talis non fuit nec est de necessitate salutis, quando admiserunt quod saltem usum habentibus traderetur. Ecce quam aperte constat

Nor did Friar John Capistran, a religious having zeal for   10
God together with knowledge,[4] nor did anyone else assert
that the Compacts contained heresy; but it has been consis-
tently denied that such things were conceded in the Compacts as are being falsely suggested to you. You can, if you
wish, easily convince your seducers from those Compacts
themselves. For since there is no salvation outside the universal Church, called the Catholic Church in Greek, as they
themselves cannot deny, look in the Compacts for where the
Catholic Church is mentioned, and you will find it written
in the heading of the first article that the Kingdom of Bohemia and the March [of Moravia] should conform themselves
in faith to the Universal Church; and no other understanding can be given to this than that that is the Universal
Church to which the Kingdom and the March should conform themselves. If therefore they admit that it is the Universal Church to which the Kingdom and the March should
conform themselves, you may understand clearly that those
priests of yours who agreed to the Compacts were confessing
that you are outside the universal Church, seduced by their
ignorance. Is it not utterly clear that the Universal Church of
which the Compacts speak holds in faith that communion
under both species is not necessary for salvation for those
who do not consecrate [i.e., for the laity]? See if those who
cite the Compacts so believe, as they are required to do even
according to the text of the Compacts, and it will be manifestly shown from the Compacts themselves, where it is said
that, after "conformity of faith and rite, those who follow the
usage of communicating under both species, male and female, shall communicate" etc.[5] Those priests therefore admit
that such communion was not nor is necessary for salvation,
when they admit that it was imparted at least to those who
have the usage.[6] You see how obvious it is that God allowed

in confusionem seductoris deum sic compactata fieri permississe.

11   Velitis queso diligenter attendere quid utilitatis uobis[2] eueniret, si obedientiam non aliter quam saluis compactatis prestare uelletis. Nam si aliquid singularitatis ex ipsis habere putatis circa ritum communionis sub utraque specie, ut seductores nonnulli persuadent, legite textum et ponderate mentem concilii ex litera, et reperietis negligentia illorum sacerdotum uos omnia ibi uobis oblata perdidisse. Est enim uobis notorium quod illi tales sacerdotes nunquam ea que fieri debebant ad habendum permissionem illius communionis procurarunt aut obseruarunt, sed non obstantibus compactatis continuarunt illa que dimittere tenebantur. Ideo ex eorum negligentia permissio etiam quo ad personas que usum habebant non est sortita effectum; minus permissio de libertatione concedenda obtineri potuit a synodo, semper ob talium presbyterorum presumptam pertinaciam, qui toto tempore quo concilium sedebat, compactata nulla ex parte obseruare curarunt, et ita soluta est synodus antequam euentualis promissio fieri potuit.

12   Videte nunc queso quomodo quidem tales uestri sacerdotes in suam confusionem ad compactata refugiunt, ex quibus penitus nihil ex eorum seductorum culpa etiam quo ad eos qui usum communionis habebant estis assecuti, sic alia que in compactatis sunt. Nonne manifeste condemnant talia[3] allegantes? Ipsi enim sua sponte rure se ingerunt, et absque

the Compacts to be made to the consternation of the seducer.

Please pay careful attention to the utility that will come to   11
you if you wish to offer obedience simply by keeping the
Compacts. For if you think you have been allowed some sort
of exception with respect to the rite of communion under
both species, as some seducers persuade you, read the text
and ponder the intentions of the council literally, and you
will find you have lost everything offered you there through
the carelessness of those priests. It is well known to you that
those very priests never took responsibility for or observed
the things that should have been done to have permission for
that communion, but, notwithstanding the Compacts, they
continued to do what they were required to give up. Thus,
through their negligence, permission [to have communion in
both kinds] was not put into effect, even for persons who already
enjoyed this usage; much less could permission be obtained
from the synod for allowing [further] liberalization
[of communion], always on account of the presumptuous
pertinacity of priests like these, who, the whole time when
the council was in session, made not the slightest effort to
observe the Compacts; and so the synod was dissolved before
the eventual promise could be fulfilled.

Please look now at how these priests of yours took refuge   12
in the midst of their confusion in the Compacts. Thanks to
those who seduced them you achieved absolutely nothing,
even with respect to those who had the use of communion;
so too with the other things in the Compacts. Does this not
obviously condemn those who cite them? For these are the
ones who force themselves of their own free will on the
countryside and preach explicitly against the Compacts, and

missione expresse contra compactata predicant, et cum nullam habeant potestatem ligandi et soluendi populum decipiunt.

13   Videtisne quomodo obedientiam illam, de qua similiter in compactatis, quo ad suum seruant romanum pontificem? Ex his intelligitis compactata nihil singularitatis uobis prestare, sed solum confusionem eorum qui sua presumptione seducti uos seduxerunt, exprimere, ut ore suo iudicentur. Quare merito, ad instar aliorum fidelium, obedientiam puram, simplicem, ueram et effectualem, que solum deo grata uobis utilis et salutaris existit, suademus in legati aduentu alacri animo acceptare et nos de illa certificare, per quam solam ab illa liberalissima apostolica sede indubie omnia que salutis et pacis sunt, potius sine pacto quam cum pacto, quamtocius in laudem poteritis obtinere.

14   Datum Ratispane sub nostro sigillo die XXVII Iunii Anno a natiuitate domini millesimo quadringentesimo quinquagesimo secundo pontificatus sanctissimi in Christo patris et domini nostri domini Nicolai diuina prouidentia pape quinti anno sexto.

15   Et quanquam in pactis inter nos et oratores ex regno qui Ratispane constituebantur habebatur nostris mittendis conductum in regno dari debere, tamen per capellanum nostrum de quo in littera saluus conductus impetrari nequiuit, inde euenit quod premisse littere non potuerunt ubilibet presentari, neque earum gerulus in credentia audiri. Fuimus autem ad sic scribendum inducti rationibus illis quibus et sanctus Bernardus mouebatur quando Mediolanensibus tunc scismatis epistolam misit, que in corpore epistolarum suarum reperitur, incipiens, *Ciuibus Mediolanensibus*, etc.

since they have no power to bind and loose, they deceive the people.

Don't you see how they keep their oath of obedience to the Roman pontiff in their own cases, an obedience like that called for in Compacts? On these grounds you will understand that the Compacts do not make any exceptions for you. They simply expose the confusion of those who, seduced by their own presumption, have seduced you, so that they might be judged by their own statements. Wherefore, like the rest of the faithful, we rightly urge you to accept with alacrity, when the legate comes, an obedience pure, simple, true and effectual, the only obedience that is pleasing to God and useful and healthful for you. We urge you to assure us of that obedience unconditionally, for only through obedience can you obtain as quickly as possible and to your credit everything from that most liberal Apostolic See that indubitably conduces to salvation and peace. 13

Given at Regensburg under our seal on the 27th day of June in the year from the nativity of the Lord 1452 in the sixth year of our most holy father in Christ and lord, Lord Nicholas V, pope by divine providence. 14

And although it is agreed in the pacts made in Regensburg between us and the envoys from the Kingdom that a safe conduct should be given to our emissaries to the kingdom, nevertheless, it turned out that the aforesaid letter could not be presented anywhere by our chaplain, for whom it was impossible to request a letter of safe conduct; nor could its bearer be heard anywhere with trust. But we were led to write thus by the same reasons that moved Saint Bernard to send a letter to the Milanese, who were then in schism: the letter is found in the corpus of his letters and begins *To the citizens of Milan*.[7] He argues that they should not 15

Suadet enim ne acquiescant pseudoprophetis sed attendant quod causam nullam habent non simpliciter obediendi apostolice sedi cui resistere est ordinationi diuine resistere, ac quod finaliter ei resistere nequeunt, quodque in ipsa sit plenitudo potestatis et auctoritatis, et ideo dare potest priuilegia etiam pallii et tollere. Unde Mediolanenses bene consulti sic fecerunt (de quo uideatur epistola illa et alia sequens eandem) et reperitur nos sane et iuste consuluisse. Sed ad hanc nostram salutiferam monitionem non recepimus responsum, nisi quorundam assertorum sacerdotum oppidi Clatoniensis, ad quos rescripsimus ut sequitur.

16   Nicolaus miseratione diuina tituli sancti Petri ad uincula sacrosancte Romane ecclesie presbiter cardinalis apostolice sedis legatus episcopus brixinensis Martino et reliquis sacerdotibus Clatoniensibus spiritu duci saniori.

17   Expectauimus ut ad nostra scripta que ad manus uestras peruenire uos obedientes responderetis, atque quod prestitam uestro et aliorum nominibus obedientiam romano pontifici realiter et cum effectu seruaretis. Nunc uero contrarium in uestris litteris reperimus, in quibus multa contra catholicam fidem, clauium potestatem, propria uestra promissa, in regni infamiam et animarum uestrarum periculum plus presumptuose quam sapienter dolenter relegimus. Nam in nostris literis, ubi de seductoribus populi loquimur, non credebamus uos offensos. Habemus enim meliorem estimationem de uobis quam uestra scripta ostendunt.

18   Scribitis nos omne ingenium adhibuisse ad compactata. Fatemur, sed ad illum certe finem, ut uos et uobis complices qui ad compactata confugitis, detectis his que scripsimus,

trust pseudo-prophets but should note that they had no reason not simply to obey the Apostolic See, to resist which is to resist a divine ordinance, and that in the end they could not resist that See, and that that See possessed plenitude of power and authority, and thus it can give or take away the privilege of the pallium.[8] Hence the Milanese took good counsel and did as advised (on this you may consult that letter and the one following), and it was found that we [orthodox Roman Catholics] had given them sound and just counsel. But we [i.e., Cusanus, in writing to the Bohemians, as above] did not receive a response to this salutary admonition of ours, except from certain self-proclaimed priests of the town of Klatovy, to which we replied as follows:

Nicholas, by divine mercy Cardinal Priest of San Pietro in Vincoli of the Holy Roman Church, Legate of the Apostolic See, Bishop of Brixen, bids Martin and other priests of Klatovy that they be led by a sounder sprit.   16

We expected that you would respond as obedient men to our letters that came into your hands and that you would observe really and effectively the obedience to the Roman pontiff that you offered in your own name and in that of others. Now, however, we find the contrary in your letters, in which it pains us to reread many things, written with more presumption than wisdom, that are opposed to the Catholic faith, the power of the keys and your own promises, to the infamy of the Kingdom [of Bohemia] and the peril of your souls. Indeed in our letter, where we speak of seducers of the people, we did not think that we insulted you. For we have a better opinion of you than your letters show.   17

You write that we employ all our wits against the Compacts. We admit it, but surely to this end: that you and your accomplices, who take refuge in the Compacts, once what we   18

cautius ageretis, quoniam in ueritate potius uobis aduersan-
tur quam seruiant. Ubi autem nobis culpam asscribitis, quasi
uos seductores et omnes, licet non reperiantur 'omnes' in
nostris litteris, seductos asseramus, non nobis sed uestris
compactatis, que nitimini cunctis inculcare usque etiam ad
iniuriam summi pontificis nostri, rectius imputaretis.

19   Ipsis enim presuppositis, hec sequi, que scripsimus, nemo
ratione utens ambigere potest, neque uos euaditis per hoc
quod scribitis nos respexisse ad id quod ponitur in ipsis, scilicet quod Bohemi usum habentes communicabunt auctoritate Christi et ecclesie, uere sponse eius. Mirandum est quod
uos, ut nobis impingatis ignorantiam, non uidetis uos ruere
in heresim maximam, quasi sit alia ecclesia catholica et alia
sponsa christi, ita quod si non sitis de prima, sitis de secunda. Non opus est declarare hunc errorem qui ex symbolo
fidei notorius est.

20   Deinde admiramini quomodo auctoritate ecclesie communicare et extra ecclesiam esse se compatiantur, neque nos id
dicimus neque credimus, et compactata docent uos autoritate ecclesie non communicare potuisse, nisi prius fuissetis in
ecclesia catholica per conformitatem fidei et rituum. Docent
itaque compactata que amplius declinare non potestis, post
sigillationes, allegationes, et uaria scripta uestra, quod sine
autoritate ecclesie illicite communionem duplicis speciei
usurpastis. Nam non dicunt compactata quod autoritate
Christi et ecclesie, sponse eius, communicastis in preteritum,

wrote had been made known, would act more cautiously, since in fact the Compacts harm you more than they help you. Where, however, you blame us, as if we called you seducers and all of you seduced (although "all" is not found in our letters), you would be more correct to blame not us, but your Compacts, which you strive to impress upon everyone, even to the point of doing injustice to our supreme pontiff.

This being presupposed, no rational person can doubt that what we wrote logically follows, nor does what you write let you escape the fact that we took account of what was posited in them, that is, that the Bohemians who had the usage [of taking communion in both kinds], will take communion by the authority of Christ and the Church, His true spouse. We wonder that you, even as you thrust the charge of ignorance on us, do not see that you are falling into the greatest of heresies, [behaving] as though there were another Catholic Church and another spouse of Christ, so that if you were not of the first, you were of the second. There is no need to declare this an error, which is notorious from the creed of the faith.[9]

Next, we wondered how they could allow themselves to take communion by the authority of the Church and [at the same time] be outside the Church. We neither say that nor believe it, and the Compacts teach that you could not communicate by the authority of the Church unless you first were in the Catholic Church through conformity with her faith and rituals. And so the Compacts also teach that, despite all your sealed documents, citations and various writings, you cannot evade the fact that you have usurped illicitly, without the authority of the Church, [the right to give] communion under both species. For the Compacts do not say that you communicated in the past by the authority of

19

20

aut communicatis in presens, sed, premissa conformitate
fidei et rituum cum catholica ecclesia, communicabunt in futurum illi et ille etc.

21   Ex quo constat manifestissime secundum intentionem
concilii, uti etiam postea synodus in decreto de communione
declarauit, uos illam communionem absque autoritate
Christi et ecclesie illicite usurpasse. Fuisset tamen tunc demum facta licita illi et illis, etc. autoritate Christi et ecclesie,
si conditio conformitatis prius fuisset adimpleta, que [cum]
nunquam sedente synodo adimpleta reperitur, quamquam
sepe sollicitati fueritis, ut scripturis per manus bone memorie tunc legati et domini Iohannis Polemar scriptis, que
apud nos sunt, ostendere poterimus.

22   Per uos igitur stetit ut uosipsi negare non potestis; manet
ergo illicita. Quomodo ergo in ecclesia esse potestis, quando
in illicite uestra propria presumptione usurpato uosipsos ab
ecclesia separastis? Neque euadere potestis nisi alia periculosiori heresi inuoluamini, quemadmodum in scriptis uestris
uos inuolutos reperimus, ubi quandam fingitis ecclesiam mathematicam, de qua uos esse dicitis, etiamsi neque cum papa,
neque cardinalibus, neque cum toto mundo sitis, asserentes
adhuc uos in templo domini esse, nisi Christus uos repellat,
quod est potius insanire quam errare.

23   Neque ita est, ut scribitis, nos compactata ignorare, nam
illa aliquam correctionem nobis tunc presidentibus in na-

Christ and the Church, His spouse, or that you communicate in the present, but that, once you have conformed in faith and ritual with the Catholic Church, you will communicate in the future, male and female, etc.

It follows with utter clarity, according to the intention of 21 the council, as even the synod afterwards declared in the decree on communion,[10] that you illicitly usurped that form of communion without the authority of Christ and the Church. Nevertheless, it might at last have been made licit for one and all, etc., by the authority of Christ and the Church, if the condition of conformity had first been fulfilled, which never was shown to be fulfilled while the synod was in session, although you often were solicited to do so, as we could show from the writings we have with us, written in the hand of the late legate,[11] and the lord Juan de Palomar.[12]

You are therefore the ones responsible and you cannot 22 deny it yourselves; hence [communion in both kinds] remains illicit. How then can you be in the Church when you have separated yourselves from the Church through the illicit usurpations brought on by your own presumption? And you cannot evade this conclusion unless you involve yourselves in another, more dangerous heresy, such as we found you in your own writings to be involved in, where you pretend the Church is a mathematical entity,[13] and say you belong to it even if you are not with the pope, the cardinals or the whole world, while asserting that you still are in the Lord's temple unless Christ expels you — a view more insane than erroneous.

Nor is it the case, as you write, that we are ignorant of the 23 Compacts; indeed they received some correction at the time

tione germanica receperunt, maxime in capitulo de libertatione communionis, ubi apponi fecimus facultatem in euentum dari sacerdotibus, posse communicare populum modo
quo ibi ponitur. Videte ergo quid populus fidelis, etiam si
cuncta per uos que fieri debebant fuissent adimpleta, obti-
nuisset, et an ex compactatis hoc uerum sit, quod communiter et in scriptis uestris ad nos datis asserere non cessatis,
communionem duplicis speciei sic per uos Basilee deductam
et euangelica ueritate probatam: quod illi doctores qui dicuntur Basilee fuisse rationibus conuicti eam admiserunt. Nam
si libera facultas dabatur tantum sacerdotibus dandi in euentum completionis appositarum conditionum, nonne manifestum est nequaquam hoc subsistere posse quod uos dicitis?
Atque quod illi doctores nequaquam fuerunt uestris rationibus et autoritatibus inducti ad quicquam concedendum, docet processus et diffinitio trigesime sessionis. Sepissime in faciem audistis quod non unicum saltem doctorem allegastis,
qui ex intentione necessitatem illius communionis probaret.

24   Propterea nonne, postquam promisistis et sigillastis compactata, et sepius per scripta et oratores concilii sollicitati,
non curastis ea seruare. Nouem petitiones obtulistis Basilee,
quarum prima erat, ut libertas euentualiter oblata, quo ad
sacerdotes tradendi et populum recipiendi, transiret in preceptum. Habemus manibus legati et auditoris prefatorum
responsum negatiuum, quod et uos, Martinum, non latet,

when we [personally] were presiding over the German nation, especially in the chapter about the liberalization of
communion, where we caused a faculty to be added, in the
event [of compliance with the Compacts], giving priests the
power to give communion to the people in the way posited
there. So see what the faithful people had obtained, even if
all the conditions that ought to have been fulfilled by you
had been implemented, and look in the Compacts to see
whether it is true — as you ceaselessly assert in general and in
your writings sent to us — that communion under both species was demonstrated by you at Basel and proved from the
Gospel so convincingly that even the university professors,
who are said to have been convinced at Basel by your arguments, admitted it. But, if the unfettered capacity [to give
communion in both kinds] was given to priests only in the
event of fulfilling the appropriate conditions, is it not evident
that this never could have happened as you say it did? That
those doctors were never compelled by your arguments and
authorities to concede anything may be learned from the
proceedings and definition of the Thirtieth Session.[14] You
heard over and over, in person, that you had not cited a
single doctor who had the intention of proving that sort of
communion.

Moreover, after you promised and sealed the Compacts,   24
did you bother to observe them, even though you were often
requested to do so in writing and by envoys of the council?
You presented nine petitions at Basel,[15] the first of which
was that the liberty conditionally given for priests to give
and the people to receive [communion in both kinds] might
be turned into a command. We possess, written in the hands
of the legate and the auditor,[16] a negative response to the
aforesaid request, as you, Martin, well know, since (as we

qui ut audiuimus pro sollicitatione responsi missus eratis Basileam. Si igitur compactata in que consensistis non dederunt que optastis, neque ex post obtinuistis a synodo, quare adhuc non cessatis asserere id quod nobis quasi ignoranti scribitis. Multa sunt apud nos munimenta concilii illius et testamentaria quedam scripta relicta legati et auditoris, que nos optime de singulis instruunt. Ita quod nihil nos quasi ignorantem latere potest. Volumus tamen pro nunc patienter ferre iniurias uestras ob spem melioris.

25 Quod autem tantum scripsimus de compactatis in aliis nostris literis causa fuit, quia legimus scripta ex regno ad principes nostros regno propinquos transmissa, in quibus ecclesiam et pontificem de non obseruantia premissorum compactatorum arguere nisi estis. Considerauimus igitur ad nos spectare, qui tenemur honorem pontificis ecclesie pro posse defensare, uobis manifestare compactata nihil tribuere, nec ad tales nos, ad quales ille littere nos prouocarunt,[4] descendimus particularitates refallendas. Sperantes quod deus concederet unionem in ecclesia sua, pro qua cum omnibus nostris tam in oriente quam in occidente fideles impendimus labores, eam turbare non uolumus, quamuis nobis synodalia gesta sacrorum generalium conciliorum ostenderent rem istam humanitus impossibilem, experimento aliorum qui de ecclesia abierunt quos raro humana diligentia comperimus uere rediisse.

26 Et ne totum legationis tempus, quemadmodum multi ex preteritis legatis, inaniter uobiscum perderemus, circa reformationem Alamanie aliquantisper uacauimus, qua pro parte

have heard) you had been sent to Basel to ask for a response to the request. If therefore the Compacts to which you consented did not give you what you wished for, and you did not obtain this afterwards from the synod, why have you not yet stopped asserting what you write to us, as though we were ignorant of it? There has been left in our hands by the legate and the auditor many records and much eyewitness evidence of that Council, which provide us with excellent and detailed information. So nothing can be hidden from us as though we were ignorant of it. Nevertheless, we wish for now to suffer patiently under your injuries in the hope of better things.

There was a reason, however, why we wrote so much 25 about the Compacts in our other letters. It was because we read writings sent from the Kingdom [of Bohemia] to our princes who are neighbors of the Kingdom in which you try to accuse the Church and the pontiff of not observing the aforesaid Compacts. We have considered therefore that it belongs to us, who are bound to defend the honor of the pontiff of the Church as far as possible, to show you that the Compacts give you nothing. Nor shall we descend to refuting the kind of particular points to which those letters provoke us to respond. Hoping that God will grant union in his Church, for which we have undertaken faithful labors in both East and West, we do not wish to disturb it, although the synodal records of the holy general councils show this very thing to be humanly impossible, from the experience of others who left the Church. We find that such people rarely have returned to the Church by means of human effort and care.

And so as not to waste the whole term of our legation 26 uselessly with you, like many legates in the past, we have absented ourselves for a short time to address matters relating

nobis possibili expedita, nouo apostolico recepto mandato incepimus. Utinam feliciter et durante mandato non deficiemus, parati omnia exequi pontificis iussa pro regni pace et salute! Nequaquam putetis nos ad ea que prius scripsimus, ob que a uobis de imprudentia arguimur, sine pontificis nostri iussu processisse. Si enim simpliciter modo quo alii Christiani obedire recusatis, ad placitandum uobis[5] nemo ab apostolica sede mittetur. Non est enim consuetudinis nec iuris quod Christi uicarius et iudex fidei se subiiciat et placitationem cum suis subditis ineat, sed quod obedientibus in his, que salutis et pacis sunt, gratiose liberaliter et paterne condescendat, prout nos in priori epistola in fine id ipsum scripsimus et obtulimus. Ad quod certe potius respicere et oblationem magis quam compactata uestra magnificare debeatis.

27   Admonemus uos, pro credito nobis legationis officio, ut amplius desistatis ab his modis inuectionis et humiliamini, uti decet christianos sacerdotes, obediendo prepositis uestris secundum legem dei et sanctorum instituta realiter et cum effectu, prout ex premisso et de iure diuino et humano tenemini, et alios ad idem inducatis, nos de hoc certificantes, et tunc sentietis, preter spem quam de persona concepistis, omnem cordialem affectum ad queuis inclito regno, uobis et singulis, salutaria. Datum Brixine decimasexta Decembris etc.

28   Ex his satis ostendi putamus Iacobellianos ex compactis pro se allegatis conuictos sua confessione extra catholicam ecclesiam esse,

to the reform of Germany; having expedited these as much as we could, we have begun again, having received a new mandate from the pope. May we be fortunate and not fail while our mandate lasts, standing ready as we do to execute all the pope's commands for the peace and salvation of the Kingdom! You should by no means think that we have proceeded without our pope's command to undertake the matters I wrote about previously, on account of which you criticize us for lack of prudence. If you simply refuse to obey as other Christians do, no one will be sent by the Apostolic See to placate you. It is neither a matter of custom nor of right that the Vicar of Christ and judge of the faith should subject himself and strive to placate his subjects. Rather he condescends graciously, freely and paternally to those who obey him in matters pertaining to salvation and peace, just as we wrote and offered at the end of the previous letter. Certainly you should look to that offer and prize it more than your Compacts.

We admonish you, on behalf of the office of the legation entrusted to us, that you should desist from now on with these kinds of invective, and humble yourselves as befits Christian priests by obeying really and effectually those placed over you, in accordance with the law of God and what has been laid down by the saints, as you are required to do by the aforesaid and by divine and human law. And you should persuade others to do the same thing, informing us of this; and then you will feel, beyond any hope which you have received personally, all cordial affection for anything salutary to the Kingdom and to you individually. Given at Brixen, 16 December, etc. 27

We think that we have sufficiently shown from the letter above that the Jacobellians, convicted by their own confession from the 28

que est sponsa Christi, et nobis solum sufficit sic ostendisse pro nostra contra eos uictoria, etiamsi in omnibus sacramentis nobiscum concurrerent, ut elegantissime arguit magnus Augustinus *Contra Rogatistas et Donatistas* in multis locis et late de catholica ecclesia, et premissis in epistola, quam ipse et Siluanus[6] senex, Valentinus, Aurelius, Innocentius, Optatus et ceteri episcopi de concilio Zertensi scripserunt ad Donatistas, cuius initium est *Cum in auribus nostris fama crebresceret.* Et quod illa sit catholica que unitur successori Petri apostoli et quod anathema sit aliam esse, ostendit Augustinus in epistola quam ipse et Fortunatus ad Generosum scripserunt, et probatur in capitulo *Pudenda,* et capitulo *Scisma,* XXIIII, questione I, et XCIII distinctione, *Qui cathedram,* et in multis aliis locis.

29   Audiant etiam Iacobelliani quid ait idem Augustinus in epistola ad Bonifacium comitem, que incipit, *Laudo et gratulor et admiror,* circa finem. Sic enim dicit: 'Isti autem cum quibus agimus non sunt desperandi' — adhuc enim sunt in corpore, scilicet suo mortali — sed non adquirent spiritum sanctum 'nisi in corpore Christi, cuius habent foris sacramentum, sed rem ipsam non tenent intus, cuius illud est sacramentum, et ideo sibi iudicium manducant et bibunt. Unus enim panis est sacramentum unitatis; quoniam, sicut Apostolus dicit, unus panis et unum corpus multi sumus. Proinde ecclesia catholica sola corpus est Christi, cuius ille caput est, saluator corporis sui. Extra hoc corpus neminem uiuificat spiritus sanctus.' Hec et plura de hoc ibidem. Et idem Augustinus in epistola ad Paulinum que incipit *Quod de peruentione,* etc., ostendit quod in sacramento altaris, quod est uotum, 'predicatur nostrum aliud[7] maximum uotum quo nos uouimus in Christo esse mansuros, utique in compage corporis Christi, cuius rei sacramentum

Compacts cited on their own behalf, are outside the Catholic Church, which is the spouse of Christ; and to have shown this alone is enough for us to have the victory over them, even if they concur with us on all the sacraments, as the great Augustine argued in many places in *Against the Rogatists and Donatists*,[17] and broadly of the Catholic Church. He set this out in the letter[18] which he and the elderly Silvanus, Valentinus, Aurelius, Innocent, Optatus and other bishops wrote about the Council of Sirte to the Donatists, whose beginning is, *Cum in auribus nostris fama crebesceret*. And that that church is Catholic which is united to the successor of Peter, and that it is anathema for there to be another church, Augustine shows in the letter that he and Fortunatus wrote to Generosus. This is proved in c. *Pudenda* and c. *Schisma* [in Gratian] C. 24 q. 1 [cc. 33 and 34], [and idem] D. 93 c. *Qui cathedram* [c. 8], and many other places.

Let the Jacobellians also hear what the same Augustine[19] says in   29
the letter to Count Boniface, which begins, *Laudo et gratulor et admiror*, near the end. For there he says, "Yet these with whom we deal are not to be despaired of" — for they are still in the body, i.e. their mortal one — but they do not take on the Holy Spirit "unless they are in the Body of Christ, whose outward sacrament they have, but they do not hold inwardly to that thing of which that Body is the sacrament, and therefore *They eat and drink judgment to themselves*.[20] The one bread is the sacrament of unity; *Since*, as the Apostle says, *there is one loaf, we who are many are one body*.[21] Wherefore the Catholic Church alone is the body of Christ, whose head he is, *the Savior of his body*.[22] The Holy Spirit gives life to no one outside this body." And the same Augustine in the letter to Paulinus that begins *Quod de perventione*, shows that in the sacrament of the altar, which is a vow, "there is declared [that] greatest of vows by which we vow to remain in Christ, joining in every respect the body of Christ, Whose Substance the sacrament is."[23] The same thing is found in [Gratian] *De consecratione* D. 2 c. *Qui*

est.' Hoc ibi. De quo idem *De consecratione*, distinctione II, *Qui manducat* in fine, et capitulo *Qui discordat*, iuncta glosa. Pretereamus nunc illa que Iacobelliani sepissime, licet surda aure, audiuerint Basilee et alibi, atque legere possunt si uolunt.

30   Nunc ad aliam partem praxis nos conuertamus, ex quo conuentio, que in Egra in festo sancti Galli sperabatur, per uos nobis nunciatur recusata. Velitis rogamus impigre que sequentur lectitare, si ueritatem scire diligitis, et reperietis nos uerum dixisse in literis nostris preinsertis. Nam ignorantia hystoriarum et scripturarum decepit Iacobellum et sequaces sacerdotes qui plerosque hactenus seduxerunt. Est igitur aduertendum quod Christus non nisi discipulis suis legitur dedisse corpus suum et sanguinem, qui, ut Lucas ait, dixit: Si quis non renunciauerit omnibus que possidet, non potest meus esse discipulus. In primitiua igitur ecclesia omnes Christiani qui quotidie communicarunt, siue sub una siue sub duplici specie, fuerunt discipuli qui omnibus resignarunt, ut scribit sanctus Iheronimus *De illustribus uiris* in capitulo de Philone, dicens: 'In primitiua ecclesia omnes fideles resignasse omnibus ut suo tempore religiosi, sicut etiam in Actibus Apostolorum legitur.' Et, ut scribit Honorius in libro qui *Gemma anime* dicitur, 'hic modus quo ad religiosos omnibus diebus communicandi suo tempore et ante, tempore scilicet sancti Benedicti, seruabatur'. Sic, ut scribit Crisostomus *Super epistolam ad Hebreos*, post communionem ministrorum altaris qui sancti reputantur, et intra sanctasanctorum circa altare communicant apud sacrum ostium, ubi ad sanctasanctorum intratur, per dyaconum sancti ex populo uocabantur ad communionem, quod et hodie apud Grecos seruatur. Et quia pauci se sanctos presumunt, raro aliqui ueniunt. Et in decretis Anacleti pape, per sanctum Petrum in presbiterum ordinati, legitur 'omnes qui intererant consecrationi communicasse'. Dicit enim

manducat [c. 58] at the end and c. *Qui discordat* [c. 65], with the gloss. For the present we may pass over what the Jacobellians heard very often at Basel and elsewhere, although with a deaf ear; they can read about it if they wish.

Now we turn to the other part, about praxis, from the time when it was announced that the agreement that was hoped for at Eger on the feast of Saint Gall had been renounced by you. Please, would you read what follows carefully if you would like to know the truth, and you will find out that we spoke the truth in the letter of ours we inserted above. For ignorance of history and the Scriptures deceived Jacobellus and the priests who follow him, who hitherto have seduced many. It should then be noted that Christ is said to have given His Body and Blood only to his disciples. As Luke says, *He said, If anyone does not renounce everything he possesses, he cannot be My disciple.* Thus in the Primitive Church all Christians who communicated daily, whether under one or two species, were disciples who had forfeited all, as Saint Jerome writes in *On Illustrious Men* in the chapter on Philo, where he says: "In the Primitive Church all the faithful forfeited everything, being the religious of their time, as we also read in the Acts of the Apostles."[24] And, as Honorius[25] writes in the book called *The Gem of the Soul,* "This way was observed with respect to the religious who communicated every day in their time and before, that is, in the time of Saint Benedict." And, as Chrysostom[26] writes in his *Commentary on the Epistle to the Hebrews,* after the communion of the ministers at the altar, who were regarded as holy—and they communicated at the altar within the Holy of Holies before the sacred gate where the Holy of Holies is entered—those who were holy from among the people were summoned by the deacon to communion, a custom preserved even today by the Greeks. And because few presumed themselves to be saints, they rarely came. And in the decrees of Pope Anacletus, who was ordained a priest by Saint Peter, we read, "All who were present at the consecration commu-

30

textus decreti prout in originali et Burcardo habetur: 'Peracta autem consecratione omnes communicent qui noluerunt ecclesiasticis carere liminibus. Sic enim apostoli statuerunt, et sancta Romana tenet ecclesia, et si hoc neglexerint, degradentur.' Ecce dicit 'degradentur'; non igitur intelligitur nisi de illis sanctis qui consecrationi intererant et ad sanctasanctorum admittebantur, sicut sunt in sacris ordinibus constituti. Pars huius textus habetur *De consecratione*, distinctione I, *Episcopus deo*. Idem probatur ex capitulo *Tribus*, iuncta glosa, et capitulo *Sacerdotum*, *De consecratione* distinctione II, et sunt primi Clementis successoris sancti Petri. Et non reperitur alios tunc sub utraque specie communicasse. Ita uidetur sanctus Dyonisius dicere in libro *De ecclesiastica ierarchia*, et reperitur Romanam ecclesiam antiquitus sic seruasse, ut Guilelmus in *Rationali diuinorum* dicit, scilicet quod presbiteri concelebrarunt pape et communicarunt. Ita hodie seruat ecclesia Constantinopolitana. Quando enim patriarcha solemniter celebrat, omnes presbiteri conueniunt ad concelebrandum et communicant, etc.

31   Est similiter attendendum quod antiquitus Eucharistia dabatur ad manus communicandi, et hoc etiam ex epistola sancti Cypriani, ubi tractat de miraculo calicis et puelle, patet, et sacerdos grecus dat Eucharistiam hodie ad manum. Calicem autem nemo ministrabat nisi dyaconus, ut ibidem ex Cypriano. Et Iheronimus ad ipsum dicit, 93 distinctione, *Dyaconi sunt*. Et in legenda sancti Laurentii et sancti Syxti, *Quo progrederis*, etc., reperitur. Et sic adhuc seruat Romana ecclesia, papa celebrante solenniter, et Constantinopolitana. Nam diaconi, pape et patriarche calicem ministrant. Et in concilio Rothomagensi, de quo in Borcardo libro III, capi-

nicated." The text of the decree, as we read in the original and in Burchard, says: "The consecration having been enacted, all communicated who did not wish to be absent from the ecclesiastical threshold. The apostles decreed this, and so the Roman church holds, and if [Christians] shall neglect this, they are degraded."[27] Notice that he says "they are degraded."[28] The decree is therefore understood only of those saints who were present at the consecration and were admitted into the holy of holies, as being in holy orders. Part of this text is found in [Gratian] De consecratione D. 1 c. Episcopus deo [c. 59]. The same is proved from [idem] c. Tribus with the added gloss and c. Sacerdotum, [in idem] De consecratione D. 2 [cc. 23 and 30]; and these are texts of Clement I, the successor of saint Peter. And it is not found that others communicated under both species. So Saint Dionysius seems to say in the book On the Ecclesiastical Hierarchy.[29] And the Roman church is found to have preserved [this custom] from antiquity, as William [Durand the Elder] says in Rationale of the Divine Offices, that is, that priests concelebrated with the pope and communicated.[30] This custom is today observed by the church of Constantinople. For when the patriarch celebrates solemnly, all the priests gather to concelebrate and communicate.

And similarly one should note that in ancient times the Eucharist once was given into the hands of the communicant, and this too is apparent from the letter of Saint Cyprian where he treats of the miracle of the chalice and the girl,[31] and today a Greek priest puts the Eucharist into the hand. No one but the deacon administers the chalice, however, as is clear from Cyprian in the same passage. And Jerome speaks to this in [Gratian] D. 93 c. Diaconi sunt [c. 23 ⊄ 3], and it is found also in the legend of Saint Lawrence and Saint Sixtus at Quo progrederis, etc.[32] And the Roman church still preserves this custom when the pope celebrates solemnly, and the church of Constantinople. For deacons, popes and patriarchs administer the chalice. And in the Council of Rouen, for which

31

tulo LXXVII,[8] fuit statutum contra sacerdotes qui laicis et mulieribus dabant calicem, precipiendo ne amplius talibus calicem tradant, quoniam corpus domini nesciunt diiudicare neque inter cibum spiritalem et carnalem discernere, sed quod sacerdotes ‹non› sumant, diaconus uel subdiaconus, qui sunt ministri altaris, colligenda tradant, ita tamen quod sacerdotes eos suis propriis manibus communicent. Et subditur: 'Sacerdos autem nulli laico aut femine Eucharistiam in manibus, sed tantum in os eius, cum his uerbis ponat: Corpus domini et sanguis prosit tibi ad remissionem peccatorum et ad uitam eternam. Si quis hec trangressus fuerit, quia deum omnipotentem contemnit et, quantum in ipso est, inhonorat, ab altari remoueatur'. Hec ibi. Sic adhuc hodie sancta romana tenet ecclesia. Nam diaconus et subdiaconus de manu pape corpus sumunt, et residuum colligunt in calice, et laicis non traditur Eucharistia ad manus, sed in os. Erat autem quedam constitutio facta in concilio Turonensi, quod Eucharistia que dabatur in os communicandi intincta esset in sanguine ad hoc, quod presbiter ueraciter dici posset in tradendo, Corpus et sanguis domini proficiat tibi. Sed hec constitutio per Romanam ecclesiam non fuit recepta, ut patet in capitulo *Cum omne*, *De consecratione* distinctione II, ubi Iulius papa intinctum panem prohibuit. Nec illa ratio allegata in concilio Turonensi fuit ualida, quia nihilominus ueraciter dici potest in tradendo Eucharistiam in specie panis, Corpus domini nostri Iesu Christi et sanguis proficiat tibi, ubi enim corpus, ibi et sanguis, ut Innocentius Tertius in *Summa* sua declarat, et quod sacramentum sub specie panis secundum eundem Innocentium dicatur 'sacramentum corporis et sanguinis Christi'. Videtur textus in capitulo *Deus qui*, in fine *De penitentiis et remissionibus*, ubi

see Burchard, Book 3, Chapter 76,[33] there was a decree against priests who give the chalice to laymen and women, instructing them no longer to give the chalice to persons like that, since they do not know how to discern the Body of the Lord nor to distinguish between the spiritual and the carnal; but what the priests do not consume, the deacon or subdeacon, who are ministers of the altar, should hand over for collection. Nevertheless the priests should give them communion with their own hands. And the decree adds: "No priests, however, are to place the Eucharist in the hands of a layman or a woman, but let him place it in their mouths with these words, 'May the Body and Blood of the Lord be of benefit to you for the remission of sins and eternal life.' If someone has transgressed in this, because he contemned God and dishonored him, in so far as he was able, let him be removed from the altar." This practice is kept by the Holy Roman Church still today. For the deacon and subdeacon receive the Body from the hand of the pope, and they place the rest in the chalice; and the laity is not given the Eucharist in their hands, but only in the mouth. There was, however, a certain constitution of the Council of Tours[34] to the effect that the Eucharist that was given in the mouth of the communicant might [first] be dipped in the Blood, so that the priest might truly say when giving the host, "The Body and Blood of the Lord be of benefit to you." But this constitution was not accepted by the Roman church, as in clear in [Gratian] c. *Cum omne, De consecratione* D. 2 [c. 7], where Pope Julius prohibited intincture of the Bread. Nor was the reason cited in the Council of Tours valid, since it can still truly be said, in giving the Eucharist under the species of bread, "The Body of our Lord Jesus Christ and the Blood be of benefit to you," for where the Body is, there too is the Blood, as Innocent III declares in his *Summa*, and the sacrament under the species of bread, according to the same Innocent, may be called "the sacrament of the Body and Blood of Christ."[35] The text is found at the end of [the *Decretals* of Gregory

uiaticum taliter nominat. Sed licet secundum eundem in ratione 'esus' non dicatur nisi corporis sacramentum, est tamen uerum quod etiam laicis aliquo tempore dabatur Eucharistia sub utraque specie, sed non reperitur hoc crebriter in anno, et aliter quam solenniter per pontificem, et in eius presentia deque eius precepto factum.

32   Greci enim laici consueuerunt tempore Chrysostomi et Ambrosii uix semel in anno communicare, ut ipse Chrysostomus *Super epistolam ad Hebreos*, et Ambrosius libro V *De sacramentis* testantur, quamuis statutum esset per Fabianum papam ut omnes laici saltem ter in anno communicarent, scilicet in festis Pasche, Penthecostes et Natalis domini, alias pro Christianis non haberentur. Propterea reperitur preceptum diocesanis quos infirmitas non excusat quod illa tria festa cum suis episcopis in ciuitatibus celebrent ad accipiendum communionis uel benedictionis gratiam, et qui hoc neglexerunt communione priuabantur, ut reperitur in libro antiquo qui *Corrector* pretitulatur, in quo diriguntur sacerdotes quomodo plebem curare debeant. Et ex Dyonisio reperitur hoc fuisse ab initio, et ex gestis concilii Calcedonensis contra Ybam continue obseruatum.

33   Et hodie in cathedralibus ecclesiis calices magni et antiqui reperiuntur, forte ad illum usum tunc ordinati, et seruaba‹n›tur Rome. Nam solus pontifex romanus usque ad proxima tempora in festo Pasche laicos, quibus ipse sua manu corpus domini tradidit, permisit accedere ad susceptionem sanguinis de manu diaconi, sed nequaquam alii laici in parrochiis ad susceptionem sanguinis reperimus admissos. Communicabant autem Romani fideles tempore sancti Hyeronimi semper corpus Christi accipiendo, ut ipse Hye-

IX] c. *Deus qui* [X 5.38.8], *De penitentiis et remissionibus*, where he calls it the viaticum. Although, according to the same Innocent, [the word] "eating" is reasonably used only of the sacrament of the Body, it is nevertheless true that at one time the Eucharist was given even to the laity under both species. But this was not done often during the [liturgical] year, and only at solemn pontifical masses, in his presence, and by his command.

The Greek laity, indeed, at the time of Chrysostom and 32 Ambrose were accustomed to communicate scarcely once a year, as Chrystostom[36] in his *Commentary on the Epistle to the Hebrews* and Ambrose[37] in Book 5 of *On the Sacraments* testify, although it was decreed by Pope Fabian[38] that all the laity should communicate at least three times a year, that is, on the feasts of Easter, Pentecost and the Nativity of the Lord, otherwise they would not be regarded as Christians. That is why the command is given to diocesan priests that infirmity does not excuse them from celebrating those three feasts with their bishops in their own cities in order to receive the grace of communion and benediction, and whoever neglects this was deprived of communion, as is found in the ancient book that is entitled the *Corrector*,[39] in which priests are directed how to care for the people. And from Dionysius[40] we learn that this was true from the beginning, and from the acts of the Council of Chalcedon[41] against Ibas we find that the practice was continuously observed.

Even today chalices of great antiquity, perhaps ordained then 33 for that use, are found in cathedral churches and are preserved at Rome. For down to the recent times only the Roman pontiff on the feast of Easter permitted the laity, to whom he himself gives the Body of the Lord with his own hand, to approach and receive the Blood from the hand of the deacon. But we never find other laymen in parish churches admitted to receive the Blood. However, the Roman faithful used to communicate in the time of Saint Jerome by always accepting the Body of Christ, as Jerome himself

ronimus testatur, et in illa quotidiana communione de sanguine nullam fecit ibidem mentionem. Dicit enim: 'Scio Rome esse consuetudinem ut fideles semper corpus Christi accipiant'.

34 Et Ambrosius, Augustinus atque alii omnes exponentes uerba illa, Panem nostrum quotidianum, de communione fidelium dicunt cotidianam illam communionem esse corporis Christi, nullam de sanguine mentionem facientes. Christus enim docet nos petere panem illum supersubstantialem quotidie; sufficit igitur si impetratur. Est consequenter attendendum quod communio est sacramentum unitatis et pacis. Ideo cuncto populo christiano loco quotidiane communionis successit communio pacis, ut dicitur in *Rationali*, et dabatur communio Eucaristie dominicis diebus, et ad hec, plus aucto populo, dabatur loco Eucaristie dominicis diebus panis benedictus, qui *eulogia* dicitur, Greci adhuc sic seruant: excindunt peciam panis in forma crucis quam consecrant pro sanctis, residuum panis benedicunt simpliciter et non consecrant et distribuunt populo.

35 Romana ecclesia fermentum panem benedixit pro populo, azimum consecrauit. Et Romani pontifices per acolitos diebus dominicis miserunt fermentum sacerdotibus qui tunc in titulis celebrabant, ne saltem pro illis diebus communione pontificis carerent, ut in antiquis obseruantiis legitur. Fuit enim statutum quod saltem in dominicis misse dicerentur in parrochiis. Ideo tunc sacerdotes erant in titulis et communicabant cum pontifice per fermentum, et sicut pontifex misit sacerdotibus intra[9] urbem, ita archidyaconi sacerdotibus extra urbem. Una autem ecclesia non habebat nisi unum sacerdotem, et cessauit rigor primitiue ecclesie. Nam, ut dicit Dyonisius, post euangelium omnes qui non fuerunt parati ad perceptionem Eucaristie expellebantur ab ecclesia. Unde post hoc

testifies; and he never mentions the Blood in that passage on daily communion. For he says, "I know at Rome it is the custom for the faithful always to receive the Body of the Lord."[42]

And Ambrose, Augustine and all the others, expounding those 34 words, [*Give us this day*] *our daily bread*, concerning the communion of the faithful, say that daily communion is with the Body of Christ, and make no mention of the Blood. Christ then teaches us to ask daily for the supersubstantial bread; it suffices therefore to ask for it. And consequently it must be noted that communion is the sacrament of unity and peace. Thus the communion of peace succeeded daily communion for all Christian people, as is said in the *Rationale*.[43] And communion of the Eucharist was given on Sundays; and in place of the Eucharist on Sundays blessed bread, which is called *eulogia*, is given because of the greater number of people. The Greeks still preserve this custom. They cut the crust of the bread that they consecrate for the saints in the form of a cross; the rest of the bread they simply bless and do not consecrate, and they distribute it to the people.

The Roman church has blessed leavened bread for the people 35 and consecrated unleavened. The Roman pontiff sent the leavened bread on Sundays by means of acolytes to the priests, who then celebrated at their titular churches so that they would not on those days be bereft of communion with the pontiff, as is read in the ancient observances. For it was decreed that, at least on Sunday, masses should be said in the parishes. Thus at that time there were priests in the titular churches, and they used to be in communion with the pontiff by means of leavened bread. Just as the pontiff sent it to the priests inside the city, so the archdeacons did to the priests outside the city. Each church, however, had only one priest, and the rigor of the primitive church came to an end. For [in the primitive church], as Dionysius says, after the Gospel [was read in the office of the Mass], all who were not prepared for the reception of the Eucharist were expelled from the church. But

fuerunt etiam non dispositi admissi ad communionem orationis, et tales ad communionem pacis, eulogiorum et benedictionis finalis admittebantur. Si uero fuerunt excommunicati, tunc non admittebantur ad communionem orationis, et per consequens ad nullam communionem, quia extra omnem communionem positi, ut in uersu: 'Os, orare, uale, communio, mensa negatur'.

36   Est etiam aduertendum quod a principio ecclesie reperimus apud sacerdotium fuisse liberam iudiciariam potestatem in distributione huius sacramenti Eucaristie, nam excommunicatio semper fuit et est medicinalis. Paulus enim excommunicauit Corinthum ut spiritus saluaretur, et quisque pontifex ex credita potestate potuit excludere a communione ob reuerentiam dei, uti Cyprianus hystriones, aut ad edificationem ecclesie et horrorem peccati, ut synodus fecit Sardicensis in capitulo *Osius, De electione*, que quosdam delinquentes perpetuo exclusit a communione. Et synodus Eleberitana que metham perpetuo exclusit. Et ante Innocentium Primum lapsi post baptismum ad penitentiam admittebantur, sed nunquam etiam in extremis ad communionem, et hanc seueritatem mitigauit ipse papa et synodus Nicena, que concessit uiaticum. Et consuluit beatus Augustinus, quod qui post baptismum peccasset capitaliter non accederet, nisi publica penitentia peracta, iudicio sacerdotis reconciliatus, aut priuata in religione, ut *De ecclesiasticis dogmatibus* scribit. Et [quia] in libro beati Dyonisii *De ecclesiastica ierarchia* reperitur quomodo adulti per episcopum baptizati admittebantur ad communionem. Quidam pontifices etiam infantes baptizatos communicarunt, etiam sub specie uini, et alii ob reuerentiam sacramenti et uomitum puerorum non fecerunt, ut in penitentiali Roberti de Sancto Victore. Alii etiam mortuis infude-

thereafter, even those who were unprepared were admitted to the communion of prayer, and such persons were [also] admitted to the communion of peace, the *eulogia*, and the final blessing. If however they were excommunicate, then they were not admitted to the communion of prayer, and consequently to no form of communion, since they had been excluded from all communion. As the verse says, "Utterance, prayer, benediction, communion, [and] the table are denied [to the excommunicate]."[44]

It must also be noted that, from the beginning of the Church, 36 we find that there was a discretionary power in the hands of the priesthood for the distribution of the sacrament of the Eucharist, for excommunication always was and is medicinal. Paul excommunicated the Corinthian so that his soul could be saved.[45] And any pontiff can exclude from communion by the power entrusted to him out of reverence for God, as Cyprian[46] did the actors, or to build up the Church and from horror of sin, as the Synod of Sardica did in c. *Osius,* [of the *Decretals* of Gregory IX], *De electione* [X 1.6.2], perpetually excluding certain delinquents from communion. And the Synod of Elvira perpetually excluded an adulteress.[47] And before Innocent I,[48] those who lapsed after baptism were admitted to penance but never, even *in extremis,* to communion. And that pope and the Nicene synod,[49] which conceded the viaticum, mitigated this severity. And Saint Augustine counseled that whoever sinned mortally after baptism could not approach the altar unless, having done public penance, they were reconciled by the judgment of a priest or set apart in religious life, as he writes in *On Ecclesiastical Dogmas.*[50] And in the book of Dionysius *On the Ecclesiastical Hierarchy*[51] we find that adults baptized by the bishop are admitted to communion. Some pontiffs even communicated baptized infants, even under the species of wine, whilst others, out of reverence for the sacrament and the tendency of children to vomit, did not do this, as in the penitential of Robert of Saint Victor.[52] Others even forced the Eucharist on the dead,

runt Eucaristiam, quod etiam fuit synodaliter prohibitum, et multe reperiuntur uarietates rituum. Ut etiam ex apostolo Paulo et Dyonisio trahitur, unus consueuit tantum panis consecrari, et ille frangebatur et distribuebatur omnibus, et unus calix tantum benedici per unum pontificem et distribui, et forte hic panis ex oblata farina conficiebatur, ut uult Iohannes Beleth, sed hic ritus nec in orientali nec in occidentali ecclesia hodie seruatur. Non enim potuit aucto populo christiano seruari. Legitur in libris Homberti, apocrisarii sedis apostolice, in disputatione contra Nicetam grecum de azimo, sanctum Iacobum primum episcopum Iherosolimorum modum tenuisse in azimo et forma panis. De quo *De consecratione*, distinctione prima, *Iacobus frater*, quem hodie et semper tenuit romana ecclesia. Et in *Rationali* dicitur apostolos Petrum et Paulum instituisse. Sed Greci a sancto Iohanne apostolo se dicunt habere quod semper fermento confecerunt.

37   Hoc est autem singulariter attendendum quod sacerdotes nunquam sine diacono celebrarunt, et in omni missa diaconus de manu sacerdotis recepit Eucaristiam sub specie panis, et sacerdos de manu diaconi calicem, ut glosa in capitulo *Peruenit*, XCIII distinctione, ponit causam, et ita preceptum fuit seruari, et ut in missali ponitur: 'Sumpsimus, domine, sacramenta'. Tunc clare uidetur plures semper communicasse, quia seruabatur illa ordinatio cui nunc uidemus in romana ecclesia, excepto solenni papali officio, derogatum. Et Guilelmus in *Rationali* dicit hoc modo, licet sit scriptum non seruari. Fuit etiam ante Innocentium III obseruantia quod tempore interdicti non concedebatur uiaticum, sed tantum penitentia et baptismus, quia uiaticum non reputabatur sacramentum necessitatis, ut hec habentur in textu et glosa et concordantiis

which was prohibited synodally; and many varieties of the rite are found. In extracts from Paul and Dionysius we find the custom that one [eucharistic minister] only would consecrate the bread, and he broke it and distributed it to all, and one chalice only was blessed by one pontiff and distributed, and perhaps this bread was made out of flour that had been offered, as John Beleth says;[53] but this rite is observed today neither in the eastern nor in the western church. Nor could it be observed once the numbers of Christian people increased. One reads in the book of Humbert, the envoy of the Apostolic See, in the disputation against Nicetas the Greek about unleavened bread, that Saint James, the first bishop of Jerusalem, held to the way of unleavened bread.[54] On this see [Gratian] *De consecratione*, D. 1, c. *Jacobus frater* [c. 47]; to this way the Roman church holds today and has always held. And in the *Rationale*[55] it is said that the apostles Peter and Paul instituted this. But the Greeks say they have the custom from the Apostle John of always consecrating leavened bread.

But this must be particularly noted: that priests never cele- 37 brated without deacons, and in every Mass the deacon received the Eucharist from the hand of the priest under the species of bread; and the priest received the chalice from the hand of the deacon, as the gloss[56] to c. *Pervenit* [in Gratian] D. 93 puts the case, so the command was observed and placed as it is in the missal: "We have received the sacraments, O Lord." Thus it seems clear that a plurity of persons always communicated, because that ordinance was observed which now we see repealed in the Roman church, except at a solemn papal service. And William [Durand the Elder] speaks in this way in the *Rationale*, although it is written that it is not to be observed.[57] Even before Innocent III[58] there was the practice during times of interdict of not granting the viaticum, but only penance and baptism, since the viaticum was not regarded as a necessary sacrament, as these things are found in the text and gloss[59] — and in the texts cited as agreeing with them — in [the

allegatis in capitulo *De sponsalibus, Non est.* Sed Innocentius III addidit uiaticum, ut in capitulo *Quod in te, De penitentiis et remissionibus,* licet non esset necessitatis, ut in glosa ibidem. Viaticum autem
semper sub specie panis reperitur reseruatum, ut idem Innocentius laudat in libro suo de officio misse, qui *Speculum ecclesie* nominatur, et textu iuncta glosa *De consecratione,* distinctione II, *Presbyter.*

38   Finaliter ipse Innocentius III in ultimo anno uite sue, scilicet
1215, congregauit synodum Rome apud Lateranum, que fuit
uniuersalis et plenissima, et in qua fuerunt duo patriarche ex
oriente per se et duo alii per suos apocrisarios, et primates, archiepiscopi et episcopi et abbates numero 1216, et omnium regum et
principum oratores; forte ante illam synodum nulla adeo plena reperitur. In illa synodo inter alia, capitula *Firmiter* et *Damnamus, De
summa trinitate* capitulum I, *De custodia Eucharistie* capitulum *Antiqua, De priuilegiis* capitulum *Omnis utriusque sexus, De penitentiis et remissionibus,* cum aliis multis edita reperiuntur. Et ibi satis clare
diffinitum reperitur in capitulo *Firmiter,* ⁋ *Una,* quod una est ecclesia, extra quam non est salus etc.; in capitulo *Antiqua* quod in illa
una ecclesia sancta Romana ecclesia principatum tenens est, omnium magistra; in capitulo *Omnis utriusque* quod fidelis in annis
discretionis constitutus confiteri ad minus semel in anno et recipere sacramentum Eucharistie tenetur, nisi de consilio sui sacerdotis abstineat. Mandatur etiam ibidem quod illa constitutio crebrius
publicetur. Illa constitutio, ut de se patet, non ligat pueros, quia
dicit de constitutis in annis discretionis; non ligat pluries quam semel in anno ad perceptionem sacramenti Eucharistie; non ligat
nisi ad sacramentum et non ad sacramenta; neque ligat ad integra

Decretals of Gregory IX], c. *Non est* [X 4.1.11], *De sponsalibus.* But Innocent added the viaticum, as in c. *Quod in te, De penitentiis et remissionibus* [X 5.38.11], although it was [still] not a necessary sacrament, as in the gloss there.[60] The viaticum, however, always is found reserved under the species of bread, as the same Innocent mentions in his book on the office of the Mass,[61] which is called the *Mirror of the Church*, and [it is also mentioned] in the text joined with the gloss at *De consecratione* [in Gratian] D. 2 c. *Presbyter.*[62]

Finally, Innocent himself, in the last year of his life, that is, 38 1215,[63] gathered a synod that was universal and plenary at the Lateran in Rome, at which there were two patriarchs from the East present and two others represented by their envoys, and primates, archbishops, bishops and abbots, 1,216 in number, and envoys of all the kings and princes. Perhaps there had never before been such a plenary council. In that council, among other texts, there were promulgated [the canons] c. *Firmiter* and c. *Damnamus, De summa Trinitate* [found in the *Decretals* of Gregory IX, X 1.1.1 and 2], *De custodia eucharistiae* c. 1 [ibid., X 3.44.1], c. *Antiqua, De privilegiis* [ibid., X 5.33.23], c. *Omnis utriusque sexus, De penitentiis et remissionibus* [ibid. X 5.38.12]. And there it is found quite clearly defined in c. *Firmiter ❡ Una* [X 1.11.3] that the Church is one and outside it there is no salvation; and in c. *Antiqua*, that one Church, the holy Roman church, holding the principate, is the teacher of all; and in c. *Omnis utriusque*, that the faithful person who has arrived at the age of discretion is bound to confess at least once a year and to receive the sacrament of the Eucharist unless he abstains on the advice of his priest. In the same text it is commanded that that constitution should be published frequently. That constitution, as is self-evident, does not bind children because it speaks of those who have arrived at the age of discretion; it does not bind [adults] to the reception of the sacrament of the Eucharist more than once a year; it binds only to the *sacrament*, and not to the *sacraments*; nor does it bind to the sacraments in their en-

sacramenta, ut dicit textus *Comperimus*, *De consecratione*, distinctione II, uel totum Eucharistie sacramentum, ut dicit textus Innocentii *De penitentiis et remissionibus* ex parte. Et concilium Nicenum nomine 'sacramenti' intelligit sub una specie et nomine 'sacramenta' sub duplici, ut in capitulo *Peruenit*, XCIII distinctione, iuncta glosa, et frequenter omnes missarum complende in plurali loquuntur: Prosint quesimus domine nobis sacramenta, etc. Ideo qui recipit sub specie panis, corpus scilicet domini nostri, satisfacit statuto. Recipit enim sacramentum Eucharistie, XCIII distinctione, *Presente*, quod neque Iacobelliani negant; satisfacit igitur.

39   Probatur etiam communionem non esse de precepto Christi, quia dicit constitutio, 'nisi de consilio sacerdotis ad tempus abstineat'. Pendet igitur a consilio sacerdotis communio talis, sic et Nicena synodus post concessionem uiatici adhuc hoc remisit ad curam et probationem episcopi, XXVI, questio VI, *De his* in fine. Non est ergo de precepto Christi nisi eo modo quo ecclesia auctoritate Christi precipit. Papa autem est summus sacerdos et magister omnium, ut diffiniuit illa synodus Lateranensis in capitulo *Antiqua*, et omnia alia concilia que precesserunt, quare ad eius consilium[10] est in hoc maxime recurrendum et ei acquiescendum.

40   Quod autem illa fuit intentio synodi, scilicet non esse hominem obligatum ad sumptionem Eucharistie nisi sub specie panis, que dicitur corpus Christi, patet primo ex capitulo primo *De custodia Eucaristie* eiusdem synodi, iuncto capitulo *Presbiter* cum glosa *De consecratione*, distinctione II, et capitulo *Officium*, *De officio archipresbiteri*, et in capitulo *De his que fiunt a maiori parte capituli*, etiam sy-

tirety, as the text of [Gratian] says at c. *Comperimus* [c. 12], *De consecratione*, D. 2; or to the full sacrament of the Eucharist, as the text of Innocent says in part at *De penitentiis et remissionibus* [in the Decretals of Gregory IX, X 5.38.12]. And the Council of Nicaea understands by the noun "sacrament," under one species, and by the noun "sacraments," under both, as in [Gratian] c. *Pervenit* D. 93 with the added gloss.[64] And frequently all parts of the Mass to be fulfilled are spoken of in the plural. "Lord, we ask that the sacraments should be useful to us." Thus, whoever receives the Body of our Lord under one species satisfies the statute. He receives the sacrament of the Eucharist ([Gratian] D. 93 c. *Presente* [c. 18]), which not even the Jacobellians deny. Therefore, [communion in one kind] is satisfactory.

It is proved also that communion [under both kinds] is not 39 commanded by Christ, because the constitution says, "unless he abstains for a time on the advice of his priest." Therefore, such a communion depends on the counsel of a priest; and the Nicene synod, after the concession of the viaticum, still remits this to the care and approval of the bishop ([Gratian] C. 26 c. 6 c. *De his* [c. 9] at the end). Therefore, it is not commanded by Christ unless in the way in which the Church commands with the authority of Christ. The pope, however, is the high priest and the master of all, as that Lateran synod defined in c. *Antiqua* [X 5.33.23], and all the other councils that preceded it. Therefore, one must have recourse most of all to his counsel in this matter, and one must acquiesce to it.

That this was the intention of the synod, namely, that a man 40 was not obligated to receive the Eucharist except under the species of bread, which is called the Body of Christ, is apparent, first, from *De custodia eucharistiae*, c. 1 [in the Decretals of Gregory IX, X 3.44.1] of the same synod, joined to c. *Presbyter* with the gloss at *De consecratione* D. 2,[65] and c. *Officium, De officio archipresbyteri* [ibid., X 1.24.3], and also in the canon of the Lateran synod in *De his que*

nodi Lateranensis. Et sic omnes de ordine mendicantium, qui tunc inchoarunt, et omnes doctores, qui post illam synodum fuerunt, intellexerunt, et uniuersalis catholica ecclesia, in qua crebriter constitutio illa *Omnis utriusque sexus* est publicata, et etiam Pragensis prouincia, que tempore Arnesti archiepiscopi suis constitutionibus prouincialibus hanc sepedictam ordinationem *Omnis utriusque sexus* inseruit; ex praxi ita se intellexisse ostendit. Fuit in illa synodo sanctus Dominicus, et illo tempore Hugo illius ordinis postillator solemnis totius Biblie, post hoc per Innocentium quartum ad cardinalatum promotus, qui talem intellectum exprimit, et post illum sanctus Thomas qui in quarto *Sententiarum*, distinctione IX, ait: Fideles ex illo statuto ecclesie ad recipiendum corpus Christi semel in anno obligari. Post quem archidiaconus in allegato capitulo *Comperimus*, et Iohannes Andree in *Clementinas*, *Ad nostram*, *De hereticis*. Sic et omnes alii doctores et magistri quotquot post synodum illam fuerunt. Similiter et Honorius Innocentii pape immediatus successor, ut in capitulo *Permittimus*, *De sententia excommunicationis*. Et tota catholica ecclesia sic intellexit illam constitutionem et in ea quieuit.

41 Etiam ecclesia in regno Bohemie usque ad Iacobellum, qui sibi ipsi uisus est omnibus aut prudentior aut sanctior. Ipse enim ob ueritatem euangelicam asseruit ritum communionis sub utraque specie quo ad laycos repetendum et ad uerba illius. Ex cuius predicatione multi multorum errorum occasionem receperunt, ut ipsemet in quodam sermone suo confessus est. Inconsulto romano pontifice et ecclesia catholica, assumptus est quidam ritus communionis sub utraque specie per plures laycos in regno Bohemie, nunquam tali modo in dei ecclesia practicatus. Quomodo deo grata esse posset talis presumptio, quando ipsi sacramentum unitatis re-

fiunt a maiori parte capituli [X 3.11.1].⁶⁶ That was the way everyone who belonged to the mendicant orders, which began at that time, and all the doctors who came after that synod understood the text, and the universal Catholic Church, wherein that constitution *Omnis utriusque sexus* was regularly published—and even the province of Prague, which at the time of Archbishop Arnest inserted this often-mentioned constitution *Omnis utriusque sexus* in its provincial constitutions,⁶⁷ showing from its praxis that it understood it in this sense. Saint Dominic was present at that Lateran synod; and at that time Hugh [of St.-Cher] of his order, the Solemn Annotator of the whole Bible, who was promoted afterwards to the cardinalate by Innocent IV, expressed such an understanding, and after him Saint Thomas,⁶⁸ who says at D. 9 of the Fourth Book of the *Sentences* that the faithful are obligated by that statute of the Church to receive the Body of the Lord once in a year. After him, the Archdeacon,⁶⁹ in the cited c. *Comperimus*, and Johannes Andreae⁷⁰ on the Clementine decree *De hereticis*, c. *Ad nostram*, say this, and so say all the doctors and masters who were after that synod. Similarly, Honorius, the immediate successor of Pope Innocent, says so in c. *Permittimus*, *De sententia excommunicationis* [in the *Decretals* of Gregory IX, X 5.39.57]. And so the entire Catholic Church understands that constitution and finds rest in it.

Even the church in Bohemia understood the text in that way, 41 up to the time of Jacobellus, who seemed to himself to be either wiser or holier than everyone else. He himself asserted, on the basis of Gospel truth, that the rite of communion under both species had to be restored to the laity, and according to the words of the Gospel. From his preaching many received occasion for many errors, as he himself admits in one of his sermons.⁷¹ Without consulting the Roman pontiff and the Catholic Church, a rite of communion under both species, never practiced in that way in God's Church, was adopted by many lay people in the Kingdom of Bohemia. How can such presumption be pleasing to God, when they

cipiunt in scissura ab apostolica romana ecclesia, quasi ipsi omnibus qui sunt aut fuerunt sint sanctiores, quando eo modo quo sancti Domini sacerdotes, quibus solum conceditur sanctasanctorum intrare, quasi quotidie communicare presumunt? Si quis attendit quomodo etiam romanus pontifex post sumptionem sanguinis bina lotione oris, ne quid remaneat in ore ex speciebus sacramentalibus, utitur ob reuerentiam tanti sacramenti, non potest illam irreuerentiam laycorum nisi detestari, etiam si horribiliora dietim non intercederent, que uitari in multitudine non possunt.

42   Contra cuius Iacobelli presumptionem in ipso regno boni et mali, etiam Wicleniste, et extra regnum multi doctissimi magistri, eum insanire dicentes, plura scripserunt, et due synodi Constantiensis et Basiliensis diffinierunt talem communionem non esse de ueritate precepti euangelici quo ad laycalem populum, et quod non licet contra ritum ecclesie rationabiliter introductum alicui illum sua sponte usurpare, prout nunc homo utique a deo missus, cui nomen frater Iohannes de Capistrano, uir religiosissimus, potens opere et sermone, non cessat ex fundatissimis scripturis errantes Iacobellianos ad ueritatem indefessis laboribus reuocare.

43   Ex his clare potest unusquisque intelligere Iacobellianos non ambulare modo quo decet humiles et obedientes Christianos, quando sensum suum preferunt uniuerse ecclesie et normam non sequuntur apostolice sedis, unde et fidem receperunt. Errant igitur. Omnes enim qui hanc regulam refutant, quam beati Petri sedem uident docere et obseruare, errare conuincuntur, XI distinctione, *Nolite*, et capitulo *Quis nesciat* cum infinitis similibus. Dicant Iacobelliani an lex diuina precipiat impossibile. Si hoc dixerint, blasphemant. Si igitur lex est possibilium, et non est in potestate

receive the sacrament of unity in schism from the apostolic Roman church, as if they are more holy than every Christian who exists or who has existed? They presume to communicate almost daily, just like the holy priests of the Lord, to whom alone it is granted to enter the holy of holies. If someone notes that even the Roman pontiff, out of reverence for so great a sacrament, washes his mouth twice after receiving the Blood, lest something of the sacramental species remain in his mouth, he cannot but detest that irreverence of the laity, even if they were not falling into more repellent practices on a daily basis, which cannot be avoided in the multitude.

Against the presumption of Jacobellus, the good and the bad in 42 that kingdom, even the Wycliffites, and learned men outside the kingdom, declaring him insane, have written a great deal. And the two synods, those of Constance and of Basel, defined communion in both kinds for the laity to be not in accordance with the Gospel's command, and that it was not permitted to anyone to usurp it to himself by his own will, contrary to a rite of the Church reasonably introduced. Now a man sent by God, whose name is John Capistran, a most religious man, powerful in work and word, unceasingly calls the erring Jacobellians back to the truth with his tireless labors, using the most reliable written authorities.

From this anyone can understand clearly that the Jacobellians 43 do not walk in a way that befits humble and obedient Christians when they prefer their own opinion to the universal Church and do not follow the norm of the Apostolic See, whence they received the faith. They are therefore in error. All who refuse this rule, which they observe the See of St. Peter teaching and observing, are convicted of error ([Gratian] D. II c. *Nolite* [c. 3] and c. *Quis nesciat* [c. II] with an infinite number of similar texts). Let the Jacobellians say that divine law commands the impossible. If they say that, they blaspheme. If therefore the law is concerned with possible things and it is not in the power of the laity to have the

laycorum habere Eucaristiam nisi eo modo quo eis ministratur, quomodo potest lex ipsos astringere ad sumptionem sub duplici specie, si eis non ministratur sub una aut duabus? Non igitur possunt obligari nisi ad modum quem assequi possunt. Et quia consecrans per se recipere potest sacramentum sub utraque specie, hinc ad hoc ipse tantum obligatur. Deinde, si quis dixerit sacerdotium obligari ad tradendum laicis sub utraque specie, esto quod sic sit, et non tradat: nonne laici sunt securi, si sunt fideles, et per eos non stat quo minus assequantur? Dicere igitur quod communio quo ad laicos fideles sit de necessitate salutis est insanire potius quam errare. Sed quod neque sacerdotes obligentur de necessitate salutis ad tradendum sub duplici specie patet, nam sacerdotes habent potestatem ligandi et soluendi in edificationem.

44 Tenentur igitur uigore credite potestatis ad omnia illa que indicauerint ad honorem et reuerentiam dei et animarum salutem conferre. Sunt enim medici animarum, et propter hoc habent claues discernendi inter lepram et lepram et potestatem faciendi id quod secundum creditam eis legationem uiderint secundum hominem, rem, locum et tempus oportunum. Quare si uniuersum sacerdotium aut saltem maior pars cum cathedra Petri, que secundum sanctum Cyprianum errare non permittitur a deo, uno tempore sic, alio aliter, propter edificationem ecclesie aut baptizaret aut sacramenta ministraret, quia omnia hec fiunt ob dei reuerentiam et animarum salutem, non potest ibi cadere deceptio, qualescunque fuerint persone. Ut elegantissime in multis passibus sanctus Augustinus, et alii catholici doctores, qui dicunt ex uoluntate dei sic fieri, hoc ostendunt ex euangelio super uerbo, Que dicunt facite, et Qui uos audit, me audit, et Sicut misit me uiuens

Eucharist except in the way in which it is administered to them, how can the law bind them to reception under both species if it is not administered to them under one or both? Therefore they cannot be obligated except in a way they can follow. And because the one who consecrates can receive the sacrament under both species through his own agency, he himself is obligated to do this only. Then if someone should say the priesthood is obliged to give the laity communion under both species, suppose this is so but the priesthood doesn't give communion in this way. Aren't the laity safe if they are faithful, and is it their fault that they are not able to take communion this way? To say then that communion is necessary for the salvation of the faithful laity is insanity, not error. But it is clear that neither are priests obligated, as necessary to their salvation, to give communion under both species, for priests have the power to bind and loose for the building up of the Church.

They are bound, therefore, in the strength of power entrusted   44
to them to grant all that they judge useful for the honor and reverence of God and for the salvation of souls. For they are physicians of souls, and for this reason they have the power of discerning between leper and leper[72] and the power to do what they see to be right, according to the representative function entrusted to them, with respect to person, thing, place and the appropriate time. Therefore, if the universal priesthood, or at least the greater part, with the See of Peter, which, according to Saint Cyprian is not permitted by God to err,[73] at one time baptizes or administers the sacraments thus, at another time otherwise, in order to build up the Church, because all these things are done out of reverence for God and for the salvation of souls, deception cannot occur there, whatever kinds of persons they might be. As Augustine and other Catholic doctors so eloquently say in many places, these things are done by the will of God. They show this from the Gospel at the passage, *What they say, do,* and *Whoever heeds you, heeds Me,* and *Just*

pater, ita mitto uos, et Vobiscum sum omni tempore usque ad consummationem seculi, et Fidelis seruus quem constituit dominus super familiam suam, ut det illis in tempore tritici mensuram.

45   Et maxime hec potestas credita est Petro et eius successoribus. Pro Petro enim rogauit Iesus ne deficeret fides eius, et obtinuit quod porte inferi non preualebunt aduersus ecclesiam cui Petrus preest. Fecit Innocentius tres sermones quos misit Arnoldo abbati Cisterciensi, ubi facto Petri exponit, quomodo ad ipsum et eius successores spectat singulariter ex precepto Christi pascere Eucharistia fideles. Et quoniam ad pastores spectat pascere, non mactare, non debent ministrare Eucharistiam in iudicium sed in uitam, et non debent margaritas proiicere ante porcos, sed debent fideles esse dispensatores, respiciendo ad mentem illius cuius uices agunt et eius honorem et ad commissi populi salutem. Quod maxime ad papam spectat, cui singulariter ecclesia est commissa.

46   Est autem istud ex praxi ecclesie etiam in formis sacramentorum manifestum. Apostoli baptizabant in nomine Iesu, alio tempore ecclesia in nomine Trinitatis. Aliter greca ecclesia hodie quam latina baptizat, et semper effectualiter. Conficiebant apostoli sacramentum Eucharistie dicendo Pater Noster, ut uult sanctus Gregorius, et uarie adhuc forme interu‹en›erunt[11] antequam scholasticus esset qui illam composuit quam hodie habet ecclesia, que etiam uaria est secundum aliquos in uariis sedibus. Nos uero qui sub Romana degemus ecclesia, ordinationem misse ab ipsis Romanis recepimus pontificibus, qui successiue addiderunt unus post alium, usque ad perfectum officium deuentum existit. Sed fides ecclesie non decipitur, quo ad animarum salutem, in rituum diuersitate. Unde ab apostolis baptizati fuerunt uere baptizati, quamuis

as the living Father sent me, so send I you, and, *I am with you all days even to the consummation of the world,* and *The faithful servant whom the master set over his household to give them a measure of wheat in due season.*[74]

And this power is entrusted especially to Peter and his successors. Jesus prayed for Peter that his faith would not fail and secured [the promise] that the gates of hell would not prevail against the Church over which Peter presides.[75] Innocent wrote three sermons which he sent to Arnold the Cistercian abbot in which he explains through the case of Peter how it is especially the responsibility of Peter and his successors, by Christ's command, to feed the faithful with the Eucharist.[76] And since it belongs to a shepherd to feed them, not kill them, they should administer the Eucharist not in judgment but in life; and they should not cast pearls before swine, but they should be faithful stewards, heeding the mind of Him on Whose behalf they act and having regard to His honor, and looking to the salvation of the people committed to them. This especially belongs to the pope, to whom especially the Church is entrusted.

It is manifest in the praxis of the Church, even in the forms of its sacraments. The apostles baptized in the name of Jesus; at another time the Church did so in the name of the Trinity. Today the Greek church baptizes otherwise than the Latin church does, and always with effect. The apostles confected the Eucharist while saying the Our Father, as Saint Gregory[77] says, and there were various forms between that time and the time of the scholar who composed the rite the Church uses now.[78] We, however, who are subject to the Roman church, have received the order of the Mass from the Roman pontiffs, who one after another in succession added to it, until they arrived at the finished office. But the faith of the Church is not deceived, in what pertains to the salvation of souls, by the diversity of rites. Hence those who were baptized by the apostles were truly baptized, although Christ said, *Baptizing*

45

46

Christus dixisset, Baptizantes in nomine Patris et Filii et Spiritus Sancti. Non fuerunt enim contra Christi preceptum qui in nomine Iesu baptizarunt. Nam in idemptitate fidei noluit Christus eos astringere, quin conuenientibus uerbis iuxta locum et tempus in edificationem ecclesie uterentur. Ministerium enim eis creditum respiciebat edificationem ecclesie, et ad illum finem, salua ueritate fidei, sine quo nemo potest esse membrum Christi et de corpore eius, quod est ecclesia, omnia potuerunt apostoli et possunt successores. Ait enim Cyprianus: 'manente concordie uinculo et perseuerante ecclesie catholice indiuiduo sacramento, actum suum disponit unusquisque episcopus, rationem propositi sui domino redditurus'. Et sanctus Augustinus in epistola ad Vincentium hoc dictum tanquam elegantissimum allegat.

47   Ex premissis constat quod tota catholica ecclesia non potest ad literam scripturarum obligari, licet semper ad spiritum. Quando enim litera non seruit edificationi et spiritui, recipit id quod magis seruit spiritui. Ita Paulus apostolus se aiebat ministrum noui testamenti, non litera sed spiritu. Et ideo qui cum humanis rationibus ex litera ecclesiam nituntur impugnare, errant. Nam ecclesia sine litera fuit aliquando ante Moysen, et etiam antequam apostolus Iohannes euangelium uel Paulus epistolas scripsit. Et Christus ecclesiam edificauit sine litera, quia nihil scripsit. Non est igitur litera, que per tyrannum penitus deleri possit, de essentia ecclesie, sed spiritus est, qui uiuificat. Quare nec mirum si praxis ecclesie uno tempore interpretatur scripturam uno modo, et alio tempore alio modo. Nam intellectus currit cum praxi; intellectus enim qui cum praxi concurrit est spiritus uiuificans. Origenes enim et quidam alii textum, Si quis non resignauerit omnibus que possidet non

them in the name of the Father and of the Son and of the Holy Spirit. For those who baptized in the name of Jesus did not act contrary to Christ's command. Though identical in their faith, Christ did not wish to constrain them in such a way that they might not use fitting words according to time and place to build up the Church. The ministry entrusted to them looks to the building up of the Church, and to that end — saving the truth of the faith, without which no one can be a member of Christ and belong to His body, which is the Church — the apostles and their successors after them could do all things. Cyprian says, "Remaining in the bond of harmony and persevering in the undivided sacrament of the Catholic Church, each bishop disposes his actions, in order to give an accounting of his purpose to the Lord." And Saint Augustine cites this saying as a particularly fine one in his letter to Vincent.[79]

From the aforesaid it is evident that the entire Catholic Church 47 cannot be bound to the letter of the Scriptures, although always to the spirit. For when the letter does not serve both building up and the spirit, it accepts that which better serves the spirit. Thus Paul called himself a minister of the New Testament not by the letter but by the spirit.[80] Thus those who dare to attack the Church with human arguments from the letter are in error. For the Church was without the letter for a long time before Moses, and before the Apostle John wrote his gospel or Paul his letters. And Christ built the Church without the letter, for He wrote nothing. Therefore, it is not the letter, which could be abolished entirely by a tyrant, that is of the essence of the Church, but the spirit, which gives life. Therefore, one should not wonder if the praxis of the Church at one time interpreted the Scripture in one way but in another at another time. For its interpretation conforms to its praxis, for the interpretation which conforms with praxis is the spirit giving life. Origen[81] and some others understood the command, *Whoever does not give up all he possesses cannot be My disciple*[82] according to the praxis of the primitive church. But when large numbers of persons

potest meus esse discipulus, secundum praxim primitiue ecclesie intellexerunt preceptum esse. Intrante autem multitudine non fuit possibile omnes resignare, et nihilominus, contra praxim tunc ecclesie, apostolici steterunt in intellectu quod textus ille haberet necessitatem precepti, et damnati sunt ab ecclesia tanquam heretici. Ita potest dici de aliis consimilibus scripturis, etiam de illa *Nisi manducaueritis* etc. Ecclesia igitur, sicut recepit scripturam, ita et interpretatur. Sequuntur igitur scripture ecclesiam que prior est, et propter quam scriptura, et non econuerso. Et qui ad hoc non respexerunt impugnarunt ecclesiam frustra et se segregarunt ab ecclesia, et hec pertinax segregatio, per quam quis sensum suum quem habet de scripturis preponit ecclesie, *heresis* grece dicitur, quod latine 'diuisio' potest interpretari. Et quia iam precesserunt doctissimi uiri qui hec latissime uerissima esse ostenderunt, neque possunt per aliquem rationem habentem difficultari, satis sit proposito nostro, scilicet non esse possibile sacerdotium necessitari ad dandum communionem laycis sub utraque specie, sed quod ministratio sacramenti credita est illis illiminate eo modo quo ad ecclesie edificationem, scilicet dei honorem et animarum salutem, pro loco et tempore iudicauerunt expedire.

48   Diceret forte aliquis, sicut quis seipsum probans et peccatorem reperiens debet abstinere ab accessu ad communionem, sic etiam tradens debet abstinere ne tradat etiam publico peccatori, sed alias non. Dicimus quod ob reuerentiam sacramenti et edificationem ecclesie semper ecclesia denegauit tradere cathecuminis fidelibus, etiam per quos non stetit quin baptizarentur, licet essent de corpore Christi, quia fideles. Similiter et existentibus in penitentia, licet essent deo reconciliati per contritionem. Similiter et energumi-

entered the Church, it was not possible for everyone to give up all they possessed. Nevertheless, the "apostolic ones" stuck to the interpretation that that text had the necessary force of a command, although they were contrary to the praxis of the Church of that time; and they were condemned by the Church as heretics.[83] The same can be said of other similar scriptures, even of the one that says, *Unless you eat,* etc.[84] The Church thus interprets Scripture the way it received it. Therefore, the Scriptures follow the Church, which is prior to them and for the sake of which the Scripture exists, and not the converse. And those who do not respect this impugn the Church in vain and separate themselves from it. This pertinacious separation, by which someone places his own understanding of the Scripture before that of the Church, is called *haeresis* in Greek, which is interpreted in Latin as "a division." And since highly learned men have already gone before us who showed this to be most true in the broadest possible way, and no difficulties can be raised by anyone having reason, we have enough for our present purpose, that is, [to show] it is impossible that the priesthood is required to give communion to the laity under both species, but that the administration of the sacraments was entrusted to them without restrictions in whatever way they judge expedient for the building up of the Church, that is, for the honor of God and the salvation of souls, in accordance with time and place.

Perhaps some will say: just as anyone testing and finding himself a sinner should abstain from coming to communion, so the one who gives it should abstain from giving it to a public sinner, but otherwise not. We say that, owing to its reverence for the sacrament and the need for building up the Church, the Church always refused to give the sacrament to faithful catechumens, even when it was not their fault that they were not baptized, although they belonged to the body of Christ, being faithful. Similarly, even to those who were doing penance, although they were reconciled

48

nis, ut patet ex Dyonisio. Unde constat ecclesiam ab initio usam fuisse libera potestate ad edificationem in ministrando hoc sacramentum.

49 Adhuc manifeste declarabitur Iacobellianos pro se nullas habere scripturas. Nam negare nequeunt omnia Christi uerba in euangeliis scripta eque uera esse, neque negare possunt Christum in omnibus tenere principatum, qui primo ascendit ad celos. Reperitur igitur Abraam, Ysaac et Iacob, prophetas, apostolos, uirgines etc. habere eternam uitam, sed nemo ante Christum ‹baptizatus fuit›. Sed Christus dixit: Nisi quis renatus fuerit ex aqua et spiritu sancto, non intrabit regnum celorum. Dixit etiam: Qui crediderit et baptisatus fuerit, saluus erit; qui uero non crediderit, condemnabitur. Oportet igitur quod hoc uerificetur de omnibus sanctis. Non potest igitur hoc intelligi de uisibili baptismo, sed de renascentia inuisibili et spirituali que fit per fidem, eo enim modo tantum illud dictum potest uerificari de omnibus sanctis Veteris et Noui Testamenti. Homo enim ex Adam natus, ut sit filius hominis; si debet denuo nasci, ut sit filius dei per gratiam, oportet quod hec filiatio fiat in uero filio naturali dei, qui sibi naturam filiationis ex Adam uniuit, ut sit filius dei et hominis. Quando igitur homo per fidem se filio dei unit, transeundo in adoptionem per gratiam dei patris cui credit et filio eius, sic in unitate spiritus sancti spiritum suum per fidem firmam se uniendo deo, credens se posse sic ad filiationem dei pertingere in filio dei, qui est eiusdem nature humane secum, tunc denuo nascitur in spiritu.

50 Unde una est sola fides, una scilicet renascentia et filiatio per quam omnes sancti renati sunt et renascentur. Illa non potest esse uisibilis et sensibilis, quia ut sic, non est eque ab omnibus sanctis

to God by contrition. Similarly, even to those who were possessed by a demon, as is evident from Dionysius.[85] Therefore, it follows that the Church had from the beginning used its free power to build up the church in the administration of this sacrament.

Besides, it will be demonstrated manifestly that the Jacobellians have none of the Scriptures on their side. For they cannot deny that all Christ's words written in the Gospels are equally true, nor can they deny that Christ, Who first ascended to the heavens, held the principate in all things. Thus we find that Abraham, Isaac, Jacob, the prophets and virgins have eternal life, but no one [was baptized] before Christ. But Christ said, *Unless you are reborn of water and the Holy Ghost, you will not enter the kingdom of heaven.*[86] He also said: *Whoever believes and is baptized will be saved. Whoever does not believe, however, will be condemned.*[87] It must be the case, therefore, that this will be shown to be true of all the saints. Christ's words cannot, therefore, be understood of visible baptism, but of invisible and spiritual rebirth, which is effected by faith, for only in this way can Christ's words be shown to be true of all the saints of the Old and New Testaments. For man is born of Adam that he may be a son of man. If he must be born again, that he may be a son of God by grace, it is necessary that this filiation be accomplished in the true, natural Son of God, Who united to Himself the nature of sonship from Adam, so that He is Son of God and Son of Man. When, therefore, a man unites himself by faith to the Son of God by crossing over in adoption by the grace of God the Father, in Whom, and in Whose Son, he believes, and he thus unites his spirit to God in the unity of the Holy Spirit by means of firm faith, believing himself thus able to attain the sonship of God in the Son of God, Who is of the same human nature with him, then he is born again in the spirit.

Hence there is only one faith, that is, one rebirth and sonship through which all the saints were and are reborn. This cannot be a visible and sensory [rebirth and sonship], because as such all the

49

50

417

participabilis, sed necessario est spiritualis et intellectualis, uti una
ueritas in multis intellectibus, et ‹sic ab omnibus sanctis› recepti-
bilis. Ob hoc Paulus aiebat patres nostros omnes baptizatos, licet
non baptismate Christi uisibiliter sicut Christiani, sed in baptismate Christi inuisibiliter, in nube uero uisibiliter. Sic ubi Christus
dicit, Nisi manducaueritis carnem filii hominis et biberitis eius
sanguinem, non habebitis uitam in uobis, necesse est quod, si de
omnibus sanctis debet uerificari qui habent uitam illam diuinam,[12]
non intelligatur de uisibili seu sacramentali manducatione, sed de
spirituali. Nam renatus per fidem in uerbo non potest cibari nisi
uerbo; ex his enim, ex quibus sumus, ex his nutrimur. Unum est
uerbum per quod renascimur et unum est uerbum per quod renati
pascimur, et est uerbum uite intellectualis, scilicet ueritas ipsa, que
solum pascere potest renatum intellectum per fidem. Et nos homines non possumus hunc cibum, per quem incorporamur uite intellectuali, scilicet ueritati, participare, nisi in eo in quo nostra natura
est in unitate persone unita ipsi uerbo, quod est ueritas.

51   Hinc Petrus aiebat Christum habere uerba uite eterne; hoc quidem habere est esse. Nam hoc uerbum est uita, ut ait de se Iesus:
Ego sum uia ueritas et uita. Ita Paulus dicebat patres nostros eandem escam spiritualem comedisse et eundem potum spiritualem
bibisse. Et non potest esse aliter uerum, quod sit una et eadem
esca plurium, nisi illa sit spiritualis, neque est alia esca sanctorum
quam panis uite et intellectus, neque alius potus quam aqua sa-
pientie, et non est alius panis uiuus nisi qui de celo descendit,
quem qui manducat non morietur, sed uiuet in eternum. Neque
alius est cibus uite eterne in hoc mundo, et alius in regno, nisi ‹in›

saints would not be able to participate equally in it, but of necessity it is spiritual and intellectual, as there is one truth in many intellects, and [for this reason it is] receivable [by all the saints].[88] On this account Paul said all our fathers were baptized, although not visibly with the baptism of Christ like Christians, but in the baptism of Christ invisibly, although visibly in the cloud.[89] Thus where Christ says, *Unless you eat the flesh of the Son of Man and drink of His blood, you shall not have life within you*,[90] it is necessary that, if it cannot be shown to be true of all the saints who have that divine life, it is not understood of visible or sacramental eating, but of spiritual. For he who is reborn by faith in the Word cannot be fed unless with the Word. For we are made of those things from which we are nourished. One is the Word through which we are reborn, and one is the Word by which we, reborn, are fed, and this is the Word of the life intellectual, that is Truth itself, which alone can feed the reborn intellect by faith. And we men cannot participate in this food by which we are incorporated into the life intellectual, that is, the Truth, except in Him in Whom our nature is united in unity of person with the Word Himself, that is, the Truth.

Hence Peter said Christ had the words of eternal life;[91] to have this is to exist. For this word is life, as Jesus says of Himself: *I am the way, the truth and the life*.[92] So Paul said our fathers ate the same spiritual food and drank the same spiritual drink.[93] And it cannot be true otherwise that there is one and the same food for many [before Christ's institution of baptism] unless that food is spiritual; neither is there another food of the saints than the bread of life and of the intellect, nor another drink than the water of wisdom. And there is no other living bread except that which descends from heaven, whereof whosoever eats shall not die but shall live eternally. Nor is there one food of eternal life in this world and another in the Kingdom [i.e. in Heaven], except insofar as that food is not attained here except in the way that this world permits, 51

quod hic non attingitur, nisi modo quo hic mundus permittit, qui est sensibilis. Unde non attingitur uita que est ueritas sensibiliter nisi per fidem, sicut discipulus non attingit doctrinam magistri nisi credat in sensibilibus uerbis magistri ueritatem doctrine contineri. Sed in alio regno intellectuali cibat ueritas, non per fidem et signa sensibilia, sed per seipsam. Nam ibi ueritas seipsam, uti est, prebet, cibum uite intellectualis. Unde postquam Iesus Christus, qui de uita eterna et cibo uite plura aperuit apostolis, recedere uoluit de hoc mundo, dixit: Vado uobis parare mensam, ut bene et clare intelligerent cibum uite esse illum quem ipse in mensa per eum paranda in recessu de hoc mundo, in alio transiens ministrabit.

52 Adhuc aliter Qui crediderit et baptizatus fuerit, saluus erit, quod est uitam habere eternam. Sed nisi quis manducauerit carnem filii hominis et biberit eius sanguinem, non habebit uitam. Igitur credere et baptizari est manducare et bibere, ut dicit Augustinus et habetur *De consecratione*, distinctione V, *Qui passus*. Et qui credit habet uitam. Credere igitur baptizari manducare et bibere, et quicquid similiter per Christum dicitur, non habet in spirituali intellectu differentiam, sed unum solum est quod per omnia talia uarie exprimitur, scilicet Quotquot receperunt, eum dedit eis potestatem filios dei fieri his qui credunt, etc. Eleganter igitur Beda ait super Iohannem, quod 'panis qui manducatur in regno dei non iuxta *cherinton* corporalis intelligendus est cibus, sed ille utique qui ait: Ego sum panis qui de celo descendi, si quis manducauerit ex hoc pane uiuet in eternum, id est, si quis mee incarnationis sacramento perfecte incorporatus mee diuine maiestatis uisione frui meruerit, hic perpetua uite immortalis beatitudine gaudebit.' Hec ille. Hic est enim cibus qui non perit, quem filius hominis dat, quem signauit pater esse filium suum, qui est cibus uerus nobis in

which is [under] sensible [species].[94] Therefore, the life which is truth is not attained in the senses except through faith, just as the disciple does not attain the teaching of the master unless he believes the truth of his teaching is contained in the sensible words of the master. But in the other, intellectual kingdom the truth feeds not on faith and sensible signs but on itself. For there the truth presents itself as it is, as the food of the life intellectual. Hence once Jesus Christ, Who revealed to the apostles many things about eternal life and the food of life, wished to depart from this world, He said, *I go to prepare a table for you*,[95] so that they might understand well and clearly that He is the food of life, which He will serve himself at the table prepared by Him in departing from this world and passing to another.

Besides, [Christ's words,] *He who shall believe and is baptized will* 52 *be saved*, that is, have eternal life, [are to be understood] in another way. But *Unless you eat the flesh of the Son of Man and drink of His Blood, you shall not have life within you*. Therefore, to believe and be baptized is to eat and drink, as Augustine holds [in Gratian] *De consecratione* D. 2 c. *Quia passus* [c. 36]. Whoever believes has eternal life. To believe, therefore, is to be baptized, eat and drink; and similar [metaphors] used by Christ are not to be taken differently in their spiritual understanding, but there is only one thing that is being expressed in different ways through all such [metaphors], that is, *To as many as received Him, to them gave He power to be made sons of God, to those who believe in His name*. Thus, says Bede neatly in his commentary on John, "The bread that is eaten in the kingdom of God is food, not to be understood according to corporeal *cerinthum* [or bees' bread], but certainly in the way of Him Who says, *I am the Bread of Life which comes down from heaven. Whoever eats of this Bread will live forever*. That is, whoever is incorporated perfectly by the sacrament of My incarnation will merit enjoying the vision of My divine majesty. He will enjoy the perpetual beatitude of eternal life."[96] This is indeed the Bread that does not per-

nostra natura datus a patre qui de celo descendit, qui est cibus uiuus et uerus et potus uerus, et lux uera omnem rationem illuminans et uitis uera. Et quia ueritas, igitur nihil de mixto habet iste cibus qui est uita. Quare non est uisibilis nec temporalis, sed prestat immortalitatem, et est hec necessaria omnium doctorum sententia, quoniam impossibile est aliter omnia Christi uerba eque uera esse, si non intelligantur, ut sunt spiritus uiuificans, pro quo facit textus qui ponitur *De consecratione*, distinctione V, *Inquit apostolus*.

53   Sed si quis dixerit: Nonne quidam hunc textum, *nisi manducaueritis*, exponunt de esu sacramentali, scilicet quod quamuis intelligatur de spirituali esu, tamen in hac ecclesia constare debet Christianum sub signis sacramentalibus confiteri Christum esse esum et potum uite? Sic edens spiritualiter, quasi corde credens ad iusticiam, etiam tenetur ad esum sacramentalem, quasi confessio oris fiat ad salutem, sicut et de baptismo fidelis dicitur. Tenetur igitur in uoto habere esum sacramentalem. Aliquando ergo debet communicare ut arguit sanctus Thomas.

54   Fatemur hoc sic se habere, sed non potest quis obligari ex uoto ad impossibile. Ideo eo modo tantum obligabitur ad executionem uoti quomodo ecclesia tradit, si ipse per se sumere nequit. Et iste est uerus intellectus sancti Thome, qui ait uoto ex precepto dei, *Nisi manducaueritis* etc., executionem precepto ecclesie per capitulum *Omnis utriusque* fidelem ad communionem obligari.

55   Adhuc forte diceret aliquis, Christus dixit: Hoc facite in meam commemorationem. Precipit igitur sacramentalem communionem fieri in sui memoriam. Non negamus preceptum Christi esse, ut

ish, which the Son of Man gives, Whom the Father marked out as His Son. He, Who descended from heaven, is the true food given to us in our nature by the Father. He is the living and true food and the true drink, and the true light illuminating all reason, and the true vine. And because He is the truth, that food which is life has nothing of mixture in it. Hence it is neither visible nor temporal but grants immortality. And this is the necessary opinion of all the doctors, since it is impossible otherwise for all Christ's words to be equally true if they are not understood so that they are the life-giving spirit. The text that is placed at [Gratian] *De consecratione* D. 2 c. *Inquit apostolus* [c. 81] argues for this view.

But suppose someone says, Are there not some who expound   53 this text, *Unless you eat*, of sacramental eating, that is, although it may be understood of spiritual eating, nevertheless, in this Church it should be evident that a Christian confesses Christ under sacramental signs to be the food and drink of life? Thus the one who eats spiritually, as if believing in the heart unto justice, is also bound to sacramental eating, as if the confession of the mouth works for salvation, just as the faithful person is said to do in the case of baptism. Therefore, he is bound by his vow to sacramental eating. He ought therefore to take communion from time to time, as Saint Thomas argues.

We confess this to be so, but no one can be bound by a vow to   54 the impossible. Therefore, he is only obligated to the execution of the vow in the way that the Church teaches, if he himself does not wish to receive in his own person. And this is the true understanding of Saint Thomas, who says that the faithful person is obligated to execute his vow, [derived] from God's command *Unless you eat*, by taking communion according to the Church's precept in c. *Omnis utriusque.*[97]

Again, perhaps someone will say, "Christ said, *Do this in memory*   55 *of Me*. He instructs us therefore that sacramental communion be performed in memory of him." We do not deny the command to

hec sic fiant in ecclesia uti ipse fecit, et sic fit per successores illorum quibus precepit. Nam episcopi et sacerdotes qui succedunt
discipulis, quibus hoc preceptum reperitur, gratias agunt, benedicunt, accipiunt, manducant, et bibunt Eucaristiam in memoriam
Christi, nec hec fieri possunt per aliquos quam tales. Nemo enim
potest per se accipere et manducare Eucaristiam nisi qui consecrauit. Simul hic traditur potestas consecrandi et accipiendi per se
et tradendi aliis. Unde dicit Augustinus et habetur in capitulo *Liquido*, *De consecratione*, distinctione V, eos potestatem circa modum
sacramenti habuisse, sed facultas tradendi aliis potestatem aut dis-
tribuendi non est preceptum. Christus enim elegit illos quibus tradidit. Dicit enim Guilelmus in *Rationali* quod per traditionem calicis signauit discipulos suos, sic et ipsis discipulis eandem dedit
potestatem, scilicet eligendi quibus tradant similem potestatem et
quibus communionem. Unde quia ipsi discipuli ad hoc constituti
fuerunt, ut ex uerbo Hoc facite constat, manifestum est eos sacerdotes sacerdotum aut pontifices creatos. Hinc qui in eorum uices
succedunt habent potestatem hoc faciendi, eo modo quo ipsi et
ante eos Christus pontifex Noui Testamenti fecit, scilicet constituendi pontifices qui omnia talia possunt per se, et tradendi potestatem electis sacerdotibus hoc faciendi, scilicet gratias agendi, be-
nedicendi, et accipiendi, simul et aliis dignis tradendi, uti
elegantissime diuinus tradit Dyonisius obseruatum. Ex nullo igitur textu habetur quod laici necessitentur recipere aliter quam eis
traditur, aut quod episcopi seu sacerdotes necessitentur eis sic tradere modo quo Christus discipulis tradidit, quorum laici uices
non gerunt.

be Christ's, that such things should be done in the Church as He Himself did, and were thus to be done by the successors of those He instructed. For the bishops and priests who succeeded the disciples, to whom this command was given, give thanks, bless, take, eat and drink the Eucharist in memory of Christ. Nor can these things be done by others than by persons like them. No one can take and eat the Eucharist by himself except the one who consecrated it. The power of consecration and taking by oneself and giving [communion] to others is here passed on simultaneously. Hence Augustine says, and this is found in [Gratian] c. *Liquido* [c. 54], *De consecratione* D. 2, that they have power over the manner [of giving] the sacrament, but the ability of handing over the power to others, or of distribution, is not in the command. Christ chose those to whom He gave it. William [Durand the Elder]⁹⁸ says in the *Rationale* that by the giving of the chalice He marked out those who would be His disciples. So he gave that power to His disciples, that is, of choosing to whom they would grant a similar power and to whom they would give communion. Hence, because those disciples were commissioned for this purpose, as is evident from the words, *Do this*, it is obvious that they were created priests or pontiffs of priests. Hence those who succeed to their place have the power of doing this in the way they and Christ, the pontiff of the New Testament, did before them, that is, of establishing pontiffs who can do all these things in their own power, and of conferring power on chosen priests of doing this, that is, giving thanks, blessing and taking, and at the same time of giving to others who are worthy, as the divine Dionysius most aptly observed in his teaching.⁹⁹ From no text, therefore, does one learn that the laity are required of necessity to receive the Eucharist other than as it is given them, or that bishops or priests have to give it to them in the way in which Christ—on Whose behalf lay persons do not act—gave it to His disciples.

56   Neque Paulus dissentit ab euangelistis quando scribit Corin-
theis. Nam forte Corintheorum sacerdotes intellexerunt Christum
cum suis discipulis ad ultimam cenam conuenisse, et primo accepisse panem, gratias egisse, benedixisse, fregisse et cenantibus
dixisse, Accipite et comedite etc. Et sic putabant cenam a fractione
panis inchoatam. Et quod postquam cenauit Christus accepisse calicem, gratias egisse, benedixisse et dixisse: Bibite ex hoc omnes;
hic est enim etc., et hunc morem sequi uolebant. Et in hoc Paulus
non reprehendit eos, sed in hoc quod mysticum esum non intellexerunt, sed se dederunt ad conuiuia, ibi finem ponentes. In hoc
non laudat eos, sed duxit eos de errore littere ad spiritum et mentem Christi instituentis sacramentum. An autem fuerunt laici in
illo conuiuio et mulieres, non potest clare ex textu haberi, sed
quod non fuerunt, maxime per finem textus uidetur, ubi ait:
Itaque fratres mei cum conuenitis ad manducandum etc. quod de
sacerdotibus concelebrantibus potius potest intelligi. Alii, ut ex
Dyonisio habetur, non conueniebant cum sacerdotibus nec uidere
poterant mysteria. Et non sine magno misterio alia uerba ponit
Paulus circa sumptionem corporis Christi et alia circa sumptionem
sanguinis. Nam dicit circa sumptionem corporis, Hoc facite in
meam memoriam etc. Sed circa sumptionem sanguinis dicit: Hoc
facite, quotienscunque biberitis, in meam commemorationem.
Quotienscunque enim sanguis ex calice bibitur, per quemcunque
bibatur tunc in memoriam Christi fieri debet. Non enim cadit preceptum in sumptionem, sed in memoriam, ut quando sumetur,
quod in memoria sumatur maxime calix, et diligenter aduertenti
clarissime constabit hanc esse intentionem Pauli ex uerbis que sequuntur, Quotienscunque enim etc. Et probet se homo. Que
uerba clare exprimunt preceptum non cadere in sumptionem, sed
in memoriam sumptionis tempore contra consuetudinem malam

Nor did Paul dissent from the evangelists when he wrote to the   56
Corinthians. For perhaps the priests of the Corinthians understood Christ to have met with His disciples at the Last Supper,
and first He took bread, gave thanks, blessed it, broke it, and said
to those dining with Him, *Take and eat.* And so they thought the
supper began with the breaking of the bread. And after Christ had
dined, He took the chalice, gave thanks, blessed and said, *Drink
you all of this. This is* etc., and wished to follow this custom. And
Paul does not rebuke them for this, but only in so far as they did
not understand mystical eating, but gave themselves up to revelry,
finding their purpose there. In this he did not praise them but led
them from the error of the letter to the spirit and to the mind of
Christ, Who instituted the sacrament. Whether, however, there
were lay men and women at [the Corinthians'] banquet cannot be
understood readily from the text; but it seems that there were not,
especially from the end of the text, where it says, *And so, my brothers, when you come together to eat,* which makes better sense in regard
to concelebrating priests. Others, as we learn from Dionysius,[100]
did not come together with the priests, nor could they see the
mysteries. And not without great mystery does Paul use other
words about consuming the Body of Christ, and still others about
consuming His Blood. For he says about consuming the Body, *Do
this in memory of Me,* while about consuming the Blood he says, *Do
this whenever you drink in memory of Me.* Whenever the Blood is
drunk from the chalice, it should be done by whoever does it in
memory of Christ. The command does not apply to the consuming but to the remembering, so that when it is taken, the cup
is taken most of all in memory. And to the one who heeds this
carefully it becomes utterly clear that this is Paul's intention from
the words that follow, *Whenever* etc., [i.e.] *And let a man examine
himself.*[101] These words clearly express that the precept does not
apply to consuming but to remembering at the time of consuming,

Corintheorum qui ad corporales delicias trahebant dominicam cenam.

57   Arbitramur nunc satis competenter per hanc prolixiorem epistolam cuncta, que Iacobelliani pro sui erroris fomento et palliatione tam ex scriptura quam praxi et compactatis assumunt, potius contra eos esse ostendisse, rogantes iterum atque iterum omnes qui in Iacobelli sectam sub suasionibus sunt inducti, et propterea a sancta Romana et catholica ecclesia segregati, ut prioribus nostris monitis, si uitam assequi cupiunt immortalem, quamtotius acquiescant. Hoc si fecerint, ut speramus, habebunt piissimum pontificem qui sit omnibus compati fidelibus. Vosque alios fideles, qui in fide parentum et ritu catholice ecclesie diuino munere hactenus perseverati[13] estis, admonemus ut Iacobellianos inducatis ad eam redire conformitatem quam aut ipsi aut eorum parentes uobiscum obseruarunt. Hoc cedit in maximum meritum animabus uestris, quod sic acquieuerint, lucrati eos estis et gaudebunt uobiscum, et cum tota catholica ecclesia esse pacifice unitos, nosque non solum amicissimum fautorem omnium et singulorum, sed et diligentissimum solicitatorem et fidelem cooperatorem offerimus in omnibus que honori et utilitati incliti regni et singulorum cadere poterunt, ut et sic tandem ex Christiane milicie catholica ecclesia una pariter ad triumphantem pertingere mereamur, gratia domini et saluatoris nostri Iesu Christi semper benedicti. Amen.

58   Datum in ciuitate nostra Brixinensi die XI, mensis octobris, anno a natiuitate domini millesimo quadringentesimo quinquagesimo secundo, pontificatus sanctissimi in Christo patris et domini nostri domini Nicolai diuina prouidentia pape quinti anno sexto.

contrary to the bad custom of the Corinthians, who were bringing the Lord's Supper down to the level of corporeal enjoyments.

Now, I think, I have shown competently enough by means of this very long letter, both from the Scripture and from praxis, and from the Compacts (as they call them), that everything that the Jacobellians take in evidence to mitigate and palliate their error is in fact against them. We ask again and again that all who have been led into the sect of Jacobellus by his arguments and are therefore separated from the holy Roman and Catholic Church to acquiesce to our prior warning as quickly as possible if they wish to attain immortal life. If they do this, as we hope, they will have a most merciful pontiff who knows how to sympathize with all faithful persons. We admonish you and the other faithful who up to now have persevered in the faith of their ancestors and the rite of the Catholic Church by divine gift to compel the Jacobellians to return to that conformity that they or their ancestors observed with you. This will result in the greatest merit to your souls. If you win them over, you will have been enriched and will rejoice to be peacefully united with them and the whole Catholic Church, and we offer ourselves to be the most friendly supporter of each and every one of you, but also a most gentle caregiver and faithful partner in all things that accrue to the honor and utility of an outstanding Kingdom and of each one of you, so that together we may merit equally attaining the Church Triumphant in the one Catholic Church of the Christian soldiery by the grace of our Lord and Savior Jesus Christ ever blessed. Amen. 57

Given in our city of Brixen on the 11th day of October in the year of the Lord's Nativity, 1452, in the sixth year of our most holy father in Christ and lord, Lord Nicholas V, pope by divine providence. 58

Epistola ad Rodericum de Trevino[1]

1 Vir doctissime mihi plurimum venerande, domine Roderice de Arevalo, Archidiacone de Trevino, ad hoc ut in his ecclesiae perturbationibus, ubi multorum opinione vulgi doctissimorum sententias in utramque partem fluctuare conspicis, ultimam verioremque coniecturam secundum regulas doctae ignorantiae venari valeas. Notato (quoniam de papa et de concilio ecclesiam repraesentante quaestio est) quod quoniam omnia in verbo Dei sunt, per quod omnia in esse prodierunt, tunc verbum ipsum est omnia complicans, et omnia per ipsum explicata sunt in varietate alteritatis, ipsum verbum participantia. Unitatem insuper alterni[2] verbi omnia complicantis omnia creata participant explicative, varie quidem, ut verbum ipsum, quod uti est participari nequit, in varietate multitudinis participantium meliori quidem modo quo potest, participetur. Omnia igitur in tantum sunt, in quantum ipsam verbi entitatem participant. Fluit ergo esse omnis creaturae ab illa absoluta entitate immediatissime, quoniam omnibus aeque praesens est, sed in alteritate participantium exoritur alteritas creaturarum.

2 Pari passu progredere, affirmando gratiam quae naturae superadditur, ita se ad Christum habere. Nam omnis creatura rationalis, in natura rationali humana, per gratiam in Christo Jesu divinitati hypostatice unita gratiam elevationis ad unionem Dei, quae est ultima foelicitas, consequi potest. Propter quam Jesus benedictus omnes tales beatificandos est complicans. Omnes igitur rationales

Letter to Rodrigo Sánchez de Arévalo

Most learned man, to whom I owe great reverence, lord Rodrigo   1
[Sánchez] de Arévalo, archdeacon of Treviño,[1] I am writing to you
in order that, during these disturbances in the Church in which
you see the settled views of many learned men being tossed from
one side to the other by the opinion of the vulgar, you may be able
to hunt down a final and truer conjecture according to the rules of
learned ignorance. You will observe that (seeing that the subject of
inquiry is about the pope and a council representing the Church),
since all things are in the Word of God, through which all things
came into existence, that Word then enfolds all things and
through It all things are unfolded in a diversity of difference,
participating[2] the Word Itself. All created things participate, in an
unfolded, indeed varied way, the unity of the eternal[3] Word, which
enfolds all things, so that the Word Itself, although as such it is
imparticiple, is participated in the variety of a multitude of participants in the best way possible. All things, therefore, only exist
in so far as they participate the existence of the Word. The existence of every creature, therefore, flows from that absolute existence in the most immediate manner, since it is present equally to
all things; but the diversity of creatures arises from the diversity of
all things participating.

Proceeding *pari passu*, by affirming the grace which is added   2
over and above nature, they are related thus to Christ. For in rational human nature, every rational creature hypostatically united
to divinity by grace in Christ Jesus can attain the grace of elevation
to union with God, which is the ultimate happiness. Consequently, the blessed Jesus is the enfolding of all such natures made
blessed. All rational creatures, therefore, can achieve the ultimate

creaturae non aliter quam participatione gratiae Jesu foelicitatem ultimam consequuntur. In omnibus ergo gratiam ipsam participantibus est gratia Jesu in varietate participantium explicata. Et hoc quidem modo gratia Jesu est omne id, quod est in omnibus Deo gratis, et omnes Deo grati in Jesu sunt omne id, quod sunt Deo grati. Una est igitur gratia Jesu ab omnibus salvatis varie participata. Hoc Petrus, omnium theologorum summitas, nobis insinuare volens, ut Lucas in Actibus refert, de veteribus patribus referens aiebat: 'Per gratiam Domini nostri Jesu Christi credimus salvari, quemadmodum et illi'. Et haec est sancti evangelii manifestatio et divini Pauli doctrina, quoniam Christus in omnibus est principatum tenens et caput omnis ecclesiae.

3   Sunt autem homines rationales peregrinantes in spe salvationis, quibus revelata est veritas huius gratiae per Christi incarnationem. Et hi quidem in fide sunt veritatem agnoscentes et in spe expectantes felicitatem medio charitatis, qui militantem constituunt ecclesiam, quae omnia habet per gratiam Jesu Christi, quae ad hoc sunt necessaria, ut post militiam in triumphantem transcendat et beatitudinem in Jesu Christo consequatur. Haec quidem ecclesia est, in qua est gratia Jesu explicata secundum istius mundi participantem naturam, quia, cum non possit corruptibilis homo veritatem intueri ob suae naturae conditionem sine aenigmate et speculo, saltem ipsam in aenigmate et speculo seu fide attingat.

4   Quapropter fideles seu in fide appraehendentes, in spe peregrinantes adhaesivo amore participare suo quidem modo, in varia alteritate, constat gratiam unicam Jesu Christi esse. Unde et hanc ecclesiam Christi corpus dicimus mystice quidem, quia non est nisi gratia Jesu Christi explicata. Quoniam autem haec est ipsa unica columba, sponsa sine macula, quae habet pontificem maxi-

happiness in no other way than by participating the grace of Jesus. In all those participating that grace, therefore, the grace of Jesus is unfolded in a variety of participants. In this way the grace of Jesus is everything which is in all who are pleasing to God; and all those pleasing to God are, in Jesus, everything that is pleasing to God. The grace of Jesus, therefore, is one thing which all the saved participate variously. Thus Peter, the culmination of all theologians, wishing to teach us (as Luke says in Acts, referring to the ancient fathers), said that "We believe we are saved, as they [our fathers] are, through the grace of our Lord Jesus Christ."[4] This is the manifestation of the Holy Gospel and Saint Paul's doctrine, since Christ is the one holding the principate in all things and the head of the whole Church.

There are rational men, however, wayfarers in hope of salvation, to whom the truth of this grace was revealed through the incarnation of Christ; and these indeed are the men who, acknowledging the truth through faith and awaiting in hope the happiness which comes through charity, make up the Church Militant, which through the grace of Jesus Christ has all things necessary for this, so that, after its military service, it may pass over to the Church Triumphant and find blessedness in Jesus Christ. This is the Church in which the grace of Jesus is unfolded according to the participatory nature of this world, because, although corruptible man, on account of the condition of his nature, cannot understand the truth without enigma and mirror image, at least he touches it through enigma and mirror image, or faith.[5]

On this account the faithful, or those who lay hold of the faith, wayfaring in hope with unifying love, evidently participate in their own way, in their varied diversity, the unique grace of Christ's being. Hence we call this Church mystically the body of Christ, because it is nothing but the grace of Jesus Christ unfolded. Since, however, this is that one dove, the spotless bride,[6] who has as her high priest Jesus, who entered the heavens, whose confession she

mum Jesum qui coelos penetravit, cuius tenet confessionem, Christo adhaerens in spiritu, qui occultatus remanet in hoc sensibili mundo, tunc haec Christi occultata ecclesia in sua sensibili particularitate membrorum cum sciri nequeat, quis hanc teneat confessionem et amore dignus existat, sed solum in vi rationis quadam universalitate rationis attingitur. Sicut enim triumphantium ecclesia supra rationem in simplicitate intelligentiae tantum accessibilis est, ita et haec militans in rationis universalitate. Oportet autem in sensibili mundo sensibilibus signis de ipsa Christi ecclesia coniecturam sumere, cum aliter attingi nequeat rationis veritas. Quapropter coniecturalis illa ecclesia in hoc sensibili mundo, secundum huius mundi contractam cognitionem, vera quidem ecclesia est, licet intra suam coniecturam ex signis receptam admittat tam Christo in spiritu adhaerentes quam non. Constituitur haec huius sensibilis mundi ecclesia ex iis, qui sensibilibus signis se Christum participare demonstrant, uti sunt Christum filium Dei confitentes. Quapropter haec ipsa ecclesia sacra quaedam habet signa ad hoc instituta, ut per ea cognoscamus eos qui Christi sunt eo quidem modo, quo ex signis coniecturalis trahi cognitio potest.

5   Dico igitur, quod haec ecclesia Christi huius coniecturalis modi iudicio sancta censetur, etiam si mali et ficti sub signis sacris se intermisceant, quorum signa quae sacra sunt, tantum coniectura attingit. Non igitur omnes Christo adhaerentes includit haec ecclesia. Qui enim nullo sensibili signo manifesti fiunt, penitus hoc iudicio exclusi remanent. Sic nec omnes de hac ecclesia Christo adhaerent, qui bonos tantum ad unionem admittit. Quoniam autem huius vitae conditio talis est, quod hanc ecclesiam ita esse oportet, ipsam a Christo optimo quidem modo, quo ipsa ut sic ordinari potuit, ordinatam non haesitamus. Qua ex re, sicut haec

keeps,[7] adhering to Christ in the Spirit, she who remains concealed in this sensible world—since this concealed Church of Christ, then, cannot be known in its sensible particularity of members, someone may hold this confession and remain worthy of love, but he only grasps her, by the power of reason, through a certain universality in reason. Just as the Church Triumphant, above reason, is accessible only in simplicity of understanding, so also this Church Militant is accessible only in generality of reason.[8] It is therefore necessary in the sensible world to try conjecturing about Christ's Church through sensible signs, since otherwise the truth of reason could not be grasped. For this reason that conjectural Church in this sensible world, according to the limited understanding of this world, is the True Church, although within this conjecture, received from signs, it contains both those who adhere to Christ in the Spirit and those who do not. This Church of this sensible world is constituted of those who show by sensible signs that they participate Christ, as they are those who confess that Christ is the son of God. For this reason this Church has sacred signs instituted for this purpose, so that we may know through them those who are Christ's, in the way in which conjectural knowledge can be obtained from signs.

I say, therefore, that this Church of Christ is regarded as holy, 5 judged in this sort of conjectural way, even if evil and hypocritical men intermingle themselves under these sacred signs, whose signs, which are sacred, only conjecture reaches. Therefore not all who adhere to Christ are included in this church, for those who have been made manifest through no sensible sign remain entirely excluded by this [conjectural] judgment. Thus neither do all who are of this Church adhere to Christ, Who admits only the good to union. Since, however, the condition of this life is such that the Church has to be this way, we do not hesitate to say that it was ordered by Christ in the best manner in which it could be, as it is now. Thus, just as the Church is perfect in its own way, in this

ipsa ecclesia perfecta est suo quidem modo, ita et caput habet. Sensibilem enim ecclesiam sensibile caput habere convenit. Et ob hoc caput huius ecclesiae sensibile est pontifex, qui ex hominibus assumitur. In quo est haec ipsa ecclesia complicative ut in primo uno confessore Christi. Petrum autem primum Christi confessorem scimus inter homines, et ob hoc Petrus, a confessione petrae quae Christus est nomen accipiens, complicatam in se ecclesiam explicavit verbo doctrinae primo omnium. Non est igitur aliud ecclesia, quae a Petro initium cepit superna revelatione, quam unio fidelium in Petri confessione. Explicatio igitur Petri a petra dicti ecclesiam complicantis est ecclesia una eandem confessionem in alteritate multitudinis credentium participans.

6 Quomodo autem multitudo unitatem non nisi in varia alteritate potest participare, non potuit ecclesia nisi in varia participatione unitatis subsistere. Quapropter varia esse membra unius corporis ecclesiae necesse fuit, in quibus una illa confessio tota in toto et in qualibet eius parte existeret. Unitas igitur in varia alteritate ecclesia existit. Et sicut unitatis virtus non nisi in participata alteritate attingi potest, sic nec complicantis principii virtus aliter quam in explicatis principiatis potest apprehendi. Non enim virtus unitatis naturae Adae, complicantis patris, aliter quam in explicatis a se hominibus attingitur; sic nec creatoris nisi in ipsis creaturis. Hoc insuper modo Petri capitis ecclesiae huius complicativa virtus non nisi in explicata a se ecclesia potest apprehendi. Quando enim varietatem potestatum, ordinum et praelationum in unitate fidei in ecclesia esse conspicimus, illa omnem varietatem ordinatissimam atque decoram in Petro complicatam originaliter conspicientes, ad coniecturas de Petri admirabili potentia et virtute erigimur, et plenitudinem omnium possibilium in ecclesia pro eius conservatione

way it has a head. For it is fitting for the sensible Church to have a sensible head; and, for this reason, the sensible head of this Church is the pontiff, who is chosen from among men. In him this Church exists in an enfolded manner as in the first confessor of Christ. We know that Peter was the first confessor of Christ among men; and for this reason Peter, who received his name from confessing the Rock who is Christ, unfolded the Church enfolded in himself first of all through the word of doctrine.[9] There is not, therefore, any other Church than the union of the faithful in the confession of Peter, which has its inception from Peter through supernal revelation. The unfolding of Peter, therefore, who is named after the Rock and who enfolds the Church, is one Church participating the same confession in a varied diversity of believers.

Since, however, a multitude can participate unity only in a var- 6 ied diversity, the Church cannot subsist, consequently, except in a varied participation of unity. For this reason it is necessary for there to be various members of the one body of the Church, in whom there is that one whole confession in the whole and in every part of it. The Church, therefore, exists as a unity in a varied diversity. And just as the virtue of unity cannot be attained except in a participated diversity, so the virtue of the enfolding principle can be grasped only in things unfolded from the principle. For the unitary virtue of Adam's nature, enfolded in him as father, is not grasped otherwise than in the men unfolded from him; so neither is the the virtue of the Creator except in his creatures. In this way, moreover, the enfolded virtue of Peter as the head of the Church cannot be grasped except in the Church unfolded from him. Thus, when we behold the variety of powers, orders, and prelacies in the unity of faith in the Church, seeing in it the entire well-ordered, seemly variety originally enfolded in Peter, we are alerted to conjectures concerning the admirable power and virtue of Peter; and we grasp the plenitude of all things possible in the Church for its

et directione unicam Petri appraehendimus potestatem. Non enim est unitas in multitudine explicabilis, tanquam unitatis virtus complicative maior existat. Hinc principatum universalem, omnem particularem principatum originaliter complicantem, inexhauribilem multiplicatione particularium cognoscimus. Si igitur in ecclesia sunt patriarcharum, archiepiscoporum, metropolitanorum, episcoporum, presbyterorumque potestates, has quidem contractas esse constat. Contractum autem ex se ortum non habet, sed ex absoluto dependet. Quare potestas primi et supremi in sua plenitudine ambit omnem omnium potestatem; immo non est potestas nisi una et primi, quae in alteritate rectorum varie participatur, a nullo tamen maxime. Imparticipabilis enim est uti est.

7   Vides nunc, prudentissime pater, quam inepte dicitur potestatem particularium rectorum aequari aut eminere posse potestati universalis principis. Vides divinum dictum Leonis papae, quomodo omnis potestas primo quidem ab absolutissima illa divina potestate esse recipit, sed in ecclesia per Petrum, caput et principem ecclesiae. Adverte igitur, quomodo non est potestas principis absoluta, nisi Dei summi. Sed principatus omnis varie hanc in alteritate contractionis participat. Principatus enim in hac ecclesia absolutus quidem est suo modo, quoniam in ipso ecclesia complicatur. Ita quidem principatus quicumque absolutionem suo modo participat, cum supra populum, cui principatur, constituatur. Unde irrationabiliter dicitur principem in eo regno, ubi est princeps, praeesse pariter et subesse. Ratio enim contradictoriorum coincidentiam non admittit. Quod sapientissimi quidam intellexerunt, qui principem solutum legibus et non posse a subditis iudicari dixerunt. Ideo satis tibi patere potest, quam execrabile delictum sit scissura obedientiae et unitatis, et praesumptuosum

preservation and the unique power of Peter for its direction. There is no unfoldable unity in the multitude, as though a greater virtue of unity exists in an unfolded way. We know this universal principate, originally enfolding every particular principate, to be inexhaustible through multiplication of particular principates. If, therefore, there are in the Church the powers of patriarchs, archbishops, metropolitans, bishops, and priests, it is evident that these powers are contracted.[10] The contraction, however, does not originate with itself but depends on the absolute. Hence the power of the first and supreme one embraces in its plenitude every power of all others. Thus there is no power except one, that of the first, which is participated variously in a diversity of prelates — by none, however, maximally. For it is imparticipable as it [really and fully] exists.

You see now, most prudent father, how incorrect it is to say that the power of particular prelates can equal or surpass that of the universal prince. You understand the divine dictum of Pope Leo, that every power first receives its being from that most absolute divine power;[11] but in the Church this is received through Peter, the head and prince of the Church. Note, therefore, how there is no absolute power of the prince, except that of the most high God. But every principate participates variously this absolute power in the diversity of the contracted power. The principate in the Church, therefore, is absolute in its own way, since in it the Church is enfolded. Thus any principate participates in its own way this absoluteness, since it is set above the people over which it rules. Therefore, it is unreasonable to say that a prince in his kingdom, where he is prince, is preeminent in like measure as he is subordinate. The principle of non-contradiction does not permit such a coincidence of power. Some wise men, who said the prince is not bound by the laws and cannot be judged by his subjects, understood this.[12] Therefore, it should be sufficiently clear to you what an execrable crime it is to break up obedience and unity and

iudicium subiectorum contra sacrum principem, sub quocumque colore istud fiat. Vides etiam sacrum principatum omnem in ecclesia sub primo subsistere, inquantum in ipso complicatur et non aliter. Nam sacer principatus universalis ad aedificandam ecclesiam existit. Quare omnis principatus, sive spiritualis, sive temporalis, inquantum huic fini subservit, in ecclesia esse potest. Et in quantum huic fini resistit, non est principatus in ecclesia, cum non participet unicam ecclesiasticam universalem potestatem, quae in omni potestate quae in ecclesia est, est id quod est ipsa, contracte.

8   Vides per coincidentiam in unitate universalis potestatis differentes, et spirituales et temporales potestates, in ecclesia distincte explicatas. Non est tibi nunc difficile intelligere, quomodo sacro principi ecclesiae omnis fidelis subiectus esse debeat, sive rex sive praeses aut alius, inquantum ipsi de ecclesia esse velint, quam illa potestas universalis ambit. Et hoc quando princeps ecclesiae, secundum principatus ipsius virtutem, praecepta discernit. Ubi vero ipse princeps ea fieri mandaret, quae ad finem aedificationis ecclesiae illi creditae non tenderent, non procederet iussio a principatu; quare ei tunc obedire non esse necesse. Si vero dubium esset, et de mente sacri principis non constaret, pro sacro principe praesumendum est, quod recte credita potestate utatur, et ipsi obediendum est.

9   Cum ergo intelligamus in ecclesia, ubi sunt boni et mali, sacrorum principem etiam et bonum et malum esse posse, et videamus potestatem eius ecclesiae obesse non posse, cum in his, quae in ipsa potestate non complicantur, ei non subsit quisquam, et in dubiis obediendo nihil sit periculi, sed periculum magnum non obediendo—hinc ait Augustinus nullam posse causam dari, ob quam

how presumptuous it is for subjects to pass judgment against the sacred prince, under whatever pretext this might be done. You also see that every sacred principate in the Church exists under the first, in so far as it is enfolded within it and not otherwise; for the sacred universal principate exists to build up the Church. Therefore, every principate, spiritual or temporal, in so far as it serves this end, can be in the Church; and in so far as it resists this end, the principate is not in the Church, since it does not participate the sole universal ecclesiastical power, which, in every power which is in the Church, is that which it is in a contracted way.

You see different powers, spiritual and temporal, unfolded 8 clearly within the Church by coinciding in the unity of the universal power. It is not difficult now for you to understand how every faithful person, whether king or ruler or any other power, must be subject to the sacred prince of the Church, insofar as they wish to be part of the Church which that universal power encompasses. And this is true when the prince of the Church, in accordance with the virtue of his principate, discerns precepts. Where, however, the prince himself commands that things be done which do not tend to the end of building up the Church entrusted to him, the commanding does not proceed from the principate; hence it is not necessary to obey it. If, however, there is a doubt and the prince's intention is not clear, it must be assumed of the sacred prince that he has used correctly the power entrusted to him, and he must be obeyed.

Since we understand, therefore, that in the Church, where there 9 are good and bad people, the prince of things holy can also be good or evil, and we see that the power [of an evil prince] cannot form an obstacle for the Church, since in those things which are not enfolded in that power, no one is subject to him, and there is no peril in obeying in doubtful matters, but great peril in not obeying — hence Augustine says that no reason can be given why it

necessarium sit ad schisma pervenire—quare schisma diabolicum inexcusabile crimen existit.

10   Adverte pater, quomodo explicata ecclesia primitiva et contracta re ipsa universali Petri potestate, varie secundum varias particulares superintendentias quilibet rector, in sua particularitate Petri potestatem contracte participans, eandem (salva contractione) quam Petrus habet potestatem. Unde quia in hoc omnes Petri sunt successores, qui dominici gregis curam gerunt, visum est sapientibus universalem potestatem sacri principis ecclesiae super istam cuiusque particularem non esse nisi secundum sacri principatus conditionem, scilicet ad aedificationem—ita scilicet, quod ipse (est!)³ qui est universalis successor Petri in particularem Petri successorem non habeat potestatem, per quam potestas aedificatoria particularis in sibi subiectis immutationem capiat aut impediatur. Secus autem, quando superintendit sacer princeps universalis, ne rector credita potestate in aedificationem abutatur in destructionem subiectae ecclesiae.

11   In hoc video murmurationes exoriri, quae facile tolluntur universali sacro principe advertente se Petri successorem post ecclesiam a Petro explicatam, non quasi ipse sit alter Petrus a petra dictus, super quam petram ecclesia erat aedificanda cum ordine suo. Nam tollere ordinem et statum universalis ecclesiae explicare, non est sequi Petrum. Omnis enim Romanus et primus pontifex in explicatum ecclesiae ordinem et statum a Petro non habet potestatem, quoniam haec explicatio per Petri potestatem in aedificationem ecclesiae iam facta per ipsum reperitur, quando ad Petri principatum natus in ecclesia filius sublimatur. Quia ita ea quae explicata reperiuntur in ecclesia per Petri successores modo nunc

is necessary to come to schism[13] — schism is on this account a diabolical, inexcusable crime.

Note, father, how, since the primitive Church was unfolded and 10 contracted in fact from the universal power of Peter, any prelate, in accordance with his various particular superintendencies, who participates in his particularity the power of Peter in a contracted way has the same power which Peter had, except for its contraction. Therefore, because in this respect all who have care of the Lord's flock are Peter's successors, it seemed good to the wise that the universal power of the sacred prince of the Church cannot be above any particular power except in accordance with the condition of the sacred principate, that is, [as far as is necessary to its role in] building up the Church — in other words, he who is Peter's universal successor may not have power over any particular successor of Peter through which the particular power of building up, in those subject to him, suffers any change or is impeded. It is otherwise, however, when the sacred universal prince acts to oversee so that a prelate may not abuse the power entrusted to him for the building up of the Church in order to destroy a church subject to him.

From this I see murmurs arising, which are easily removed by 11 noting that the universal sacred prince is Peter's successor after the Church was unfolded from Peter, [and] not his successor in the sense that he is another Peter, [also] called after the Rock on which the Church with its order had to be built. For [a successor of Peter] to undermine the order and status of the universal Church is to unfold, not to follow Peter. Every Roman and supreme pontiff, indeed, in the unfolded order and state of the Church does not have power from Peter, since this unfolding is known to have already been done for him through the power of Peter for the building up of the Church, since a son born in the Church is raised up to the principate of Peter. So because those things which are found unfolded now in the Church by Peter's

dicto, sunt ea quae ex universalis principis potestate prodierunt,
non est conveniens illa per eandem potestatem nunc in electo pontifice complicatorie existente quovismodo infringi, sive illae sint regulae, sive ordo statuum, aut alia universalia quaecumque, nisi in
casu quo pontifex ipse videret aut epiciam aut immutationem utilem pro aedificatione ecclesiae; quo in casu advertere habet, ne
cum utilitatem procurare studet, fratres offendat et scandalizet.

12   Eo quidem modo sapientiores semper intellexerunt, quod
quamvis sacri principis ecclesiae manus ad aedificationem ex-
tensae, nulla observantia aut regula patrum, etiam in conciliis, inhiberi impedirique possent, non est tamen apud ipsum libera potestas reiciendi semel per Petri explicatam potestatem, salubriter
pro regimine ecclesiae ordinata‹m›,[4] quamdiu illa ad aedificationem praestat adiumentum. Sed nullam sedem magis oportet sanctorum patrum bene statuta inviolabiliter exequi quam[5] verum Petri successorem, in iis quae ex eadem Petri potestate explicatorie
prodiere.

13   Vides nunc, quando sacer princeps ecclesiae contra sanctorum
patrum statuta aliquid praesumeret, ubi non constaret eum ex
causa utilitatis aut necessitatis moveri sed potius ex aliqua particulari non digna causa, quomodo tunc in ipsa priora eiusdem Petri
mandata offendit, exiens vires potentiae suae. Quapropter non esset inconveniens, si pertinaciter in hoc persisteret, ab eo recedi
posse per ecclesiam, quando recessus ipse unitati ecclesiae, sine
qua ecclesia esse nequit, scissuram non inferret. Eo quidem modo
pontificem canonibus sanctorum patrum subesse intelligendum
est, quasi in eo non sit potestas bene ordinatis pro libito abutendi,

successors in the aforesaid way are those which originate from the power of the universal prince, it is not appropriate for that same power, now existing unfoldedly in the elected pontiff, to infringe them in some way, whether they be rules or an arrangement of ranks or other universal things of this sort, except in the case in which the pontiff himself discerns either [an issue of] equity or a useful change for the building up of the Church; in this case he has to be careful that he does not, in attempting to make useful changes, offend and scandalize his brothers.

In the same manner, wiser men have always understood that, although the hands of the sacred prince, when stretched out to build up the Church, cannot be inhibited or impeded by any respect for or rule of the Fathers, even in councils, he does not possess, nevertheless, the freedom to cast off a power once it has been unfolded through Peter, a power that has been ordained in a salubrious way for the rule of the Church, as long as that power provides help in the building up of the Church. But it befits no see more to execute what was established inviolably by the holy Fathers than it befits the true successor of Peter, in those things which proceed in an unfolded manner from the same power of Peter. 12

You see now that, when the sacred prince of the Church presumes to do anything against the statutes of the holy Fathers, where he does not seem to be moved by reason of utility or necessity but rather from some particular, unworthy cause, in such a manner that he then offends in it against the previous mandates of Peter himself, he exceeds the remit of his power. For this reason it would not be inappropriate, if he should persist in this pertinaciously, for one to withdraw from him by means of the Church, when that withdrawing would not bring a split in the unity of the Church, without which the Church cannot exist. It is in this way that the pontiff must be understood to be subject to the canons of the holy Fathers, as if there were in him no power of abusing as he wished things well ordered; and, if he should persist in this perti- 13

et si in hoc pertinaciter persisteret, quod tunc se sacro principatu, quem in abusum parvifaceret, indignum constitueret.

14   Quemadmodum enim Petrus in universali successore vivit, ita et in canonibus patrum, quoniam patres ipsi et universa‹lis›⁶ ecclesia in patribus. Sic et Petrus in ecclesia in ipsis sanctorum regulis vivere dicitur, quamdiu illa utilitati aedificandae ecclesiae praestat adiumentum. Et hoc est iuxta regulam intellectualem doctae ignorantiae, in pontifice esse ecclesiam complicative et ipsum esse pariter in ecclesia, hoc est, cum ipsa in suis sacris ordinationibus consentanee vigilare.

15   Haec, si ad liquidum extendantur, intellectum aperiunt, ut aliquorum ineptissimae scripturae facile spernantur. Videatur quam apertissime s‹anctissimum› d‹ominum› n‹ostrum› nulla cuiuscumque synodi constitutione prohiberi potuisse, quando concilium pro reductione orientalis ecclesiae in eo loco, ubi magis rebus agendis congruebat, institueret atque ob hoc omnes alias congregationes dissolveret, et patres a Basilea absolveret, ut ad tam sanctam unionem libere concurrere possent. Nam sicut non est potestas pontificis ad destructionem bene actorum per patres, ita non est potestas sub coelo, quae eius possit auctoritatem minuere, quominus errantes ad ovile reducat. Visi sunt illi obcaecatissimi viri in spiritu furoris fuisse extra omnem sensum, quando supra sacrum principem ecclesiae, nescio qualem iudiciariam sibi vendicabant potestatem et horridum! nefas! attentarunt in sacrum principem suum saevientes, seipsos ab eodem et universa per orbem catholica ecclesia perniciosissime secantes. Nunc satis est, quoniam gesta tibi res notissima est.

16   Habes etiam illuminatum clare intelligentiae oculum, ut sophisticas palliationes eorum optime conspicias nulla auctoritate aut ratione fulciri. Patet etiam universo orbi, cui viri illi desperati virus

nacity, then he would show himself unworthy of the sacred principate which he diminishes through abuse.

Just as Peter lives in his universal successor, so also he lives in 14 the canons of the Fathers, since the Fathers themselves and the universal Church live in the Fathers. Thus Peter is said to live in the Church in those rules of the holy Fathers, so long as that power helps the purpose of building up the Church. And this is according to the intellectual rule of learned ignorance, that the Church is in the pontiff in an enfolded manner, and the sacred prince in like manner is in the Church, that is, when he keeps watch over her in her holy ordinances in an appropriate way.

These principles, once they become evident, open the intellect, 15 so that the highly incorrect writings of some are easily spurned. It may be seen in the most obvious way that our holy lord cannot be stopped by any ordinance of any synod if one considers how he laid it down that the Council of Union with the eastern Church should be held in the place most convenient for its business; and how he dissolved all other assemblies gathered for that purpose; and how he absolved the fathers from [their obedience to] Basel, so that they might concur freely in that holy union. For just as the the pontiff has no power to destroy things done well by the Fathers, so there is no power under heaven which can diminish his authority to bring the erring back to the fold. Those purblind men seem to have been utterly senseless when in a spirit of madness they usurped to themselves heaven knows what sort of judicial power over the sacred prince; and — the horror! the wickedness! they tried to savage their own prince, cutting themselves off in the most destructive way from him and from the universal Catholic Church throughout the world. That is enough for now, since what they did is well known to you.

Clearly you have the illuminated eye of intelligence so that you 16 can see very well that their sophistical excuses are supported by no authority or reason. Their vain ambition and apostate rebellion is

pessimum inicere tanta diligentia et cura sategerunt, eorum vanissima ambitio et apostatica rebellio, et maxime serenissimo maximarumque laudum dignissimo regi Castellae et Legionis, qui (te medio) Deo amabilem sollicitudinem conservandae unitati in his longe distantibus Germaniarum regionibus tanto zelo impendit, ut nihil occupatissimo regi in quotidiana Agarenorum depressione infestius dietim occurrat, quam tales christianae reipublicae inimicissimos sub periculosa quadam conniventia tolerari per eos, quos ipsi temerario ausu cum Christi vicarii[7] anathemate ferire conati sunt. Reportabit princeps ille clementissimus pro sua interna devotione immarcessibilem gloriam. Non enim poterit inconsolatus a Deo et ecclesia relinqui vir sanctissimorum desideriorum. Nec poterunt vota sacratissima eius tua circum spectissima agitatione in hac praeclara invictissimi Romanorum regis et gloriosissimorum electorum sacri Romani imperii constituta dieta, tanquam e coelo missa non acceptari, ut sic in Domino gaudens omnia foeliciter peracta relaturus revertaris. Quod tibi tanto cordialius advenire opto, quanto me nosti annis multis pro eodem ferventius laborasse. Vale.

clear to the whole world, into which those desperate men strove with great effort to inject the worst of poison — particularly their rebellion against the most serene king of Castile and Leon,[14] a man worthy of the highest praise, who (through your agency) showed a zealous and loving solicitude towards God in conserving unity in these far distant regions of the Germanies. The result was that no more ferocious attacks were made daily against that king, heavily preoccupied as he was with the incursions of the Saracens,[15] than the ones those enemies of Christendom tolerated by turning — perilously — a blind eye to them, whom they themselves with rash daring had tried to strike down with the anathema of Christ's vicar. That most clement prince will win imperishable glory for his inward devotion. A man of such holy desires cannot be left unconsoled by God and the Church. Nor can his most holy vows with regard to your highly respectable activity not be acceptable in this distinguished and heaven-sent Diet of the unconquered King of the Romans[16] and the most glorious electors of the sacred Roman Empire, so that, thus rejoicing in the Lord, you may go back and report all the things happily accomplished. I wish most cordially that this will happen to you, the more so since you know I have labored for this same thing with great fervor for many years. Farewell.

Sermo CXXVI: Tu es Petrus

1453 Brixinae in die Petri et Pauli apostolorum

1 'Tu es Petrus.' Matthaei 16 et in evangelio; cui alludit Johannes in Apocalypsi: 'Vincenti dabo' 'manna absconditum et' 'calculum candidum et in calculo nomen novum scriptum, quod nemo scit, nisi qui accipit.' Apocalypsis 2°.

2 'Petrus' a petra, petra calculus. 'Vincenti dabo calculum.' Si vincit Simon, quia confitetur illa, quae nec caro nec sanguis revelare queunt, fit Petrus. Nam datur sibi ‹calculus candidus›, a quo nominabitur.

Calculare est inquirere ignotum, et hoc via rationis seu numeri. Et quia per calculos fiebat sicut hodie per certos denarios ad hoc factos, tunc unus calculus ex inquisitione peracta recipit 'nomen novum', scilicet, quia sunt supra hunc mundum, quae vocatur centum vel mille. Nam colligit in se ex loco omnes numeros et sortitur nomen novum. Et 'nemo scit, nisi qui accipit' id, quod ratio ostendit.

Puta ratione facta datur mihi calculus, et secundum calculum recipio id, quod merui: Servivi tibi decem diebus, et pro die dabis decem denarios. Facta calculatione teneris mihi centum. Calculus, quem tradis, habet in se 'nomen novum', quod 'nemo scit, nisi' ego, ‹qui accipio› ex ‹calculo› centum. Habet enim alius calculum, et non significat centum, sed mille. Alius habet, et significat quattuor, et ita de singulis. Et non est ‹calculus› sine novo ‹nomine›, et

Sermon 126: "Thou art Peter"

1453 at Brixen on the day of the Apostles Peter and Paul [29 June]

Thou art Peter, Matthew 16[:18] and in [today's] gospel. John al-   1
ludes to this in Apocalypse 2, *To him that overcometh, I will give the*
hidden manna, and I will give him a white stone, and in the counter, a
new name written, which no man knoweth, but he that receiveth it, Apocalypse 2[:17].

Peter, from *petra*, stone. *To him that overcometh, I will give a white*   2
stone. If Simon overcomes because he confessed those things which
neither flesh nor blood are able to reveal, he becomes Peter. For he
is given a white stone after which he is named.

To calculate is to seek an unknown, and this by way of reason
or number. And, because there used to be done by means of
stones what today is done for this purpose by means of certain
coins, then one stone, as a result of an inquiry carried through, receives *a new name* (that is, because they are above this world),
which is called 100 or 1,000. For it gathers into itself all numbers
from anywhere, and it receives a new name. And *no man knoweth*
but he that receiveth it, which reason shows.

Suppose that I am given a stone when an accounting is made,
and I receive what I deserve according to that stone. I have served
you for 10 days, and you give me 10 coins for each day. When the
calculation has been made, you will owe me 100. The stone which
you will give me has on it *a new name* which *no man knoweth* except
I who receive 100 on account of the stone. Another has a stone;
and it does not signify 100, but 1,000. Another has one, and it
signifies 4; and so on in each case. There is no stone without a
new name; and *no man knoweth, but he that receiveth it*. Therefore,

'nemo scit, nisi qui accipit.' Unde calculus secundum locum, ubi in tabula abaci recipitur, nomen novum rationis accipit.

Sic Christus in credentibus, sicut radius solis in piro pirum, in pomo pomum etc.

3   Nota: Dicit 'vincenti.' Datur igitur calculus candidus militibus, qui vicerunt. Victoria autem est tanto maior, quanto adversarius potentior. Christus vicit principem mundi et mundum, qui dixit: 'Confidite, quia ego vici.' Petrus vicit, quia vicit carnem et sanguinem. Paulus vicit, et omnes sancti, quia Christus prior vicit. Recepit calculum et 'factus est in caput anguli.' Petrus vicit et factus est fundamentum, et alii sunt superaedificati, etc.

Et nota, quo modo Christus est ‹lapis vivus› conectens parietes ‹domus›, quae construitur vivis ex lapidibus. Nam haec est theologia suprema, quam Pater, ut ex evangelio patet, Petro, et Petrus nobis, revelavit, scilicet Christum esse lapidem angularem.

4   Fuit religio Judaica, quae Deum absolutum ab omni quod videtur et sentitur venerabatur, et dixerunt Gentiles Judaeos adorare id, quod numquam conceperunt in sensu, imaginatione aut intellectu, et deridebant eos.

Fuerunt Gentiles, qui colebant Deum, prout experimento eius bonitatem et potentiam in sensibilibus experiebantur, dando sibi secundum hoc varia nomina secundum opera, ut Saturnum, Venerem, Iunonem, etiam Pacem, Concordiam etc. nominando.

Et quia Judaei non colebant Deum nisi absolutum ab omni quod concipi potest, et Gentiles non colebant Deum, nisi ut contracte relucet in rebus, Judaei deridebantur a Gentilibus quasi fatui, qui colerent, quod ignorarent, Gentiles deridebantur a Judaeis quasi fatui, quia colerent sensibile, quod est corruptibile.

the stone, according to where it is placed on the abacus, receives a new name of reason.

So Christ is in believers like a ray of the sun, the pear in a pear, the apple in an apple etc.

Note that he says, *To him that overcometh.* A white stone, therefore, is given to soldiers who have overcome. Victory, however, is the greater the more powerful the foe. Christ, Who said, *Have confidence, I have overcome the world,*[1] overcomes the prince of this world and the world itself. Peter overcame because he overcame flesh and blood. Paul overcame, and all the saints, because Christ overcame first. He received a stone and *is become the head of the corner.*[2] Peter overcame and was made the foundation, and the others are built upon him, etc.[3]

And note how Christ is the living stone connecting the walls of the house, which is built of living stones.[4] For this is supreme theology, which the Father, as is apparent from the gospel, revealed to Peter — and Peter to us — that is, that Christ is the cornerstone.

It was the Jewish religion that venerated God apart from everything which is seen and sensed. And the Gentiles said that the Jews adore that which they never conceived in sense, imagination or intellect; and they derided it.

It was the Gentiles who worshipped God as they experienced goodness and power by experience of sensible things, giving Him various names according to His works, naming [those works] Saturn, Venus, Juno, even Peace, Concord etc.

And because the Jews did not worship God except apart from everything which can be conceived, and the Gentiles did not worship God except as He is reflected in a contracted way in things, the Jews were derided by the Gentiles as fools who worshipped what they knew not. The Gentiles were derided by the Jews as fools because they worshipped the sensible, which is corruptible.

5   Venit Jesus tamquam pacificator et mediator, in quo est unita natura, quam colebant Judaei, scilicet Dei, et natura deificata per eos, quam colebant Gentiles. Concurrunt igitur in Jesu omnia, in quibus Judaei et Gentiles posuerunt culturam et fidem. Nam si Judaei naturam, ex qua omnia, coluerunt, et sine qua nihil, et Gentiles naturam coluerunt, quam experiebantur ad vitam necessariam, sive in Saturno, sive in Venere etc., tunc Christus coli debet tam per Judaeos quam Gentiles.

Omnis enim ratio culturae in Christo reperitur: Si Deus colendus, quia creator, Christus colendus, quia ipse est, per quem facta sunt omnia; si homo colendus est, quia in eo relucent divinae operationes, Christus maxime colendus est, quia in eo maxime relucent. Nam in eo habitat divinitas corporaliter, id est secundum omnem perfectionem longitudinis, latitudinis et profunditatis.

6   Unde ut Petrus in canonica sua nos instruit de Christo lapide, qui ab omnibus sacerdotibus Judaicis et Gentilibus, qui sunt aedificantes in suis religionibus, reprobatus est et persecutionem passus, 'factus est in caput anguli.' Prout dixit, quod quando exaltatus foret, traheret ad se omnia, sic ex Judaeis et Gentilibus aedificata est ecclesia Christi.

Et haec est aedificata per primum sacerdotem Petrum, qui recepit ‹revelatione Patris› confessionem, in qua est fundamentum huius aedificii, scilicet Christum esse 'filium Dei vivi,' ita quod in Christo absoluta divina natura assumpsit humanam contractam in unitate suppositi, sicut in homine intellectualis natura unitur sensibili.

7   Unde, si est aliqua ratio culturae Judaeorum aut gentilium, illa reperitur in Christo Jesu, ita quod, si quis est ex Judaeis, qui

Jesus came as the peacemaker and mediator in whom is united 5
[the absolute, unconceived] nature, which the Jews worshipped,
namely the nature of God, and the nature the Gentiles worshipped, [namely] the natural world deified. Therefore, all the
things which the Jews and Gentiles worshipped and believed in
come together in Jesus. For, if the Jews worshipped the nature
whence all things originated, and without which nothing exists,
and the Gentiles worshipped the nature they were experiencing
that was necessary for life, whether in Saturn or in Venus, etc.,
then Christ must be worshipped as much by the Jews as by the
Gentiles.

Indeed, every reason for worship is found in Christ. If God is
to be worshipped because He is the creator, Christ must be worshipped because He is the one by Whom all things were made.[5]
If a man should be worshipped because the operations of the divinity are reflected in him, Christ must be worshipped maximally,
because they are reflected maximally in Him. For in Him divinity
lived in a bodily way,[6] that is, according to every perfection of
length, breadth and depth.[7]

Hence, as Peter in his canonical epistles instructs us about 6
Christ the stone Who was rejected by all the priests, Jewish and
Gentile (who are builders in their own religions) and suffered persecution, *He is become the head of the corner.*[8] Just as He said that,
when He was lifted up, He would draw all things to Himself,[9] so
the Church of Christ is built up from Jews and Gentiles.

And the Church is built by the first priest, Peter, who received
by the Father's revelation the confession in which is the foundation
of this edifice, that is, that Christ is *the Son of the living God,*[10] so
that in Christ the absolute divine nature took on a human nature,
contracted in the unity of an underlying substance, just as in man
the intellectual nature is united to the sensible.

Hence, if there is any explanation or reason for the worship of 7
the Jews or the Gentiles, it is found in Christ Jesus, so that any

Christum non recipit, hic a vero cultu Judaeorum longe abest. Sic si quis ex Gentilibus Christum non recipit, hic longe abest a vero cultu Gentilium. Nam neque verus cultus Judaeorum exclusit Christum, neque verus cultus Gentilium exclusit Christum.

Loquor de vero cultu. Fuit enim fallacia tam in cultu Judaeorum quam Gentilium, et deceptiones leguntur et divisiones atque haereses in illis sectis. Verus autem cultus Gentilium numquam fuit sine ratione, ut scilicet sibi ipsi contradiceret, ita quod crederet creaturam esse creatorem, aut creatorem non esse praeferendam creaturae, aut Deum non esse optimum, licet ipsum in operibus honorarent.

Et si quis attendit, tunc Christus est omnis culturae verae veritas, perfectio et complementum. Nemo enim colit Deum, nisi qui credit eum optimum et remuneratorem. Ob hoc Judaei credunt simul et Gentiles ab immortali Deo se posse consequi immortalitatem naturae suae et resurrectionem a mortuis etc. Sed quo modo sine Christo est hoc possibile, in quo natura humana unita est immortalitati, scilicet divinae naturae? Ideo si omnium hominum natura seu humanitas, quae una est, in Christo unita divinae naturae resurrexit, et omnes homines resurgent. Si autem hoc non credit Judaeus aut Gentilis possibile, scilicet quod natura humana sit unita divinae in Christo Jesu, inanis est fides ‹increduli›. Sic si Judaeus credit se posse consequi vitam aeternam, necesse est, ut credat naturam humanam posse uniri immortali, quae Deus est. Solus enim Deus inhabitat immortalitatem, hoc est, quod solus est illa natura, quae est immortalitas. Credit igitur, sive velit sive nolit, Christum. Non enim est aliud Christus quam unio naturae nostrae cum natura immortali. Et plura de hoc dici possent, quae idem ostendunt. Et ob hoc fides Judaica implicite semper Chris-

Jew who does not receive Christ is far from the true worship of the Jews. So any Gentile who does not receive Christ is far from the worship of the Gentiles. For neither does the true worship of the Jews exclude Christ, nor does the true worship of the Gentiles exclude Christ.

I am speaking of true worship. For there was falseness in both the worship of the Jews and that of the Gentiles; and we read of deceptions, divisions and heresies in those sects. However, the true worship of the Gentiles was never without reason, so that, in other words, it might contradict itself and believe that a creature was the creator, or the creator was not to be ranked before a creature, or that God was not the best, although they honored Him in His works.[11]

And if anyone takes heed, then Christ is the truth, perfection and fulfillment of all true worship. No one, then, worships God except he who believes Him to be the best and the one who repays. On account of this, the Jews and Gentiles together believed that they could obtain from the immortal God the immortality of their nature and resurrection from the dead etc. But how is this possible without Christ, in Whom human nature is united to immortality, that is, to the divine nature? Thus, if the nature of all men, or humanity, which is one, united to the divine nature in Christ, rose again, all men shall rise again. If, however, the Jews or Gentiles do not believe this to be possible, that is, that human nature is united to the divine in Christ Jesus, the faith of the unbeliever is vain. Thus, if a Jew believes that he could obtain eternal life, he must of necessity believe that human nature can be united to the immortal one, which is God. God alone inhabits immortality,[12] that is, He alone is that nature which is immortality. The Jew therefore believes in Christ whether he wishes to or not. There is no other Christ than the unity of our nature with the immortal nature. And much could be said on the subject that shows the same thing. And on this account the Jewish faith always implicitly

tum continebat, quem Christum seu Messiam futurum videbant prophetae sive videntes.

8   Nos autem scimus ipsum venisse, quia 'opera' sua ipsum patefecerunt, scilicet illa opera, quae solum per Christum fieri possunt. Nam videntes ‹et›[1] prophetae qui praeviderunt ipsum futurum, declararunt quibus signis cognosceretur. Et ita in illis repertus est. Imperabat enim mari, ventis, febri, mortuis, etc., tamquam potestatem habens divinam etc. Unde virtus illa divina, quae apparuit in operibus Christi, se ipsam ostendit mundo.

Inter quae hoc unum maxime attendendum, quia pauperes et indoctos piscatores fecit summos evangelistas. Fuit igitur lux illuminans et pellens omnem ignorantiam. Duo autem sunt, per quae sapientia magistri pellit ignorantiam ab intellectu discipuli, scilicet verbum et veritas. Instruit per verbum, et in verbo veritas pascit intellectum. Ob hoc fuit Christus Verbum et Veritas, Verbum Creatoris et Veritas omnium scibilium.

Verbum Creatoris seu Patris solum est potens momentanee transmutare penitus ignorantem in penitus doctum. Et non caperetur verbum in intellectu, nisi foret veritas. Nam quidquid intellectus appetit, veritas est. Et si pascitur fallacia, non tamen nisi sub specie veritatis. Unde veritas est vita intellectus. Est igitur Verbum, 'Veritas et Vita' ille, qui de Petro piscatore fecit summum theologum, quem sanctus Dionysius dicit ipsam summitatem omnium theologorum.

Est enim Christus 'manna absconditum.' Venit enim de caelo manna uti Christus, et habet in se suavitatem sive suavem pascentiam intellectus circa suam humanitatem et divinitatem indignis absconditam. Quam si quis degustaret, ille diceret ad alios: 'Gustate et videte, quoniam' suavis 'est Dominus! Beatus vir, qui sperat

contained Christ, whom, as the Christ or the Messiah, their prophets or seers foresaw.

We, however, know that He came, because His works revealed 8 Him, that is, those works which only can be done by Christ. For the seers or prophets who foresaw His coming, declared by what signs He would be known. And thus He was found [to be the Christ or Messiah] in those signs. For He commanded the sea, the winds, fever, the dead etc. like one having divine power, etc.[13] Hence that divine potency which appeared in Christ's works revealed itself to the world.

Of these works, one should especially note the one whereby He made poor and untutored fishermen into supreme evangelists. He was, therefore, the light illuminating and dispelling all ignorance. There are two ways, however, that the wisdom of a master dispels ignorance from the mind of his disciple, that is, by the word and by the truth. He instructs by means of the word, and the truth in the word feeds the mind. For this reason Christ was the Word and the Truth, the Word of the Creator and the Truth of all things knowable.

The Word of the Creator or of the Father is the power to transmute in an instant the entirely ignorant into the entirely learned. And a word would not be grasped by the intellect unless it were the truth. For whatever the intellect desires is truth. And, if falsity is nourished, it is only under the appearance of truth. Hence truth is the life of the intellect. Christ is therefore the Word, *the Truth and the Life*,[14] Who made of Peter the fisherman the supreme theologian, whom Saint Dionysius calls the summit of all the theologians.[15]

Christ, then, is *the hidden manna*.[16] For manna came from heaven as Christ; and He has in Himself sweetness or sweet food for the intellect on account of His humanity and divinity hidden from the unworthy. If anyone taste it, he says to others, O *taste, and see that the Lord is* sweet! *Blessed is the man that hopeth in Him*.[17]

in eo.' Hanc dulcedinem degustavit Petrus, qui in canonica sua
aperit secundo capitulo, quod Christus non potest degustari nisi
deposita omni malitia, dolo et simulatione, invidia et detractione.
Nam, ut de se patet, illa omnia sunt contraria Veritati. Unde
oportet evacuare omnia de anima, quae contrariantur Veritati, et
tunc evacuatur omnis animalitas et quod ex terreno Adam con-
traximus. Et erimus 'quasi modo geniti infantes, rationabiles sine
dolo,' et 'concupiscimus lac' illud veritatis, si saltem ipsum degustavimus, quoniam, si degustavimus, ut ipse ait, reperimus, 'quoniam
dulcis' est 'Dominus.' Quare hanc dulcedinem non possumus ‹attingere›[2] nisi semper ‹concupiscere›.

9   Et ita 'accedimus ad lapidem vivum ab hominibus quidem re-
probatum', scilicet ab illis, quia ex carne et sanguine sunt, sed 'a
Deo electum et honorificatum.' Et tunc nos ipsi tamquam lapides
vivi superaedificabimur in domos spirituales, in 'sacerdotium sanctum, offerre spiritales hostias, acceptabiles Deo per Jesum Christum.' Subiungit Petrus: 'Propter quod continet Scriptura: Ecce
ponam in Sion lapidem summum angularem, electum pretiosum,
et qui crediderit in eum, non confundetur. Vobis autem honor credentibus; non credentibus autem lapis, quem reprobaverunt aedificantes, hic factus est in caput anguli et lapis offensionis et petra
scandali his qui offendunt Verbo nec credunt, in quo et positi
sunt,' etc.

Vide quam admirabilis est iste theologus, qui nobis aperit virtutes illius lapidis, qui Christus est! Nam quamcumque virtutem vo-
lueris habere lapidem, illam habet, si credideris. Et si credideris,
non confunderis. Et non est virtus, quae appeti possit per intellectum extra hunc lapidem. Quidquid impendis ei, recipies: Si amorem, amorem; si honorem honorem; si misericordiam, misericordiam; si pietatem, pietatem. Sic si offendis, offenderis; si
maledicis, maledicere; si inhonoras, inhonorareris; si accusas, ac-
cusaberis; si spernis, sperneris; si iudicas, iudicaberis; et sic de
aliis.

Peter tasted this sweetness — he who revealed in the second chapter of his canonical epistle that Christ cannot be tasted except by setting aside all malice, guile, dissimulation, envy, and all detraction.[18] For, as is self-evident, all such things are contrary to the truth. Hence one must empty from the soul all things contrary to the truth, and then shall be emptied out everything of our animal nature and [the disease of sin] we contracted from the earthly Adam. And we shall be *As newborn babes, reasonable, without guile,* and *we desire that milk* of Truth if we have at least tasted Him, since if we have tasted, as he himself says, we have found *that the Lord is sweet.*[19] Therefore we cannot attain this sweetness unless we always desire it.

And so we arrive at *the living stone, rejected indeed by men,* that is, by them because they are of flesh and blood, but *chosen and made honorable by God.* And then we are built up like living stones into spiritual houses, into *a holy priesthood, to offer spiritual sacrifices, acceptable to God by Jesus Christ.*[20] Peter adds, *Wherefore, it is said in the Scripture: Behold I lay in Sion a chief cornerstone, elect, precious. And he that shall believe in Him shall not be confounded. To you, therefore, that believe, He is honor; but to them that believe not, the stone which the builders rejected, the same is made the head of the corner; and the stone of stumbling, and a rock of scandal to them who stumble at the Word, neither do believe, whereunto also they are set.*[21]

See how admirable is this theologian who reveals to us the virtues of that stone, which is Christ. For whatever potency you wish the stone to have, it has, if you believe.[22] And, if you believe, you will not be confounded. And there is no potency which could be desired by the intellect apart from this stone. Whatever you pay to it, you will receive back. If love, love; if honor, honor; if mercy, mercy; if piety, piety. Thus if you offend, you will be offended; if you curse, you will be accursed; if you dishonor, you will be dishonored; if you accuse, you will be accused; and so on in other cases.

9

Nam lapis est vivus et est Veritas. Hinc eo modo vera fit reflexio, quo modo aut accedis aut impingis, sicut exposcit veritas. Est enim lapis candidus specularis, quia speculum sine macula et vivus. Hinc prout tu te ei repraesentas, sic tibi respondet, sicut, si sensibile speculum foret rectum et vivum, tunc eo modo te respiceret, quo modo tu te eidem repraesentares.

Sic diligentes diligit, et misericordes misericordiam consequuntur. Quidquid das, dabitur tibi et accipis retributionem centuplam, quia in possessione seu regno vitae fit retributio. Id, quod tu das alicui indigenti propter ipsum, sibi das. Quidquid enim feceritis minimo eius propter ipsum, ei facitis. Quidquid facitis filio regis propter regem, regi facitis. Immo quidquid cani regis facitis propter regem, regi facitis. Sed rex non retribuet nisi ut rex secundum regnum suum; ita Deus, rex regum secundum regnum suum, quod est regnum veritatis et perpetuae vitae.

10   Adhuc circa lapidem illum plura occurrunt dulcissime speculanda. Nam virtus inest lapidibus. Alius enim lapis reddit hominem omnibus amorosum, alius victoriosum, alius sanum custodit, alius pellit morbum, alius phantasma, alius spiritum malignum, alius dirigit nautas per viam ad intentum, et sunt indicibiles virtutes lapidis. Reperiuntur in lapidibus virtutes caeli, imagines herbarum, arborum, hominum, piscium, leonum et ceterorum animalium cum mirabilissimis virtutibus. Unde valor lapidum pretiosorum excedit valorem auri in infinitum. Parvus diamas multum valet auri.

Considera igitur, quo modo in pretioso lapide est materia, quae est dura et difficulter resolubilis, tactui grata et transparentia lucida varie terminata. Et terminus est color oculo gratissimus.

For the stone is living and is the Truth. Hence in this way a true reflection occurs in the way you approach or collide with it, just as the Truth demands. For it is a white reflecting stone, since it is a mirror without flaw,[23] and sparkling.[24] Hence, just as you present yourself in it, so will it respond to you — just as if a sensible mirror were flat and sparkling, it would then reflect you back to yourself just as you presented yourself to it.

Thus He loves those who love, and the merciful obtain mercy,[25] whatever you give will be given to you,[26] and you will receive your reward an hundred fold,[27] because you will be rewarded in possession or in the kingdom of [eternal] life. That which you give to some needy person for His sake, you give to yourself. For whatsoever you do to the least of His for His sake, you do to Him.[28] Whatever you do to the king's son for the king's sake, you do to the king. Indeed, whatever you do to the king's dog for the king's sake you do to the king. But the king will not reward except as king according to his kingdom; thus [will] God [reward us], the King of kings, according to His kingdom, which is the kingdom of truth and perpetual life.

Numerous delicious speculations, besides, arise in connection 10 with the stone. For there are potencies in stones. One stone makes a man loveable by all; another, victorious; another preserves health; another dispels illness; another, phantasms; another, an evil spirit; another directs sailors on the way to their destination; and there are unsayable potencies in stones. The virtues of heaven are found in stones, images of herbs, trees, men, fish, lions and other animals with wondrous virtues. Therefore, the value of precious stones infinitely exceeds the value of gold. A small diamond is worth more than gold.

Consider, therefore, how there is material in a precious stone which is hard and difficult to shape, pleasing to the touch and transparent, transforming light in various ways. And the result is

Deinde est vis in lapide, quae est super omnem sensum, quam ex operibus experimur.

11   Considera igitur, si foret ‹calculus› parvus candidus seu lucidus, qui haberet in se complicite omnem omnium lapidum pretiosorum virtutem, ille certe calculus, quamdiu virtus eius non foret cognita, pro nihilo haberetur et quasi petra scandali sperneretur. Sed si quis crederet alicui magno et doctissimo magistro, qui ostenderet calculum et annuntiaret virtutem eius, ille postquam crederet, reperiret ita esse. Talis poneret lapidem illum super omnes lapides in Sion.

Sic dicitur Christus per similitudinem lapis, qui reprobatus factus est in caput anguli. Ille autem, qui ostendit primo calculum, fuit Johannes Baptista (Joh. 3°). Et ostendit ipsum ex revelatione Patris et ostendit ipsum ut sacerdos maximus et completio sacerdotii Veteris Testamenti. Ille, qui ostendit ipsum post hoc, fuit Petrus, sacerdos ex revelatione Patris, in quo est complicatio sacerdotii Novi Testamenti, ut ex evangelio hodierno.

12   Unde attende quod, sicut lapis candidus ex purissimis guttulis elementaribus in terra virtute caelesti coagulatur ita, quod lapis pretiosus incomparabiliter excedit matrem et non habet alium patrem quam virtutem caelestem, sic Christus ex purissimis guttulis virginis gloriosae compactus virtute Altissimi exsistit. Et habet calculus ille materiam ex terra virginea, candorem seu animam lucidam seu rationalem, quia lux ratio, de caelo lucidissimo.

Caelum lucidissimum est sapientia seu ratio aeterna, per quam omnia facta. Nihil enim est, cuius ratio, ut esset, non exsistit. Habet virtutem, quia candor ille animae rationalis est in luce originis suae, et ita suppositatur in virtute, quae est causa omnis virtutis, et ita est virtus divina.

Et sic habes corpus, animam et deitatem optime figurari in calculo.

color most pleasing to the eye. Then there is force in a stone which is suprasensual but which we experience from the stone's effects.

Consider, therefore, if there were a small stone, white or clear, 11 which had in itself in an enfolded manner all the potency of all precious stones, certainly that stone, as long as its potency were not known, would be regarded as worthless and would be spurned as a stumbling block. But if someone should believe in some great and most learned master, who displayed the stone and announced its potency, the person who believed would afterwards find it to be so. Thus he would prize that stone above all the stones in Zion.[29]

Thus Christ is said by similitude to be the stone which was rejected [and] was made the cornerstone. He, however, who first displayed the stone was John the Baptist. And he displayed Him by means of the Father's revelation, and he displayed Him as the high priest and the fulfillment of the priesthood of the Old Testament. The one who displayed Him after this was Peter, the priest by means of the Father's revelation, in whom is the enfolding of the priesthood of the New Testament, as is found in today's gospel.

Hence, note that, like a white stone that is coagulated out of 12 the purest elemental droplets, so that a precious stone incomparably exceeds its mother and has no father except celestial virtue, so Christ existed, compacted of the purest droplets of the glorious Virgin by the power of the Most High. And He, the stone, has His matter out of the virgin earth, whiteness or a clear — or rational — soul (because light is reason) from the clearest heaven.

The clearest heaven is wisdom — or eternal reason — through which all things were made.[30] For there is nothing which does not have a reason for being. It has potency because that whiteness of the rational soul is in the light of its origin, and so it is presupposed in a potency which is the cause of every virtue; and thus it is divine virtue.

And so you have the body, the soul and deity figured excellently in the stone.

13   Unde non est hic ‹calculus› nominabilis, quia omnium lapidum nominibus nominari deberet secundum virtutem eius, quae est omnium virtutum complicatio. Sed, qui accipit eum, reperit in eo lapide nomen scriptum, sed non est illud alteri communicabile. Sicut Paulus, quando in tertium caelum raptus accepit calculum: bene scivit Paulus, quod recepit. Non potuit hoc fieri, nisi reperisset nomen eius inscriptum in eo, quod recepit.

Nomen enim est omnibus rebus inscriptum, et quicumque intellectualiter ‹accipit› quamcumque rem, ille reperit nomen eius in re, quia nomen est notitia. Intellectus si ‹accepit›, cognoscit seu intelligit. Simul igitur cum re recipit nomen; alias non accipit, nisi simul nomen videat in re, quam accipit. Accepit igitur Paulus calculum et vidit nomen, sed non potuit revelare, quia non est possibile, quod reveletur nisi recipienti calculum. Ac si aliquem fructum incognitum prius degustasset Paulus, cuius sapor omnem saporem complicaret, non posset Paulus tibi saporem, quem degustasset, revelare per omne ‹nomen› tibi cognitum, quia nullum ipsum nominaret. Sed postquam degustasses fructum illum, tu reperires in gustu ‹nomen› non dicibile aliis.

14   Sic Johannes in Apocalypsi manna absconditum vidit cum calculo candido dari vincenti. Et nota, quod Judaei ‹nesciverunt, quid esset manna›, nec alter alteri dicere potuit saporem eius. Hinc nominarunt 'man hu', hoc est: 'Quid est hoc?' Omnem enim saporem in uno sapore complicatum repererunt, et secundum desideria cuiusque reperiebatur sapor. Sic Christus, qua fide capitur, ea satiat; et quisque experitur ‹secundum mensuram fidei› se assequi desideria in Christo Jesu Domino nostro semper benedicto.

Therefore this is not a stone which can be named, because it ... 13
should be named by the names of all stones on account of its potency, which is the enfolding of all potencies. But one who receives
Him finds a name written in that stone, but it is not one which
can be communicated to another. Just so Paul, when he was taken
up to the third heaven,[31] received the stone. Paul knew well what
he received. This could not have been done unless he found His
name written on what he received.

For the name is written on all things; and whoever receives anything intellectually finds His name on the thing, because a name is
knowledge. The intellect knows or understands when it receives.
Simultaneously, therefore, he receives the name with the thing; he
does not receive otherwise unless he simultaneously sees the name
in the thing which he receives. Therefore, Paul received a stone
and saw a name; but he could not reveal it, because it is not possible to reveal it except to one who receives the stone. And if Paul
first tasted some unknown fruit whose taste enfolded all tastes,
Paul could not reveal to you the taste which he has tasted by
means of any name known to you, because he could not name it.
But after you had tasted that fruit, you would find in the taste a
name which you cannot tell others.

Thus John in the Apocalypse saw the hidden manna with the ... 14
white stone to be given to the victorious.[32] And note that the Jews
did not know what manna was, nor could one tell another its
taste. They name this [in Hebrew] *man hu*, which means: *What is
it?*[33] For they find every taste enfolded in that one taste, and the
taste is discovered according to the desires of each. Thus Christ,
grasped by faith, satisfies these desires; and whoever tests this according to the measure of his faith will attain what he desires in
Christ Jesus, our ever blessed Lord.

Sermo CXLIV: Tibi dabo claves regni caelorum

1454 Brixinae in die cathedrae sancti Petri

1 'Tibi dabo claves regni caelorum.' Est considerandum, quo modo
agimus festum cathedrae Petri, et est festum exsecutionis promissi
Christi in hoc evangelio. Ait Optatus Milevitanus ecclesiam habere cathedram et angelum; de quo alibi.

2 Primo attende, quo modo Christus est, qui dat claves regni caelorum. Christus autem est Veritas. Non errat ianitor, si Veritas
sibi claves aperiendi ministrat. Sed si Veritas non ministrat, errat,
ut Hieronymus dicit.

De supercilio et praesumptione etc.

Quando igitur Veritas ministrat clavem, iam annuit, ut ianua
aperiatur. Sine igitur Christo, qui Veritas est, non potest quisquam aperire, et qui aperit, ex Christi commissione aperit. Et
Christus est ille pontifex noster immortalis, ‹cui data est omnis
potestas›, qui per se aperit sine commissario et per commissarium.
Omnis igitur sacerdos in exercitio clavium Christi vices agit et est
vicarius Christi. Et tantum facit absolvendo, quantum lavando seu
baptizando, scilicet exsequitur commissionem. Committens autem
est, 'qui operatur omnia in omnibus,' scilicet Christus pontifex
pontificum. Petrus autem singulariter dicitur commissarius et vicarius Christi, quia commissarius commissariorum.

Sermon 144: "I shall give thee the keys to the Kingdom of Heaven"

Brixen, 1454 on the Feast of Peter's Chair [18 January]

I shall give to thee the keys of the kingdom of heaven.[1] We must consider   1
how we are to celebrate the Feast of Peter's Chair. It is the feast of
the keeping of Christ's promise in the Gospel. Optatus of Milevis[2]
says that the Church has a chair and an angel. More about this
elsewhere.[3]

First attend how Christ is the one Who gives the keys of the   2
kingdom of heaven. Christ, however, is the Truth.[4] The door-
keeper [i.e., the pope] does not err if the Truth furnishes him
with the keys that open. But, if the Truth does not furnish them,
he can err, as Jerome says.[5]

Concerning superciliousness and presumption etc.

When, therefore, the Truth furnishes the key, he has already
approved of the door being opened. Without Christ, Who is the
Truth, therefore, there cannot be anyone to open; and he who
opens does so by Christ's commission. And Christ is our immortal pontiff, to Whom all power is given,[6] Who can open by Himself, with or without an agent. Every priest, therefore, in the exercise of the keys acts on Christ's behalf and is a vicar of Christ.
And he executes a commission as much by absolving as by washing (or baptizing). The one who commissions, however, is He
Who works all things in everyone,[7] in other words, Christ the Priest
of Priests. But Peter, especially, is called the agent and Vicar of
Christ, because he is the agent above all agents.

Item attende, quo modo dicit: 'Tibi dabo.' Unde omnis, qui habet claves, in Petro recepit. Alibi de hoc.

3   Item dicit 'claves.' Unde duae ad minus esse debent, si debent esse 'claves' in plurali numero. Per unam clauditur regnum et ligantur animae, per aliam aperitur regnum et solvuntur animae. Reperimus animam ligari praestigiis daemoniorum, ita quod non potest in actus rationales et caret vita et luce, quae est ratio, quia alligata est principi tenebrarum, a quo vexatur. A quo vinculo absolvitur per pontificem, qui catechizat, et tradit pontifex illam potestatem sacerdotibus, ut in baptismo, et exorcistis.

Item aliquando traditur homo Satanae, ut Paulus tradidit Corinthium. Et tunc ligat pontifex animam et eam anathematizat. Ita Christus misit spiritum in porcos.

4   Nota, quantum refert inter verba pontificis in cathedra, id est pontificaliter procedentis, et inter illa, quae non in cathedra, sed private fiunt. Nam in cathedra iudicat ex commissione Christi. Iudex autem in sede iudiciaria cum intentione iudicandi absolvit unum et ligat alium, et sententia eius habet exsecutionem ex officio et sede. Et ideo potestas illa divina est. Nam homo non habet ut homo potestatem alium hominem ad mortem condemnandi. 'Par in parem non habet imperium,' sed 'homo praeest bestiis.' Ideo Pilato iudici Christus dixit: 'Non haberes in me potestatem, nisi data tibi foret desuper.'

Sic cathedra est, quae ostendit sedentem non esse privatum hominem, sed commissarium. Et verba in cathedra sunt committentis, qui loquitur per commissarium. Unde Veritas adhaeret cathedrae. In cathedra sedet, ut iudicet quis admittendus et quis

Again, pay attention how He says, *I shall give to thee*. Hence anyone who has the keys receives them in Peter etc. More about this elsewhere.

Again, He says, *keys*. Hence they should be at least two in number if one says "keys" in the plural number. With one the kingdom is closed and souls are bound; with the other the kingdom is opened and souls are loosed. We find that the soul is bound by the deceptions of demons so that it cannot perform rational acts and lacks life and light, that is, reason, because it is bound to the prince of darkness, by whom it is vexed. It is released from this chain by the pontiff who catechizes; and the pontiff confers that power on priests, as in baptism, and on exorcists.

Again, [it is bound] when a man is handed over to Satan, as Paul told the Corinthians.[8] And then the pontiff binds his soul and anathematizes it. Thus did Christ send the evil spirit into the pigs.[9]

Note the relationship between the words of the pontiff spoken from his chair, that is proceeding pontifically, and those that are not spoken from it but are uttered privately. For from his chair he judges by Christ's commission. The judge on his judgment seat with the intention of judging looses one and binds another, and his sentence is executed on account of his office and see. And so that power is divine. For a man does not have, *qua* man, the power of condemning another man to death. "Equal does not have power over equal," but "a man has charge of beasts."[10] Therefore, Christ said to Pilate, the judge, *Thou shouldst not have any power against Me, unless it were given thee from above*.[11]

Thus it is the chair which shows that the one sitting on it is not a private person but one commissioned. And the words spoken from the chair are those of the One Who commissions, Who speaks through the one commissioned. Therefore, Truth inheres in the chair. He sits on the chair to judge who is to be admitted and who is to be driven away; and, having discerned, he opens to

471

repellendus, et facta discretione uni aperit, alteri claudit. Auctoritas in discernendo, potestas in exsequendo.

Una clavis et plures: una in essentia, plures in respectu ad res, quia exsecutio praesupponit sententiam. Petro fuerunt datae plures claves, quia 'in medio ecclesiae aperuit os eius, et ideo implevit eum,' etc.

5   Attende, quod Petro, quia prae ceteris agnoscens. Cognovit enim Christum esse 'filium Dei vivi,' et haec cognitio est vita aeterna, non cognitio medicorum aut iuristarum. 'Naturaliter omnis homo scire desiderabat,' et ad audiendum nova inclinamur. Apprehensio igitur veritatis et sapientiae, quae habitabat in sua plenitudine in Christo, est apprehensio vitae purae, quae est ipsum ultimum desiderium spiritus et id, quod amat in omni eo, quod amat. Nec est alia sapientia, quae vitam nobis possit dare immortalem, nisi illa, quae fuit menti Christi unita, neque ad illam pervenire possumus, nisi per Christum, qui est ‹magister unicus›, qui habet 'verba vitae aeternae.'

6   Petrus habuit prae ceteris apostolis benevolentiam caritatis, quia praeceptum Christi amavit. Et hoc experimur in proprietatibus amoris, quas in ipso fuisse reperimus. Nam amor gravia facit levia, amor non laborat; sicut ignis aquam resolvit in levem vaporem ascendentem, quae fuit gravis. Petrus supra aquas ambulavit ad Christum aliis discipulis navigantibus.

Anima per amorem in devotionem venit, ita quod in lacrimas resolvitur. Nam est ut ignis, qui cum virido ligno applicatur, tunc ardet in una parte, in alia humectatur. Sic fit de anima frigida. Petrus, quando de Christo cogitabat, lacrimabatur.

In omni congregatione, quamdiu durat amor, tamdiu ordo, sive in familiis, civitatibus, regnis, monasteriis etc. Amor igitur causa est ordinis, quo cessante cessat ordo. Sicut in corpore, durante

the one and closes to the other. The authority to discern is the power to execute.

The keys are one and many: one in essence; many in respect to things, because execution presupposes a sentence. Peter was given many keys, because *in the midst of the Church he opened his mouth, and therefore God filled him* etc.[12]

Note that [the keys were given to Peter] because he recognized 5 Christ before the others. For he knew Christ to be *the Son of the living God.*[13] And this knowledge is eternal life, not the knowledge of physicians or jurists. "By nature every man desires to know,"[14] and we are inclined to hear new things. Therefore, apprehension of truth and of the wisdom that dwells in its fullness in Christ is the apprehension of pure life, which is the ultimate desire of the spirit and is that which it loves in everything that it loves. Nor is there another wisdom that could give us immortal life than that which was united to the mind of Christ. Nor can we come to it except by way of Christ, who is the only teacher,[15] who has *the words of eternal life.*[16]

Peter had the benevolence of charity beyond all the other apos- 6 tles, because he loved the command of Christ.[17] And we experience this in the properties of love, which we find to have existed in it. For love makes heavy things light; love does not labor. Thus fire turns water, which was heavy, into a light vapor ascending. Peter walked on the water to Christ while the other disciples remained in the ship.[18]

Love turns into devotion by way of love, so that it is dissolved in tears. For it is like a fire that is applied to green wood, which burns one part while leaving another moist. Thus does love act upon the frigid soul. Peter wept when he thought about Christ.[19]

In every group, whether in families, cities, kingdoms, monasteries etc., as long as love lasts, order does too. Therefore, love is the cause of order. When it ceases, order does too. Just as in a body, as long as love between the humors endures, a man is temperate, but,

amore inter humores, homo est temperatus, sed cessante concordia et amore distemperatus. Sanctus Petrus valde ordinatus, ideo sibi ecclesia fuit commissa.

Amor est quidam calor spiritualis. Et ideo est sollicitus et non sinit aliud cogitare. Et numquam quiescit, sicut calor naturalis numquam quiescit, sicut nec cor, in quo est sedes eius. Sic Petrus de Christo sollicitus semper fuit. Dixit: 'Etsi oportuerit me mori' etc. Et dicit sanctus Augustinus, quod Dominus noluit ei ostendere Judam traditorem, quia statim eum interfecisset.

Item amor contentam facit animam. Qui enim ferventer amat, non nisi amatum appetit. Petrus de pane et olivis et tunica cum pallio contentabatur, quia Deum habuit. Quem qui habet, omnia habet, et cui ille non sufficit, multum avarus est.

7 Prae ceteris Petrus habuit efficaciam virtutis: eo loquente 'cecidit Spiritus Sanctus,' Tabitam suscitavit, paralyticum etc., et eius umbra sanavit.

Prae ceteris habuit excellentiam dignitatis: 'Tibi dabo claves.'

'In omni multitudine unius generis reperitur unum, in quo est plenitudo respectu omnium,' sicut in Christo plenitudo gratiae, quae descendit in omnes sanctos, quia 'de plenitudine eius omnes accepimus.'

In virgine Maria plenitudo misericordiae, et dicitur mater misericordiae, de qua descendit misericordia in omnes peccatores. Bernardus: 'Maria omnibus sinum aperit, de plenitudine eius sumant universi.'

In caelo primus motus, a quo omnes motus recipiunt, ut sint. Sic in sole plenitudo lucis et in igne plenitudo caloris. In corde plenitudo vitae, in capite plenitudo sensus, in imperatore plenitudo civilis imperationis.

once concord and love cease, his humors are out of balance. Saint Peter was well ordered; therefore, the Church was committed to him.

Love is a kind of spiritual heat. And thus it is solicitous and does not admit another thought. It never rests, just as natural heats never rests, just as the heart, wherein love has its seat, never rests. Thus Peter always was solicitous about Christ. He said, *Though I should die,* etc.[20] And Saint Augustine says that the Lord did not wish to reveal to him Judas' treachery, because Peter would have killed him.[21]

Likewise, love makes a soul content. Whoever loves fervently desires only the beloved. Peter was content with bread and olives, a tunic with a cloak, because he had God. Whoever has Him has everything; and the one for whom He does not suffice remains very greedy.

Beyond the rest, Peter had the exercise of power. When he spoke, *the Holy Spirit fell upon* them. Tabitha was resuscitated, and the paralytic, etc., and his shadow healed.[22]

Beyond the rest he had the excellence of dignity, *I will give to thee the keys.*

"In every multitude of one genus there is found one which has fullness with respect to all,"[23] just as in Christ there was plenitude of grace that descended upon all the saints, since *of His fullness we have all received.*[24]

In the Virgin Mary there is plenitude of mercy; and she, from whom mercy descends upon all sinners, is called the Mother of Mercy. Bernard says, "Mary opened her bosom to all; from her plenitude all receive."[25]

In heaven, there is a first moved, from which all receive motion, so that they exist. Thus in the sun is fullness of light, and in fire is the fullness of heat. In the heart is the fullness of life; in the head is the fullness of the senses; in an emperor is the fullness of civil rule.

Sic in Petro plenitudo auctoritatis a Christo commissae, quae descendit in omnes pontifices et sacerdotes in ecclesia. Et ideo illis datae sunt claves, iuxta illud: 'Quaecumque alligaveritis,' sed per Petrum, cui dictum fuit: 'Tibi dabo'.

8   Nota, quod cum regnum caelorum sit cognoscere Deum, tunc Petrus habuit clavem scientiae, ut ex evangelio: 'Tu es Christus,' etc. Et ideo datis sibi clavibus 'in medio ecclesiae,' illis usus est. Nam 'in medio ecclesiae aperuit os eius,' congregavit sibi ecclesiam, quae est 'congregatio rationabiliorum unitorum in observantia legis, pacis et laudis.' Non est laus communis, nisi ubi pax Dei; non est pax, nisi ubi mandata servantur. Congregatio, quae ista non habet, est synagoga seu bestialium congregatio. Spiritus, qui ponit extra ecclesiam est ‹divisor›, quia est spiritus bestialis canis et porci, rabidi et gulosi atque luxuriosi etc.

Thus in Peter is the fullness of authority, conferred by Christ, which descends to the other pontiffs and priests in the Church. And therefore the keys are given to them, according to the words, *Whatsoever you shall bind.*[26] But this is done by way of Peter, to whom was said, *I shall give thee,* etc.

Note that, since the kingdom of heaven is knowing God, then   8 Peter had the key of knowledge, as is found in the gospel, *Thou art the Christ,* etc.[27] And therefore the keys were given to him *in the midst of the Church* so that he might use them. For *in the midst of the Church he opened his mouth;* he gathered the Church around him, which is "the gathering together of rational persons united in the observance of the law, peace and praise."[28] For there is no common praise except where God's peace abides; and there is no peace except where the commandments are observed. The gathering that does not have these things is a synagogue or a gathering of beasts. The spirit that places itself outside the Church is a divider, because it is a bestial spirit of dog and the pig, rabid and gluttonous and wanton etc.

Sermo CLX: *Tu es Petrus*

1 'Tu es Petrus.' Quomodo Petrus sit agnoscens; quo modo Petrus sit lapis fundamentalis aedificii; quo modo sit *bet ros*, id est caput domus; quo modo tota ecclesia sit explicatio Petri.

2 Nam Petrus primus fidelis, primus sacerdos, primus pontifex, primus patriarcha, primus papa. Et melius: Quo modo Petrus sit primus fidelis et princeps fidei. Ideo omnes Christiani sicut a Christo Christiani, sic a Petro dicuntur fideles seu agnoscentes. Et nemo potest intrare regnum caelorum, nisi sit in unitate cum Petro. Et omnes principes in ecclesia participant de principatu Petri sicut omnes fideles de fide Petri.

3 Petrus est lapis aedificii ecclesiae, in quo totum complicatur aedificium sicut in lapide fundamenti, sine quo esse nequit aedificium, et in quo sistit aedificium. Unde non potest esse nisi una ecclesia, quia non est nisi unus Petrus. Non potest esse nisi unum sacerdotium in illa ecclesia, quia non nisi unus Petrus. Non potest esse nisi unum sacrificium, quia non est nisi unum sacerdotium ab uno Petro. Non potest esse nisi ‹unus episcopatus› per orbem diffusus, quia non nisi unus Petrus apostolorum primus. Non potest esse nisi unus principatus in ecclesia, quia non nisi una ecclesia, unum sacerdotium, unus pontificatus seu episcopatus, et sic non nisi unus principatus Petri. Non potest esse nisi una potestas ligandi et solvendi, quia unus Petrus. Et licet una illa potestas participetur a multis, tamen non est nisi una Petri potestas.

4 Et ob hoc qui in unitate cum Petro non est, nec ligare potest nec solvere etc.

Sermon 160: "Thou art Peter"

[Probably delivered on June 29, 1454 at Bruneck]

Thou art Peter.[1] How Peter is the one who recognizes; how Peter is 1
the cornerstone of the edifice; how he is *bet ros*, that is, the head of
the house; how the whole Church is the unfolding of Peter.[2]

For Peter is the first of the faithful, the first priest, the first 2
pontiff, the first patriarch, the first pope. And better: How Peter
is the first of the faithful and the prince of the faith.[3] Therefore,
all Christians, just as they are called Christians from Christ, are
called faithful or "recognizers" from Peter. And no one can enter
the kingdom of heaven unless they are in union with Peter. And
all princes in the Church participate in the principate of Peter, just
as all the faithful participate in the faith of Peter.

Peter is the cornerstone of the Church, in whom is enfolded the 3
whole edifice, just as in a foundation stone, without which there
would not be an edifice and on which the edifice rests. Therefore,
there can be only one Church, because there is only one Peter.
There can be only one sacrifice in that Church, because there is
only one priesthood derived from Peter. There can be only one
episcopate diffused throughout the world, because there is only
one Peter, first among the apostles. There can be only one
principate in the Church, because there is only one Church, one
priesthood, one pontificate or episcopate, and thus there is only
one principate, that of Peter. There can be only one power to bind
and loose, because there is one Peter. And, although many participate in that one power, nevertheless, there can be only one power
of Peter.

And for this reason no one who is not in union with Peter can 4
bind or loose etc.

Viget spiritus apostolicus et vivit secundum Hieronymum in cathedra Petri. Quare necesse est quemlibet esse unitum sedenti in Petri cathedra, si vult in ecclesia esse, in qua est potestas ligandi et solvendi. Oportet enim per successiones pontificum venire in Petrum, qui a Christo recepit potestatem ligandi et solvendi.

Et tunc certum est nos esse in ecclesia, si sumus in ecclesia cui praesidet successor Petri, neque ad nos attinet, si malus est, qui successit, quia hoc est suum. Veritas autem quae pro me est, est alligata cathedrae, ut dicit Augustinus. Nam non diceret Christus: 'super cathedram Moysi' etc., 'quae dicunt, facite!' nisi veritas esset alligata cathedrae.

Non enim est alius, qui ex cathedra praecipit, quam Christus, qui audiendus est. Nec diceret: 'quae faciunt, facere nolite!' nisi illa duo starent simul, scilicet veritas doctrinae et perversitas vitae.

5   Nota, quam firma est ecclesiae aedificatio, quia nemo decipi potest etiam per malum praesidentem. Mandat Christus, quod ipsos praelatos audire debeamus, quia eos audiendo Christum audimus: 'Qui vos audit, me audit.' Si igitur ex praecepto Christi oboedire debeo praelato et praeposito, etiam discolo, ut dicit Petrus apostolus, non possum igitur decipi, quando adimpleo praecepta Christi.

6   Item, si vis esse agnoscens seu Petrus, oportet sequi in Petrum, qui peccavit, et quo modo rediit et 'flevit', et quo modo 'dilexit multum', et quo modo ‹vicit mundum› et mortuus est in cruce.

According to Jerome, the apostolic spirit thrives and lives in the see of Peter.[4] Hence it is necessary for anyone to be united to the one sitting in Peter's seat if he wishes to be in the Church, in which is the power to bind and loose. For through the succession of the pontiffs one must come to Peter, who received from Christ the power to bind and loose.

And then it is certain that we are in the Church if we are in the Church over which the successor of Peter presides. Nor does it matter if that successor should be bad, because that is his affair. The truth which matters as far as I am concerned is bound to [Peter's] see, as Augustine says.[5] For Christ would not have said, [*The scribes and Pharisees sit*] *on the seat of Moses* etc., *what they say, do* etc., unless the truth were bound to the see.[6]

There is no one other who teaches from that see but Christ, who must be heeded. Nor would He have said, *Do not do what they do,* unless two things could coexist, that is, the truth of teaching and perversity of [the teacher's] life.

Note how firm is the building up of the Church, because no   5 one can be deceived, even by a bad leader. Christ commands that we should heed those prelates, because by heeding them, we heed Christ: *Whoever hears you hears Me.*[7] If, therefore, according to Christ's teaching I should obey a prelate and a person set over me, even a difficult one,[8] as the Apostle Peter says, I cannot then be deceived when I fulfill Christ's commands.

Again, if you wish to be a "recognizer" like Peter, it is necessary   6 to follow after Peter, who sinned; and [to imitate] how he went out and *wept,*[9] and how he *loved much,*[10] and how he overcame the world and died upon a cross.[11]

Sermo CCLXXXVII: *Beatus es, Simon Bar Iona*

1457 in Insbruka die apostolorum Petri et Pauli

1 'Beatus es, Simon Bar Iona.' In evangelio, cuius expositionem aliqualiter habes supra, Simon est oboediens, Bar Iona filius columbae. Anima enim oboediens, tali oboedientia quae generatur ex columbina simplicitate illa, est beata, sicut est anima rationalis, quae oboedit fidei. Illa dici potest Petrus, id est agnoscens. Oportet enim quod anima beata sit agnoscens; nam anima quae non potest esse agnoscens, uti est bestialis, non potest assequi beatitudinem. Consistit enim beatitudo in agnitione. Lapis enim, etsi haberet esse incorruptibile, quia non cognosceret se habere, non est beatus. Sola natura, cuius esse est intelligere seu cognoscere, capax est beatitudinis.

2 Sed cognitio beatificans non oritur ex sensibilibus neque ex vi naturae creatae, quoniam est cognitio principii. Nihil potest sui ipsius principium, scilicet unde et quomodo venit in esse, agnoscere nisi revelatione. Puer in insula positus in infantia ex se ipso non perveniret, ut cognosceret patrem et modum quomodo natus. Intellectualis natura revelatione suum principium cognoscit. Et cognoscere est esse. Et ita dum intelligit, intra se habet principium sui esse, quare est in beatitudine immortali. Sicut si stagnum aliquod intra limites suos constitutum exortum a vivo fonte in eo centraliter ebulliente esset naturae intellectualis et cognosceret intra se fontem vivum suae emanationis, esset ut stagnum beatum, quia cognosceret se habere esse incorruptibile.

3 Habemus autem ex evangelio quomodo Christus est revelatio principii seu Patris, non modo quo vulgus concipit videntes seu

482

Sermon 287: "Blessed art thou, Simon Bar-Jona"

1457 in Innsbruck on the day of the apostles Peter and Paul

Blessed art thou, Simon Bar Jona.[1] In the gospel, whose exposition   1
you have just heard above, Simon means "obedient," Bar Jona, "son
of the dove." For the obedient soul, by such obedience as is born
from the simplicity of the dove, is blessed, just like the rational
soul, which obeys faith. It can be called Peter, that is, "he who recognizes" [or knows][2] It is necessary that the blessed soul be knowing, for the soul which cannot be knowing is like the bestial soul
and cannot achieve blessedness. Blessedness, then, consists in
knowledge. A stone, even if it had incorruptible being, because it
does not know it has being, is not blessed. Only a nature to whom
it belongs to understand or know is capable of beatitude.

But beatifying knowledge does not originate from things sensi-   2
ble nor from the force of created nature, since it is knowledge of a
beginning [or principle]. Nothing can know its own beginning,
that is, from where and how it came to be, except by revelation. A
boy placed on an island in infancy would not by himself come to
know his father and how he was born. Intellectual nature knows
its own beginning by revelation. And knowing is being. And so,
when one understands, one has within oneself the beginning [or
principle] of one's own being, whence one is in immortal beatitude. Just so, if some pool, set within its limits, arisen from a living fountain bubbling up in its center, were of an intellectual nature and knew within itself the living fountain from which it
emanated, it would be a blessed pool, because it would know that
it was incorruptible.

We know from the Gospel how Christ is the revelation of the   3
beginning or of the Father, not in the way in which the crowd con-

prophetas revelare, sed modo quo Filius, qui est imago et figura substantiae Patris, revelat. Iohannes, ultimus veteris testamenti sacerdos, revelavit primo Christum, Petrus, primus novi testamenti, similiter revelavit Christum, sed ex revelatione Patris. Totum igitur vetus testamentum concluditur in revelatione Christi, et totum novum testamentum ibi initiatur. Unde medio Iohannis et Petri Pater de caelis primo omnes attraxit in revelationem Filii sui. Bene dicebat Iesus: 'Nemo potest venire ad me, nisi Pater meus traxerit eum.'

4   Nemo autem potest venire ad Patrem nisi revelatione Filii. Si igitur receperimus confessionem Petri sibi a Patre revelatam, scilicet quod 'Christus Filius Dei vivi,' beati sumus; nam Petrus confitetur Iesum esse 'Christum, Filium Dei vivi'. Christus dicit hanc esse revelationem Patris. Si primum admittimus, secundum est indubitatum, quia Filius Dei hoc dixit, qui est veritas. Et si Pater revelat Petro occultam veritatem, quomodo non revelaret Filio omnia?

5   Attende igitur, ut saepius habuisti: Qui Christum recipit esse Filium Dei, ille utique credit ei, et credit ipsum esse missum Dei Patris et loqui verba Dei. Certe ille non peccat, quia mandata servat. Quis non servaret mandata Filii Dei, quae promittunt vitam aeternam et quod mori huic mundo sit vivere in regno Dei? Signum igitur, quod faciliter quis peccat, est quia non credit Christo uti verbo Dei. Si autem quis veraciter credit, ille in se habet verbum Dei, quia non loquitur in eo nisi Christus, cui oboedit, qui est rex ipsum regens et perducens ad promissam hereditatem vitae.

6   Nota quomodo ecclesia fundatur in confessione Petri. Nam ecclesia est corpus Christi mysticum, quod in se habet Christum

ceives that seers or prophets reveal things, but in the way in which
the Son, who is the image and figure of the substance of the Father, reveals it. John, the last priest of the Old Testament, first revealed Christ; Peter, the first priest of the New Testament, similarly revealed Christ, but from the revelation of the Father. The
whole Old Testament, therefore, is concluded in the revelation of
Christ; and the whole New Testament begins there. Hence
through the medium of John and Peter, the Father from heaven
draws all into the revelation of His Son. Jesus said very well, *No
man can come to me, except the Father draw him.*[3]

No one can come to the Father unless by the revelation of the   4
Son. If, therefore, we receive the confession of Peter, revealed to
him by the Father, that is, that He is *Christ, the Son of the living
God,*[4] we are blessed. For Peter confessed Jesus to be *Christ, the Son
of the living God.* Christ says this was a revelation from the Father.[5]
If we admit the first, the second cannot be doubted, because the
Son of God, Who is the truth, said it. And, if the Father revealed
to Peter the hidden truth, how could He not reveal all things to
the Son?

Pay attention, therefore, as you so often have. He who receives   5
Christ as the Son of God both believes in Him entirely and believes Him to be the one sent by God the Father to speak the
words of God. Surely he did not sin, since he observed the commandments. Who would not observe the commandments of the
Son of God, which promise eternal life; and [who does not know]
that dying to this world is living in the kingdom of God? The
sign, therefore, that someone can sin easily is that he does not believe in Christ as the Word of God. If, however, someone truly believes, he has the Word of God in himself, because there speaks in
him no one but Christ, Whom he obeys, Who is the king ruling
him and leading him to the promised heritage of life.

Note that the Church is founded on the confession of Peter.   6
For the Church is the Mystical Body of Christ, which holds

esse Filium Dei vivi. In illo corpore est omnis potestas ligandi et solvendi, quae potestas est in Christo a Patre. Sicut enim Christus est verbum Dei incarnatum, in se omnem Patris includens potestatem, ita verbum Christi in Petro omnem Christi includens potestatem. Dico 'verbum Christi,' prout capitur Christus pro vere et mystice; nam prout capitur mystice, scilicet pro ecclesia, quae est corpus Christi mysticum, in hoc corpore Petrus caput exsistens, habet omnem corporis potestatem, quia rector qui regit per revelationem verbi Dei.

7 Habet etiam Petrus omnem Christi potestatem, ut aedificare possit ecclesiam nondum aedificatam. Sicut Christus dixit: 'Super hanc petram aedificabo ecclesiam,' sic Petrus aedificat in verbo Christi et ecclesiam gubernat. Hoc est dicere quod Christus aedificat ecclesiam medio Petri et regit aedificatam medio Petri.

8 'Petrus' etiam capitur pro omni fideli; nam omnis fidelis non habet nisi fidem Petri. A Christo igitur Christiani, a Petro fideles dicimur. In Petro est complicatio omnium fidelium et omnis principatus et omnis potestas ligandi et solvendi. Et ideo vocatur beatus, et nemo potest esse beatus, nisi sequatur patronum nostrum Petrum, qui est patronus universalis ac huius nostrae Brixinensis ecclesiae.

within it that Christ is the Son of God. In that body is all the power of binding and loosing, a power in Christ from the Father. Just as Christ is the incarnate Word of God, including in Himself all the power of the Father, so the word of Christ in Peter includes all the power of Christ. I say "the word of Christ" as Christ is understood truly and mystically. For as it is understood mystically, that is, standing for the Church, which is the Mystical Body of Christ, Peter, existing in this body as head, has all the power of the body, because he is the rector who rules by the revelation of the Word of God.

Peter has all the power of Christ, so that he can build up the 7 Church not yet built up. Just as Christ said, *Upon this rock I will build My church*,[6] so Peter builds on the word of Christ and governs the Church. That is to say, Christ builds the Church through the medium of Peter and rules what is built up by means of Peter.

"Peter" is also understood to stand for every faithful person, for 8 every faithful person has no faith but that of Peter. From Christ, therefore, we are called Christians; from Peter, the faithful. In Peter is the enfolding of all the faithful and every principate and all power of binding and loosing; and, therefore, he is called *blessed*, and no one can be blessed unless he follows our patron, Peter, who is the patron of the universal Church and of this our church of Brixen.

Sermo CCLXXX: *Ego sum pastor bonus*

1457 Brixinae lunae post dominicam Misericordias Domini

1 Ministrat nobis, fratres, sancti evangelii lectio pabulum huic sacrae synodali conventioni congruum, ut non sit opus alibi pastum quaerere, quo reficiamur, qui sub Christo pastore ad vitae pascua ducimur atque ad pascendi artem, qua creditas nobis pascamus oves dirigimur. Dicebat Christus: 'Ego sum pastor bonus.'

2 Saepissime audistis naturam, quae per sapientiam pascitur, ob ipsam capacitatem sapientiae incorruptibilem. Intellectualis enim natura quae sola est apta pasci sapientia seu veritate, numquam potest in nihilum redigi. Et ut latum et laetum pascentiae pratum intremus, ubi uberes herbas inveniamus, attendamus quomodo Christus post sanationem caeci nati dixerat: 'In iudicio ego in mundum hunc veni, ut qui non vident, videant, et qui vident, caeci fiant.' Verbum Dei ignorantes et caecas mentes illuminat, quae suam caecitatem recognoscunt et a Christo, qui lux est, illuminari desiderant. Praesumentes vero se lucem intelligentiae habere excaecat, quia peccatum in illis manet. Nam praesumptio non sinit eos accedere, ut illuminentur, quando se videntes esse iactant. Et quoniam Pharisaei et pastores aliorum, praesumentes se videntes, alios ducere nitebantur lumine suae intelligentiae, subiungit Christus, quod ipsi tales sunt seductores, quia 'non intrant per ostium.'

Sermon 280: "I am the Good Shepherd"

1457 on the Monday after Misericordia Domini Sunday[1]
at Brixen in the Synod

Brothers, the reading from the holy gospel provides fitting nour-   1
ishment to this holy synod, so that there is no need to seek elsewhere the sustenance by which we are refreshed, we who are led
by Christ the shepherd to the pastures of life and to the art of pas-
turing, by means of which we feed the sheep entrusted to us.[2] For
Christ said, *I am the good shepherd.*[3]

Very often you have heeded [your intellectual] nature, which is   2
fed by wisdom, on account of its incorruptible capacity for wisdom. For intellectual nature, which alone is apt to be fed by wisdom or truth, never can be reduced to nothing. And so that we
may enter the wide and rich pasture for feeding, where we may
find rich grass, let us note how Christ, after the healing of the man
born blind, said, *For judgment I am come into this world; that they who
see not, may see; and those who see, may become blind.*[4] The word of
God illuminates ignorant and blind minds which recognize their
own blindness and desire to be illuminated by Christ, who is the
light. But those who presume that they have the light of intelligence He blinds, because sin remains in them. For presumption
does not let them draw near that they might be illuminated, when
they boast that they are seers. And since the Pharisees and the
shepherds of others, presuming themselves to be seers, strive to
lead others by the light of their own intelligence, Christ adds that
such men are those who lead others astray, because *they do not enter
through the gate.*[5]

3   Dat exemplum de pastore ovium, qui per ostium intrat ad ovile,
fures vero et latrones aliunde ascendunt. Explanat, in quo deprehenditur pastor, scilicet quia eius vox est nota ovibus et oboediunt
atque ipsum sequuntur, alienum fugiunt, quia vocem eius ignorant. Post hoc revelat se ostium, per quod intrant pastores, et quomodo qui per ipsum non intrant, sunt fures et latrones. Dicit se
deinde ostium ovium, qui non venit ut alii pastores, quorum finis
est ut demum oves mactent et perdant, sed ut vivant abundantius.

4   Dixit igitur sic: 'Ego sum ostium, per me si quis introierit, salvabitur, et ingredietur et egredietur et pascua inveniet. Fur non venit, nisi ut furetur et mactet et perdat. Ego veni, ut vitam habeant
et abundantius habeant.' Habemus igitur iuxta vaticinium Ie-
remiae 3° pastores christiformes pascere in scientia et doctrina et
quod ideo nos pastores, si quaerimus pascere creditas nobis oves,
in prata sacrae scripturae eas ducere debemus, et hoc per ostium
quod Christus est; nam verus introitus est per Christum, de quo
loquuntur scripturae. Id enim quod pascit animam in prato scripturarum, verbum Dei, est sub littera contentum. Sicut enim sub
diversis herbis pabulum invisibile ovium continetur, per quod solum sensibilis vita pascitur, sic sub varia scriptura spiritus latitat
mentem pascens. Unde spiritalis pastus, vivificans et illuminans,
non deprehenditur nisi medio Christi, qui est ostium vivum se ipsum aperiens pulsanti et claudens praesumenti.

5   Et nota quomodo mens rationalis quae se Christo subiecit, cognoscit vocem et mediante voce verbum occultatum in voce et sequitur ipsum. Tanta est dulcedo verbi Dei, ad quod mens cognitione pervenit, quae Christo se per fidem subiecit, quod nullum

He uses the example of a shepherd of sheep, who enters the   3
fold by the gate; thieves and robbers, however, climb in elsewhere.
He explains how the shepherd is known, that is, because his voice
is known to the sheep; and they obey and follow Him. They flee
the stranger, because they do not know his voice. After this, He
reveals Himself to be the gate through which shepherds enter, and
how those who do not enter through Him are thieves and robbers.
Then He says that He is the gate of the sheep, Who did not come
like other shepherds, whose goal is to kill and destroy the sheep,
but [His goal is] that they might live abundantly.[6]

That is why he spoke thus: *I am the door. By Me, if any man shall*   4
enter in, he shall be saved: and he shall go in and out, and shall find pas-
ture. The thief cometh not, but to steal, and to kill, and to destroy. I am
come that they may have life, and may have it more abundantly.[7] We
learn therefore, according to the prophecy of Jeremiah 3[:15], that
Christiform shepherds feed upon knowledge and doctrine, and
that in this way we shepherds, if we seek to feed the sheep entrusted to us, should lead them into the pasture of Sacred Scripture, and this through the gate which is Christ. For the true entry
is through Christ, of Whom the Scriptures speak. Indeed, that
which feeds the soul in the field of the Scriptures, the word of
God, is contained beneath the letter. Just as the invisible food of
sheep, through which alone life in the senses is fed, is contained
under different herbs, so the Spirit lies concealed under various
writings, feeding the mind. Hence spiritual food, life-giving and illuminating, is not found except by means of Christ, Who is the
living door, opening Himself to the one who knocks and closing to
the presumptuous man.

And note how the rational mind which submits itself to Christ   5
recognizes his voice and, by means of the voice, the Word hidden
in the voice, and follows Him. Such is the sweetness of the Word
of God, which comes to the mind in thought — the mind that submits itself in faith to Christ — that it follows no one except Him.

nisi ipsum sequitur, et qui alia verba loquitur, eius vox est sibi aliena et incognita, et fugit ab eo. Quando enim Christus interrogavit Petrum et alios apostolos, an ipsi abire vellent, respondit: 'Quo ibimus? Verba vitae aeternae habes.' Cognovit ille qui credidit Christum Filium Dei vocem et in voce verbum et quod verbum fuit verbum vitae aeternae, et non potuit abire.

6 Si igitur quaerimus salvare eos, quorum curam suscepimus, per ostium ducamus. Fures et latrones aliunde intrare docent, ut perdant; nam seducitur a via veritatis et vitae, qui Christi doctrinam spernit.

7 Ecce quod solus ille salvabitur, qui intrat per ostium quod Christus est, qui est via et vita. Si quaeris ostium ad vitam, ipse est; si quaeris vitam, ipse est; si quaeris pascua vitae, ipse est. Quis est autem ille Christus? Certe ipse est, qui est dator vitae spiritalis, quia veritas et sapientia et lux rationis omnem hominem illuminans, et venit ut vivant et abundantius vivant. Sicut sol nunc venit, ut arbores et animalia vivant, et propius ad influendum suam virtutem venit, ut arbores quae in hieme sine fructifera vita erant et tamen non erant penitus mortuae, nunc vivant et abundantius etiam ad fructificandum vivant, Christus sol iustitiae cum luce intelligentiae et calore caritatis sic ad nos venit, in quo virtus Dei.

8 Et ostendit se ostium paradisi, scilicet sacrae scripturae. Nam si per medium Christi intras ad domum intelligentiae scrutando scripturas, ipsum in omnibus pabulum vitae invenies. Si exis per hoc ostium, explanando scripturas et enodando pascua invenies. In Vetus Testamentum intras per Christum. De Veteri exis in Novum per Christum.

9 Adhuc aliter considera quomodo Christus est ostium, in quo ut in ostio ingressus et egressus coincidunt. Ostium enim est ad egre-

And the voice of the man speaking other words is alien and unknown to it; and it flees from him. For when Christ questioned Peter and the other apostles whether they wished to leave, Peter replied, *To whom shall we go? Thou hast the words of eternal life.*[8] He who believed Christ to be the Son of the Living God[9] knew his voice and, in the voice, the Word, and that the Word was the Word of eternal life; and he could not leave.

If, therefore, we would save those whose care we have undertaken, let us lead them through the door. Robbers and thieves teach them to enter elsewhere, so that they are lost. For whoever spurns Christ's doctrine is seduced from the way of truth and life. 6

Behold, he alone will be saved who enters through the gate, that is, Christ, Who is the way and the life.[10] If you seek the gate to life, it is He. If you seek life, it is He. If you seek the pasture of life, it is He. Who, however, is that Christ? Surely it is He Who is the giver of spiritual life, because He is truth, and wisdom, and the light of reason, enlightening every man; and He comes so that they might live and live more abundantly. Just as the sun now comes so that trees and animals may live, and comes nearer to pour out its power, so that trees, which in the winter were without fruitbearing life and yet were not entirely dead, may now live and live more abundantly, even to the point of bearing fruit — so Christ, *the sun of justice*[11] with the light of understanding and the heat of charity, in Whom is God's strength, comes to us. 7

And He shows Himself to be the door of paradise, that is, of the Sacred Scriptures. For if by means of Christ you enter the house of understanding, scrutinizing the Scriptures, you will find the very food of life in them all. If you go through the gate, explaining and expounding the Scriptures, you shall find pasture. In the Old Testament you enter through Christ. From Old Testament you go out into the New Testament through Christ. 8

Consider besides, in another way, how Christ is the gate in which, as in a gate, going in and coming out coincide. The gate, 9

diendum simul et ad ingrediendum. Christus est ostium, per quod omnis creatura egreditur in esse, quia est ratio rerum, per quam omnia facta sunt et sine ea nihil. Est et ostium, per quod omnia redeunt in causam seu rationem suam tamquam ad suum principium. Est ostium creationis simul et salvationis seu effluxus et refluxus.

10   Si quis per intellectum profunde considerat, quomodo Christus est via, per quam omnis creatura fluit in esse, ut id sit quod est, quodque Christus qui est via, est etiam terminus creationis, quia in ipso terminatur et perficitur creatio, et cum hoc attente meditatur quomodo ipse est via, per quam necessario omnis creatura complet circulum refluxus et revertitur ingrediendo in primam causam, et est terminus refluxus, ille videt ipsum sic esse medium, fluxus et refluxus, quod etiam est principium et finis. Tales pascua invenient semper pascentia.

11   Christus igitur si cognoscitur, omnia in ipso cognoscuntur. Christus si habetur, omnia in ipso habentur. Ad nos igitur spectat evangelizare Christum, ut cognoscatur, quia in eius nomine seu cognitione consistit salus et vita, neque est aliud nomen aut cognitio salvans intellectualem naturam, quae vivit ex cognitione, nisi illa. Unde Christus est veritas illa quae quaeritur, ut cognoscatur per omnem intellectum; quae cum habetur, habetur ultimum desideriorum; et gaudium illud de apprehensa veritate est vita aeterna.

12   Diceret aliquis ex simplicioribus: Quomodo debemus evangelizare Christum, ut cognoscatur, cum ipse dicat, quod nemo cognoscit Filium nisi Pater et nemo cognoscit Patrem nisi Filius? Respondeo, quod per ostium humanitatis debemus ipsum evangelizare, ut ad cognitionem eius nostros subditos perducamus. Quae

then, is to be entered and exited at the same time. Christ is the gate through which every creature goes forth into being, because He is the pattern of things, through which all things were made, and without which nothing exists.[12] And He is the gate through which all things return to their cause or pattern, as if to their beginning. He is at once the door of creation and of salvation, or of flowing out and flowing back.[13]

If one considers deeply with the intellect how Christ is the way 10 through which every creature flows into being so that it may be what it is, and that Christ Himself Who is the way is also the term of creation, because creation ends and is perfected in Him; and when one meditates carefully upon how He is the way through which every creature necessarily completes the cycle of flowing back and returns by regressing to the first cause, and that he is the end of this flowing back, one will see that he is thus the means, the flux and reflux [of creation] because He is also the beginning and the end. Men who meditate thus will always find pastures to feed upon.

Therefore, if Christ is known, all things are known in Him. If 11 Christ is possessed, all things are possessed in Him. It belongs to us, therefore, to preach Christ, so that He may be known, because salvation and life consist in His name or in knowledge of Him. Nor is there any other name or knowledge that saves the intellectual nature, which lives by knowledge, than that knowledge. Therefore Christ is that truth which is sought so that He may be known by the entire intellect. When this is possessed, the ultimate among desires is possessed. And that joy from apprehending the truth is eternal life.

One of the simpler sort might say, "How should we preach 12 Christ so that He may be known when He says that no one knows the Son except the Father and no one knows the Father except the Son?"[14] I reply that we should preach Him through the gate of humanity, so that we may lead those subject to us to

cognitio est fides in nobis illa, quae sufficit nobis ad salutem. Nam Deus Pater etsi non potest cognosci uti est nisi per Filium—nemo enim Patrem ut Patrem cognoscit nisi Filius, et nemo cognoscit Filium ut Filium nisi Pater—, tamen Pater et Filius cognoscuntur revelatione fidei. Si enim pervenerimus, ut Christum Filium Dei habeamus per fidem, ipse nobis revelat Patrem. Ad hoc autem ostium habemus humanitatis, quia dum ea quae Christus homo gessit, inspexerimus, reperiemus in homine virtutem divinam supra omnem hominem, ex quibus sibi credimus, in eo enim quod se dicebat Filium Dei esse et missum Patris. Testimonia enim efficacissima atque certissima produxit, ita quod nemo in hoc haesitare potest, qui ratione utitur.

13   Dicimus igitur populo, quomodo Christus venit natus de virgine, quae miracula operatus, quae docuit, quae promisit, quomodo mortuus est, ut testimonium perhiberet veritati per ipsum. Praedicate, quomodo resurrexit a mortuis, quomodo apparuit post resurrectionem et quomodo illi, quibus apparuit, receperunt Spiritum Sanctum, in quo confortati testimonium perhibuerunt resurrectioni usque ad mortem inclusive, et non solum illi, sed et alii infiniti! Ex illis enim ascendimus usque ad fidem, scilicet quod ille homo fuit etiam Filius Dei et quod ei ut Filio Dei oboediendum atque credendum sit.

14   Deinde convertimur ad evangelizationem, doctrinam et mandata ipsius Filii Dei et quomodo aperuit scripturas, quia ostendit se esse illum, de quo loquuntur scripturae, et quomodo recipiendo ipsum per fidem formatam, oboediendo doctrinae et praeceptis eius et respiciendo ad ipsum tamquam ad exemplar viae nostrae sperare debemus sibi conformari et beatitudinem secum possidere. Et ita est Christus evangelizandus ut praemittitur. Tunc si creditur Filius Dei, ratio concludit sibi credendum et quod sicut docuit

knowledge of Him. That knowledge is the faith within us, which suffices for us for salvation. For God the Father, even if He cannot be known as he is except through the Son — for no one knows the Father as Father except the Son and no one knows the Son as Son except the Father — nevertheless, the Father and the Son are known by the revelation of faith. If we come to grasp the Son of God through faith, He reveals the Father to us. For this we have the gate of humanity, because, when we have inspected what Christ the man did, we find divine power beyond every man in the man, and on this account we believe in Him, in that He said that He was the Son of God and the one sent by the Father. He produced these most efficacious and most certain testimonies so that no one who uses reason can waver in this.

We tell the people, therefore, how Christ comes, born of the 13 Virgin, what miracles He worked, what He taught, what He promised, how He died, so that He might bear witness by Himself to the truth. Preach how He rose from the dead, how He appeared after the Resurrection and how those to whom He appeared received the Holy Spirit and were comforted by it, so that they bore witness to the Resurrection even unto death, and not only they alone but infinite others too! By means of this testimony we ascend even to faith, that is, that He was both man and the Son of God, and that He must be obeyed and believed in as God's Son.

Thereafter we turn to evangelization, teaching and the com- 14 mands of God's own Son, and how He opened the Scriptures, because He showed Himself to be the one of Whom the Scriptures speak, and how, by receiving Him by means of an informed faith, by obeying His doctrine and commands, and by looking to Him as to the exemplar of our life, we should hope to be made like Him and to possess beatitude with Him. And so Christ must be preached, as we have said. Then, if he is believed to be the Son of God, reason concludes that He must be believed and that He

oboediendum et quod via sua est forma omnium ad aeternam vitam tendentium.

15   Diceres adhuc: Quomodo praedicabo populo Christum esse
viam seu ostium ad paradisum seu regnum vitae aut deliciarum?
Dices: Christus est via seu ostium ad immortalitatem, nam Christus fuit humilis, mitis, verax, iustus, misericors, oboediens et Patrem amans et eius praecepta servans usque ad mortem, et ita de
singulis virtutibus. Ipse autem dicit se viam, qui tales habuit altis-
simas et immortales virtutes. Quando igitur dicimus Christum
viam ad immortalitatem, intelligere debemus quod, qui viam virtutum tenet, Christum imitatur et sequitur et secum intrat in regnum immortalitatis.

16   Si igitur resolvis viam in iustitiam aut aliam virtutem, clare in-
telligis; nam tantum est dicere: Ego sum ostium seu via, ac si diceret: Ego sum iustitia seu veritas seu humilitas seu virtus ipsa quae
ducit ad pascua vitae, uti ait propheta: 'Omnes viae tuae veritas,' et
alibi: 'Universae viae tuae misericordia et veritas,' et Apocalypsis
15°: 'Iustae et verae sunt viae tuae.' Illae sunt viae aeternae, quia virtutum numquam deficientium. Unde qui habet veram iustitiam,
habet viam quae Christus est, ad salutem; et ita de omnibus virtutibus, quoniam Christus qui est via, est omnis virtus seu virtus
vera quae in se complicat omnes virtutes.

17   Diceres: Est igitur omnis iustus in via, quae Christus est? Dico:
Omnis iustus qui est vere iustus, est in via, quae Christus est. Iustitia autem vera non potest esse nisi apud fidelem Christianum,
qui solus habet iustitiam iustificantem. Christus enim qui creditur
esse redemptor et iustificatio peccatorum, est ille qui per gratiam
fideles ipsum imitantes iustificat. Opera enim nostra non iustifi-
cant nos sine fide, sed Christus per gratiam illos iustificat, qui ipsum sequuntur. Unde non est virtus vera quae sit via ad supremam
beatitudinem, nisi illa quae Christus est. Et ideo qui tenet Chris-

must be obeyed as he taught, and that His life is the form of those straining toward eternal life.

You might still say, "How shall I preach to the people that 15 Christ is the way or the gateway to paradise or to the kingdom of life or of delights?" Try saying, "Christ is the way or the gate to immortality, for Christ was humble, mild, truthful, just, merciful, obedient and loving towards His Father, obeying His commands even to death," and so on of the individual virtues. But He Who had those loftiest and immortal virtues says that He is the way. When, therefore, we call Christ the way to immortality, we should understand that whoever adheres to the way of the virtues imitates and follows Christ and enters with Him the kingdom of immortality.

If, therefore, you analyze the way to justice or to another virtue, 16 understand clearly that to say, *I am the gate* or *the way*, is tantamount to saying, I am justice, or truth, or humility, or that virtue which leads to the pasturage of life, as the prophet says, *All Your ways are truth*, and, elsewhere, *All Your ways are mercy and truth*.[15] And, in Apocalypse 15[:3], *Just and true are Thy ways*. Those are the eternal ways, because they are the ways of virtues that never fail. Hence whoever has true justice has life, which is Christ, unto salvation; and so of all the virtues, since Christ, Who is the way, is all virtue or the true virtue which enfolds all virtues in itself.

Perhaps you might say, "Is every just person on the way which 17 is Christ?" I say, "Every just person, who truly is just, is on the way which is Christ." Justice cannot be true except with the faithful Christian, who alone has the justice which justifies. Christ, Who is believed to be the redeemer and justification of sinners, is the one Who justifies the faithful who imitate Him through grace. Our works do not justify us without faith; but Christ justifies those who follow Him through grace. Therefore, there is no true virtue which is the way to supreme beatitude except that which is Christ. Therefore, the one who holds to Christ, although he might

tum, etsi videatur iustus et misericors, non tamen ex operibus suis iustificatur coram Deo. Non est enim iustitia nisi una, quae est iustificans ad immortalem beatitudinem, et est forma, quae dat esse iusto. Iustitia enim Filii Dei dat esse omni iusto, ut sit etiam filius Dei seu immortalis vitae. In conspectu enim Dei non iustificatur omnis vivens sine illa iustitia quae Christus est, in qua Deus habet complacentiam.

18   Prosequamur consequenter textum evangelii: Dicit enim: 'Ego sum pastor bonus.' Qui dixit se ostium, ille dicit se pastorem. Pastor igitur per se ipsum ad pascua ducit oves suas. Ponderemus verba: Dicit enim 'Ego sum.' 'Ego' proprie convenit Deo. Omnes enim rationales substantiae se nominant per 'ego,' sed soli Deo propriissime convenit; nam dicit meram substantiam ante omnem dependentiam sine accidente, genere vel specie. Unde non est extra Deum praecisa substantia, sed omnis talis potest esse substantialior. Solus Deus substantia substantialissima, quae non potest esse perfectior nec maior nec minor. Ideo soli Deo convenit 'ego.'

19   Sic etiam verbum 'sum' Deo convenit. Nulla enim creatura proprie dicere potest 'ego sum,' quia principio, a quo omne id quod est habet, ut sit, proprie convenit dicere 'ego sum.' Deus est ipsum absolutum esse, causa omnis esse.

20   De istis duobus, scilicet 'ego' et 'sum,' ait Deus per prophetam: 'Singulariter sum ego,' et Exodi 3°: 'Sum qui sum,' et 'qui est misit me.'

21   Pastor proprie Deus qui omnia pascit. Et similiter quod sit bonus, solus ille dicere potest, qui est Deus, nam 'nemo bonus nisi Deus,' Lucae ‹18°›. Simpliciter bonus per essentiam Deus est, per participationem creatura, sicut ignis simpliciter calidus, alia calida per participationem. Bonus pastor est Christus; pastor quidem quia caput ecclesiae, bonus vero quia Filius bonitatis sive Dei.

seem just and merciful, is nevertheless not justified before God by his works. There is only one justice which justifies for eternal beatitude, and that is the form which give being to the just person. The justice of the Son of God gives being to every just person, so that he too can be a son of God or of immortal life. In the sight of God no one living is justified without that justice which is Christ, with which God is pleased.

Let us follow now in order the text of the gospel. For He says, *I* 18 *am the good shepherd.* The one Who called Himself the gate calls Himself the shepherd. The shepherd therefore leads his sheep to pasture through Himself. Let us ponder the words he says: *I am. I* properly pertains to God. All rational substances name themselves using the word *I*, but it pertains most properly only to God, for it expresses pure substance prior to all dependency, without accident, genus or species. Hence there is no substance without remainder outside of God; but all extradeical beings are able to be more substantial. God alone is the utterly substantial substance, which cannot be more perfect, nor greater, nor lesser. Therefore, *I* pertains to God alone.

So too the word *am* pertains to God. No creature can properly 19 say, *I am*, because properly it pertains to the principle from which everything has its being to say, *I am.* God is that absolute being, the cause of every being.

God says of these two things, that is, *I* and *am*, through the 20 mouth of the prophet, *I alone am*,[16] and Exodus 3[:14], *I am Who I am*, and *He Who is has sent me.*

God, properly speaking, is the shepherd Who feeds all things. 21 Similarly only He Who is God can say that He is good, for *None is good but God alone*, Luke 18[:19]. God simply is good through His essence; the creature, by participation, just as fire simply is hot, others things are hot by participation. The good shepherd is Christ: he is a shepherd because he is the head of the Church, good because he is the Son of Goodness or of God.

22   Attendamus nunc quid requiratur ad bonum pastorem. Dicit enim: 'Bonus pastor animam suam dat pro ovibus suis.' Utique non potest esse pastor tantae bonitatis nisi Filius Dei; nam ita bonus non est nisi ille unus qui melior esse nequit.

23   Notate: dicit quod 'animam suam dat pro ovibus.' Se ipsum interimi sinit, ut pascat subditos. Mira bonitas pastoris dicentis: Vos subditi esuritis et egetis et deficitis penitus, nec est modus vos reficiendi nisi me faciam cibum. Moriar igitur, ut pasci possitis.

24   Notemus, fratres, quomodo creditum gregem pascere tenemur, non nostram, sed eius vitam quaerendo. Quomodo sumus boni pastores, qui non solum animam non damus pro ovibus, sed nullam etiam iniuriam propter eas pati volumus? Ne offendamus homines, negligimus gregem. Quis nostrum hodie pascit gregem verbo et exemplo, et quid patimur pro vita et pascentia eius? Nonne omnia operamur, non ut oves, sed nos ipsi potius vivamus? Nonne sumus mercenarii? Dicit enim Christus: 'Mercenarius' autem 'et qui non est pastor, cuius non sunt oves propriae, vidit lupum venientem et dimittit oves et fugit, et lupus rapit et dispergit oves. Mercenarius autem fugit, quia mercenarius est et non' spectat 'ad eum de ovibus.'

25   Hoc experimento manifeste constat, quam pauci sunt hodie pastores et quam multi mercenarii, quia veniente adversario tamquam illi qui sua quaerunt, paene omnes fugiunt. Sed si forent pastores, tunc haberent oves non ut alienas sed suas.

26   Minus fugit pastor ab ovibus quam pater a filiis aut mater ab infante uteri sui. Pastor enim plus affici debet Christianis sibi commissis, ut eos servet, quam parens. Quantum studium adhibuit pastor ille noster qui dixit, quod non perdidit quemquam sibi commissum.

Let us attend now to what is required in a good shepherd. He says, *The good shepherd giveth his life for his sheep.*[17] Assuredly there cannot be a shepherd of such goodness except the Son of God, for no one is so good except the one Who cannot be better.   22

Note: He says that He *giveth his life for his sheep.* He permitted Himself to be killed in order to feed His subjects. Wondrous is the goodness of the shepherd Who says, "You, my subjects, hunger and are needy and you fail utterly. There is no way to feed you unless I make Myself into food. I shall die, therefore, so that you may be fed."   23

Let us note, brothers, how we are bound to feed the flock entrusted to us, seeking not our but its life. How are we good shepherds, we who not only do not give up our lives for our sheep but do not even want to suffer any injury for them? We neglect the flock lest we offend men. Who among us feeds our flock by word and example, and what do we suffer for its life and feeding? Do we not do everything so that not the sheep, but rather we ourselves might live? Are we not hirelings? *For Christ says, But the hireling, and he that is not the shepherd, whose own the sheep are not, seeth the wolf coming, and leaveth the sheep, and flieth: and the wolf catcheth, and scattereth the sheep. The hireling fleeth, because he is an hireling, and careth not for the sheep.*[18]   24

By this test it is evident how few shepherds there are today and how many hirelings, because, when the foe comes, just like those who look after their own interests, almost all flee. But, if they were shepherds, then they would treat the sheep not like another's but like their own.   25

A shepherd flees less from his sheep than a father from his children or a mother from the babe of her womb. For the shepherd should be more bound to the Christians entrusted to him, so that he might serve them, than is a parent. How much zeal our Shepherd displayed Who said that He would not lose any of those entrusted to Him.[19]   26

27   Adhuc, fratres, non solum plures, qui nomen habent pastoris, sunt mercenarii se habendo, quasi ad eos non spectet de ovibus, sed sunt lupi rapaces. Non pascunt sed devorant. Rapiunt enim quaecumque habere possunt, etiam de quibus vivere deberent subditi, et quantum in ipsis est illos privant vita, quos pascere deberent. Dico etiam spiritualiter, nam quos verbo et doctrina pascere deberent, mala sua vita et exemplo atque blanditiis et complacentiis interimunt. Quid est, fratres, horribilius quam quod plures complacendo absolvunt a gravibus delictis, non aggravando, sed palpitando seu excusando, parva aut nulla paenitentia iniuncta, ut favorem et lucrum reportent? Utique mactant animas, ut devorent terrena.

28   Notemus, fratres, quae est proportio pastoris ad gregem: illa certe quae hominis ad ovem. Tanta debet esse discretio et sapientia in pastore, quod ipse super subditos emineat quasi homo super pecudes. Quae vigilia, quae assiduitas, quae circumspectio requiratur, ut quis sit pastor bonus animarum, docet diligentia pastoris ovium, qui est custos, medicus et director. Deinde nonne qui substantialiter pascit, Deus est qui dat iumentis escam ipsorum? Sic et pastor animarum dirigit gregem, ut ad interiora deserti perveniat, ubi pascatur a verbo Dei. Transeo multa quae ex his quisque facile intelligere poterit.

29   Docemur consequenter, quis est pastor bonus. Sic enim ait Christus: 'Ego sum pastor bonus et cognosco oves meas, et cognoscunt me meae. Sicut agnovit me Pater et ego agnosco Patrem.' Utique non est nisi unus bonus pastor, qui est sapientia Dei Patris, ut non erret, et est homo, ut ex sua infirmitate iudicet quomodo infirmum hominem pascat.

30   Christus est pastor pastorum. Ipse est lex et lux pastorum. Ipse est via pascendi et vita quae finis pascentiae et est veritas perma-

Besides, brothers, not only are many of those who bear the   27
name shepherd hirelings, acting as if the sheep did not belong to
them, but they are ravening wolves. They do not feed, but they
devour. They carry off whatever they can, even from those who
should live as their subjects; and, as far as they can, they, who
should feed them, deprive them of life. I speak in a spiritual sense,
for those whom they should feed with the word and doctrine, they
destroy with their bad life and example, and with flattery and favors. What, brothers, is more horrible than that they complacently
absolve many of grave sins, not rebuking them, but stroking (or
excusing) them, enjoining little or no penance on them so that
they might gain favor and profit? Certainly they rend souls so that
they might devour earthly things.

Let us note, brothers, what is the proportion of the shepherd to   28
his flock. Surely it is that of a man to a sheep. There should be
such discretion and wisdom in the shepherd that he stands out
from his subjects like a man from herd animals. The diligence of a
shepherd of sheep, who is a guardian, physician and leader,
teaches what wakefulness, what continual attention, what circum-
spection is required to be a good shepherd of souls. Then too, is
not God, Who feeds substantially, the one Who gives their food
to the beasts? Thus the shepherd of souls leads the flock so that it
may come to the inner parts of the desert, where it may be fed
upon the Word of God. (I will pass over many things which anyone easily can learn from these reflections.)

Next we are taught Who is the good shepherd. For Christ says,   29
*I am the good shepherd; and I know Mine, and Mine know Me. As the
Father knoweth Me, I too know the Father.*[20] Certainly there is only
one good shepherd, Who is the Wisdom of God the Father, so
that He err not, and is man, so that He might judge from His
infirmity how to feed frail mankind.

Christ is the shepherd of the shepherds. He is the law and the   30
light of the shepherds. He is the way of feeding and the life, which

nens. In omnibus ipse primatum tenet. Sed sic fuit dominus et magister quod 'humilis' omnium minister. Ita quidem minister quod etiam ultimum ministerium, scilicet pedes, extremam hominis partem, lavando, perfecit. Non est pastor bonus nisi in cuius summa praesidentia coincidit summa humilitas, et in summa eius iustitia misericordia, et in summa eius clementia disciplina et correctio, et ita de reliquis, ut sit in ipso omnis virtus quae est in coincidentia extremorum, et aequalitas essendi, ut omnes formam in ipso habeant eius, qui se omnibus conformat, ut ad aequalitatem sui omnes attrahat.

31   Attendamus quomodo primo et ante omnia Christus se dicit pastorem bonum et cognoscere oves suas. Solus ille pastor qui est et dator vitae, cognoscit, quibus paratum est regnum ab initio et qui sunt praedestinati. Et illi ipsum ut pastorem cognoscunt, quia ut Filium Dei audiunt. Alii pastores non cognoscunt in veritate ut Christus, sed in coniectura, et quanto magis studium adhibent ut cognoscant, tanto christiformiores.

32   Cognitio igitur arguit pastorem bonum. Oportet medicum cognoscere illum, qui subditus est curae suae. Oportet pastorem cognoscere oves, ut sciat quomodo pasci debeant. Non cognitione vaga publica et coniecturali, sed vera et secreta, sic scilicet cognoscere sicut pater filium. Et haec cognitio subinfert cognitionem ovium, scilicet qui tenentur cognoscere pastorem ut filii patrem.

33   In cognitione pastorali est coincidentia consideranda. Sicut enim in ordine illo divini principatus, quae hierarchia dicitur, coincidit in descensu principatus ascensus subiectionis — nam haec coincidentia est medium conexionis, in quo subsistit ecclesia — sic in cognitione, nam hoc est cognoscere oves in pastore ut pastore,

is the end of feeding; and He is the enduring truth.[21] He holds the primacy in all things. But he was the lord and master in this way because he was the humble servant of all. So much was he a servant that he even performed the ultimate service, that is, washing the feet, the lowest part of a man. There is no good shepherd except the One in Whom supreme humility coincides with supreme rule, and mercy with supreme justice, and discipline and correction with His supreme clemency, and so of the rest, so that every virtue, which is in the coincidence of opposites, is in Him; and equality of being, so that all might have His form in him, Who conforms Himself to all, so that He might draw all things to His equality.

Let us note how Christ, first and before all, calls Himself the 31 good shepherd and says that He knows His sheep. He alone, Who is the shepherd, Who is the giver of life, knows for whom the kingdom is prepared from the beginning,[22] and who are the predestined. And they know Him as the shepherd, because they hear the word of God. Other shepherds do not know in the truth as Christ does, but by means of conjecture; and the more they exert themselves to know, the more Christiform they are.

Therefore, knowledge reveals the good shepherd. A physician 32 needs to know the person subject to his care. It is necessary for a shepherd to know his sheep, so that they may know how to be fed. Not by vague public and conjectural knowledge but by true and secret knowledge, that is, as the Father knows the Son. And this knowledge entails knowledge of the sheep, that is, of those who are bound to know the shepherd as sons know their father.

Coincidence must be considered in pastoral knowledge. Just 33 as in that order of the divine principate which is called hierarchy the ascent of the subject coincides with the descent of the principate — for this coincidence is the medium of the connection in which the Church subsists — so too in knowledge. For the sheep knowing the shepherd as shepherd is the shepherd knowing his

quod est cognoscere pastorem in subditis ut subditis. Si cognoscit pastor pascendos paterne, cognoscunt pascendi pastorem filialiter. Quis est pater, qui est adeo negligens, quod non cognoscit filios? Et quis filius adeo negligens, quod non cognoscit patrem suum, illum scilicet, qui se sibi ut patrem ostendit?

34   Quanta debet esse amicitia inter pastorem et subditos, ex hoc docemur; nam prima amicitia est patris ad filium, quae tenet principatum amicitiarum. Nulla autem talis est, si non praecedit cognitio, scilicet quod se cognoscant. Cognitio igitur quae initio praecedit amicitiam, quae esse debet prima et maxima, debet esse ut patris et filii cognitio. Pastor igitur pater subditi filii, et esse debent subditi ut unus filius, quia faciunt ex unitate unum corpus mysticum pastoris. Quemlibet enim ex subditis ut unicum debet habere filium.

35   Et quomodo debet esse pastor pater? Certe ut Deus pater est, qui sic est pater quod, nulla paternitas potest esse ei aequalis, quia omnis paternitas alia minor est illa. Nam de se et sua essentia sic generat filium, quod ei totam tribuit essentiam, nihil sibi reservando, quod non tribuat filio. Sic et Filius Dei est ita filius, quod nullus filius potest ei esse aequalis. Est enim omnis filius minus filius sui patris quam Filius Dei. Pastor vero sic debet esse pater sicut Pater caelestis et subditus sic subditus sicut Filius Dei Deo.

36   Dixit autem magister, quomodo cognitionis Patris et Filii est cognitio pastoris et ovium similitudo; nam Deus Pater cognoscendo generat Filium. Sic pastor de supremitate cognitionis quae est fides, debet generare filium. Sicut enim una est fides baptizantis et baptizati, sic in spiritu pastoris debet esse fides, in qua Christus, quae debet generare filios spirituales aequales, scilicet generando de fide sua fidem in spiritu subditi, ut formetur in fideli

subjects as subjects. If the shepherd knows how to feed paternally, those who are to be fed know the shepherd filially. What father is so negligent that he does not know his sons, and what son is so negligent that he does not know his father, that is, the one who shows himself to be his father?

We are taught by this how great the friendship should be between shepherd and subjects. For the first friendship is that of a father for his son, which holds first place among friendships. However, there is none such if knowledge does not precede, that is, that they know one another. The knowledge, therefore, that initially precedes the friendship which should be the first and the greatest should be like the knowledge of father and son. Therefore, the shepherd should be a father to his subject son; and the subjects should be like one son, because from their unity they make up the single mystical body of the shepherd. He should regard any of his subjects as an only son.

And how should the shepherd be a father? Certainly as God is a father, Who is a father such that no fatherhood can be equal it, because every other fatherhood is lesser. For He so begets the Son of Himself and His essence that He gives Him His entire essence, reserving nothing for Himself that He does not give to the Son. So too the Son of God is a son to whom no son can be equal. Every son, then, is less the son of his father than is the Son of God. The shepherd, however, should be a father like the celestial Father; and a subject should be subject like the Son of God to God.

The Master, however, says that the knowledge of the pastor and the flock is a similitude of the knowledge of the Father and the Son. For God the Father generates the Son by knowing. Thus the shepherd from the supremacy of his knowledge, which is faith, should beget a son. Just as there is one faith shared by baptizer and baptized, so should there be faith in the spirit of the shepherd—faith in Christ—which should beget equal spiritual sons, that is, by begetting faith in the spirit of the subject from his own

34

35

36

Christus. Ecce pastor bonus habet in se per fidem pastorem bonum, scilicet Christum, et generat in subdito per fidem pastorem, scilicet Christum. Pastor quando via agnitionis generat Christum in subdito, facit quod subditus in se habet pastorem, qui ipsum regit et pascit. Subditus enim semper secum habet pastorem, ad quem si respicit, non deviat sed semper ad pascua eius medio pervenit.

37 Non debet cessare pastor a generando temporaliter, sed semper generare verbo doctrinae Christum, quousque formetur aeternaliter in resurrectione. Quamdiu enim vivimus, non est cessandum. Sicut enim Pater Deus in aeternitate semper generat Filium et non cessat esse Pater generans Filium, sic pastor in hoc mundo in tempore cessare non debet.

38 Attente considera quomodo Christus est 'omnia in omnibus': in pastore est ut pastor, in subdito ut subditus et oboediens. In pastore Christus est verbum Dei docens praeesse, in subdito verbum Dei docens parere et subici, in divite docens humilitatem et misericordiam, in infirmo patientiam, in iudice iustitiam, et ita de omnibus. Nam quidquid virtutis est, docet hoc verbum. Et pro exemplo doctrinae producit humanitatem suam, ut homo in ipsam respiciat et sic verbo et exemplo pascatur.

39 Consequenter consideremus quae ad pastorem requirantur. Primo, ut dictum est, cognitio, deinde facere, ut sequitur. Ait enim Christus: 'Et animam meam ponam pro ovibus meis.' Intelligo animam iuxta officium vivificationis, uti animal vivum ab anima dicitur. Dicit 'pro ovibus meis'; nam hoc est primo necessarium, ut oves sint Christi pastoris, alias inutiliter poneret pro eis animam. Ideo sequitur: 'Et alias oves habeo, quae non sunt ex hoc ovili, et illas oportet me adducere, et vocem meam audient, et fiet unum

faith, so that Christ may be formed in the believer. Behold, the good shepherd has in himself the Good Shepherd, that is, Christ; and he begets in the subject through faith the Shepherd, that is, Christ. When the shepherd begets Christ in the subject via knowing, he causes the subject to have in himself the Shepherd Who rules and feeds him. For the subject always has the Shepherd with him. If he looks toward Him, he does not stray, but by means of Him he always comes to pasture.

The shepherd should not cease from begetting temporally, but 37 he should always be in the process of begetting Christ by the word of his teaching, until he is formed eternally in the Resurrection. As long as we live, this must not cease. Just as God the Father begets the Son in eternity forever and does not cease to be the Father begetting the Son, so the shepherd in this world should not cease [begetting Christ] in time.

Consider attentively how Christ is *all in all,*[23] in the shepherd as 38 a shepherd, in the subject as a subject and as obedient. In the shepherd Christ is the Word of God teaching how to preside; in the subject, the Word of God teaching how to obey and be subject; in the rich man, teaching humility and mercy; in the infirm, patience; in the judge, justice; and so of the rest. For this Word teaches whatever belongs to virtue. And He brings forth His humanity as a teaching example so that man may look to that humanity and so be fed by word and example.

Next let us consider what is required of shepherds. As it is 39 said, first knowledge, then action, as follows. Christ says, *I lay down My life for My sheep.*[24] I understand "life" [anima, or soul] in connection with the function of giving life, as a living creature is said to be alive from his life [or soul]. He says *for My sheep.* For it is necessary, first, that the sheep belong to Christ the shepherd. Otherwise He would lay down His life for them uselessly. Thus there follows, *And other sheep I have, that are not of this fold: them also I must bring, and they shall hear My voice, and there shall be one fold and*

ovile et unus pastor.' Pastor auget gregem et alias oves habet elec-
tas nondum adductas quas adducet. Et tunc adducuntur, quando
audiunt vocem pastoris; sequuntur enim vocem, si audiunt inter-
naliter. Et tunc ex omnibus fiet unum ovile et unus pastor.

40   Deinde sequitur: 'Propterea me Pater diligit, quia pono animam meam' pro ovibus meis, 'ut iterum sumam eam.' Quid hoc
est aliud nisi quod nemo diligitur a Deo Patre, qui est pastor, nisi
sit verus et bonus pastor? Deus non diligit mendacium et malitiam, quia ipsa bonitas. Sed verus pastor et bonus extra ipsum
pascere non habet vitam, sicut nec visus extra videre et intellectus
extra intelligere. Unde pascentia est forma divina dans pastori vi-
tale et delectabile esse. Ideo nihil est ei carius illa forma, immo
omnem vitam sensibilem animalem sive animam atque omne esse
et quidquid dici potest pro nihilo habet, ut maneat pastor bonus.

41   Sed attendamus quare superius dixit primo: 'Bonus pastor animam suam ponit pro ovibus suis.' Deinde subsumit: 'Ego sum
pastor bonus' et cetera 'et animam meam pono pro ovibus.' Nunc
tertio addicit: 'Pater me diligit, quia pono animam meam pro ovibus meis, ut iterum sumam eam. Nemo eam tollit a me, sed ego
pono eam a me ipso. Potestatem habeo ponendi eam, et potestatem habeo iterum sumendi eam. Hoc mandatum accepi a Patre
meo.' Ille est admirandus pastor, a quo nemo potest animam tollere, et tamen quia est verissimus et optimus pastor, ponit animam
suam, ut iterum sumat eam. Et haec potestas in eo est mandatum
Patris.

42   Quod nota: quoniam impossibile non praecipitur a Deo, ideo
praeceptum eius dat etiam potestatem parendi, puta si praeciperet
homini, ut volaret, daret eo ipso potestatem, per quam posset. Similiter quia dat potestatem, quod possumus esse filii Dei recipiendo in nos Christum, qui est forma filiationis, ideo etiam man-

one shepherd.[25] The shepherd enlarges the flock and has other sheep chosen but not yet brought into it, which He will bring in; and they are brought in when they have heard the shepherd's voice, for they follow his voice if they hear it within them. And then one fold and one shepherd will be made of them all.

Then follows, *Wherefore doth the Father love Me: because I lay down My life, so that I may take it again.*[26] What can this mean but that no one who is a shepherd is loved by God the Father unless he is a true and good shepherd? God does not love falsehood and malice, because He is goodness itself. But the true and good shepherd does not have life apart from His feeding, just as there is no sight apart from seeing, nor intellect apart from understanding. Therefore, feeding is a divine form giving vital and delectable being to the shepherd. Therefore, nothing is dearer than that form, indeed he holds as nothing all sensible life, animal or animate, and all being and whatever can be said, in order that he may remain a good shepherd. 40

But let us note why He said above, first, *The good shepherd giveth his life for his sheep*, and then added, *I am the good shepherd.*[27] Now He adds, in the third place, *Wherefore doth the Father love Me: because I lay down My life, so that I may take it again. No man taketh it away from Me: but I lay it down: and I have power to take it up again. This commandment have I received of My Father.*[28] He is a wonderful shepherd from Whom no one can take away His life; and, nevertheless, because He is the truest and best shepherd, He lays down His life so that He may take it up again. And this power is in Him by the Father's command. 41

Note that, since God does not command the impossible, His command thus confers the power to fulfill it. For example, if He were to command a man to fly, He would give him the power by means of which he could do it. Similarly, because He confers the power that we can be sons of God by receiving in ourselves Christ, Who is the form of divine sonship, He thus also commands that 42

dat, ut faciamus. Nam eo ipso quod dat potestatem, etiam praecipit et mandat. Sicut enim frustra praeciperet, nisi adderet potestatem adimplendi, sic frustra daret potestatem, nisi etiam mandaret illam adimpleri. Deus nihil agit frustra. Ideo Pater diligit Christum, quia ponit animam suam, ut iterum sumat eam.

43 Exponit Iohannes in canonica sua, I^{ae} Iohannis 3°, quomodo ponere animam suam intelligit dicens: 'In hoc cognovimus caritatem Dei, quoniam ipse pro nobis animam suam posuit.' Pastoris ut pastoris bonitas est plus diligere gregem quam se, ideo ponere animam suam (hoc est omne quod habet) pro ovibus, est praeferre gregem animae. Unde si pastor non facit ultimum, scilicet quod det animam pro liberatione gregis, etiam si subditi essent in vinculis Luciferi in inferno, non est pastor bonus.

44 Christus descendit ad infernum, ut gregem suum de vinculis eius liberaret, ut nuper aliqui vestrum a me audiverunt. Sic Moyses pastor dicebat: 'Dimitte eis hanc noxam aut dele me de libro, in quo me scripsisti.' Et David ad angelum dicebat, ut ovibus innocentibus parceret et in ipsum gladium verteret, quia peccasset. Paulus pastor optabat 'anathema' esse 'pro fratribus,' sicut Christus factus est anathema sive maledictum pro nobis, quia 'maledictus omnis qui pendet in cruce,' ut nos a maledicto redimeret.

45 Et nota quod pastor bonus debet pascere sicut agnus paschalis qui dat animam suam, ut vivant filii Israel. Sic Christus verus agnus dedit animam seu vitam suam, ut nos vivamus. Sed agnus per sensibilem mortem transit in rationalem, quando convertitur in homine in naturam aliti. Non sic ponit Christus animam, quam nominavit spiritum, dum obiret et diceret: 'In manus tuas commendo spiritum meum,' ut sumat aliam meliorem animam seu meliorem spiritum, sed ut iterum sumat illam, quia ponit animam

we do so. For, by the very fact that He gives us power, He also orders and commands. Just as He would order in vain unless He added the power to comply, so He would give power in vain unless He also commanded that compliance. God does nothing in vain. Therefore, the Father loves Christ, because He lays down His life so that He may take it up again.

John expounds in his canonical letter, 1 John 3[:16] how he understood the laying down of His life, saying, *In this we have known the charity of God, because He hath laid down His life for us.* The goodness of a shepherd as shepherd is in loving his flock more than himself; therefore, in laying down his life, that is, all that he has, for his sheep, he is preferring the flock to his own life. Hence, if the shepherd does not do the ultimate thing, that is, give his life for the liberation of the flock, even if his subjects were in Lucifer's bonds in Hell, he is not a good shepherd.

Christ descended into Hell to liberate His flock from its chains, as some of you heard from me not long ago. Thus Moses the shepherd said, *Either forgive them this trespass, or strike me out of the book Thou hast written.*[29] And David said to the angel that it should spare the innocent lambs and turn the sword upon him, because he had sinned.[30] The shepherd Paul wished to be *anathema for his brethren,*[31] just as Christ was made anathema or accursed for our sakes,[32] because *Cursed every is one that hangeth on a cross,*[33] so that He might redeem us from the accursed one.

And note that the good shepherd should feed like the paschal lamb, who gives his life that Israel's children might live. So Christ, the true lamb, gives His soul or life so that we might live. But the lamb passes by way of sensible death into a rational one, when it is converted in a man in the nature of something eaten. Not so did Christ lay down His life, which He called His spirit, when he met [death] and said, *Into Thy hands I commend My spirit,*[34] that He might taken up another, better soul or better spirit, but so that He might take up that [same] soul again, because He lays down His

515

seu spiritum vitae, ut pascantur animae vita spiritus sui, non ut transeat in naturam aliti, sed sumat iterum animam seu vitam, in quam transivit qui recepit.

46   Sicut cum sol splendorem mittit in aërem, non ut convertatur in tenebram aëris, sed ut ad se convertat tenebram, ut sic sumat iterum in se cum lucro et fructu emissum splendorem, sic facit pastor illuminans subditos ponendo fidem, quae est vita iusti — 'iustus enim ex fide vivit' —, in cordibus subditorum, ut sint credentes in ipso unum, et coincidit in ponere iteratio sumptionis. Et sic bonus pastor qui Christum induit, ponit spiritum vitae seu animam continue, ut iterum sumat, ut cum lucro sumat eam. Et illum Pater ideo diligit, quia pascit oves suas.

47   Hunc 'spiritum vitae,' qui est 'spiritus Christi' seu sapientiae et veritatis, quod idem est, quem in se habet pastor, nemo potest artare, quia est spiritus libertatis, seu violenter tollere ab eo, sed ipse potest per verbum a se ipso ponere seu emittere, discipulos suos instruendo vitaliter, et iterum sumere ad vivificandum se ipsum. Qui enim alios docet per verbum Dei, potest et se ipsum per idem denuo sumptum verbum instruere.

48   Attendamus, fratres, quomodo praeceptum pastoris boni, descripti etiam in Veteri Testamento, qui promissus est, non potuit verificari nisi in uno pastore, qui est Christus. Nam quis est pastor ita bonus, quod se det in mortem pro ovibus, nisi ille solum, qui non potest esse melior? Et hic est Christus. Errant itaque illi, qui non putant scripturas de Christo loqui nisi ubi de rege Messia redemptore mentio habetur. Immo et omnis scriptura quae visitato-

life, or the spirit of life, so that lives are fed with the life of His spirit, not so that He might pass into the nature of being eaten, but that he might take up His soul or life again into which he who received Him passes.

Just as when the sun diffuses its splendor through the air, not so that it may be converted into the darkness of the air, but so that it may convert the darkness into itself and thus take up again into itself the splendor emitted with increase and fruit, so the shepherd acts to illuminate and instill faith in the hearts of his subjects, faith which is the life of the just — *The just man liveth by faith*[35] — so that those who believe in Him are one; and the repetition of feeding coincides with laying down life. And thus the good shepherd who puts on Christ lays down the spirit of life or his soul continually, so that he may take it up again, so that he may take it up again with increase. And, therefore, the Father loves him, because he feeds his sheep. 46

This *spirit of life*, which is the *spirit of Christ*,[36] or of wisdom and truth, which is the same thing, which the shepherd has in himself, no one can curtail, because it is the spirit of liberty, nor violently take away from him; but he can by means of the Word lay it down or diffuse it by himself, instructing his subjects vitally, and take it up again in order to vivify himself. Whoever teaches others by means of God's Word can instruct himself by means of the same Word received anew. 47

Let us take heed, brothers, how the command of the good shepherd, described even in the Old Testament, Who is the promised one, cannot be found true except in the one shepherd, Who is Christ. For who is so good a shepherd that he gives himself for his sheep except He alone Who cannot be better? And this is Christ. And so they err who do not think the Scriptures speak of Christ except where mention is made of the king, the Messiah. Indeed every Scripture which promises a visitor, a shep- 48

rem et pastorem et redemptorem et illuminatorem et vivificatorem
atque salvatorem promittit, de Christo loquitur.

49   Christus enim est ille promissus pastor qui cognoscit illos, qui
sunt sui, et illi audiunt illum ut Christum Filium Dei, et illis dat
vitam aeternam, et non peribunt in aeternum, ut sequitur in eodem capitulo. Nam nulla est potentia, quae possit rapere de manu
illius pastoris gregem, quia quid Pater dedit Christo maius est omnibus. Si Pater dedit sapientiam aliquibus, sapientia, quam dedit
Christo, maior est omnibus, quia non potest esse maior. Si virtutem dedit, maior est virtus, quam dedit Christo; si potestatem,
maior illa, quam dedit Christo. Nam esse Filium Dei est maius
omnibus, per quem Pater se revelat.

50   Filius est revelatio Patris. Ideo dicitur 'imago' et 'figura substantiae eius,' quia per ipsum accedit omnis intellectualis natura ad
invisibilem Deum, quia est notitia sive via sive sapientia sive veritas et cetera huiusmodi, quae revelant Deum Patrem. Ipse est medium, per quod Pater creator omnia operatur, quia omnia operatur propter se ipsum, ut ostendatur gloria eius et cognoscatur.
Ideo Filius est verbum, per quod se ostendit Pater creando et ope-
rando. Unde Christus se dicit Filium, quia Pater per ipsum opera
facit; quae opera cum sint creatoris et fiunt per ipsum, ideo concludit ipse se esse legatum et Filium Dei.

51   Unde ex hoc intellige, quomodo tibi formabis conceptum de
Christo, quoniam ille est Christus, cui Pater id dedit, quod est
maius omnibus. Notitia enim Dei est maius omnibus, et ideo
quamdiu exspectabatur maius donum, quam aliquis habuit, quia
nemo habuit donum, quo non possit dari maius, tamdiu exspectabatur Christus, ut donum Dei veniret ad ultimam perfectionem.
Et hoc est donum sublationis ignorantiae Dei, ut ait Paulus
Actuum 17°.

herd, a redeemer, an illuminator, a life-giver and a savior speaks of Christ.

Christ then is that promised Shepherd Who knows His own; and they heed Christ as the Son of God, and He gives them eternal life, and they shall not perish forever, as follows in the same chapter.[37] For there is no power which can snatch the flock from the hand of that Shepherd, because what the Father gave Christ is greater than all. If the Father gave wisdom to some, the wisdom which He gave to Christ is greater than that of all, because it cannot be greater. If He gave strength, the strength which He gave to Christ is greater. If He gave power, that which He gave Christ is greater. For to be the Son of God is a greater thing than everything, the Son through whom the Father reveals Himself. 49

The Son is the revelation of the Father. Thus He is called "the image" and "the figure of His substance,"[38] because, by means of Him, every intellectual nature reaches the invisible God, because He is awareness or the way or wisdom or truth, and other things of this sort, which reveal God the Father. He is the means through which the Father, the creator, works all things, because He works all things for His own sake, so that His glory might be revealed and known. Therefore, the Son is the Word through which the Father shows Himself by creating and working. Hence Christ calls Himself the Son, because the Father did all his works by means of Him. These works are the Creator's and are done by Him, so He proves that He is the ambassador and God's Son. 50

Hence you can understand from this how you will form for yourself a concept of Christ, since He is the Christ to Whom the Father gave the gift of being greater than all. The awareness of God is greater than all other things; and thus, as long as a greater gift than anyone had is expected, because no one had the gift than which nothing greater could be given, so long Christ was expected, so that God's gift would come to final perfection. And this is the gift of taking away ignorance of God, as Paul says in Acts 17[:30]. 51

52   Considera haec attente, scilicet Christum esse notitiam sive
scientiam aut cognitionem Dei, et intelligere poteris evangelium
Iohannis et Paulum et alios. Et tunc etiam intelliges, quomodo
Christus dicit: 'Ego et Pater unum sumus,' quia scientia et scitum
sunt unum, et scientia in scito et scitum in scientia. A scito et
scientia procedit scire, quod similiter est unum. Scitum, scientia et
scire unum sunt in essentia, licet scitum non sit scientia nec scire.
Coincidunt autem in essentia, quia non est aliud scitum a scientia
et a scire in intellectualibus.

53   Dubitaret forte aliquis, quomodo intelligatur, quod pastor se
det etiam ad mortem et poenas inferni pro grege suo, cum nemo
teneatur dare animam suam rationalem in mortem pro vita alterius. Dico sic hoc intelligendum, quod pastor non debet ad se respicere, dummodo qualitercumque in pascendo ea faciat, quae
Deus praecipit pastori bono, etiam si propterea conciperet se in inferno damnandum. Nam si quis tantae caritatis esset, ille utique
non esset damnatus in inferno. Iustus enim in inferno non habet
poenam iniustorum. Quare pastor quanto fuerit maioris caritatis
et paratior magis pati pro grege, tanto maiorem gloriam assseque-
tur. Si igitur se non curat vivere, dummodo subditi vivant, qui
sunt corpus eius mysticum, tunc quanto hoc fuerit verius, tanto
melius vivet, quia non solum ipse vivet in subditis, sed ipsi vivent
in eo, qui suam vitam obtulit pro eis. Ac si caput habens debilia
membra omnia patitur, ut membra sua sanentur, tunc ex sanitate
membrorum, quae per eius passionem recuperata est, ipse homo
etiam in capite in sanitate et vita augetur, et caput per tristitiam et
passionem non reperit nisi gaudium.

Consider these things attentively, that is, that Christ is the   52
awareness or knowledge or cognition of God, and you will be able
to understand the Gospel of John, and Paul, and the others. And
then too you will understand how Christ says, *I and the Father are
one*,[39] because knowledge and the thing known are one, and knowledge is in the thing known, and the thing known is in knowledge.
From knowledge and the thing known proceeds [the act of] knowing, which likewise is one. The thing known, knowledge and
knowing are one in essence, although the thing known is not
knowledge or knowing. They coincide, however, in essence, because the thing known is nothing other than knowledge and
knowing in intellectual matters.

Perhaps someone might doubt how it may be understood that a   53
shepherd may give himself for his flock even to death and the
pains of Hell, since no one could be obligated to give his rational
soul for the life of another. I say this should be understood as follows. A pastor ought not to consider his own situation so long as
in feeding in one way or another he does what God commands a
good shepherd to do, even if he could imagine himself condemned
to Hell on that account. For if someone possessed such great charity, he certainly would not be condemned to Hell. For the just
man does not suffer the pains of unjust men in Hell. Hence the
more charity a shepherd has and the readier he is to suffer for his
flock, the greater will be the glory he will attain. If, therefore, he
does not care whether he lives as long as his subjects live, the
members of his mystical body, then the truer this will be, the
better will he live, because not only will he live in his subjects, but
they will live in him who offered his life for them. And if the head,
having infirm members, suffers all things so that his members are
healed, then from the health of his members that have recovered
by means of his suffering, that man too will know increase as head
in his health and life; and the head will find only joy through his
sorrow and suffering.

54   Quanto enim animam suam seu vitam magis perdit propter caritatem, tanto magis invenit. Nam quanto magis perdit ex caritate,
tanto caritas maior; quanto caritas maior, tanto vita spiritus maior,
cum caritas sit vita spiritus intellectualis. Nam ex notitia Dei caritas procedit, quae est motus delectabilis seu vita, gaudium scilicet
de apprehensione. Qui enim Deum noscit, non haesitat sibi usque
ad ultimum oboediendum, et operatur omnia ex caritate. Unde actus, per quem caritas ostenditur maior, ostendit maiorem vitam in
spiritu.

55   Sic spiritus qui se dat ad humilitatem ultimam, ut quantum in
eo est, in nihilum resolvatur propter caritatem, ille dum videtur ire
in nihilum, transit in perfectius esse. Et propterea Christus dicebat
superius, quod pastor ponit animam, ut iterum sumat. Nam ponere vitam sive deponere, illud non est perdere, sed invenire, non
est minuere, sed augere, quia et proposito et voluntate sua moria-
tur, tamen sic mori est vivere.

56   Ecce immortalitatem spiritus, qui moriendo invenit vitam.
Omne id quod moriendo vivit, deficere nequit, sed transit de
morte ad vitam, scilicet ad conformitatem Dei, 'qui solus immortalitatem inhabitat.'

57   Ex quo igitur experimur in nobis spiritum intellectualem esse,
qui ad absolute et per essentiam bonum, verum, iustum et cetera
quae sunt nomina Dei, inclinatur, et Deum tanto plus diligit,
quanto eius maiorem notitiam habuerit. Diligit, quia notitiam ipsam rationali dilectione ⟨habet⟩, quae est concreata sibi et naturalis. Tunc scimus spiritum nostrum capacem vitae aeternae; quae
vita non est nisi caritas Dei.

58   Et nota quod Christus, cum non sit nisi verbum Dei Patrem
ostendens, ideo ipse est cuius doctrina subinfert spiritum vitae.
Nam ex notitia Dei Patris, quam Christus revelat in nobis, procedit caritas a Patre et notitia eius, quae est verbum seu Filius eius,

The more he loses his soul or life on account of charity, the 54
more he will find it. For the more he loses for the sake of charity,
the great the charity; the greater the charity, the greater the life of
his spirit, since charity is the life of the intellectual spirit. For charity proceeds from knowing God, which is delectable motion or
life, or in other words the joy that comes from comprehending.
For whoever knows God does not shrink from ultimate obedience;
and he does all things for charity's sake. Hence the act through
which charity is shown to be greater shows greater life in the
spirit.

So the spirit which gives itself over to ultimate humility, so 55
that — as far as it can — it is reduced to nothing for charity's sake,
when it seems to pass into nothing, passes into more perfect being.
And on this account Christ said above that the shepherd lays
down his life in order to take it up again. For to lay it down or put
it down is not to lose but to find, it is not to diminish but to increase, because he dies for a purpose and of his own will; nevertheless, to die thus is to live.

Behold the immortality of the spirit which by dying finds life. 56
All that which lives by dying is unable to fail; but it passes from
death to life, that is, to conformity with God, *Who alone inhabits
immortality.*[40]

From this, then, we experience in ourselves the intellectual 57
spirit, inclined to what is absolutely and essentially good, true, just
etc., which are the names of God; and the more he loves God the
greater will be his knowledge of Him. He loves God because he
has that knowledge through rational love, which co-creates itself
and is natural. Thus do we know that our spirit is capable of eternal life, a life which does not exist except as the charity of God.

And note that Christ, since He does not exist except as God's 58
Word, revealing the Father, so exists Himself as the one by whose
teaching the spirit of life is added. For from knowledge of God the
Father, which God reveals to us, charity proceeds from the Father

et in nostrum diffunditur spiritum et est vivificans eum, quia ipsum movet motione gaudiosa quae est vita, quia est motus cordialis sive centralis amorosus causatus a Deo amato, qui est intra ipsum mansionem faciens.

59 Verbum igitur illuminans animam, ut iustitiam et veritatem, quae sunt quaedam nomina seu notitia Dei, cognoscat, Christus est, qui est notitia revelans Patrem. Ideo Christus spiritum nostrum parat ad receptionem spiritus seu caritatis Dei, quem Deus Pater Christi mittit in nomine seu notitia sui, quae Filius est, et in nomine Filii, scilicet notitia notitiae, in spiritum intellectualem, et Christus dat illum, sicut notitia boni influit eius amorem. Unde patet Christum Patris revelatorem sive clarificatorem mittere Spiritum vitae sive caritatem in corda fidelium, quia in Filio Pater. In notitia quae Filius est, est Pater qui noscitur seu revelatur. Et tam ex noto quam notitia oritur caritas.

60 Ac si absoluta pulchritudo quae in his, quae non sunt pulchra per essentiam sed participationem, per rationalem spiritum amatur, Filium suum unigenitum de essentia sua mitteret ad revelandum pulchritudinem sive Patrem suum in sua veritate et essentia. Iste averteret rationalem spiritum ab amore participatae et corruptibilis pulchritudinis ad amorem seu caritatem absolutae et immortalis pulchritudinis, cuius natura est, quod numquam potest satis amari, quia semper amabilior est quam ametur.

61 Ideo spiritus ille qui ex amore in amando fortificatur, pascitur et crescit, unitive seu adhaesive aeternam laetitiam adipiscitur. Et sicut de pulchritudine dixi, ita de sapientia aut iustitia aut veritate concipe, quia sunt nomina Dei, qui est ipsa absoluta amabilitas quae dicitur et bonitas, veritas, sapientia et cetera, quae amantur

and His knowledge, which is the Word or His Son, and He is diffused into our spirit, making it live, because He moves it with a joyful motion, which is life, because it is a heart-felt or inner amorous motion caused by a beloved God, Who is within it, building his mansion.[41]

Therefore, the Word, illuminating the soul, like justice and   59 truth, which are names as it were or the awareness of God, is Christ, Who is the awareness revealing the Father. Therefore, Christ prepares our spirit to receive the spirit or charity of God, which God the Father of Christ sends into his intellectual spirit in His [own] name or in the awareness of Himself, which is His Son, and in the name of the Son, that is, in the awareness of awareness; and Christ gives [the spirit of God], just as awareness of the good flows into His love. Hence it is clear that Christ, the one who reveals or illuminates the Father, sends the spirit of life or charity into the hearts of the faithful, because the Father is in the Son. In awareness, which is the Son, is the Father, Who is known or revealed. And charity originates from awareness and that of which one is aware.

And if absolute beauty, which is in those things which are not   60 beautiful by essence but by participation, is loved by a rational spirit, He sends His only-begotten Son from His own essence to reveal beauty or His Father in His truth and essence. He turns the rational soul from love of participated and corruptible beauty towards the love or charity of absolute and immortal beauty, whose nature is that it never can be loved enough, because it is always more loveable than loved.

Therefore, that spirit which is fortified, fed and grows by love   61 in loving obtains eternal happiness unitively or adhesively. And imagine what I said of beauty to be so of wisdom, justice or truth, since they are names of God, Who is that absolute lovability which is called goodness, truth, wisdom etc., which are loved by a

per spiritum rationalem, qui quidem rationalis amor est intellectualiter vivens et ad differentiam amoris brutalis caritas appellatur.
Haec nunc sufficiant.

rational spirit. This is a rational love living intellectually, and it is called charity to differentiate it from the love of beasts.

Let this now suffice.

Sermo CCXC: Dum sanctificatus fuero in vobis

1459 Romae 'sabbato ante Invocavit'

1 'Dum sanctificatus fuero in vobis,' 'congregabo vos de universa terra,' 'et effundam super vos aquam mundam, et mundabimini' etc. Haec sunt verba, quae verbum Domini loquebatur per Ezechielem prophetam, ut legitur Ezechielis 36° capitulo, et audivimus illa in introitu missae decantari, quae nobis introitum dabunt ad officium, quod nunc Deo dirigente peragi cepimus. Possunt, fratres dilectissimi, haec prophetica verba non inepte sumi quasi de hac nostra synodali conventione dudum praedicta, scilicet Deum nostrum nobis insinuasse, quomodo tempore hoc sacro, quando in nobis fuerit per oboedientiam ieiunii et paenitentiae sanctificatus, de universa terra ista nos congregare instituit et effundere super nos aquam mundam, et quod mundabimur ab omnibus inquinamentis nostris, et 'dabit nobis spiritum novum.'

2 Fratres, haec ita esse pro nostra salute sperare poterimus, cum solo Deo inspirante, a quo bonum omne datur, hodie cum sancto proposito convenerimus, qui nobis haec verba in introitu officii contulit quasi summam brevem agendorum. Ego enim, dum praevidere vellem, quomodo hac die synodum dirigerem et missale aperirem, haec quae praemisi verba primo contuitu visum sistere fecerunt, ut intelligerem in illis me instrui. Sic eunucho librum Isaiae aperiente verba occurrerunt ad suam salutem scripta. Accidit et Augustino similiter codicem apostolicum aperiente, ut in libro *Confessionum* scribit.

3 Arbitror ex toto corde Deum quaerentem, si, qua via ad ipsum pergere debeat, inquirit, sacro codice aperto mox reperire, dummodo firmiter crediderit verba quae se offerunt Dei voluntatem

Sermon 290: "When I shall be sanctified in you"

1459 in Rome on the Saturday before Invocavit

When I shall be sanctified in you, I will gather you together out of all coun- 1
tries. I will pour upon you clean water, and you shall be cleansed. These
are the words which the Word of the Lord spoke through Ezekiel
the prophet, as read in Ezekiel chapter 36[:23–25]; and we have
heard them sung at the Introit of the Mass that gives us entry into
the office which now, under God's direction, we have begun to exercise.[1] We can, dearest brothers, understand the prophetic words
not unsuitably as predicting long ago the meeting of our synod. In
other words, Our God is suggesting to us how in this sacred time,
which has been sanctified for us by the obedience of fasting and
penance, He resolved to gather us from all the earth and to pour
clean water over us, that we might be cleansed of all our stains,
and He *shall give us a new spirit.*

Brothers, we can hope that this is for our salvation, since by the 2
sole inspiration of God, from whom all good things come,[2] we are
come together today with a holy purpose. God it was who gave us
these words upon my entry into office, like a precis of what we are
to do. When I wished to look ahead at how I would direct this
synod today and I opened the missal, on my first glance the words
I have just set out imposed themselves on my sight so that I might
learn from them. Thus the eunuch, opening the book of Isaiah,
found the words which were written for his salvation.[3] It happened to Augustine in a similar way when he opened the Bible, as
he wrote in the book of his *Confessions.*[4]

I think that anyone seeking God with a whole heart, if he asks 3
by which route he ought to come to Him, should open the sacred
volume. He will soon find out what he should do, so long as he

continere quam scire cupit, ut faciat. Dicebat Iohannes Climacus, dum monachus dubitat, alium aliquem quaerere debere et eius responsa quasi divina recipere. Nam, dum cum hac fide interrogat loco Dei hominem, non homo, sed Deus per hominem respondit. Similiter de sacra scriptura, quae aperienti codicem se oculis ingerit, credi poterit. Deus enim omnibus ipsum pro sua salute interrogantibus respondet modo, quo ipsum invocantes sibi firma fide responderi exspectant.

4   Diceres: Nonne prohibitum est non quaerere per sortem responsa in Psalterio? Dico: Immo, sed refert inter curiosa et salutaria animae. Diceres: Fortassis dii sic arbitrati sunt sacerdotibus templorum in libris Sibyllinis et divinationum respondere. Dico libros sortium in plerisque templis pro sacris veneratos, et idolatrae responsa ibi dari per deum templi putaverunt, quae erant frequenter ambigua, cum spiritus illi maligni futurorum, quae in Dei tantum potestate erant, nullam certitudinem haberent. De his alibi latius. Sufficiat scire christianum pro animae suae salute sollicitum non deseri a magistro, qui est verbum in scriptura divina contentum. Nam 'quae ibi scripta sunt ad nostram doctrinam utique scripta sunt,' et ita ad cuiuslibet instructionem, etiam si scriptura se ad unum aliquem videatur determinasse, dicente magistro: 'Quod uni dico omnibus dico.' Concedat igitur Christus noster nos vere dicere posse, dum abhinc hodie recedemus, quemadmodum ipse dixit, dum aperuisset librum Isaiae, ut legitur Lucae 4°, dicens scilicet: 'Quia hodie completa est haec scriptura in' oculis 'vestris.'

5   Receptis igitur sacris verbis introitus quasi divino responso, ad agenda pondus verborum exquisite pensemus, primum attendentes ad ea quae supponuntur, dum dicitur: 'Dum sanctificatus fuero

believes firmly that the words which present themselves to him contain the will of God that he desires to know. John Climacus, when a monk was in doubt, used to say that he should ask some other man and accept his reply as though it was a divine message. For when with this belief he questioned a man in the place of God, not the man but God replied. A similar thing can be believed of Holy Scripture, which presses itself upon the eyes of anyone who opens the book. God then answers all who question Him for their own salvation in such a way that those who invoke Him with firm faith can expect a reply.[5]

You might say: Is it not prohibited to seek a reply in the Psalter by casting lots? I say: Certainly, but one may distinguish between curiosity and what is good for the soul. You say: Perhaps the gods were thought by the priests of the temples to reply thus in the Sybilline books and other books of divination. I say: Books of divinations were venerated as sacred in many temples, and idolaters thought responses were given there by the god of the temple. These replies frequently were ambiguous, since those malign spirits had no certitude about the future, which is in God's power alone. I have written more about these things elsewhere. It suffices to know that the Christian concerned about the salvation of his soul will not be abandoned by the Master, who is the Word contained in the divine Scripture. *For the things written there certainly were written to teach us*[6] and thus are for the instruction of anyone, even if the Scripture seems to have been directed to one person. As the Master says, *What I say to you, I say to all.*[7] Our Christ, therefore, granted us the power to speak truly when we go forth from here today, just as He Himself said when He had opened the book of Isaiah, as we read in Luke 4[:21], *This day is fulfilled this Scripture in your ears.*

Receive, therefore the holy words of the Introit as a divine reply, 5 and let us weigh nicely the force of the words in order to guide our actions, first attending to the things which are hidden beneath the

in vobis.' Haec verba, prout Ezechielis 36° leguntur, dixit Deus per Ezechielem ad eos, qui de populo Israelitico intra gentes habitabant ut ipsi de Israel, scilicet Deum videntibus. Ipsis enim erat notus Deus tantum, ut ait propheta David: 'Notus in Iudaea Deus' etc. Per sanctificationem gentibus Deum innotescerent. Quod si hoc facerent, promisit eis quod ipsos 'congregaret de universa terra et effunderet' etc.

6   Primum attendamus verbum fieri ad fideles et electos a Deo, inter inimicos et persecutores fortes, et multos dispersos, et fuit verbum de sanctificatione Dei. Hic primum dubitatur, quomodo potest Deus in tempore sanctificari in creatura, cum sit aeternus et incomprehensibilis; dicit enim: 'Dum sanctificatus fuero' etc. Puto intelligendum tunc ipsum in fidelibus temporaliter sanctificari, quando ut sanctus sanctorum formata fide recipitur. Convertit enim sic ad se animam, quae sanctificata sanctificat sanctificantem, sicut calor receptus in calefactibili ad se calefactibile convertit, ita quod de calefacto nihil spiratur nisi vis caloris recepta. Frigidus, qui delectabiliter calefit, non potest sufficienter laudare calorem, qui ipsum de inimico vitae, scilicet frigore, liberavit et conservavit, atque tutatur ab eo, quamdiu manserit cum ipso. Laudes illae caloris et cura ipsum aeternaliter ut datorem vitae omni studio tenendi est ut sanctificatio. Non quod sanctificator det aliquid, sed recognoscat se ab ipso datore recepisse illa quae ipsum sanctificant.

7   Vide, quomodo Deus est finis omnium suorum operum. Sanctificat ut sanctificetur, instruit ut intelligatur, iustificat ut iustificetur, clarificat ut clarificetur, amat ut ametur, et ita de singulis. Ideo

letter when it is said, *When I shall be sanctified in you*. These words, read in the 36th chapter of Ezekiel, God spoke through Ezekiel to those of the people of Israel who lived among the Gentiles as Israelites, i.e. as those who saw God. For only to them was God known; as the prophet David says, *In Judea is God known* etc.[8] They made God known among the Gentiles through santification. But if they did this, He promised them that He will *gather* them *out of all countries* and *pour* etc.[9]

First let us note that the word was done to the faithful and cho- 6 sen of God, many of them scattered amidst their enemies and strong persecutors, and the word was of God's holiness. Here, first, we can wonder how God could be sanctified in time and in a creature, when He is eternal and incomprehensible.[10] Ezechiel says, *When I shall be sanctified [in you]*. I think He must be understood as sanctified in time in the faithful at the time when He is received as the Holy of Holies by a well-formed faith. For God converts the soul to Himself, which, by being made holy, sanctifies the sanctifier, just as heat received into something capable of being hot converts the heatable thing into [a thing like] itself, so that no [heat] is thrown off by the heated object unless it has received the power of heat. The cold object, which is made warm so pleasantly, cannot praise sufficiently the heat, which liberated it from the cold, the enemy of life, and guards it and preserves it, and which will keep it safe from the cold, as long as it remains with the source of the heat. Those praises of heat and the concern to preserve it zealously and forever as a giver of life are like sanctification. Not that the man who sanctifies [God] will contribute anything [to God's sanctity], but he acknowledges himself to have received from the Giver that which makes the Giver holy.

See how God is the end of all His works. He confers holiness, 7 so that He might be [acknowledged as] holy. He teaches so that He may be understood. He justifies so that He may be justified. He illuminates so that He may be illuminated. He loves so that

e converso amantes Deum amantur, scientes sciuntur, sapientes sapiuntur et nescientes nesciuntur, ignorantes ignorantur, in capitulo *Si iuxta*, XXXVIII distinctionem. Qui enim vidit Deum sanctum in omnibus operibus suis, vidit ipsum sanctificari in omnibus. Sanctificare autem est sibi omnem honorem dare omnium spiritualium bonorum, in quibus spiritus deliciatur, qui appetit munda et immaculata atque praecisa, pura et perfecta. Talia enim sancta dicimus. Nihil igitur nisi spiritum sanctificationis habet, qui haec se diligere opere ostendit et horum datorem tantum sanctificat.

8 Evenit autem sanctificatio ex indubitata cognitione, quae est per certam fidem. Dei igitur sanctificatio ostendit sanctificantem indubiam fidem habere. Quare qui habet talem fidem, si Iudaeus est credens verba prophetarum esse verba Dei, utique scit quod illis oboedire tenetur et oboediendo sanctificat illum ‹et›[1] esse magnum Deum, cuius imperio per prophetam ab eo missum publicato ostendit, usque ad mortem oboediendum. Sic prae omnibus Christus Patrem suum sanctificavit, qui ei ʼoboediendum usque ad mortem crucisʼ in se ipso ostendit.

9 Et si acute respicis, sanctificare et sanctificari coincidere vides, quomodo in maximo sanctificare coincidit maxime sanctificari et in minimo minime. Hinc maxime Deum sanctificantem scimus maxime a Deo sanctificatum. Sanctificatur et Deus in eo quod verbis Christi, quae credimus esse verba Dei Patris, oboedimus, omnia in eius comparatione penitus pro nihilo habentes.

He may be loved, and so on in the case of each divine activity. Therefore, in return, those who love God are loved; those who know God are known by God; the wise are made wise. Those who do not know God are not acknowledged; those who ignore God are ignored by God,[11] as is said in [Gratian] c. *Si ea* D. 38 [c. 10].[12] Whoever sees that God is holy in all His works sees Him being made holy in all of them. [For God] to be made holy is to give all honor to him for all spiritual goods, which delight the spirit, the spirit that loves the clean, stainless and well-ordered, the pure and the perfect. Such things we call holy. The man, therefore, who shows through his work that he loves these things and acknowledges only the holiness of the One Who gives them has nothing but the spirit of sanctification.

Sanctification [in this sense] derives from the doubt-free 8
knowledge which comes from unshakeable faith. The sanctification of God shows that the sanctifier has a faith free from doubt. Hence a man who has such faith, if he is a Jew and believes the words of the prophets to be God's words, surely knows that he is obliged to obey them and that by obeying, he sanctifies God, and shows that God is great, Whose command was announced by the prophet He sent, requiring obedience even unto death. Thus Christ beyond all others sanctified His Father, who showed in Himself that *he had to be obeyed, even to the point of dying on the cross.*[13]

If you reflect on this with penetration, you will see that sancti- 9
fying and being sanctified coincide, so that in its maximum, sanctifying coincides maximally with being sanctified, and in its minimum, minimally. Hence we have our knowledge of the God who sanctifies maximally from the God Who is sanctified maximally. God is also sanctified in our obeying the words of Christ which we believe to be the words of God the Father, regarding all things as nothing in comparison with Him.[14]

10   Diceres: Christus nos docuit in oratione petere sanctificationem
nominis Dei Patris. Hoc dicitur de sanctificatione Dei. Dico: Nomen notitiam affert, ut Christus Paulum dixit 'portare nomen
suum coram regibus,' id est notitiam. Patris notitia seu nomen notitiae est Filius, quem 'nemo scit' ut Patrem 'nisi Filius,' et ideo in
sanctificatione nominis Patris seu Filii confitemur nos ad notitiam
Patris accessisse nobis per Filium revelatam. Haec est causa sanctificationis. Per sanctificationem igitur nominis notitiae verbi seu
Filii, qui Deus est, sanctificamus Patrem in Filio. Aliter enim recte
non sanctificatur, quia non cognoscitur, sicut non est possibile paternitatem ut paternitatem sanctificari, si ignoratur; tunc autem
ignoratur, quando non revelatur per Filium. Quem enim ignoro
habere filium, ignoro esse patrem. In Filio vero, in quo video opera
ut Filii, video Patrem ut Patrem, a quo Filius omnia habet. Quare
Filius opera sua dicit esse Patris sui et etiam sua ut Filii, dicens:
'Pater meus usque modo operatur, et ego operor.'

11   Diceres: Quomodo intelligi potest quod Iesus Patrem revelando
se Dei Filium ostendit? Dico Christum venisse a Deo missum
cum omni potestate, etiam creativa Dei, quasi universalis heres
cum omni plenitudine, ut apostolus ad Hebraeos deducit, et hoc
ostendunt opera. Sed rex quoscumque legatos mittat, nemo habet
potestatem regiam per omnia regi aequalem, quin superest aliquis,
qui mitti potest regi coniunctior. Filio vero nullus coniunctior Patri. Qui igitur mittitur cum omni plenitudine potestatis, propter
aequalitatem omnimodam, qua nec filiatio maior esse potest, recte,
in eo quod missus, dicitur mittentis Filius, aequalis essentiae et
naturae.

You might say: "Christ taught us in the Lord's prayer to seek   10
the sanctification of God the Father's name.[15] This is spoken
about God's sanctification." I say: A name implies knowledge, as
Christ told Paul to *bear His name before kings*, that is, to make it
known.[16] The Son is the knowledge of the Father, or the name of
knowledge, the Father whom *no one knows* as Father *except the Son*,
and thus in sanctifying [or hallowing] the name of the Father or
the Son we confess that we have come near to a knowledge of the
Father revealed to us by his Son. This is the reason for sanctifying
[God's name]. Thus by sanctifying the name of the knowledge of
the Word or Son, who is God, we sanctify the Father in the Son.
For otherwise we do not sanctify [that name] rightly, because it is
not known, just as it is impossible for his paternity to be sanctified
[or acknowledged][17] as paternity if it is unknown; and his paternity remains unknown unless it is revealed by His Son. If I do not
know someone to have a son, I cannot know him to be a father.
But in a son in whom I see the works of a son, I see a father as father, from whom the son has all things. Hence the Son says that
his works are those of His Father and also His own, as works of a
son, when he says: *My Father worketh until now, and I work.*[18]

You will say: "How can it be understood that Jesus manifests   11
the Father by revealing Himself as the Son of God?" I say: Christ
was sent by God with all power, even the creative power of God,
like a sole heir with full powers, as the Apostle brought out in his
letter to the Hebrews,[19] and His works show this. But whomso-
ever the king sends as his envoys, none has a royal power equal to
that of the king in all things, such that there does not remain
someone else who could be sent who is even closer to the king. No
one, however, is closer to the Father than the Son. He who is sent,
therefore, with complete fullness of power, owing to his equality in
every way — than which no greater sonship can exist — is rightly
called, in that he is sent, the Son of the One who sent Him, equal
to Him in essence and nature.

12   Sicut si papa legatum posset mittere cum plenitudine papalis potestatis, utique iste foret eius papalis naturae et non aliud in essentia et natura, nec minor sed una et eadem utriusque dignitas, auctoritas et indivisa papalitas, quae est ob suam maximitatem immultiplicabilis, licet alia foret persona mittentis et alia missi. Unde, cum Iesus solum 'sine omni macula conversatus in hoc mundo' se Filium Dei Patris omnibus incogniti, ut quem 'nemo umquam viderit,' per opera, quae soli Patri Iudaeorum fides ascribit, se Filium verum manifestaverit, incognitum Patrem omnium creatorem revelavit, cuius se verbum seu virtutem ostendit.

13   Adhuc dicta verba introitus nos christiani applicemus ad Christum. Credimus Christum sic nobis loqui: 'Dum sanctificatus fuero in vobis' ut Filius Dei, 'congregabo' etc. Et haec est evangelii summa, scilicet credere Iesum Filium Dei in fide viva et formata et inhaesitabili, ita ut Deus Dei Filius in nobis sanctificetur. Tunc certissime haec faciet, quae sequuntur in themate. In eo enim, in quo sic Christus sanctificatur, non vivit nisi Christus. Hic in Christum mutatus spiritu Christi movetur ad complementum omnium quae evangelium praecipit. Qui enim verba Christi credit esse verba Filii Dei, scit esse 'verba vitae aeternae,' et non abit retro, sed sequitur Christum usque in mortem. Hic est totus lucidus, et dum 'lucent opera sua coram hominibus, glorificant homines Patrem qui in caelis est,' et haec glorificatio est clarificatio sive sanctificatio quam Deus requirit.

14   Diceres: Cur requirit a nobis sanctificationem? Dico quia lux, in qua non sunt tenebrae ullae, lux scilicet spiritualis seu intellectualis. Sicut enim sensibilis lux, quanto nobilior, tanto melior et se ipsam remotius diffundit ex natura suae perfectae bonitatis, sic de

To make an analogy, if the pope could send a legate with the   12
fullness of papal power, he would certainly share the nature of the
pope and he would be identical in essence and nature, and there
would be one and the same rank, authority and undivided papality
in both. For papality is unmultipliable owing to its maximal
nature, although the sender and the sent are different persons.
Hence, when Jesus alone, *dwelling without stain in this world*, showed
Himself to be the Son of God the Father, unknown to all, whom
no man hath seen at any time,[20] by His works, which the faith of the
Jews ascribed only to the Father, He manifested Himself to be the
true Son. He revealed the unknown Father, creator of all, whose
Word or strength He showed Himself to be.

Now let us Christians apply the words of the introit to Christ.   13
We believe Christ to have said to us, *When I shall be sanctified in
you*, as the Son of God, *I will gather* etc. And this is the sum of the
Gospel, that is, to believe with well-formed and living and unhesi-
tating faith that Jesus is the Son of God, so that God, as the Son
of God, is sanctified in us. Then most certainly will he do the
things that follow in the text. For in him in whom Christ is thus
sanctified, Christ alone lives. This person, being changed into
Christ by the spirit of Christ, is moved to the fulfillment of all
things which the gospel teaches. He who believes the words of
Christ to be the words of the Son of God knows them to be *the
words of eternal life*, and he does not turn back, but follows Christ,
even unto death. He becomes entirely a source of light, and *when
his works shine before all men, men glorify the Father who is in heaven*.[21]
And this glorification is the clarification or sanctification which
God asks of us.

You might say: "Why does God require to be sanctified by us?"   14
I say: Because of the light in which there are no shadows of darkness, namely spiritual or intellectual light. Just as visible light, the
nobler it is, diffuses itself that much better and further by the nature of its perfect goodness, so in the case of intellectual light. For

luce intellectuali. Vult enim intellectus intelligi et cognosci. Sicut enim rex magnus, si non cognoscitur in gloria sua, non est plus rex quam privatus, et ideo regia celsitudo cognosci desiderat in gloria sua quia rex, sic intellectus, qui est rex regum (id enim quod regit in omni vere regente intellectus est), vult cognosci et, quanto nobilior, tanto magis, ut in libris experimur doctorum. Sic conditor intellectus, cum sit infinite bonus, cognosci volens, quia intellectus infinitus, omnia creavit, ut cognoscatur seu videatur in gloria sua et sanctificetur. Sicut si sol visum lucidum produceret, ut ipse sol in sua claritate videretur et glorificaretur seu sanctificaretur. Deus igitur quia vult sanctificari, ideo haec omnia sunt, quae creavit. Vult autem hoc quod vult, quia Deus.

15   Diceres: Cum sanctitas sit deiformitas, quomodo acquiritur? Dico: In christiformitate. Nam, cum Deus sit nobis incognitus, ut nos ad deiformitatem attraheret, misit Filium in nostram naturam, qui, cum sit homo, accedi per nos potest, ut, sicut ipse induit nostram naturam mortalem ab omni vitio separatam, sciamus nos, si vitio caruerimus, ipsum induere posse, et sic, sicut ipse factus est filius hominis, nos fiamus filii Dei. Tunc enim mundi sumus, quando vitio caruerimus. Carere vitio est esse sanctum et immaculatum, et hoc est, quando spiritum Christi habuerimus, scilicet qui non est de hoc mundo, quia, si de hoc mundo esset, utique mundus eum diligeret et ipse ea quae mundi.

16   Diceres: In quo cognoscitur spiritus ille? Dico: In paupertate secundum mundum carnis, quae est abundantia secundum mundum spiritus. Nam nihil penitus huius mundi possidere ut suum dicitur paupertas. Spiritus ille nullo amore coinquinatus est nec

the intellect wants to be known and understood. Just as a great king, if he is not known in his glory, is no more a king than a private individual, and so desires his royal highness to be known in its glory because he is a king, so the intellect, which is the king of kings — for that which rules in every truly ruling thing is an intellect — wishes to be known, and the nobler that intellect is, the more it wants to be known, as we experience in the books of the learned. Thus the Creator of the intellect, since He is infinitely good, wished it to be known that His infinite intellect created all things so that He might be known or seen in His glory and sanctified. It is just as if the sun should produce a shining object of sight so that the sun itself might be seen in its brightness and glorified or sanctified. Because therefore God wishes to be sanctified, all these things thus exist that He has created. He wishes what he wishes because He is God.

You might say: "Since holiness is conformity to God (*deiformitas*), how can it be acquired?" I say: By conformity to Christ (*Christiformitas*). For, since God is unknown to us, in order to draw us into conformity with Him, He sent His Son into our nature; since He is man, we can draw near to Him, so that, as He put on our mortal nature free from every vice, we may know that if we ourselves shed our vices, we can put on Him. And so, just as He was made a son of man, we may be made sons of God. We are pure when we shed our vices. To shed our vices is to be holy and clean; and this is when we shall have the spirit of Christ, namely, of Him Who was not of this world.[22] If He had been of this world, then the world would surely have loved Him; and He would have loved the things of the world.

You say: "How shall we know that spirit?" I say: We shall know it in its poverty by the standards of the fleshly world — which is abundance according to the world of the spirit. For to possess absolutely nothing of this world as one's own is called poverty. That spirit is not defiled by any love of praise, temporal

laudum nec bonorum temporalium nec carnalitatum, sed mundo utitur ut navi, per quam mare navigat, ut celeriter et sane portum attingat. Et hoc est signum spiritum illum, qui sine amoris motu non est, ad aeternorum dilectionem conversum. Unde cum, ut dicit Dionysius, in Deum transire appetamus, hoc quisque agere intendit, ut similis Deo pro viribus efficiatur.

17   Sed quia Deus, qui spiritus est, non nisi per spiritum adiri potest, noster autem spiritus, qui habet potentiam intellectivam et volitivam, non potest per intellectivam transire in Deum, quoniam omnem intellectum exsuperat, nec per volitivam sive amorem, cum incognitum non ametur, patet quod per se non poterit pervenire ad transitionem in Deum; ideo per mediatorem. Nam Deus Pater mediante mediatore attrahit spiritum nostrum sicut desideratum desiderantem. Quando enim spiritus recipit verbum et doctrinam Iesu et sermones eius servat, Christum uti Dei Filium diligit et in eo Patrem, et Pater diligit ipsum per Filii dilectionem, ut habet evangelium. Deus autem caritas est, quae amore cognoscitur et cognoscendo amatur. Ita pergit spiritus in Deum in unitate utriusque potentiae praedictae.

18   Adhuc, fratres, attendamus, quomodo Petrus iubeat Dominum Iesum in cordibus nostris sanctificari, qui et paratos nos reddere rationem de ea, quae in nobis est spe et fide. Quod, cum magis de nobis intelligi debeat, qui sacerdotes sumus et doctores, ideo aliqua de hoc subiungamus. Consideremus officium nostrum sanctissimum, qui Christi legatione utimur. Dixit enim: 'sicut misit me vivens Pater, ita mitto vos,' quoniam per manus impositionem recepimus spiritum Christi, scilicet veritatis, ita quod evangelizare et rationem fidei reddere teneamur. Primum ante oculos ponamus, si recte intravimus et cum quo voto et cum qua commissione.

goods or the pleasures of the flesh. Rather it uses the world like a
ship to sail the seas, so as to reach harbor swiftly and safely. And
this is the sign that that spirit, which is not without the motion
imparted by love, has been converted to the love of things eternal.
Hence when, as Dionysius says, we desire to pass into God, each
person aims to do this so that he may be made as like unto God as
his strength allows.

But since God, Who is spirit, cannot be approached except   17
through spirit, our spirit, which has powers of will and intellect,
cannot pass into God by intellect, since He surpasses all intellect,
nor by will (or love), since what is unknown may not be loved. It
is therefore clear that our spirit could not make on its own the
passage into God; thus it does so through a mediator. For God the
Father draws our spirit to him by means of a mediator, just as the
beloved draws the lover. When the spirit receives the word and
teaching of Jesus and follows His teaching, it loves Christ as the
Son of God, and the Father in Him; and the Father loves our
spirit through the love He has for his Son, as the gospel proclaims.[23] God, however, is charity,[24] charity known by love and
loved by knowing. Thus the soul reaches God in the unity of both
of its aforesaid powers.[25]

Besides, brothers, let us note how Peter commands us to sanc-   18
tify the Lord Jesus in our hearts and to be ready to give an accounting for the faith and hope which is in us.[26] But because we
who are priests and teachers ought to understand more about ourselves, let me add a few remarks on this subject. Let us consider
our most holy office, we who engage in representing Christ. For
He said, *As the Father hath sent Me, so send I you,*[27] because we have
received by laying on of hands the spirit of Christ, that is of truth,
so that we are obliged to preach the Gospel and give an accounting
of our faith. First, let us visualize whether we have rightly entered
[upon our representative office], and with what vow and with
what commission. Then let us consider how we are bound to put

Deinde, quomodo Christum induti teneamur Deum corde, id est, omni conatu desiderii et voluntatis, sanctificare, et quod tunc rectam rationem fidei et spei, quae in nobis est, omni poscenti rationem reddamus opere et sermone. Qui enim fidem et omnia consequentia ad ipsam et sacras litteras ita interpretatur quod toto corde Deum velit sanctificare, lucidas habet rationes.

19   Quod nota. Nam sic dicit Petrus patronus noster: 'Dominum autem Christum sanctificate in cordibus vestris, parati semper ad satisfactionem, omni poscenti vos rationem reddentes de ea quae in vobis est spe' et fide, 'sed cum modestia et timore, conscientiam habentes bonam' etc. Sacerdotes Christum repraesentant. Non enim ipsi sunt qui operantur sacerdotalia mysteria, sed in ipsis Christus, in quo Pater. In sacerdotibus ergo spiritus Patris loquitur, ut ait Christus: 'Non enim vos estis qui loquimini, sed spiritus Patris vestri, qui loquitur in vobis.' Quis baptizat, quis confirmat, quis consecrat, quis evangelizat in legato ut tali? Certe ille qui eum misit. Quis spiritus seu auctoritas legati apostolici? Certe Petri, quia auctoritas papae, in qua spiritus apostolicus, ut Hieronymus dicit spiritum apostolicum numquam deficere in sede Petri. Sicut enim est una auctoritas unius sedis, ita uno apostolico spiritu vegetatur. Apostolicus spiritus est legationis Christi. Sicut igitur Christus fuit legatus Patris cum plena potestate Patris — omnia enim dedit in potestate eius –, sic Christus Petro plenam potestatem. Aliis apostolis dedit similiter suam potestatem Christus, sed addidit Petro principatum dicendo: 'Tu es Petrus,' id est, caput domus.

20   Est enim quaedam genealogia, sed regalis et sacerdotalis domus, peculiariter Dei domus sive apostolica ecclesia dicta, quae est in regno Christi seu ecclesia catholica, quae non est ex propagatione naturae, sed ex gratia ad sortem Dei electa, ut evangelium Christi

on Christ in our heart, that is, to sanctify him with every effort of desire and will, and how through our works and our speech we should give a right account of the faith and hope that are in us to everyone who seeks it. He who has interpreted the faith and all the things consequent upon it and sacred literature, so that he wishes to sanctify God with his whole heart, will be able to give a clear account.

Bear this in mind. For Peter, our patron,[28] says, *But sanctify the Lord Christ in your hearts, being ready always to satisfy everyone that asketh you a reason of the hope* and faith *which is in you. But with modesty and respect, having a good conscience* etc.[29] Priests represent Christ. They do not enact the priestly mysteries with their own powers; but Christ, in whom is Father, enacts the mysteries through them. In the priests, therefore, the spirit of the Father speaks; as Christ says, *For it is not you who speak, but the Spirit of your Father that speaketh in you.*[30] Who baptizes, confirms, consecrates and proclaims the gospel through a legate as such? Surely the one who sent that legate. Whose spirit or authority does a legate of the Apostolic See possess? Surely Peter's, since his authority is the pope's, and in that authority the apostolic spirit dwells. As Jerome says, the apostolic spirit never can fail in the see of Peter.[31] Just as the authority of a single see is undivided, so it is animated by one apostolic spirit. The apostolic spirit belongs to the legate of Christ. Just as Christ was His Father's legate with the full power of the Father — for He gave all things into Christ's power — so Christ gave Peter full power. Similarly, Christ gave His power to the other apostles, but he gave the principate to Peter besides, saying, *Thou art Peter* [etc.],[32] that is the head of the household.

For this is a kind of genealogy, but of a royal or priestly house, named in particular God's house or the Apostolic Church, which is in the kingdom of Christ or the Catholic Church, which is not descended by natural propagation but by the grace of God's election,[33] so that it might administer the Gospel, to which adminis-

19

20

habeat in administratione, cui Deus dedit omnem potestatem. Et huius domus pater familias Petrus est et qui Dei dono ei succedit. Ille autem, qui per domum illam pro successore tenetur et colitur, pro successore habendus est.

21 Omnes in hac domo exsistentes divinam sortem secuti sunt, succedentes in hereditatem Dei, quam sibi servavit, scilicet in decimis, oblationibus et primitiis, et apostolicam sive legationis domum inhabitant et vivunt de bonis Christi, pro quo legationis officio funguntur. Nisi enim fuerimus degeneres filii, utique Christum in cordibus nostris sanctificare tenemur, cum nihil simus sine ipso. Consideremus quid agit per nos Christus, quomodo transfert per nos suos legatos homines ad ipsum, ut in ipso sint, ut[2] filii Dei adoptivi et coheredes eius, quomodo filii Adae veniunt ad conformitatem Christi, quomodo eucharistia est veritas sacramentalis, ubi substantia panis transsubstantiatur in corpus Christi manentibus sensibilibus signis, et significat sic fideles transire spiritaliter in corpus Christi mysticum. Neminem igitur nisi Christum sanctificare poterimus, qui hoc in nobis operatur, cuius est et sacerdotium nostrum. Haec igitur est sanctificatio, quae omni poscenti rationem fidei nostrae redditur, quando Christo damus honorem omnium sacerdotalium operationum.

22 Nunc attendamus quae sunt nobis Deum sanctificantibus promissa. Primo congregatio de universa terra. *Agios* dicitur 'sanctus,' et est dictum quasi 'sine terra.' Sancti de terra separati sunt, quae est faex lucis et ideo opaca tenebra et immunda in lucis respectu. Electi igitur de terra separantur et in lucem congregantur, quae est lux intellectus, scilicet illuminans intellectum et dans parvulis sapientiam vivificantem, sicut famosus intellectus congregat de uni-

tration God gave all power. And the paterfamilias of this house is Peter and the man who succeeds Peter by the gift of God. The man who is regarded and revered as his successor by that house, must be regarded as Peter's successor.

All who live in this household inherit by divine election, suc-   21
ceeding to the inheritance of God that has maintained them, namely tithes, gifts and first fruits. They dwell in the apostolic house, or the house of legation, and they live off the property of Christ, for whom they exercise the office of legate. Unless we are degenerate sons, we are obliged to sanctify Christ in our hearts in every way, since we are nothing without Him. Let us consider what Christ does through us, how He brings men to Himself through us, His legates, so that they are in Him and are made adoptive sons and co-heirs of God. Let us consider how through us in Christ the sons of Adam come into conformity with Christ; how the Eucharist is the sacramental truth, where substantial bread is transubstantiated into the body of Christ, although the sensible signs of bread remain. The Eucharist signifies the means by which the faithful are transformed spiritually into the mystical body of Christ. We therefore can sanctify no one but Christ, Who works in us, Whose priesthood we exercise. This therefore is sanctification, which renders an account of our faith to all who demand one, when we give the honor to Christ for all our priestly works.

Now let us attend to what God promises those who sanctify   22
him. First, there is the gathering of the saints from all the earth. *Hagios* means holy [in Greek], as though to say "without earth," unworldly.[34] The saints are separated from this earth, which is the dregs of light, and therefore it is opaque shadow and uncleanliness compared to the divine light. The elect, therefore, are set aside from the earth and are gathered in the light, which is the light of the intellect, that is, illuminating the intellect and granting life-giving wisdom to children, just as a famous thinker gathers dis-

versa terra discipulos, ut illuminet congregatos ad sui apprehensionem. Fundit 'aquam sapientiae salutaris' in eloquio, quasi in rore descendente de caelo, vivificatio terrae nascentium, et secundum naturam aquae sequitur mundatio sive clarificatio. Munda enim mundat, viva vivificat, sapientialis sapientificat, et ideo sermo Dei mundat quasi aqua mundissima. Quare Christus apostolis dixit: 'Vos mundi estis propter sermonem quem' audistis.

23   Post omnium inquinamentorum detersionem ab ipsa anima, quae capax facta est divini spiritus, datur spiritus novus. Et dicitur novus, quia numquam deficere poterit, quando semper est novus. Sic ignis est incorruptibilis et radius solis, quia semper innovatur, sicut spiritus qui amor dicitur praesente infinito amabili semper innovatur in motu amoroso delectabilis vitae. Dum haec anima audit in se ipsa Christum loquentem, assurgit in gaudiosam hymnizationem dicens: 'Benedicam' ergo 'Dominum in omni tempore. Semper laus eius in ore meo.' Et dum Deo trino gloriam decantavit, resumit verba salvatoris sui dicens: O quam bonus et suavis es, Domine, dicens: 'Dum sanctificatus fuero' etc.

ciples from the whole earth, so that He might enlighten those gathered with his own insight. God pours out *the water of saving wisdom*[35] in His eloquence, like dew come down from heaven. Life is given to what springs from the earth, and according to the nature of water, purification or clarification follows. It purifies the pure; it gives life to the living; the wise it makes wise; and therefore the Speech of God purifies like the purest water. Hence Christ said to the apostles, *Now you are pure by reason of the word which you heard.*[36]

After the cleansing of all defilement from the soul, which is 23 made able to receive the divine spirit, a new spirit is given. It is called new because it never can fail, since it always is new. Therefore, it is incorruptible fire and the sun's ray, because it always is renewed, just as the spirit, which is called love, by the presence of infinite Love is renewed always in the loving motion of a life of delight. When this soul hears Christ speaking within it, it rises into a glorious singing of hymns, saying, *I shall bless the Lord at all times. His praise shall be ever in my mouth.*[37] And, when he has sung the glory of the Triune God, he will take up again the words of his Savior, saying, *O how good and sweet is thou art, o Lord,*[38] saying, *When I shall be sanctified in you,* etc.

Reformatio generalis concepta per sanctae memoriae reverendissimum
dominum Nicolaum de Cusa, cardinalem Sancti Petri ad Vincula

‹Praefatio›

1 Ut haec nostra reformatio capiatur per cuiuslibet intellectum esse
iusta et necessaria ad salutem, quaedam ex alto praemittere convenit, causam scilicet, cur homo creatus exsistat, quam apostolus
Paulus sapientibus Graecis, dum Athenis in Areopago evangeliza-
ret, asseruit esse propter 'quaerere Deum, si forte attractent et in-
veniant.' Neque hoc aliud est quam quod homo creatus est, ut
Deum videat in gloria sua. Videmus enim, naturam intellectualem, Dei bonitatem participantem, inclinari ad sui ostensionem et
participationem, quemadmodum nos docent libri sapientum qui
propter hoc editi sunt, ut quisque suum intellectum ostendat et ad
eius participationem dociles vocet; sic divina bonitas intellectualem creavit naturam, ut se ei visibilem praebeat. Ideo et alia omnia
propter intellectualem creavit naturam quasi librum, in quo quaerat intellectus ipsam Dei sapientiam, per quam omnia sic facta
sunt, habens sensum visus et alios sensus tamquam organa et in-
strumenta, ut admiretur et concitetur ad quaerendum eam et
ipsam attractet, si possit. Sed homo, ignorans linguam seu verbum
Dei per quod scriptus est liber creationis, non potuit ex omni sua
virtute sapientiam seu artem creativam attingere, nisi verbum illud
sibi notum fieret. Unde, quemadmodum ignorans linguam seu
verbum alicuius libri potest facere sibi plures coniecturas de libri
continentia, tamen veraciter nihil scire potest sine magistro: om-

A General Reform of the Church

The general reform conceived by Nicholas of Cusa, Cardinal of St. Peter in Chains, of holy memory

[Preface]

So that this reform of ours is understood by anyone's intellect 1
to be just and necessary for salvation, it is fitting to begin with
something from on high, that is, the reason why created man exists. The apostle Paul asserted to the Greek wise men, when he
preached at the Areopagus in Athens, that this reason was *to seek
God. If they seek Him, perchance they may find Him.*[1] In other words,
mankind was created that he might see God in his glory. For we
see that intellectual nature, participating in the goodness of God,
is inclined to revelation of and participation in him, just as the
books of the wise written for this purpose teach us that anyone
should display his intellect and summon those who are teachable
to participate in him. Divine goodness created intellectual nature
so that he might reveal himself to it visibly. Thus He created all
other things for the sake of intellectual nature, like a book in
which the intellect may seek the very wisdom of God, through
which all things were made, having the sense of sight and the
other senses like organs and instruments, so that it wonders and
is spurred to seek that wisdom and lay hold of it, if it can. But
mankind, ignorant of the speech or Word of God in which the
book of creation was written, could not with all his strength attain
wisdom or creative art, unless the Word should make itself known
to him. Thus mankind is like a person ignorant of the language or
word of some book, who can make for himself numerous conjectures about the contents of the book, yet can have no true knowl-

nes igitur homines, qui natura scire desiderant, potuerunt bene con-
iicere, quod magisterium creationis est immortalis ars et sapientia
et lux, illuminans et intellectum ad perfectum adducens, beatum
et felicem faciens, qui finis desiderii. Sed Deus videns ignorantiam, quae omnes errare fecit a scientia Dei, et suae sapientiae
compatiens homini, desideratum illum magistrum, quem omnes
summopere videre cupiebant, misit in hunc mundum, qui ignorantiam tolleret et omnes ad ipsum venientes illuminaret; quem oportebat esse Verbum ipsum et magistrum, in quo omnes thesauri desideratae scientiae absconditi essent.

2   Misit igitur Deus Verbum caro factum, dilectum Filium suum
'plenum gratia et veritate,' mandans eum audiri, dans potestatem
omnibus, qui ipsum receperint, filios suos fieri, 'his qui credunt in
nomine eius,' et hoc est unicum Dei Patris praeceptum, scilicet
ipsi suo Filio et legato, qui et Verbum eius, credere, scilicet in nomine eius; qui enim ipsum ut talem recipit, utique in ipsum credit,
et scit omnia quae annuntiat vera esse, quia Filius et Verbum Dei.
Venit itaque Christus et elegit de mundo discipulos et aedificavit
ecclesiam ex sibi fidelibus, quae eius doctrina et spiritu vegetatur
et vivit, in qua omni tempore manebit. Est itaque fidelium unio in
ipso ecclesia eius, cuius ipse caput. Qui in hac fide vivit et movetur, quod ipse Jesus Christus Mariae virginis filius verax, immo
ipsa veritas est, sic 'habens verba vitae aeternae': haec fides est
dans omnem sanctitatem et scientiam et iustitiam ac quidquid
beatificat. Quicumque enim hoc veraciter credit, utique mandata
eius servat et non peccat. Nam malignum atque mundum ille vicit
et concupiscentias eius, sciens non esse vitam nisi in promissis
Christi, atque quod nemo iustificatur nisi quem ipse in merito
mortis suae iustificaverit. Hic et cum Apostolo dicere poterit se nihil scire 'nisi Christum et hunc crucifixum,' in quo adeptus est su-

edge of it without a teacher. All men, therefore, who by nature desire to know,[2] can conjecture well that the teaching authority of creation is immortal art, wisdom and light, illuminating and leading the intellect to be perfect, making it blessed and happy, which is the end of desire. But God, seeing that ignorance which made all men stray from knowledge of God, and of his wisdom taking pity on mankind, granted the Teacher it desired, Whom all desired exceedingly to see, Who would take away ignorance and illuminate all who come to Him. This Teacher had to be the Word Itself, in which are hidden all the treasures of knowledge that can be desired.[3]

God, therefore, sent the Word made flesh, his beloved Son, *full* 2 *of grace and truth*, commanding that he be heard, giving power to all who received him, *to those who believe in his name*, to become God's sons.[4] And this is the only precept of God the Father, that they should believe in His Son and legate, who is His Word, that is, believe in His name. Whoever receives Him as such, in fact, believes entirely in Him and knows all which He announces to be true, because He is the Son and Word of God. Thus Christ came and chose disciples from the world and built from those faithful to Him the Church, which He invigorated and enlivened with His doctrine and Spirit, and in which He will remain for all time. Thus the union of the faithful in Him is His Church, whose head He is. Whoever lives and moves in this faith, that this Jesus Christ, true son of the Virgin Mary, is indeed is the Truth, *having the words of eternal life*.[5] This faith is that which gives all sanctity, knowledge and justice, and it beatifies all things. Whoever believes this truly keeps His commandments entirely and does not sin. For he vanquishes evil, the world and its desires, knowing there is no life except in Christ's promises and that no one is justified except the one whom He has justified by the merits of His death. Here he can say with the apostle that he knows nothing *except Christ and*

premam et completam scientiam, fidem scilicet, per quam iustus vivit.

3   Quoniam autem ecclesiam Dei, iam super firmam petram optime fundatam, regendam recepimus, non circa aliam fidem neque alias formas, quam a Christo capite et sanctis apostolis atque eorum successoribus ecclesiae rectoribus recepimus, inquirere necessitamur; sed tantum operam dare tenemur, ut quanto superno dono fieri conceditur, abiecta pravi huius mundi concupiscentia, quae non est de regno Christi — transibit enim mundus iste cum concupiscentia eius — omnes Christiformes efficiamur et quisque in ordine suo, ut sic simus haeredes Dei in participatione regni immortalis vitae, et ipsius Christi Dei unici Filii cohaeredes. Ipse enim 'cum in forma Dei esset,' qui solum inhabitat immortalitatem, nostram assumpsit mortalem naturam servilemque formam, ut ipsam sic suae divinae naturae uniret, quod in eius immortalitatis formam transiret. Unde, cum una sit humanitatis natura, Christi capitis nostri et nostra, quae in ipso solo formam Dei induit, non est possibile hominem ad regnum immortalitatis aliter posse pertingere, nisi ipsius Christi Domini formam induat. Haec forma imitatione acquiritur. Unde ait Apostolus, in quo Christus formatus loquebatur: 'Imitatores mei estote, filii carissimi, sicut et ego Christi.'

4   Quoniam igitur in locum apostolorum successimus, ut alios nostra imitatione forma Christi induamus, utique prioriter aliis Christiformes esse necesse est. Humana vero natura a Deo habet docilitatem prae cunctis huius mundi creaturis, quam concreavit homini, ut possit felicitari; ideo 'erunt omnes docibiles Dei.' Videmus autem virtutes incorruptibiles, et unam a multis usu et doctrina participari. Christus autem rex noster et Dominus virtutum, ideo et rex gloriae, est viva illa virtus, quae omnibus ipsam participantibus dat requiem aeternam, 'in quo omnes thesauri sapientiae

him crucified,[6] in whom he attains the highest and fullest knowledge, that is faith, by which the just man lives.[7]

Since we have received responsibility for ruling the Church of God, already well founded on a firm rock, we need not inquire about any other faith nor any other tenets than those we received from Christ, the holy apostles and their successors, the rulers of the Church; but we are required to do such work as is given us to be done by gift from above, having set aside the lust of this evil world, which is not part of Christ's kingdom—for the world with its lusts will soon pass away—and we shall all be like unto Christ (*Christiformes*), each in his order, so that we may be heirs of God, participating in the kingdom of immortal life and coheirs with Christ Himself, the only Son of God.[8] For He, *although he was in the form of God*,[9] Who alone inhabits immortality, assumed our mortal nature and servile form, so that He could unite it to His divine nature, so that it could pass over into the form of His immortality. Wherefore, since there is one nature of humanity, that of Christ, our head, and ours, which has put on the form of God in Him alone, it is impossible for mankind to attain the kingdom of immortality otherwise than if it takes on the form of Christ our Lord. This form is acquired by imitation. Hence the Apostle, in whom the form of Christ spoke, says, *Be imitators of me, beloved children, as I am of Christ.*[10]

Since, therefore, we succeeded to the place of the apostles, so that we can put the form of Christ on others through imitation of us, it is entirely necessary, first of all, to be Christlike to others. Human nature has from God a teachability above all creatures of this world, a teachability which he created together with the creation of humanity, so that it could be happy; thus *All will be teachable by God.*[11] We see, however, incorruptible virtues and One participated in by many through practice and doctrine. Christ, our king and the Lord of Virtues, thus also the King of Glory, is that living virtue, which gives that eternal rest to all participating in

et scientiae sunt absconditi.' Clamat igitur magister ad nos omnes eius discipulos, qui in eius formam transire cupimus, dicens: 'Discite a me, quia mitis sum et humilis corde, et invenietis requiem animabus vestris.' Et alibi cum opere lotionis pedum se humilem ostenderet, aiebat: 'Exemplum enim dedi vobis, ut quemadmodum ego feci, et vos faciatis.' Ipse enim faciendo docuit. 'Coepit enim facere et docere,' volens ostendere, non omnem moralem virtutem dare vitam perpetuam, sed ipsam, quae sic est viva, quod hunc corruptibilem mundum vincit, uti in ipso mundi victore, Christo, primo. In omni autem Christoformi virtus ita vivere debet, quod propter virtutem, quae est vita spiritus, haec sensibilis vita nihili pendatur.

5   Haec est enim ipsa caritas Christi: adeo habere caram virtutem, quod pro ipsa dare mundum et mori parvum credatur et gloriosum. Omnis autem scriptura divinitus inspirata non aliud revelare nobis nititur quam Christum formam virtutum et vitae immortalis ac felicitatis aeternae ab omnibus desideratae, quem ut unicum magistrum vitae recipientes fide et opere sic formati sunt, quod aeternae vitae capaces exsistunt. Neque capaces eo ipso eam habent, sed necesse, quod eis eam Christus communicet et donet, qui eam non solum merito virtutis obedientiae habet, ut sit in gloria Patris, sed etiam ut capacibus donare possit, ut ex merito eius habeant et ex iustitia eam vendicent et possideant. Ex gratia enim vocamur ad haereditatem, quam nisi ex iustitia meritorum Christi assequamur, non possumus ultimum felicitatis gradum assequi. Ideo ipse pro nobis factus est iustitia, quando se pro omnibus in mortem obtulit, in quo omnes mortui iusto Dei iudicio vivunt aeternaliter. Deus enim Pater remunerator iustissimus omnibus, qui propter eum obedire moriuntur in Christo, retribuit vitam immortalem. Omnia igitur ad perfectam felicitatem necessaria, sive sit gratia,

Him, *in whom are hidden all the treasures of wisdom and knowledge.*[12]
The Teacher therefore calls out to all of us, his disciples, who wish
to change into his form, saying, *Learn from me, for I am meek and
humble of heart; and you will find rest for your souls.*[13] And elsewhere,
when He wished to show his humility by washing His disciples'
feet, He said, *I gave you an example, that you should do what I did.*[14]
He taught them by doing, *He began to do and to teach,*[15] wishing to
show, not that every moral virtue can give eternal life, but that that
virtue can which is so alive that it vanquishes this corruptible
world, as it did first in the case of Christ, the victor over this
world. In every Christlike person, virtue must live so that, because
of virtue, which is the life of the Spirit, this sensate life is valued as
nothing.

This, then, is the charity of Christ: to hold virtue so dear that 5
to give up the world for that virtue is believed a thing of small consequence, and to die for it glorious. Every divinely-inspired scripture strives to reveal to us nothing else than Christ, the form of
the virtues, of eternal life and of the eternal felicity desired by all.
Those receiving Him as the only teacher of life by faith and works
are formed so that they are capable of eternal life. Nor are they capable of it by that fact alone; but it is necessary that Christ should
communicate it and confer it on them, He Who has it not just by
merit of obedience, that He might be in the glory of the Father,[16]
but also so that He might give it to those capable of having it, so
that by His merit they may have it and justly lay claim to it and
possess it. By grace we are called to His inheritance and, unless we
succeed to it by the justice of Christ's merits, we cannot attain the
utmost grade of felicity. Therefore, he was made justice for us,
when He gave himself up to death for all; in Him all the dead live
eternally by God's just judgment. For God the Father, the most
just, who rewards all who die in Christ in order to obey him, rewards them with life immortal. Therefore all things necessary for
perfect felicity, whether from grace or justice, we cannot have

sive iustitia, sine ipso habere nequimus. Ipse igitur est solus mediator, in quo omnia et sine quo impossibile est nos veraciter felicitari.

6   Nos igitur, qui cunctos Christianos reformare cupimus, utique aliam nullam possumus eis formam, quam imitentur proponere, quam Christi, a quo nomen receperunt. Illa est lex viva et forma perfecta, in qua fit iudicium vitae et mortis aeternae. Conformes ei sunt filii vitae benedicti, qui vocantur ad possessionem regni Dei. Difformes vero, quia filii mortis, maledicti in gehennam abiicientur. Esse igitur debet omne studium nostrum, ut abluamur poenitentia et reinduamus formam innocentiae, quam in lavacro Christi recepimus; tunc enim, quando Christus in gloria Dei Patris apparuerit, similes ei erimus, eiusdem scilicet formae, quae solum in regno Dei, ad quod tendimus, reperitur.

7   Quoniam autem ecclesia Dei est corpus Christi mysticum, recte per Apostolum corpus hominis ei assimilatur, in quo in spiritu vivificante omnia membra uniuntur, ut vivant, sicut in toto corpore ecclesiae spiritu Christi omnia membra vivificantur, cui in hoc mundo omnes fideles per fidem adhaerent. Diversitas autem membrorum ecclesiae quodam amoris vinculo sive glutino Christi constringitur, et diversa sortiuntur officia in aedificationem corporis, et sunt membra de membro, quorum quodlibet contentatur id esse, quod est, dummodo adsit spiritui vivificanti. Sunt autem oculi, per quos singula membra visitantur et ad sua officia adaptantur, et illi oculi si lucidi fuerint, totum corpus lucidum erit. Nam visitant corpus et singula membra et non sinunt aliquam foeditatem aut turpitudinem tenebrosam ipsis adhaerere. Si vero oculus fuerit tenebrosus, totum corpus tenebrosum erit. In ecclesia igitur, si oculi,

without Him. He therefore is the only mediator, in whom all is possible and without whom it is impossible for us truly to be happy.

We, therefore, who wish to reform all Christians, can inevitably 6 propose to them no other form than that they imitate the form of Christ, from whom they have received their name. He is the living law and the perfect form by which judgment is made concerning eternal life and death. Those conformed to Him are the blessed children of life, who are called to possess the kingdom of God. Those not conformed, however, because they are the children of death, are cast down into Gehenna accursed. Therefore all our zeal ought to be directed to cleansing ourselves by penance and putting on again the form of innocence, which we have received in Christ's baptismal bath. For then, when Christ appears in the glory of God the Father, we shall be like Him, of His same form, which is found only in the kingdom of God, toward which we direct our course.

Since, however, the Church of God is the mystical body of 7 Christ, rightly likened by the Apostle to the human body, in which, in the life-giving Spirit, all members are united, so that they might live, just in the whole body of the Church all members are given life by the Spirit of Christ, to whom all the faithful in this world adhere through faith. The diversity of members of the Church, however, is bound together by a certain bond of love, the glue of Christ; and diverse offices are allocated for the building up of the body.[17] And they are members of each other, of whom each is content to be what he is, that is, as long as he has access to the life-giving Spirit. They are the eyes through which individual members are visited and adapted to their duties; and those eyes, if they are clear, enlighten the whole body,[18] for they visit the body and its individual members and they do not permit any foulness or dark ugliness to adhere to them. If, however, the eye were darkened, the whole body would be darkened. In the Church, there-

qui lucerna corporis esse debent, tenebra sunt, utique ex hoc certum est, totum corpus esse tenebrosum. Notum autem est, corpus ecclesiae hoc tempore valde declinasse a luce et die, et umbris obscuris involvi, ex eo maxime, quia oculi, qui lux eius esse deberent, in tenebras degenerarunt. Et quoniam oculus, qui aliorum maculas videt, suas non videt, ideo oculus se visitare nequit, sed oportet, ut se subiiciat alii visitatori, qui ipsum visitet, corrigat et mundet, ut sic aptus fiat ad visitandum corporis membra.

8   Duo igitur elicimus in nostro proposito necessaria, scilicet quod nos, qui oculi sumus, subiiciamus nos sanum visum habentibus, ne nobis ipsis quasi lucidos oculos habeamus credentibus, decipiamur in nostram et ecclesiae per nos visitandae perniciem. Secundo, quod post hoc in totum ecclesiae corpus lucidos oculos convertamus et singula membra per nos aut nostras vices gerentes sollerter visitemus, tamquam Deo de nostro officio, credita ecclesia et animabus omnium districtam rationem reddituri, nisi omnem possibilem in hoc fecerimus diligentiam. Et in hoc a nostra ecclesia Romana et curia incipiemus et consequenter visitatores ad singulas provincias mittemus. Regulas autem, quas tenere debent visitatores, qui nostras vices agent, hic annotare decrevimus.

9   Tres volumus eligere et deputare visitatores graves et maturos viros, in quibus forma Christi clare resplendeat, qui veritatem cunctis praeferant, zelum Dei scientiamque ac prudentiam habeant opportunam nihilque amplius honoris et divitiarum habere exspectent, ut sint in iudicio, cogitatione et opere liberi et mundi, neminem gravantes, sed victu et vestitu secundum iuris determinationem contenti atque per iuramentum ad ista astricti. Illis tradimus subscriptas quatuordecim regulas.

fore, if the eyes, which should be the lamps of the body, are dark, inevitably the whole body would be dark. It is notable, however, that the body of the Church in this age has declined greatly from the light and the day, becoming enveloped in dark shadows, especially because the eyes, which should be its light, have fallen into darkness. Since the eye which sees the stains of others does not see its own,[19] therefore, the eye is unable to visit itself; but it should submit itself to another visitor,[20] who will visit, correct and cleanse it, so that it can visit the members of the body.

Two things, therefore, we recommend as necessary for our proposal, that is, that we who are the eyes should submit ourselves to those having sound vision, lest we, as though believing ourselves to have clear eyes, should be deceived to our detriment and that of the Church to be visited by us. Second, that after this, we turn clear eyes on the whole body of the Church and visit the individual members skillfully by ourselves or through others acting for us, as though we shall have to render to God a strict accounting of our office, the church entrusted to us and the souls of all, unless we show all possible diligence in this. We shall begin this visitation with our Roman church and the Curia; and, thereafter, we shall send visitors to individual provinces. We have decided to set down here, however, the rules which the visitors, who act on our behalf, should follow. 8

We wish to choose and depute three grave and mature men as visitors, in whom the form of Christ clearly shines forth, who may show forth the truth to all. They should have zeal for God, knowledge and appropriate prudence; and they should expect to receive no additional honors or riches, so that they may be more free and pure in judgment, thought and work, burdening no one, but being content with food and clothing, according to the law's determination,[21] and bound by oath to do these things. To them we give the following fourteen rules. 9

‹Regulae visitationum›

10 Primo volumus, quod ipsi actum visitationis devotis adhibitis cae-
remonialibus cum Dei timore et verbo Dei solemniter et publice
incipiant; ad quid venerint exponant; visitandos ad obedientiam
adaptent, eis formam Christi proponentes. Et post haec ante omnia tres eligant viros maturiores ex visitandis, quos publice iurare
faciant de observantiis et consuetudinibus dicere veritatem; et singulos de his examinent, et quae audiverint, notarius scribat, ut
cum sic fuerint informati de statu et modo, qui in usu exsistit, meliorem formam, si opus videbitur, aut introducant aut bonam,
quam reperiunt, laudent et confirment. Deinde ad singulares personas visitandas descendant et quae sui officii fuerint expediant.

11 Secundo volumus, quod ipsi visitatores curam habere debeant,
reformandos ad formam primam reducere, puta generaliter omnes
Christianos ad formam quam induerunt in baptismate, dum fierent Christiani. Praelatos ultra hoc ad formam quam receperunt,
dum fierent praelati, reges et principes similiter ad formam quam
tempore suae constitutionis induerunt, sic de sacerdotibus et beneficiatis, sic de religiosis et generaliter de omnibus officialibus et
aliis, qui ultra formam baptismatis, ad quam se, ut Christiani essent, solemniter astrinxerunt, etiam in publicis dignitatibus, offi-
ciis et religionibus aliam formam priori addiderunt, ad quam voto,
iuramento aut promissione quacumque se Deo astrinxerunt. Et
quia omnia licita et honesta Deo promissa de necessitate salutis
servanda sunt, ideo necesse est visitatores talium transgressores

[Rules for Visitations]

First, we wish that the visitors should begin the visitation by celebrating devout ceremonies solemnly and publicly with fear of God and by the word of God, explain the purpose for which they have come, preparing those to be visited for obedience by placing the form of Christ before them. And, after this, before doing anything else, they should choose three mature men from among those being visited, whom they may cause to swear publicly to tell the truth about [local] observances and practices. They should examine each of these individuals on these subjects; and a notary should write down what they hear, so that, when they have been informed about the conditions and manners then in use, they may introduce a better form, if it seems necessary, or praise and strengthen the good form which they find. Then they may descend to examining individual persons and doing whatever is necessary for their task.

Second, we wish that these visitors should take care to bring back those being reformed to their original form, returning Christians generally to the form which they put on in baptism, when they became Christians. Beyond this, they should bring prelates back to the form which they received when they became prelates; kings and princes, similarly to the form they received at the time of their institution. The same should be done in the case of priests, beneficed clergy, and religious, and generally for all officials and others who, beyond the form received in baptism, in which they bound themselves solemnly to be Christians, added another form to the previous baptismal one in public dignities, offices and religious orders, to which they bound themselves solemnly through a vow, an oath or some sort of promise to God. Since all things licit and honorable promised to God are of necessity to be observed for salvation, it is therefore necessary that the visitors bring transgressors back to their form or eject them [from their offices].

aut ad illam formam reducere aut eiicere. Oportet igitur visitatores formas illas scire iuramentorum, votorum et promissionum, et ideo ante omnia undique illas habere procurent.

12 Tertio volumus, quod si forte dictae formae sint neglectae in certis provinciis ex mala consuetudine et incuria, quod tunc visitatores formas, quas in iure reperiunt observari debere, introducant: puta religiosi non profitentur, episcopi et sacerdotes nihil iurant vel promittunt tempore ordinationis nisi[1] talia, sicut canones et libri pontificales continent. Et quia tales non minus obligantur ad observantiam regularum et canonum, ideo canon, qui mandat, illa etiam promitti, omnino recipi mandetur, et transgressores, cum non sint ex mala consuetudine ab observantia canonum absoluti, non minus quam in priori casu, ad formam in canone et pastorali scriptam reducantur aut eiiciantur.

13 Quarto. Ultra haec iuramenta et vota ac promissa, quae omnino strictissime debent observari, et ad hoc per visitatores quosque cogi volumus et compelli, quisque etiam iuxta ethymologiam nominis sui et eius causam canonice vivat. Diffinitur enim vita cuiuslibet in nominis eius diffinitione. Qui enim aliter se habet quam nomen eius designat, utique falso sic nominatur et indignus est nomine, cuius vita eius significato contradicit. Quomodo enim veraciter dici potest quis Christianus, cuius vita Christo adversatur? Aut quomodo religiosus, qui apostata, quomodo monachus, qui in urbibus discurrit, quomodo canonicus, qui irregularis, quomodo sacerdos, qui profanus, quomodo curatus, qui curam fugit, quomodo rector, qui absens, quomodo episcopus, qui commisso gregi non superintendit, quomodo dux, qui seductor, quomodo rex, qui tyrannus? Et ita de singulis.

14 Quinto. Singularius ad beneficiatos descendentes volumus, quod visitatores ordinent, quod ipsi in habitu, tonsura, castitate, conversatione, officio et servitio divino canones servent. Item volu-

The visitors, therefore, must know those forms of oaths, vows and promises; and thus they should arrange to have copies of such things in advance.

Third, we wish that, if perhaps the aforesaid forms are neglected in certain provinces because of bad habits and carelessness, the visitors should then impose observance of the forms they find in law; for example, religious should not profess — nor bishops and priests swear at the times of their ordinations — anything other than what the canons and books of papal decrees contain. Because such men are no less obliged to observance of their rules and the canons, they should be commanded to embrace entirely the canon which commands those things which they have promised. Transgressors, since they are not absolved by bad habits from obedience to that canon, no less than in the preceding case, should be brought back to the form written in the canon and pastoral instruction or be driven out.

Fourth, beyond these oaths and vows which should be observed entirely and most strictly, we also wish that each visitor should insist on everyone living canonically according to the etymology of his name and the reason for it. Anyone's life is defined in the definition of his name. Whoever acts differently from what his name designates is certainly named falsely and is unworthy of that name, whose meaning his life contradicts. How can someone be called a Christian whose life is contrary to Christ? How can a man be called a religious who is an apostate; a monk, if he runs around in cities; a canon, if he is irregular; a priest, if he is profane; a curate, if he flies from care of his flock; a ruler, if he is absent; a bishop, if he does not supervise the flock committed to him; a leader, if he is a seducer; a king, if he is a tyrant? And so forth in each case.

Fifth, looking more particularly at beneficed clergy, we wish that the visitors should ordain that they observe the canons in their habit, tonsure, chastity, dealings with others, office and di-

mus, quod omnia beneficia habeant debitum suum secundum primaevam eorum institutionem, quantum hoc fieri poterit. Decla-
rantes, quod omnes nostrae et praedecessorum nostrorum
incorporationes, dispensationes et commendae, ubi non apparet
expressa exstinctio prioris ordinationis in fundatione beneficii
factae, intelliguntur, et ita per omnes et visitatores ipsos intelligi
debere declaramus, scilicet sine diminutione divini cultus, sicut et
illud in apostolicis litteris inseri consuevit. Non est enim nobis
ecclesia Christi credita in destructionem et diminutionem, sed in
aedificationem et augmentum eius et divini cultus. Ideo statuimus,
quod ubi visitatores viderint in aliquo beneficio propter nostram
aut predecessorum[2] nostrorum dispensationem ad[3] incompatibilia
aut incorporationem sive commendam divinum cultum negligi,
nisi ad statum cultus ipse restauretur ibidem, uti erat ante nostram
dispensationem, incorporationem vel commendam, quod mox visitatores illi beneficio nostra auctoritate, tamquam actu vacet, legi-
time provideant. Volumus autem, nomine beneficii hoc loco intelligi generaliter omnes ecclesiasticos proventus, qui cedunt titulum
habenti propter officium illi beneficio ex fundatione aut alias de
iure et consuetudine debitum, sive illud fuerit dignitas quaecumque, etiam abbatia seu praepositura vel alia inferior, sive ecclesia curata sive alia dignitas seu beneficium residentiam personalem
requirens, cuiuscumque conditionis seu valoris.

15 Sexto volumus, quod si visitatores invenerint divinum cultum
ob hoc diminutum, quia aliquis, qui plura habet etiam compatibilia beneficia, in certis, quae habet, negligit per se vel alium exsol-
vere debitum quod beneficium requirit, quia non decet quemquam
etiam plura compatibilia beneficia occupare in diminutionem divini cultus, quod tunc curent, ut titulum habens servitium per se

vine worship. Likewise, we wish that all benefices should receive their due according to their original institution, as far as possible. All the unions, dispensations and trusts,[22] made by us or our predecessors, where there does not appear to be an explicit expiry of the original arrangement made in the foundation of the benefice, are to be understood; and we declare that these things should be understood by all and by those visitors thus: "without diminution of divine worship," as it is usual to insert the phrase in apostolic letters.[23] The Church of Christ is not entrusted to us for its destruction and diminution, but for its building up, for its augmentation, and that of divine worship. Thus we lay it down that, wherever the visitors shall see in any benefice, through our dispensation or that of our predecessors,[24] neglect of divine worship through incompatibility or combining of benefices or entrusting them to absentees, unless the right order of worship can be restored there, as it was before our dispensation, union or entrusting, visitors may immediately provide a new occupant for that benefice, legitimately by our authority, as though that benefice were actually vacant. We wish, however, by the term "benefice" in this place to be understood generally all ecclesiastical revenues which accrue to the one having title to the benefice by reason of his duty to that benefice, due from its foundation or otherwise by law and custom, of whatever rank that benefice may be, even an abbacy or capitular provostship, or some inferior rank such as a church with cure of souls, or any other rank or a benefice requiring personal residence, of whatever condition or value.

Sixth, if the visitors should find divine worship diminished because someone who has several compatible benefices[25] neglects in some of them to perform those services which tenure of a benefice entails, directly or through another,[26] since it is wrong that someone have several compatible benefices in diminution of divine worship, we direct them to see to it that the one having the title should perform services by himself or through another;

15

vel alium peragat. Alioquin de alio nostra auctoritate provideant, ac si actu vacarent, sicut et nos, divino cultu sic neglecto, talia vacare decernimus. Et nomine beneficii hic omnia talia intelligi volumus, quae ex consuetudine possunt sine apostolica dispensatione simul obtineri.

16 Septimo praeposituram, decanatum, archidiaconatum, scholastriam, thesaurariam et quaeque talia, sive nominentur dignitates sive officia in cathedralibus seu collegiatis ecclesiis: volumus cum aliis talibus in alia ecclesia collegiata incompatibilia esse, cum quis non possit in utroque loco simul et semel esse et satisfacere, et divinus cultus et eius decor per hoc imminuatur. Ideo volumus, ut ubi aliquem plura talia in diversis locis tenere invenerint, agant, ut unum locum eligat, ubi serviat, et alium dimittat alteri, qui satisfacere possit; alioquin ipsi provideant visitatores, etiam dispensatione quacumque aut contraria consuetudine non obstante.

17 Octavo volumus quod, ubi visitatores invenerint alicui ecclesiae cathedrali vel collegiatae sive monasterio parochiales ecclesias incorporatas, quoniam illae incorporationes factae sunt in augmentum divini cultus ipsis ecclesiis cathedralibus, collegiatis et monasteriis, sine eo quod in parochia negligatur, et non invenerint divinum cultum maiorem esse post incorporationem quam ante fuit, aut non invenerint horas canonicas nocturnas et diurnas cum officio altaris devote peragi, curent quod in parochialibus ecclesiis omnes fructus, ac si nulla facta fuisset incorporatio, pro divino cultu augendo teneantur et exponantur. Non enim sunt incorporationes factae ut canonici aut religiosi lautius vivant et otientur, sed ut numerus augeatur Deo ibidem die noctuque devote famulantium.

18 Nono volumus, quod si qui religiosi visitatores non admiserint aut non audierint, et habuerint ab Apostolica Sede privilegia,

otherwise, visitors may appoint another by our authority, as if they were actually vacant, just as we too declare such benefices vacant if divine worship be thus neglected. We wish the term "benefice" to be understood to include all those things which can be obtained at the same time by custom without a papal dispensation.

Seventh, we wish any provostship, deanship, archdeaconry, precentorship, schoolmastership, treasurership and the like, whether called dignities or offices in cathedrals or collegiate churches,[27] to be incompatible with like offices in any other collegiate church, since one cannot be in two places at once and give satisfactory service, and divine worship and its seemliness is diminished by absenteeism. Therefore, we wish that, where they find anyone holding several such offices in different places, the visitors should compel him to choose one place in which to serve; and let him give up the other to someone who will give satisfactory service. Otherwise, the visitors can themselves appoint [someone to that benefice], notwithstanding any dispensation or contrary custom.

Eighth, where visitors shall find parish churches united with a cathedral, collegiate church or monastery, since those unions were made to augment divine worship in cathedrals, collegiate churches or monasteries without its being neglected in the parish, should they not find divine worship greater after the union than before or should they not find the canonical hours, day and night, devoutly celebrated, together with Mass, let them take care that all income in the parish churches should be retained and laid out as if the union never occurred, so as to augment divine worship. Unions are not made so that canons and religious persons may live in style and enjoy luxury, but so that the number of those serving God devoutly day and night should be increased.

Ninth, if some religious do not admit the visitors or heed them, and have privileges, exemptions or the like from the Apostolic See,

16

17

18

exemptiones aut alia, quoniam illa non sunt eis concessa nisi ut humilibus et obedientibus et tamquam dilectis Deo et Apostolicae Sedi propter regulae observantiam et ut illam cum maiore pace observare possint: ideo nisi mox obediant et observantiam regulae resumant et continuent, apostolica privilegia nostro nomine per ipsos visitatores revocari mandamus.

19   Decimo volumus, quod si visitatores cathedrales seu collegiatas ecclesias invenerint habere apostolicas exemptiones et incorporationes ecclesiarum aut alia quaecumque privilegia apostolica seu ordinaria, quae non velint visitationem atque emendationem admittere, quia tales non merentur quamcumque gratiam ob eorum rebellionem et incorrigibilitatem, ideo omnia istorum privilegia, tam quae a nobis quam ‹ab› ordinariis habent, nostra auctoritate revocentur, et ipsis divina per visitatores interdicantur.

20   Undecimo volumus, quod si quos sive religiosos sive alios visitatores invenerint, qui sua proterva audacia censuras sive a iure sive a nobis sive a legatis nostris aut ordinariis latas contempserint, divinis contra prohibitionem iuris vel hominis se immiscendo, volumus illos irregulares clavium contemptores suis beneficiis privari et ad altaris mysterium inhabiles declarari, eisdem ingressum ecclesiae inhibendo, quodque cum hoc visitatores omnibus Christianis prohibeant sub poena damnationis aeternae et excommunicationis latae sententiae, ne illos foveant aut missas eorum audiant seu eis intersint; alioquin absque alia declaratione ut excommunicati a cunctis Christianis habeantur et vitentur.

21   Duodecimo curam habeant visitatores circa hospitalium reformationem, quod eleemosynae iuxta primaevam institutionem, testamenta et legata pauperibus cedant et ratio fiat per eos, qui eis praesunt; sic et circa ecclesiarum fabricas, ne fraudes committantur, atque circa quaestuarios, qui populum decipere, ubi possunt,

since these were given to them only as humble and obedient men and as men beloved by God and the Apostolic See for the observance of their rule and so that they can observe it with greater peace, we order that those apostolic privileges be revoked in our name by these visitors, unless these religious immediately obey and resume observance of their rule and continue to observe it.

Tenth, if the visitors find cathedrals or collegiate churches possessing apostolic exemptions, unions of churches and other apostolic and episcopal privileges[28] which do not wish to accept correction or emendation, since they do not merit any favor owing to their rebellion and incorrigibility, we direct that all of their privileges, whether they have them from us or from the bishops, therefore be revoked by our authority, and the visitors may place them under interdict. 19

Eleventh, if the visitors find any religious or others who out of impudent audacity have held in contempt the censures imposed by law, by us, our legates or their bishops and are holding divine services against the prohibitions of the law or of man, we wish that these irregular persons, contemptuous of the power of the keys, be deprived of their benefices and declared incapable of the mystery of the altar [i.e. saying Mass], and forbidden from entering church. At the same time, let the visitors forbid all Christians, on pain of eternal damnation and automatic excommunication,[29] to support them or to hear or participate in their Masses. Otherwise, let them be held excommunicate without any other decree and shunned by all Christians. 20

Twelfth, visitors should concern themselves with the reform of hospitals, seeing to it that alms are given to the poor in accordance with their original intent, wills and legacies, and that those in charge of them give an accounting. Visitors should also see to the construction of churches,[30] so that fraud is not committed, and not overlook alms seekers who deceive the people when they can. 21

non omittunt; sic et circa monialium clausuras et reformationes districte vigilent propter tollere multa scandala et magnam iram Dei, quando illae, quae se in sponsas Christi solemni voto dedicarunt, turpi excessu multos ecclesiasticos et saeculares secum trahunt in baratrum, prout de his omnibus in iure sufficienter provisum exsistit. Quas provisiones ad praxim ponentes districte faciant observari.

22   Decimo tertio volumus, quod visitatores, dum ecclesias, sacraria, ornamenta, libros, calices et cetera visitant, non negligant reliquias examinare et causam scientiae, quod sint verae reliquiae, investigare, et ubi repererint easdem reliquias in diversis locis, cum utrimque esse nequeant, et dubium sit, ubi sint verae, tunc adhibeant bonam discretionem de tollendo scandalo a populo, et potius ostensionem inhibeant quam scandalum permittant. Advertant etiam, quod nec de reliquiis, nec de miraculoso sanguine hostiarum fiat quaestus; est enim quaestus causa, cur saepe falsificantur talia ab avaris. Unde ubicumque ob quaestum viderint homines ad ostensionem reliquiarum aut talium hostiarum currere, aut inhibeant ostensionem aut sub poena gravi oblationem. Sic, si cursus aliquis ad aliquam imaginem vel locum fit, quasi miracula ibi fiant aut facta sint, inhibeant aut cursum aut oblationem. Nam frequenter avaritia falsa pro veris introducit, ut deceptione acquirat, quae per veritatem habere nequit. Sufficiat populo Christiano habere Christum veraciter in sua ecclesia in divinae Eucharistiae sacramento, in quo habet omne quod desiderare potest ad salutem. Reliquias veras veneretur, sed longe plus Christum, caput omnium sanctorum, et caveat, ne dum Christo et reliquiis plerique in suum

The visitors should be strictly vigilant with regard to the cloisters of nuns and their reforms so as to take away any occasions for scandal and the wrath of God when those who dedicate themselves as brides of Christ by solemn vows draw many clerics and laymen with them into the pit by foul excess, implementing what is sufficiently provided for in law in all these cases. They should see to it that those provisions be put into practice and strictly observed.

Thirteenth, we wish that visitors, while exercising visitation 22 over churches, sacristies, ornaments, books, chalices and the like, not neglect to examine relics and to investigate how it is known that they are true relics. And where they find the same relics in different places, since they cannot be in both places and there is doubt where the true ones are, they should show discretion about removing scandal from the people; and it would be better to prohibit their display than to permit scandal. Let them also take note that gain is not to be made either from relics or from miraculous blood coming from hosts; for gain is a reason why such things are often faked by the greedy. Hence, wherever they see men running after the display of relics and bleeding hosts for the sake of gain, either they should prohibit, under grave penalty, their display or the making of offerings [to relics and hosts]. Thus, if there is a concourse of people to such an image or place, as if miracles might occur there or had occurred, let the visitors forbid either the concourse or the making of offerings. For avarice often substitutes false things for true, so that it may acquire by deception what it cannot get through truth. It suffices for a Christian people to have Christ truly in its church in the sacrament of the divine Eucharist, in which it has all it could want for salvation. True relics may be venerated, but Christ, the head of all the saints, should be venerated much more; and let it beware lest numerous persons abuse Christ and [true] relics for their temporal convenience, turning re-

temporale commodum abutuntur, religionem in quaestum verten-
tes, divinae offensioni fomentum praebeant, si non correxerint.

23   Decimo quarto circa exstirpationes publicorum usurariorum,
adulterorum et contemptatorum mandatorum ecclesiae diligenter
vigilent; partialitates damnent et eliminent; purgent omnia loca a
sortilegiis et incantationibus et a cunctis talibus peccatis, per quae
divina maiestas et res publica Christiana valde offenditur. Et curent facere ecclesiam sponsam mundam, Deo placentem, uti fuit
ecclesia primitivorum, quae mereatur de militanti in triumphantem transferri et ibi perpetua felicitate potiri.

24   In his quatuordecim regulis visitatores formam reperient
quosque reformandi, cui omnis sana mens acquiescet, nec quisquam bonus vir rebellis reperietur, cum nemo nisi ad id reducatur,
quod ipsemet esse elegit et publice professus est et suae professio-
nis nomine accepit et nominatur. Contradicentes igitur visitatoribus sibi ipsis contradicent et audiendi non sunt, sed coercendi.

‹Visitatio pape et curiae papalis›

25   Nos autem, qui vicariatum Christi, licet immeriti, super suam ecclesiam militantem tenemus, ad professionem et observationem
atque custodiam orthodoxae fidei Christianae atque ad omnia, ad
quae nostri praedecessores se reperiuntur obligasse dum ad papatum sumerentur, et ad ea quae nobis dum assumeremur proposita
fuere et admisimus, profitemur astrictos. Scimus enim nos papam
nominari, quia esse debemus pater patrum; et patriarcham, quia
ad quae omnes patres sunt astricti, nos principalius obligamur;

ligion into gain, offering kindling for divine displeasure, if they do not correct these abuses.

Fourteenth, they should keep watch diligently over the extirpa-   23
tion of public usurers, adulterers and persons in contempt of the Church's mandates; they should condemn and eliminate partisanship; they should purge every place of divination, sorcery and all such sins through which Divine Majesty and Christendom are offended greatly. They should take care to make the Church a pure bride, pleasing to God — just as the Church of the original disciples was — which may deserve to be translated from the Church Militant to the Church Triumphant and there to partake of perpetual felicity.

In these fourteen instructions visitors will find a way to make   24
reforms in each case, a way or form to which any person of sound mind shall acquiesce, nor shall any good man be found to be a rebel, since no one [is good] unless he returns to this form, which he chooses voluntarily and professes publicly, and accepts and is named by the name of his Christian profession. Therefore those who say "Nay" to the visitors, say "Nay" to themselves and are not to be heeded, but coerced.

[Visitation of Pope and Curia]

We who, however unworthy, hold the vicariate of Christ over His   25
Church Militant, have obligated ourselves to the profession, observation and guardianship of the orthodox Christian faith and to all the things which our predecessors obligated themselves, once we were assumed to the papacy; and we confess ourselves to be bound to those things which were purposed and accepted by us when we were assumed [to the papacy]. We know ourselves to be called pope because we ought to be the father of fathers; and patriarch, because we are more directly obligated to do the things all fathers have been bound to do; also archbishop, because we hold the

etiam archiepiscopum, quia inter diligenter superintendentes episcopos nos principatum tenere oportet; episcopum nos etiam nomi-
namus, quia attentius superintendere divino gregi tenemur; sacerdotem nos fatemur, quia ea, quae sacerdotalis officii sunt, maxime
ad nos spectare scimus. Ob haec omnia utique altissima et Christo
magis conformia sanctitatis nobis nomen Christiani servi Dei at-
tribuunt, quorum servorum Dei nos servum confitemur.

26   Si de his omnibus nominibus gloriamur, utique conari debemus
id esse, quod nominamur, et id ostendere actu, quod nos esse
profitemur; et ne nos in propria causa nostro iudicio fallamur,
electos vice Dei visitatores rogamus, ut nos diligenter visitent et
iudicent, certificantes eos, quia parati sumus, formam, quae nobis
eorum iudicio convenerit, quoad personam, familiam, curiam et
omnia, quae ad papalem dignitatem et officium spectant, gratis-
simo animo acceptare. Nec terreantur papam visitare, quando
eundem, quem vident vicarium Christi, vident et Christianorum
ministrum, et quem vident patrem patrum, vident etiam servum
servorum, et quem vident singulariter dignitate altissimum et
sanctissimum, vident etiam communiter cum aliis hominibus pec-
cabilem et infirmum et se pro tali cognoscentem et iuxta evangeli-
cam doctrinam profitentem, prioritatem et maioritatem non in do-
minatione, sed in ministerio aedificandae ecclesiae consistere.
Quidquid igitur in nobis invenerint, quod non aedificat, sed scan-
dalizat potius ecclesiam, nobis omnino manifestent, ut emende-
mus. Volumus enim Deo adiuvante evadere terribile iudicium
scandalizantis ecclesiam et exspectare ex nostris laboribus in terra
viventium fidelium dispensatorum optimam portionem.

27   Postquam Dei dono toto corde credito nobis officio satisfacere
optamus — et ob hoc a visitatoribus emendationem erratorum
prompto spiritu desideramus — non est indignum venerabiles fra-

principate among those who superintend the other bishops diligently. We even call ourself bishop, because we are obligated to tend the divine flock attentively. We admit to being called priest, because what pertains to the priestly office we know pertains most of all to us. Because of all these roles, which are indeed the highest ones and those most conformable to Christ, Christians, God's servants, attribute to us, who profess ourself to be servant of those servants of God,[31] the name "Holiness."

If we glory in all these names, we should strive in every way to 26 be what we are called and to show in action what we profess to be. And, lest we should act as judge in our own case,[32] we shall ask the visitors on God's behalf to visit and judge us diligently, assuring them that we are ready to accept with grateful soul the form which in their judgment is suitable to us as regards our person, household, Curia, and all things which pertain to the papal dignity and office. Nor should they be afraid to conduct a visitation of the pope, since the same man they will see as Vicar of Christ, they will also see as a minister to Christians; and whom they will see as the Father of Fathers they will also see as the servant of servants; and whom they will see as uniquely high and holy in rank they will also see as sinful and weak like other men, a man who knows himself to be such and one who professes, according to evangelical doctrine, that his prior and greater status lies not in domination but in his ministry of building up the Church. Whatever, therefore, they find in us which does not build up but rather scandalizes the Church, let them show it to us completely, so that we may amend it. We wish, with God's help, to avoid a terrible judgment for scandalizing the Church, and hope from our labors on earth among the living the best portion reserved for faithful servants.

After providing satisfaction, as we hope, with our whole heart 27 in the office given us by God's gift — and we desire correction of our errors with a ready spirit from the visitors for this reason — it

tres nostros, Sanctae Romanae Ecclesiae cardinales, atque omnem ecclesiasticum ordinem se pariformiter visitatorum emendationi subiicere. Et quamvis in generalibus regulis supra positis omnia ad visitationem opportuna complicentur, ad tria tamen singularius in cardinalibus attendere habent: primo ut habeant zelum domus Dei; secundo ut sint fideles et liberi in consilio; tertio ut sint viri exemplares, ad quos subsequentes ecclesiastici tamquam ad formam vivendi respiciant.

28   Primum utique necessarium est, cum ad hoc eorum tendat vocatio. Ad cardinalatum enim vocati firmi cardines ecclesiae esse debent, in quibus firmetur omnis motus et stabilitetur omnis fluctuatio. In ipso enim collegio est quidam totius dispersae per orbem ecclesiae consensus; ideo et eligunt pastorem ecclesiae, et in quem ipsi consentiunt, ecclesia, quae in ipsis est repraesentive, etiam consentit. Faciunt igitur nobiscum quotidianum compendiosum ecclesiae concilium quasi legati nationum, et sunt partes et membra corporis nostri mystici, scilicet, sanctae Romanae apostolicae et catholicae ecclesiae, et ipsi sunt in nobis, ut ecclesia in suo pontifice, et nos in ipsis, ut episcopus in ecclesia. Quapropter eos electos Deo gratos et gravissimos viros ab omni levitate remotos esse oportet. Unde cum non sint cardinales propter se ipsos, sed propter cooperari summo pontifici in aedificatione ecclesiae, quomodo erunt solliciti peragere suum officium sine zelo? Quem si habuerint, sollicitabunt, ut ementes et vendentes non intromittantur in templum, sed, si in eo sunt, turpiter eiiciantur. Non erunt nec sollicitatores, quod indigni promoveantur, etiam consanguinei et servitores, sed illi, qui iuxta canonicas sanctiones verbo et exemplo domum Dei aedificare possunt.

is not unfitting that our venerable brothers, the cardinals of the holy Roman church, and every ecclesiastical order, submit themselves in like manner to correction by the visitors. And although in the general rules given above all things useful for the visitation are enfolded, they have to attend, nevertheless, to three things more particularly in the cardinals: first, that they have zeal for God's house;[33] second, that they are faithful and free in counsel; third, that they are exemplary men whom all ecclesiastics beneath them may respect as models in life.

The first is surely necessary, since their vocation tends to this. 28 For those called to the cardinalate should be firm hinges[34] of the Church, in whom all motion is strengthened and all wavering is stabilized. In that college, after a fashion, is the consent of the whole Church dispersed through the world; thus they choose the shepherd of the Church, and the Church, which is in them representatively, also consents to the one to whom they consent. They therefore, like representatives of the nations, form with us a daily, comprehensive council of the Church; and they are parts and members of our mystical body, that is the holy Roman, Apostolic and Catholic Church.[35] They are in us as the Church is in the pontiff, and we are in them as a bishop in his church. For this reason, those chosen by God ought to be agreeable and extremely grave men set apart from all levity. Hence, since they are cardinals not for their own sakes but to cooperate with the supreme pontiff in building up the Church, how will they have the solicitude to perform their office without zeal? If they have zeal, they will have the solicitude to prevent buyers and sellers from entering the temple and, if they do come in, to eject them ignominiously. They will not be solicitous that the unworthy should be promoted, even if they are their kinsmen and servants, but rather will support the promotion of those who can build up God's house by word and example according to canonical norms.

29   Secundum est non minus de essentia boni cardinalis. Nam quomodo erit cardinalis, si sua consilia non sunt fidelia, et quomodo erunt fidelia, si non sunt libera? Id autem quod ligat consilia, sunt favores, odia, partialitates et huiusmodi. Si igitur cardinalis est protector nationis, principis aut communitatis propter quamcumque suam utilitatem, ligatum est consilium eius. Si ex relationibus in consistorio in favorem alicuius faciendis munera sperat, conductus est. Oportet igitur, perfectum cardinalem sibi ipsi firmam legem imponere munera spernendi, nihil tunc plus exspectare, quando tria milia aut quatuor florenos habuerit annue, et omnia huius mundi blandimenta vitare, quae eum a fideli et libero consilio retrahere possent.

30   Tertium utique requiritur ad aedificationem ecclesiae. Nam cum cardinales magis exemplo quam verbis aedificare possint universalem ecclesiam, utique ad vitam exemplarem propter loci prioritatem plus aliis obligantur. Vita enim gradui debet correspondere. Contenti igitur esse debent de honesto statu competenti et honesta familia et equitaturis non nimium numerosis, quemadmodum statuerunt nostri praedecessores, ita quod in curia familia numerum quadraginta personarum et vigintiquatuor bestiarum non excedat, et taliter in omnibus, quod nec de nimia pluralitate titulorum beneficialium nec de ruina ecclesiarum et diminutione divini cultus in locis, ubi sunt beneficiati, possint reprehendi. Utique supra quam dici potest laudabile foret cardinali, de unico cardinalatus sui titulo contentari, et quod quodlibet eius beneficium proprio intitulato gauderet, qui de quota fructuum iuxta beneficii qualitatem annue responderet. Per hoc se a multa cura et oblocutione liberaret.

31   Utique nullus decor ornatior in cardinali, quam ut se in exteriori habitu, statu et decentia Christi servum ostendat, pompam omnem spernat, quae ex diabolo est. Unum est cardinalium colle-

The second point is no less of the essence of a good cardinal. 29
For how will he be a cardinal, if his counsels are not faithful and
how will they be faithful, if they are not free? Those things which
inhibit counsel, however, are favors, enmities, partisanship and the
like. If, therefore, a cardinal is protector of a nation, prince or
community[36] for the sake of some interest of his own, his counsel
is inhibited. If he hopes for gifts on account of speeches to be delivered in the consistory[37] in favor of someone, he is a mercenary.
It befits the perfect cardinal, therefore, to impose on himself a firm
law of spurning gifts, not expecting to have more than three or
four thousand florins a year, and to eschew all the blandishments
of this world, which can deter him from free and faithful counsel.

The third point of visitation is surely required for building 30
up the Church. For since cardinals might build up the universal
Church more by example than by words, they are surely obliged
more than others by their exalted position to live an exemplary
life. One's life should correspond to one's rank; they should therefore be content with maintaining an honorable, appropriate status, a decent household and not too many horsemen. As our
predecessors decreed, in the Curia a household should not exceed
forty persons and twenty-four animals; and likewise in all things,
the cardinals should take care that they cannot be criticized for
excessive pluralism in titles to benefices, nor for the dilapidation of
churches and the diminution of worship in places where they have
benefices. It would be beyond all praise for a cardinal to be content with the single title of his cardinalate; and for him to be
happy with annual income produced by the benefice of his titular
church.[38] In this way he may free himself from much care and
obloquy.

Certainly no ornament is seemlier in a cardinal than showing 31
himself a servant of Christ in his external dress, way of life and
decency of conduct, and spurning all pomp, which is of the devil.
There is only one college of cardinals; why are there so many

gium; cur sunt tot capparum varietates? Estne religio S. Petri laxior quam alicuius sancti, quasi illis, qui se non alligarunt ad ordinem alicuius alterius religionis, etiam si sint religionum omnium duces et conservatores, liceat nunc in rubeis, tunc in flavis et sicut libuerit cappis in publico comparere? Credimus, formam cappae signum religionis esse et singulos sacri collegii fratres de uno aliquo colore sacerdotibus in canone indulto merito debere contentari, quemadmodum religiosi alii, qui in collegio sunt, habitum, quem religio deposcit, non immutant. Disparitas enim habituum levitatis videtur signum et plurimum detrahit tantorum virorum gravitati. Sic et in vestibus familiarium nihil quod offendat aut levitatem arguat, reperiri convenit, ut qualis dominus est, consociantes ipsum cunctis ostentent.

32   De mensa cardinalis, quae taliter regulata esse debet, ut solum refectioni necessaria sine gulosa ferculorum multitudine videatur, et lectione, dum comeditur, et disputatione post gratias visitatores cuncta moderentur et rite disponant. Sic et circa ornatum aularum et camerarum, sublatis superfluis, quae munditiae serviunt permittantur, proviso quod locus oratorii atque cappellae, ubi quotidie aut legere cardinalis aut devote debet missam audire, sit in laudem Dei devotissime adornatus.

33   Haec sic succincte visitatoribus rememoravimus, reliqua ad ipsos remittentes, ut agant, secundum quod invenerint, taliter quod catholica ecclesia gaudeat de tam sacro et divino collegio et dignissimis cardinalibus, Christianae religionis praeducibus, merito imitandis.

34   Post haec ad divinum cultum in urbe Romana reformandum visitatores per suprapositas regulas manum apponant, et primo principales papales basilicas adeant, deinde cardinalium titulos,

kinds of capes? Is the religious observance of Saint Peter more lax than that of any other saint, as if it were permissible for those who do not bind themselves to the observance of any other religious order — even if they are leaders and guardians of all orders — to appear in public now in red capes, now in golden ones, as they please? We believe the form of the cape is a sign of religious observance and that it would be right and appropriate for individual brothers of the sacred college to content themselves with a cape of some one color permitted to priests in canon law, just as other religious who belong to a college may not change the habit that their order demands. Disparity of clothing seems a sign of levity and detracts greatly from the gravity of such important men. Likewise, it is appropriate that nothing be found in the dress of their households which offends or suggests levity, so that those who associate with him show what sort of man their master is.

Visitors should regulate and dispose with due ceremony all   32
things concerning a cardinal's table, which ought to be so well regulated that only what is necessary for refreshment is seen, without a gluttonous multitude of dishes, and with reading during meals[39] and discussion after grace. Thus also with regard to the decoration of halls and chambers: all things superfluous should be removed; and [only] those things that preserve neatness and cleanliness should be allowed, with the proviso that the place of prayer and worship, where the cardinal daily should read or devoutly hear Mass, should be ornamented most devoutly for the praise of God.

We remind visitors briefly of these things, leaving the rest to   33
them, so that they may take action in accordance with what they find, in such a way that the Catholic Church may have joy of so holy and divine a college and of such worthy cardinals, the princes of the Christian religion, who must deserve to be imitated.

After this, visitors should set about reforming divine worship in   34
the city of Rome according to the aforesaid rules. First, they should go to the principal papal basilicas,[40] then the titular churches

post haec religiosos; demum hospitalium non obliviscantur. Nec opus est, ad dictas regulas quidquam adiicere, cum sufficiant. Quando enim quisque quod iuravit seu vovit sincere servaverit et devote peregerit, congruis temporibus canonicis horis et divino missae officio vacaverit et creditam curam vigilanter peregerit, habitum et tonsuram, ut iura et religio praescribit, gesserit, adhuc nisi se inutilem servum Dei aestimaverit, non iactet se perfecte reformatum.

35   Advertant visitatores, quod mundi sint servi Dei ab omni carnis foeditate, et nequaquam concubinarios de eleemosyna Christi concupiscentiarum suarum illecebritates continuare patiantur.

36   Circa librorum ad divinum cultum necessariorum etiam curam convertant, non solum quod non deficiant, sed quod sint emendati et Romano ordini concordantes; sacerque ornatus divina mysteria celebrantium integer et mundus sit; ecclesiaeque, quantum fieri potest integrae et taliter clausae et reparatae, ut sint divinis serviis aptae et devotae.

37   Circa personas quae in nostra curia reperiuntur, advertant visitatores an sint de necessariis, uti sunt cardinales et officiales, an alii praeter istos, et investigent causas cur in curia degant. Quod si non repererint iustas et necessarias, et fuerint episcopi, abbates aut alii beneficiati, non patiantur eos in curia nostra tempus terere, sed ut Deo serviant ad loca sua remittantur. Non enim decet curiam nostram dare praelatis beneficiatis et religiosis evagandi libertatem et ambiendi maiores dignitates et beneficiorum pluralitatem perniciosam occasionem. Valde enim indecens est, quod episcopus vel abbas, qui iam habet sponsam sibi in fide desponsatam, cuius de-

of the cardinals, then the religious houses; likewise they should not forget the hospitals. And there is no need to add anything to the aforesaid rules, since they suffice. For when anyone shall observe sincerely and carry out devoutly what he swore or vowed to do, when he shall free himself at fitting hours to say the canonical hours and the divine office of the Mass and shall fulfill vigilantly his assigned task, and when he shall wear fitting garb and a tonsure, as law and religion prescribe, he will still not boast that he is perfectly reformed, unless he reckons himself useless as a servant of God.[41]

Visitors should take care that God's servants are clean of all foulness of the flesh, nor should they suffer clerics who keep concubines to continue living on Christ's alms while reveling in their lusts.   35

They should turn their attention also to the care of the books necessary for divine worship, not only seeing to it that they are not lacking, but also that they are correct copies and conform to the usage of Rome. The holy ornaments of those celebrating the divine mysteries ought to be complete and clean; and churches, as far as possible, should be completed, well-enclosed and in good repair, so that they are useful for and consecrated to divine services.   36

Concerning the persons who are found in our Curia, the visitors should investigate whether they belong to the necessary personnel, as are the cardinals and the officials, or whether there are others beyond these, and let them investigate the reasons why such person stay in the Curia. If no just and necessary reasons are found, and the curialists are bishops, abbots or others with benefices, they should not permit them to waste time in our Curia, but they should send them back to their own places so they can serve God. It is not fitting that our Curia give beneficed prelates and religious the freedom to wander about and pernicious occasion to canvass for higher offices and more benefices. It is utterly unseemly for a bishop or abbot who has already taken a bride in   37

sponsationis annulum gestat, illam vel deserere per absentiam vel cum illa adhuc aliam sponsam habendi in curia operam dare, et ut sua desideria impleat, non solum cardinalibus servire et blandiri, sed et minoribus officialibus, quos sibi favorabiles esse tam munere obsequii quam manus procurat, qui pontificem in qualibet vacatione alicuius gratae dignitatis pro eo vexare non desistant. Avaritia enim talium, quae est idolorum cultus, non debet foveri, sed exstingui. Omnibus talibus praelatis de avaritia et ambitione suspectis merito praeferri debent in promotionibus illi, qui circa suas ecclesias resident tamquam graves et iusti et Deo amabiles fideles dispensatores.

38   Si qui vero se asserunt principum missos et ambasciatores, et sub tali colore curialibus venationibus insistunt, peracta ambasciata aut dato competenti termino, ut se expediant, ad ecclesias suas remittantur.

39   Fatemur, praelatos saepe auxilio Romani pontificis indigere; sed dum iuxta praestitum per eos iuramentum de visitandis liminibus apostolorum Romam venerint, illa poterunt convenienter expedire, neque nos volumus, quod beneficiati curiam sine necessitate, sed propter cupiditatem sequentes, gaudeant privilegiis de perceptione fructuum et aliis praerogativis curialibus indultis. Non est nostra intentio allicere beneficiatos et curiam augere cum offensa Dei et divini cultus imminutione. Omnes autem, qui ex iustis causis in curia manent, volumus ut in moribus, vita, habitu, tonsura et in legendis canonicis horis, ut ius disponit, se habeant; et si qui curiales, etiam laici, reperti fuerint lenones, concubinarii, lusores et deceptores ab honestate declinantes, illos a nostra curia omnino eiici mandamus.

faith[42] to seek to annul that marriage, or to desert his bride by absence, or to strive in the Curia to have still another bride along with the one he already has; to fulfill his desires, he dances attendance on and flatters not only cardinals but even lesser officials, whom he renders favorable to himself as much by his fawning as by doing them services, so that they may ceaselessly vex the pope on his behalf about any vacancy in an office they would like. For greed about such offices, which is the worship of idols,[43] should not be kindled but stamped out. To all such prelates, suspect for their greed and ambition, visitors would be right to prefer in promotions those who reside in their churches like grave, just and faithful stewards, who are beloved of God.[44]

Those who claim that they are emissaries and ambassadors of 38 princes and who insist on hunting benefices in the Curia under some such pretense should be sent back to their churches after fulfilling their embassies or after giving them a suitable terminal date for extricating themselves.

We confess that prelates often need the aid of the Roman 39 pontiff; but when in accordance with an oath sworn by them they shall come to Rome to visit the thresholds of the apostles,[45] they can be suitably released from their vows. We wish that beneficed clerics who follow the Curia without need but merely on account of their greed should not enjoy the privilege of receiving income [from their benefices] and other privileges granted to members of the Curia. It is not our intention to entice beneficed clerics and to increase the Curia to God's offense and the diminution of divine worship. All, however, who remain in the Curia for just reason we wish to behave in manners, life, dress, tonsure and in the reading of the canonical hours as the law disposes. If any curialists, even lay ones, are found to be procurers, keepers of concubines, gamblers and deceivers fallen into dishonor, we command that they be expelled entirely from our Curia.

40   Ad officia curiae se visitatores convertentes, imprimis poeniten-
tiariam examinent et secundum praemissas regulas convocatis omnibus membris officii coram summo poenitentiario, praemisso
verbo ad visitationem et animorum praeparationem opportuno,
eligant, ut regula habet, tres practicos ex ipsis, per quos de officio,
personis, statutis, iuramento et observantiis se informent; deinde a
capite visitationem inchoent et, an debita gravitas, zelus, scientia,
diligentia, experientia, mundicies manuum, vigilantia et cura tam
sancto officio debita in ipso capite reperiantur. Post cum duodecim
minoribus poenitentiariis similiter agant, quos de omnibus natio-
nibus Romam pro suarum animarum salute confluentibus esse necesse est, ut confitentes eis intelligant et patriam eorum penitus
non ignorent. Quos et peritos esse oportet tam in sacra scriptura
quam in canonibus; etiam ipsos canones poenitentiales et poeni-
tentias tam solemnes quam publicas et privatas a sanctis patribus
et praedecessoribus nostris designatas scire oportet, ut confitenti-
bus peccatorum conditiones ex ordinatis poenitentiis sciant aggra-
vare. Quod si poenitentiarios illos repererint leves aut ignorantes
aut transgressores iuramentorum et statutorum, non habentes zelum animarum, sed lucris deditos in eo officio, ubi receptio dono-
rum abominabilis est omnibus bonis, sine difficultate eiiciantur.
Omnino iniungentes, quod peregrinos homicidas et mutilatores
membrorum in sacris exsistentium sic ad propria cum littera re-
mittant, quod ipsi teneantur omni anno publice poenitentiam re-
petere cum aliquo actu humilitatis et devotionis, ita quod per hoc
ad omnium notitiam per poenitentiam deducatur peccati immani-
tas. Sic et in aliis publicis criminibus, homicidio et superiori, de-
scribendo in littera poenitentiam et non remittendo totaliter ad
ordinarios, qui forte talem iniungere non auderent. Oportet enim,

Turning now to the Curial offices, visitors first should examine   40
the Penitentiary.[46] Let them summon all the members of the office
in the presence of the major penitentiary, according to the aforesaid rules, and having said something appropriate about the visitation and the preparation of souls, they should choose, as the rules
of the Penitentiary require,[47] three experienced persons from
among them, through whom they may inform themselves about
the office, staff, statutes, oath and observances. Then, beginning
with the head official, let them inquire whether due gravity, zeal,
knowledge, diligence, experience, clean hands, vigilance and the
care befitting so holy an office may be found in that head. Afterwards, they should do the same with the twelve minor penitentiaries, who necessarily represent all the nations who flock to Rome
for the salvation of their souls, so that they may understand those
who confess to them and not be entirely ignorant of their home
countries. They ought also to have knowledge of Holy Scripture
as well as of canon law; and they ought to know especially the
penitential canons and the penances, solemn, public and private,
designated by the holy fathers and our predecessors, so that they
know how to weigh the conditions of those confessing their sins
according to the assigned penances. If they find the penitentiaries
to be flippant, ignorant or breakers of their oaths and statutes,
lacking zeal for souls but dedicated to making profit from their
office, wherein the receiving of gifts is abominable to all good
men,[48] they are to be summarily ejected. Let the visitors enjoin
upon them that they should send back to their homes aliens guilty
of homicide and bodily injury to clerics with letters saying they are
obliged every year publicly to repeat their penances, with some act
of humility and devotion, so that through the penance all may receive notice of the enormity of their sin. Thus also with regard to
other public crimes, homicide and the above, let the penitentiaries
describe the penance in the letter and not leave it entirely to the
bishops, who perhaps may not dare impose such a penance. It is

quod in publicis peccatis appareat de poenitentia publica ad aedificationem ecclesiae. Et maxime cavere habent, ne facilitas veniae
augeat potius delicta quam imminuat. Super omnia apud ipsos
non reperiatur personarum acceptio, qui vices Christi tenent.

41   Scriptores vero litterarum poenitentiariae sint per se scribentes
et intelligentes quae scribunt, et nisi sint honesti et mundi, suum
iuramentum servantes et taxam laborum suorum per nostros praedecessores factam non excedentes, eiiciantur. ‹Non›⁴ liceat etiam
unicuique supplicationes facere, porrigere et litterarum expeditio-
nem sollicitare per se aut alium quemcumque, sive fuerit procurator poenitentiariae sive non, et illi, qui se ingerunt ad hoc et peregrinos decipiunt et gravant, puniantur et de curia eiiciantur.

necessary that, in public sins, public penances should contribute to building up the Church. Let them beware especially lest ease of pardon should increase crimes rather than decrease them. Above all, there should not be any regard for persons among those who act on Christ's behalf.

The letter writers of the penitentiary should write their own   41
letters and understand what they write; if they are not honest and pure, following their oath and not exceeding the fees set by our predecessors for their work, they are to be expelled. It is also not permitted that they should make supplications for anyone, offer or solicit written exemptions for themselves or anyone else, whether they are a procurator of the Penitentiary or not, and those who conduct themselves in this way, deceiving and burdening pilgrims, should be punished and ejected from the curia.

Note on the Texts and Translations

꽃ᏕᎴᎢᲮ

Where possible, the translations in this book were made from the Heidelberg Academy's authoritative edition, *Nicolai de Cusa opera omnia* (Leipzig and Hamburg: Felix Meiner Verlag, 1932–2005).[1] The texts based on the Heidelberg edition are:

1. *De usu communionis*, ed. Hans Gerhard Senger, vol. 15, fasc. 1, in press
8. Sermon 21, ed. R. Haubst and M. Bodewig, in vol. 16, part 3, pp. 318–329;
11. Sermon 126, ed. R. Haubst and H. Paul, in vol. 18, part 1, pp. 20–27;
12. Sermon 144, ed. H. Paul, in vol. 18, part 2, pp. 103–107;
13. Sermon 160, ed. H. Paul, in vol. 18, part 2, pp. 183–185;
14. Sermon 287, ed. H. D. Riemann, in vol. 19, part 7, pp. 641–643;
15. Sermon 280, ed. H. D. Riemann, in vol. 19, part 6, pp. 585–598;
16. Sermon 290, ed. H. D. Riemann, in vol. 19, part 7, pp. 658–667.

The exceptions are (text 2) *Is the Authority of the Holy Councils Greater Than That of the Pope?*, edited by Erich Meuthen in *Cusanus Texte*, 2.2 (Heidelberg: Heidelberger Akademie, 1977); (text 3) *On Presidential Authority in a General Council (De auctoritate praesidendi)* edited by Gerhard Kallen in *Cusanus-Texte*, 2.1 (Heidelberg: Heidelberger Akademie, 1935–36); (text 4) *Oration at the Diet of Frankfurt* and (texts 5–6) *Two Memoranda against Neutrality*, both in *Acta Cusana: Quellen zur Lebensgeschichte des Nikolaus von Kues*, edited by Erich Meuthen and Hermann Hallauer, 1.2 (Hamburg: Felix Meiner Verlag, 1976); (text 7) *A Dialogue against the Amedeists*,

edited by Erich Meuthen in *Mitteilungen und Forschungsbeiträge der Cusanus Gesellschaft* 8 (1970): 78–114; (text 9) *Letter to the Bohemians on Church Unity*, in *Nikolaus von Kues Werke*, edited by Paul Wilpert, 2 vols. (Berlin: De Gruyter, 1967) 2.2, fol. 13v-22r; (text 10) *Letter to Rodrigo Sánchez de Arévalo*, edited by Gerhard Kallen in *Cusanus-Texte*, 2.1 (Heidelberg: Heidelberger Akademie, 1935–36); (text 17) *A General Reform of the Church*, edited by Stephan Ehses, "Der Reformentwurf Kardinals Nikolaus Cusanus," *Historisches Jahrbuch* 32 (1911): 281–297.[2] All texts are used by kind permission of the publishers. I am most grateful to Dr. Hans Gerhard Senger for allowing me to make use of his edition of Text 1 before publication. Some minor changes of punctuation, capitalization and orthography have been made silently in order to make the texts more accessible; the few more substantial changes are indicated in the Notes to the Text. Banal typographical errors have been corrected silently.

The translations attempt to make Cusanus' texts accessible without making them more fluent than they were in the original. The author's Latin was awkward, especially in the early works, and some of them are studded with references to sources. In cases where Cusanus descends into elliptical language and legalese the translations sometimes supply words within square brackets to make the thought clearer. Other texts, especially the sermons, contain passages that are little more than notes, presumably to be filled out *ex tempore* by the preacher; these have been rendered as literally as is consistent with correct English.

The conventions for citing legal texts are explained under Abbreviations in the Notes to the Translation; the latter notes contain citations from other, non-legal sources as well. (Some of Cusanus' sources seem to have been quoted from memory, and some of the citations have no obvious relevance to the issue under discussion.) A few references were not possible to trace, and these cases have been noted individually. I have relied heavily for the

identification of sources on the *apparatus fontium* of the Heidelberg editors and the editors of the other texts reprinted here, and gratefully acknowledge the work of these scholars.

The early works should be read along with Paul Sigmund's translation of *The Catholic Concordance*. Later works should be read alongside translations of *On Learned Ignorance* and *On Conjectures*.[3]

Editorial additions to the Latin text are indicated with ‹ › and deletions with [ ]; editorial additions to the English translation are indicated with [ ].

NOTES

1. When completed, the Heidelberg Academy edition will have twenty-three volumes, including three index volumes. Publication dates for vol. 15 and for the later fascicules of vol. 19 have not been announced.

2. New editions of Texts 10 and 17 are forthcoming in the vol. 15, part 2, of the Heidelberg Academy edition.

3. Both can be found in Volume 1 of *Complete Philosophical and Theological Treatises of Nicholas of Cusa,* translated by Jasper Hopkins (see Bibliography).

Notes to the Text

꙰꙳꙰

I. TO THE BOHEMIANS

1. absque *ed.*
2. *Perhaps emend to* primatu
3. et *ed.*
4. ecclesiastiae *ed.*
5. caperet *ed.*
6. ministrans *ed.*

2. AUTHORITY OF THE HOLY COUNCILS

1. antiquitas *ed.*
2. *a second* quod *after* sunt *ed.*
3. dicit *ed.*
4. civitatem *ed.*

4. ORATION AT THE DIET OF FRANKFURT

1. *Not in ed., but compare* §25.
2. Ad hoc *ed.*
3. congregata *Gratian*
4. qui a *ed.*
5. *sc.* Anulinum
6. *supplied from Augustine*
7. quibus *after* aliis *ed.*
8. *sc.* De potestate ecclesiastica

9. *an otiose* quod *after* igitur *ed.*

10. invitus *ed.*: invitis *supplied from Gratian*

5. NEUTRALITY OR INDECISION

1. *emendation (not in ed.)*

6. AGAINST SUSPENSION OF ALLEGIANCE

1. Condictio *ed.*

7. A DIALOGUE AGAINT THE AMEDEISTS

1. liberato *ed.*

2. *a conjecture: not in ed.*

3. *a conjecture:* tunc *ed.*

4. *a second clause corresponding to the first* aut *clause is evidently missing.*

5. uti *after* ista *ed.*

6. furore *Augustine*

7. *words supplied from Augustine*

9. LETTER TO THE BOHEMIANS ON CHURCH UNITY

1. et *ed.*

2. nobis *ed.*

3. tales *ed.*

4. prouacarunt *ed.*

5. nobis *ed.*

6. Sibuanus *ed.*

7. illud *Augustine*

8. *sc.* LXXVI

9. infra *ed.*

10. concilium *ed.*

11. Interuerunt *(sic) ed.*

12. *a second* quod *after* divinam *ed.*

13. preseruati *ed.*

10. LETTER TO RODRIGO SÁNCHEZ DE ARÉVALO

1. *Title in ed.*: Epistola Nicolai de Cusa ad Rodericum de Trevino, archidiaconum, oratorem regis Castellae. In dieta Francofordiensi. Anno 1442, die 20 Mai.

2. *One should perhaps read* aeterni

3. *So in ed.; the word should probably be deleted*

4. ordinata *ed.*

5. tamquam *ed.*

6. universa *ed.*

7. vicario *ed.*

11. SERMON 126

1. *not in ed.*

2. *not in ed.*

16. SERMON 290

1. *not in ed.*

2. ipse *after* ut *ed.*

17. A GENERAL REFORM OF THE CHURCH

1. aut non *ed.*

2. successorum *ed.*

3. *Perhaps* aut *should be read*

4. *Supplied word not in ed.*

Notes to the Translation

꽃삶꽃

The Bible is quoted from the Douay-Rheims version. The ordinary gloss is cited from *Biblia sacra cum glossa ordinaria . . .* 6 vols. (Douay and Antwerp: Baltazar Bellervs, 1617). Church canons are cited by Cusanus under their Latin incipits, e.g., *Haec est fides*. The references added by the translator use the following style in citing texts from *Corpus Iuris Canonici*, ed. Emil Friedberg, 2 vols. (Leipzig, 1879):

Gratian's *Decretum:*

D. c. = Distinction and chapter [e.g., D. 40 c. 6]

C. q. c. = Causa, question and chapter [e.g., C. 24 q. 1 c. 1]

Gratian's *dicta* or notes following a chapter are cited as p.c. [*post capitulum*].

Decretal collections are cited by Latin name, book and title (subject heading). The collections cited are:

X = *Decretals of Gregory IX* or *Decretales Gregorii IX,* known as the *Liber Extra* (1234)

VI = *Sixth Book of Decretals* or *Liber Sextus Decretalium* (1298)

Clem. = *The Decretals of Clement V* or *Clementines* (1317)

Extrav. commun. = *Additional Decretals* or *Extravagantes Communes.*

All are cited by book, title and chapter [e.g., X 1.1.1]. The symbol ℭ is used where the edition cites a paragraph within a chapter.

I. TO THE BOHEMIANS

1. Psalm 5:9.

2. *On the Grace of Christ and Original Sin against Pelagius and Celestine, PL* 44: 397–398.

3. Leo I, *On the Heresy and History of the Priscillianists, PL* 55: 1033.

4. Letter 2, *PL* 16: 887.

5. Action 13 of the Third Council of Constantinople, which references a letter of Sophronius, in Mansi 11: 571.

6. *Letter to the Catholics against the Donatists, Commonly Called "On the Unity of the Church," PL* 43: 393.

7. This reference does not match Sermon 321, *PL* 38: 1443.

8. Mansi 12: 1089.

9. John 14:6.

10. For example, if someone at the point of death is converted but there is not time to perform the rite of baptism, Catholic theology understands that in this special case the mental act of conversion can stand by itself as a sign or sacrament of conversion.

11. Luke 10:33.

12. Exodus 20:8.

13. John 3:16–17.

14. Referring to the common practice of following the administration of any of the other sacraments with a Mass.

15. John 6:54.

16. I.e., he had that sign, baptism, of which the Eucharist is a sign. The Hussite argument stipulates that the Eucharist is less necessary when used simply as a confirmation of other sacraments.

17. This would later become the principle of union with Greek Orthodox Christians during the Council of Ferrara-Florence, "one religion in a variety of rites" (*una religio in varietate rituum*).

18. John 6:54.

19. Luke 14:33.

20. Homily 16, *PG* 12: 251.

21. *Dialogue against the Pelagians under the Names of Atticus the Catholic and Critobulus the Heretic, PL* 23: 551.

22. *On Heresies to Quodvultdeus, PL* 42: 32.

23. *On Baptism against the Donatists,* CSEL 51, 170–171, which gives the number of bishops as eighty.

24. Letter 93, *PL* 33: 343. The letter actually is to Vincent concerning the Rogatists.

25. *On the Unity of the Church*, CCSL 3: 265.

26. Matthew 16:18.

27. Letter 53, *PL* 33: 195–197.

28. Letter 26, *PL* 16: 1042–1046.

29. Letter 102, *PL* 33: 373–376.

30. Letter 199, *PL* 33: 904–925.

31. John 3:3 and Matthew 28:19, respectively.

32. The translators of the Hebrew Scriptures into Greek, who produced the Septuagint.

33. Book 18 c. 42, CCSL 48: 638.

34. The specific statements in the Apostles' Creed often were attributed to individual apostles.

35. *Against the Letter of Mani That is Called Fundamental*, PL 42: 176.

36. Ephesians 5:27.

37. John 14:6.

38. *Explanations of the Psalms*, Explanation 2 of Psalm 33, Sermon 1, CCSL 38: 193. See also Sermon 183, *PL* 39: 2091–2092.

39. See the Solemn Prayers for the Good Friday Liturgy in the Roman Missal.

40. *On Baptism against the Donatists*, PL 43: 155. See also, ibid., PL 43: 241.

41. John 14:18 and Matthew 28:20, respectively.

42. That is, impediments, including degrees of blood relationship or consanguinity.

43. Affinity was contracted by sexual intercourse, licit or illicit.

44. *PL* 23: 625–630.

45. Matthew 16:18.

46. Matthew 23:2–3.

47. Pseudo-Ambrose (Ambrosiaster), *On Paul's Letter to the Galatians* 2.7–8, *PL* 17: 349.

48. *On the Holy Spirit to the Emperor Gratian*, PL 16: 776.

49. Letter 69, *PL* 4: 406.

50. Cyprian, *Epistles* 69.8, *PL* 4:406.

51. *Against Jovinian*, *PL* 23: 247.

52. 1 John 3:24.

53. Legalese for the proposition that a Church tribunal cannot *command* an illicit act on the basis of a defective legal decision, but it can *prohibit* someone from performing a licit act on defective grounds because of the overriding importance of obedience in the Church. In the latter case, any graces that might have accrued to the defendant from the foregone licit act may be acquired directly from God. For example, if someone is excommunicated by a Church tribunal on the basis of corrupt testimony, that person is bound to obey the Church even though the decision was wrongly taken, but he may approach God directly in prayer to obtain the graces of communion. Cusanus' point presumably is to show that the Church's power to prevent someone from taking communion is not limited even in extreme cases where a sentence of excommunication is the result of a unjust plea. Restricting the laity to communion in one kind would then *a fortiori* be licit.

54. 1 Corinthians 5:5.

55. Burchard of Worms, *Decretum*, *PL* 140: 754.

56. Arnulf of Beauvais, *Epistle on the Sacrament of the Altar*, printed as *Epistola de sacramento altaris, seu Responsiones ad varias Lamberti quaestiones de sacramento eucharistiae*, in *Spicilegium, sive Collectio veterum aliquot scriptorum qui in Galliae bibliothecis delituerant*, ed. Jean Luc d'Achéry, vol. 3 (Paris: Apud Montalant, 1723), pp. 470–474 at pp. 471.

57. 1 Corinthians 11:24.

58. Matthew 28:19.

59. Partial quotation of Arnulf, *Epistle on the Sacrament of the Altar*, p. 471.

60. Paraphrased from Arnulf, *On the Sacrament of the Altar*, p. 472.

61. Hinschius, pp. 109–112.

62. Ecclesiastes 31:12.

63. Paraphrased from Arnulf, *On the Sacrament of the Altar*, p. 472.

64. Paraphrased from Arnulf, ibid.

65. John 6:54.

66. Hilary of Poitiers, *On the Trinity*, PL 10: 284.

67. Matthew 4:4.

68. *On the Gospel of John*, tract CXXIV, PL 35: 1613–1614.

69. John 14:6.

70. John 6:47, 50.

71. Possibly Letter 35, to Hortonianus; see PL 16: 1074 and Hebrews 11:6.

72. *On the Lord's Sermon on the Mount according to Matthew*, PL 34: 1280–1281; *Explanations of the Psalms*, Explanation of Psalm 33, Sermon 2, CCSL 38: 290.

73. Sermon 3, PL 46: 826–28 or 834–36.

74. 1 Corinthians 11:28–29: a passage condemning those who take communion in an unworthy manner.

75. *Enchiridion to Lawrence, or On Faith, Hope and Charity*, PL 40: 258–259.

76. See above, note 71.

77. See 1 Corinthians 13:12.

78. *Apologetic Oration*, PG 35: 438–439

79. *De fide et symbolo* 10.23, PL 40: 193–194.

80. Hebrews 11:6.

81. See §15, above.

82. I.e. 1 Corinthians 11:28–29; see §44, above.

83. Ibid.

84. John 3:3.

85. *tradendi*, here evidently referring to Paul's excommunication of the Corinthian: *judicavi . . . eum . . . tradere huiusmodi Satanae in interitum carnis.*

86. 1 Corinthians 5:5.

87. PG 3: 566–567.

88. I.e. Odilbert of Milan. On this text, see Susan A. Keefe, *Water and the Word: Baptism and the Education of the Clergy in the Carolingian Empire* (Notre Dame, 2002). I, 75, 78; II, 91, 154–170.

89. The Fourth Lateran Council, held by Pope Innocent III in 1215.

90. *PL* 4: 484–486.

91. Daniel 4 contains the dream of Nebuchadnezzar, apparently irrelevant, but see Hosea 4:9: *Et erit sicut populus, sic sacerdos.*

92. *De poenitentia* D. 7 c. 5.

93. Hinschius, pp. 528, 532.

94. Hinschius, p. 267.

95. See the Second Council of Carthage in Hinschius, p. 296.

96. Hinschius, pp. 342–343.

97. Augustine quotes Cyprian in his text; see Letter 93, *PL* 33: 341.

98. Which text Cusanus consulted is unclear, but early liturgical texts make frequent mention of the roles played by deacons.

99. Innocent III, *On the Sacred Mystery of the Altar, PL* 217: 871–872.

100. AA SS Aug. II, p. 490 (BHL 4753).

101. I Corinthians 11:26.

102. Ordinary Gloss to *De cons.* D. 2 c. 93.

103. See *PL* 47: 770.

104. Not found.

105. This is one of the collects for the First Sunday in Advent.

106. Ordinary Gloss to *De cons.*, D. 2 c. 93.

2. AUTHORITY OF THE HOLY COUNCILS

1. First Nicaea (325), First Constantinople (381), Ephesus (431), Chalcedon (451), Second Constantinople (553), Third Constantinople (680–681), Second Nicaea (787), Fourth Constantinople (869–870).

2. COD 8–9.

3. Mansi 11: 207–212, 737–740.

4. Mansi II: 201–202.

5. Actually Leo IX.

6. *PL* 143: 750.

7. *COD* 99–100.

8. Cusanus is not citing a letter of Leo I, but see Hinschius, pp. 577, 609–610, 610–611.

9. Mansi 16: 140. The reference is actually to the Eighth Proceeding.

10. Anastasius the Librarian in Mansi 16: 78.

11. Hinschius, pp. 607–609.

12. Mansi II: 233–234.

13. Mansi 16: 20–24.

14. Mansi 16: 20–24.

15. *COD* 8–9.

16. Mansi II: 199–200.

17. Mansi II: 2032–4.

18. Mansi II: 233–234, 235–236, 285–286.

19. *ACO* 2.3, 7f.

20. *ACO* 2.2, 26f.

21. *ACO* 2.4, 27f.

22. This apparently is a reference to the First Proceeding of the Third Council of Constantinople; see Mansi II: 214–15.

23. Cusanus means either Fifth or Sixth Toledo; see Hinschius, pp. 374–380.

24. Mansi 3: 599–620 at col. 602.

25. Mansi II: 233–236.

26. Mansi II: 305–306, 285–316.

27. *COD* 179–180.

28. See Mansi 16: 82–83. The edition says "Fifth Proceeding."

29. No one passage in the Seventh Proceeding says this.

30. Mansi 16: 108, 110.

31. Mansi 16: 117.

32. Mansi 11: 239–242.

33. John 21:18.

34. Luke 22:32.

35. Mansi 16: 27.

36. *On Schism against the Donatists*, CSEL 26: 36–37, 39.

37. Matthew 16:18–19.

38. Canticles 4:8.

39. *PL* 139: 171.

40. C. 24 q. 1 c. 14.

41. Letter 16, CSEL 54: 69.

42. *ACO* 2.4, 19–21, 26f, 30f.

43. CCSL 95: 11, a letter addressed to the Emperor Marcian. Honorius I (625–638) sought a compromise on the issue of Monothelitism. His case was unknown in the West before Cusanus' day. Liberius (352–366) yielded under imperial pressure and tried to compromise with the Arians.

44. *On the Unity of the Church*, CCSL 3: 263–264.

45. Mansi 16: 183; *COD* 164–165.

46. *COD* 185.

47. *COD* 182.

48. Mansi 16: 140–141.

49. See above n. 47.

50. Hinschius, pp. 17–21.

51. *ACO* 2.3, 65.

52. In Mansi 11.

53. Mansi 16: 199, 200.

54. *ACO* 2.3, 61.

55. Mansi 16: 33, 84. The edition says "Fifth Proceeding."

56. Mansi 16: 32.

57. COD 182.

58. COD 174.

59. Mansi 16: 107.

60. Mansi 16: 87.

61. Mansi 16: 21.

62. Mansi 16: 117.

63. Mansi 16: 91.

64. Mansi 16: 115.

65. Mansi 16: 103–104.

66. Mansi 16: 87.

67. See above n. 61.

68. Matthew 16:19.

69. Matthew 18:18.

70. *On the Unity of the Church*, CCSL 3/1: 251–52.

71. "in act or in potency:" terms from Aristotelian physics. Either they actually do sit in judgment over the pope, or they have the power to do so.

72. COD 8–9.

73. COD 179–181.

74. First Constantinople is cited by the Council of Chalcedon in COD 99–100.

75. COD 32.

76. See Hincmar of Rheims, *Against Hincmar of Laon*, PL 126: 326.

77. ACO 2.7, 36f.

78. ACO 2. 3, 13.

79. See Hincmar of Rheims, *Against Hincmar of Laon*, PL 126: 329–332.

80. See *The Catholic Concordance*, Book 2, chapter 32.

81. D. 99 c. 1.

82. This may be a reference to D. 22 c. 2.

83. COD 8–9.

84. *Against Hincmar of Laon*, PL 126: 332.

85. AC 2.3, 506.

86. Matthew 16:18.

87. D. 21 c. 2.

88. This quotation is derived from Hincmar of Rheims, *Against Hincmar of Laon* in PL 126: 335.

89. See Galatians 2:11.

90. ACO 2.4, 73.

91. Fourth Constantinople in Mansi 16: 27.

92. Cusanus is using Rufinus' translation of Eusebius; see *Die Kirchengeschichte*, ed. Theodor Mommsen, vol. 2 (Leipzig, 1908), pp. 673–74.

93. See Bede on the Canonical Epistles in PL 93: 9.

94. PL 23: 258–529; see John 14:27.

95. Ps. Dionysius, *On the Ecclesiastical Hierarchy*, PG 3: 375.

96. Psalm 18:9.

97. Psalm 118:105.

98. Proverbs 6:23.

99. Isaiah 26:9.

100. COD 166.

101. Mansi 16: 87.

102. COD 174.

103. COD 182.

104. See Hincmar of Rheims, *Against Hincmar of Laon*, PL 126: 321–323.

105. See Hincmar of Rheims, *Against Hincmar of Laon*, PL 126: 369, 371.

106. PL 143: 751.

107. As opposed to Second Ephesus, the so-called Robber Synod of 451.

3. ON PRESIDENTIAL AUTHORITY

1. Matthew 18:20

2. Mansi 6: 627.

3. Matthew 18:20.

4. COD 408–09.

5. Not found.

6. Mansi 16: 32–33; the Biblical citation is Matthew 16:19.

7. Mansi 16: 33.

8. *Register of Letters*, CCSL 140: 332: Book 5, Letter 44.

9. Ibid. 140: 309: Book 5, Letter 37.

10. Mansi 6: 1046–47.

11. Mansi 11: 554–59.

12. Mansi 16: 189.

13. *The Catholic Concordance* 1.17.

14. Luke 22:32.

15. Matthew 28:20.

16. 1 Corinthians 11:26.

17. The edition wrongly gives the citations as "Lev. 14 and 27."

18. Matthew 28:20.

19. *The Catholic Concordance*, 1.9, citing Augustine, *On Correction of the Donatists*.

20. John 17:21.

21. *Against the Letter of Parmenian*, CSEL 26: 36: Book 2, Chapter 2.

22. *Register*, p. 50: Book 7, Letter 37.

23. COD 8–9.

24. *Against Jovinian*, PL 23: 258–59.

25. Ordinary Gloss to C. 2 q. 7 c. 35.

26. Henry of Susa (Hostiensis), *Summa aurea* (Venice, 1574; reprint, Turin, 1963), fol. 347–56.

27. Ordinary Gloss to John 21:17.

28. Ordinary Gloss to Matthew 16:9.

29. Matthew 18:20.

30. COD 7.

31. COD 179.

32. Mansi 11: 875.

33. Mansi 16: 185.

34. Acts 15:28 and Acts 4:32.

35. Mansi 16: 86.

36. Mansi 16: 80.

37. *To Glorius, Eleusis and Others*, CSEL 34: 101.

38. *Letter in the Case of Bonosus*, PL 16: 1233. Cusanus' conjecture about the authorship of this letter, found in *The Catholic Concordance*, 2.18, controversial in his own day, has not found favor since.

39. Mansi 16: 87.

40. COD 166–67.

41. *The Catholic Concordance* 2.20.

42. Hinschius, pp. 32–52.

43. VI. 1.7.1.

44. *The Catholic Concordance* 2.21.

45. Guido de Baysio, *Archidiaconus super decreto* (Lyons, 1549) [*Rosarium decreti*] at C. 11 q. 1 c. 46.

46. COD 179–80.

47. *The Catholic Concordance* 2.22.

48. For Boniface, understand Paschasinus, who did sign; see COD 102 and Mansi 6: 400–01, 983–86.

49. The edition has "C. 36."

50. Letter 33, *PL* 54: 799.

51. Damasus, Letter 1, *PL* 13: 349.

52. Letter 44, *PL* 54: 827–31.

53. *The Catholic Concordance* 2.5.

54. Mansi 11: 235.

55. Letter 44, *PL* 54: 827–31.

4. ORATION AT THE DIET OF FRANKFURT

1. Eugenius IV had declared Panormitanus (the jurist Nicolaus de Tudeschis) deposed from his see of Palermo. On Panormitanus, who was the representative of the Amedeists at the Diet of Frankfurt, see the Introduction.

2. The followers of Basel's antipope, Felix V, who had formerly been Amadeus VIII, Duke of Savoy.

3. Psalm 72:9. The quotation is inexact.

4. Ordinary Gloss to D. 23 c. 1 ₵ 7.

5. Frederick IV of Hapsburg, the German king, was crowned Holy Roman Emperor Frederick III in 1452.

6. Amadeus had gone into retirement at Ripaille in a quasi-monastic setting.

7. Second Council of Nicaea, Action VI, Mansi 23: 207.

8. John 14:6.

9. Novatian, a Roman presbyter of the third century, had gone into schism because he advocated more severe treatment of lapsed Christians and made himself antipope.

10. *Against the Letter of Parmenian* 2.9–10 (*PL* 43: 62).

11. Eugenius decreed the transfer of the council on September 18, 1437.

12. *COD* 478–82.

13. Cusanus distinguishes between a case in which there was more than one pope, as at the Council of Constance, and the present case, in which there was only one pope.

14. Canon law permitted an undoubted pope to lose his see for the crime of heresy.

15. The quotations here are from Eugenius IV, Bulls *Existimantes* (November 15, 1434) in *CF*, vol. I, pt. I, pp. 35–37 nr. 45; *Salvatoris* (May 30, 1437) in *CF*, vol. I, pt. I, pp. 64–70 nr. 66; and *Doctoris gentium* (Sept. 18, 1437) in *CF*, vol. I, pt. I, pp. 91–99 nr. 88.

16. Cristoforo Garratoni.

17. Giuliano Cesarini.

18. John VIII Palaeologus.

19. The Greeks regarded the presence of the five ancient patriarchal sees, Rome, Constantinople, Alexandria, Antioch and Jerusalem, as necessary for an ecumenical council.

20. See the majority decree of May 7, 1437 in *COD* 510–12. As Savoy was close to Avignon, it made possible the strong-arm tactic described below in §8.

21. The tithe was to support the Council of Union.

22. As opposed to promissory notes. For this memorandum of February 23, 1437, see Mansi 30.1121–22.

23. The four deputations — on faith, reform, peace and common matters — had to approve a proposal before it was brought to a general congregation.

24. Greek protests were dismissed as inspired by the pope.

25. Joseph II, patriarch of Constantinople.

26. The steering committee of the council.

27. Louis d'Aleman, whom Eugenius IV deposed from the cardinalate and Nicholas V later restored to it.

28. See the minority decree of May 7, 1437 in *COD* 512–13.

29. See Eugenius IV's bull *Salvatoris*, cited in n. 15 above.

30. Sigismund died in December of 1437.

31. Niccolò Albergati.

32. *COD* 514–17.

33. Council of Basel, Decree *Audivit* (January 24, 1438) in Mansi 29: 165–69.

34. For the decree of union with the Greeks, *Laetentur coeli* (July 6, 1439), see *COD* 523–28; for that with the Armenians, *Exultate Deo* (November 22, 1439), see *COD* 534–59; for that with the Copts, *Cantate Domino* (February 4, 1442), see *COD* 67–83; for that with the Syrian Jacobites, *Multa et admirabilia* (September 30, 1444), see *COD* 586–89; for that with the Chaldeans (or Nestorians) and Maronites, *Benedictus sit Deus* (August 7, 1445), see *COD* 589–91. The "Hyperboreans," a mythical race in antiquity associated with the Thracians or any remote people, may refer to the Kievan branch of Orthodoxy, which did not however accept the union.

35. Council of Basel, Decree *Prospexit* (June 15, 1439) in Mansi 29: 179–81.

36. Dominicus Ram.

37. Francesco Pizzolpasso.

38. Panormitanus' master, Alfonso V of Aragon, was not eager for schism.

39. Aside from his promises of obedience to the pope, Panormitanus once had represented Eugenius at Basel.

40. On November 12, 1440, Felix V had made him a cardinal.

41. Albert II was elected king of the Romans in 1438 and died in 1439.

42. The edition says C. 8. q. 3 c. 1.

43. There is nothing significant related to this subject in the Ordinary Gloss to C. 2 q. 7 p.c. 41 ℂ 10.

44. Antonius Altan.

45. March 11, 1438, see *DRTA* 13.191–95 nr. 126f.

46. Ordinary Gloss to C. 7 q. 1 c. 12.

47. Ordinary Gloss to C. 7 q. 1 c. 7.

48. Cusanus is implying that Albert's death prevented a decision against Basel.

49. Compare COD 409–10.

50. Ephesians 4:2–3.

51. Ordinary Gloss to C. 2 q. 7 c. 46.

52. Mansi 30: 1121–22.

53. This meeting began on May 15, 1437.

54. Johann von Gelnhausen.

55. The argument of the Amedeists was that the choice of site made by the committee appointed by the presidents of the council (see §10 above) would never have been accepted by a majority vote had it been presented to the general congregation of the council.

56. Ordinary Gloss to X 1.6.42.

57. Juan Palomar; Giovanni Berardi da Tagliacozzo, archbishop of Taranto; Johann von Gelnhausen, abbot of Maulbronn.

58. Second Council of Nicaea, Action VI, Mansi 23: 207.

59. COD 482.

60. Eugenius IV's bulls *Alta nos cure* (December 15, 1433), in Mansi 29: 576–77, and *Cum sacrum* (December 16, 1433), ibid. 29: 578.

61. Eugenius IV's bull *Salvatoris*, cited in n. 15 above.

62. COD 466–69.

63. See above n. 59.

64. Compare Mansi 29: 236–67 at col. 264 and 245.

65. COD 472.

66. For the nineteenth session, see above n. 59; for the twenty-fourth session, see COD 507–09.

67. Ordinary Gloss to D. 17 c. 5.

68. See above n. 59.

69. Fifth Council of Toledo (633), c. 4, in Hinschius, p. 375.

70. Venice.

71. *On Baptism against the Donatists*, CSEL 51.178.

72. See above n. 59.

73. *COD* 409–10.

74. See the decree of union *Laetentur coeli*, cited in n. 34 above.

75. Eugenius IV's bull *Doctoris gentium*, cited in n. 15 above.

76. Ordinary Gloss to D. 40 c. 6.

77. For the decree, see above n. 62. For Eugenius IV's bull *Dudum sacrum*, see Mansi 29: 78–89.

78. *COD* 438–39.

79. Cf. *COD* 472.

80. Second Council of Nicaea, Action VI, Mansi 23: 207.

81. Cusanus keeps insisting on the fact of the pope being "unchallenged and undoubted" in order to avoid appeal to the decrees of the Council of Constance (1414–18), where three rival popes had been deposed by the Council's authority.

82. Hinschius, pp. 456–61.

83. Hinschius, pp. 223–26.

84. Sermon 4, c. 3 in *PL* 54.151.

85. *On Schism against the Donatists*, CSEL 26.39 and CSEL 26.44.

86. *PL* 143.751.

87. Ordinary Gloss to C. 2 q. 5 c. 10 v. *Potuissem*.

88. See Hinschius, p. 449, where the text says 277.

89. Ps. Dionysius, Letter VIII in *PG* 3.1083–100 at col. 1087.

90. *To Glorius, Eleusis and Others*, CSEL 34.113–14.

91. See above, n. 76.

92. *To Glorius, Eleusis and Others*, CSEL 34.101.

93. Pseudo-Augustine, *Book of Questions on the Old and New Testaments*, CSEL 50.135.

94. CSEL 34.152–54.

95. CSEL 53.29; *PL* 43.610 (§16.28).

96. *Against the Letter of Parmenian*, CSEL 51.29.

97. Council of Pavia-Siena (1423–1424).

98. *On the Only Baptism*, CSEL 51.178.

99. Luke 22:32 ("But I [Christ] have prayed for you, that your faith may not fail.")

100. Ordinary Gloss to C. 24 q. 1 c. 6.

101. *On Marriages and Concupiscence* 1.24 in *PL* 44: 435, CSEL 42.250–51.

102. Ephesians 5:27.

103. Mansi 29: 261.

104. Mansi 29: 251.

105. Mansi 16: 185.

106. Fourth Council of Toledo (633), c. 4, in Hinschius, p. 365.

107. Mansi 10: 875.

108. Actually *Canons in the Cases of Apian*, c. 2, found as the Third Council of Carthage in Hinschius, p. 297.

109. *COD* 179.

110. See above n. 59.

111. Mansi 16: 147.

112. First Council of Carthage (349), c. 14, in Hinschius, p. 294.

113. Mansi 16: 188.

114. Ordinary Gloss to D. 65 c. 3. The edition has *Episcoporum*. Arguments against majority rule have been made above at §23 ff.

115. Ordinary Gloss to D. 17 c. 5.

116. Ordinary Gloss to D. 66 c. 1.

117. Guido de Baysio, *Archidiaconus super decreto* (Lyons, 1549) [*Rosarium decreti*] at D. 24 c. 6.

118. Ordinary Gloss to 1 Cor. 10.13.

119. *On the Only Baptism*, CSEL 51.180–81.

120. Isaiah 11: 2.

121. *COD* 409.

122. The iconoclast synod of Hiereia (754) preceded the Second Council of Nicaea (787).

123. Second Council of Nicaea, Action VI, Mansi 23: 207.

124. Augustinus Triumphus, *On Ecclesiastical Power*, q. 101; the title is given incorrectly as *On the Equity of Power* in the Latin.

125. I.e., their idea of majority rule is an abstraction that takes no account of the qualitative differences among persons and their offices, the actual needs of the Church and the need for consensus among representatives.

126. The bulls of Martin V and Eugenius IV read at the first session are in Mansi 29: 111–13.

127. Ordinary Gloss to C. 5 q. 4 c. 1.

128. Five came from Amadeus VIII's former domains.

129. Mansi 29: 178–79.

130. *COD* 529–34.

131. Eugenius IV's bull *Etsi non dubitemus* (1441), in CF 1, pt. 3, pp. 24–35 nr. 248.

132. For Panormitanus' role in this debate, see Aeneas Sylvius Piccolomini, *De gestis Basiliensis concilii commentariorum libri II*, ed. D. Hay and W. K. Smith (Oxford, 1967), pp. 92–138, 172–180.

133. *AC* vol. 1, pt. 2, pp. 375–76 nr. 519.

134. In the decree *Haec sancta*, for which see n. 140 below.

135. See above, n. 126.

136. The so-called Robber Synod (449); see the decree in *COD* 533.

137. Matthew 7:16.

138. See the end of §51.

139. See above, nn. 130 and 131.

140. The decree *Haec sancta* of 6 April 1415, which stated that a council had its authority immediately from Christ and that popes were bound to obey it in matters pertaining to faith, schism and reform, was issued by the Council of Constance under the authority of the French and Pisan obediences before the submission of Pope Gregory XII, who was head of the Italian obedience; this circumstance provided later popes with grounds to deny its authority. The document is quoted in Text 7, §4, below.

141. See above, n. 130.

142. CSEL 3.779.

143. Cesarini left on January 9, 1438.

144. Mansi 29: 409.

145. COD 170–71.

146. Second Council of Nicaea, Action VI, Mansi 23: 207.

5. NEUTRALITY OR INDECISION

1. The Nicene Creed.

2. *Unam sanctam* [Extrav. Commun. 1.8.1].

3. C. 24 q. 1 c. 18.

4. C. 24 q. 1 c. 34 ⁋ 2.

5. The princes' first declaration of neutrality was issued at the Diet of Frankfurt in March of 1439.

6. The followers of Felix V, formerly Amadeus VIII of Savoy.

6. AGAINST SUSPENSION OF ALLEGIANCE

1. The Acceptation of Mainz, decreed on March 26, 1439, before the proclamation of Felix V as pope by the Council of Basel in November, 1439.

2. The translation of the Council of Basel to Ferrara was decreed by Eugenius on September 18, 1437.

3. A reference to the Nicene Creed, which confesses belief in "one, holy, catholic and apostolic church."

4. Literally *extravagans*, a text "wandering" outside the official collections of canon law. The bull *Unam sanctam* was the famous bull of 1302 in which Boniface VIII asserted the rights of the pope over the king of France and declared that membership in the Church was contingent on obedience to the pope.

5. Ordinary Gloss to C. 24 q. 1 c. 34 ℂ 4.

6. Apocalypse 3:16.

7. A DIALOGUE AGAINST THE AMEDEISTS

1. Eugenius IV's bull *Moyses* in CF 1/2: 101–06 nr. 210; COD 505–510.

2. See DRTA 16: 432.

3. See Mansi 29: 239–267.

4. Cusanus is assigning the date of the fifth session to the fourth; see COD 385–386. For the decree *Haec sancta* see Text 4, n. 140, above.

5. See Mansi 27: 811–824.

6. See Mansi 29: 239–267 at 264.

7. The Council of Chalcedon (451) condemned the so-called Robber Synod of Ephesus (449).

8. COD 455.

9. See the decree *Frequens* in COD 438–439.

10. COD 456.

11. See Mansi 29: 10 and 13.

12. See COD 476.

13. See COD 458.

14. Actually a meeting of the electors in August of 1439.

15. See DRTA 14: 320–323.

16. Because at the time the Church was divided among three obediences, each with its own pope.

17. See COD 455.

18. See Mansi 29: 247.

19. See Mansi 29: 248.

20. Mansi 29: 260–261, citing C. 25 q. 1 c. 1 and D. 15 c. 2.

21. See Mansi 29: 249–250.

22. See Mansi 29: 248.

23. See Mansi 29: 6–10.

24. COD 438–439.

25. Psalm 72:9.

26. See Mansi 29: 244.

27. COD 478–482.

28. See Mansi 29: 245.

29. See Mansi 29: 482–492.

30. Mansi 29: 264.

31. See Mansi 29: 74.

32. Henricus Kalteisen, O. P., in Mansi 29: 1001, citing *On Consideration,* Book III, c. 4; see *S. Bernardi opera,* ed. J. Leclerq and H. M. Rochais, vol. 3 (Rome, 1963), p. 445.

33. Kalteisen in Mansi 29: 1007, citing John 21:17.

34. Kalteisen in Mansi 29: 1011, citing *Summa on Ecclesiastical Power;* see the Augsburg, 1473 edition at q. lxiv.

35. Kalteisen in Mansi 29: 1053–54.

36. Kalteisen in Mansi 29: 1054, citing a Pseudo-Cyril text found in Thomas Aquinas's *Catena aurea* or *Golden Chain,* an anthology of texts commenting on the gospels.

37. Kalteisen in Mansi 29: 1056 alluding to Job 41:24.

38. Kalteisen in Mansi 29: 1073, citing *On Consideration,* Book IV, c. 8, in ed. cit., p. 423.

39. Book I, CSEL 42: 250–251.

40. That is, the Council as it was before being declared schismatic by Eugenius IV.

41. Not found.

42. *On Marriage and Concupiscence*, 1.33, PL 44: 435, citing Ephesians 5:27.

43. The Synod of Rimini (359), supposedly attended by 830 bishops, favored Arianism.

44. John of Ragusa, O. P., in Mansi 29: 790, citing 1 Tim 3:15 with "Ambrosiaster" on that text (CSEL 81/3: 270).

45. 1 Timothy 3:15.

46. Letter 105, CSEL 34: 609.

47. *Against the Letters of Petellian*, 2.51.118, CSEL 52: 87 = PL 43: 300, citing Matthew 23:2–3.

48. Mansi 30: 624–25.

49. This letter is cited in the synodal letter *Cogitanti*; see Mansi 29: 261.

50. An impossible supposition *ex hypothesi*, since it is a principle of canon law that Christ made sufficient provision for the eternal life of the Church.

51. See Mansi 29: 1054. See also D. 40 c. 6.

52. See above, n. 47.

53. Matthew 18:20.

54. Matthew 18:19.

55. Psalm 35:7.

56. Compare Wisdom 17:1.

57. I.e., it would require special divine grace to accomplish.

58. On Cusanus's idea of church concord, balancing hierarchy and consent, see his treatise *The Catholic Concordance*.

59. *Against the Letters of Petellian*, 2.38.91, in CSEL 52: 75 = PL 43: 292, citing Acts 1:7–8.

60. Letter 93, PL 33: 333, citing Luke 24:46.

8. SERMON 21

1. Matthew 2:11.

2. The first part, *How the Magi entered the house*, is omitted in the MSS.

3. Ordinary Gloss to C. 7 q. 3 c. 3.

4. See *The Catholic Concordance* 1.1.

5. 1 Corinthians 13:12.

6. Bonaventure, *Hexameron*, coll. 1, in his *Opera* 5 (Quarrachi), p. 329.

7. See *The Catholic Concordance* 1.3.

8. Proverbs 16:4.

9. Proverbs 9:1.

10. Proverbs 9:5.

11. John 17:11–12.

12. I.e., the souls in Purgatory.

13. Letter 16, CSEL 82: 116, 118 and 120–121.

14. See *The Catholic Concordance* 1.5.

15. (Pseudo) Dionysius, *On the Celestial Hierarchy*, PG 3: 531–538.

16. Psalm 25:5.

17. 1 Peter 3:19–20.

18. COD 527–528.

19. Ephesians 5:27.

20. See Ambrose on Psalm 118:1, CSEL 62: 7.

21. Genesis 2:21–24 with Ephesians 5:22.

22. See Jerome in Letter 23, CSEL 56: 84.

23. Expressions traditionally interpreted as referring to the Church in Romans 5:19; 1 Corinthians 15:45 and Apocalypse 1:5.

24. (Pseudo) Dionysius, *On the Ecclesiastical Hierarchy*, PG 3: 374–375, 499–503, 529–538.

25. Correctly, Leo IX.

26. Leo IX, *Letter to Michael, Patriarch of Constantinopole, and Leo Bishop of Archida*, in PL 143: 767.

27. I.e. *The Catholic Concordance*.

28. See *The Catholic Concordance* 1.6.

29. See (Pseudo) Dionysius, *On the Ecclesiastical Hierarchy*, PG 3: 427.

30. 1 Corinthians 13:12.

31. *Sacramentum* here means "sign" in relationship to "thing;" see Augustine, *On the Gospel of John* 26.6, CCSL 36: 267–68.

32. See (Pseudo) Dionysius, *On the Ecclesiastical Hierarchy*, PG 3: 499–503, 529–538.

33. See Gregory Nazianzen, *Second Dogmatic Oration*, c. 3, translated by Rufinus, CSEL 46: 8–9.

34. Matthew 5:14 and 13.

35. See (Pseudo) Cyprian, *On the Gamester*, CSEL 3/3: 93.

36. Letter 55, CSEL 3/2: 642 cited in C. 7 q. 1 c. 6.

37. PL 23: 258.

38. See *The Catholic Concordance* 1.2.

39. 2 Corinthians 5:20.

40. John 20:21.

41. Isidore of Seville, *Etymologies* 7.5.

42. See *The Catholic Concordance* 1.6.

43. *On Schism against the Donatists*, CSEL 26: 36.

44. C. 24 q. 1 c. 33, citing Augustine, Letter 53.

45. See *The Catholic Concordance* 1.6, 11 and 14.

46. Matthew 16:18.

47. For the Aristotelian theory of regimes, see the Preface to *The Catholic Concordance*.

48. See Augustine, *On the Faith and the Creed*, CSEL 41: 281.

49. The MSS say D. 83.

50. Gregory I, *Forty Homilies on the Gospels*, Homily 19, PL 76: 1154.

51. See *Roman Breviary*, Antiphon at the Benedictus at Lauds on Epiphany.

52. Matthew 2:1–2.

53. Extrav. Commun. 1.8.1.

54. See *The Catholic Concordance* 1.14.

55. An antiphon in the office for the dedication of a church; see *CAO*, no. 2998.

56. See Thomas Aquinas, *Summa theologiae* III q. 66 aa. 1, 11, and 12, and q. 67 a. 7.

57. Ibid. III q. 72 aa. 5, 8 and 11.

58. Apocalypse 14:4.

59. See *The Catholic Concordance* 1.4, 6.

60. Matthew 2:11.

61. See *The Catholic Concordance* 1.5.

62. Note that the word for soul, *anima*, is feminine.

63. 1 Corinthians 9:27.

64. Psalm 131:7.

65. The correct reference is to Deuteronomy 13:1–5.

66. See William Perauld, *Summa on the Vices*, Tract 9, *On the Sins of the Tongue* 2.1.

67. Ibid. (308).

68. Ibid. (304).

69. I.e., the first five of the Ten Commandments.

70. *Codex Iuris Civilis* 9.7.1.

71. Ibid., *Novellae* 72 c. 1.

72. Perauld, *Summa* (307–08).

73. *Dialogues* 4.18 (PL 77: 349), cited by William Perauld (305).

74. Stephan of Bourbon, *On Diverse Materials for Preaching*, part 4, cited in X 5.7.10; *On the Gift of Fortitude*, Title 9, ed. A. Lecoy de la Marche in *Anecdotes historiques, légendes et apologues* (Paris, 1877), pp. 341–342.

75. Not found.

76. 2 Timothy 4:7.

77. Isaiah 46:7.

78. See Augustine, *On the Spirit and the Soul*, PL 40: 816–817.

79. Ibid., *PL* 40: 800.

80. Psalm 39:13.

81. 2 Kings 7:27.

82. *Roman Breviary*, Response 1 for the Fourth Day of the Week after the Octave of Pentecost; see *CAO* no. 7372.

83. Ephesians 3:17.

84. Augustine, *On the Spirit and the Soul*, PL 40: 791.

85. Psalm 37:9.

86. 2 Corinthians 1:12.

87. Matthew 6:10.

9. LETTER TO THE BOHEMIANS ON CHURCH UNITY

1. The Compacts of Prague, dated November 30, 1433, were negotiated between the Hussites of Bohemia and representatives of the Council of Basel. The compacts allowed the Bohemians and Moravians communion in both kinds to all adults who wished for it; free preaching was granted under condition that the Church must approve the preachers and that preachers should defer to the local bishop and to papal authority. The Compacts were confirmed by the Bohemian Diet of Iglau in 1436 and had the force of law. They were finally declared invalid by Pope Pius II in 1462.

2. Nicholas is, in short, requesting a simple, unconditional submission, and wishes the Compacts negotiated with the Council of Basel to be set aside as voided by the failure of the Bohemians to keep them.

3. Isaiah 1:2.

4. St. John Capistran (1385–1456), a famous preacher and reformer, was appointed apostolic nuncio to the Holy Roman Empire in 1451 and converted thousands of Bohemian Hussites to Catholic orthodoxy.

5. G. G. Leibnitz, *Codex iuris gentium diplomaticus*, Mantissa (Hannover, 1700), 2: 138.

6. I.e., the Council's ability to concede utraquist communion to the Bohemians in itself shows, by its contingency, that such communion is not necessary to salvation. This is an example of Cusanus' typical practice of finding in works used as authorities by his opponents conclusions that disprove their own theses; other examples can be found in II.8, above, and in his *Sifting of the Koran (Cribatio Alkorani)*.

7. Letter 131, *PL* 182: 286–287; Letter 134, *PL* 182: 289.

8. I.e., the privilege the Milanese enjoyed of having an archiepiscopal see in their city.

9. I.e., from the Nicene Creed, which includes the statement, "I believe in one, holy, catholic and apostolic Church."

10. Mansi 29: 158.

11. Giuliano Cesarini (1398–1444), a leader in the Council of Basel who later, like Cusanus, abandoned the Basel fathers and submitted to Pope Eugenius IV.

12. A Spanish canon lawyer, archdeacon of the Cathedral of Barcelona, who held the post of Master Auditor at the Council of Basel.

13. Compare Text 4, §§41, 48, above.

14. Mansi 29: 158–159.

15. Which petitions Cusanus means is unclear, but the request for communion under both species was made during the Bohemian visit to Basel in 1432. The article on communion was first formulated in 1420; it can be found in Mansi 29: 385.

16. Palomar was an auditor of the Roman Rota.

17. Letter 93, *PL* 33: 321–347.

18. Letter 141, *PL* 33: 577–582.

19. Letter 185, *PL* 33: 792–815 at col. 815.

20. 1 Corinthians 11:29.

21. 1 Corinthians 10:17.

22. Ephesians 5:23.

23. Letter 159, *PL* 33: 630–645 at col. 637.

24. *On Illustrious Men*, *PL* 23: 627.

25. *The Gem of the Soul*, *PL* 172: 564.

26. *Explanations of Hebrews*, Homily XVII, PG 63: 131–132.

27. There is no mention of communion in the letters of Anacletus in Hinschius, pp. 66–87, nor in the passages from these letters in Burchard's *Decretum*.

28. Cusanus assumes that the reference to grades implies that communicants are members of the ecclesiastical hierarchy and therefore clerics, not lay persons.

29. Pseudo-Dionysius the Areopagite, *On the Ecclesiastical Hierarchy* chap. III actually refers to communion with both bread and wine.

30. *Rationale of the Divine Offices*, Book IV, c. 41 ℂ 50, CCCM 140.461.

31. *PL* 4: 606–607.

32. B. Mombritius, *Sanctuarium seu Vitae Sanctorum* (Hildesheim, 1978), 2: 542 (BHL 7801).

33. *PL* 140: 689–90.

34. See Mansi 1: 91.

35. Innocent III, *On the Holy Mystery of the Altar*, *PL* 217: 854.

36. *Explanations of Hebrews*, Homily XVII [c. 10], PG 63: 131–132.

37. But see *PL* 16: 452, where Ambrose says the Greeks receive daily.

38. See *De consecratione*, D. 2 c. 16.

39. Cusanus applies the title *Corrector* to the entirety of the *Decretum* of Burchard of Worms, not just Book XIX; see, however, *PL* 140: 639 for this reference from Book II.

40. *On the Ecclesiastical Hierarchy* chap. III ℭ xiv, discusses communion and church order. Cusanus believed Dionysius the Areopagite to have been the disciple of St. Paul mentioned the Acts of the Apostles, though the writings that circulate under his name are now regarded as pseudonymous, possibly the work of a sixth-century Monophysite monk.

41. This may be a botched reference to the condemnation of the letter of Ibas by the Second Council of Constantinople (553); see *COD* 121–122.

42. Letter 48, *PL* 22: 506.

43. *Rationale*, Book IV, c. 53 ℭ 3, CCCM 140: 544–545.

44. See *PL* 66: 510 (a commentary on the *Rule of St Benedict*) and 77: 553 (St. Gregory the Great, *Register* 2.18).

45. 1 Corinthians 5:1–5.

46. Letter 61, *PL* 4: 362–364.

47. Hinschius, p. 340, c. VII.

48. Hinschius, p. 528, c. VII.

49. *COD* 12.

50. See Gennadius of Marseilles (pseudo-Augustine), *On Ecclesiastical Dogmas*, *PL* 58: 994.

51. *On the Ecclesiastical Hierarchy* chap. II ℭ 2.

52. See Robert of Flamborough, *Liber poenitentialis*, ed. J. J. F. Firth (Toronto: Pontifical Institute of Mediaeval Studies, 1971), pp. 268–269.

53. Beleth discusses the eucharistic bread more generally in *On Ecclesiastical Offices*, c. 41, CCCM 41: 76.

54. Humbert of Mourmoutiers, *Response to the Blasphemies of Nicetas*, *PL* 143: 983–1000, does not mention James.

55. *Rationale*, Book IV, c. 41 ℭ 11, CCCM 140: 462.

56. Ordinary Gloss to D. 93 c. 14.

57. Not found in the *Rationale*.

58. Innocent III, *On the Holy Mystery of the Altar*, *PL* 217: 903.

59. Text and Ordinary Gloss to X 4.1.11.

60. Ordinary Gloss to X 5.38.11.

61. Innocent III does not discuss the viaticum in these terms in *On the Holy Mystery of the Altar*.

62. Text and Ordinary Gloss to *De consecratione*, D. 2 c. 93.

63. Innocent III died in 1216.

64. Text and Ordinary Gloss to D. 93 c. 14.

65. Text and Ordinary Gloss to *De consecratione*, D. 2 c. 93.

66. I.e., the Third Lateran Council.

67. Arnest de Pardubiz (1343–1364) held this council in 1346. For the reenactment of *Omnis utriusque sexus*, see Mansi 26: 101–104.

68. *Opera omnia*, vol. 7 (Parma, 1857; New York, 1948), p. 604.

69. Guido de Baysio, *Archidiaconus super decreto* (Lyons, 1549) [*Rosarium decreti*] at *De consecratione*, D. 2 c. 12.

70. Ordinary Gloss to Clem. 5.3.3. Johannes Andreae (d. 1348) was an Italian expert on canon law.

71. The sermons of Iacobellus have not been edited.

72. Deuteronomy 17:8.

73. See D. 93 c. 3.

74. Matthew 23:3; Luke 10:16; John 6:58; Matthew 28:20; Matthew 24:45.

75. Luke 22:32 and Matthew 16:18.

76. Innocent III's letter to Arnold Amalricus, Abbot of Cîteaux, precedes copies of his sermon collection; see *Between God and Man: Six Sermons on the Priestly Office*, tr. C. J. Vause and F. C. Gardiner (Washington, DC: The Catholic University of America Press, 2004), pp. 1–6.

77. See the "Ancient rite for celebrating Mass" appended to the Gregorian Sacramentary in *PL* 78: 254.

78. See John the Deacon, *Life of Saint Gregory the Great*, *PL* 75: 95.

79. Letter 93.10.41, *PL* 33: 341, quoting Cyprian's Letter 53.

80. 2 Corinthians 3:16.

81. Not in the Ordinary Gloss to Luke.

82. Luke 14:33.

83. Cusanus may mean a sect found near Cologne in the time of Bernard of Clairvaux.

84. John 6:54.

85. *On the Ecclesiastical Hierarchy* chap. III ❡ 6.

86. John 3:5.

87. Mark 16:16.

88. Cusanus' argument, briefly, is that baptism must be essentially spiritual because only in this way can the fact that there were Old Testament saints who were saved before the institution of baptism by Christ be reconciled with Christ's statements in §49 making salvation conditional on baptism.

89. See 1 Corinthians 10:2: "I would not have you ignorant, brothers, that all our fathers were under the cloud [in the desert] and all crossed the sea, and all were baptized in Moses in the cloud and in the sea."

90. John 6:54.

91. John 6:68.

92. John 14:6.

93. 1 Corinthians 10:3–4.

94. I.e., there is no distinction between the food of the spirit in heaven and in this life except that in the latter case, spiritual food is taken under the sensible forms of communion.

95. John 14:2, but the passage reads "I go to prepare a place for you;" Cusanus is perhaps conflating this passage in memory with Psalms 23:5.

96. Homily 16, *PL* 94: 302.

97. *Opera omnia*, p. 604.

98. *Rationale*, Book IV, c. 54 ❡ 9, CCCM 140: 550.

99. *On the Ecclesiastical Hierarchy* chap. I ❡ 1.

100. *On the Ecclesiastical Hierarchy* chap. III, ℭ 3.

101. 1 Corinthians 11:28.

10. LETTER TO RODRIGO SÁNCHEZ DE ARÉVALO

1. Rodrigo Sánchez de Arévalo (1404–1470), a canon lawyer, served as the secretary of Juan II of Castile and Léon and later as an envoy to the Council of Basel. Cusanus expected him to attend the 1443 Diet of Frankfurt at which conciliar versus papal power was to be debated by the princes of the Empire. Rodrigo rejected conciliarism and became an ally of Cusanus in establishing the authority of Eugenius IV.

2. The word *participare*, participate, is transitive in Latin; following a common practice in philosophical translation, the English equivalent "participate" is here treated as transitive verb. *Participare* is a technical term in the Platonic tradition, meaning "to derive being and essence severally from" some Form or Idea. Here Form or Idea is replaced by the Word, Jesus Christ, the Second Person of the Trinity in his function as exemplary and creative force; see John 1:1–3.

3. Reading *aeterni* for the edition's *alterni* ("opposed").

4. Acts 15: 10.

5. See 1 Corinthians 13:12.

6. See Canticle 6:8; Ephesians 5:27.

7. Paraphrasing Hebrews 4:14.

8. Cusanus distinguishes in the Platonic way between *intelligentia*, noetic reason or direct, timeless intuition, and *ratio* or discursive reason, a reasoning process that takes place in time.

9. Matthew 16:18–19.

10. Cusanus uses the metaphysical term "contracted," which is used to indicate the manner in which a universal exists in a particular thing. Here the universal is "the absolute," that which is free from particularity, for example, courage considered in the abstract, apart from any courageous act.

11. D. 19 c. 7.

12. *Corpus iuris civilis, Digest* 1.3.31.

13. C. 23 q. 1 c. 19.

14. Juan II, king of Castile 1406–1454, was a weak king ruled by those around him. His policies favored Eugenius IV over the Council of Basel.

15. Literally, the children of Hagar, the mother of Abraham's son Ishmael.

16. Frederick III.

II. SERMON 126

1. John 16:33.

2. Psalm 117:22.

3. Ephesians 2:20.

4. 1 Peter 2:4.

5. John 1:3.

6. Colossians 2:9.

7. Ephesians 3:18.

8. 1 Peter 2:4–7.

9. John 12:32.

10. Matthew 16:16.

11. I.e., the fact that pagan religion was falsifiable showed that it had a rational basis.

12. 1 Timothy 6:16.

13. John 5:36.

14. John 14:6.

15. (Pseudo) Dionysius the Areopagite, *On Divine Names*, chap. 3 ℂ 2.

16. Apocalypse 2:17.

17. Psalm 33:9; Cusanus changes "good" (*bonus*) to "sweet" (*suavis*).

18. 1 Peter 2:1.

19. 1 Peter 2:2–3.

20. 1 Peter 2:4–5.

21. 1 Peter 2:6–8.

22. Ephesians 2:20.

23. Wisdom 7:26.

24. Cusanus plays on the double sense of *vivus* as "living" and "sparkling;" a *lapis vivus* (literally "living stone") is a stone that will emit sparks when struck.

25. Matthew 5:7.

26. Luke 6:38.

27. Matthew 19:29.

28. Matthew 25:40.

29. Romans 9:33; 1 Peter 2:6.

30. John 1:3.

31. 2 Corinthians 12:2.

32. Apocalypse 2:17.

33. Exodus 16:15.

12. SERMON 144

1. Matthew 16:19.

2. *On Schism against the Donatists*, CSEL 26: 36.

3. See the translation of Sermon 21 (Text 8, above).

4. John 14:6.

5. C. 24 q. 1 c. 20.

6. Matthew 28:18.

7. 1 Corinthians 5:1–5.

8. 1 Corinthians 5:1–5.

9. Matthew 8:31–32.

10. See, respectively, X 1.6.20 and Aristotle, *Politics* 1.5.

11. John 19:11.

12. Ecclesiasticus 15:5.

13. Matthew 16:16.

14. Aristotle, *Metaphysics* 1.1.

15. Matthew 23:10.

16. John 6:69.

17. §§6–7 are indebted to a sermon on the feast of St. Peter's chair by Aldobrandinus de Tuscanella, preserved in a manuscript in Brixen, the bishopric occupied by Cusanus.

18. Matthew 14:28–41.

19. Matthew 26:75.

20. Matthew 26:35.

21. See Hugh of St. Cher, Postilla to John 13:28, in his *Postillae*, vol. 6 (Cologne, 1621), fol. 368ra.

22. Acts 11:15, 9:36–41, 5:15.

23. Aristotle, *Metaphysics* 2.1, 993b.

24. John 1:16.

25. Bernard of Clairvaux, *Sermon on the Sunday after the Assumption*, in *Opera*, ed. J. Leclerq and H. Rochais, vol. 5 (Rome, 1968), p. 263.

26. Matthew 18:18.

27. Matthew 16:18.

28. Bonaventure, *Hexameron*, coll. 1, n. 2, in *Opera*, vol. 5 (Quarrachi, 1891), p. 329.

13. SERMON 160

1. Matthew 16:18.

2. See Jerome, *On the Interpretation of Hebrew Names*, CCSL 72: 141. Peter is called "the one who recognizes" here because in Matthew 16:16 he is the first of the disciples to recognize that Jesus is the Christ or the Anointed, "the son of the living God." The verses that follow are the ones upon which the Petrine claim to primacy are based.

3. *Princeps* carries the sense both of precedence and of leadership or rulership.

4. Jerome, Letter 15, CSEL 54: 62–64.

5. Augustine, *Against the Letters of Petilian*, CSEL 52: 88.

6. Matthew 23:2–3. See Text 7.29 above.

7. Luke 7:47.

8. 1 Peter 2:18.

9. Luke 22:62.

10. Luke 7:47.

11. John 16:33.

14. SERMON 287

1. Matthew 16:17.

2. See note 1 to Text 13.

3. John 6:44.

4. Matthew 16:16.

5. Matthew 16:17.

6. Matthew 16:18.

15. SERMON 280

1. Second Sunday after Easter. The synod was held on May 2, 1457.

2. Cusanus is addressing other priests and clergy at a diocesan synod.

3. John 10:11.

4. John 9:39.

5. John 10:1.

6. John 10:1–10.

7. John 10:9–10.

8. John 6:69.

9. Matthew 16:16.

10. John 14:6.

11. Malachi 4:2.

12. John 1:3.

13. Cusanus is interpreting Christ in terms of the metaphysical dynamics of Christian Neoplatonism; he sees in Christ the cause and pattern (*ratio*, meaning reason, pattern, explanation) of creation, the source or pattern of all essences, and the goal of creation, to which all creation ultimately reverts as to its source.

14. Matthew 11:27.

15. Psalm 118: 151; Psalms 24:10.

16. Psalm 140:10.

17. John 10:11.

18. John 10:12.

19. John 10:28.

20. John 10:14–15.

21. John 14:6.

22. Matthew 25:34.

23. 1 Corinthians 15:28.

24. John 10:11.

25. John 10:16.

26. John 10:17.

27. John 10:11.

28. John 10:17–18.

29. Exodus 32:31–32.

30. 2 Samuel 24:17.

31. Romans 9:3.

32. Romans 9:13.

33. Galatians 3:13, citing Deuteronomy 21:23.

34. Luke 23:46.

35. Habbakuk 2:14 in Romans 1:17.

36. Romans 8:2 and 1 Peter 1:11.

37. John 10:27–28.

38. Image: 1 Corinthians 11:7, 2 Corinthians 4:4, Colossians 1:15. Figure of His substance: Hebrews 1:3.

39. John 10:30.

40. 1 Timothy 6:16.

41. See John 14:2.

16. SERMON 290

1. Cusanus is playing upon the idea of entry in the introit, the entry rite of the Mass; entrance upon his legatine office in Rome; and perhaps also on the name "Invocavit", a summoning-in, the name for the second Sunday in Lent, the day in the liturgical year on whose vigil this sermon was given. The sermon was given at the opening of a synod he held as legate in the papal chapel at St. Peter's in Rome (later the Sistine Chapel).

2. Compare James 1:16–17.

3. Acts 8:26–40.

4. *Confessions*, 8.12, CSEL 33: 194–195.

5. Cusanus is recommending the *sors biblica*, picking a Biblical text at random to use as an oracle, which (despite the example of Augustine) was condemned as a superstitious divinatory practice by Aquinas; see his *Opuscula theologica*, ed. R. A. Verardo (Rome, 1954), 1: 165–7. Versions of this practice were condemned throughout the Middle Ages; see W. E. Klingshirn, "Defining the Sortes Sanctorum: Gibbon, Du Cange, and Early Christian Lot Divination," *Journal of Early Christian Studies* 10.1 (2002): 77–130. This method of divination is related to the late antique pagan practice of *sors virgiliana*, opening the *Aeneid* at random in search of an inspired reply.

6. Romans 15:4.

7. Mark 13:37.

8. Psalm 75:2.

9. Ezekiel 36:24 (paraphrased).

10. Cusanus here explores the paradox that God, the holiest of beings and the source of sanctification, could in some sense be Himself made holy.

11. 1 Corinthians 14:38.

12. The manuscript says c. *Si iuxta* (c. 9), but the actual text is from the following chapter.

13. Philippians 2:8.

14. 1 Corinthians 7:19.

15. Matthew 6:9. The first line of the Lord's Prayer in the Vulgate is "Pater noster, qui es in caelis, sanctificetur nomen tuum" (Our Father, who are in Heaven, let your name be sanctified).

16. Acts 9:15.

17. Cusanus plays here and elsewhere on the close relation between *sanctificare*, sanctify, and *sancire*, to sanction or acknowledge as legitimate.

18. John 5:17.

19. Hebrews 1:2.

20. John 1:18.

21. Matthew 5:16.

22. Cusanus plays on the word *mundus*, which means both "clean" and "world."

23. See John 14:21.

24. 1 John 4:8.

25. §17 is Cusanus' eirenic solution to the scholastic debate among the religious orders about whether the will or the intellect was the highest human act, and the closely related debate whether beatitude consists in knowing God through the intellect (Dominicans) or enjoying God in love (Franciscans and Augustinians).

26. 1 Peter 1:15.

27. John 20:21.

28. Cusanus was cardinal priest of the titular church of San Pietro in Vincoli.

29. 1 Peter 3:15–16.

30. Matthew 10:20.

31. C. 24 q. 1 c. 14.

32. Matthew 16:18.

33. 1 Peter 1:23.

34. Cusanus invokes a common false etymology of *hagios* from *a-gaia*, "without earth."

35. Ecclesiasticus 15:3.

36. John 15:3.

37. Psalm 33:1.

38. Wisdom 12:1.

17. A GENERAL REFORM OF THE CHURCH

1. Acts 17:27.

2. Aristotle, *Metaphysics* 1.1.

3. Colossians 2:3.

4. John 1:14, 12.

5. John 6:69.

6. 1 Corinthians 2:2.

7. Romans 2:4.

8. Romans 8:17.

9. Philippians 2:6.

10. 1 Corinthians 4:16, 11:1.

11. John 6:45.

12. Colossians 2:3.

13. Matthew 11:29.

14. John 13:15.

15. Acts 1:1.

16. Philippians 2:6.

17. 1 Corinthians 12:12–20.

18. Matthew 6:22–23; Luke 11:33–36.

19. Luke 6:39–42.

20. In canon law, visitation is an inspection by a superior power to correct abuses.

21. A legate could extract "procurations" to support his mission.

22. Benefices were supposed to be united only when too poor to support a tenant. Dispensations to hold benefices incompatible because of pastoral responsibilities were common in the fifteenth century. Entrusting or "commending" an abbey to an absentee, titular abbot also was common.

23. I.e., any alterations to the composition of church offices should be made on the principle that conditions for worship should thereby be maximized, and not (for example) to increase the income of a prelate.

24. The translation follows the variant reading *predecessorum*, not the edition's *successorum*.

25. Two benefices without cure of souls could be held simultaneously, or one with and one without pastoral responsibilities.

26. An absentee pastor was supposed to hire a substitute out of the revenues of the benefice.

27. Cathedral chapters varied. In Italy, a provost presided; in England, a dean; collegiate churches are churches of a rank higher than ordinary parish churches, and are usually administered by canons.

28. The bishop had "ordinary," i.e. presumptive jurisdiction over his flock.

29. Excommunication *latae sententiae* was incurred automatically without any formal proceedings.

30. The *fabrica* of a church was the body (in Italy usually a civic body) charged with the ongoing work of constructing, decorating and maintaining a church, especially cathedral churches in towns.

31. Gregory the Great first called the pope "servant of the servants of God."

32. The inability of anyone to judge his own case was an established legal principle.

33. Psalm 69:9.

34. A false but popular etymology of "cardinal," which originally referred to the schedule of clergy serving at the major Roman basilicas, not to a *cardo* (hinge).

35. In the fifteenth century the major political powers of Europe had a presumptive, though informal, right to representation in the College of Cardinals; the college also performed high-level administrative, legal and financial roles in the papal court.

36. Cardinals were assigned as protectors of city-states, religious orders and others to promote their interests in the Curia.

37. The pope's audiences were modeled on those of the later emperors, who sat enthroned with their advisers standing nearby.

38. Each cardinal was assigned a see near Rome or a church in the city, and was thus known by the name of his "titular" church.

39. It is a monastic practice to read some work of piety during meals.

40. San Giovanni in Laterano, San Pietro in Vaticano, Santa Maria Maggiore and San Paolo fuori le Mura are the major papal basilicas. All were visited by pilgrims.

41. Luke 17:10.

42. According to ancient belief, a bishop married his church.

43. Colossians 3:5.

44. Luke 12:42.

45. Bishops still are required to make *ad limina* visits to Rome to pay their respects to the pope and to report on the state of their dioceses.

46. The Papal Penitentiary was a curial office that developed in the later Middle Ages to handle absolutions from ecclesiastical censures and dispensations reserved to the pope. It was famously corrupt and incompetent.

47. Books of rules and privileges for the Penitentiary were compiled in the later Middle Ages.

48. Pursuit of gain in such a sensitive office was a form of simony, the buying and selling of spiritual gifts.

Bibliography

EDITIONS

Acta Cusana: Quellen zur Lebensgeschichte des Nikolaus von Kues. Edited by Erich Meuthen and Hermann J. Hallauer. 4 vols. Hamburg: Felix Meiner Verlag, 1976–2000.

Nicolai de Cusa omnia iussu et auctoritate Academiae Litterarum Heidelbergensis. 19 vols. Hamburg: Felix Meiner Verlag, 1932–.

TRANSLATIONS

Nicholas of Cusa. *The Catholic Concordance.* Edited and translated by Paul E. Sigmund. Cambridge: Cambridge University Press, 1991.

Nicholas of Cusa. *Complete Philosophical and Theological Treatises.* Translated by Jasper Hopkins. 2 vols. Minneapolis: A. J. Banning Press, 2002. On line at: http://cla.umn.edu/sites/jhopkins/.

Nicholas of Cusa. *Selected Spiritual Writings.* Translated by H. Lawrence Bond. Mahwah (New Jersey): Paulist Press, 1997.

Piccolomini, Aeneas Sylvius [Pius II]. *De gestis Concilii Basiliensis commentariorum libri II.* Edited and translated by Denys Hay and W. K. Smith. Oxford: Clarendon Press, 1967.

Piccolomini, Aeneas Sylvius. *Reject Aeneas, Accept Pius: Selected Letters of Aeneas Sylvius Piccolomini (Pope Pius II).* Introduced and translated by Thomas M. Izbicki, Gerald Christianson and Philip Krey. Washington, DC: Catholic University of America Press, 2006.

SECONDARY LITERATURE

Biechler, James E. "Nicholas of Cusa and the End of the Conciliar Movement: A Humanist Crisis of Identity." *Church History* 44 (1975): 5–21.

Black, Antony J. *Council and Commune: The Conciliar Movement and the Fifteenth-Century Heritage.* London: Burns and Oates, 1979.

Black, Antony J. *Monarchy and Community: Political Ideas in the Later Conciliar Controversy, 1430–1450.* Cambridge: Cambridge University Press, 1970.

Bond, H. Lawrence, Thomas M. Izbicki and Gerald Christianson. "Nicholas of Cusa: On Presidential Authority in a General Council." *Church History* 59 (1990): 19–34.

Casarella, Peter J., ed. *Cusanus: The Legacy of Learned Ignorance.* Washington, DC: Catholic University of America Press, 2006.

Christianson, Gerald. *Cesarini: The Conciliar Cardinal—The Basel Years, 1431–1438.* St. Ottilien: EOS-Verlag, 1979.

Gill, Joseph. *The Council of Florence.* Cambridge: Cambridge University Press, 1961. Reprint New York: AMS Press, 1982.

Gill, Joseph. *Eugenius IV: Pope of Christian Union.* Westminster (Maryland): Newman Press, 1961.

Bellitto, Christopher M., Thomas M. Izbicki and Gerald Christianson, eds. *Introducing Nicholas of Cusa: A Guide to a Renaissance Man.* Mahwah (New Jersey): Paulist Press, 2004.

Izbicki , Thomas M. "An Ambivalent Papalism: Peter in the Sermons of Nicholas of Cusa." In *Perspectives on Early Modern and Modern Intellectual History: Essays in Honor of Nancy S. Struever*, ed. Joseph Marino and Melinda W. Schlitt, pp. 49–65. Rochester (New York): University of Rochester Press, 2001.

Izbicki, Thomas M. "The Church in the Light of Learned Ignorance." *Medieval Philosophy and Theology* 3 (1993): 196–214.

Izbicki, Thomas M. "Representation in Nicholas of Cusa." In *Repraesentatio: Mapping a Keyword for Churches and Governance: Proceedings of the San Miniato International Workshop, October 13–16 2004*, ed. Massimo Faggioli and Alberto Melloni, pp. 61–78. Münster: Lit Verlag, 2006.

Jacob, E. F. "The Bohemians at the Council of Basel." In *Prague Essays*, ed. R. W. Seton-Watson, pp. 81–123. Oxford: Clarendon Press, 1949.

Oakley, Francis. *The Conciliarist Tradition: Constitutionalism in the Catholic Church, 1300–1870.* Oxford and New York: Oxford University Press, 2003.

Sigmund, Paul E. *Nicholas of Cusa and Medieval Political Thought.* Cambridge (Massachusetts): Harvard University Press, 1963.

Stieber, Joachim W. *Pope Eugenius IV, the Council of Basel and the Secular and Ecclesiastical Authorities in the Empire: The Conflict over Supreme Authority and Power in the Church.* Leiden: E. J. Brill, 1978.

Sullivan, Donald. "Nicholas of Cusa as Reformer: The Papal Legation to the Germanies." *Medieval Studies* 36 (1974): 382–428.

Tierney, Brian. *Foundations of the Conciliar Theory: The Contribution of the Medieval Canonists from Gratian to the Great Schism.* Enlarged new edition. Leiden: E. J. Brill, 1998.

Tillinghast, Pardon E. "An Aborted Reformation: Germans and the Papacy in the Mid-Fifteenth Century." *Journal of Medieval History* 2 (1976): 57–79.

Watanabe, Morimichi. *Concord and Reform: Nicholas of Cusa and Legal and Political Thought in the Fifteenth Century.* Edited by Thomas M. Izbicki and Gerald Christianson, Aldershot: Ashgate, 2001.

Watanabe, Morimichi. *The Political Ideas of Nicholas of Cusa.* Geneva: Librairie Droz, 1963.

Index of Biblical and Canon Law Citations

༄༅༔

Italicized numbers in entries for biblical books refer to chapter and verse. Double numbers refer to number and paragraph of works included in this volume. Page numbers with *n* (e.g., 640n15) refer to page and note number in the Notes to the Translation.

General Index

ॐ॥॰॥ॐ

Lowercase roman numerals refer to pages in the Introduction. Double numbers refer to number and paragraph of works included in this volume. Arabic numbers with *n* (e.g., 619n1) refer to page and note number in the Notes to the Translation.

Council of Ferrara-Florence
(1438–1445), viii, xi, vii, 4.6–16,
4.21, 4.26, 4.28–37, 7.1, 7.12,
7.14, 7.23, 10.15, 610n17, 613n21
Council of Nicaea, 1.53, 2.2, 2.3,
2.5, 2.18, 2.23–27, 3.5, 3.7, 4.35,
4.36, 9.38, 9.39, 605n1; Second,
605n1
Council of Pope Martin I, 3.8
Council of Rimini, 3.14, 622n43
Council of Rouen, 9.31
Council of Sardica, 1.53, 3.7, 4.35,
9.36
Council of Siena, 7.12, 7.22, 7.30
Council of Sirte, 9.28
Council of Toledo, 2.5, 4.29, 4.43
Council of Tours, 1.36, 9.31
Council of Union. See Council of
Ferrara-Florence
councils: authority of, 1.15, 1.17,
1.57, 2.1, 2.11–21, 2.24, 2.31–34,
4.23–26, 4.29, 4.32–62, 6.2,
7.2–37; presidents and legates
of, 3.1–2, 3.11–13, 4.5, 4.7, 4.14,
4.23–26, 4.29, 4.32, 4.39, 4.46,
4.50, 4.55, 7.10–14, 7.22, 7.30;
representing Church, 2.12, 3.2–
3, 3.8, 3.10, 4.5, 4.25, 4.30,
4.47, 4.57, 7.6, 7.9–15, 7.18–19,
7.26, 7.37, 10.1; transfer and
dissolution of, 4.14, 4.20, 4.22–
26, 4.32, 4.51–54, 7.1, 7.14,
7.22–23, 10.15; types of, 2.2–6,
2.11–12, 3.2, 3.7, 4.30, 7.12
Critinus, Theodore, 1.2
Cyprian, 1.12, 1.13, 1.22, 1.25, 3.7,
4.58, 4.60, 6.3, 6.7, 7.10, 9.31,

9.36, 9.44, 9.46; Concerning the
Lapsed, 1.52; letter to
Antoninus, 1.53; letter to
Antonius (quoted by Augus-
tine), 1.53; letter to Florentius
and Puppianus, 3.5; letter to
Novatian, 1.13, 2.10, 2.22. See
also pseudo-Cyprian

Damasus, Pope, 3.9, 3.14
David, King, 2.31, 15.44, 16.5
Diet of Frankfurt (1442), xi–xii,
xiv, 619n5, 632n1
Diet of Iglau, 626n1
Diet of Mainz, 7.12
Diet of Regensburg, 9.5
Dionysius the Areopagite. See
pseudo-Dionysius
Dioscorus, 3.2, 3.16
Dishypatus, John, 4.9
Dominic, Saint, 9.40
Donatists, 9.28
Durand, William (the Elder),
Rationale of the Divine Offices,
9.30, 9.34, 9.36, 9.37, 9.55
Dursmit, John, 9.5

Eger, 9.30
Eighth General Synod, 1.2
Elias, vicar of Jerusalem, 1.2
Ephesus, See of, 2.29
Eucharist, 1.2–14, 1.31, 1.36–45,
1.49–57, 8.6, 9.2, 9.10, 9.19–24,
9.29–48, 9.50–58, 16.21,
17.22
Eugenian party, xii
Eugenius III, Pope, 7.24

Publication of this volume has been made possible by

The Myron and Sheila Gilmore Publication Fund at I Tatti
The Robert Lehman Endowment Fund
The Jean-François Malle Scholarly Programs and Publications Fund
The Andrew W. Mellon Scholarly Publications Fund
The Craig and Barbara Smyth Fund
for Scholarly Programs and Publications
The Lila Wallace–Reader's Digest Endowment Fund
The Malcolm Wiener Fund for Scholarly Programs and Publications